Landscape and Prehistory of the East London Wetlands

Investigations along the A13 DBFO Roadscheme, Tower Hamlets, Newham and Barking and Dagenham, 2000-2003

by Elizabeth Stafford

with Damian Goodburn and Martin Bates

and other contributions by

Alistair Barclay, Catherine Barnett, Edward Biddulph, Barry John Bishop, John Crowther, Denise Druce, Stuart Foreman, Andrew Haggart, Richard Macphail, Jacqueline McKinley, Frank Meddens, Lorraine Mepham, Rebecca Nicholson, Sylvia Peglar, Ruth Pelling, Louise Rayner, Edward Rhodes, Alison Sheridan, David Smith, Lena Strid, Charlotte Thompson, John Whittaker

illustrated by

Elizabeth Stafford, Hannah Kennedy, Mark Gridley and Magdalena Wachnik

Oxford Archaeology Monograph No. 17

2012

The publication of this volume has been generously funded by Transport for London

Published by Oxford Archaeology as part of the Oxford Archaeology Monograph series

Designed by Elizabeth Stafford and the Oxford Archaeology Graphics Office

Edited by Rebecca Nicholson

Front cover: Alder (*Alnus glutinosa*) wet woodland, Brownsea Island, Poole Harbour, Dorset (photograph by David J. Glaves, all rights reserved)

Back cover: Early Bronze Age barbed and tanged arrowhead from Movers Lane, RIR01 1033 (photograph by Magdalena Wachnik)

ISBN 978-0-904220-70-4

This book is part of a series of monographs which can be bought from all good bookshops and internet bookshops

For more information visit www.thehumanjourney.net

Typeset by Production Line, Oxford

Printed in Great Britain

Contents

List of Figures

List of Tables

List of Plates

Summary

This report presents the results of archaeological investigations carried out during improvements to five key junctions along a stretch of the A13 trunk road through the East London Boroughs of Tower Hamlets, Newham and Barking and Dagenham. The A13 at this location runs parallel to the River Thames, traversing the very edge of the Thames gravel terraces and alluvial floodplain. Previous archaeological work has shown the Thames gravel terraces to be one of the most intensively occupied regions of Southern England during the prehistoric period and locations on or adjacent to the terrace edge have high potential for preserving organic remains such as timber structures and palaeoenvironmental evidence in waterlogged conditions.

The archaeology recorded covers a wide chronological range representing intermittent activity spanning the Mesolithic through to the post-Roman period. Regionally important evidence of Neolithic activity included artefact assemblages of pottery and worked flint. A rare cache of charred emmer wheat recovered during evaluation at the Woolwich Manor Way site provides definitive evidence of early Neolithic cereal cultivation in the vicinity, and a fragment of belt slider made from Whitby jet attests to long distance exchange networks. The greatest concentration of activity, however, dates to the 2nd millennium BC and includes several Bronze Age timber stake-built structures and brushwood trackways with associated wetland edge occupation.

The A13 structures add to the corpus of regional evidence for trackway building and marshland exploitation during this period. The broadly north-south orientation would suggest they were built to maintain access to the Thames floodplain during a period of increased wetness. This may have been to exploit a range of natural resources and to herd animals to seasonal pasture. To the west, at Freemasons Road, a double row of large oak piles may represent the remains of a wooden footbridge linking the drier ground of the terrace to an island on the Lea floodplain. The piles are among the most substantial known in the region and are of similar form to those from Runneymede Bridge and Vauxhall. The bridge structure seems to have been associated with a series of gullies and postholes representing some form of enclosure perhaps associated with the corralling of animals. At Movers Lane a burnt mound deposit and associated pits located at the edge of a palaeochannel appear to post-date trackway construction and date to the latter part of the 2nd millennium BC, as does a cremation deposit and series of linear features that may define boundaries or drainage systems.

Evidence during the later periods was sparser and probably relates to a period of marine incursion, with the spread of saltmarsh environments and tidal creeks making the area unsuitable for activity. Extensive geoarchaeological and palaeoenvironmental sampling carried out during the lifetime of the project provides an important record of landscape evolution and periods of major change can be detected, both natural and anthropogenically induced. As well as providing a context for the archaeology along the A13, this raises a number of issues regarding the interaction of local communities with the natural environment, how they responded to change and to a certain extent exploited it. Ultimately this is of relevance not only to understanding the past but also to current concerns regarding environmental management along the Thames estuary.

Acknowledgements

The A13 improvements were undertaken under a Design, Build, Finance and Operate (DBFO) contract on behalf of Transport for London (TfL) Street Management, by Road Management Services (A13) plc (RMS). The DBFO contract was awarded in April 2000. Due to the long-running and complex nature of the construction project, the A13 archaeological programme saw an unusually complex interaction between project sponsor, construction contractor and the various archaeological consultants and contractors. The archaeological work was funded by RMS and Transport for London.

Particular thanks are due to Mike Wright and Aidan Murray of the Department's Agent/ Department's Representative (DA/DR) A13 DBFO Site Team for their patience and skill in steering the archaeological project through stormy contractual waters on behalf of Transport for London. The archaeological advisor to the DA/DR team (representing the Project Sponsor, Transport for London) was Oxford Archaeology, who were responsible for supervising the tendering process and monitoring the DBFO construction contractor (RMG) for compliance for the terms of the contract. OA was represented by George Lambrick during the tender evaluation phase, Tim Allen during the preliminary design, Phase I and Phase II evaluation, and Stuart Foreman during the Phase III 'Further Archaeological Works' and post-excavation phases.

External monitoring during the fieldwork, on behalf the local authorities, was undertaken by Nick Truckle of English Heritage (EH) Greater London Archaeological Advisory Service (GLAAS) during the fieldwork, and during the post-excavation by David Divers. Jane Sidell (EH) provided much valuable advice throughout the project.

Chris Place, acting on behalf of Chris Blandford Associates, was appointed Project Archaeologist by RMG in July 2000. He prepared designs for the Phase I and II evaluations and the watching briefs, with detailed input from Ken Whittaker of the main Archaeological Contractor, Gifford and Partners (GP). Martin Bates (University of Wales Trinity Saint David), as sub-consultant to GP, provided key specialist advice in formulating the schemewide research strategy, and subsequently coordinated geoarchaeological activity during the fieldwork and post-excavation assessment phases. Paul Falcini (Wessex Archaeology) took over as Project Archaeologist in June 2001 and produced the Phase III 'Further Archaeological Works Designs'.

All Phase I and Phase II archaeological works (evaluation test pits and trenches) were undertaken by GP, for the most part under the direction of Ken Whittaker (latterly Simon Blatherwick). Pre-Construct Archaeology (PCA) were employed by GP as fieldwork sub-contractor. Phase III of the investigation, comprising a series of formal excavations (including preparation of assessment reports) was split between GP and Wessex Archaeology (WA) for contractual and financial reasons, the former working on Prince Regent Lane and Woolwich Manor Way, the latter on Movers Lane.

In a project beset by numerous practical challenges, special thanks are due to John Brace of RMG for arranging the plant and temporary works that ensured the field teams were able to operate efficiently in a safe working environment. Other staff of RMG who arranged much logistical assistance for the archaeological teams included Brian Patfield (Prince Regent Lane and Movers Lane) and Doug Pratt (Freemasons Road).

Marion White and Mark Beasley coordinated the fieldwork on behalf of GP, under the direction of Ken Whittaker. The Phase I and II evaluations at all sites, and the Phase III fieldwork at Freemasons Road Underpass, were supervised by Alistair Douglas (PCA) who also wrote the assessment reports. Prince Regent Lane was supervised by Mark Beasley and Gary Evans (PCA) while Tim Carew (PCA) supervised the excavation at Woolwich Manor Way. Alistair, Mark, Gary and Tim prepared the context index, archaeological phase descriptions and matrix diagrams and contributed to the assessment reports for their respective sites. The site plans and sections from the PCA sites were prepared by Josephine Brown, Jo Thomas, Cate Davies, Sally Pickard and Cheryl Blundy (PCA). The surveyor was Giles Hammond and the photographer was Richard Young (PCA). Noreena Shopland (GP) prepared the finds catalogue and coordinated the production of the finds assessment reports. Specialist assessments were completed for GP/PCA by Damian Goodburn (worked wood), Louise Rayner and Charlotte Thompson (pottery), Barry Bishop (worked flint), Jane Liddle (animal bone), John Giorgi (plant remains), John Whittaker (microfossils) and John Crowther (soil chemistry). Staff at Royal Holloway, University of London, completed the pollen and diatom assessments, under the direction of Nick Branch. Martin Bates coordinated the geoarchaeological work.

The Phase III excavation at Movers Lane was supervised by Vaughan Birbeck (WA), who also prepared the assessment report. Mike Allen (WA) coordinated palaeoenvironmental assessments for this site, in discussion with Martin Bates (geoarchaeology); in some cases building on work previously undertaken by the GP/PCA specialist team for the Phase II evaluation trenching. John Whittaker assessed the microfossils. Mike Allen and Mark Robinson the charred plant remains and Rob Scaife the pollen.

For the purpose of this project, the DBFO contractors' responsibilities for analysis and reporting were discharged on completion of the post-excavation assessment phase for the individual sites. A scheme-wide Post-Excavation Project Design (PEPD) was prepared by Stuart Foreman and Elizabeth Stafford of Oxford Archaeology (OA), who coordinated the post-excavation specialist analyses and publication, reporting directly, on behalf of the funding body, Transport for London, drawing on the results of the detailed assessment reports produced by GP/PCA and WA. The reasons for this exceptional arrangement were contractual/financial, and provided the only viable means of analysing and reporting on the fieldwork results in an integrated manner, as envisaged in the Project Design.

The main text and associated specialist reports incorporate the work of the following specialists: Radiocarbon dating was undertaken by Beta Analytic Inc. and the Scottish Universities Environmental Research Centre (SUERC). Optically Stimulated Luminescence (OSL) dating was undertaken by Edward Rhodes (then at the University of Oxford). Prehistoric pottery reports were by Alistair Barclay (WA) and Louise Rayner (Archaeology South East, formerly at MoLA). Edward Biddulph (OA) wrote the Roman pottery report and Barry John Bishop the worked flint report. Alison Sheridan (National Museums of Scotland) contributed a report on the jet belt slider from Movers Lane and she thanks Terry Manby for providing information on the Boltby Moor and Blubberhouses Moor sliders. Lorraine Mepham (WA) Charlotte Thompson (MoLA) and Louise Rayner contributed reports on the fired and unfired clay. Pollen from Freemasons Road was analysed by Denise Druce (OA), pollen and diatoms from Woolwich Manor Way by Andrew Haggart (University of Greenwich) and the pollen from Movers Lane by Sylvia Peglar. Ostracods and foraminifera were analysed by John Whittaker (Natural History Museum) and insects by David Smith (University of Birmingham). Waterlogged and charred plant remains were analysed by Ruth Pelling (now at English Heritage). Wood charcoal, waterlogged wood species and age analyses were undertaken by Catherine Barnett (WA). Animal bone was analysed by Lena Strid and Rebecca Nicholson (OA). Human bone from Movers Lane was assessed by Jacqueline McKinley (WA). The sediment micromorphology was undertaken by Richard Macphail (University College London) and the soil chemistry by John Crowther (University of Wales, Trinity Saint David).

The monograph was compiled and designed by Elizabeth Stafford (OA); both Damian Goodburn (MoLA) and Martin Bates (University of Wales, Trinity Saint David) are acknowledged as joint authors in recognition of the central importance of the worked wood and sediment interpretations to the site descriptions, and the fact that their specialist work during the fieldwork, assessment and post excavation stages is entirely integrated within the main text of the volume.

Andy Simmonds (OA) assisted with archive collation, stratigraphic analysis and specialist liason during the early stages of the post excavation analysis. This volume is illustrated by Elizabeth Stafford, Hannah Kennedy, Mark Gridley and Magdalena Wachnik (OA). Frank Meddens (PCA), who contributed to the original project design, provided much valuable advice based on his extensive experience of archaeological work in the Thames marshes, and wrote much of the concluding chapter. Elizabeth Huckerby (OA) provided much useful feedback on aspects of the Holocene vegetation, particularly for Chapter 8. Jon Cotton (FSA, former Curator of Prehistory at the Museum of London) kindly commented on the publication text. Rebecca Nicholson (OA) edited the report. Alex Smith (OA) managed the typesetting and printing.

PART 1: INTRODUCTION AND BACKGROUND

Chapter 1: Introduction

The A13 Thames Gateway DBFO Roadscheme
(Fig. 1.1)

The A13 Thames Gateway DBFO (Design, Build, Finance and Operate) Roadscheme refers to a series of improvements along a 20km stretch of the A13 trunk road through the East London Boroughs of Tower Hamlets, Newham and Barking and Dagenham (Fig. 1.1). The £146 million project was approved as part of the Accelerated Review of the trunk road programme in 1997 and provides a vital link in the east-west transport infrastructure to assist regeneration in East London. The route is of major importance to industry located along the A13 and provides heavy goods vehicle links from Docklands and the Lower Lea Valley to the M25 and Tilbury Docks.

The A13 DBFO contract was awarded to Road Management Services (A13) plc (RMS) by the Highways Agency in April 2000. The contract was novated from the Highways Agency to Transport for London (TfL) under the terms of the Greater London Authority (GLA) Act in July 2000. As part of the 30 year DBFO contract RMS was required to undertake a series of improvements at key junctions or route sections. This included carriageway widening and an additional flyover at the Iron-bridge to Canning Town section (CT), new under-passes and slip roads at the Prince Regent Lane junction (PRL), replacement of an existing flyover and carriageway widening at the Woolwich Manor Way junction (WMW), improvement of the Old Roding Bridge (RB) and a new underpass at the Movers Lane junction (ML). The DBFO contract made provision for a programme of archaeological works to be undertaken in advance of, and during, construction works.

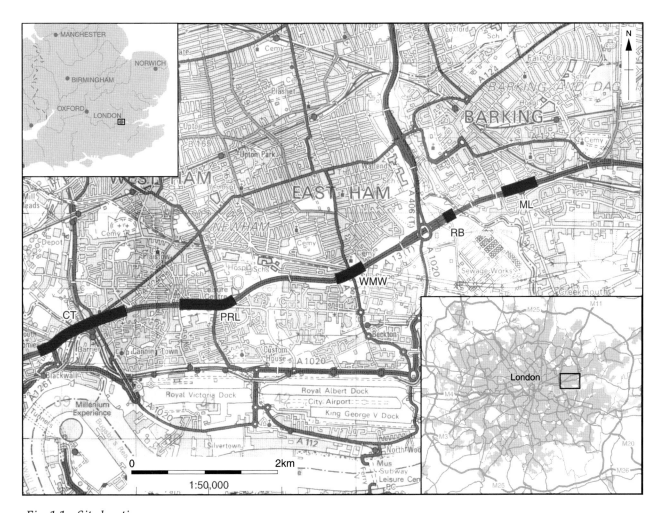

Fig. 1.1 Site location

1

Table 1.1   Summary of phased archaeological investigations

Route section		Phase I evaluation	Phase II evaluation	Phase III excavation	Phase III WB
CT	A13 Ironbridge-Canning Town	•			•
PRL	A13/A112 Prince Regent Lane	•	•	•	•
WMW	A13/A117 Woolwich Manor Way	•	•	•	•
RB	A13 Old Roding Bridge	•			
ML	A13 Movers Lane	•	•	•	•

The route of the A13 at this location runs parallel to the River Thames, traversing the very edge of the Thames gravel terraces and alluvial floodplain. Previous archaeological work has shown the Thames gravel terraces to be one of the most intensively occupied regions of southern England during the prehistoric period and locations on or adjacent to the terrace edge have high potential for preserving waterlogged organic remains, such as timber structures. Three phases of archaeological fieldwork were undertaken between 2000 and 2003 to evaluate and mitigate the impact of the road improvements on potential archaeological sites. Evaluation Phases I and II comprised a series of boreholes, test pits and trenches at five locations and Phase III a series of targeted excavations at three of the five sites, followed by watching briefs during construction work (Table 1.1).

Although not prolific in cultural material, the archaeology recorded covers a wide chronological range representing intermittent activity spanning the Mesolithic through to the post-Roman period. Regionally important evidence of early Neolithic agriculture was recovered during evaluation of the Woolwich Manor Way site, that was subsequently preserved *in situ*. The greatest concentration of activity, however, dates to 2nd millennium BC and includes several waterlogged timber structures and trackways with associated wetland edge occupation. Extensive geoarchaeological and palaeoenvironmental sampling carried out during the lifetime of the project provides an important record of landscape evolution and periods of major change can be detected, both natural and anthropogenically induced. As well as providing a context for the archaeology along the A13, this raises a number of issues regarding the interaction of local communities with the natural environment; how they responded to change and to a certain extent exploited it. Ultimately this is of relevance not only to understanding the past, but also to current concerns regarding environmental management along the Thames estuary today.

Archaeological project history

Due to the long-running and complex nature of the construction project, the A13 archaeological programme saw an unusually complex interaction between project sponsor, construction contractor and the various archaeological consultants and contractors. The responsibilities of the various parties are explained below.

The archaeological advisor to the Departments' Agent team (representing the Project Sponsor, TfL) was Oxford Archaeology (OA), who were responsible for supervising the tendering process and monitoring the Principal Contractor for compliance with the terms of the DBFO contract. OA were represented by George Lambrick during the tender evaluation phase, Tim Allen during the Preliminary Design, Phase I and Phase II evaluation, and Stuart Foreman during the Phase III Further Archaeological Works and post-excavation phases. External monitoring during the fieldwork, on behalf of the local authorities, was undertaken by Nicholas Truckle of English Heritage Greater London Archaeological Advisory Service (GLAAS), assisted by Dr Jane Sidell (English Heritage regional scientific advisor). Christopher Place, acting on behalf of Chris Blandford Associates, was appointed Project Archaeologist by RMG/RMS in July 2000. He prepared designs for the Phase I and II evaluations and the watching briefs, with detailed input from the main archaeological contractor, Ken Whittaker of Gifford and Partners. Dr Martin Bates, as subconsultant to Gifford and Partners, provided specialist geoarchaeological advice in formulating the schemewide research strategy. Paul Falcini of Wessex Archaeology took over as Project Archaeologist in June 2001 and produced the Phase III Further Archaeological Works designs.

All Phase I and Phase II archaeological works were undertaken by Gifford and Partners (GP), under the direction of Ken Whittaker (latterly replaced by Simon Blatherwick). Pre-Construct Archaeology (PCA) were employed by Gifford and Partners as fieldwork sub-contractor. Phase III further archaeological works, including preparation of assessment reports, were split between Gifford and Partners and Wessex Archaeology for contractual reasons, the former working on Prince Regent Lane and Woolwich Manor Way, the latter on Movers Lane.

For the purpose of this project, the DBFO contractors' responsibilities for analysis and reporting were discharged on completion of the post-excavation assessment phase for the individual sites. The scheme-wide post-excavation project design was prepared by Stuart Foreman and Elizabeth Stafford of Oxford Archaeology who coordinated post-excavation specialist analyses and publication, reporting directly on behalf of the funding body, TfL.

Structure of this volume

This volume is divided into three parts. Part I (chapters 1 and 2) summarises the history and aims of the project and provides a general background to contextualise the archaeological discoveries found along the route. It also includes detail of the strategies and methodologies employed during the fieldwork, assessment and specialist analytical stages. Part II (chapters 3-7) focuses on the key sites. Each site is presented as a separate chapter and includes a description of the sediment sequences and associated palaeoecological evidence, followed by a period-based description of the cultural evidence. The description of the cultural evidence primarily focuses on the structural remains, both cut features and timber structures, but also integrates the artefactual evidence where appropriate. The date ranges of the periods used in this volume are presented in Table 1.2. Part III of the volume comprises a series of thematic discussions that summarise the routewide evidence within the wider regional context. Full details of the scientific dating programme,

Table 1.2 Chronology of the archaeological periods referenced in this volume

Period	Date Range
Modern	AD 1800 - Present
Post-medieval	AD 1500 - 1799
Medieval	AD 1066 - 1499
Late Saxon	AD 850 - 1066
Mid Saxon	AD 650- 850
Early Saxon	AD 410 - 650
Late Roman	AD 250 - 410
Mid Roman	AD 150 - 250
Early Roman	AD 43 - 150
Late Iron Age	43 BC- AD 100
Middle Iron Age	400 - 100 BC
Early Iron Age	700 - 400 BC
Late Bronze Age	1100 - 700 BC
Middle Bronze Age	1500 - 1100 BC
Early Bronze Age	2400 - 1500 BC
Later Neolithic	3000 - 2400 BC
Earlier Neolithic	4000 - 3000 BC
Mesolithic	8500 - 4000 BC
Early Post-Glacial	10000 - 8500 BC
Late Glacial (Late Upper Palaeolithic)	12,000 - 10,000 BP
Upper Palaeolithic	30,000 - 10,000 BP
Middle Palaeolithic	150,000 - 30,000 BP
Lower Palaeolithic	500,000 - 150,000 BP

together with detailed specialist reports for both artefactual and palaeoenvironmental remains are included in the appendices.

Geology, topography and recent land-use
(Figs 1.2 and 1.3)

Greater London lies in the centre of the London Basin, an area bounded by the exposed Cretaceous chalk of the Chiltern Hills to the north and north-west, the Berkshire Downs to the west and the North Downs to the south-west and south (Fig. 1.2). To the east the Thames Basin opens onto the North Sea (Sumbler 1996). The chalk extends beneath the entire basin and is overlain by Palaeocene and Eocene deposits. The Palaeocene deposits consist of Thanet Sand and the Lambeth Group (Upnor, Reading and Woolwich Formations) laid down around 60 million years ago. The Eocene deposits consist of London Clay laid down 55 million years ago, in places capped by the Claygate Member and Bagshot Formation (British Geological Survey sheet 257).

Superficial drift deposits occur throughout the central part of Greater London along the course of the River Thames and its tributaries (Fig. 1.3). These deposits are all Quaternary in origin; predominately formed by fluvial or fluvial-glacial action with some periglacial deposits. Boulder clay or till of glacial origin is almost absent from the London area although localised deposits of the Lowestoft Till occur at Chigwell and Havering to the north-east and Finchley Common, Belmont and Chase Side to the west. The most extensive drift deposits are found in West London where gravels relating to a number of phases of river downcutting and terrace formation underlie most of Hammersmith to Slough and Egham. Other substantial deposits occur in the Lea Valley and to the north-east at Tower Hamlets to Havering. The terrace gravels are variably capped by expanses of Langley Silts ('brickearths') which are especially extensive and deep in the areas to the west of London. The youngest of the terrace gravels in the valley bottoms are capped by Holocene (*c* 10,000 years to present) alluvial deposits, which occur along river margins. In Central and East London these deposits are extensive from Westminster downstream, with significant deposits in the Thames, Lea, Roding, Darent and Mar Dyke valleys.

The A13 Thames Gateway route begins on the low-lying floodplain, to the north-east of the Isle of Dogs peninsular, in the London Borough of Tower Hamlets. At this point it is in the valley of the River Lea, a tributary of the Thames. From here the route extends eastwards across the London Borough of Newham, running parallel with the edge of the gravel terraces and floodplain. Exceptions to this are where the route crosses the River Roding into the London Borough of Barking and Dagenham. Recent landuse along the route predominantly comprises urban and industrial areas and in places

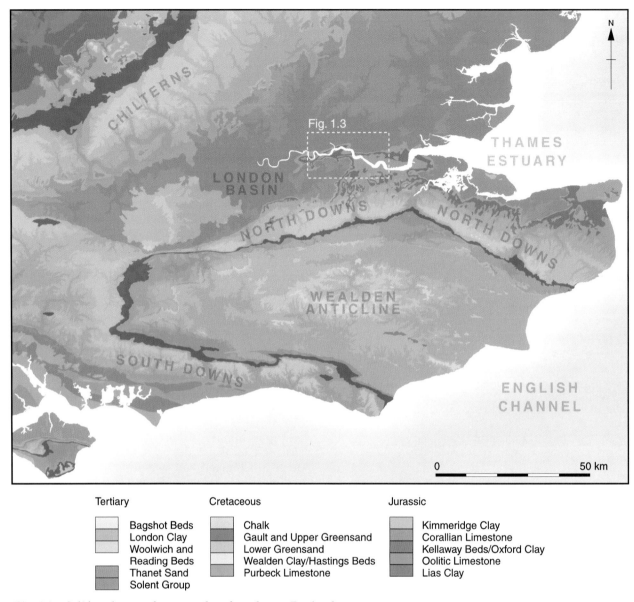

Tertiary

	Bagshot Beds
	London Clay
	Woolwich and Reading Beds
	Thanet Sand
	Solent Group

Cretaceous

	Chalk
	Gault and Upper Greensand
	Lower Greensand
	Wealden Clay/Hastings Beds
	Purbeck Limestone

Jurassic

	Kimmeridge Clay
	Corallian Limestone
	Kellaway Beds/Oxford Clay
	Oolitic Limestone
	Lias Clay

Fig. 1.2   Solid geology and topography of south-east England

a significant thickness of modern deposits mask the underlying Holocene alluvial sediments and the natural topography of the terrace gravels.

Geoarchaeological and environmental background (Fig. 1.4)

In order to understand fully the character and distribution of archaeological sites in the lower estuary area and the reasons behind major changes in settlement patterns in the past it is necessary to understand the changing nature of the estuary. The geological history of the Thames is complex. Today the estuary is characterised as "tide-dominated" (*sensu* Dalrymple *et al.* 1992) in which major sandbars occur within the outer estuary area, a marine-dominated zone, and tidal meanders in an inner mixed energy zone (Fig. 1.4, Bates and Stafford forthcoming; Bates and Whittaker 2004).

The recent geomorphologic development of the area and the establishment of the modern topography have resulted from major drainage pattern modifications during the Quaternary. The Pleistocene deposits of the Lower Thames have been extensively studied (Gibbard 1985; Bridgland 1994; 1995; Bridgland *et al.* 1995). Deposition in the Thames Valley began in the late Anglian stage (*c* 500,000 BP) and continued intermittently throughout the Pleistocene. Sediments, deposited in cold climate braided stream systems, exist as wedges of sand and gravel on the valley sides, subsequently eroded by fluvial incision during periods of lowered sea level to create terraces. The most recent episodes of gravel deposition formed the Shepperton Gravels in the valley bottom. Despite extensive research on the Pleistocene deposits however, considerable controversy exists regarding the age of some of the older aggradational units and their

4

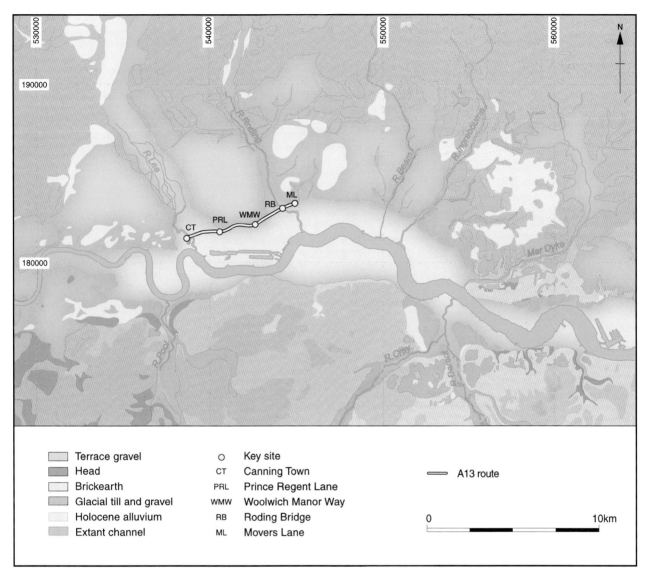

Terrace gravel
Head
Brickearth
Glacial till and gravel
Holocene alluvium
Extant channel

○ Key site
CT Canning Town
PRL Prince Regent Lane
WMW Woolwich Manor Way
RB Roding Bridge
ML Movers Lane

═══ A13 route

0   10km

Fig. 1.3   Quaternary geology of East London

correlation with the global oxygen isotope strati-graphy (Gibbard 1994; Bridgland 1994).

The surface of the valley bottom gravels formed the 'template' over which alluvial and estuarine sediments were later deposited, during the Holo-cene. The landscape during this period saw a number of changes, largely attributed to a rise in sea level caused by the continued shrinking of the polar ice caps and tectonic subsidence. The Holocene sediments form a wedge thickening downstream, from less than 2m at Tower Bridge to a maximum thickness of 35m east of the study area at Canvey Island (Marsland 1986). Within the inner estuary, Holocene sediments consist of complex sequences of minerogenic and organic clay, silts, sands and peats, deposited in a variety of environments repre-senting variously: freshwater alder carr, fen, reedswamp, intertidal saltmarsh and mudflats.

In contrast to the relatively well known sequences of the Pleistocene, the nature of the Holocene sediments deposited during the last 12,000 years are

not well understood and have, with few exceptions, only been described superficially. Over the years the most commonly adopted stratigraphic sequence for the Lower Thames has been based on work under-taken by Devoy (Devoy 1977; 1979; 1980 and 1982). Borehole stratigraphies were integrated with biostratigraphic studies to infer successive phases of marine transgressions (Thames I-V) represented by clay/silt units, and regressions (Tilbury I-V) repre-sented by peat units. Devoy constructed two age-altitude curves of relative sea level movement, one for Tilbury (outer estuary) and one for Crossness, Dartford and Broadness (inner estuary). The model suggests transgressions occurred in the Palaeolithic to early Mesolithic periods, the late Mesolithic to early Neolithic periods, throughout the Bronze Age, the middle Iron Age and at the beginning of the 4th century AD.

The 'Thames-Tilbury' model is regarded as the seminal work in this area (Haggart 1995) and has been widely applied by researchers outside the

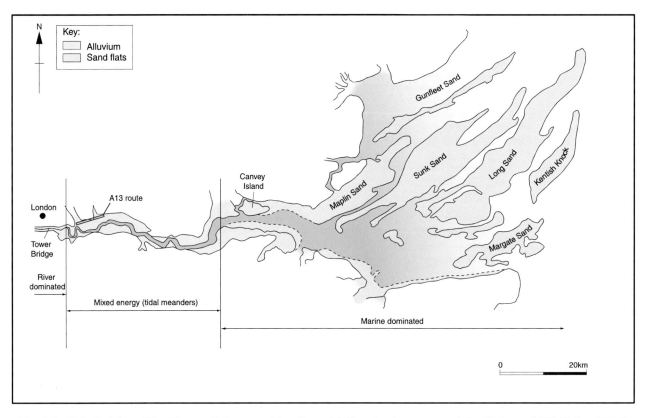

Fig. 1.4 Sub-division of the Thames Estuary and location of different estuary zones (after Bates and Whittaker 2004)

original study area. It should be noted, however, that more recent work (Bates 1999; Bates and Barham 1995; Bates and Stafford forthcoming; Haggart 1995; Sidell *et al.* 2000; Sidell *et al.* 2002; Sidell and Wilkinson 2004) has highlighted several problems, such as the need for two age/altitude curves, suggesting it cannot always be easily applied to the whole of the Thames Estuary, either in terms of lithology or age/altitude analysis. This reflects the complex nature of the floodplain environment during this period, consisting of peat forming communities, migrating channels and sand eyots (Sidell *et al.* 2000). More recently a simplified (tripartite) model for floodplain development has been presented by Long *et al.* (2000). A similar model was presented by Bates and Whittaker (2004) which examined the likely impact of these changes on human activity (Table 1.3). This latter cultural landscape model has been utilised and developed during the various stages of work on the A13 scheme in order to contextualize the archaeological remains discovered and provide a framework of investigation (Table 1.3).

Bates and Whittaker (2004) pointed out that one of the consequences of the Devoy model for archaeologists, and the use of pollen analysis to aid vegetation reconstruction and understand sea-level changes, has been a focus on the landscape at a regional scale. The nature and archaeological context of sites vary considerably across the landscape as a result of environmental as well as cultural factors (for example the location of tribu-

taries, areas of local impeded drainage and the presence of local topographic features). Consequently the scale and focus of palaeoenvironmental reconstruction may require refinement for archaeological purposes. Over the last two decades a number of detailed site-specific investigations have been undertaken, many in association with developer-funded archaeological work (Fig. 8.2), for example the Jubilee Line Extension (Sidell *et al.*. 2000), High Speed 1, formerly known as the Channel Tunnel Rail Link (Bates and Stafford forthcoming), various sites in Southwark (Sidell *et al.* 2002) and excavations at Silvertown (Wilkinson *et al.* 2000; Crockett *et al.* 2002). Many of these investigations are located at floodplain-terrace edge and tributary locations and begin to address the complex range of factors responsible for sequence accumulation.

Archaeological background (Figs 1.5 and 1.6)

The low-lying areas of the Inner Thames Estuary have been shown to contain a varied archaeological resource dating to the prehistoric period. This includes surface middens, lithic concentrations representing flint procurement, knapping and hunting camps and other features such as wooden structures. It is only relatively recently, however, that the importance of wetland contexts has been fully recognised (Bates and Barham 1995; Meddens and Beasley 1990; Merriman 1992; Rackam 1994). This is most probably due to the problems of access

Table 1.3 Lower Thames Cultural landscape model (from Bates and Whittaker 2004)

Model Stage	Time frame	Geological events	Dominant sediment type	Inferred environments	Associated archaeology
1a	15-30ka B.P.	Reworking of the East Tilbury Marshes Gravel	Sands and gravels	Cold climate periglacial slopes with active solifluction and possible loess blow	Occasional activity associated with channel margins and sporadic finds across floodplain surface. Most finds reworked
1b	10-15ka B.P.	*Downcutting* Deposition of the Shepperton Gravel	Sands and gravels	*Active erosion* Braided channels	
2	8-10ka B.P.	Landscape stability	Some sand deposition in meandering channels, elsewhere weathering of late Devensian sediments to form soils	Development of woodlands and meandering channels on floodplain	Occasional activity associated with channel margins and sporadic finds across floodplain surface. Some reworked finds
3	5-8ka B.P.	Sea-level rise resulting in transgression of marine/estuarine conditions from outer estuary into inner estuary and progressive backing-up of lower reaches of freshwater channels	Fine grained silts, clays and sands	Expanded freshwater marshland systems resulting from back-up of lower reaches of river channels giving way to estuarine channels and saltmarsh systems	Occasional activity associated with channel margins and sporadic finds across floodplain surface. Occupation becoming focused on drier ground at margins of floodplain. Mixed *in situ* and reworked finds
4	3-5ka B.P.	Expansion of semi-terrestrial wetlands and marshes giving way to coastal marshlands during phase of apparent relative sea-level fall	Peats and organic silts with minerogenic sedimentation in channels	Alder carr wetlands with replacement brackish marshland towards end of phase	Extensive occupation of the dry ground at the margins of the floodplain as well as activity on remnant 'islands' of sand and gravel within the floodplain. Construction of wooden trackways at the edges of the marsh in places. *In situ* material probably common
5	3-1ka B.P.	Expansion of brackish water conditions due to rising relative sea level.	Fine grained silts, clays and sands	Estuarine channels and saltmarsh systems	Activity sporadically throughout the flood plain with evidence for resource gathering/hunting and watercraft and infrastructure. Eventual colonisation of floodplain with land reclamation
6	1ka B.P.+	Continued rise in relative sea level	None	Managed floodplains	Drainage systems, land reclamation, construction of tidal defences. Waterside structures.

within urban and floodplain areas where the deposits are often deeply buried in waterlogged conditions

The A13 lies at the foot of the latest terrace formed between 110,000 and 13,000 BP. The few Palaeolithic stone tools that have been associated with the gravels are frequently tools that have been washed down from higher, earlier, terrace deposits (Wymer 1991; 1999; Merriman 1990; Gibbard 1994). Evidence is largely confined to isolated find spots which in the vicinity of the A13 include finds from the basal Mucking gravel at Upton Park, Forest Gate, Manor Park and Little Ilford (Wymer 1999, map 10).

During the Mesolithic period the climate gradually became warmer and as sea level rose Britain eventually became an island separated from mainland Europe. Temporary campsites or hunting sites have been excavated in the London region. The favoured locations for such sites are along the Thames itself and in tributary valleys such as the Colne and the Lea, with a particular emphasis on floodplain edges, high points within the valley floors, and areas adjacent to the main channels (see for example Lewis with Rackham 2011; Corcoran *et al.* 2011). The majority of archaeological remains recorded in the Greater London Sites and Monuments Register (GLSMR) consist of single finds of flint artefacts, although larger assemblages have also been recorded in low-lying areas to the west of the study area , for example Three Ways Wharf, Uxbridge and the B&Q site in Bermondsey. To the east of the City, Mesolithic finds are notably sparse. A few flint artefacts have been recovered from the Lower Lea Valley in Newham, including an assemblage from Stratford Market Depot, approximately 2km to the northeast of the A13/A1011 junction at Canning Town. Several axes and a disturbed knapping site have also been recorded close to the Hackney Brook some distance upstream (Lacaille 1961; Harding and Gibbard 1983). On the Thames floodplain, in Newham, a flint flake was recovered at Beckton Gasworks, approximately 1km southwest of the A13 junction with Woolwich Manor Way. Further to the east flint artefacts have been recovered along the terrace edge at Rainham and Wennington, between 7km and 10km east of the Movers Lane Junction.

The Neolithic period saw the beginnings of the spread of agriculture, which eventually led to a fundamental change both in the landscape of the Lower Thames valley and in the lifestyle of its inhabitants. Riverside occupation sites such as Runnymede to the west of London or in the east at Brookway, Rainham, have provided the earliest evidence of more permanent settlements with houses and domestic waste deposited in tree-throws, pits and middens, although the evidence does suggest that people were still relying very much on gathering local wild fruit, nuts and shellfish. To the west of Central London, however, higher areas overlooking the floodplain have been described as ritual or

monumental landscapes (Merriman 1990, 22). Excavations have revealed surprisingly large numbers of monuments which include causewayed enclosures which have been interpreted as ritual meeting places, for example at Staines (Robertson-Mackay 1987), Eton Wick (Ford 1983; 1986) and Dorney (Allen *et al.* forthcoming). A series of cursus monuments have been located under the western edge of Heathrow Airport, including the so-called Stanwell cursus, an embanked avenue some 2.5 miles in length (Framework Archaeology 2006; 2010).

Low-lying late Mesolithic and Neolithic sites predominantly occur on stable terrestrial surfaces, formed on the top of late Pleistocene deposits or the 'topographic template'. These are typically sand bodies where well-developed palaeosols exist. The environment appears to have been one of closed mixed deciduous woodland on a stable floodplain, although there was variation in terms of species composition associated with changes in local topography and hydrology (for example at Erith: Seel 2000). The surface of the Shepperton gravels was, on the whole, accessible during the Mesolithic prior to flooding caused by marine transgression which began around 6000-7000 BP. Sea-level fluctuations and hydrological changes restricted later dry land activity to increasingly smaller areas of higher valley bottom terrain. In some areas, however, this surface remained accessible in the valley bottoms until the first millennium (Bates and Whittaker 2004). Excavations in East London by the Newham Museum Service and others (in particular the Thames Valley Archaeological Service (TVAS), Pre-Construct Archaeology (PCA) and Museum of London Archaeology (MoLA)) have produced some evidence for Neolithic occupation in this area, although generally sites are still quite rare. In the vicinity of the A13, a mixed flint assemblage associated with soil horizons containing burnt flint and pottery of Neolithic and Bronze Age date was identified at Royal Docks Community School, Custom House, approximately 500m to the south of the A13 Prince Regent Lane junction on the Thames floodplain (Holder 1998) (Fig 1.5, 1). At Fort Street, Silvertown, approximately 1.5km to the south of the A13 in the same area, a wooden trackway over marshy ground seems to have been constructed, anchored with posts driven vertically into the ground (Crockett *et al.* 2002) (Fig. 1.5, 2). To the north, in the Lea Valley finds include an axe hoard from Temple Mills, Stratford (Holgate 1988, 285) and single finds of flint axes at Manor Road and Stratford Market Depot, between 4.5km and 2km to the north-east of the A13/A1011 junction at Canning Town (MoLAS 2000). A number of finds have also been located to the east of the route, along the edge of the floodplain and gravel terrace at Rainham which include pits, flintwork and pottery at Brook Way Allotments and Bridge Road (ibid.).

During the Bronze Age there is firm evidence for the establishment of field systems that replaced or appeared amongst the earlier, and still relatively

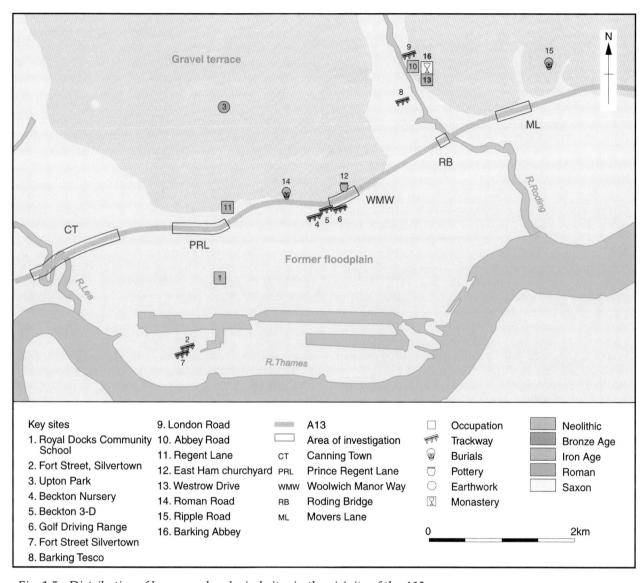

Key sites
1. Royal Docks Community School
2. Fort Street, Silvertown
3. Upton Park
4. Beckton Nursery
5. Beckton 3-D
6. Golf Driving Range
7. Fort Street Silvertown
8. Barking Tesco

9. London Road
10. Abbey Road
11. Regent Lane
12. East Ham churchyard
13. Westrow Drive
14. Roman Road
15. Ripple Road
16. Barking Abbey

A13
Area of investigation
CT   Canning Town
PRL Prince Regent Lane
WMW Woolwich Manor Way
RB   Roding Bridge
ML   Movers Lane

Occupation
Trackway
Burials
Pottery
Earthwork
Monastery

Neolithic
Bronze Age
Iron Age
Roman
Saxon

0   2km

Fig. 1.5   Distribution of known archaeological sites in the vicinity of the A13

forested, landscape. Large excavations at Heathrow and further upstream at Eton have found the remains of ditches which marked the field boundaries (Framework Archaeology 2006 and 2010; Allen *et al.* forthcoming). More direct evidence of arable agriculture has been found at sites in north Southwark and Bermondsey, where a dense patchwork of marks in the subsoil have been interpreted as ard marks (Sidell *et al.* 2002, 35-7). There is also evidence of increasing wealth in the Bronze Age as the London area became a centre for production and consumption of bronze. It seems likely that society became more hierarchical and possibly more violent too, as a warrior aristocracy emerged who controlled land and competed for wealth and prestige. Late Bronze Age defended settlements, where metalworking and exchange were probably carried out, have been identified at Carshalton and at Mayfield Farm, near Heathrow although the date of the latter site remains open (J. Cotton pers. comm.). Evidence of religious practice

comes from a few early Bronze Age burial mounds, such as that at Teddington and a number of middle Bronze Age cremation cemeteries found in West London (eg Barrett 1973). Few settlement sites have so far been located in East London. The majority of the evidence comes from the higher ground on the gravel terraces. Isolated pits and artefact assemblages have been found in the Lower Lea and Roding Valleys and in a ring ditch at Upton Park (Fig. 1.5, 3). At Rainham, a late Bronze Age ring work associated with buildings, field systems and cremation burials was excavated at Scott and Albyn's Farm, on the terrace overlooking the Ingrebourne River (Guttmann and Last 2000). Nearby and on lower lying ground on the flood-plain, evidence for animal husbandry was found in the form of a wattle enclosure fence and evidence of trampling by cattle in the sediments on the stone causeway (Meddens 1996). Further evidence of field systems has also been identified further up the Ingrebourne Valley at Hornchurch

Aerodrome and Hacton Lane, Upminster (MoLAS 2000; Howell *et al.* 2011).

A large quantity of late Bronze Age luxury metal work and some human remains have been found during dredging of the Thames: it would seem that the river was a focus for religious ritual and possibly cremation and inhumation burial towards the end of the Bronze Age (Merriman 1990; Rackham 1994). Of note are the finds of two socketed axes on the Barking marshes, some 700m south of the A13/A117 Woolwich Manor Way junction, adjacent to the River Roding (MoLAS 2000).

Recent work in East London has identified a number of trackways dating to this period, in which piles, brushwood, wattle hurdles and logs were used to build timber causeways over the wet marshland. In the vicinity of the A13 a series of wooden trackways have been located at Beckton Nursery (Fig. 1.5, 4) the Beckton 3D site (Fig. 1.5, 5) (Meddens 1996) and most recently the Golf Driving Range (Fig. 1.5, 6; Carew *et al.* 2010) between 350m and 150m south-west of the A13/A117 Woolwich Manor Way junction. Trackways have been identified in association with peat deposits at the edge of the terrace in the Roding Valley at the Barking Tesco and London Road sites, 0.5km and 1.5m north of the A13/A406 junction (Fig. 1.5, 8 and 9; Meddens 1996). Three kilometres to the east of Movers Lane, at the Hayes Storage site in Dagenham, a 'causeway' 4m wide and 0.27m deep constructed from pebbles, sandy silts and burnt flint was traced for 23m, sandwiched between peat deposits (Divers 1996). At Bridge Road, Rainham, a brushwood trackway was located on the bank of the Ingrebourne River (Meddens 1996). A number of other wooden structures have also been identified in Westminster and on the south bank of the Thames in Southwark and Bexley (Meddens and Beasley 1990; MoLAS 2000).

The gravel terraces of the Lower Thames are known to have been intensively settled in the Iron Age and Roman periods (Wilkinson 1988) with the development of London as a major provincial capital and the subsequent remodelling of the surrounding economies. The gravel terrace was still the focus for occupation and it is possible that the first elements of the marshland draining process may have begun at this time. Significant changes in this period include the growth of salt-making as an important activity along the estuarine and coastal margins (ibid.). Archaeological excavations have produced evidence of Iron Age agricultural hamlets and villages at sites such as Heathrow and Dawley in West London and Rainham in the east. Increasing numbers of defensive hillforts and settlements were built. Several are known in East London, such as Loughton Camp and Ambresbury Banks in Epping Forest and the later very large univallate enclosure at Uphall Camp on the River Roding in Ilford. The Thames during this period continued as an important transport route and a setting for ritual activities (Merriman 1990; Rackham 1994). Evidence for Iron Age occupation at the terrace edge and on the floodplain in east London is currently sparse. However, Iron Age settlement has been recorded at Abbey Road, Barking (Fig. 1.5; 10) and across the river at the Woolwich Arsenal site.

The Roman city of *Londinium* was founded soon after the Roman invasion under Emperor Claudius in AD 43; a wooden drain by the side of the main Roman road at No. 1 Poultry was dated by dendrochronology to AD 47 (Hill and Rowsome 2011). The land east of *Londinium* is crossed by several roads, including the main Roman road to Colchester (*Camulodunum*) (Brown 2008). These roads probably crossed the tributary rivers of the Thames on the higher gravels to the north of the study area. East of the River Lea, the London to Colchester highway probably follows the line of the Romford Road in Stratford where a section, assumed to be Roman by virtue of its position directly above natural gravels, was observed in 1963 in front of the Passmore Edwards Museum. Settlement evidence is associated with roads and river crossings as at Old Ford on the River Lea, 2.5km north of the A13. The area was probably agricultural land occupied by small settlements, farmsteads or villas exploiting the fertile soils of the gravels and managing the timber resource. A Roman farmstead was identified approximately 400m north-east of the A13/A112 Prince Regent Lane junction (Fig. 1.5, 11) and a pottery assemblage and building debris was also recovered from East Ham churchyard approximately 100m north of A13/A117 Woolwich Manor Way junction (Fig. 1.5, 12). Settlement evidence has also been recorded at Westrow Drive, approximately 1.4km north-west of Movers Lane (Fig. 1.5, 13) and at a number of other sites on the terraces to the east (Howell *et al.* 2011). On the gravel terraces to the east around Rainham numerous Roman period settlement sites have been excavated; these include field systems, ditched enclosures and farmsteads from sites such as Moor Hall Farm, Hunt's Hill Farm, Whitehall Wood and Manor Farm (ibid.). Roman burial sites have been found at Roman Road, East Ham, approximately 150m north of the A13, between Prince Regent Lane and Woolwich Manor Way (Fig. 1.5, 14) and at Ripple Road, approximately 1km north-east of Movers Lane (Fig. 1.5, 15).

As the city of London regained importance towards the end of the Anglo-Saxon period, the recognisable pattern and place-names of the surrounding villages began to form. The origins of East Ham and West Ham, Plaistow and Beckton probably date to this period. Much of the floodplain of East London was by now marshland as a result of the continued relative rise of the Thames. Barking and Dagenham both appear to have developed as local centres during the Anglo-Saxon period. Dagenham is first mentioned in AD 690 and an abbey of Benedictine nuns was founded at Barking in AD 666. The remains of the abbey buildings, scheduled as an ancient monument, are located

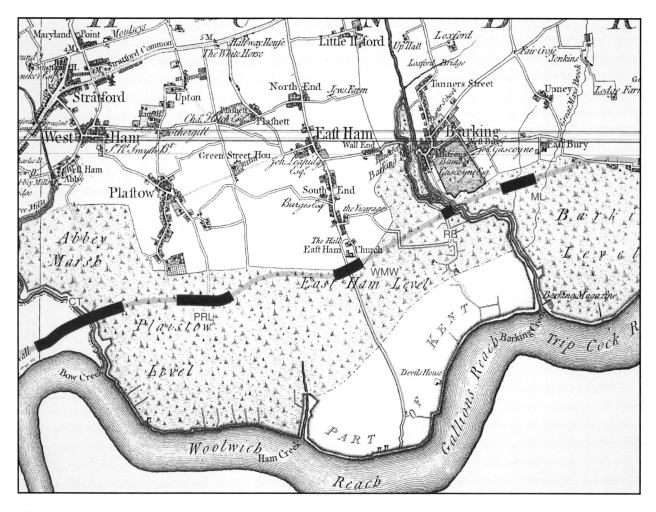

Fig. 1.6   Chapman and Andre's map (1777)

approximately 1km north of the A13 on the east bank of the River Roding (Fig. 1.5, 16). A recent evaluation in Rainham on the lower edge of the gravel terrace overlooking the River Ingrebourne, 500m north of the A13/Dovers Corner junction, revealed regionally important late Roman (AD 360-410) and early Saxon (AD 410-550) pottery, field ditches and a well (MoLAS 2000).

A number of medieval manors are known to have existed in the area. By the 13th century the marshes, which were prone to frequent flooding, were used for fishing, fowling, grazing, reed growing and tanning. There are references to floods, marshland management and river defences throughout the medieval period, although more systematic reclamation was undertaken from the 16th and 17th centuries. By the 18th century the

marshland areas in the vicinity of the Route were known as the Plaistow, East Ham and Barking Levels, as illustrated on Chapman and Andre's map of 1777 (Fig. 1.6).

As London became an increasingly important port, the East London area became a zone for industrial expansion. Former villages were swallowed up by the expansion of London: quays and later huge docks were built along the north of the River Thames and the marshland of the flood-plain began to be drained for agriculture and settlement. The historic character of the marshland over a large part of East London has largely disappeared through reclamation and recent development and at the time of the investigations most of the buildings along the A13 route were 20th century industrial or residential.

Chapter 2: Aims and Methodologies

Project aims

At the outset of the project an Outline Archaeological Strategy (OAS) was prepared which set out the general aims of the project. The over-arching aim was to consider how the unique and local patterns of prehistoric human habitation, and the environmental sequences, compare with others within the Lower Thames Valley. The project was designed to consider evidence contributing to established cultural models and mechanisms of environmental change, including the transition from hunter/gathering to agriculture, the exploitation of diverse and changing wetland environments, sea-level rise and climate change along terrace edge locations. Where possible it was intended that this generic approach should proceed to the construction of a specific historical narrative in which the relationships between past cultural events and the detailed pattern of habitation would form the subject of focused investigation. Implicit in this from the outset was a strong reliance on geoarchaeological techniques and paleoenvironmental evidence to help understand the evolution of the landscape relating to the sites.

The OAS was followed by a more detailed Preliminary Archaeological Investigation Design (PAID). The PAID included a desk-based assessment of the known archaeology along the route and set out the scheme-wide research aims and objectives and the scope of the initial field evaluation programme. The PAID was developed through consultation with English Heritage (EH) and the Greater London Archaeological Advisory Service (GLAAS). This was an ongoing process throughout the duration of the project and was structured to incorporate route-wide considerations, such as research aims, as well as site specific issues, such as exploratory hole locations and sampling strategies. Road Management Services (A13 plc (RMS)) was keen to ensure that any archaeological works were undertaken with reference to relevant emerging research frameworks (eg MoLAS 2000; Sidell *et al.* 2000). In general the aims set out in the PAID were to:

- establish, as far as reasonably practicable the locations, extent, character, date and significance of any archaeological or palaeoenvironmental remains or deposits
- assess the significance of deposits/remains and the need for Further Archaeological Works
- reduce the risk of unforeseen archaeological remains being encountered during construction

- where possible within the context of the Scheme, provide benefit to the wider community by undertaking meaningful archaeological works against a series of considered research questions.

More specifically, the archaeological works were designed to investigate potential buried channels and the terrace edge, to locate any remains of prehistoric or Roman settlement or other permanent or temporary activities such as trackways, causeways, enclosures, revetments, waterfronts and artefact concentrations, with a view to:

- determine the nature, extent and date of such activities and any shifts in location through time
- recover evidence to help understand the nature and extent of human exploitation of local riparian locations and adaptations to wetland environments
- determine whether the Becton 3-D trackway and any associated or adjacent structures continue into the Woolwich Manor Way sections of the Scheme
- recover evidence from trackways and other wood structures to determine the nature of prehistoric technology, construction techniques and woodland management
- determine whether there are any physical remains of the possible East Ham High Street Roman Road and any contemporary activity adjacent to it
- determine whether any prehistoric or Roman waterfront features are present along the River Roding
- investigate current and buried channels to locate any remains of medieval and post-medieval activity such as revetments, waterfronts and boats
- identify the surface topography of the present Floodplain Terrace and the nature of the contact between any overlying deposits
- identify the nature of past fluvial conditions and date the migration of the Thames' tidal head across the Scheme area
- characterise the changing ecology with the aim of dating general trends and specific events across the Scheme area
- identify the likely dates, causes and processes by which the prehistoric peat formed.

Following the completion of the evaluation phases the following aims were defined for the mitigation works, each applicable to all three sites:

- to describe the sequence, timing and character of prehistoric cultural and related environmental events at each site
- to resolve the phasing of landscape development through facies definition
- to define within each phase the associations and spatial arrangement between related cultural stratigraphic units and groups of units
- to describe the cultural character of each stage of landscape development in terms of function and duration
- to describe a comprehensive structural sequence and identify the relationship between periods of cultural activity in order to identify priorities for specific enquiry
- to further define the resolution for dating and analysing cultural and environmental phases and events through the recovery of stratified cultural and environmental studies
- to determine whether the character and timing of late Mesolithic/early Neolithic activities in the Lower Thames floodplain provides insights on the adaptation/adoption of an agricultural subsistence base
- to consider if the construction of trackways to access the Lower Thames floodplain during the Bronze Age is related to processes of agricultural intensification and 'rituals of reproduction' on the adjoining terraces
- to consider whether local technological, social, ritual and economic strategies/adaptations were geared to mitigate/exploit circumstances related to environmental change
- to recover evidence for the mechanisms driving local environmental change, including climate change and relative sea level rise.

As the archaeology and sediment sequences recorded during the excavations were largely as expected from the previous work, the majority of the excavation aims remained relevant for the post excavation analytical stage. However, apart from *in situ* material retrieved from T15 at Woolwich Manor Way, only a small amount of evidence was retrieved from the late Mesolithic to early Neolithic period. It was therefore thought unlikely that much could be done 'to determine whether the character and timing of late Mesolithic/early Neolithic activities in the Lower Thames floodplain provides insights on the adaptation/adoption of an agricultural subsistence base'. Although a number of Bronze Age trackways were identified at Woolwich Manor Way and Movers Lane, only a relatively small section of each was uncovered. Without knowing the origin or destination, the potential 'to consider if the construction of trackways to access the Lower

Thames floodplain during the Bronze Age is related to processes of agricultural intensification and 'rituals of reproduction' on the adjoining terraces' is restricted. However, the trackways did offer the potential to investigate the technological aspects of their construction which allows comparison with other similar structures both in the Lower Thames and elsewhere.

Fieldwork

Evaluation

The evaluation programme was split between two phases. Phase I comprised a series of 9 boreholes and 54 test pits (TPs) (Table 2.1). The aim of the investigations was to assess the potential for archaeological remains based on a description of the Holocene sedimentary facies and the characterisation of the local archaeological landscape at locations affected by the proposed construction of the A13. The fieldwork was carried out between August and November 2000.

The boreholes were drilled using a cable-percussion rig capable of drilling and casing to depths of more than 20m below ground level through a variety of sediments including made-ground, sand and gravel. Continuous sequences of U4/U100 cores were collected from suitable fine grained and organic sediments at each borehole location. Drilling was monitored at all times under the supervision of the project geoarchaeologist and a description of the sediments and sample locations recorded on pro-forma borehole description sheets.

Test pits were normally 3m x 2m in plan at their base, allowing for the insertion of sheet metal piles or shoring boxes. Access to some test pits, however, was limited where site constraints prevented the installation of shoring. All alluvial deposits were removed in spits no more than 150mm thick with organic deposits in spits of no more than 100mm. All spoil was carefully examined to recover samples of cultural material, by appropriately qualified personnel with experience of excavating alluvial sequences. Care was taken to identify deposits that may have resulted from human activity, or which displayed features indicative of human activity such as worked wood, charcoal horizons or the presence of midden or burnt mound material. Where a cultural horizon was identified during machining, machining ceased while the appropriate hand excavation, recording and sampling took place. The stratigraphic sequence in each test pit was recorded by the project geoarchaeologist and sampling was carried out as appropriate

The Phase II trial trenching comprised the excavation of 25 trenches and was intended to focus on those areas identified in Phase I to be of high archaeological potential (Table 2.1). The fieldwork was carried out at three junctions: Prince Regent Lane, Woolwich Manor Way and Movers Lane, between October 2000 and March 2001.

Table 2.1 Summary of Phase I and II preliminary investigations

| Route section | Phase I | | | Phase II | |
	Site Code	No. test pits	No. boreholes	Site Code	No. trenches
A13 Ironbridge-Canning Town	TGW00	4	4	-	-
A13/A112 Prince Regent Lane	TGW00	18	-	PGL00	7
A13/A117 Woolwich Manor Way	TGW00	16	-	WMW00	6
A13 Old Roding Bridge	TGW00	-	5	-	-
A13 Movers Lane	TGW00	16	-	MOE00	12
Totals		54	9		25

Based on the results of the Phase I investigations and limited impact of the Scheme, no Phase II trenches were excavated at Ironbridge-Canning Town and Roding Bridge; further work was restricted to a watching brief during construction. The Phase II trenches varied in size depending on the area of the proposed construction impacts. Excavation was similar to the Phase I test pits. Modern overburden and alluvial deposits were removed by machine in spits until the first archaeological horizon was encountered. At this point machining ceased while the appropriate hand excavation, recording and sampling took place. Edge support was achieved by a combination of stepping and shoring techniques.

Excavation

Phase III Further Archaeological Works comprised a series of open area excavations targeted on archaeological deposits within the limits imposed by construction impacts. At Prince Regent Lane this was conducted by cofferdam excavation at Freemasons Road Underpass (Areas A and B) to excavate the Bronze Age timber piled structure identified during the evaluation. The fieldwork was carried out between October and November 2001. Excavations at Woolwich Manor Way in May 2002 consisted of two small trenches (Areas 1 and 2) to the west of the junction to mitigate the impact of flyover abutments on a series of Bronze Age brushwood trackways. Mitigation work at Movers Lane between August and October 2001 included two open area strips (Areas 2 and 3), located to the east and west of the junction to excavate prehistoric

activity on the terrace gravels and the brushwood trackways identified during the Phase II works. A watching brief during construction was also maintained on earthworks at Ironbridge-Canning Town, Prince Regent Lane, Woolwich Manor Way and Movers Lane.

Geoarchaeological and palaeoenvironmental investigations

The facies-based approach to sediment recording

Throughout all fieldwork stages a facies-based approach was adopted towards the recording of sediment sequences. Sedimentary facies are a unique set of characteristics that relate to individual environments of deposition. Differing environments, in which sedimentation processes vary, will develop unique sets of traits that change across the landscape as the processes responsible for the sequence of development change. Consequently if analogy is used to link processes observable in modern environments to sets of properties of sediments, we can use this information to infer past conditions. The suite of sedimentary characteristics selected for inquiry can also be designed to reveal cultural components or signatures. This information can be subsequently used to describe the nature of the depositional environments, establish archaeological data potential (preservation and survival) and infer the nature of the generic landscapes of archaeological relevance, with particular reference to broader patterns of land-use.

This approach to recording sedimentary units developed as a practical reaction to the integration of

Table 2.2 Summary of Phase III investigations

Route section	Contractor	Site Code	Area
A13/A112 Prince Regent Lane (Freemasons Road Underpass)	PCA/Gifford	FRU01	Area A
			Area B
A13/A117 Woolwich Manor Way	PCA/Gifford	WMA02	Area 1
			Area 2
A13 Movers Lane	Wessex Archaeology	RIR01	Area 2
			Area 3

borehole and geotechnical test pit data with archaeological purposive trenching information, as well as the realisation that sedimentological data can significantly enhance interpretation of site specific cultural events and improve the resolution for cultural narratives across all timeframes. The facies approach also offers an opportunity to understand former landscape dynamics and provides a framework for the study of cultural processes at the sub-regional level. This relies on four key objectives: deposit characterisation, stratigraphy and chronology, describing landscape diversity and function, and understanding landscape processes. These incorporate the objectives set out in the Outline Archaeological Strategy. The primary focus of the geoarchaeological elements of the project was therefore to characterise the environments of deposition and specifically to look for evidence of pedogenesis, indirect evidence for human activity and degree of bioturbation.

In order to achieve these aims there was a need to accurately describe the sediment bodies (contexts) using standard terminology and make observations containing correct information to infer past environments. The strategy therefore considered five key requirements:

1   sediment context and resolution, in particular the vertical/lateral sediment sequences and spatial relationships between structures and adjacent deposits
2   an objective description of deposits to provide initial deposit characterisation
3   facies type assignment as the basis for primary interpretation
4   systematic sampling across vertical and lateral sequences at a number of points within the unit
5   sampling of a wide area, not just areas of interest, including 'off-site' contexts and avoiding sampling only 'problem' deposits.

The methodology of the initial investigations and assessment phases was specifically designed towards developing problem orientated analysis with explicit identification of the problem to be analysed. A process of informed interpretation was adopted where the interpretation of recovered structures, artefacts and similar was considered in light of the whole site. Adoption of a context only recording strategy was considered inappropriate because of four key weaknesses commonly encountered in archaeological recording strategies:

1   the lack of separation of pre-depositional, depositional and post-depositional attributes during context recording
2   a lack of clear criteria by which man-made stratigraphies can be separated from natural stratigraphies
3   limited recording of sedimentological structures

on site at a within context and between context scale
4   limited separation of descriptive and interpretative terminologies.

A dual approach to the recording of on-site stratigraphy was agreed. A standard archaeological recording system was used in addition to detailed geoarchaeological recording of selected site areas. This is an appropriate response to complex stratigraphies containing both anthropogenic signatures and natural processes. This dual system was coordinated through the use of summary proformas. The methodology involved the description of sediment units using standard geological terminology (Jones *et al.* 1999). These descriptions were used to define provisional sediment facies types that were further detailed following assessment. The facies types were identified after examination of Phase I test pit data, prior to more extensive trenching during Phases II and III. Further laboratory assessment was carried out before and during Phase II works creating a dual feedback mechanism, allowing further resolution of objectives both on and off site. The sediment descriptions for a representative profile of each test pit and evaluation trench was presented in the assessment report for each site, along with preliminary correlation of facies types and cross sections where appropriate.

On-site sampling and assessment

Systematic sampling across vertical and lateral sequences was undertaken at a number of locations at each site. The methodology was devised to sample a wide area including 'off-site' contexts, not just areas of interest or 'problem' deposits. In general the Phase I works focused on collecting column samples for reconstructing the environmental history of the area and enhancing identification of facies types. During the Phase II evaluations and Phase III excavations column and bulk samples were collected to provide an immediate landscape context for archaeological deposits.

A range of materials was examined during the site assessment stages from a representative series of deposits. This provided preliminary information on preservation levels, environments of deposition and changes in hydrology, local and regional vegetation patterns as well as evidence for agricultural practices and the exploitation of natural resources. Sedimentological work included determination of organic content, carbonate presence, phosphate-P levels, magnetic susceptibility and lead/zinc/copper content. The biological remains examined included pollen, plant macrofossils, insects, diatoms, foraminifera and ostracods.

Laboratory analysis

The results and recommendations from the individual site assessments were incorporated into the post-excavation project design and were considered in terms of both the site and schemewide research objectives.

Sediments

In addition to the characterisation work carried out during the assessment stages, further analytical work on the sediments targeted horizons associated with key phases of activity. Properties investigated included soil chemistry, micromorphology (thin section analysis) and magnetic susceptibility. These were used to characterise the surface of the weathered sands/land surface associated with early Neolithic artefact scatters at Woolwich Manor Way and the Bronze Age artefact scatters at Movers Lane. Also examined were sediments directly associated with the Bronze Age trackway sequences at Woolwich Manor Way and Movers Lane, along with burnt mound material sampled at the latter site.

Macroscopic plant remains and insects

Evidence of the local vegetation associated with the archaeological remains has been gained primarily from analysis of macroscopic plant remains and insects. These provide complimentary information to that gained through the study of pollen, which largely relates to the regional environment. Results at the assessment stage showed that the vast majority of the waterlogged plant remains represented wild habitats and therefore the bulk of the information obtained from these samples relates to the environmental character of the area rather than the nature of human activities. Individual plant and insect assemblages, however, in conjunction with artefactual evidence from the same samples, provided some evidence pertaining to the possible use of particular features. In total, 32 samples were submitted for the full analysis of plant remains and 13 were submitted for full insect analysis.

Charred plant remains recovered from samples have helped to elucidate the nature of the activities on the site, the wider resource base and nature of the woodland and woodland management. It had also been hoped that the plant remains would provide some information on the wider agricultural economy; however only sparse assemblages of cereal grains and associated weeds of cultivation were recovered along the route making the potential to achieve this aim difficult. In total nine samples were recommended for further work based on preservation and the archaeological significance of the associated contexts. Identification of charcoal was used to define the nature of the local woody taxa (for example to investigate whether scrub or mature woodland was present, augmenting information from both pollen and waterlogged wood) and more explicitly to define the exploitation of trees and other woody species. Management of the woodland may be elucidated from the charcoals, waterlogged wood and pollen. Nine samples were submitted for full charcoal analysis.

Pollen

Analysis of pollen provides data not only on the local vegetation but on the wider regional landscape. For the analysis, the most complete sequences with the best pollen preservation were targeted (as determined at assessment), particularly the peats and organic deposits which spanned long time periods and those containing clear evidence for environmental change. Short sequences associated with the trackways were also included; in conjunction with other environmental analyses it was hoped that the pollen could help to elucidate the environment of, and possible reasons for, their construction. In total five sequences were analysed, one from Freemasons Road Underpass (the sump sequence), two from Woolwich Manor Way (TP1 and trackway 2/14, Area 2) and three from Movers Lane (TP39 channel deposits and trackway 5268, Area 3).

Diatoms, ostracods and foraminifera

Diatoms, ostracods and foraminifera can provide information related to environments of deposition and changes in hydrological regimes. However, assessment indicated that preservation of these microfossils was very variable at the sites along the scheme and was particularly poor with regard to ostracods and foraminifera. In many cases it was considered that further detailed work would not provide significant additional information beyond what was achieved at the assessment stage. However, two sequences from Woolwich Manor Way (TP1 and Area 2) were submitted for further diatom analysis, based on the better preservation of these microfossils at this site. Additional samples from palaeochannel deposits at Movers Lane recommended at assessment for further ostracod and foraminifera work could not be investigated due to deterioration of the monolith samples in the intervening period.

Recording and sampling of waterlogged wood and timber structures

The investigation area is very low lying, well below 5m OD, with generally high water tables and dominated by recent alluvial deposits overlying bands of peat, alluvium, sands and gravels. Thus preservation of timber and roundwood structures dating from the industrial age back to at least later prehistory was expected at the outset. However, due to chance and very limited development of the wet marsh pastures up until Victorian times, the worked wood found was of later prehistoric date, without any historic material. Indeed, previous archaeological work in this region, carried out by the now defunct Passmore Edwards Museum, the Newham Museum Service, Pre-Construct Archaeology and Museum of London Archaeology, has shown that a range of roundwood trackways, fence lines and simple wooden 'platforms' have survived (Meddens 1996). By far the majority of the dated woodwork has proved to be of the Bronze Age period. The archaeological work prior to the A13 project indicated that some areas were likely to have been zones of particularly intense prehistoric activity where structures such as trackways were very likely to occur, for example in the Beckton area (Meddens 1996, 327). It is important to note that no current form of remote sensing device can locate such structures below ground; the thick clay-silt, estuarine deposits completely hide what lies below, except where found along the Thames foreshore, truncated by modern tidal action.

It is generally clear that woody materials were the main structural materials used in the changing built environments of British prehistory, from houses to livestock fences, boats and much portable equipment. This is particularly true in an area like Greater London where there is very little building stone. Wooded environments of various types formed much of the backdrop to human activity in the area in later prehistory, but very little evidence survives of the use of wood or the nature of the woodlands on typical decayed, 'dryland' excavations. Consequently archaeologists working in a wetland zone such as the Thames floodplain are obliged to extract as much information as possible from the wood found preserved there. Much of the information gained relates not just to the wetlands but also to the the drier hinterland, where such evidence no longer exists. Since there is much modern development in this area of East London the wetland resource will inevitably diminish (through de-watering for example). This, then, is also a key reason for detailed recording while the material still survives.

The approach used for the investigation and recording of the waterlogged woodwork is broadly compatible with that laid out by English Heritage (Brunning 1996). As is established practice in the field of prehistoric wetland archaeology (Coles and Orme 1980a) the wooden structures were exposed as fully as they could be within the limits of the excavation area. Then, either the whole of a small structure or a fully representative area of a larger feature was dismantled, following which the material was recorded and sampled in detail off-site. Occasionally severe weather or safety considerations limited access to the woodwork and so precluded detailed recording. Indeed, the very narrowness of the excavation trenches presented some problems in the interpretation of some of the trackway structures. The ancient woodworking specialist for the project (D. Goodburn) provided on-site advice about the interpretation, broad dating, excavation, sampling and recording of the woodwork uncovered. Site plans were made at 1:20 with some details at 1:10. Standard section drawings were also made of box sections around some *in situ* piles and stakes, and general photographs were taken. Following excavation the selected worked or 'possibly worked' wooden items were washed, closely examined and proforma

'timber sheets' filled out for those that proved to be worked. Naturally deposited wood, fragments of bark and very repetitious worked items such as abraded small wood chips were simply listed briefly and discarded, unless there was a specific need to document their non-artefactual nature. A large proportion of the lifted clearly worked material was also drawn in detail on gridded film by the specialist, highlighting technical details such as tool marks. Finally, a subset of the worked material was also photographed off-site in several formats.

A full representative sample of the worked roundwood from each investigated area was sampled for microscopic wood species identification (Barnett in Appendix 3), except for small items clearly of yew, which has visually diagnostic features even in small diameters. The larger roundwood and small amount of material split from larger logs ('timber') was sampled for wood species identification if the material did not have clear diagnostic features. In some cases a small number of samples which had been identified by a specialist were included to act as an independent check on the veracity of the visual species determinations. Most of the unidentified material was of alder, a much used wetland tree. Thus, it is important to note that the species identification tables in Appendix 3 mainly concern roundwood and somewhat under represent the oak, ash, elm and yew that were found. Slices were taken for tree-ring studies when the parent timbers appeared to have over 45 annual rings and to be from one of the oaks or yew. Samples for radiocarbon dating were taken from young roundwood or the outer parts of larger material which contain the youngest carbon, most representative of the date of cutting.

At several stages during the project the issue of dating and changes in date ranges due to the development of more refined dating methods was discussed. As tree-ring chronologies are extended back in time and ever closer radiocarbon dating of later prehistoric woodwork becomes possible, this becomes an important issue as sites, and their woodworking attributes, can be more closely compared than was true when the A13 project was initiated. Of particular significance is the closer dating of early tool marks indicating when changes in woodworking toolkits took place. The adoption of metal tools was crucial, enabling a much greater range and extent of woodworking to become possible in the lifetime of one woodworker. The impact of the seemingly rapid adoption of the new, much more effective tools must have been widespread, leaving a large imprint on pollen and other environmental sequences. The conversion of wildwood into forms of managed woodland such as woodpasture and eventually arable land must have been much accelerated by the introduction of the new tools. Recent work on a number of projects shows that the earliest use of metal axes can now be pushed back to around 2500 BC, with tree-ring dated wooden trackways with clear metal axe cut marks dating back to at least 2250 BC from Britain and Ireland (see for example Corlea 6 from central Ireland, O'Sullivan 1997).

Scientific dating

In total, 64 samples were submitted for radiocarbon dating and 62 dates have been obtained for the project schemewide, the detailed results of which are presented in Appendix 1.

Thirty samples (bulk sediment, wood and charred material) were submitted to Beta Analytic Inc., Florida, USA for standard radiometric dating during the assessment stages and 34 samples were sent to the Scottish Universities Environmental Research Centre (SUERC) in East Kilbride, Scotland for Accelerator Mass Spectrometry (AMS) dating during the post-excavation analytical phase. In general the purpose of the radiocarbon dating programme was help to refine the individual site chronologies and phasing. A range of material was selected from the sediment sequences, timber structures and trackways: dated materials included charred and waterlogged plant remains from key features, cremate bone and carbonised residues adhering to pot sherds. Where possible only clearly worked wood associated with the timber structures ,. .. submitted. With reference to the sediment sequences, waterlogged seeds or wood were the preferred material, but in some cases, where preservation was poor, a sample of organic sediment was submitted instead. Unfortunately two dates on charred residues adhering to potsherds failed.

The radiocarbon results are quoted in accordance with the international standard known as the Trondheim convention (Stuiver and Kra 1986). They are conventional radiocarbon ages (Stuiver and Polach 1977). All dates from samples submitted from this project have been calibrated using datasets published by Reimer *et al.* (2004) and the computer program OxCal (v3.10) (Bronk Ramsey 1995, 1998, 2001) (see Appendix 1). In the text the calibrated age estimates are quoted, with the radiocarbon years in parentheses. The calibrated date ranges cited in the text are those for 95.4% (2σ) confidence.

Twenty samples of wood from the timber structures were submitted to Dr Daniel Miles at the Oxford Dendrochronology Laboratory, but unfortunately the samples proved undatable by this method. Oak piles submitted from Freemasons Road derived from very fast grown, probably managed oak, which means they contained relatively few, ill-defined annual rings. In contrast, some of the other samples from natural timbers had many more annual rings deriving from very slow grown unmanaged trees, but here the rings were too closely spaced to get a match either (Miles, pers. comm).

A number of samples from the sediments were collected for Optically Stimulated Luminescence dating (OSL, Appendix 1). Four of these samples were processed during the evaluation stage by Dr Edward Rhodes at the luminescence dating laboratory, University of Oxford, to help define the facies interpretations of the late Pleistocene and early Holocene sequences. No further samples were processed during the post-excavation stage as key phases associated with the periods of archaeological activity could be adequately dated by radiocarbon assay.

Chapter 3: Canning Town

Introduction (Figs 3.1 and 3.2)

The site at Canning Town lies 700m to the north of the River Thames and crosses the valley of the tidal River Lea. The River Lea, at this point called Bow Creek, is shown on the early 18th century maps, from where it is possible to trace its gradual movement in ox-bows across the floodplain. This movement, the tidal regime and the presence of marsh such as the Plaistow Level to the east, resulted in little development of the area until the beginning of the 19th century (Fig. 1.6). The West and East India Docks were constructed at this time and the New Iron Bridge was constructed across the

River Lea in 1810. The present bridge and road crossing was constructed during 1930-1933. The area on the south-west side of the site was leased to the Great Eastern Rail Company and later used as a LNER wharf. The east side of the River Lea was previously used by the Woolwich Branch of the Great Eastern Railway. More recently the Docklands Light Railway has been constructed alongside the Lea. The location of the site in or close to the low-lying floodplain has resulted in little occupation or settlement during most of the historical period. The medieval villages of Bromley and Poplar were situated further north and west on the higher

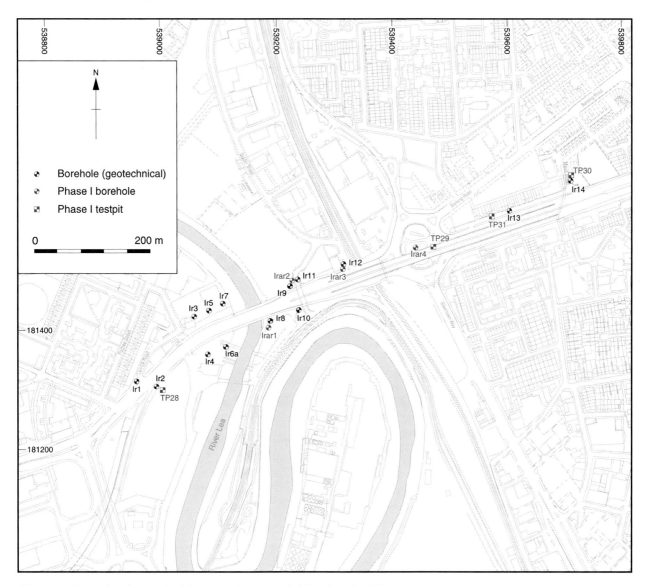

Fig. 3.1   Plan of archaeological interventions, Ironbridge-Canning Town

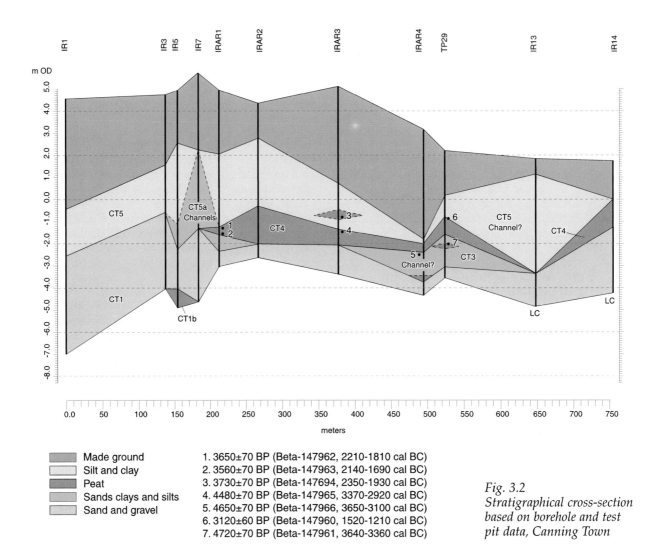

Made ground
Silt and clay
Peat
Sands clays and silts
Sand and gravel

1. 3650±70 BP (Beta-147962, 2210-1810 cal BC)
2. 3560±70 BP (Beta-147963, 2140-1690 cal BC)
3. 3730±70 BP (Beta-147694, 2350-1930 cal BC)
4. 4480±70 BP (Beta-147965, 3370-2920 cal BC)
5. 4650±70 BP (Beta-147966, 3650-3100 cal BC)
6. 3120±60 BP (Beta-147960, 1520-1210 cal BC)
7. 4720±70 BP (Beta-147961, 3640-3360 cal BC)

Fig. 3.2
Stratigraphical cross-section based on borehole and test pit data, Canning Town

ground. The settlement pattern may have been significantly different in the Bronze Age and earlier periods when lower sea-levels may have allowed exploitation and occupation of the river banks and eyots. The River Lea is likely to have been used as both a navigable route and possibly for ritual deposition.

The Stage I evaluation involved the excavation of four test pits; *c* 3m x 4m and 5m deep (TP28-TP31) and four boreholes (Irar 1-4) (Fig. 3.1). In addition to the archaeological records, the assessment of stratigraphy drew on archive geotechnical borehole logs (Ir 1-14). Overall five broad sediment units were identified at Canning Town (Fig. 3.2). Pockets of fibrous peat, dark brown organic clay and soft brown clay within the basal part of the Pleistocene gravel sequence may date to the Late Glacial period (see below). A variable sequence of Holocene deposits occurred beneath the recent fills including an intermittent peat bed sandwiched between minerogenic alluvium. Assessment of the sediments recovered from three locations (Irar 2, Irar 4 and TP29) identified enriched phosphate levels including vivianite precipitate as well as fragments of charcoal; however no direct evidence

of cultural activity was identified during the test pitting. Between 3m and 5m of modern fill occurred to the east and west of Iron Bridge, raising the levels of the ground along Bow Creek. Similar efforts to raise land levels have not been necessary to the east of Silvertown Way, where the depth of fill is between 0.5 and 1.5m. The depths of recent fill and the relatively limited scale of impact at Ironbridge-Canning Town did not warrant Phase III investigations. A watching brief carried out during construction did not identify any further evidence of human activity.

Sedimentary architecture and environments of deposition

The pre-Holocene sediments and basement topography

Fluvial gravel (CT1)

At Canning Town poorly sorted coarse flint gravel lay between the Holocene soft sediment sequence and the London Clay bedrock. These deposits were only penetrated to *c* 0.5m to 1.0m by the purposive geoarchaeological drilling, although the geotechnical investigations managed to reach bedrock. These sediments typically accumulated in cold climate braided river conditions during the late Pleistocene. The height datums indicate that they probably correlate with the Shepperton Gravels, deposited between 10,000 and 15,000 BP.

Organic clay and peat (CT1b)

This group of sediments was only identified in the geotechnical borehole logs and no samples were available for closer examination. The deposits all lie at the base or within the main gravel aggradation phase and comprise soft brown clay (Irar 3), pockets of fibrous peat (Irar 4) or dark brown organic clay (Irar 6a). These organic sediments are probably indicative of lower flow velocities and small-scale channel infill features of probable Late Glacial date. Similar deposits were most recently identified during borehole work at the Olympic Park in Stratford spanning both the Windermere Interstadial (warm phase) and Loch Lomand Stadial (cold phase) at *c* 11,000–13,000 BP (Corcoran *et al.* 2011, 150).

The early Holocene topographic template

A major temporal unconformity is likely to be represented by the surface of the terrace gravels, in other words the early Holocene topographic template. The surface therefore represents the Mesolithic/ Neolithic land surface. Inundation of this land surface during the early to mid Holocene appears to have commenced under freshwater conditions and is represented by the lower alluvial sediments described below.

The Holocene sediments (Fig. 3.3)

Freshwater sand and clay silts (CT3)

This group of sediments directly overlay the Pleistocene gravels and consisted of minerogenic sandy-silts or clay-silts. The sequence is well represented in TP29 by contexts 200 and 201 (Fig. 3.3). The fine-grained nature of the sediments suggests deposition in a relatively low-energy environment. Pollen was only preserved at the top of this unit immediately below the overlying peat where pollen of grasses contributed the highest proportions. The presence of *Bithynia* sp., a mollusc that prefers flowing water conditions, along with a tooth from a cyprinid (Cyprinidae: carp family) and amphibian bones suggests these deposits accumulated in freshwater conditions in or adjacent to an active channel. Debris from a number of different habitats and activities appears to have accumulated in this location, including microscopic charcoal. Age estimates in TP29 from a peat layer towards the top of this unit suggests much of the lower alluvial sequence predates at least *c* 3600 cal BC.

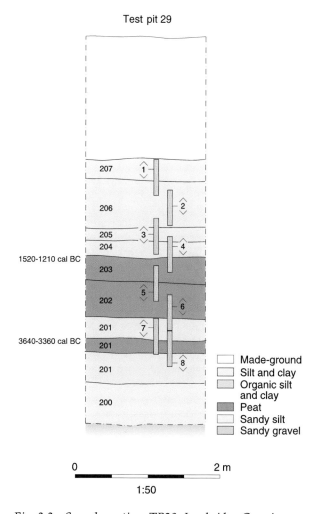

Fig. 3.3 Sample section, TP29, Ironbridge-Canning Town

Freshwater peat and organic silt (CT4)

This group of sediments are dominated by highly organic silts and peat. The peat directly overlay the Pleistocene gravels, or the lower alluvium where present, and was sealed by a further extensive unit of minerogenic alluvium. Differentiation from the last, however, proved difficult due to the high organic content of the silts. The peat unit varied from firm humified peat to wood peat, but the presence of fine silty material within the peat implies that frequent low-energy flood episodes occurred throughout the period represented by it. Radiocarbon age estimates from TP29 indicate that accumulation occurred between the early Neolithic and the middle Bronze Age at 3640-3370 cal BC (Beta-147961: 4720±60 BP) and 1520-1210 cal BC (Beta-147960: 3120±60 BP).

Pollen was well preserved in these sediments. Alder dominated, with oak, lime and hazel also present. Grasses and sedges were also represented which suggests that a damp alder carr may have existed in the vicinity with an understorey of grasses, sedges and ferns. Samples from TP29 contained seeds from a wide range of plants of river-bank, ditches and marshes, including sedge, gypsywort and branched burweed. Charcoal fragments in TP29 and TP30 may indicate cultural activity, but the lack of any corroborative evidence means that it could also have resulted from natural fires. The phosphatic mineral vivianite was present in the organic silts in borehole Irar 2. Stratigraphically this corresponds with the vivianite in the lower part of the overlying alluvium in borehole Irar 4 (see below) and may suggest a discrete area of cultural activity.

Freshwater and estuarine clay silt (CT5)

This sedimentary complex was dominated by minerogenic clays and silts containing variable quantities of organic material and zones dominated by laminated sediments. In some instances, such as Irar 1, coarser flint gravel horizons were also present. The deposits typically underlay 19th century made ground and the accumulation in TP29 post-dates *c* 1500-1210 cal BC. The deposit thickness varied from less than 1m to over 4m, with an upper surface occurring at *c* -1.0 to +2.0m OD.

These deposits represent a period of inundation leading to the development of an intertidal wetland system. Sediments at the base of this sequence in TP29, immediately above the peat, contained a range of microfossils including freshwater bivalves and gastropods. However brackish water ostracods (*Cytherura gibba*) and minute foraminifera (*Haynesina germanica, Ammonia limnetes* and *Elphidium williamsoni*) were also present and increased up-profile. The pollen was dominated by grains from grasses and sedges, which suggest an increase in the importance of reedswamp vegetation up-profile. Significant levels of goosefoot pollen may indicate areas of local saltmarsh. These factors indicate that the environment of deposition was probably brackish but that sediment input was also received from both upstream (freshwater) and downstream (brackish,

tidal) sources. Interestingly the uppermost levels of this sequence contained a pollen spectra suggesting a return to a more wooded environment dominated by alder and willow, with oak, lime and hazel in drier habitats. Various possible cultural indicators occurred in isolation, often near the base of the deposits. Ceramic fragments were identified in one borehole (Irar 1), along with gravel, as matrix supported clasts within the clay silt. These were extremely fragmented and provide evidence of the fluvial reworking of deposits associated with cultural activity, rather than *in situ* activity. The phosphatic mineral vivianite was also present within the lower part of the unit in borehole Irar 4, and enriched phosphate levels also occurred higher in the sequence in TP29 at *c* 2.20m bgl. The depth and ages ascribed to the sediments levels containing vivianite suggests the activity in Irar 1 may be of middle to late Bronze Age date, whilst those in TP29 are most likely to be later, probably post-Roman.

Fluvial gravel (CT5a)

In addition to the fine grained clays and silts the geotechnical logs recorded localised accumulations of sand and gravel. This group of sediments is very restricted in distribution and was only recorded in two boreholes (Ir 5 and Ir 7). No sediment was available for examination and these deposits were not observed in the purposive geoarchaeological boreholes. The deposits were described as clay units containing significant quantities of sand and gravel, with an upper surface occurring between -1.1m and 2.0m OD. Superficially the description is similar to some of the thinner gravel horizons identified within the clay silts. Coarse sand and gravel are indicative of generally higher flow velocities and may represent sediments deposited closer to the former main channel through this area, contemporary with deposition of the finer grained alluvium.

Chapter 4: Prince Regent Lane

Introduction (Figs 4.1-4.4)

The Stage I evaluation at the Prince Regent Lane site involved the excavation of 27 test pits (TPs 50-76). This was followed by 8 evaluation trenches (T20-T27) as part of the Stage II works; 3 to the north-east of the Prince Regent Lane junction and 5 to the south-west (Fig. 4.1).

T20, T22-24 and T27 all lay within the Newham, formerly Beckton, recreation ground, laid out in the 1890s. The earliest maps of the district (Roque 1746; Chapman and Andre 1777) show the local area as open fields and pasture surrounded with drainage ditches. The area of the present park was known as the Plaistow Levels, which suggests that even in the 18th century the area was still marshy and prone to periodic flooding. The Chapman and Andre map shows the edge of the marshland considerably further north, on the line of the current Barking Road (Fig. 1.6). The area remained predominantly rural in 1896 when two small farms still existed to the north of the present Newham Way. Before 1840 Prince Regent Lane was known as Trinity Mills Lane and was certainly in existence in 1819. Prince Regent Lane, along with Tollgate Road, is one of the oldest roads in the area. T25 and T26 lay within the grounds of the Terence Macmillan leisure centre. Previously this side of the Newham Way was taken up with housing which dated mostly to the beginning of the 20th century. These were partly destroyed during the Blitz and were finally demolished in the 1970s to make way for the new sports complex.

Geoarchaeological modelling of the test pit data revealed that beneath the modern overburden the surface of the Pleistocene sands and gravels, forming the edge of the terrace, lay at relatively high elevations over much of the site, sealed by a shallow deposit of silty clay alluvium. Deeper alluvial and peat sequences, however, were noted in the far western end of the site (TPs 50, 51, 53 and T23) where the Pleistocene deposits rapidly shelved away (Fig. 4.2).

Archaeological remains identified during the evaluation work were dated to the Neolithic, Bronze Age and Roman periods. On the higher ground activity appears to have been concentrated in the central area of the site in the vicinity of T20, T21 and T24. This included artefact scatters of mixed date on the weathered surface of the Pleistocene deposits, sealed beneath the alluvium. A series of middle to late Bronze Age and Roman linear features may represent the remains of field systems or boundary ditches. In the western part of the site discrete localised features occurred within and beneath the deeper alluvial sequences and included a timber structure in T23, defined by two substantial timber piles and an accumulation of woodworking debris. One of the piles produced a radiocarbon date within the first half of the 2nd millennium BC.

To mitigate the impact of the proposed Freemasons Road Underpass, Phase III investigations consisted of the detailed excavation of the timber structure identified in T23. To enable the

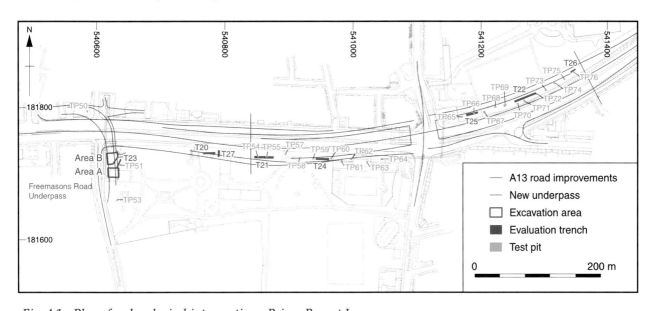

Fig. 4.1 Plan of archaeological interventions, Prince Regent Lane

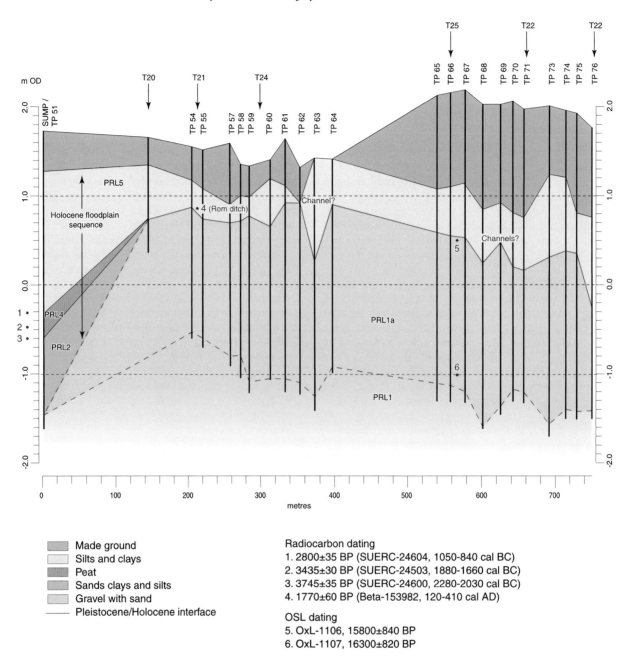

Fig. 4.2   Stratigraphical cross-section based on evaluation test pit data, Prince Regent Lane

excavation two temporary cofferdams of sheet piles were constructed: Area A (17m x 14m) and Area B (17m x 17m) (Plate 1). The modern overburden and underlying alluvium was removed by mechanical excavator to the first archaeological horizon, after which excavation proceeded by hand. A land surface formed on alluvial deposits was exposed in the base excavations and produced a mixed assemblage of flint artefacts and pottery dating from the Neolithic and middle to late Bronze Age periods. A series of features, concentrated on the slightly higher ground in Area B, truncated this surface and included stake holes, postholes, ditches and pits. The timber structure was further exposed in Area A and formed a double row of piles with associated artefact scatters.

A total of about 250 worked, or possibly worked,

wooden items were exposed and lifted at this site, some deriving from the evaluation phase but most coming from the cofferdam excavations (Areas A and B). Following washing of the material off-site, unworked bark and twig fragments were listed and discarded together with small broken fragments of wood chips. Fifty two items were recorded on pro-forma timber sheets with sketches and 23 items were drawn to scale. Subsequently a small selection were retained for conservation and 10 items were photographed in detail. In total, 23 samples were taken for species identification and 11 for tree-ring studies. This assemblage is 'medium sized' if compared nationally but is large by the standards of other London sites, and is the second largest assemblage from the A13 project.

Plate 1 Coffer dam excavation, Freemasons Road (FRU02, Area A)

Palaeoenvironmental work during the evaluation stage focused on characterising the deeper sediment sequence exposed in T23. Further examination of biological remains from the sediments excavated during the Phase III works at Freemasons Road Underpass was carried out as part of the post-excavation assessment stage (Fig. 4.3). Unfortunately the key monoliths examined during the assessment phases were not available to carry on to full analysis. For this reason the samples retrieved from a small drainage sump excavated immediately to the south of Area A have been the subject of detailed pollen work (Druce, Appendix 3). The sequence of deposits in the sump has been correlated with the main excavation through comparison of stratigraphy and dating evidence (Fig. 4.4). A total of 13 samples from a range of deposits were processed for radiocarbon dating. Overall the assessment indicated that the preservation of ostracods, foraminifera and diatoms was very poor and conse-

quently no detailed analytical work was carried out. The results of the assessment, however, have provided useful information in terms of characterising the environments of deposition associated with the sediments. Macroscopic plant and insect remains were variably preserved and detailed analysis has been carried out on a representative selection of the richest bulk samples available from the main excavation areas (see Appendix 3).

Sedimentary architecture and environments of deposition

The pre-Holocene sediments and basement topography

Fluvial gravel (PRL1)

The basal part of the investigated sequence comprised poorly-sorted coarse flint gravel, varying

27

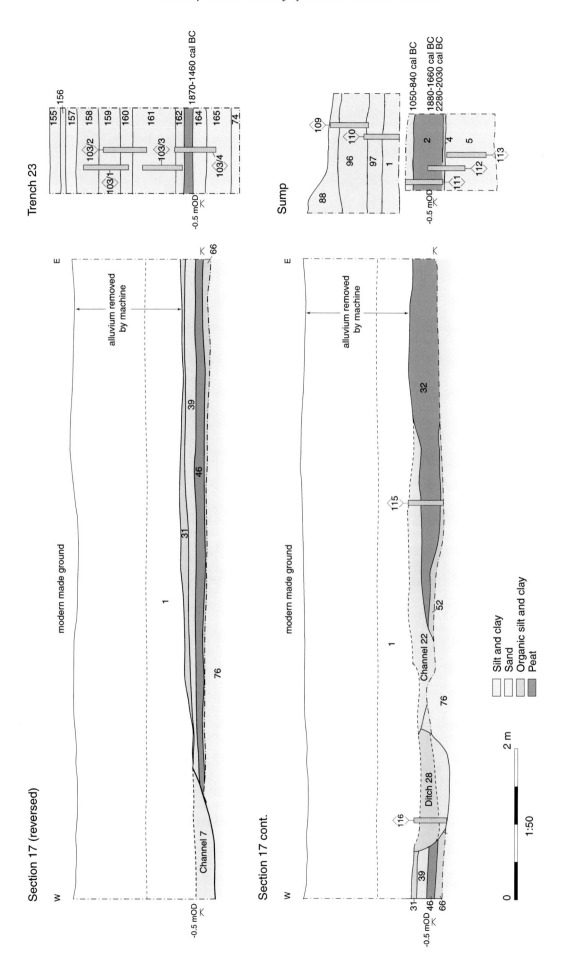

Fig. 4.3 Sample sections, Freemasons Road

Atmospheric data from Reimer et al (2004);OxCal v3.10 Bronk Ramsey (2005); cub r:5 sd:12 prob usp[chron]

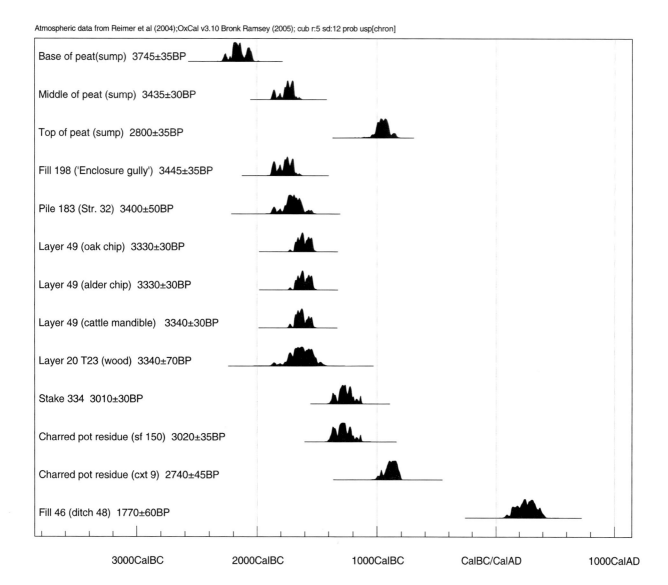

Fig. 4.4   Radiocarbon dates, Prince Regent Lane and Freemasons Road

from less than 10mm in diameter to clasts in excess of 100mm. In places these deposits were interbedded with sands. The gravels were exposed in most of the test pits, but were only penetrated to a maximum depth of about 0.3m. They are typically associated with high-energy rapid sedimentation in braided channels during Pleistocene cold climate episodes. The oldest parts of the sequence exist beneath a series of dated colluvial deposits (see below) and by implication would exceed 30,000 BP. The more recent sediments exist below the modern floodplain (as in T23) and probably date to 12,000-15,000 BP.

Colluvial sand and gravel (PRL1a)

Extensive deposits of sand overlay the fluvial gravels across much of the site (TP54–TP76 and T20-26), although the transition between the two units was gradational. The sands were not examined in detail as the excavations were prone to flooding and the

sections unstable. However, considerable variation was noted in the structure of these deposits where they exhibited clear bedding of sands, sandy-gravels and silts. OSL age estimates from TP66 produced results ranging from 15800±840 BP to 16300±820 BP. There was an absence of associated palaeoenvironmental material, but sedimentological information coupled with the known age of the sediments indicates that these deposits are likely to have been laid down by colluvial and solifluction processes during intervals of severe cold with frozen ground dominant. These sediments would have accumulated on a slope southwards towards the contemporary braided channel system of the Thames. Periodic washing of the surface and erosion of sands from higher gravel terraces is likely to have contributed to the accumulation of the sediment stack here, although erosional episodes probably alternated with times of more stable landsurface generation.

The early Holocene topographic template

The early Holocene topographic template at Prince Regent Lane is represented by the surface of the Pleistocene sediments. Examination of the shape of the template reveals the highest elevations, up to +0.90m OD, occur in the central part of the site. Elevations gradually reduce eastwards to around -0.2m OD, and more rapidly westwards to about -1.5m OD in the vicinity of Freemasons Road Underpass. This surface, where exposed, was generally described as weathered or 'dirty' sand. In the lower lying areas associated cultural material generally dates to the Neolithic and Bronze Age. On the higher ground the relatively late date for alluvial inundation resulted in features of prehistoric and Roman date occurring at this level.

The Holocene sediments

Freshwater sand and clay-silt (PRL2)

Minerogenic sediments dominated by blue grey clay-silts or sandy-silts occurred directly above the Pleistocene gravels. These sediments are indicative of the earliest processes taking place as an indirect result of sea level rise during the early Holocene resulting in backing up of waters in river valleys. Sedimentation appears to have occurred at the margins of the site; in the low-lying areas on the relict undulating Late Glacial landsurface (TP50-TP53, Area A and Area B). Some erosion and redeposition of sands on the steeper slopes underlain by the Pleistocene colluvial sediments may also have occurred, particularly near the break of slope. Low-energy environments of deposition are indicated by the sediment grain size. Accumulation appears to have taken place under freshwater conditions as indicated by the presence of charophyte oogonia (calcified fruiting bodies of stonewort), water flea eggs and fish remains which included 3-spined stickleback and eel (fish remains identified by S. Parfitt) although the last two also inhabit estuaries and coastal waters (Nicholson pers. comm). Unfortunately these sediments contained no diatoms, ostracods or foraminifera and pollen preservation was poor.

In both Areas A and B at Freemasons Road this surface appeared to have been eroded and scoured by alluvial action leaving an irregular undulating surface. With only a difference of *c* 0.10m between the highest levels recorded in Area B and Area A, there seems to be only a very gradual incline south towards the Thames. The upper layers of these deposits were often described as weathered sand or 'dirty' soil suggesting a subsequent drier period and surface stability. Cultural artefacts and features cut into this surface date from the early Neolithic to middle Bronze Age periods.

The pollen spectra for equivalent deposits in sump sequence, below -0.68m OD, predating *c* 2000-2300 BC, indicates a local environment of damp alder carr and sedge, with lime, hazel and oak

woodland growing on the drier slopes or interfluves. Arboreal pollen is relatively well represented although areas of disturbed or lightly grazed ground are indicated by the presence of dandelion and plantains. There was also evidence of possible cereal cultivation, with one or two cereal-type pollen grains although this remains equivocal. A temporary decline in arboreal pollen was noted at very top of the weathered silty sand, together with a corresponding increase in grass pollen. This may suggest a clearance episode; however lime woodland appears to be most affected, decreasing from 25% to 15% of total land pollen (TLP) with both alder and hazel showing very little change.

Freshwater peat and organic silt (PRL4)

Typically these deposits rest on the alluvial deposits described above and were only present in the test pits at the western end of the site; in T23 and the excavations for Freemasons Road Underpass. Levels of contained organic matter in these contexts were low and they are in no way true peats. Rapid lateral changes in the composition of this unit and the decrease in organic content (relative to minerogenic content) moving towards the drier, higher ground may indicate greater inputs of minerogenic sediment from the terrace edge and the mobilisation of the Pleistocene colluvial deposits. At Freemasons Road the earliest organic sedimentation appears to have occurred in the slightly lower lying hollows on the surface of the alluvium in Area A (organic clay layer 66 and 52 in Area A and layer 4 in the sump). This was followed by more widespread peat formation (layer 2 in the sump, layers 46, 47 and 32 in Area A and layers 123, 105, 101, 102 and 108 in Area B). Radiocarbon dating of the base of the peat in the sump suggests accumulation commenced in the south-eastern area during the early Bronze Age at 2280-2030 cal BC (SUERC-24600: 3745±35 BP) at *c* -0.60m OD and ceased during the late Bronze Age at 1050-840 cal BC (SUERC-24604: 2800±35 BP). In other slightly higher areas peat accumulation probably started a little later as evidenced by the presence of pottery sherds and radiocarbon dates from the first half the 2nd millennium BC from timber and animal bone scattered on the surface of the underlying alluvium.

The pollen spectra from the sump sequence initially indicates a similar environment to that described above with damp alder carr and sedge, and lime, hazel and oak woodland growing on the drier ground. Up-profile, however, there is evidence that conditions became rapidly wetter and much more open. Damp species-rich sedge fen and grassland developed immediately at the site and freshwater pools and streams were prevalent with green algae, aquatics and bulrushes. A radiocarbon determination at -0.48m OD dates the onset of this period of sedge fen development to the later part of the early Bronze Age at 1880-1660 cal BC (SUERC-24598: 3435±30 BP). It is during this period that the timber bridge or jetty (Str. 32) was constructed at

Freemasons Road (see below). On the drier ground the pollen indicates woodland cover also declined which may be related to human activity. A slight increase in bracken may indicate increased grazing (Behre 1986) and cereal-type pollen is recorded once more.

The macroscopic remains from the peat and organic feature fills provided a broadly similar picture to that obtained from the pollen. Seeds and cones of alder and fruit of branched bur-reed indicate carr or fen conditions. Aquatic species included crowfoots, water-plantain, water-pepper and occasional seeds of duckweed, as well as oogonia (calcified fruiting bodies) of stonewort and the larval cases of caddisfly. These last three items are particularly indicative of standing water. The insect fauna was also dominated by beetles associated with slow flowing or stagnant water, typified by the predatory 'diving beetle' *Agabus bipustulatus* and the small hydreanid *Octhebius*. *Tanysphyrus lemnae* which feeds on duck weed was also present, together with *Liosoma deflexum* which is often associated with the marsh marigold. Episodic higher energy flooding is indicated, however, by Elmid species such as *Oulimnius* spp. and *Elmis aenea* which are normally associated with flowing water crossing over sands and gravels. Seeds of waterside vegetation which might have included species growing within the shallow muddy water include branched bur-reed, club-rushes, water dropwort, fool's water-cress, gypsywort and water-mint. The beetles *Donacia simplex* and *Plateumaris sericea* are particularly associated with branched bur-reed and other vegetation such as reeds and sedges. Seeds of elder and bramble may indicate shrubby disturbed ground and certainly disturbed habitats and nitrogen rich soil are suggested by fat hen, stinging nettle, black nightshade, hairy buttercup and docks. Wet or damp grassland is indicated by meadow species including possible meadow rue, ragged robin, and buttercups. There was also some indication of the openness of the landscape from the 'click beetle' *Adelocera murina* commonly associated with grassy ground and woodland edges, as well as from the presence of *Aphodius*, a 'dung beetle'.

Freshwater and estuarine clay silt (PRL5)

The upper alluvial deposits sealing the peat are dominated by minerogenic sediments, predominantly clay and silt-sized fractions, mottled in places and containing abundant traces of modern roots. This group of sediments, where present, typically underlay the modern made ground and varied in thickness from less than 0.3m to 2.65m. A radiocarbon date of 1050-840 cal BC (SUERC-24604: 2800±35 BP) was obtained from the top of the underlying peat in the sump sequence, implying that the change to minerogenic sedimentation at Freemasons Road dates to the late Bronze Age or early Iron Age. This is confirmed by pottery sherds recovered from features cut into the top of the peat

and filled with clay silt in the main excavation area. Higher up on the gravel terrace these sediments directly overlay Pleistocene colluvial deposits but also sealed features of Roman date. This implies the higher ground remained relatively dry ground well into the historical period. The pollen from the sump sequence at Freemasons Road immediately above the peat interface shows little change apart from a slight rise in pollen of the goosefoot family, which does include species that grow on saltmarshes. Other than this there was very little in the pollen assemblage to suggest a major increase in saline conditions as yet, although the sedimentary changes seen here are likely to be related to shifts in the morphology of the river during the period of estuary expansion.

Several erosion channels were recorded cutting into the top of the peats in the main excavation area. The clay-silt fills of these channels and the overlying alluvium indicates they were laid down under aqueous conditions and they show evidence of strong weathering and pedogenesis. This sub-aerial weathering is also indicated by the decalcification of the diatoms and the presence of earthworm granules. Ostracods from the upper fill of one of the channels included a few specimens of the freshwater *Candona* group. The presence of sponge spicule fragments, as well as marine and brackish diatoms, however, suggests encroaching estuarine conditions.

The upper part of the alluvium from the excavations was not analysed in detail but pollen work from the evaluation stage in T23 indicated the gradual development of open saltmarsh vegetation with freshwater marshes on the inland edge. Foraminiferal and ostracod evidence suggests mixed brackish and freshwater conditions where the introduction of freshwater species probably derives from influxes of freshwater from streams draining the inland marshes.

The cultural evidence from the gravel terrace (Fig. 4.5)

Mesolithic and Neolithic

Evidence for Mesolithic and Neolithic activity identified during the evaluation stages on the higher ground of the gravel terrace is largely inferred by the presence of a small amount of worked flint characteristic of these periods on the weathered surface of the Late Glacial colluvial sands and gravels, as well as residual components in later features. The condition of the flint was frequently described as chipped or abraded and is consistent with material that has resided in the soil for a long period. Artefactual material of Bronze Age date was also often found in the same contexts. The quantity of material perhaps suggests small scale and intermittent activity. No evidence of any intentional 'patterned' or structured deposition was identified, and in general the material suggests

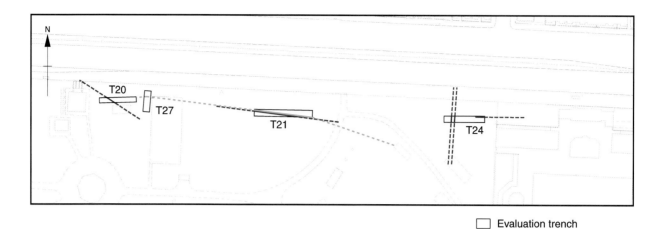

*Fig. 4.5   Plan of linear features identified
on the gravel terrace, Prince Regent Lane*

deposition through casual loss and/or accidental redeposition. A single sherd of impressed decorated Peterborough Ware pottery was also recovered from a Bronze Age pit fill (95) in T21. A number of ephemeral features cutting the weathered sand were initially thought to be of Neolithic date. Many of these features, however, were quite irregular and are likely to be of natural origin. Artefactual evidence, where present, comprised occasional fragments of burnt flint and undiagnostic struck flint and cannot be securely dated to this period given features of later date also occur at this horizon.

Middle to late Bronze Age

Along with the Neolithic material, the evaluation identified a general scatter of middle to late Bronze Age pottery and worked and burnt flint lying on the surface of the Late Glacial colluvial sands and gravels. The condition of the material was better than that from the earlier periods and more indicative of an *in situ* assemblage, with limited reworking. This, together with a small number of features perhaps suggests a focus of settlement activity on the higher terraces during this period. The features comprised a series of linear ditches, probably the remains of field systems or boundary ditches, and a small number of shallow pits concentrated in the centre of the site in T20, T21 and T24 (Fig. 4.5). The features were generally filled with minerogenic silty clay and artefactual material included worked flint, burnt flint, animal bone and pottery dated to the middle to late Bronze Age. The primary fill of the ditch in T21 (context 91) produced a single sherd of a Deverel-Rimbury bucket urn and a fragment of burnt clay, possibly a loom weight of cylindrical type, was recovered from a pit in the same trench (fill 95). An interrupted ditch in T20 may represent a boundary defining activity to the east, and re-cutting of the north-south ditch in T24 suggests that some of these alignments

were of enough importance to maintain. The study area, however, is, too small to infer the nature or extent of any associated settlement.

In addition to the archaeological features a number of possible small channels were also identified in the eastern part of the site in T22 and T26. The channel in T26 not only showed evidence of re-cutting/braiding, but the complex fills also demonstrated changing flow patterns and rates. There was some indication of human activity associated with these channels. Flint flakes and burnt flint were recovered from the channel fills and from the weathered sand between the channels in T22.

Roman

A series of linear features of Roman date were identified during the evaluation. It is likely that three ditches recorded in T20, T21 and T27 form part of the same ditch (Fig. 4.5), and a further ditch section was recorded in T26. Although a number of sherds of middle to late Bronze Age pottery was recovered from these features along with worked flint, these are likely to be residual. A fragment of charcoal from the ditch in T21 (context 46) yielded a radiocarbon date of cal AD 120-410 (Beta-153982: 1770±60 BP) and a single sherd of Oxfordshire Red Colour-coated (OXRC) dated to about AD 270-400 was also recovered from the same feature (context 39). The Roman activity may represent the edge of a field system or boundary ditch aligned along the edge of the gravel terrace and appears to reinforce aspects of the earlier terrace edge landscape broadly coinciding with the Bronze Age features.

Post Roman

Evidence for occupation following the Roman period was largely absent. The only post Roman pottery was 19th century and came from an early 20th century cut in T21.

The cultural evidence from the wetland zone (Freemasons Road Underpass)

Mesolithic and Neolithic

Artefacts from the weathered sands and later deposits

Similar to the gravel terrace, evidence of activity for the earlier periods at Freemasons Road is largely inferred by the presence of a small assemblage of worked flint and pottery located on the weathered surface of the lower alluvium (layers 76, 81 and 106, Fig. 4.6), as well as residual material in later features. The finds from the weathered surface also included artefacts of Bronze Age date suggesting a prolonged period of activity on a relatively stable land-surface with little sedimentation. A possible enclosure ditch and associated postholes, thought perhaps to be Neolithic during the assessment stage, has subsequently been radiocarbon dated to the 2nd millennium BC (see below). A number of ephemeral irregular features cutting the weathered silt are likely to be of natural origin and generally contained occasional artefactual material of mixed date.

Indication of the earliest presence at the site is provided by a residual Mesolithic micro-burin from a middle Bronze Age ditch (feature 183). No other certain Mesolithic material was identified. The struck flints were concentrated on the western side of Area B, suggesting a discrete scatter that continued to the west. A number of these pieces are likely to have been detached from the same cores but refitting exercises were not profitable. Technologically, the material recovered is predominantly blade based. There was a relatively low proportion of knapping waste and a high proportion of retouched pieces (scrapers and edge-retouched cutting flakes and blades), and potentially useable flakes exhibiting micro-wear damage. This suggests that, although some core reduction was occurring, the assemblage primarily represents tool use rather than production. A bifacially worked flake (layer 106) may indicate attempts at arrowhead manufacture and other possible arrowhead blanks were found as residual material in later phases at Freemasons Road. The material from the features that cut the silts includes a number of blades and blade-like flakes but these generally appear to have been residually incorporated and are very fragmented and include many burnt pieces. Retouched pieces include two edge-retouched flakes, both probably used as cortically backed knives (natural feature 163, fill 162 and layer 66), a side-and-end scraper (layer 66), a bifacially worked flake (gully 169, fill 168) and an invasively retouched flake (ditch 132, fill 141). The last two may represent very early stages in arrowhead manufacture (Bishop, Appendix 2).

Nine sherds of early Neolithic pottery were also recovered from similar contexts, including a rolled rim (natural feature 137, fill 136) and a decorated body sherd, possibly from a Mildenhall style bowl

(layer 81, SF98, Fig. A2.1, 7). Middle Neolithic Peterborough Ware comprised two sherds with impressed twisted cord decoration (layer 76/40 SF46 and layer 49 SF114). A single sherd is from the neck of a probable 'barbed wire' decorated Beaker (layer 49, SF77, Fig. A2.1, 21). It is from a straight or gently shouldered vessel rather than the globular form of the East Anglian style (Barclay and Rayner, Appendix 2).

Early to middle Bronze Age

The 'enclosure' (Area B)

A number of features cutting the surface of the lower alluvial silts in Area B, based on radiocarbon dating, appear to date to the first half of the second millennium BC (Fig. 4.7). This included an east-west linear gully (cut nos 199, 169, 165 and 190), 0.27m to 0.48m deep, with a possible return to the north (cut no. 254). The 1.50m gap between cuts 169 and 199 may mark the location of an entrance. Cut 190 was truncated to the east and west by later intrusions. The gully was characterised by steeply sloping or near vertical sides falling to a slightly concave base and was filled by a mid grey sandy silt. The only artefact retrieved was a single struck flint from fill 168 (cut 169), but a fragment of wood from fill 198 (cut 199) produced a radiocarbon date of 1890-1660 cal BC (SUERC-24599: 3445±35 BP).

Immediately to the north of this gully, and probably associated with it, was a series of five postholes (cut nos. 151, 153, 157, 159 and 155) forming an east-west alignment covering a distance of 4.30m. All five postholes were filled with a similar soft mid grey brown silty sand. Postholes 151, 153 and 157 were spaced approximately 1.5m apart, while posthole 159 extends the line a further 1m to the east. Posthole 155 interrupts this regular spacing as it was set 0.65m to the east of 153. The five postholes were set out on an east–west alignment covering a distance of 4.30m. The presence of cut features appears to suggest that ground conditions in the slightly raised northern part of Area B during this period were dry enough to carry out certain activities. The gully and associated postholes (Plate 2) may represent a field enclosure or other land division or perhaps a foundation trench or drip gully of a structure. This group of features may demarcate a parcel of land to the north and east that continues beyond the limits of the excavation.

Timber structure 32 (Area A)

In Area A a large timber structure, defined by a double row of oak piles (Str. 32) appears to have been constructed during the same period as the 'enclosure' in Area B (Fig. 4.7 and 4.8 (A); Plates 3 and 4). One of the piles (pile 183) produced a radiocarbon date of 1880-1600 cal BC, at 90.4% (Beta-152738: 3400±50 BP). Analysis of the site stratigraphy and reconstruction of the ancient

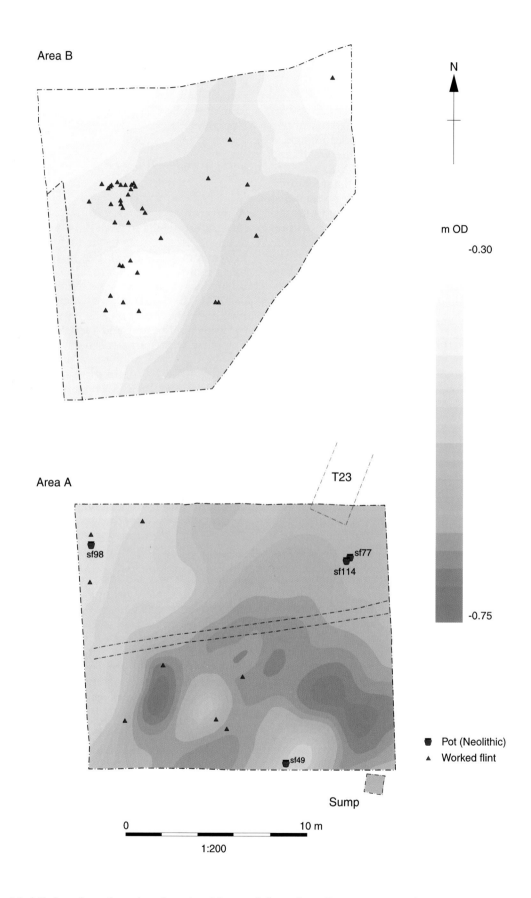

Fig. 4.6   *Modelled surface of weathered sands with recorded artefacts, Freemasons Road*

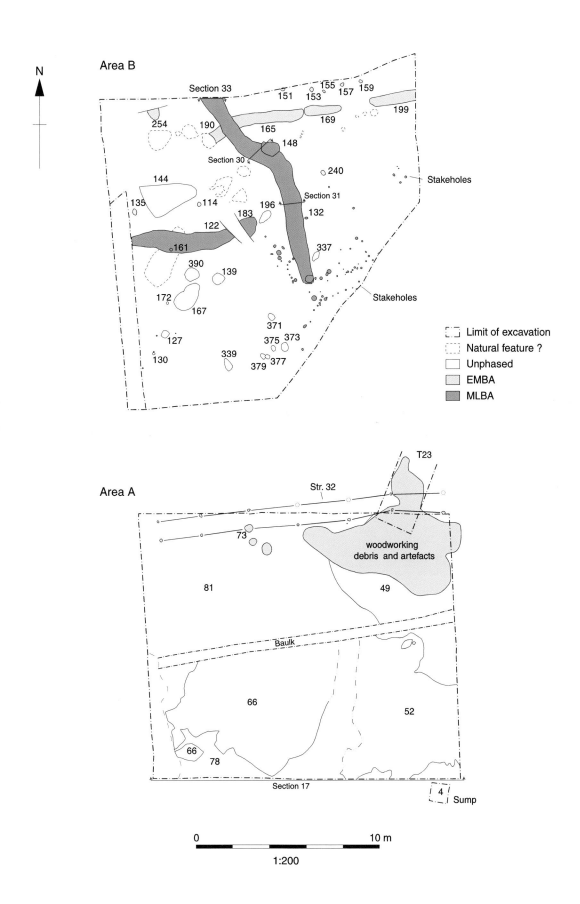

Fig. 4.7 Plan of Bronze Age features, Freemasons Road

Plate 2 'Enclosure' gully and associated postholes, Freemasons Road (Area B)

topography tends to support the interpretation that this structure was a bridge or jetty running from the higher ground out into a wetland zone. It also appears to have been built during a period of increasing wetness which the pollen studies suggest coincided with a phase of reduction in woodland and increased open grazing and agriculture. Recent topographic modelling work in the Lea Valley suggests that during the early Bronze Age a large floodplain island existed immediately to the east of Freemasons Road. It is possible the pile structure at Freemasons Road linked the drier ground of the terrace to this island (Fig. 4.8 (B); Corcoran *et al.* 2011).

The structure was traced for over 16m on an east-west alignment but was obviously longer, continuing beyond the edges of the excavation area. A total of ten *in situ* piles were excavated and recorded (Plate 3), including two identified in T23. They were arranged in a fairly regular pattern, in pairs. With

the implied location of additional piles, a total of seven pairs of vertically set timbers could be measured at between about 2.2m and 2.8m apart with the centres of each pair around 1.0m to 1.1m apart. The piles were cut from fast or medium growth timber having a maximum of about 50-70 annual rings. The comparative youth of the parent trees has prevented successful tree-ring dating but does indicate that they derive from oaks growing fairly fast in rather open, probably managed woodland of some form.

Most of the piles were round whole logs between 150mm and 210mm diameter with the bark removed but two were cleft out of larger logs. Pile 57 was a cleft 1/8th section and pile 79 a 1/4 log section (Fig 4.9; Plate 4). They were all truncated by ancient rot and measured between 0.61m and 0.96m in length with the highest standing to -0.18m OD. All the piles had multi-facetted 'pencil type' points and most had fairly

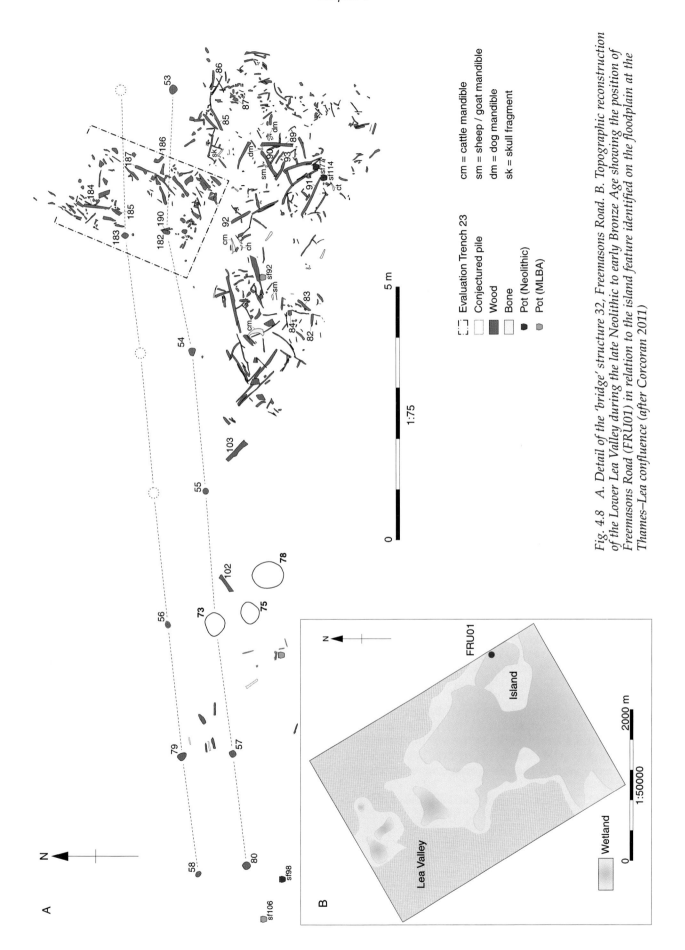

Fig. 4.8 A. Detail of the 'bridge' structure 32, Freemasons Road. B. Topographic reconstruction of the Lower Lea Valley during the late Neolithic to early Bronze Age showing the position of Freemasons Road (FRU01) in relation to the island feature identified on the floodplain at the Thames–Lea confluence (after Corcoran 2011)

Plate 3   Excavation of timber pile 55 from 'bridge' Structure 32, Freemasons Road (Area A)

well-preserved tool marks. These were smooth, with some incomplete examples up to 65mm wide, implying the use of a rounded axe blade of about 70mm wide. Such tool marks have been found to be typical of large scale woodwork of the middle Bronze Age. Earlier Bronze Age axe marks are generally wider and later Bronze Age marks substantially narrower (Sands 1997, 79; Goodburn 2003a, 104; 2004, 132). The late early to middle Bronze Age radiocarbon dating thus broadly confirms this emerging pattern. Although none of the marks were exactly the same in terms of any small features left by nicks in the axe blades used ('signature marks') the axe marks on piles 79 and 56 were so similar that they could have been cut with the same tool.

Post pit 73, 0.42m in diameter and 0.43m deep, probably marks the original location of a further pile that was later removed. The pit was characterised by steeply sloping sides falling to a pointed base and was filled with a dark brown clayey sandy silt (fill 72) containing a flint flake, a trimming flake and a quantity of burnt flint. A small assemblage of bone fragments included frog/toad bones and a spine from a three-spined stickleback (identified by J. Liddle). Some 0.20m to

the south of pile 54 a smaller cleft alder stake (context 94) may be associated with Structure 32. In addition, to the south of pit 73, two circular features were recorded (cut nos. 75 and 78). These were very shallow (0.08m and 0.07m deep) with sloping sides falling to a slightly concave base and both were filled with a loose light brownish grey silty sand. Burnt flint, struck flint, animal bone and indeterminate prehistoric pottery were recovered from feature 75 (fill 74).

Layer 49 (Fig. 4.7 and 4.8; Plate 5) on the east side of the trench comprised a dark brown organic clay silt up to 0.20m thick overlying the surface of the natural sand that appears to have built up around the piles of Structure 32. It covered an area of some 6-7m east-west and 5m north-south extending east of the trench edge. From this layer an assemblage of pottery, burnt and struck flint, daub, worked wood and animal bone was recovered. Three radiocarbon dates from layer 49 add support to the view that much of the material is likely to be directly associated with the use of Structure 32. This includes an oak 'sliver' type chip and an alder chip (93) which produced identical calibrated dates of 1690-1520 cal. BC (SUERC-27349: 3320±30 BP and SUERC-27362: 3330±30 BP)

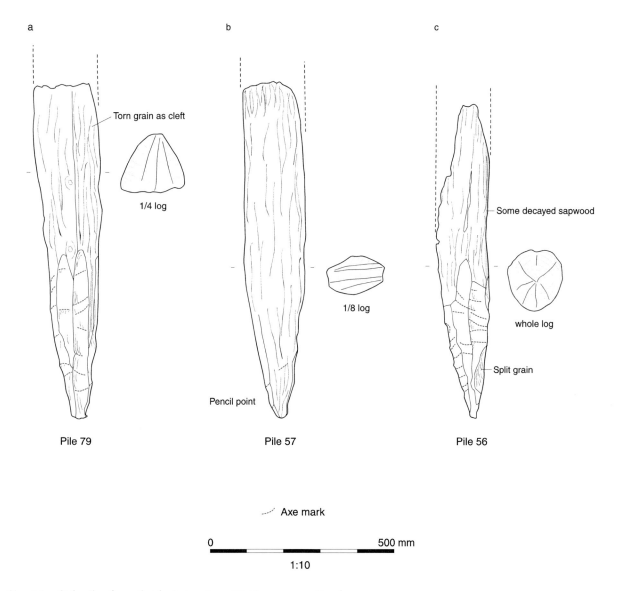

a

Torn grain as cleft

1/4 log

Pile 79

b

Pencil point

1/8 log

Pile 57

c

Some decayed sapwood

whole log

Split grain

Pile 56

Axe mark

0   500 mm

1:10

Fig. 4.9   Oak piles from 'bridge' structure 32, Freemasons Road

as well as a cattle mandible which was also dated to 1690-1520 cal BC at 94% (SUERC 27345: 3340±30 BP).

The small number of pottery sherds recovered from layer 49 were of mixed date comprising four residual Neolithic sherds and a single middle to late Bronze Age sherd. The lithics mostly comprised preparation flakes, flake fragments and cores, and suggest waste discard rather than tool use. The few blades that were present are thought to be residual. The majority of the flints showed technological characteristics dateable to the middle Bronze Age or later. The animal bone included a mix of cattle, sheep/goat (including a goat horncore), pig and dog. Heavy chop marks were evident on the goat horncore, seemingly produced by a metal blade, and a cattle horncore and limb bones also showed cut marks. The dog bones included a partial skull and a pair of mandibles, possibly indicating that an entire head was dumped or redeposited away from the rest of the body. Charcoal fragments from layer

49 derived predominantly from oak and alder with some hazel and ash. Pomaceous fruit wood and six pieces of lime/linden (*Tilia* sp.) were also recovered.

The large amount of waterlogged wood debris mainly consisted of compressed roundwood and bark fragments. Some of the roundwood bore cut marks but much of the material showed no signs of having been worked. It may be that much of the material was deposited naturally or that the wood had been collected, perhaps for firewood, and then dropped. However, the debris also contained elongated wood chips, mainly of oak 'sliver' type, suggesting that the trimming of boards or planks took place near by. Similar elongated slivers and chips were produced during the experimental production of oak planks as part of research into the Dover Boat (Goodburn 2004, 125). They appear to be particularly associated with the use of middle Bronze Age axe blades or 'palstaves' hafted as adzes to smooth very wide planks working along the grain. It was possible to recover a number of the

Plate 4   Excavated timber piles 56 and 57 from 'bridge' Structure 32, Freemasons Road (Area A)

fragile lath-like chips, the longest of which was item 82 (450mm x 75mm x 3mm; Fig. 4.10b). Others were shorter, like wood chip 87 (90mm x 45mm x 4mm). Totally fresh or 'green' oak chips do not normally float in slow moving fresh water and would accumulate near where they were dropped. It is possible that the chips were associated with the preparation of cleft and hewn planks that would have been used for the walkway of such a bridge. The slightly irregular planks would have required

trimming whilst fitting to sit firmly on cross bearers between the pile heads. If that was done working out from the 'land' on the east side of the channel it is quite possible that some of the green heartwood chips would fall and be trapped in sediment where they fell. This phenomenon was recorded at the tidal frontage of the 3rd century AD Roman quayside at Vintners Place City of London (Goodburn 1990). Other timber of fair size was also being cleft and trimmed nearby as shown by

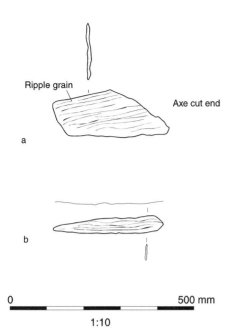

Ripple grain

Axe cut end

a

b

0

500 mm

1:10

fragment 65 which was a radially cleft alder fragment (*c* 320mm long x 125mm x 10mm thick; Fig. 4.10a). Alder could have been used for decking the bridge or jetty but would not have lasted long in the wind and rain.

One item of worked wood appears to have been a portable artefact rather than structural woodwork or woodworking debris. Timber 95 was located to the south of the 'bridge' structure on the surface of an organic clay (layer 52). Although one end of the timber was broken off it was identified as a radially cleft piece of oak, trimmed to a 'D' shape in cross section (95mm x 35mm). The original end was bruised as if it had been used as a crow bar or for digging, or, alternatively, it might have been the upper end of a robust fence pale or gatebar.

Fig. 4.10 (left) A sample of woodwork debris from layer 49, Freemasons Road a) alder cleft debris (65) b) oak shaving (82) radially faced

Plate 5 (below) Excavation of debris layer 49 associated with 'bridge' Structure 32, Freemasons Road (Area A)

Middle to late Bronze Age

Artefacts from the weathered sands

The Bronze Age artefact assemblage retrieved from the surface of the alluvial silts (layers 76, 88 and 106) at the base of the excavation comprised a small amount of Deverel Rimbury pottery, struck flint, animal bone and fragments of worked and unworked timber. The pottery was confined to the northern part of Area A (layer 81) and includes a decorated (combed) body sherd from a globular urn (Fig. A2.1, 22) and a base sherd from a bucket urn.

Features in Area B

A number of features dated to the middle to late Bronze Age appear to be concentrated in Area B (Fig. 4.7). The dating is largely based on the pottery assemblage. The presence of Deverel Rimbury pottery and radiocarbon dating suggests much of this activity occurred during the later half of the 2nd millennium BC. Although a few of these features displayed intercutting relationships hinting at a prolonged period of activity, a larger number did not which makes more detailed phasing difficult.

Butt-ended ditch 132, in the central part of the Area B, measured at least 11m long, 1m wide and about 0.50m deep and clearly truncated the earlier 'enclosure' (Plate 6). The ditch was aligned north-south with a dog-leg curve veering to the west approximately two thirds along its length and continuing north beyond the edge of excavation. The sides of the ditch sloped steeply to a slightly concave base (Fig. 4.11). The basal deposit infilling this feature to the north (fill 140) comprised mid grey blue sandy silty clay with occasional lenses of orange sand. To the south the basal deposit (fill 170) consisted of a dark brown silty peat. The upper deposits (fills 146 and 133) consisted of dark brown silty or clayey peat and contained struck flint, burnt flint, animal bone and pottery. The pottery included sherds from a Deverel Rimbury bucket urn and the bone assemblage comprised six fragments from cattle and sheep/goat. Butchery cut marks and dog gnawing were evident on cattle bones.

Located in the central part of Area B was east-west aligned linear feature 122. This feature measured 5.66m in length, 1.28m wide and 0.20m deep and was characterised by steeply sloping sides falling to a concave base. The fill (121) was a soft dark greyish brown clayey silty peat from which were retrieved a single sherd of middle to late Bronze Age pot, burnt flint, struck flint and goat/sheep and cattle bone. The feature continued west beyond the edge of excavation and was truncated to the east by a modern drain. Beyond the drain, what may have been the eastern end of the feature was recorded as feature 183.

Ditch 132 was truncated by a small pit on its eastern side. Pit 148 was at least 0.57m deep and characterised by near vertical sides falling to a flat

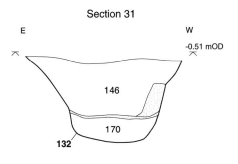

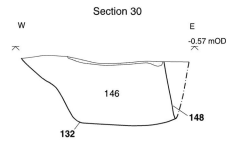

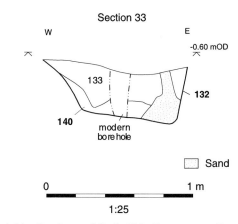

Fig. 4.11   Sections of ditch 132, Freemasons Road

base. The basal fill (192) consisted of dark brown organic clayey silt. This was overlain by a bluish grey silty clay (191) and dark brownish grey clayey sandy silt (147) which contained struck flint and middle to late Bronze Age pottery.

The stakeholes in Area B

In the south-east corner of the trench there was a concentration of postholes and stakeholes that may represent the locations of animal pens or fence lines (Figs 4.7 and 4.12). The pattern of these stakeholes is difficult to discern perhaps suggesting a number of repairs or replacement structures. What can be identified is an arc of stakeholes about 4.70m long in the southern area and perhaps a rectangular struc-ture just to the north. Within this a number of align-ments appear to form circular structures, for example features 201, 211, 328 and 330 represent a group of possible postholes forming a circle roughly

Plate 6   Ditch 132 and later stakeholes, Freemasons Road (Area B)

0.40m in diameter. Within the circle, and central to the group, was a fifth posthole (332) although this was notably larger and shallower than the surrounding features. Stakeholes 222, 224, 226, 242 and 244 on the eastern margin of the trench also appear to form a coherent group. Many of the stakeholes appear to have been set in close pairs and if contemporary may have clasped off-cut branch wood and small stems to form a 'dead hedge'. Whether they supported a wattle fence or dead hedge it is possible the structures were used to control livestock or wild herbivores. Another possibly less likely use might have been to hold and straighten freshly cut bark or cleft planks that often separate in a slight curve (Stewart 1984, 43).

In a few of the stake holes stake tips had actually survived and comprised either roundwood (*c* 55-70mm diameter) or cleft poles. All of the stake tips were identified as alder, apart from 334 which was of hazel and produced a radiocarbon date of 1390-1120 cal BC (SUERC 24291: 3010±30 BP). A pottery sherd from posthole 304 derived from a Deverel Rimbury bucket urn. In the southern part of the trench timbers 342 (not illustrated) and 214 were large oak branches driven into the earth at an acute angle. However, close examination revealed no cut

marks and the 'points' consisted of torn sapwood and bark (Fig 4.12a). Observations in modern wet woodland environments show that dying trees often shed large branches which, on occasion, have sharp wind-broken ends that become embedded in the ground almost vertically and resemble structural piles (Goodburn 1995).

Flood deposit 125

Evidence of a flood episode in Area B prior to the commencement of peat formation is apparent from a spread of eroded branch-like or drift wood timbers (wood spread 164) covering some of the stakeholes (Fig. 4.13). The wood was in turn overlain by a discrete spread of dark brownish grey silty sand (layer 125) 0.17m thick, and a layer of loose orangey brown silty sand (layer 107).

The finds from these two contexts included struck and burnt flint and animal bone and pottery, although the abraded condition of much of this material suggests it has been reworked from its original position by the flood waters. The burnt and struck flint may represent knapping waste rather than tool use and discard. Although some of the flints showed similar technology to that employed during the earlier phases of activity, a substantial

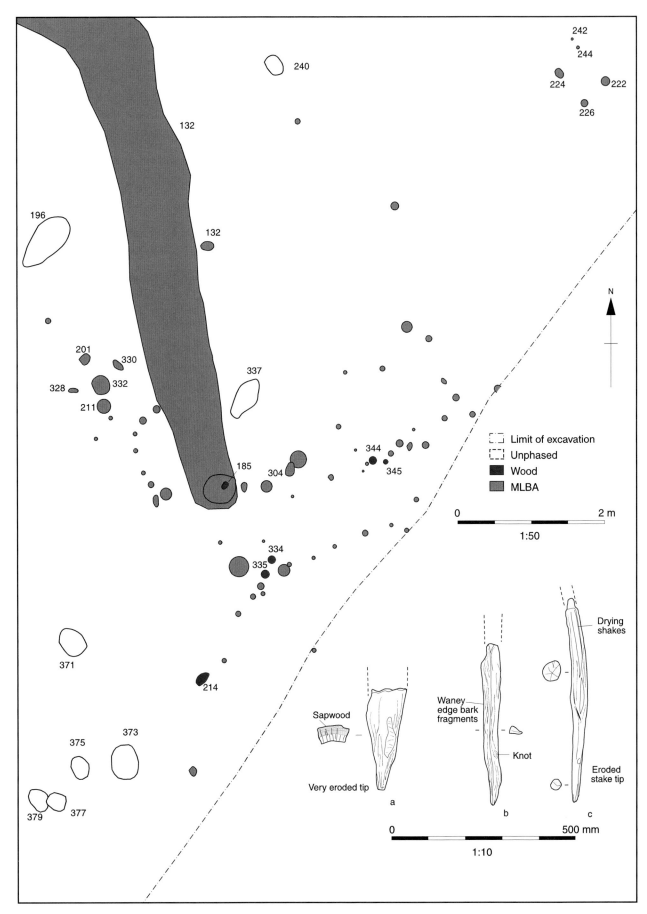

Fig. 4.12   Detail of the middle Bronze Age stake alignments, Freemasons Road a) timber (214) naturally shed oak branch b) stake (344) from a cleft eighth section c) roundwood stake (345)

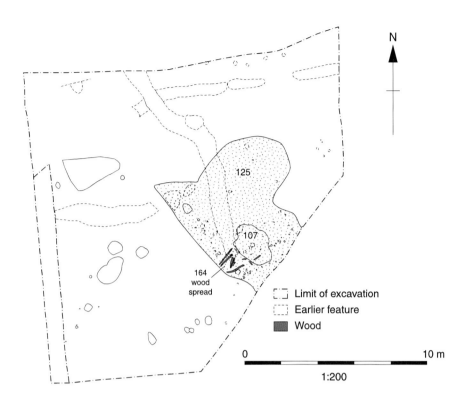

Fig. 4.13   Plan of flood deposit 125, Freemasons Road

proportion showed reduction techniques more typical of those employed during the middle Bronze Age and later. The pottery assemblage comprised 104 sherds (70% of all the pottery recovered from Freemasons Road) and included the fragmentary remains of several plain vessels considered as either transitional between the Deverel-Rimbury and post-Deverel-Rimbury (PDR) traditions (1200-1100 cal BC) and/or belonging to the initial PDR 'plain ware' phase (1150-950 cal BC, Barclay and Rayner Appendix 2). Charred residues within the bases and on the interior surfaces of a number of body and rim sherds indicate that these vessels were used to cook food over a hearth or within an oven. The animal bone from layer 125 comprised 20 fragments and included a partial disarticulated dog skeleton. Cattle bones with evidence of dog gnawing and sheep/goat bones were also recovered. Layer 107 contained cattle skull fragments likely to have derived from the broken remains of a single partial skull (Strid and Nicholson, Appendix 3).

Artefacts from the peat

It appears that peat formation on the surface of the sands had begun in the lower-lying ground in the southern part of Area A during the latter part of the third millennium BC. During the middle Bronze Age this appears to have encroached northwards (peat layers 46, 47, 32), sealing the artefactual material in layer 49. The peat appears to have extended into Area B (peat layers 123, 105, 101, 102 and 108) sometime towards the end of the 2nd

millennium BC judging from the date of the pottery retrieved from the underlying flood deposit 125.

A spread of wooden branches (wood spread 48) in the north of Area A appeared to form a linear arrangement and may have been deliberately laid down, perhaps to consolidate the underlying peat (layer 47) to support human or animal traffic. However, none of the wood showed any signs of being worked and the deposit may have a natural origin. One wooden item (SF1), however, retrieved from peat layer 32 that directly overlay layer 49, was a section of split and axe trimmed yew wood, *c* 25mm square in cross section and over 0.44m long, tending towards a point at both ends (Fig. 4.14). This piece resembles similar double pointed cleft sticks from Woolwich Manor Way and another middle Bronze Age trackway site on the floodplain at Erith in North Kent (Bennell 1998, 26). The function of these items is unclear but it is likely they were used in food preparation (see Chapter 10).

The majority of the burnt flint and nearly a third of all the struck flint recovered at Freemasons Road came from these peat deposits (Bishop, Appendix 2). The material was concentrated in Area A, especially in the lower peat horizons, suggesting that the peat was traversed and probably relates to the activity recorded in Area B during this period. The quantities of burnt flint suggest dumping in, or the consolidation of, the peat horizons or possibly that a 'burnt mound' type feature was

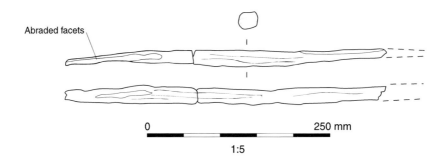

Fig. 4.14   A cleft yew wood object pointed at both ends, Freemasons Road

located in the vicinity. Analysis of the lithics suggests that both use and discard was occurring throughout the period. The majority of the tools were scrapers perhaps indicating that animal processing was occurring, although a variety of other tools would suggest that other activities were also being carried out. That actual knapping was also being carried out, is evidenced by the collection of quantities of preparation flakes, flake fragments and cores. Only minor differences were noted amongst the struck flint recovered from Areas A and B. Area B did contain a higher proportion of useable flakes but less retouched implements than Area A. This may be an indication of the presence of different activity areas. Whilst the peaty deposits may have formed under wet conditions, i.e. standing water, the lithic evidence and perhaps the timber consolidation of the surface of the peat recorded in Area A suggests that there were at least times when the peat was drier and it may have been possible to walk on it.

A quantity of cattle, sheep/goat and pig bones, some of which exhibited butchery marks, was recovered from the peat deposits. The presence of infant and juvenile cattle and sheep/goat bones is an indication that the breeding and/or rearing of these animals occurred in the vicinity. Some of the bones showed signs of dog and rodent gnawing. Interestingly a dog atlas, the first vertebra from the skull, showed approximately three fine chops indicative of an attempt at decapitation (Strid and Nicholson, Appendix 3).

Late Bronze Age to early Iron Age (Fig. 4.15)

The change to minerogenic sedimentation in Area A appears to have occurred early in the first millennium BC. A thin deposit of light brownish grey clay silt (layer 39) overlay the peat and a small quantity of burnt and struck flint, cattle, sheep and pig remains were recovered from the layer. In the central part of the trench a patchy layer of orange/yellow sandy silt with occasional fragments of charcoal and charred wood (layer 34) was recorded that may represent either *in situ* burning or a dump of burnt material. Analysis of the charcoal revealed it to be entirely composed of hazel roundwood. In

the north of the trench a single feature was recorded; pit 45. The pit was at least 0.16m deep was filled with reddish brown clayey silt (fill 44) with occasional fragments of charcoal and pottery dated to the late Bronze Age to early Iron Age.

Overlying these features was a layer of organic dark greyish brown clayey silt alluvium (layer 31). In the north of the trench the irregularity of the surface suggested possible poaching by cattle hooves (Fig. 4.15). Layer 31 was truncated by a north-south linear feature (6.70m x 1.20m), 0.38m deep (cut no. 42/38). The cut was characterised by slightly concave sides sloping to a flat and level base. The fill (fill 41/37) was dark bluish grey organic silt from which two fin spines from a three-spined stickleback were retrieved, evidence that the ditch contained water. Animal bone, including a gnawed cattle bone, and two flint flakes were also recovered. Layer 31 was also truncated by pit 36 (1.25m x 0.40m), 0.30m deep. The pit was filled with a dark greyish brown sandy clayey silt (fill 35), containing a single flint flake. Both pit 36 and ditch 42/38 were truncated by a north-south curvilinear ditch (10.10m x 1.90m), 0.38m deep (cut no. 28) that continued south beyond the limits of the excavation. The basal fill (fill 33) consisted of a dark grey peaty silt from which only small fragments of daub were recovered. The upper fill (fill 27) was a dark brown clayey peat from which burnt and struck flint, daub, butchered cattle and sheep bones and part of a pig skull were recovered. It may be that the ditches recorded here were field boundaries and/or were an attempt to drain the land.

In the north-west quadrant of Area A, a group of five features of possible natural origin were also recorded (cut nos. 24, 30, 19, 21 and 25). All of these features were relatively shallow and irregular with sandy clay fills containing occasional burnt and stuck flint and fragments of animal bone.

Two natural channels that appeared to drain to the south were recorded in Area A (cut nos. 22 and 7). The channels were sealed by alluvium at least 1.20m thick which was excavated by a mechanical excavator. Channel 22 was 5.5m wide, at least 0.40m deep and ran north-south across the whole length of the trench for 14m continuing beyond the limits of

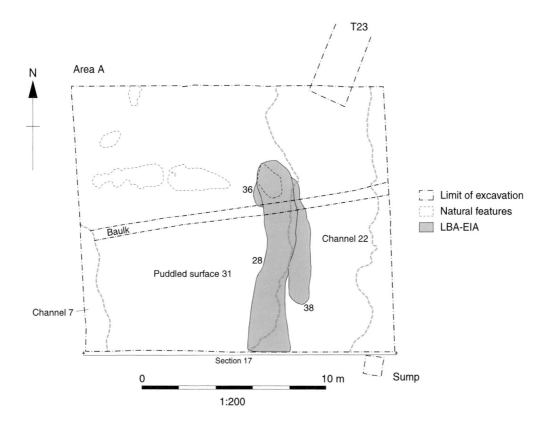

Fig. 4.15 Plan of features within the upper alluvium, Freemasons Road

the excavation both to the north and south. The channel was filled by a sequence of alluvial deposits of clayey and sandy silts. The complex sequence of fills probably resulted from changing flow patterns and rates, which would have caused differing rates of deposition and erosion. On the western side of the trench another natural watercourse, channel 7, was partly exposed (6.7m x 1.5m wide) 0.40m deep, and continued to the west and south beyond the edge of excavation. Again the channel appeared to have silted up naturally.

Natural and unphased features

A number of features were recorded truncating the surface of the lower alluvium in Area B, although most these had irregular profiles suggesting they could be the result of natural root action or perhaps tree-throw holes (Fig. 4.7). This included a group of features to the west of ditch 132 which were filled with dark brown peaty or organic silts and clays and produced occasional struck flint, burnt flint and pottery dated to the middle to late Bronze Age. Two larger features were recorded to the south of this group that appear to intercut, and were themselves cut by ditch 122. These features were quite shallow at 0.15m and 0.42m deep and produced burnt flint, struck flint and bone.

A number of features thought to be of anthropogenic origin truncating the surface of the lower alluvium may relate to any of the phases of Bronze Age activity. A group of possible postholes, scattered across Area B and filled with a similar soft, mid grey brown sandy silt, were provisionally associated with the 'enclosure' gully during the assessment. They were thought to represent fence lines for animal pens, with the gaps perhaps supporting wattle hurdles. Some of these features, however, were quite widely spaced and could relate to later phases of activity. The only artefactual material recovered was a small amount of burnt flint from posthole 130. Postholes 135, 114 and 240 form an east-west alignment over a distance of 10.40m, 3.0m to the south of the 'enclosure'. To the south and at approximate right angles was a north south alignment of three further postholes: 130, 161 and 172, regularly spaced at 2.90m intervals over a distance of 5.60m. In the south-east corner of Area B was a further cluster of four small pits or possibly postholes (cut nos. 371, 373, 375, 377 and 379). All these features were filled with dark grey brown clayey silt.

In the central part of the trench two possible post-pits (cut nos 196 and 337) were initially thought to be associated with the group of middle Bronze Age stake holes. Both features were filled by greyish brown sandy silt containing burnt and struck flint. Approximately 0.70m to the north of the ditch 122 was a large (3.10m x 1.70m) sub-triangular shaped pit 0.22m deep (cut no.144). The feature was filled with mid greyish brown sandy silt from which burnt flint was also retrieved (fill 143). To the south of the ditch was a cluster of four small pits. Pits 167 and 390 were filled with a dark brown peaty clay containing burnt and struck flint, as well as sheep/goat teeth in the case of pit 167 and also pit 127 in this cluster.

Chapter 5: Woolwich Manor Way

Introduction (Figs 1.6, 5.1-5.4)

The early historical maps (for example Roque's map of 1754, Chapman and Andre's map of 1777 and Milne's 1800 map) show that the area around the A13 and Woolwich Manor Way junction comprised undeveloped marsh and low-lying marginal land. The marsh was known as the East Ham Level and lay between the River Thames and the higher ground occupied by settlements such as East Ham and West Ham (Fig. 1.6). The Level was crossed by numerous small streams and, subject to frequent flooding, remained unsuitable for settlement into the 19th century. The Northern Outfall Sewer was constructed across East Ham Manor Way in 1865 and remains beneath the present junction with its crown lying at +7.7m OD. The development of the marshes accelerated with the construction of the Royal Victoria Dock (opened 1855), followed by the

Royal Albert Dock (opened 1880) and the King George V Dock (opened 1921). A Tar and Liquor Works (opened 1879) was located 300m to the east, and Roman Road was built in 1897. The rest of the area remained agricultural land with fields and allotment gardens, although the land northwest of the junction was later developed into terraced housing. The most significant evidence for prehistoric activity in the immediate vicinity of Woolwich Manor Way are the Bronze Age timber structures and trackways at Beckton Nursery, Beckton 3-D (Meddens 1996) and the Golf Driving Range site (Carew *et al.* 2010). The latter site lies immediately to the south of the A13 sites. The alignment of East Ham High Street and Manor Way may also mark the line of a Roman road leading from the higher ground to the north, perhaps to a ferry crossing at North Woolwich, which is of at least medieval origin.

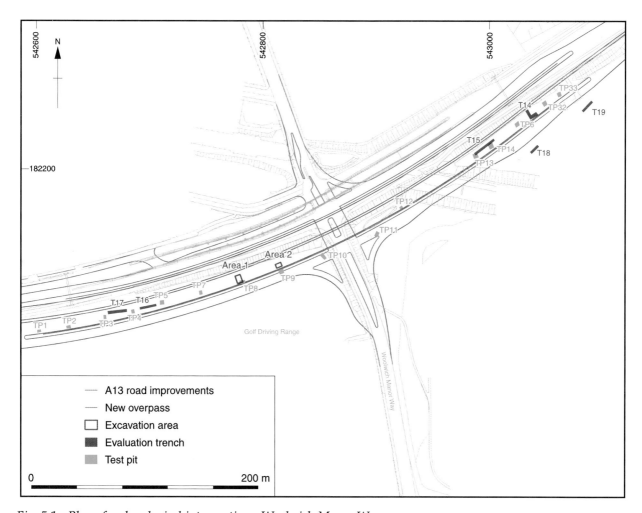

Fig. 5.1   Plan of archaeological interventions, Woolwich Manor Way

The Phase I evaluation at the Woolwich Manor Way site involved the excavation of 16 test pits (TPs 1-14, 32 and 33). This was followed by 6 evaluation trenches (T14-T19) as part of the Phase II works; four to the northeast of the Woolwich Manor Way junction and two to the southwest (Fig. 5.1) (Plate 7). Geoarchaeological modelling of the test pit data revealed that beneath the modern overburden the highest elevations in the surface of the Pleistocene sands and gravels occurred at the far eastern end of the site, dropping westwards. A deep alluvial sequence including a major peat bed was present in the west, thinning eastwards against the rise of the terrace (Fig. 5.2). Archaeological remains identified during the evaluation work were dated to the Neolithic, Bronze Age and Roman periods. One of the most significant discoveries was a scatter of early Neolithic worked flint (Bishop in Appendix 2),

pottery (Barclay and Rayner in Appendix 2) and charred cereal grain (Pelling in Appendix 3) in T15 in the eastern part of the site. These deposits were subsequently preserved *in situ*. To the west, preserved within the peat, were the remains of a series of Bronze Age timber structures (TP8 and TP9). A Roman pottery assemblage was also recovered from the upper alluvial sequence. Phase III investigations focused on the area to the west of the junction. The works comprised targeted excavation to mitigate the localised impact of flyover abutments on the timber structures. Two areas were excavated; Area 1 (5m x 7m) and Area 2 (7m x 3.5). In both trenches, near the top of the peat, were the well-defined remains of three relatively simple trackways. At the south end of Area 1, one of the trackways was cut away by a natural channel and another structure, perhaps a trackway or a platform, had been built over the fill.

Plate 7   Excavations at Woolwich Manor Way (WMA02, Area 2 in the foreground)

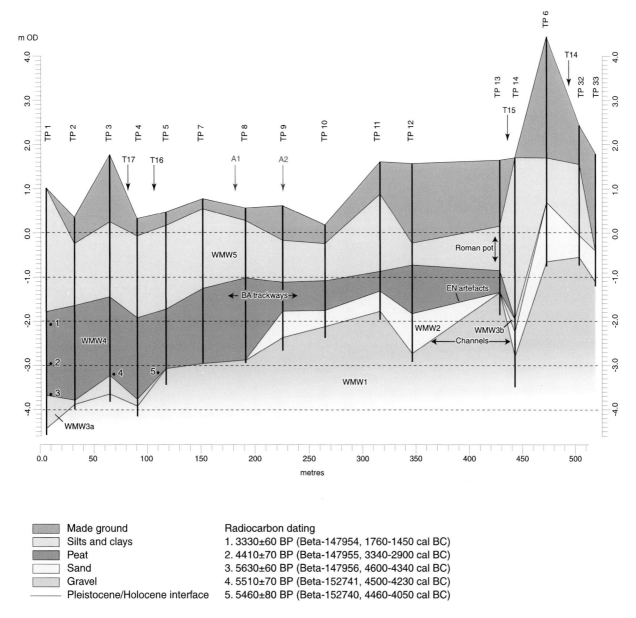

Radiocarbon dating
1. 3330±60 BP (Beta-147954, 1760-1450 cal BC)
2. 4410±70 BP (Beta-147955, 3340-2900 cal BC)
3. 5630±60 BP (Beta-147956, 4600-4340 cal BC)
4. 5510±70 BP (Beta-152741, 4500-4230 cal BC)
5. 5460±80 BP (Beta-152740, 4460-4050 cal BC)

Fig. 5.2   Stratigraphical cross-section based on test pit data, Woolwich Manor Way

A small amount of waterlogged wood was excavated and lifted as part of the evaluation phase but the vast majority derives from the excavation of Areas 1 and 2. A total of 201 items were lifted for examination and recording as potentially worked material, although 168 were small bags of un-worked material and bark chips and a small number of items were fragments of worked wood such as broken wood chips. This material was briefly listed and discarded. For the remainder of the material, following washing off-site, 39 timber sheets with sketches were completed. A total of 21 worked items were drawn to scale and a small proportion was also photographed in raking light to pick out tool marks. The total number of samples taken for dendrochronology was four, two of oak and two of yew; additionally 154 wood samples

were taken for species identification and age. Due to resource limitations and the condition of some samples the multiple samples from the same contexts were sub-sampled and a total of 92 were examined (Barnett in Appendix 3). This assemblage must be considered medium sized by national standards but is moderately large compared to assemblages from the small excavations typical in the London wetlands.

Palaeoenvironmental work during the evaluation stage focused on characterising the deep sediment sequence exposed in TP1. Further examination of biological remains from the sediments excavated during the Phase III investigations was carried out as part of the post-excavation assessment. Overall the assessment stage indicated that the preservation of ostracods and foraminifera was very poor and no

51

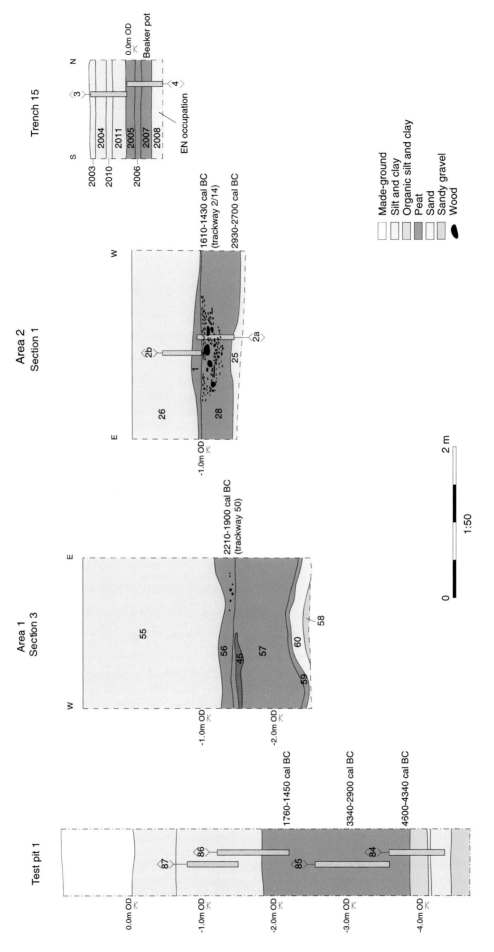

Fig. 5.3 Sample sections, Woolwich Manor Way

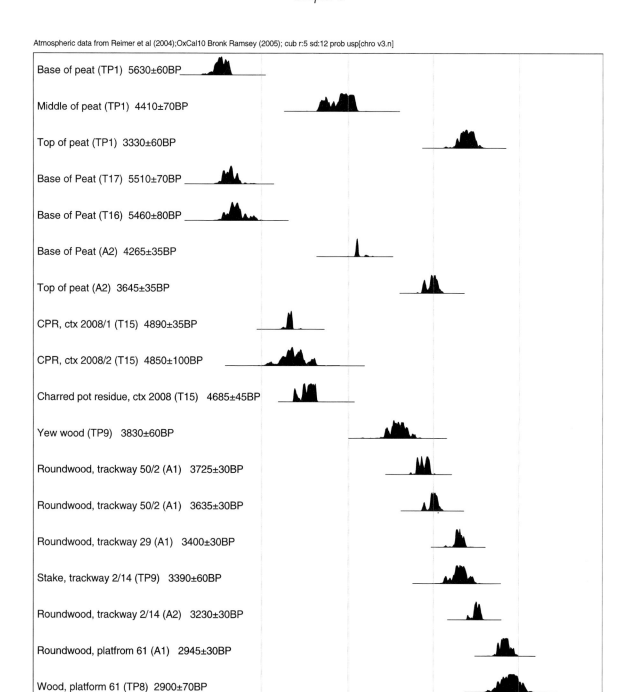

Atmospheric data from Reimer et al (2004);OxCal10 Bronk Ramsey (2005); cub r:5 sd:12 prob usp[chro v3.n]

Fig. 5.4   Radiocarbon dates, Woolwich Manor Way

detailed analytical work has been carried out. The results of the assessment, however, do provide useful information in terms of characterising the environments of deposition associated with the sediments. Further detailed work on the pollen and diatoms has been carried out on the sequences from Area 2 and TP1 (Fig. 5.3) (Haggart in Appendix 3), and plant and insect remains from a representative

selection of the richest bulk samples were analysed (Smith in Appendix 3; Pelling in Appendix 3). Thin sections for micromorphology were processed from the early Neolithic landsurface in T15 and through the Bronze Age trackway levels in Area 2 (Macphail and Crowther in Appendix 3). A total of 18 samples from a range of deposits were submitted for radiocarbon dating (Fig. 5.4; Appendix 1).

Sedimentary architecture and environments of deposition

The pre-Holocene sediments and basement topography

Fluvial gravels (WMW1)

The basal part of the investigated sequence comprised poorly bedded coarse flint gravels and sands. These deposits were not examined in detail as the excavations were unstable and prone to rapid flooding. They were, however, recorded at the base of most of the test pits across the site and are typically associated with high-energy rapid sedimentation in braided channels during Pleistocene cold climate episodes.

The early Holocene topographic template

The early Holocene topographic template at Woolwich Manor Way is represented by the surface of the Pleistocene gravel. Examination of the shape of the template reveals the highest elevations, up to -0.5m OD, occur in the eastern part of the site in the vicinity of TP32. Elevations gradually reduce westwards over a distance of about 400m to c -4.4m OD in TP1. Localised dips in elevation in the vicinity of TP12 and TP14 may indicate the locations of early Holocene channel features.

The Holocene sediments

Freshwater sands (WMW2)

The earliest Holocene sediments were encountered in the central and eastern areas of the site. Here sand bodies exhibited a similar surface trend to that of the underlying gravel body. Differentiation between the sands and the underlying gravels was difficult where the sand contained gravel beds or lenses. Similar sandy facies have been identified elsewhere in the Thames system and are thought to have accumulated as sand bars within an early Holocene meandering channel system (Wilkinson *et al.* 2000).

The upper surface of the sands appeared weathered indicating that the sands were exposed as a land surface prior to inundation as a consequence of sea-level rise and flooding. This weathering occurs later than the original deposition of the sands and the archaeological evidence suggests the surface was accessible throughout the early and mid Holocene. A regionally significant sequence of charred plant remains consisting of several hundred charred cereal grains, chaff, weeds seeds and hazel nuts were recovered from T15 (Pelling in Appendix 3), along with concentrations of early Neolithic pottery and worked flint (Barclay and Rayner; Bishop in Appendix 2). Thin section analysis revealed a mature occupation soil, latterly modified by a brief episode of alluviation prior to peat formation (Macphail and Crowther in Appendix 3). The

soil showed no sign of phosphate enrichment but did contain much fine anthropogenic material (burnt flint and charcoal). The homogenous fabric and the presence of dusty clay void coatings may be ascribed to compaction by trampling and/or perhaps cultivation. Bronze Age ploughsoils of similar character are recorded from the fens and under Thames alluvium at Bermondsey (French 2003; Macphail *et al.* 1990; Merriman 1992; Sidell *et al.* 2000).

Estuarine silts and clays (WMW3)

In the lower-lying western part of the site grey or brown clay-silt units occurred above the gravel. These deposits became increasingly organic up-profile. In TP1 the clay-silts lay between c -4.4m and -3.7m OD but thin and wedge eastwards against the rising gravel surface. In TP14 a unit of thin dark grey organic clay lying within a possible channel above the early Holocene sands probably represents a lateral equivalent.

Overall these deposits appear to have accumulated under conditions arising from the initial submergence of these lower-lying areas as a consequence of rising sea-levels. Radiocarbon age estimates from the overlying peat suggest the deposits in TP1 accumulated during the Mesolithic period, prior to around 4600 cal BC. The lower part of the sequence in TP1 comprised dark greyish brown silty clay. Organic content was quite low with LOI values at c 9%. The pollen assemblages, although poorly preserved, suggest that while the eastern part of the site remained relatively dry ground, a wetland environment began to develop in the western part of the site during the late Mesolithic period. Sediment accumulation initially appears to have occurred under rather open conditions with the vegetation dominated by sedges and grasses, with some bracken and ferns. Pine was the dominant tree pollen, although this is often over-represented in estuarine clays (Godwin, 1975). The occurrence of pollen of goosefoot family together with dinoflagellate cysts, sponge spicule fragments and a single example of the brackish diatom *Cyclotella striata*, hint at the proximity of intertidal conditions. Towards the interface with the overlying peat the sediment became much more organic (28% loss on ignition value). Alder began to dominate the pollen assemblages with secondary willow and hazel, suggesting the development of a carr environment with perhaps oak growing at slightly higher elevations.

Freshwater peat and organic silts (WMW4)

Overlying the sands and clay silts at Woolwich Manor Way was a major peat unit. Sediments assigned to this unit varied considerably along the route corridor. The thickest sequences occurred in the west comprising a lower woody peat and an upper amorphous peat. This graded into more minerogenic sandy sediments as the peat thinned approaching the higher ground of the gravel terrace to the east. Radiocarbon age estimates in TP1 indicate that peat formation at the lowest elevations to the west began during the late Mesolithic at 4600-4340 cal BC (Beta-147956: 5630±60 BP). Two further dates from the base of the peat in T17 and T16 produced similar results at 4500-4230 cal BC (Beta-152741: 5510±70 BP) and 4460-4050 cal BC (Beta-152740: 5460±80 BP) respectively. Here scatters of burnt flint indicate that late Mesolithic cultural activity within the floodplain corresponds with the early stages of peat development. The peat appears to have accumulated throughout the Neolithic and Bronze Age, gradually encroaching onto the higher ground to the east. In Area 2 accumulation began during the later Neolithic at 2930-2700 cal BC (SUERC-25563: 4265±35 BP) and in T15 further to the west Bronze Age Beaker pottery was recovered from the base of the peat that sealed the earlier Neolithic activity.

The sediments from the sequence recorded in TP1 comprised a very dark brown peat varying to silty peat that was moderately to well-humified with abundant wood and plant fragments in places. Occasional pockets of dark greyish-brown organic silt were also noted. The pollen assemblages suggest alder carr continued to develop in the western part of the site. There are some indications from the base of the peat of a period of quite dry or 'semi-terrestrial' conditions. Loss on ignition (LOI) measurements of organic matter increase to about 74% and of note was the presence of fungal spores indicative of mesotrophic conditions, perhaps with abundant dry leaf litter. Lime (*Tilia* sp.) pollen was very well represented but this could well be the result of destruction of less robust grains under oxidising conditions.

Further up the sequence alder pollen increases in abundance suggesting the alder carr became very dense, although oak and hazel were still present, probably growing on the slightly elevated drier areas. Overall the carr appears to have been quite species rich. Although lime occurred at much lower frequencies, willow, yew, buckthorn and viburnum were also present along with sedges and grasses. Cereal-type pollen was sporadically noted and may relate to cultivation on the higher ground of the terrace. Peat accumulation appears to have occurred in predominantly freshwater conditions and increases in algal spores hint at areas of shallow stagnant water. Episodic estuarine influxes, however, are also indicated by rare valves of the marine and brackish water diatoms (*Pseudostelligera westii, Cyclotella striata, Diploneis didyma* and *Actinoptychus senarius*) as well as sponge spicule fragments.

The pollen assemblages from the late Neolithic to early Bronze Age peat from the excavation areas further to the east produced similar results to TP1. In addition a diverse range of seeds of wetlands plants: sedges, crowfoots, water dropwort and water pepper/mite, were recovered from the lower part of the peat profile in both Area 1 and T15. Preservation of plant remains was generally poorer below the

Bronze Age trackway structures, although the assemblages included similar wetland species. Disturbed ground species were also present and included chickweeds, black nightshade and brambles. The insect assemblage included water beetles suggestive of slow flowing or stagnant waters (*Ochthebius* spp., *Cercyon sternalis, Laccobius* spp. and *Dryops* spp.), along with species associated with decaying wood (*Melasis buprestoides, Cerylon histeroides* and *Grynobius planus*). A single wing case of an *Aphodius* 'dung beetle' was also recovered, although when present in small numbers these beetles may represent no more than a very routine part of the 'background fauna' found on most archaeological sites (Kenward 1975; 1978).

In T15 the weathered sand surface was overlain by a thin layer of sandy peat that graded upwards into a black woody peat. Thin section analysis revealed a possible brief period of alluviation, evidenced by clay inwash, prior to the main period of peat formation. There was also evidence of fluctuating water tables leading to peat decay (ripening) and associated insect burrowing, as evidenced by organic excrement-replacement of the original peat sediment. The pollen from this sequence was not examined in detail; however, bulk samples from the base of the profile produced diverse wetland plant assemblages similar to those in Area 1.

Towards the top of the peat profiles examined in TP1 and Area 2 increases in pollen of plantains (including sea plantain) and pondweeds suggest a gradually rising water table around the middle of the 2nd millennium BC, probably triggered by rising sea-levels. In TP1 this occurs around 1760-1450 cal BC (Beta 147954: 3330±60) and is accompanied by a substantial drop in organic content with LOI values at around 54%. Diatom assemblages were better preserved in these levels and were dominated by estuarine species common in tidal channels (such as *Cyclotella striata*) and upper saltmarsh environments (for example *Diploneis interrupta*). In Area 2 the increased surface wetness appears to be associated with the construction of the brushwood trackway in this trench (Str. 2/14), dated to 1610-1430 cal BC (SUERC-24292: 3230±30 BP). A range of fruits and seeds of wet ground species were recovered from the peat at this level, particularly water pepper/mite, but also clustered dock, gypsywort, spikerush, branch bur-reed and water plantain. Diatoms were poorly preserved but there were a few examples of estuarine forms (*Cyclotella striata.* and *Navicula navicularis*). A minor phase of brackish water incursion within the upper part of the peat is also represented by channel 53 recorded in Area 1. A mixture of brackish and freshwater diatoms was recovered from the fill of this channel indicating the presence of a former small saltmarsh creek perhaps extending into the freshwater wetland. The fill of this channel is overlain by a timber 'platform' (Str. 61) dated to 1270-1040 cal BC (SUERC-24504: 2945±30 BP), implying this marine incursion in Area 1 occurred sometime during the middle Bronze Age.

This period is also characterised by a gradual decline in arboreal pollen, most notably alder and oak, and in Area 2 there is an increase in pollen of grasses and goosefoots as well as seeds of meadow buttercup and rushes, suggesting more open areas of damp grassland. The changing hydrological conditions at the site would undoubtedly have affected vegetation, while further possible evidence of cereal cultivation in the pollen spectra along with an increase of microscopic charcoal and seeds of disturbed ground species, such as nettle and bramble, may also indicate clearance and cultivation, perhaps on the higher terraces.

Estuarine silts and clays (WMW5)

A thick sequence of clay silts sealed the peat across the whole site area. Radiocarbon age estimates from the top of the underlying peat suggests the change to minerogenic sedimentation occurred during the mid to late 2nd millennium BC. Accumulation appears to have continued throughout the later prehistoric and into the historic period with evidence of Roman occupation occurring within the alluvium in T15 and TP13 in the east of the site. The environmental evidence indicates that these deposits formed high in the tidal frame of a predominantly open estuarine environment of tidal creeks and saltmarsh, with freshwater environments co-existing close-by.

In TP1, at -1.78m OD, a dense dark greyish-brown silt to clay-silt which was slightly organic in places, overlay the peat. This graded upwards into a blocky yellowish brown clay-silt. Compared to the underlying peat, the organic content of the clay-silt unsurprisingly dropped markedly with LOI values at aproximately 13-15%. Pollen was not preserved in these sediments. The diatom assemblages, however, were generally indicative of tidal mudflats and saltmarsh. Once again the estuarine form *Cyclotella striata* was most frequent, although subtle changes in the proportions of species that prefer freshwater conditions *(Navicula menisculus, Cocconeis disculus, C. placentula* and *Staurosirella pinnata)* suggest brief periods when freshwater input increased, probably from streams issuing from the gravel terrace. Foraminifera and ostracods recovered from the clay-silt tend to support this. The ostracods were typical of both freshwater *(Candona neglecta, Candona* sp, *Darwinula stevenson* and *Limnocythere inopinata.)* and brackish environments *(Cyprideis torosa, Cytherura gibba* and *Leptocythere porcellanea)* suggesting deposition in creeks towards the limits of tidal reach. Similar deposits examined in Area 2, at -0.70m OD, consisted of very dark grey silty clay grading upwards into orangey brown and grey mottled silty clay with iron mineralization in root channels. Diatoms were less well preserved, but both brackish *(Cyclotella striata)* and fully marine forms *(Triceratum favus)* were noted. The pollen assemblages in Area 2 were very similar to the underlying peat. Grasses

and sedges were the most abundant plants and alder continued to decline, suggesting quite an open environment. Towards the top of the sampled sequence the percentages of goosefoots and bracken increased markedly.

The cultural evidence

Early Neolithic (Figs 5.1 and 5.3)

Neolithic activity was identified in T15 in the eastern part of the site on the surface of a 'dirty' layer of weathered sand (context 2008, unit WMW2) (Figs 5.1 and 5.3). The sand was 0.10 to 0.15m thick, lying at -0.73m to -0.45m OD, and was sealed by a sequence of peat deposits. Thin section analysis has confirmed that the sand probably represents an occupation soil that may have been subject to trampling and/or cultivation. The cultural material recovered from this surface was densest in the north-eastern part of the trench and included a concentration of early Neolithic pottery, struck flint, burnt flint and a spread of charred plant remains and charcoal. The condition of the struck flint and conjoined pottery supports the interpretation of a relatively in situ assemblage. The occurrence of a single sherd of Beaker pottery, however, suggests that the surface was subsequently exposed for a considerable period of time. Cut into this horizon were three small circular or sub-circular features. They contained no finds, were too shallow to hold timbers, and probably represent natural rootholes.

The lithics consisted of 102 struck pieces, including blades, flakes, utilised flakes, cores, two scrapers, two serrated blades and six utilised flakes, probably of early Neolithic date (Bishop, Appendix 2). The pottery assemblage comprised 85 sherds that collectively could be accommodated within the Mildenhall style of the decorated bowl tradition of the mid 4th millennium BC. Three sherds had been either overfired or refired. One thickened semi-rolled rim was decorated with rows of `horseshoe`-shaped motifs, probably made with the articular surface of a bird or small mammal bone to give oval-shaped impressions (Fig. A2.1.2). Other sherds belong to a fine black burnished shouldered bowl with thickened surface broken just below the rim (Fig. A2.1.1). This sherd had sooty and charred residue below the rim and had therefore probably been used as a cooking pot; the residue produced a radiocarbon date of 3630-3360 cal BC (SUERC-24830: 4685±45 BP) (Barclay and Rayner, Appendix 2).

Significant numbers of charred plant remains were recovered from bulk samples from layer 2008. This included charred grains of emmer wheat *(Triticum dicoccum)* and associated spikelet forks and glumes, as well as occasional weeds and hazel nut shells. Preservation of the material was exceptionally good for a deposit of this antiquity and in total 470 grains were counted. A small number of grains showed characteristics of einkorn *(Triticum monococcum)*, but may simply derive from single seeded emmer wheat. The limited weed flora included typical ruderal species, mostly spring germinating, which tend to be found associated with early prehistoric cereal remains such as fat hen (*Chenopodium album*), black bindweed (*Fallopia convolvulus*), small seeded medick/trefoil/clover type (*Medicago/Trifolium/Lotus* sp.) and grasses (Pelling, Appendix 3). An initial radiocarbon date on the grain from the assessment stage provided a date of 3950-3350 cal BC (Beta-153983: 4850 ±100 BP). A second, AMS, date obtained during the analysis produced a more precise date of 3770-3630 cal BC (SUERC-24597: 4890±35 BP).

Analogous sand and sandy gravel deposits in TP13 (context 1517) and T16 (context 2080) produced a small number of artefacts including burnt flint, occasional animal bone, a single sherd of flint-tempered pottery and a flint scraper. In T17 a similar 'dirty' gravel layer (context 2073) produced a considerable concentration of burnt flint.

Early to middle Bronze Age (Figs 5.5-5.9)

The early to middle Bronze Age period at Woolwich Manor Way is largely represented by a series of simple roundwood trackways recorded within the peat (unit WMW4) in excavation Areas 1 and 2. The earliest of these was located in Area 1 and dates to the late 3rd millennium BC (Str. 50) with other structures dating up until the mid 2nd millennium BC

(Str. 29 and 2/14). The structures occur in close proximity and on similar north-south alignments to the trackway (Str. 107) recorded immediately to the south at the Golf Driving Range (Fig. 5.5) (Carew *et al*, 2010).

Trackway 50 (Area 1)

The earliest trackway in excavation Area 1 was Structure 50 located in the northwest corner of the trench (Fig. 5.6). Radiocarbon dating of roundwood produced two dates of 2210-2030 cal BC (SUERC-24292: 3725±30 BP) and 2130-1900 cal BC (SUERC-27350: 3635±30 BP). The structure was aligned north-south and was visible for just over 2m within the trench. It was fairly narrow at 0.60m wide and comprised small rods and branch wood laid side by side (context 49). The species were a mix of oak, alder, ash, and elm with diameters ranging between approximately 30mm to 50mm. The material was very compressed and weathered and too small to preserve clear axe-marks. Several cut ends were, however, recorded *in situ*. The rods and branches were mainly broken into rather short lengths of under 0.6m, which may have happened as a result of compaction as the wood began to decay after a couple of years and became brittle. A large oak axe cut chip was also found lying on the trackway surface that must have derived from hewing a knotty oak log at least 150mm in diameter. The structure was quite slight in construction being only one

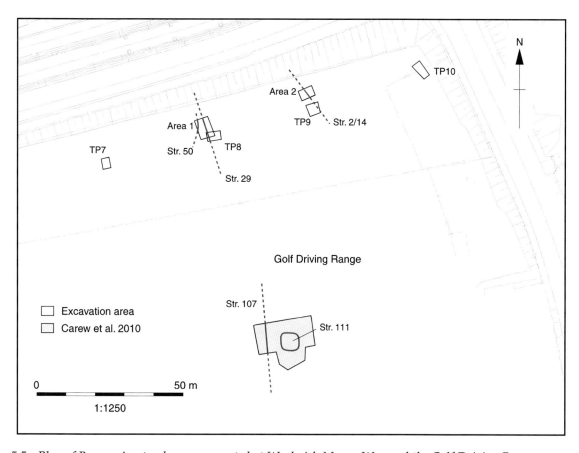

Fig. 5.5   Plan of Bronze Age trackways excavated at Woolwich Manor Way and the Golf Driving Range

or two rods thick and was most likely used for human foot passage and possibly light livestock. No stakes were found associated with the structure. This may suggest that the builders did not expect high water levels to disturb it. The tight outline of the trackway edges also suggests that it was little affected by water erosion before it was buried by the peat growth. It seems unlikely, however, that such a trackway could have survived much use, and it may have been intended as a temporary measure only. It is not quite parallel to the later Trackway 29 in the same trench and appears to have curved off to the

west at its southern extent within the limit of excavation, although this may be an artificial impression given by some horizontal truncation at its southern end. A physical relationship between the two trackways in Area 1 could not be determined.

A thin (roughly 5mm) layer of orange burnt sand with frequent charcoal inclusions (layer 45) was found in a 1m² area in the north-west corner of Area 1, extending beyond the limit of excavation. This has been phased with the trackway on the basis of parity within the peat sequence. It would seem unlikely that the sand could have been deposited

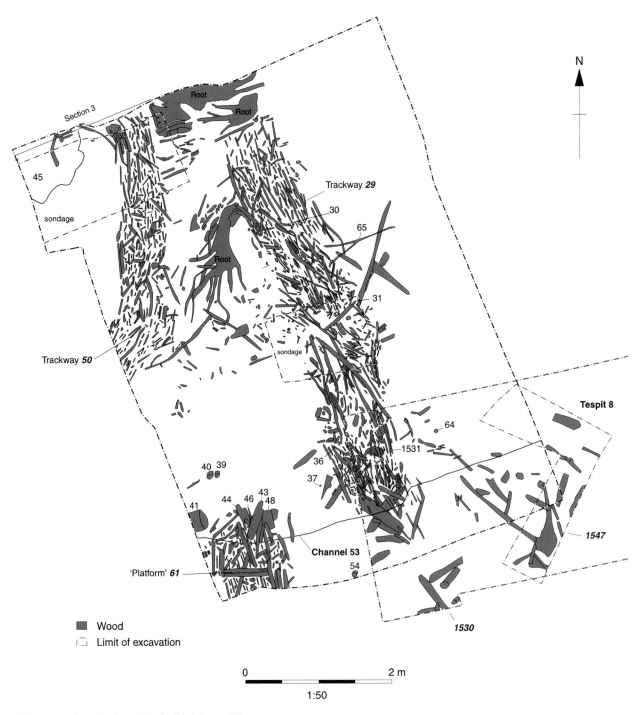

Fig. 5.6   Area 1 plan, Woolwich Manor Way

there naturally, as the layer was many times too thick for a minerogenic lens within the peat. In addition, it was only found in a discrete area and did not appear to contain significant organic material. As wood seems to have been the favoured material for consolidation of the soft, wet peaty ground surface, the introduction of this sand may have been associated with the formation of a hearth or cooking surface, or that the deposit represents casual or ritual disposal of rake-out from nearby domestic activity on the terrace edge. If the deposit were burnt *in situ,* it would appear to represent the first direct evidence of such domestic use of the marshland fringe on the north Thames marshes. Such domestic activity is more normally found on dry terrace edge locations.

Trackway 29 (Area 1)

Trackway 29 was much more substantial, running NNW-SSE the length of the trench for about 6m. It was truncated at the south end by later channel 53 (Fig. 5.6; Plate 8). A piece of roundwood from this trackway produced a date of 1770-1610 cal BC (SUERC-24297: 3400±30 BP). A small area of the southern end of trackway 29 was found in TP8 during the Phase I work (recorded as Str. 1531). The

structure was approximately 0.9m to 1.0m wide and made from relatively uniform small roundwood rods (context 62) which had been laid side by side to a depth of over 100mm in the centre. The rods varied from about 24mm diameter to small 'poles' at about 60mm diameter and there were a very small number of larger elements. The uniformity, small size, and straightness of the rods suggests that they were largely sourced from coppiced or pollarded trees. The ends of the rods were cut with small, rounded metal axe blades into wedge shapes, but the ancient weathering prevented the survival of very clear axe marks including signature scratches created by small nicks in the blades of the axes used. Three rod ends were lifted for more detailed examination (rods 30, 31 and 36). The first two were wedge pointed and of alder (Fig. 5.7a), and the third was of willow or poplar and was pencil form. A small group of rotten yew stem fragments may also have been casually reused as 'makeup' material beneath the freshly cut material.

The pattern of stakes possibly associated with the trackway is not clear. Up to three stakes (stakes 33, 37 and 64, see Fig. 5.7b) identified as ash and alder, could have been part of the structure, although stakes 64 and 37 were offset to the side. It is possible

Plate 8   Trackway 29, Woolwich Manor Way (Area 1)

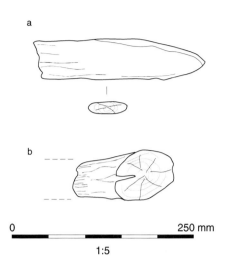

Fig. 5.7 Worked wood from trackway 29, Woolwich Manor Way. a) cut rod end (30), b) stake (33)

that they were marker stakes showing the edge of the trackway at times of high water level. The lack of variation in the material in the trackway suggests that if it was repaired it was with similar material throughout its life and the weathering suggests it was probably in use for at least a couple of years. A small number of worked wood items appeared to have been dropped on the surface on the track. The most well-preserved was a 'Y' shaped branch

section of yew (timber 65, Fig. 5.6). The shape was probably arbitrary but the resemblance to a modern water divining stick is clear.

Trackway 2/14 (Area 2)

The trackway structure in Area 2 was the most substantial of the three trackways excavated at Woolwich Manor Way (Fig. 5.8; Plates 9 and 10). Two radiocarbon dates were obtained, the first from evaluation TP9 at 1880-1520 cal BC (Beta-153984: 3390±60 BP) and the second from Area 2 at 1610-1430 cal BC (SUERC-24292: 3230±30 BP). The structure ran NW-SE across the trench and was about 1.20m in width. It was of the same general form as the other two trackways described above, but was much more substantial. It was mostly made of roundwood rods and branches of about 15-50mm in diameter (context 21), the majority of coppiced alder. However, the trackway also contained a high proportion of heterogeneous material from a variety of species which is unusual compared to other simple 'brushwood' type trackways known from the London region. This included sections of poles, cleft timbers, small logs and worked old timbers. This material was generally in the upper part of the make-up of the trackway. The mix of materials and the variable condition of the wood suggests that the trackway was probably open for some time and repaired *ad hoc* with whatever was to hand. It would appear that when in use the middle of the trackway

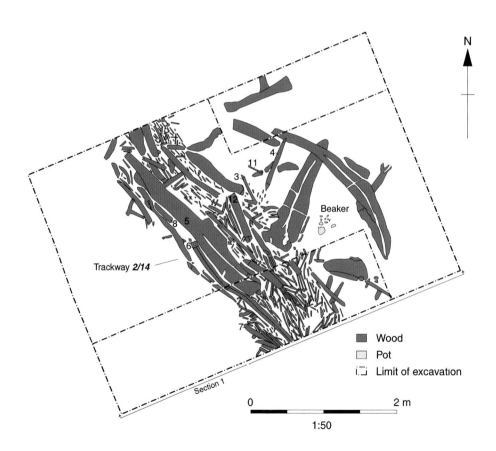

Fig. 5.8 Area 2 plan, Woolwich Manor Way

Plate 9   Trackway 2/14, Woolwich Manor Way (Area 2)

Plate 10   Section through trackway 2/14, Woolwich Manor Way (Area 2)

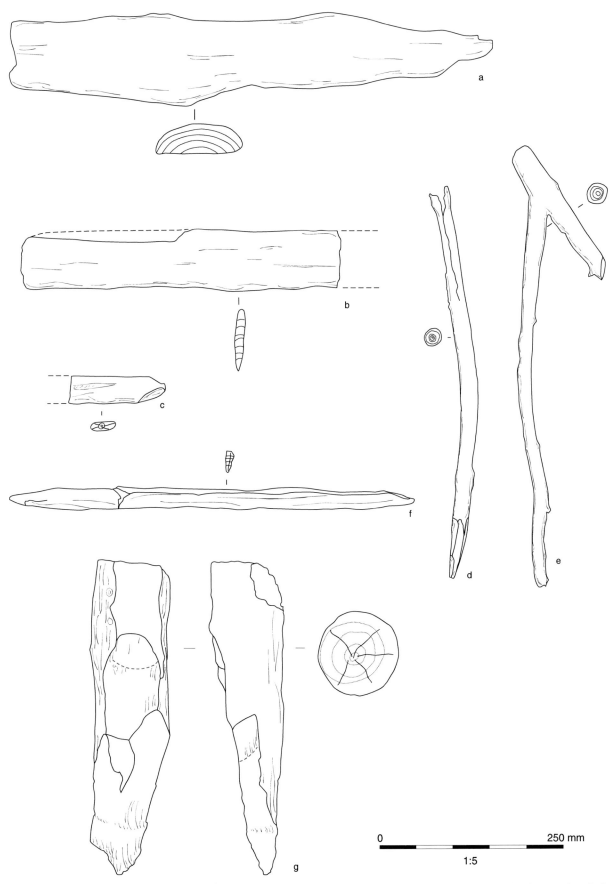

Fig. 5.9   Worked wood from trackway 2/14, Woolwich Manor Way. a) weathered half ash log (12), b) reused radially cleft oak pale (7), c) cut rod end (13), d) pointed yew stick (11), e) hooked yew peg (3), f) radially cleft timber pointed at both ends (4), g) hazel roundwood stake from TP9

became depressed into the soft peat and that area was then built up again. This resulted in a lentoid cross section up to near 400mm thick in the middle (Section 1, Fig. 5.3). It appears no retaining stakes were used. To the east of the trackway lay several naturally fallen, decayed alder logs which may have provided a slight rise in the peaty deposits that was used to advantage by the trackway builders.

The vast majority of the wooden elements were laid parallel with the long axis of the structure but a few were laid cross wise and a small number were rather crooked small branches. Five small round-wood worked ends (35-37mm diameter) were lifted and found to have weathered chisel or wedge form ends (Fig. 5.9). The majority of the roundwood items submitted for identification comprised alder and ash with larger pole sized sections of the same species. A small number of items were identified as willow/poplar, elm and holly, the last of which is very rare in prehistoric assemblages from the London region. The more curved of the larger material (approximately 80mm diameter) was clearly of branch origin and species included alder, elm and yew. Larger material in the form of small whole or cleft half logs were also used. The largest was timber 5 (about 2.6m long by 300mm wide) which, although heavily eroded, was probably a cleft half log of alder. Timber 12 (0.65m long by 120mm wide and *c* 40mm thick) was another cleft half log, this time of ash (Fig. 5.9a). Such a short cleft log was probably an off cut from the production of long timbers for use elsewhere. Several other items had been more elaborately worked and included two smoothed cleft oak pales (about 85mm wide and 15mm thick, Fig. 5.9b). It is likely that these were reused items but their original function is uncertain. Several worked wood objects were also found dropped or placed on the top, or just to the east, of the trackway surface. These included a neatly axe cut section of a crooked yew branch (timber 3, 0.585m x 38mm) with one metal axe facetted pointed end and one abraded end (Fig. 5.9e). Such small hooked pegs are still occasionally used in the English countryside today and used for many purposes: holding down snares and nets, layering coppice stems and holding woodland craft equipment temporarily in place. These uses would not have been out of place at the time the trackway was in use. A peg of yew would have been the equivalent of one of metal today as, along with holly, it is the hardest and strongest of the wood species that would have been available. Another small pointed yew peg (item 11, Fig. 5.9d) had a truncated top so it was not possible to determine whether it had had a hooked terminal or not. A radially cleft log (timber 4, Fig. 5.9f) derived from a straight slow grown log (0.56m x 37mm x10mm), pointed at both ends, which appears to have been a similar object to SF71 from Freemasons Road.

In addition to the items of worked wood, a number of Beaker sherds were recovered next to trackway 2/14 (Fig. 5.8). It was possible to refit the majority of the sherds and it appears they derive from a single East Anglian style or globular shaped vessel with zonal decoration (Fig. A2.1, 17; Plate 26). The pot lay in an inverted position in the peat, although the base had been broken off sometime in antiquity. The Beaker was located within 0.40m of the eastern edge of the trackway, and was found at the same level (-1.05m OD) while the peat was being peeled away to reveal its timbers. It may represent a placed deposit rather than a casual disposal. There is some overlap between the date ranges of the Beaker (2500-1600 BC) and the initial radiocarbon date for trackway 2/14. An overlap of the dates for the Beaker and trackway is not an essential condition for an association, as the Beaker may have been curated before deposition. The position of the trackway and Beaker may be coincidental and it is equally possible that it relates to the earlier activity recorded in Area 1.

Middle to late Bronze Age (Figs 5.6, 5.10)

'Platform' structure 61 (Area 1)

In the southern part of Area 1 the peat and trackway 29 was truncated by east-west linear feature 53, probably a natural channel (Fig. 5.6). The profile of the channel was only partially exposed as it extended beyond the edges of the excavation. It was recorded to a depth of at least 0.40m and filled with a dark brown silty clay with frequent small wood inclusions (fill 52). The channel fill was overlain by Structure 61 which was partially exposed over an area of 1m x 1m in the south-western corner of Area 1 (Plate 11). This may represent a later phase of trackway building, consolidation deposits over the soft channel fills or perhaps part of a 'platform' structure. The latter is the preferred interpretation due to the varied assortment of woody material incorporated into this structure as well as what appears to be a discrete 'corner' identified in plan. It is likely that the uppermost layers of the platform that were presumably occupied had decayed or been eroded being at a higher level than the foundation level recorded in the trench. A piece of hazel roundwood from the structure produced a middle to late Bronze Age radiocarbon date of 1270-1040 cal BC (SUERC-24504: 2945±30 BP).

The 'make-up' material consisted of a remarkable heterogeneous mix of woody material including cut roundwood, small logs and fragments of re-used cleft and hewn timbers (Fig. 5.10). The roundwood elements (context 63) included oblique cut ends, mostly under 50mm in diameter, from a wide range of species such as elm, willow, alder and ash. The short lengths and form of the wood suggests that all or much of the material was of branch origin. Many of the larger elements, mostly on the upper surface of the structure, were a mix of oak, elm and ash. The largest single element, partially exposed at the edge of the excavation, was a log of slow grown elm (timber 41) about 280mm in diameter which

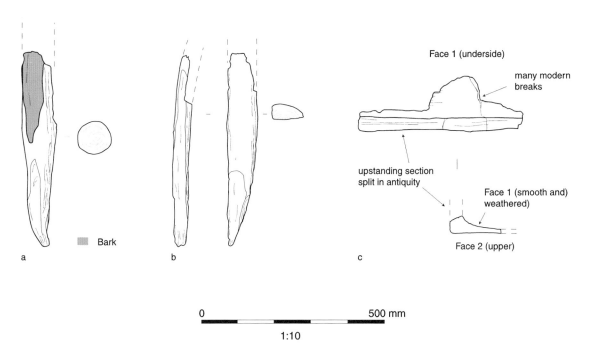

Face 1 (underside)

many modern
breaks

upstanding section
split in antiquity

Face 1 (smooth and)
weathered)

Face 2 (upper)

Bark

a

b

c

0   500 mm

1:10

Fig. 5.10   Worked wood from platform structure 61, Woolwich Manor Way, a) alder round wood stake with pencil end (43), b) half log ash stake (1535), c) re-used oak planking fragment (44)

Plate 11   'Platform' Structure 61, Woolwich Manor Way (Area 1)

perhaps formed a 'kerb'-like' edge to the northern limit of the structure. Most of the other larger elements were of cleft half logs or poles, or more carefully trimmed plank-like sections of oak or alder. The planks occurred in rather short lengths and may have been left-over off-cuts from other operations or perhaps reused timbers. The cleft alder logs were not very elaborately worked, however the reused cleft oak timbers (timbers 43, 44 and 46) were all tangentially faced, worn, and may have come from the same object. The most interesting was timber 44 (440mm x 140mm) which although slightly damaged by machine excavation, appeared to have been hewn into an 'L'-shaped cross section which tapered to a thickness of approximately 25mm (Fig. 5.10c). The simplest explanation of the shape is that it derives from a large broken up dugout trough or possibly a dugout boat. Unfortunately no clear axe 'stop marks' survived on the woodwork of this assemblage, just very worn rounded facets. If the radiocarbon date range is accurate the structure may have overlapped with the changeover from broader palstaves to the narrower socketed axes.

The pattern of stakes possibly associated with Structure 61 is not entirely clear. Two small stake tips along the eastern edge of the platform may have acted as retainers, and about 0.6m to the north and east a scatter of stakes (stakes 40, 39, 37. 1534, 1535 and 54) of various sizes and forms may be the remains of an outer hurdle fence or dead hedge. Identified species included alder, ash and elm. Stake 40 (510mm x 95mm) was quite typical and was made from alder roundwood with an irregular pencil point created by repeated shallow axe blows working around most of the outside of the pole (Fig. 5.10a). Stake 1535 (510mm x 85mm x 45mm) was more unusual in that it was from a very slow grown ash pole, cleft in half and hewn along one edge, perhaps suggesting it was cut from a second-hand timber (Fig. 5.10b). The stakes were in quite a poor condition and although no complete stop marks survived the facets appeared to be relatively small and rounded. The narrow, concave facets recorded

on stake 39, up to 45mm wide, are typical of late Bronze Age socketed axe marks found in the south-eastern region (Goodburn 2003a, 104)

Less well-defined groups of timbers were recorded in the south-east corner of Area 1 and across TP8 (Str. 1530 and 1547) although the density was insufficient to have supported any significant weight on such soft ground. It is most likely that these were discarded pieces, although some may have been redeposited from Structure 29. A radiocarbon date from a plank fragment from Structure 1530 produced a date of 1310-900 cal BC (Beta-152738: 2900±70 BP) which is consistent with the date for Structure 61.

Artefacts from the peat above the timber structures (Areas 1 and 2)

Above the timber structures, in both Areas 1 and 2, peat continued to form, but only as a thin layer prior to the deposition of the minerogenic clay silts (layers 1 and 56). Two struck flints and occasional pieces of burnt flint provide some evidence for low-level activity in the area following the abandonment of the timber structures.

Roman (Figs 1.5, 5.1, 5.2, 5.11)

Evidence of Roman activity at Woolwich Manor Way was restricted to the evaluation phases of work; in T15 and TP13 in the east of the site (Figs 5.1, 5.3 and 5.11). Here, significant quantities of pottery were found in association with a possible consolidation surface within the upper minerogenic alluvium (Biddulph in Appendix 2). This indication of a domestic presence is relevant to other sites in the vicinity (outlined in Chapter 1, Fig. 1.5), and a postulated Roman road that may have followed the line of East Ham High Street and Manor Way, linking the Thames at North Woolwich to the London to Colchester road to the north (Hanson 1996, Watson 1988).

In T15 occasional pottery sherds were recovered from a disturbed amorphous dark brown peat with frequent wood fragments (layer 2005), 0.05 to

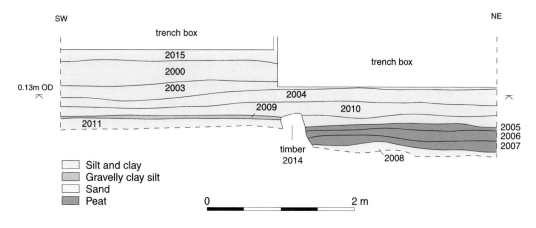

Fig. 5.11   Section through alluvial sequence, T15 (western), Woolwich Manor Way

0.10m thick, with an upper surface lying at -0.40m to -0.11m OD. A number of struck and burnt flints recovered from this deposit are likely to represent residual material. Sealing the peat layer was a 0.10m to 0.30m thick layer of silty clay alluvium (layer 2011) which also contained pottery sherds. Layer 2011 was thinnest at the north-western end of the trench (Fig. 5.11) and appeared disturbed, probably by activity associated with the deposition of the overlying gravelly layer. Layer 2009 appeared to butt up against an unworked tree trunk (timber 2014) and consisted of a gravelly clay silt, up to 0.05m thick, which produced a much larger quantity of pottery (179 sherds). Jars dominated the group, but dishes made an important contribution and deposition from the mid-3rd century is likely. The latest piece was an incipient bead-and-flanged dish (Going B5) in black burnished ware dating from about AD 240 to 300/330. An East Gaulish ware dish was probably deposited after the currency of the form (up to AD 240) but it need not have been out of use for very long. The deposit may represent the casual disposal of domestic waste, but it could also be an intentional spread of aggregate material over the alluvium to consolidate it. This would not have been sufficient to make the surface stable for protracted or heavy use, but may have been sufficient for some lighter or temporary purpose.

The overlying alluvial deposits (layers 2010 and 2004) also contained Roman material, including a 1st century coin from layer 2010. Layer 2003 comprised a grey compact, slightly sandy, clay silt with frequent flint fragments and pebbles. Along with a small quantity of residual worked flint, the deposit produced 21 sherds of Roman pottery as well as six highly abraded small sherds of medieval to post medieval date. Given the quantity of Roman finds, both from this sequence and from TP13 (see below) and the quality of the later material, it is possible these finds are intrusive, either as a result of trample or from the installation of the trench boxes.

In TP13 two layers of silt clay alluvium were recorded. The lowest of these (layer 1514) was a dark greyish brown clay silt, 0.25m deep, overlain by a layer of mid greyish brown silty clay (layer 1515) 0.63m deep. These two layers broadly equate to layers 2003, 2004 and 2010 in T15, where hand excavation was able to define the sequence more thoroughly. A total of 257 Roman pottery sherds were recovered from layer 1514 along with a small quantity of probably residual burnt flint and a single highly abraded sherd of medieval pottery (AD 1080-1200). In view of the size of the Roman assemblage and the retrieval method (hand sorting of the spoil heap) the latter may reasonably be considered intrusive. The pottery assemblage may represent a midden spread and contained a wider range of material than context 2009 in T15. Jars similarly dominated the group, but dishes were restricted to a single bead-and-flanged vessel. Bowls were marginally better represented than dishes, although vessels present were residual. The dish and bowl-jar (cf. Going 1987, 21-2), supported by Much Hadham ware and Nene Valley colour-coated ware, date deposition to after AD 250 and up to the mid 4th century, but it is possible that groups 1514 and 2009 were contemporaneous.

Layer 1513 was cut by two features, also containing a small quantity of Roman pottery. The first of these was a small ovoid pit (1507) measuring 0.73m x 0.65m and 0.22m deep. This was filled with grey fine silt (fill 1505) and mid brown silty sand (fill 1506). The second cut was curvilinear ditch (1508) measuring 2.10m x 0.80m and 0.25m deep and running east to west across the trench. This was filled with a mid bluish grey clay silt (fill 1509), a mid grey coarse sandy gravel (fill 1510) and a mid blue grey clay silt (fill 1511).

In general, the presence of South and Central Gaulish samian, Verulamium-region white ware, and South Essex shelly ware amongst the pottery assemblage from T15 and TP13 indicates later 1st and 2nd-century occupation in the vicinity of the Woolwich Manor Way site. However, no context group is certain to date earlier than the mid-3rd century, confining deposition at site to the late Roman period.

The dominance of jars suggests that the vessel class served multiple functions, including storage, cooking and dining, and points to low-level adoption of forms, such as dishes and mortaria, that typify continental-style dining practices. However, the presence of a possible Much Hadham ware flagon (represented by body sherds from layer 2004, T15) and decorated samian Drag. 37 bowl and dishes in various fabrics, suggests that the inhabitants were familiar with certain continental practices and had access to appropriate material.

Post Roman

More recent cultural activity in the vicinity of Woolwich Manor Way appears to have been largely absent until the construction of drainage ditches associated with floodplain management, which probably begins with a post medieval ditch discovered in T19. Ditch 2025 was orientated north-south measured 2.10m wide and 0.95m deep and was filled with a lower peaty deposit (fill 2024) and upper silty clay alluvium (layer 2023). A single sherd of pottery was recovered from fill 2023 dated to AD 1270-1500. Extensive deposits of modern made-ground occurred to the east of Woolwich Manor Way and are associated with 19th century urban expansion.

Chapter 6: Roding Bridge

Introduction (Figs 1.6, 6.1-6.2)

The site is located on the banks of the River Roding (also known as Barking Creek) approximately 1.4km north-west of the River Thames. The existing crossing of the River Roding represents the most recent truncation of deposits associated with the site. The early maps (Chapman and Andre 1777; Milne 1800) show the River Roding and the adjacent areas of marsh known as the East Ham Level and Barking Level (Fig. 1.6). The river is shown as having several braided channels at Barking; further downstream a single channel is shown. There is little or no occupation along the lower reaches of the river at this time. The nature of the river floodplain and the marginal land either side resulted in very little activity until well into the 19th century. By the 1900s the London, Tilbury and Southend railway line was constructed to the north of the site and the

Northern Outfall Sewer to the south. Alongside the River Roding a road was constructed to Creek-mouth and a few isolated buildings were associated with the road. Modern development of the area of the site has included industrial sites and workshops on either bank of the Roding, but much of the site remains undisturbed.

The Phase I evaluation involved the excavation of 5 boreholes (Rdar 1-5) along a 50m transect on the west bank of the River Roding (Fig. 6.1). A sequence of Holocene peat and clay silts occurred beneath 2m to 4m of recent fill (Fig. 6.2). The sequence superficially resembles the tripartite sequence found throughout the Lower Thames, with thin peat overlying Pleistocene gravel. No archaeological horizons were encountered and stratigraphic assessment did not reveal sedimentological indica-

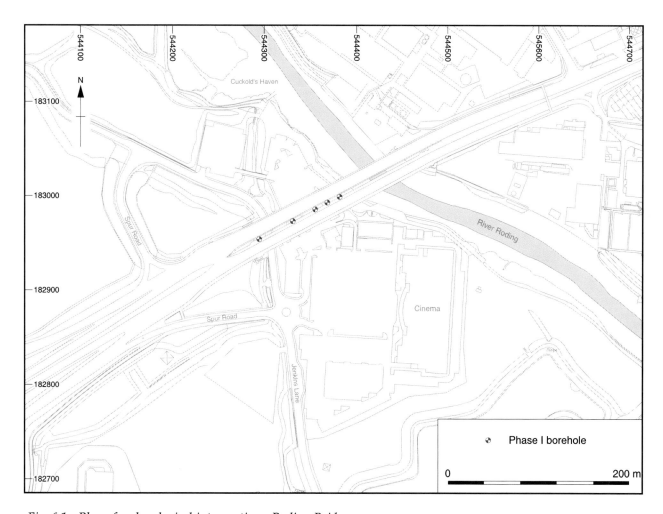

Fig. 6.1 Plan of archaeological interventions, Roding Bridge

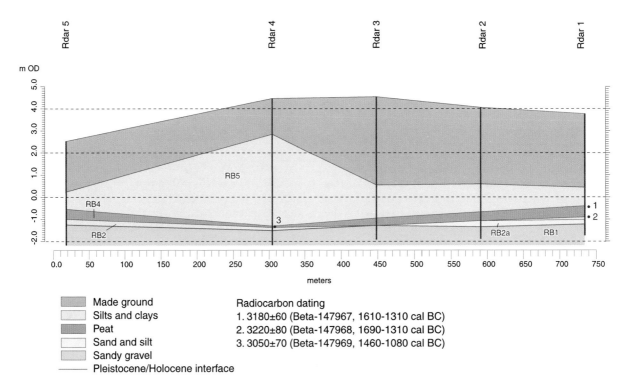

Fig. 6.2 Stratigraphical cross-section based on borehole data, Roding Bridge

tors of local cultural activity. The depths of recent fill and the relatively limited scale of impact did not warrant Phase II investigations. The results of the borehole assessment carried out during the evaluation are presented below. A limited programme of environmental work and radiocarbon dating was carried out from the cores retrieved from borehole Rdar 1.

Sedimentary architecture and environments of deposition

The pre-Holocene sediments and basement topography

Fluvial gravel (RB1)

At Roding Bridge poorly sorted coarse flint gravel grading upwards into sandier deposits lay between the Holocene soft sediment sequence and the London Clay bedrock. These deposits were only penetrated by around 0.5m to 1.0m by the purposive geoarchaeological drilling. These sediments typically accumulated in cold climate braided river conditions during the late Pleistocene. The height datums indicate that they probably correlate with the Shepperton Gravels which were deposited between 10,000 and 15,000 BP.

The early Holocene topographic template

A major temporal unconformity is likely to be represented by the surface of the terrace gravel, in other words the early Holocene topographic template. The surface therefore represents the Mesolithic/

Neolithic land surface. Examination of the shape of the template reveals relatively consistent levels of around -1.25m OD. Due to the relatively high elevations inundation of this land surface appears to have occurred later than other parts of the route, probably during the middle Holocene.

The Holocene sediments

Freshwater sand and clay silts (RB2)

This group of sediments directly overlay the Pleistocene gravel and consists of minerogenic sandy-silts or clay-silts becoming increasingly organic up-profile approaching the interface with the overlying peat. The fine-grained nature of the sediments suggests deposition in a relatively low-energy environment. Environmental remains were poorly preserved in the deposits examined in Rdar 1, although pollen was recovered from the lower sandier part of the sequence (RB2a). The assemblage was dominated by pondweeds which, together with spiked water millfoil, suggests a freshwater environment, perhaps adjacent to an active channel. The low values for trees and presence of plantains, including ribwort plantain, indicates it was probably a relatively open environment with grassland nearby. Pollen of the goosefoot family perhaps hints at saltmarsh environments in the vicinity, although the poor preservation compared to the other taxa suggests the freshwater component may better represent the actual conditions on site during deposition. Age estimates from the base of the overlying peat in

Rdar 1 suggests this lower alluvial sequence predates at least about 1700 cal BC.

Freshwater peat and organic silt (RB4)

This group of sediments are dominated by highly organic silt and peat which lay directly over the Pleistocene gravel, or the lower alluvium where present, and was sealed by an extensive unit of minerogenic alluvium. Although the peat was mapped as continuous across the site the maximum thickness was only around 0.5m, lying at elevations between *c* -0.5m and -1.4m OD. Differentiating between the different units of alluvium and peat, however, proved difficult as the alluvium was frequently quite organic. Localised units ascribed to this group vary from firm humified peats to peats containing well-preserved wood and twig fragments. Towards the west, in the vicinity of Rdar 5, the peat graded laterally into a peaty clay silt. The consistent presence of fine mineral material may imply frequent flood episodes. Radiocarbon age estimates from the base and top of the peat in borehole Rdar 1 produced dates of 1690-1310 cal BC (Beta-147967: 3220±80 BP) at -0.90m OD and 1610-1310 cal BC (Beta-147966: 3180±60 BP) at -0.60m OD. Pollen was generally poorly preserved although suggestive of an alder carr environment.

Estuarine clay silts (RB5)

This sedimentary complex is dominated by minerogenic clays and silt containing variable quantities of organic material. This group of deposits typically underlies the 19th century made ground and post-dates about 1300 cal BC in the eastern part of the site (Rdar 1). The deposits contained zones dominated by laminated or bedded sediments and represent a period of inundation leading to the development of an intertidal wetland system. In Rdar 1 the sediments contained frequent brackish water ostracods (*Cyprideis torosa* and *Cytherura gibba*) and occasional freshwater species (*Candona* sp.). Unfortunately pollen was absent from these deposits.

Chapter 7: Movers Lane

Introduction (Figs 1.6, 7.1-7.5)

The site lies on low-lying ground, immediately east of the River Roding and north of the Thames and the proximity of the two rivers resulted in the area remaining as marginal land for much of its history. The early historical maps (Chapman and Andre 1777; Milne 1800) show the River Roding and the area of marsh known as the Barking Level (Fig. 1.6). The site lies at the northern edge of the Barking Level, later named as the Eastbury Level. Several tributary streams to the Roding and Thames, including Mayes Brook, ran close to the position of the modern road junction. The area remained undeveloped during the later medieval and post-medieval period, although part of the length of Movers Lane was established by 1805. This was associated with Movers House situated just to the north of the junction. By the later 19th century a greater amount of residential and industrial development took place following the construction of the London, Tilbury and Southend Railway. In the vicinity of the site this included an expansion of the road pattern and terraced housing. The north-west side of the junction is currently occupied by Greatfields Park. On the south-east side is the Lyon Business Park, but elsewhere residential housing is present.

The Phase I evaluation at the Movers Lane site involved the excavation of 16 test pits (TP15-26 and TP36-39). This was followed by 12 evaluation trenches (T1-10, T12 and T13) as part of the Phase II works; 4 to the east of the Movers Lane junction and 8 to the west (Fig. 7.1). Geoarchaeological modelling of the test pit data revealed that beneath the modern overburden the surface of the Pleistocene sequence lay at elevations of up to about +1.2m OD in the central part of the site but dropped rapidly in the west and east where evidence of former channel activity was noted. Deeper alluvial sequences overlying the gravels coincide with the lowest elevations and include a major peat bed in the eastern area of the site (Fig. 7.2).

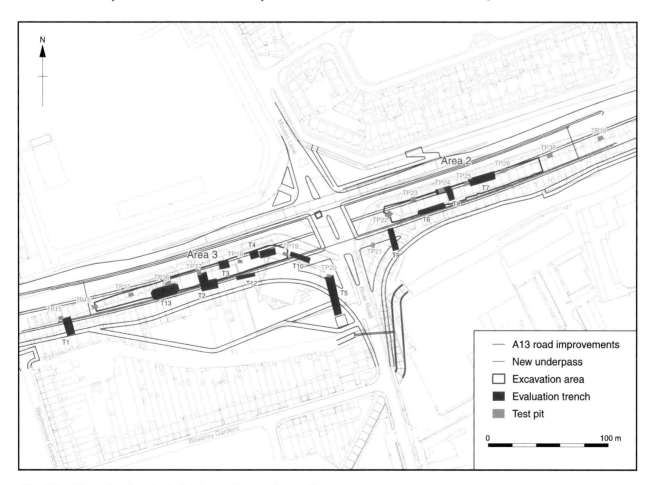

Fig. 7.1   Plan of archaeological interventions, Movers Lane

71

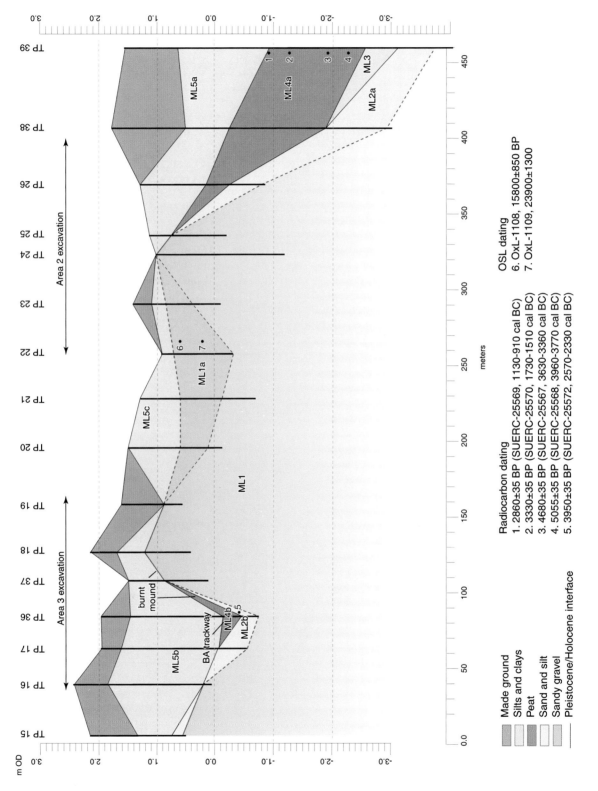

Radiocarbon dating
1. 2860±35 BP (SUERC-25569, 1130-910 cal BC)
2. 3330±35 BP (SUERC-25570, 1730-1510 cal BC)
3. 4680±35 BP (SUERC-25567, 3630-3360 cal BC)
4. 5055±35 BP (SUERC-25568, 3960-3770 cal BC)
5. 3950±35 BP (SUERC-25572, 2570-2330 cal BC)

OSL dating
6. OxL-1108, 15800±850 BP
7. OxL-1109, 23900±1300

Made ground
Silts and clays
Peat
Sand and silt
Sandy gravel
Pleistocene/Holocene interface

Fig. 7.2 Stratigraphical cross-section based on test pit data, Movers Lane

Plate 12   Excavation of Area 2, Movers Lane (RIR01, view from the west)

Plate 13   Excavation of Area 3, Movers Lane (RIR01, view from the west)

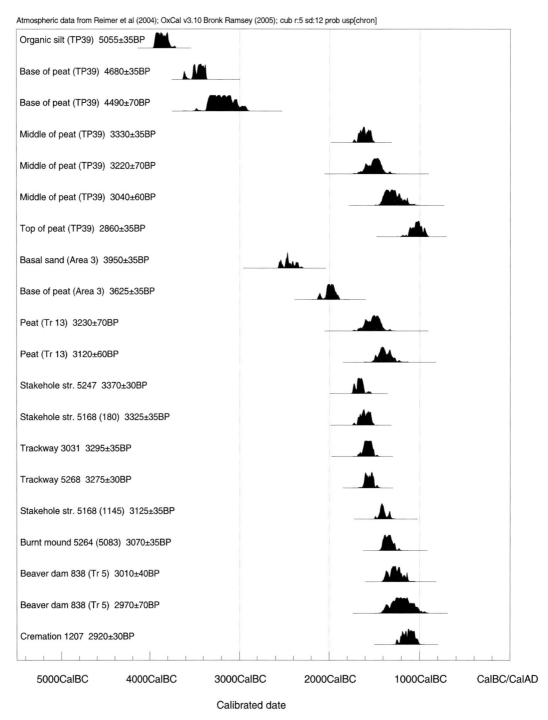

Atmospheric data from Reimer et al (2004); OxCal v3.10 Bronk Ramsey (2005); cub r:5 sd:12 prob usp[chron]

Organic silt (TP39) 5055±35BP	
Base of peat (TP39) 4680±35BP	
Base of peat (TP39) 4490±70BP	
Middle of peat (TP39) 3330±35BP	
Middle of peat (TP39) 3220±70BP	
Middle of peat (TP39) 3040±60BP	
Top of peat (TP39) 2860±35BP	
Basal sand (Area 3) 3950±35BP	
Base of peat (Area 3) 3625±35BP	
Peat (Tr 13) 3230±70BP	
Peat (Tr 13) 3120±60BP	
Stakehole str. 5247 3370±30BP	
Stakehole str. 5168 (180) 3325±35BP	
Trackway 3031 3295±35BP	
Trackway 5268 3275±30BP	
Stakehole str. 5168 (1145) 3125±35BP	
Burnt mound 5264 (5083) 3070±35BP	
Beaver dam 838 (Tr 5) 3010±40BP	
Beaver dam 838 (Tr 5) 2970±70BP	
Cremation 1207 2920±30BP	

5000CalBC   4000CalBC   3000CalBC   2000CalBC   1000CalBC   CalBC/CalAD

Calibrated date

Fig. 7.3   Radiocarbon dates, Movers Lane

Archaeological remains identified during the evaluation work included artefact scatters of late Mesolithic to early Neolithic date which marks the beginning of a long sequence of habitation stretching into the late Bronze Age. The discovery of a beaver dam in T5 illustrates the nature of the late prehistoric wetland during the later periods of extensive floodplain submergence.

The Phase III excavations were designed to mitigate the impact of the Movers Lane underpass and were divided into two areas (Areas 2 and 3)

totalling approximately 3500m² (Plates 12 and 13). A total of 20 samples from a range of deposits from the site have been radiocarbon dated (Fig. 7.3, Appendix 1). Late Mesolithic and Neolithic activity was represented by a substantial quantity of worked flint and pottery largely located on the area of higher ground within the central part of the site, although these appeared to be almost entirely residual material in later contexts. A notable find was a fragment of a jet belt slider of probable early Neolithic date, associated with Peterborough ware pottery which was recovered from an alluvial deposit in Area 3 (layer 5074, Sheridan in Appendix 2). Evidence of later *in situ* activity was more extensive. Large palaeochannels located to the extreme eastern and western ends of the excavation areas probably mark former courses of the Mayes Brook and the River Roding, respectively. Within these palaeochannels were found two simple trackways, three possible stake built structures, a root system (a possible utilised platform) and artefact scatters dateable to the early to middle Bronze Age. On the higher ground in the central part of the site lay artefact scatters, a possible burnt mound, a cremation deposit and a series of linear ditches dating to the middle and late Bronze Age. The vast bulk of the waterlogged wood was excavated during Phase III excavations (Areas 2 and 3). The degree of preservation of the worked wood varied greatly, from almost pristine material with surviving fine signatures marks to decayed crushed material that could only just be recognised as worked. Much of the material was also pierced by small later root holes which left sub-rectanguler holes, a typical feature of horizontal prehistoric woodwork from the Thames floodplain in this region. Here, there is also the added complication that some of the cut wood found was 'worked' and deposited by beavers rather than humans. Some of the smaller material was sub-sampled from the broad context from which it came such as small sections of possibly cut small twigs. The area also had many spreads of broken bark fragments which often took rectangular form remarkably like some types of axe cut wood chips; large sub-samples of some of this material were also taken on-site. In all, including the small amount of lifted beaver cut wood, around 750 items were scanned after the excavation but the vast majority proved to be, in fact, unworked bark fragments. A total of 62 bags of bark fragments, not clearly worked material and fragmentary, repetitive, worked fragments were examined, cleaned and simply listed rather than fully recorded. The principal specialist record for the key woodwork of this area are detailed scale drawings of 38 worked items each of which also had a pro-forma timber sheet. The assemblage is moderately large by London region standards but nationally would be considered medium sized to small.

Palaeoenvironmental work during the evaluation stage focused on characterising the deeper sediment sequence exposed in TP39 in the eastern palaeochannel. Further examination of biological remains from the sediments excavated during the Phase III works was carried out as part of the post-excavation assessment stage. Overall, this assessment indicated that the preservation of ostracods and foraminifera was very poor in the sediments from the eastern part of the site, but samples from the western palaeochannel produced better results although deterioration of the key assessment monoliths precluded more detailed work. The results of the assessment, however, have provided useful information in terms of characterising the environments

of deposition associated with the sediments (Whittaker in Appendix 3). Diatoms were similarly poorly preserved (Haggart in Wessex Archaeology 2003); some information was gleaned from the lower part of the sequence in the eastern palaeochannel although these deposits clearly predate the key periods of activity at the site. Pollen preservation was far better and further detailed work has been carried out on three sequences from the eastern (TP39, Fig. 7.4) and the western palaeochannels (Fig. 7.5) (Peglar in Appendix 3). Analysis of plant macrofossil and insect remains was also undertaken on a representative selection of the richest bulk samples (Pelling in Appendix 3, Smith in Appendix 3). Thin sections for sediment micromorphology were also processed from Bronze Age occupation horizons, trackway levels and burnt mound in Area 3 (Macphail and Crowther in Appendix 3).

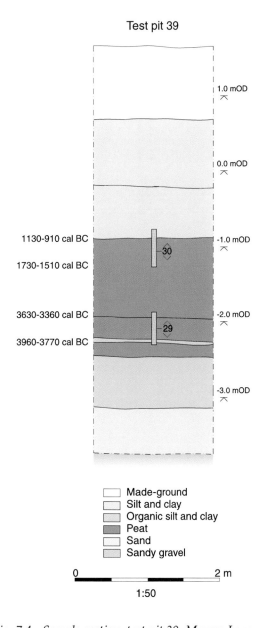

Fig. 7.4   *Sample section, test pit 39, Movers Lane*

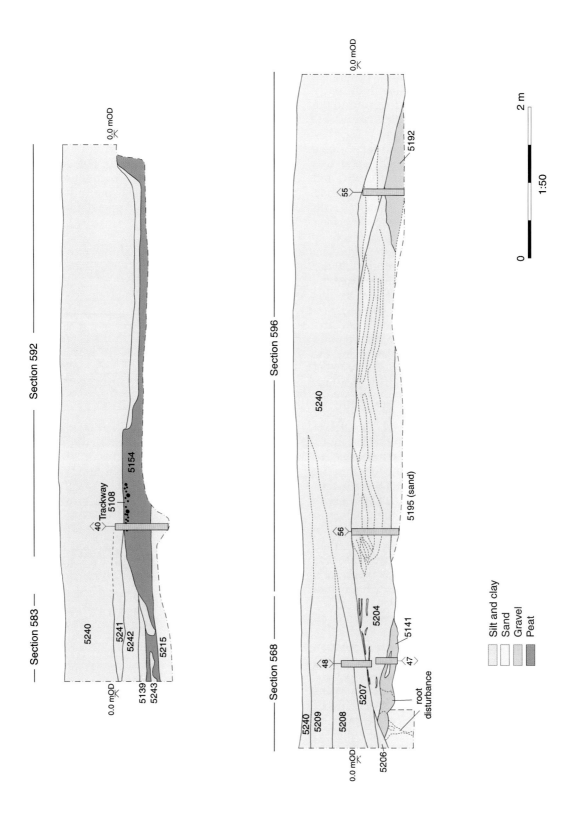

Fig. 7.5   Sample sections through the western palaeochannel (Area 3), Movers Lane

Sedimentary architecture and environments of deposition

The pre-Holocene sediments and basement topography

Fluvial gravels (ML1)

Poorly sorted coarse flint gravels formed the base of the exposed sediment sequence across the site. These deposits were not exposed extensively due to the rapid entry of ground water when the base of the overlying alluvium was penetrated. More detailed observations of these deposits were made during the works at Woolwich Manor Way and Prince Regent Lane and are typically associated with braided channel systems during late Pleistocene cold climate episodes.

Colluvial sand and gravel (ML1a)

A complex sequence of well-stratified, poorly sorted yellowish red to yellowish brown sandy gravels, becoming sandier up-profile, overlay the fluvial gravels in the western part of Area 2. OSL age estimates from T6 range from 15,800±850 BP to 23,900±1,300 BP clearly indicating accumulation immediately prior to and following the Glacial Maximum at 18,000-19,000 BP. These age estimates are too young to associate the sediments with the East Tilbury Marshes Gravel and too old to be associated with the Shepperton Gravel. They are considered to have accumulated as a result of reworking of sediments of the East Tilbury Marshes Gravel either by surface run-off or colluvial processes during phases of climatic instability and landscape degradation. The upper parts of this sequence are, however, of more recent origin (as indicated by the presence of later prehistoric artefacts within these levels). This indicates that further reworking of the sediments derived from the East Tilbury Marshes Gravel occurred, perhaps in relation to landscape instability associated with sea-level rise during the Holocene (see below).

The early Holocene topographic template

The early Holocene topographic template at Movers Lane is represented by the surface of the Pleistocene deposits. Examination of the shape of the template reveals the highest elevations up to +1.20m OD occur towards the central part of the site. The lowest elevations occur to the far east of Area 2, recorded at -3.85m OD in TP39, and to the west at -0.75m OD in the vicinity of TP17 and TP36. A further dip in elevation is also noted in the central area and to the south of the main excavations in the vicinity of TP20-23 and T5. The lowest elevations both to the west and east probably correspond to the position of major palaeochannels that appear to have been active throughout much of the early and mid Holocene. It is possible that the palaeochannel in the east is a former channel of the Mayes Brook, which now flows along the southern edge of the site, and the palaeochannel in the west represents the prehistoric course of the River Roding, which presently lies approximately 300m to the south-west.

The Holocene sediments

Freshwater sands (ML2)

Yellowish brown, sometimes weakly laminated, sands and sandy silts directly overlay the Pleistocene sequence. The thickest deposits occurred in the lower lying areas forming the basal fills of the palaeochannels. These deposits probably accumulated during the early to middle Holocene under conditions of sand bar sedimentation in freshwater meandering channels. Thin spreads of sandy silt located on the higher ground in the central sector may relate to episodic overbank flood events.

The sands were well exposed and sampled at the base of the Holocene sequence in TP39 in the eastern palaeochannel where they grade upwards into greyish brown slightly organic sandy silt (ML2a). The maximum thickness was about 1.38m, with the base at -3.85m OD. Unfortunately environmental remains were poorly preserved. No diatoms or foraminifera and only one species of poorly preserved freshwater ostracod were recovered from these deposits. Pollen concentration was low and preservation was poor, with a high proportion of the determinable pollen being broken or folded suggesting mechanical damage. The pollen taxa included alder and oak with hazel, grasses and sedges also present. Microscopic charcoal levels were also quite high with a concentration of about 160,000/cm^3. In the western palaeochannel similar sandy silt units were noted at the base of TP17 and TP36 and during the excavations in Area 3 (ML2b), although these were not excavated to any significant depth due to problems with flooding and trench collapse. Radiocarbon determination on a wood fragment from the upper part of this unit in the vicinity of TP36 produced a late Neolithic to early Bronze Age date of 2570-2330 cal BC (SUERC-25572: 3950±35 BP). This is significantly later than the eastern palaeochannel and may indicate sand mobilisation in the western area was occurring during the period of peat formation in the east (see below).

Estuarine silt (ML3)

A gradual change from sand to organic silt in TP39 suggests a shift to slow moving conditions. On the basis of the radiocarbon dates from the overlying peat this occurred in the eastern part of the site during the Mesolithic, prior to around 4000 BC. The pollen assemblage was similar to that described above, although the presence of pollen of goosefoots, together with dinoflagellates and pollen preservation evidence, perhaps suggests some marine influence with local saltmarsh environments and some coastal woodland.

Freshwater peat and organic silt (ML4)

A substantial unit of peat overlay the sands in the far eastern and western areas of the site. The most extensive deposits occured infilling the eastern palaeochannel in Area 2 (ML4a). These deposits increased in thickness eastwards and were sampled in TP39, east of Area 2. Accumulation at this location spans a considerable time period between the early Neolithic and late Bronze Age. Thinner deposits occurred at the edge of the western palaeochannel in Area 3 although these appear to have accumulated over a much shorter period during the early to middle Bronze Age and were clearly truncated laterally by channel activity (ML4b). Generally, the evidence suggests the peat formed in a freshwater environment of dense alder carr although the later stages are characterised by more open wetter conditions with the development of freshwater reedswamp, marsh and areas of grassland.

In TP39 the peat had a maximum thickness of about 1.7m. Here, the lower part of this unit contained a high silt content and thin discontinuous bands of organic silts indicate periodic higher energy flooding. Radiocarbon dating suggests accumulation occurred between 3960-3770 cal BC (SUERC-25568: 5055±35 BP) and 3630-3360 cal BC (SUERC-25567: 4680±35 BP) broadly corresponding with the evidence for early Neolithic activity identified across the site. The pollen from the lower silty peat was not well preserved, however tree and shrub pollen dominated with alder being the most abundant. Other important tree taxa included lime, oak and hazel. There was very little elm in the assemblages suggesting that this unit is post 'elm decline' but pre 'lime decline' Ferns were also present and charcoal particles were quite high. Overall, this suggests that during the early Neolithic freshwater alder carr was growing locally in wet places and along riverbanks, with deciduous woodland on the drier ground. There was some evidence for open areas with grassland, possibly used for pasture with perhaps some cereal cultivation. There was no evidence in the pollen assemblages for the growth of freshwater aquatic taxa or of taxa associated with saline water. The diatom assemblage include *Pinnularia* sp. fragments, however, and some of the *Pinnularia* in the lower silty peat was tentatively assigned to the *P. aestuarii* indicating an environment high in the tidal frame.

Further up-profile in TP39 the peat contained abundant woody material. The overall minerogenic component was much reduced, although intermittent lenses of silt suggests that episodes of flooding continued. Age estimates indicate peat accumulation continued throughout the Neolithic and Bronze Age at this location. Unfortunately, only the very base and top of the wood peat was sampled. The pollen from the base was similar to the silty peat below although few herbs and ferns were noted and there was an overall increase in the abundance of

alder suggesting the alder carr became quite dense. A marked decline in lime pollen was noted at the junction of the silty peat and wood peat. Although this could be attributed to human activity it could also have been related to an increased water level (lime cannot survive on wet ground) or equally the thick alder carr may have prevented other pollen reaching the site. There was no evidence for cereal growth in the vicinity although the dense alder woodland may have filtered out the large cereal grains.

The upper part of the wood peat is bracketed by two radiocarbon dates; 1730-1510 cal BC (SUERC-25570: 3330±35 BP) and 1130-910 cal BC (SUERC-25569: 2860±35 BP) suggesting accumulation occurred during the early to late Bronze Age. The upper part of the peat profile in TP39 therefore corresponds with the period of trackway building (Trackway 3031) at the edge of the eastern palaeochannel in Area 2 dated to 1680-1490 cal BC (SUERC-24595: 3295±35 BP). The pollen assemblages were initially similar to that described above, but towards the top of the peat there is a rapid increase in herbs and fern spores and a concomitant decrease in tree and shrub values, mainly due to a large drop in alder and increases in grasses and sedges. Some evidence of cereal cultivation is also indicated by the presence cereal-type pollen grains. Diatoms were poorly preserved but a single valve of the brackish species *Diploneis interrupta* in the upper part of the peat profile perhaps suggests episodic influxes of brackish water.

Analysis of the plant and insect evidence from the peat directly associated with Trackway 3031 on Area 2 produced similar results to the upper part of the profile in TP39. The plant assemblage provided some evidence for alder (seeds and cones); wet ground species (such as water-dropwort, fool's water-cress, gypsywort, watermint, common spike-rush, branched bur-reed, crowfoots, water-worts, water-plantain, red-shank, meadowsweet, sedges and rushes) suggest marshy grassy conditions, and a small number of seeds of duckweeds and caddisfly larval cases may point to some open bodies of water. The drier ground species (for example bramble, fat hen, stinging nettles orache, knotgrass, cinquefoils, chickweed/stitchworts, black nightshade and thistle) were relatively limited, but indicate a background of scrubby vegetation, ruderal and disturbed habitats. The majority of the insect fauna comprised beetles associated with slow flowing water conditions and stands of waterside vegetation. *Donacia marginata* is associated with bur-reed and the 'reed beetles' *Donacia simplex* and *Plateumaris sericea* are both associated with a range of sedges, rushes and water reeds. There were a few individuals of *Aphodius* 'dung beetles' along with the 'garden chafer' (*Phyllopertha horticola*) suggesting that grassland or meadow was present in the area. There were also a number of species which are associated with deadwood such as *Cerylon* spp., the 'woodworms'

Anobium punctatum and *Hadrobregmus denticollis* and the *Curculio* 'nut weevil' which may indicate that woodland was present locally and/ or that these species were associated with the decaying trackway.

In the western palaeochannel in Area 3 the peat was much thinner and less extensive. The base of the unit was gradational with the underlying sand, developing up-profile into a very dark brown to black sandy peat. At 50-100mm, the top of the unit consisted of well-humified woody peat. Radio-carbon age estimates suggest peat accumulation was of much shorter duration but was of broadly equivalent age to the upper part of the peat profile in the eastern palaeochannel. Accumulation commenced during the early Bronze Age at 2120-1890 cal BC (SUERC-25571: 3625±35 BP) at *c* -0.40m OD in the vicinity of TP36. A date provided by timber Trackway 5268 which lay across the peat surface at roughly -0.20m OD suggests cessation by the early to middle Bronze Age at 1630-1450BC cal BC (SUERC-24288: 3275±30 BP). The environmental evidence suggests similar environments to those described above with dense alder carr giving way to more open reedswamp and marsh with some grass-land and disturbed, ruderal habitats. The presence of humans locally is evidenced by the dramatic rise in charcoal particles at the top of the profile and the occurrence of cereal-type pollen.

Freshwater and estuarine clay silt (ML5)

The upper alluvium is dominated by laterally exten-sive minerogenic sediments, predominantly clay and silt. This group of sediments typically underlay the modern made ground across the site and varied in thickness from less than 0.3m to 2.65m. Overall these deposits represent suspended load sedimenta-tion across the valley floor during the submergence of the former floodplain topography during the later prehistoric period.

In TP39 the peat was overlain by 1.60m of dark greyish brown silty clay (ML5a). Radiocarbon deter-mination of the top of the peat produced a date of 1130-910 cal BC (SUERC-25569: 2860±35 BP) implying that the change to minerogenic sedimen-tation in the eastern palaeochannel in Area 3 dates to the middle to late Bronze Age. Unfortunately only the lower part of the alluvium was sampled in TP39. Pollen evidence suggests that initially the environment was similar to that represented by samples from the top of the underlying peat; the abundance of aquatic taxa and green algae suggests freshwater wetlands and reedswamp were present locally. Further up-profile a small rise in pollen of the goosefoot family may indicate that saltmarsh was growing closer to the site, although some goosefoots are also found on dry land. Unfortun-ately no other environmental indicators were preserved in the sampled sequence although additional information is provided from the upper silty clay fill of middle to late Bronze Age ditch 1038 at the edge of the eastern palaeochannel in Area 2.

Diatoms were poorly preserved, however *Cyclotella striata* was present which is a common planktonic diatom, often abundant in estuaries, and *Triceratum favus* is a common fully marine planktonic form (Hendey 1964). Whilst these might suggest some marine influence, the low numbers make it impos-sible to be certain. The pollen assessment indicated the area surrounding the ditch during the later stages of infilling was open grassland with sedges and reed-mace and/or bur-reed in wetter areas.

Considerable complexity within the upper alluvium was noted in the vicinity of the western palaeochannel on Area 3 (ML5c). Here there was clear evidence for channel erosion. Sand and sandy gravel deposits within this channel indicates periods of higher flow velocities and additional sandy deposits overlying archaeological features on the higher ground suggest associated episodes of high energy overbank flooding. Several erosion channels were recorded cutting into the top of the peat. As well as clay and silt dominated sediments, deposits filling these channels include sand and gravelly sub-facies indicative of episodes of much higher flow velocities. Interestingly at least one cut and fill episode appears to have taken place prior to the construction of Trackway 5268 which clearly traversed both the surface of the peat and an infilled channel that truncated the peat. Discrete deposits of sandy gravel overlying the earlier sands within the main palaeochannel to the west of the trackway contained concentrations of artefactual material; worked and burnt flint, pottery and animal bone. This material may well have been eroded from activity areas on the higher ground. The majority of the pottery and worked flint was of middle to late Bronze Age date but with some earlier residual material too. These artefact rich gravel deposits were overlain by a complex series of laminated sands and silty clays, in places with a high organic component.

A note on the beaver dam from Trench 5
(Figs 7.6-7.7)

Worthy of note is the remains of a beaver dam, recorded in T5 in the very southern central area of investigation associated with an east-west channel

Plate 14   European beaver (photo by Paul Stevenson)

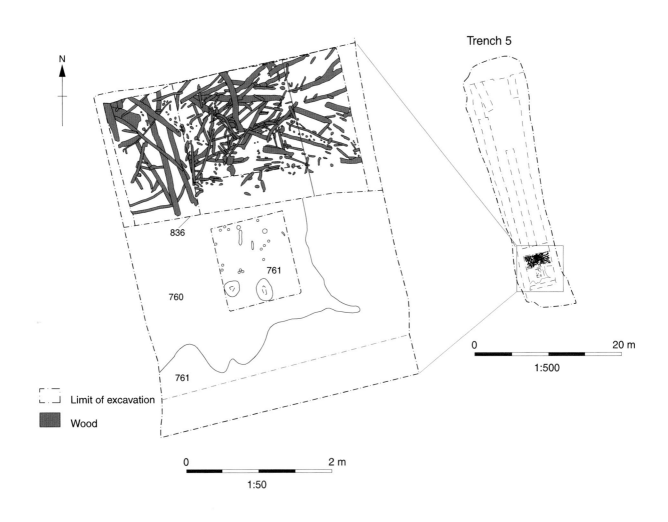

Trench 5

N

836

761

760

761

☐ ☐ Limit of excavation

Wood

0   2 m

1:50

0   20 m

1:500

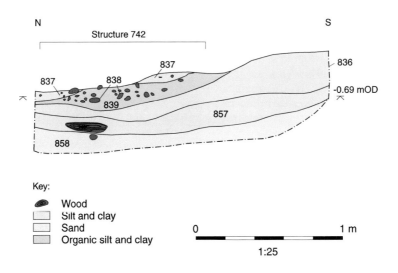

N   S

Structure 742

837

837   838   836

839   -0.69 mOD

857

858

Key:

Wood
Silt and clay
Sand
Organic silt and clay

0   1 m

1:25

Fig. 7.6 *Plan and section of the beaver dam, Trench 5, Movers Lane*

like feature within the upper clay silts (ML5). The channel was filled with a series of dark brownish grey sands, sandy silts and organic clay silts. Structure 742 was excavated in extremely difficult rainy conditions, the worst for 300 years, at the end of the period allotted for excavating the trench and with the overlying clay alluvium masking the wood surfaces. It appeared at first to have been the edge of a roundwood platform or trackway and, given the conditions, a small sondage was dug across the centre and worked wood and cut ends retained for recording off-site (Fig. 7.6). A small worn wood chip (838) and a weathered, chisel form, axe cut rod end (828) were found lying on top of the main wood accumulation.

Apart from a small rod end (829a) which had the characteristic curving shape of a probable coppiced heel (Coles and Orme 1985, 31) with faint traces of a possible axe mark, off-site examination of the sondage material revealed that the bulk of the wood was beaver cut. The structure appears to have been part of a small beaver dam, perhaps on a small tributary stream running down onto the floodplain. The humanly worked wood had probably been carried to the structure by water and become entangled there after a period of weathering. The beaver cut marks on medium sized pole ends took the form of crisp pairs of marks 4-5mm wide mostly running at around 90 degrees to the long axis of the object. Three pieces of roundwood lifted from the sondage had very clear gnaw marks 838a, 838b, and 838c. The first two were the best preserved (Fig. 7.7). In both cases they were poles or branch wood 45mm and 60mm diameter respectively with one beaver cut end and one cut for lifting. Item 838a had traces of bark adhering, whilst 838b was bark free. The species was identified as alder during the assessment phase (Anne Davis, MoLA) and two statistically consistent radiocarbon dates indicate a date at the end of the middle Bronze Age at 1390-1120 cal BC (Beta-152742: 3010±40 BP) and 1400-1000 cal BC (Beta-152743: 2970±70 BP).

Today in the Rocky Mountains of the USA beavers live and create dams, as do captive European beavers in Kent (Plate 14). Using reference samples of beaver cut wood from both modern source areas it was possible to compare the A13 material to be certain of the identification of beaver gnaw marks. The first beaver gnawed wood to be clearly recognised during the excavation of a prehistoric wetland site was in Somerset at the Neolithic Baker platform although it was initially confused with stone knife whittled material (Coles and Orme 1982, 67). The implications of finding such a feature are wide in that the action of beavers can have considerable impact on local water regimes, vegetation and sedimentation. Bryony Coles has extensively examined the literature and a number of beaver environments and found evidence of dams up to 3m high which had enormous effects on the local sedimentary regime (Coles 1992; 2006). Tentative evidence of beaver activity in the

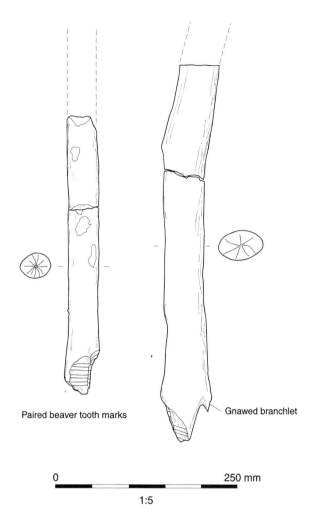

Paired beaver tooth marks — Gnawed branchlet

0   250 mm

1:5

Fig. 7.7   Examples of beaver gnawed wood, Trench 5, Movers Lane

area was first found in later prehistoric deposits on the nearby Mar Dyke tributary just to the east (Wilkinson 1988).

Beavers create a form of coppiced woodland, and can change freshwater levels by as much as a metre or even more, apart from building dams and lodges. It could be tentatively suggested that this impact is rarely considered in archaeological studies even near tributaries reaching the edge of the Lower Thames floodplain. Another key feature of this 'structure' is that it clearly shows that the local watercourse was fresh water up to a height of a little over -0.54m OD, the height as found after some compaction of the peat.

The cultural evidence

Mesolithic and Neolithic (Fig. 7.8)

Evidence of activity for the earlier periods at Movers Lane, similar to the other sites along the route, is largely inferred from the presence of worked flint and pottery, almost exclusively as residual material in later features or layers. A

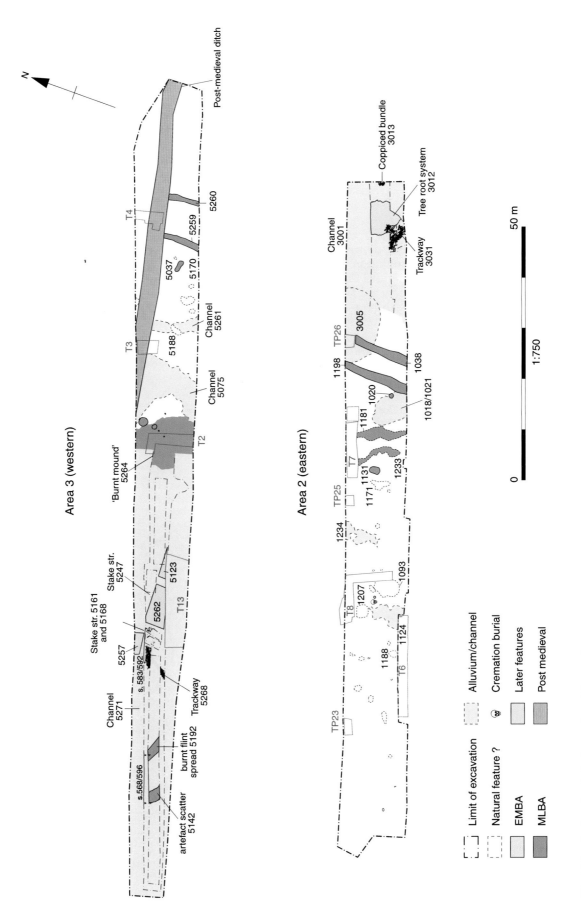

Fig. 7.8 *Archaeological phase plan, Movers Lane*

number of features (features 1188, 1171, 1093, 5188 and 5170, Fig. 7.8) cutting into the surface of the gravels produced pottery and worked flint of early to late Neolithic date, although many also produced material of later date too. The irregularity of many of these features suggests a natural origin, probably a result of tree throw or root action. Feature 1093, for example, was a large shallow hollow, possibly a very large tree throw (5.50m x 2.50m x 0.60m) that produced early Neolithic worked flint and pottery, but also included pottery sherds of middle Neolithic and middle to late Bronze Age date.

Although Mesolithic or early Neolithic struck flint was widely present across the site, few features of this date could be identified as containing *in situ* or directly associated assemblages. The lithics were manufactured from many different raw materials and their condition would indicate that they had been lying on the surface for some time before being incorporated into the features. The earliest activity at the site is indicated by the presence of a rod-shaped microlith of later Mesolithic date recovered from an unstratified context in T5. No other unequivocal Mesolithic struck flint was present but a high proportion of the overall assemblage is blade-based and characteristically Mesolithic or early Neolithic in date. Two flakes had polished surfaces suggesting the reuse of Neolithic polished implements, most probably axes. There was also a high proportion of Mesolithic or early Neolithic retouched implements comparable to the range of tools identified at Prince Regent Lane and Woolwich Manor Way, including simple edge-retouched blades, serrated implements and various types of scrapers. Hollow 1093 contained 15 struck flints, including a serrated blade exhibiting silica polishing, a small long-end scraper with blunted margins and a badly thermally-flawed opposed-platform core (Bishop in Appendix 2).

The pottery assemblage included 186 sherds assigned an early Neolithic date on the basis of fabric (Barclay and Rayner in Appendix 2). Most of these were plain body sherds but included two rolled rims from later deposits. A notable concentration was retrieved from hollow 1093 (22 sherds, fill 1094). Larger numbers of sherds were also recovered from evaluation contexts in T8 (43 sherds: layer 628) and T1 (79 sherds: layers 11 and 121) although again this was found alongside later material. Sixty eight sherds of Peterborough Ware included three rims, a shoulder and a small number of decorated sherds. A small decorated (bone impressed) everted rim could be from an Ebbsfleet style vessel (*c* 3550-3300 cal BC; Burchell and Piggott 1939; Barclay and Stafford 2008) (Fig. A2.1, 11). The fragmentary remains (55 sherds) from at least three Mortlake Ware vessels (*c* 3350-2850 cal BC: Barclay 2008; Barclay and Case 2007; Peter Marshall pers comm; Gibson and Kinnes 1997) decorated with impressed twisted cord and finger tip impressions, were recovered as residual finds from a middle to late Bronze Age alluvial deposit (layer 5074, Gp. 5070) (Fig. A2.1, 8-10). Additional Mortlake sherds were recovered from a

middle to late Bronze Age alluvial deposit 1109 (Gp. 1124) and the fill of hollow 1093 (fill 1094).

In addition to the Mortlake pottery, a fragmentary jet belt slider was recovered from alluvial deposit 5074 (Gp.5070, Sheridan in Appendix 2). This constitutes a prestigious, exotic artefact that formed part of a set of high status objects during the period *c* 3350–2900 BC, and its presence at Movers Lane is consistent with middle Neolithic depositional practices. Whether it represents a votive deposit, placed in or beside a river channel, or else the last traces of an eroded funerary deposit is uncertain; no specific association with fragments of disarticulated human bone recovered from alluvial deposits at Movers Lane need necessarily be assumed.

Late Neolithic to early Bronze Age

Worked flint dating to the later Neolithic is represented by a petit-tranchet type transverse arrowhead (Fig. A2.3, 15; Plate 25d; Green 1980), whilst Beaker/early Bronze Age industries are indicated by the presence of a finely made Sutton B or Conygar Hill type barbed and tanged arrowhead (Area 2, layer 1033 ibid.; Fig. A2.3, 16; Plate 25e). Both items were recovered as residual artefacts in middle to late Bronze Age contexts. No other truly diagnostic pieces from these periods were identified but there was a high proportion of scrapers amongst the overall assemblage and, whilst scrapers are notorious difficult to date, a number of these are characteristically later Neolithic and early Bronze Age, similar to the 'thumbnail' types that these closely resemble. A further possible implement of this period was a flaked knife made on a large curved blade and with a finely facetted striking-platform (layer 121; Fig. A2.3, 14; Plate 29a). This is a rather unusual implement but is perhaps most closely matched with the elaborate knives of the later Neolithic or early Bronze Age, such as the plano-convex types. Again, no cut features of this date contained what could be reliably considered as contemporary flintwork. Some, such as hollow 1171 on Area 2, contained a few pieces with later Neolithic or early Bronze Age characteristics but the general paucity of diagnostic implements and the real possibility of residuality means that no integral assemblages were identified (Bishop in Appendix 2).

Late Neolithic Grooved Ware pottery (*c* 2900-2400/2200 cal BC; Garwood 1999) included 6 sherds from features 5170 (fill 5169) and 5188 (fill 5189) on Area 3 (Fig. A2.1,14), with the remaining 11 sherds recovered from middle to late Bronze contexts in the western palaeochannel (layer 5142, Area 3) and gully 1038 (fill 1052, Area 2) (Fig. A2.1, 15-16). The pottery from these latter contexts closely resembles other Durrington Walls style pottery from the Middle and Upper Thames valley. Two Beaker (2450-1700 cal BC) sherds were also recovered. This included a base sherd with worn comb impressions, possibly from a globular shaped vessel, residual within a later alluvial deposit (Area 2, layer 1074, Gp. 1124) and a sherd from alluvial deposit 3005 (Fig A2.1, 18-19; Barclay and Rayner in Appendix 2).

Sandy silt alluvial deposit 3005 (Area 2, Fig. 7.8) contained a low-density artefact scatter of worked and burnt flint, animal bone, Beaker pottery and three possible very small fragments of human long bone shaft (McKinley, Appendix 3). The deposit was confined to a small area on the north-western side of the palaeochannel in Area 2 and extended into the palaeochannel itself. Test pitting showed that artefacts were confined to the top 50mm of the deposit. The worked flint assemblage was small but potentially related and may represent a scatter or dump of knapping debris and discarded tools. It included two refitting decortication flakes, three scrapers, an edge trimmed flake and a globular flake core found in association with Beaker pottery. None of the flintwork is particularly chronologically diagnostic but two of the scrapers are typical of later Neolithic and early Bronze Age types whilst the core would not be out of place in assemblages of this date.

Early to middle Bronze Age (Figs 7.9-7.10)

Trackway 3031 (Area 2)

Within the eastern palaeochannel in Area 2 a short length of trackway (Str. 3031), aligned north-west to south-east, was traced for approximately 4m from the southern limit of excavation and was truncated at its northern end by later erosion (Fig. 7.9). Alder roundwood from the trackway produced a radiocarbon date of 1680-1490 cal BC (SUERC-24595: 3295±35 BP). This was presumably constructed during the period of peat formation as it lay above a thin layer of peat (layer 3009) and below another (layer 3028).

A thin layer of sand (3030) appears to have been laid down over the surface of the peat prior to the placement of the wood. The trackway was about 1m wide with a total thickness of approximately 0.2m and was constructed out of poles, branchwood, naturally fallen debris and regular, almost certainly coppiced, rods laid end to end. There was a

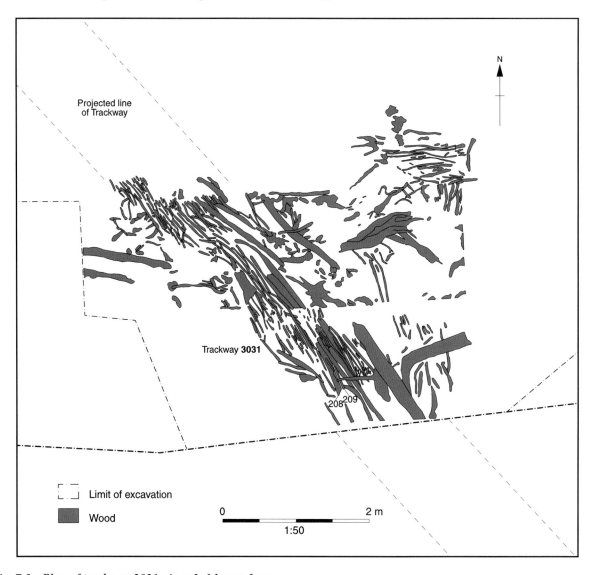

Fig. 7.9 Plan of trackway 3031, Area 2, Movers Lane

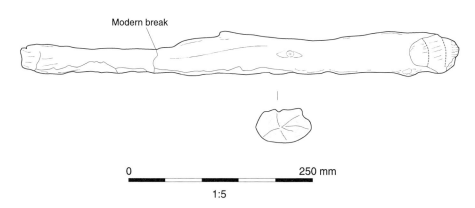

Modern break

0   250 mm

1:5

Fig. 7.10   Cut pole end 208 from eastern trackway 3031, Area 2, Movers Lane

Plate 15   Trackway 3031, Movers Lane

tendency for the larger material (3011) to have been placed along the north-east side of the structure. During excavation it was just about possible to discern armfuls or shoulder loads and some attempt was made to separate these apparent differences into separate contexts (3027 and 3010). These may have represented different phases of minor repairs to the trackway. While most samples had become desiccated and unidentifiable, detailed examination of elements of the trackway revealed that some were willow/poplar type. The largest diameter pole section lifted from the trackway from context 3010 was 90mm across and probably cut from a small alder. One lifted section was also charred and may have been left over fuel.

Unfortunately weathering and compaction had damaged the tool mark evidence, although it was clear that rounded, small metal blades had been used. One pole section (80mm diameter) from 3010 (timber 208) had the best preserved and most complete axe mark on a chisel form end (Fig 7.10). The axe stop mark was not absolutely complete but appeared to have been nearly so at 50mm wide with a very marked curve. A very similar axe stop mark was also found on the wedge shaped end of round-wood (timber 209). Very curved axe stop marks of this size have generally proved to have been typical of the late Bronze Age period in south-east England (Goodburn 2003a, 104). If the radiocarbon dating is accurate then the tool marks cannot be considered typical at least of the largest class of axe head available at the time. It might also have been the case that smaller tools were used for smaller items such as poles and coppiced rods.

The only finds associated with the trackway comprise a small assemblage of worked flint, burnt flint, animal bone and two small residual sherds of early Neolithic pottery (SF175 and SF191) which were both found on the surface of context 3011.

'Platform' 3012 (Area 2b)

Immediately to the north-east of trackway 3031, and possibly associated with it, was a second timber 'structure' (Str. 3012, Fig. 7.8 and Plate 16). When originally exposed this structure was thought to be a platform of radially laid branchwood approximately 6m in diameter. However, subsequent excavation showed that it was in fact the extensive root system of a 'drowned' tree, although it may have been utilised as some sort of platform by laying down branches and bundles of brushwood (context 3008). The upper layer had been severely weathered, although a scatter of artefacts, comprising burnt flint, worked flint, wood chips, animal bone and late Bronze Age flint tempered pottery was recovered from the surface of the underlying sandy silt clay deposit (3003) to the west, among the branchwood and degraded upper wood of the structure (3008) and within the overlying peat deposit (3004).

The small number of wood chips included examples derived from working larger cleft timbers of oak and alder. From layer 3003 came an axe cut chip of alder (70mm x 75 mm x 15mm) which had clearly been derived from the notching and reducing of the radial face of a moderately large timber. Two chips from the overlying peat layer 3004 were both of oak. Chip 188 was an off-cut from the end of a radially cleft oak timber with several partial axe stop marks up to 35mm wide and chip 189 was a small chip from 'notch and chop' hewing of an edge with sapwood. The wood chips indicate activity in the vicinity, but were not of sufficient quantity to suggest this took place on the platform itself. Another possibility is that the chips were discarded cooking fuel or kindling.

Just to the east of the platform a better-preserved bundle of coppiced wood (3013) was found. The bundle was not found tied together as a faggot but may have been so tied using a non durable material such as plant fibres as it lay in a tight discrete area. The rods, mostly of alder but also willow/poplar and oak, typically exhibited chisel shaped cut ends.

Stake structures 5161, 5168 and 5247 (Area 3)

Within the western palaeochannel in Area 3 the truncated remains of three, possibly associated, stake built structures (5168, 5161 and 5247) were preserved within peat deposit 5263. These comprised stakes that were clearly driven into the peat from above and partially truncated by channel 5271.

Stake structure 5161 is difficult to interpret due to later channel erosion (Fig. 7.11) although it appears to have been constructed within a small east-west

Plate 16 'Platform' 3012, Movers Lane

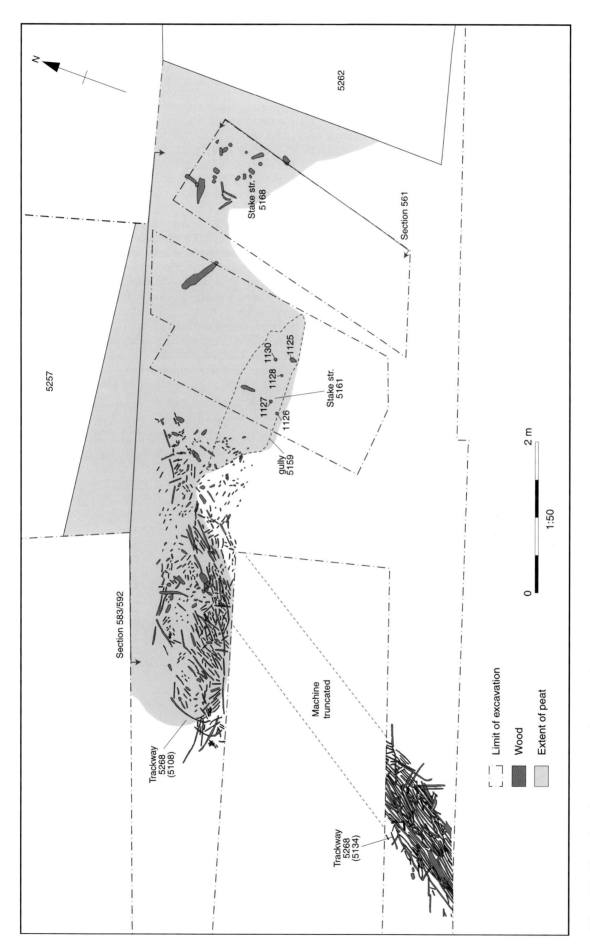

Fig. 7.11   Plan of trackway 5268 and associated structures, Area 3, Movers Lane

gully (feature 5159) and may represent a wattle fence lines or perhaps some form of earthen mass-wall laced with roundwood and timber stakes. The gully was about 0.55m wide and up to 0.30m deep with moderately steep concave sides and a concave base. The lowest fill of the gully (fill 5158) in which the stakes were found was almost indistinguishable from the surrounding peat into which the gully was cut. Overlying fill 5158 was a deposit of silty sand (fill 5147/5160) that contained possible burnt daub and some charcoal. The gully only survived for a length of some 1.6m. The stakes were quite varied and predominantly consisted of medium sized roundwood with the stake tips ranging from 25mm to 45mm. Stake tip 1127 was fairly typical exhibiting two adjacent facets. Radially cleft stake 1125, however, was unusual in that it came from a medium-sized, fairly slow grown oak log (Fig 7.12a). The stake was approximately 90 mm wide and 42mm thick, with about 70 annual rings including some sapwood. The fairly narrow annual rings and straight growth are typical of oak grown in tall dark natural wildwood. Unfortunately an attempt at tree-ring dating failed. The tip was of pencil from, shaped with a rounded metal blade,

although full axe stop marks were not preserved.

The full extent of Structure 5168 was also uncertain due to channel erosion and truncation by later features (Fig.7.11). All of the stakes and cut pieces of wood were found within the peat deposit. The upright stakes survived to a length of up to 0.35m, penetrating the underlying gravels by only 0.02m. The structure comprised a densely packed group of varied stakes, possibly set in two rough parallel lines approximately 0.5m apart, on a north-west to south-east alignment. The majority of the stakes were of roundwood and between 25mm and 55mm in diameter. The point forms varied and included chisel points, two faceted and pencil points. Roundwood stake tip 1145 was typical with a pencil form point made with small concave facets (Fig. 7.10c); this object was radiocarbon dated to 1500-1310 cal BC (SUERC-24590: 3125±35 BP). The structure also included two radially cleft stakes, one of oak (stake 1134) similar to stake 1125 described above, and the other of alder (stake 180). This latter stake produced a radiocarbon date of 1690-1510 cal BC (SUERC-24596: 3325±35 BP). Although similar, the two dates obtained on the stakes from Structure 5168 failed a chi-square test (T=16.32 at 1 df) and

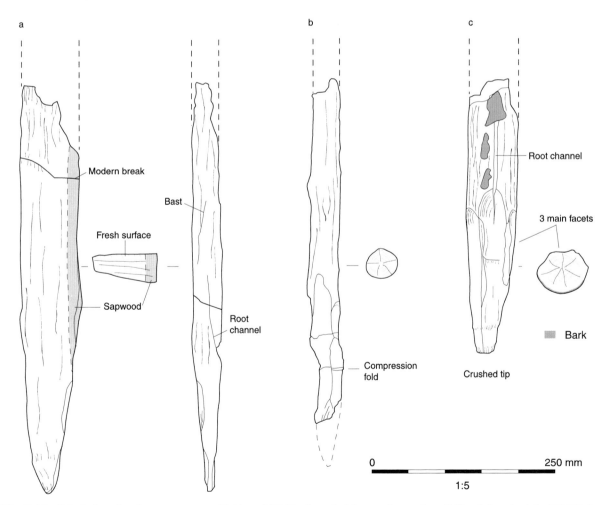

Fig. 7.12   Worked stakes from structures 5161 and 5168, Area 3, Movers Lane a) radially cleft oak stake (1125) from structure 5161, b) roundwood stake (1127) from structure 5161, c) roundwood stake (1145) from structure 5168

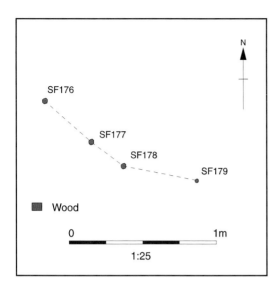

Fig. 7.13 Plan of structure 5247, Movers Lane

therefore are statistically inconsistent, an indication that these two objects are not of the same age.

A small amount of burnt flint recovered from the peat deposit and the surface of the underlying gravels may also be associated. Structure 5247 (Fig. 7.13) lay further to the east and comprised a group of four alder stakes that been driven into the peat, one of which was radiocarbon dated to 1750-1530BC cal BC (SUERC-24289: 3370±30 BP). The stakes appeared to form a slightly curvilinear line *c* 1m long although a later rectangular feature may have truncated it to the north. The diameter of the stakes varied from around 20 to 40mm and they were set approximately 0.2m to 0.5m apart. The stake tips were of pencil form with adjacent or multiple facets. The facets were concave and smooth and without complete axe stop marks.

Possible functions for the structure could include a light 'bender type' frame for a hut covered with reed mats or skins. If the arc of stakes represents the truncated remains of some form of circular structure, it would have been about 4.2m in diameter. Other functions could include stakes for holding up a fowling net or for supporting a light wattlework pen. The only associated finds include two pieces of fired clay from near the surface of the peat deposit (context 5131) and three flint flakes.

Trackway 5268 (Area 3)

Within the western palaeochannel in Area 3 a more elaborate hurdle trackway (Str. 5268), aligned north-east to south-west was traced for approximately 7.5m from the southern limit of excavation and was truncated by a later feature at its northern end (Fig. 7.11). Alder roundwood from the trackway produced a radiocarbon date of 1630-1450 cal BC (SUERC-24288: 3275±30 BP).

The trackway was about 0.7m wide with a total thickness of around 100mm and was constructed out of coppiced rods, approximately 10mm in diameter and 0.80m in length, formed into roughly woven hurdles. The weaving of the rods was much more apparent in the southern section of trackway (5134), the central part having been removed by machine. The northern part (5108) was in a much worse state of preservation and the construction was much less apparent. Here the trackway seems to spread out and merge into what is almost a thin platform of roundwood at the north-eastern end. This may be due to 5108 only having a single layer and it overlying peat rather than clay. However, several cross pieces were noted and several pieces of worked wood were recovered along with a small amount of burnt flint and a single small fragment of a human long bone shaft (McKinley, Appendix 3).

Plate 17 Trackway 5268 (5134) Movers Lane

The southern part of the trackway was 1.5m long, 0.7m wide and was constructed of three layers of hurdles secured by occasional thin stakes along either side. This may indicate repair to a relatively shallow flexible trackway that had sunk and broken under foot. The width suggests this trackway was probably intended for foot traffic and light livestock. It is probable the hurdles were originally woven round a line of stakes set in the ground about 400mm apart. No evidence of locking or binding of the weave was found. The three phases of hurdle seemed quite similar and distinctive with groups of 3-4 rods woven round slightly larger diameter roundwood stakes in an alternate weave. This is termed a 'slew' weave by basket makers today and, although easy and quick to complete, has little locking power. The general looseness of the weave suggests that the panels were probably no more than 3-4m length, but could not have been carried far and were unlikely to have been reused pieces.

The rods and stakes were very regular (31-12mm diameter) and clearly of dense coppice or, less likely, pollard origin due to lack of side branchlets. One rod from the southern section of the trackway (rod 1131) may have preserved the coppice heel on the base. Detailed examination revealed the majority of the roundwood to be of alder, although willow/ poplar and a single example of ash were also identified. Each stem was cut with a smooth oblique single blow at roughly 70 degrees, forming chisel points, presumably the result of use of a thin bronze axe blade.

Middle to late Bronze Age (Figs 7.14-7.15)

'Burnt mound' layer 5264 (Area 3)

Layer 5264 (Figs 7.14 and 7.15) was a *c* 0.10m thick deposit of black sandy silt clay with abundant burnt flint inclusions and charcoal fragments. This lay on the western side of the gravel terrace and extended for approximately 10m into the eastern side of the large palaeochannel in Area 3 and extended across the full width (north-south) of the excavation area. It appeared to be associated with a group of four post-holes (5091, 5094, 5097 and 5113) and two pits (5084 and 5088) all of which contained abundant burnt flint. It is uncertain whether this represents a deliberate spread of material used to try and stabilise the bank of the channel or the remains of a denuded burnt mound. In addition to very large quantities of burnt flint (over 73kg from a roughly 10% sample of the deposit) a small assemblage of unburnt worked flint and late Bronze Age flint tempered pottery was recovered.

Hazel charcoal retrieved from layer 5264 produced a radiocarbon date of 1430-1250 cal BC (SUERC 24594: 3070±35). Hazel was the dominant wood type found in the charcoal assemblage retrieved from the burnt flint spread and associated features. Small numbers of fragments of pomaceous fruitwood, oak, willow/poplar, elder, cherry-type and alder were also found in these contexts. This mix of wood types, is likely to reflect local gathering of fuel wood but with stands of (potentially managed) hazel particularly targeted (Barnett, Appendix 3)

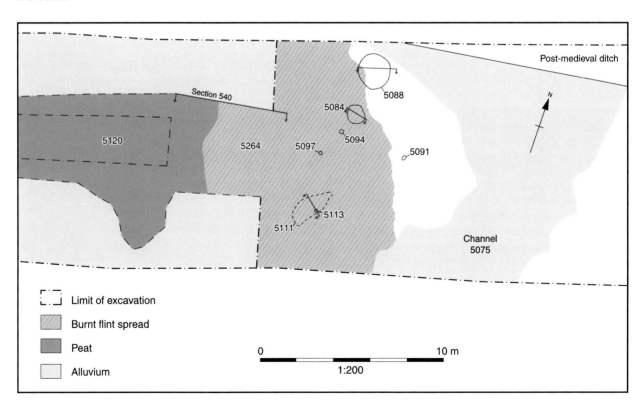

Fig. 7.14   Plan of burnt mound, Area 3, Movers Lane

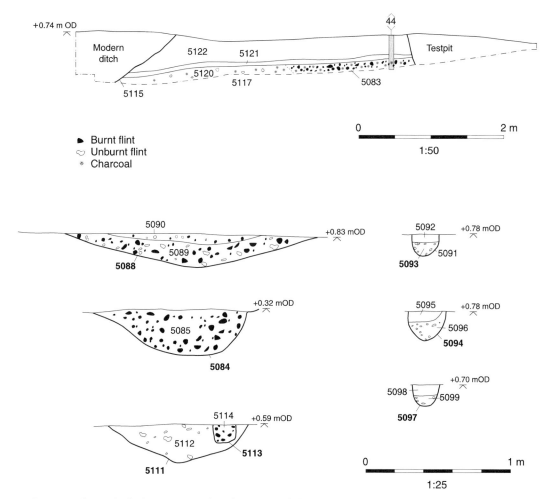

Fig. 7.15 Sections through the burnt mound and associated features, Area 3, Movers Lane

Plate 18 Burnt flint layer 5264, Movers Lane

Artefact scatters in the western channel (Area 3)

A dense, localised artefact scatter was located on what was either a sandbank close to the western side of the large river channel or the western bank of the partly silted up channel in Area 3. The artefacts, comprising late Bronze Age flint tempered pottery, animal bone, human bone (a single small fragment of a long bone shaft, McKinley, Appendix 3), worked wood, worked flint and burnt flint were all found within a *c* 0.15m thick layer of yellowish brown sandy gravelly loam (5142), possibly a truncated soil horizon. The deposit appeared to have been disturbed, possibly by root action, but more likely by the trampling of livestock (poaching). The only possible feature associated with this scatter was a small, sub-circular pit (5135). This pit was 0.54m long, 0.40m wide and 0.10m deep with shallow concave edges and a concave base. A small assemblage of burnt flint and a single piece of fuel ash slag were recovered from the bulk sample taken from the organic, silty clay fill but no other finds were recovered.

A scatter of burnt flint (5192) was located on a further sandbank, approximately 7m to the west of artefact scatter 5142. This comprised a layer of very dark brown-black silty sand up to 0.16m thick, which may represent a similar deposit to the large spread of burnt flint on the eastern bank of the river channel. A roughly 10% sample of this deposit produced a large assemblage of burnt flint (360/1725g) but no datable finds.

Parallel ditches 5259, 5260, 1038 and 1198 (Areas 2 and 3)

Ditch 5259 produced two small sherds of pottery recovered from its single fill. An approximately parallel ditch (5260), which was located some 7m to the east, contained no datable finds, but was assumed to be broadly contemporaneous. Both were between 1m and 1.2m wide and between 0.15m and 0.20m deep with slightly irregular sides and concave bases.

Two approximately parallel ditches (1038 and 1198) on a very similar north-south alignment to ditches 5259 and 5260, were located to the west of the eastern palaeochannel in Area 2. Ditch 1038 varied between 1.75m and 2.00m in width and between 0.45m and 0.75m in depth and had steep, slightly irregular sides and a sharply concave base. In general the primary fills comprised redeposited gravels, sands and silts. Above these were very organic, secondary fills, which contained relatively large quantities of branches (one of which appeared to have been cut) together with leaves and other organic material. The uppermost fills comprised very tenacious clays and silts. A small assemblage of late Bronze Age pottery was recovered from these along with small quantities of worked and burnt flint.

Ditch 1198 lay approximately 3.5m to the west of ditch 1038 and varied between 1.50m and 2.10m in width and between 0.14m and 0.35m in depth and had moderately steep, concave sides and a concave base. A small assemblage of middle-late Bronze Age pottery was recovered from its fills, along with worked flint, burnt flint and five small pieces of fuel ash slag. Ditch 1198 cut an alluvial deposit 1018/1021, as did a small circular pit 1020. This pit was 0.95m in diameter and 0.20m deep with moderate, concave sides and a concave base. The single fill contained a small assemblage of worked flint, burnt flint and animal bone, but no dateable artefacts. Analysis of environmental samples suggests that while the organic fills were forming these were open ditches with pools of stagnant water with duckweed and reeds, set in a landscape of fen vegetation, with alder, brambles and nettles on its edges and damp grassland and rushes beyond. There is some tentative evidence of grazing suggested by the presence of a few dung beetles. The upper fills show a similar environment, but possibly the development of willow locally and on the channel and ditch edges.

Two further possible north south aligned ditches were also investigated to the west of ditch 1198. Feature 1181, which was sealed below a thin layer of alluvium (1182) varied between 1.0m and 2.20m in width and between 0.28m and 0.39m in depth with very irregular sides and base. The fills comprised very mixed silty sands, silty clays and redeposited gravels, which contained a small assemblage of undiagnostic late Bronze Age pottery (2/3g) and two flint flakes, all from the upper 50mm of the fill. Although this was identified as a ditch during the evaluation (feature 595), the very irregular form and very mixed fills of this feature suggest that this is more likely to be of natural origin. The small assemblage of finds recovered could well be derived from the overlying alluvial layer (1182). Approximately 1.50m to the west of 1181 was a second linear feature (1233). This very irregular feature was aligned, very approximately, north south and had shallow, irregular sides and an irregular base. It varied between 0.70m and 2.0m in width and between 0.12 and 0.17m in depth and was traced from the northern limit of excavation for approximately 9m to where it terminated. This is assumed to be a continuation of one of the features found during the evaluation. The single silty clay fill produced a small assemblage of abraded late Bronze Age pottery and a few pieces of worked flint and burnt flint, all from the top 50mm. Although it is possible that this feature represents a ditch, its very irregular form, when compared to the broadly contemporaneous ditches to the east, suggest that this too is of natural origin. It has been noted (Coles 1992) that beavers sometimes dig "canals" between their pond and a food source. Features 1181 and 1233 were very similar in form and size to one of the few possible beaver canals recognised on an archaeological site (Coles and Orme 1982). Given the very irregular form of these features it is possible that these could be the result of beaver activity.

Cremation 1207 (Area 2)

A single cremation (1207) was recorded on the higher ground of Area 2. The cremated remains were contained within a shallow circular cut c 0.45m diameter and 0.18m deep. The cremation was of an adult, probably male. The bone weighed 189g, representing around 33% of what would be expected for a complete cremation. The bones were well burnt and quite comminuted with fragments being small and relatively abraded (McKinley in Appendix 3). No charcoal was recovered from the cremation (Wessex Archaeology 2003) which may suggest that cremated remains were collected from the pyre and placed in cut 1207. A sample of the bone was radiocarbon dated to 1260-1010 cal BC (SUERC-24290: 2920±30 BP) demonstrating that this activity clearly post-dates the use of the trackways. Although there appears to be a slight overlap with the calibrated date range from burnt mound 5264 in Area 3, at 1430-1250 cal BC (SUERC-24594: 3070±35 BP) the two dates failed a chi-square test (T=10.62 at 1df) and are unlikely to be contemporary.

'Natural' features on the gravel terrace

With the exception of the series of features described above, possible Bronze Age features recorded on the higher ground away from the channels contained few or no finds. While some of these may represent heavily truncated features (eg 1016, 1030, 1031, 1035, 1061, 1085, 1089, 1091, 1119, 1128, 1232, 5013, 5086, 5105, 5111, 5127, 5129 and 5132), their very irregular form combined with the abraded condition of the few finds recovered and the paucity of the charcoal and charred plant remains recovered from environmental samples, suggest a natural origin for most (such as tree throw hollows, root holes and variations within the

natural substrata). Some of the possible features excavated in Area 2 are likely to represent localised deposits of alluvium within small undulations in the underlying deposits.

Two possible pits (1131 and 5037) comprised irregular oval features with slightly irregular, concave sides and concave bases and were between 0.12m and 0.26m deep. Both contained small assemblages of middle to late Bronze Age pottery and small quantities of worked flint and burnt flint. Environmental sampling of pit 5037 produced a very small quantity of charcoal but very little other material. Middle to late Bronze Age pottery was also recovered from patchy alluvial deposits (contexts 1018/1021, 1124, 1182 and 1234) which were confined to the eastern part of Area 2.

Later features

Within the western palaeochannel in Area 3 a group of three large rectangular features (5123, 5262 and 5257, Fig. 7.8) with straight, vertical sides were found cutting through peat deposit 5263, partly truncating Structure 5247 and Trackway 5268. The bases of these features coincided with the base of the peat deposit. No finds were recovered from any of these features, although a single sherd of Romano-British pottery recovered from one of the lower deposits in the adjacent evaluation trench (T13, layer 832) may hint at a similar date for these features. The function of these features is uncertain. They appear to be confined to the area of the peat deposit, so peat extraction appears the most obvious function; however, the common coarse sand inclusions and general poor quality of the peat appear to make this unlikely. Apart from a large post-medieval ditch in the eastern side of Area 3, all later features recorded were clearly of 20th century date.

PART III: DISCUSSION

Chapter 8: Landscape and environment

The sediment sequences and environments of deposition (Fig. 8.1)

Several recurring sedimentary units and facies types were identified throughout the route sections during the initial fieldwork stages, correlated through detailed lithological description as well as associated features and artefactual assemblages (Appendix 2). Interpretation of the sequences was enhanced during the assessment and analysis stages with a programme of radiocarbon dating (Appendix 1), together with detail provided by the examination of palaeoecological indicators (Appendix 3).

Superficially the Holocene sequences can be correlated with the typical Thames tri-partite sequence of clay-silt, peat and clay-silt as described by Long *et al.* (2000) and in general there are similarities with profiles recorded in other areas of the Lower Thames floodplain (for example Devoy 1979; 1982). For the purposes of this discussion general correlations have been made within and between sites and with the Cultural Landscape Model (CLM) of Bates and Whittaker (2004) referred to in Chapter 2 (Table 1.3), in order to contextualise the associated archaeological remains (Table 8.1). There are, how-

ever, differences, as the sequences from the A13 sites can be traced into edge marginal sequences that abut the rising gravel terraces. The investigations have demonstrated that significant complexity exists within the sediment sequences at terrace edge locations and in the vicinity of palaeochannels, particularly at Movers Lane. Here, sequences are a reflection of complex local as well as regional factors. Figure 8.1 provides a summary of the key sample sequences examined from each site and Figure 8.2 shows the site locations.

The following section briefly describes the key characteristics of each CLM Stage as presented in Bates and Whittaker (2004), followed by a summary of the evidence recorded during the A13 investigations.

Late Pleistocene (Fig. 8.3)

The sequence of Pleistocene river terrace formation in the Thames is relatively well-documented (eg Bridgland 1994; Gibbard 1977; 1985; 1994). The deposition of sand and gravel sequences associated with the East Tilbury Marshes Gravel, which forms

Plate 19   Braided river, Denali National Park, Alaska (photo by Nick McPhee)

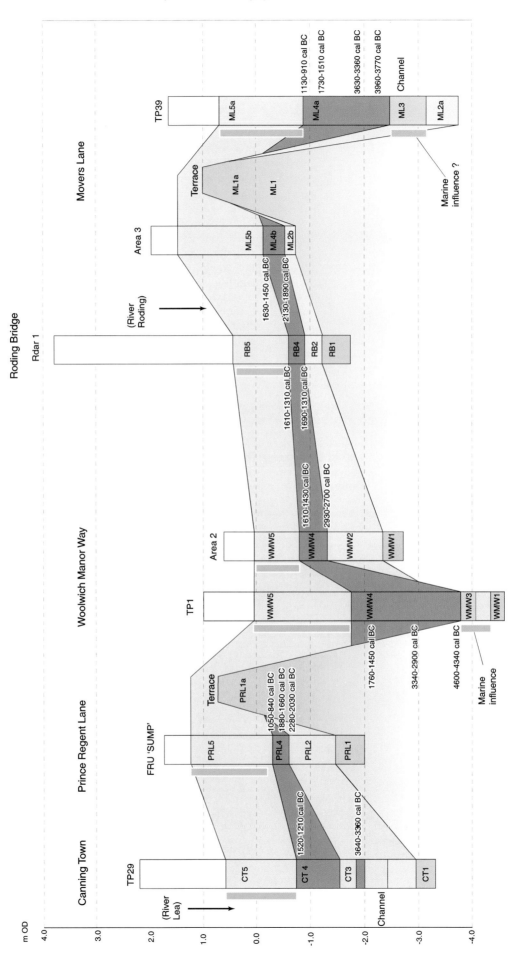

Fig. 8.1   Summary of the route-wide sampled sequences

the higher terrace in the vicinity of the A13, occurred during MIS 6 through 5e (Ipswichian Interglacial) to MIS 3. This terrace includes both temperate and cold climate deposits which accumulated in a range of environments, from braided to meandering river channels and estuarine situations. From *c* 30,000 BP (CLM Stage 1a, Bates and Whittaker 2004; Fig. 8.3), prior to and during downcutting under the sea-level

lowstand associated with the Last Glacial Maximum (LGM: 18,000-19,000 BP), reworking of the surface of the East Tilbury Marshes Gravel occurred by cold-climate solifluction processes. The Shepperton Gravel deposited following the LGM (CLM Stage 1b, Bates and Whittaker 2004, Fig. 8.3) forms the terrace that lies beneath Holocene sequences. Aggradation of the Shepperton Gravel is likely to

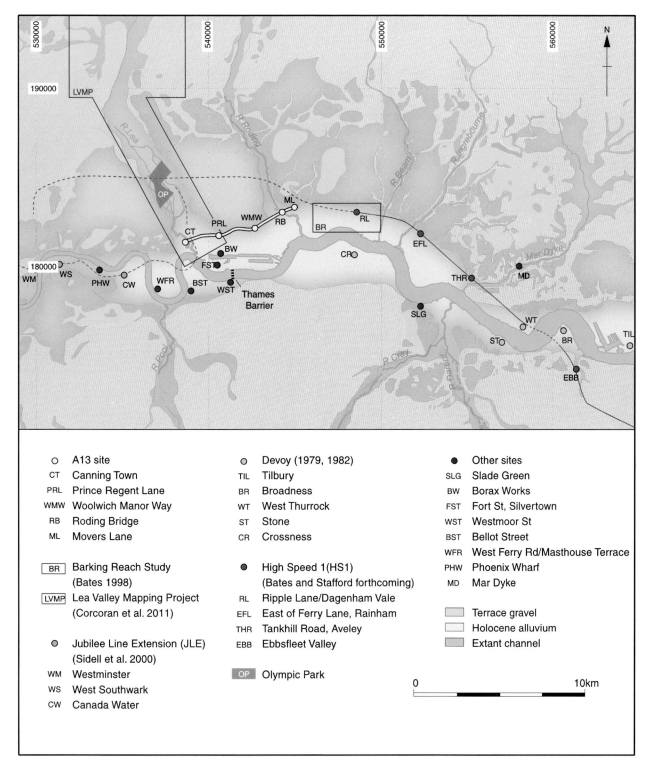

Fig. 8.2   Location of sites referred to in Chapter 8

Table 8.1 Summary of route-wide sediment sequences

Lower Thames tri-part sequence	General description	Environments of deposition	Inferred date	CLM	Sediment units					Associated archaeology
					Ironbridge-Canning Town	Prince Regent Lane	Woolwich Manor Way	Moorers Lane	Old Roding Bridge	
Upper alluvium	Blue-grey clay silt mostly structureless. Occasionally laminated with occasional coarse flint gravel horizons	Low energy wetland environment initially fresh or brackish water conditions, giving way to salt marsh/inter tidal mudflats. Possible post-depositional pedogenic activity	Post 3ka B.P.	5-6	CT5	PRL5	WMW5	ML5	RB5	Seals features of Neolithic to Roman date at higher elevations.
Organic complex	Highly variable organic silts and peats extending across low-lying area.	Alder carr wetland with phases of minerogenic input. Up-profile possibly becoming reedswamp or brackish marshland. Rapid lateral changes in sediment and vegetation/species composition.	3-6ka B.P.	4	CT4	PRL4	WMW4	ML4	RB4	BA trackways, structures and associated artefact scatters
Lower alluvium	Blue grey or light brown clays silts or sandy silts and sands, sometimes well sorted, weakly laminated sands grading upwards into silts, with occasional gravel clasts. Frequently exhibit evidence of rooting on upper weathered surface	Sand bars in meandering channel systems or sand sheets reworked by surface run-off, followed by sea-level rise resulting in sediments from backed up freshwater systems, grading upwards to salt marsh surface/inter tidal channel systems (ML and WMW). Post depositional pedogenic activity/upper surface weathered	? Pre 6ka B.P.	2/3	CT3	PRL2	WMW3 WMW2	ML3 ML2	RB2	Reworked and *in situ* artefact scatters. Mesolithic, Neolithic and Bronze Age located on upper weathered surface. A concentration of early Neolithic Neolithic flint, ceramics and charred plant remains, located on a possible sand-bar (WMW). Features cut into upper weathered surface. Particularly at higher elevations at edge of terrace. Isolated possible Neolithic features Bronze Age activity indicative of domestic and agricultural activities. Roman field system? (PRL)
Gravels	Sand and gravel horizons, clear bedding of sands, sandy gravels and silts. Occasionally grading upwards into fine silty sand	Severe cold with frozen ground. Periodic washing of erosion of higher sands, solifluction and erosion processes alternating with more stable surfaces	? Pre-15ka B.P.	1a-1b	-	PRL1a	-	ML1a	-	
	Soft brown clay, pockets of fibrous peat or dark brown organic clay	Low energy channel infill features, probably Late Glacial		-	CT1b	-	-	-	-	
	Poorly sorted coarse flint gravels	High energy fluvial environment, probably braided stream channels	>30ka to 10-15ka B.P.	1b	CT1	PRL1	WMW1	ML1	RB1	

have occurred under cold-climate conditions in high-energy fast flowing braided river channels accompanied by continued down slope erosion of the higher terrace. The braided river probably comprised a network of transient channels with sand and gravel bars, similar to those that flow in areas of Alaska today (Plate 19).

Pleistocene gravel deposits were exposed throughout the A13 route, although due to problems with ground water and trench collapse they were rarely exposed to any great extent. The deposits largely comprised coarse flint sandy gravels and sands of fluvial origin (CT1, PRL1, WMW1, RB1 and ML1), although sand, silt and gravel horizons, possibly deposited by sub-aerial erosion, were recorded at Movers Lane and Prince Regent Lane

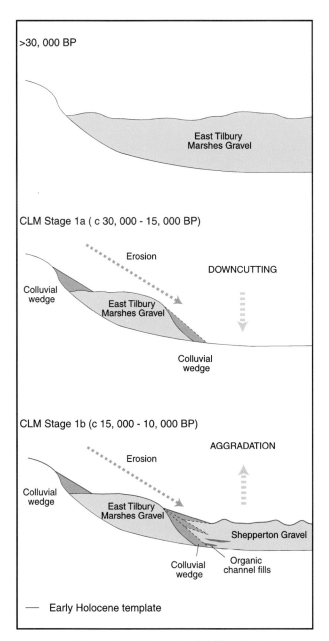

Fig. 8.3   Cultural Landscape Model (CLM) Stages 1a and 1b

(ML1a and PRL1a). Although there was an absence of associated palaeoenvironmental material within this latter group of sediments, their character suggests that they probably represent slopewash, colluviation and solifluction during intervals of severe cold when frozen ground dominated. Periodic washing of the surface and erosion of sands from higher gravel terraces is likely to have contributed to the sediment stack and slope erosion may have alternated with periods of relative surface stability. These sediments would have accumulated on a slope southwards towards the contemporary Thames channel (a braided system across the valley floor at this time) and active downward erosion would characterise this phase of fluvial activity away from the immediate site vicinity. At Movers Lane these deposits demonstrated considerable complexity grading upwards into fine silty sand and were dated by luminescence techniques from 15,800±850 BP to 23,900±1300 BP, clearly indicating accumulation immediately prior to and following the LGM. At Prince Regent Lane extensive deposits of bedded sand, sandy gravels and silts overlying the fluvial gravels were dated from 15,800±840 BP to 16,300±820 BP (see Appendix 1).

At Canning Town, a sediment unit identified at the base of gravels, or associated with the upper part of the Shepperton gravels, comprised soft brown clay, pockets of fibrous peat or dark brown organic clay (CT1b). Although these deposits were identified in geotechnical boreholes, unfortunately they were not sampled by the purposive geoarchaeological boreholes and no sediment was available for analysis. Organic deposits of similar description occur at the base of the lowermost gravels in the Lea Valley and are well known from sites in Temple Mills and Edmonton (the Lea Valley Arctic Beds described by Warren 1912; 1916; 1938). They represent severely cold climate deposits dated 21,530 to 28,000 BP, comprising broken rafts of peaty material, frequently rich in plant macrofossils and molluscs. Sediments of this type are rarely penetrated in the Lea Valley and are of considerable interest as they have the potential to provide regional palaeoenvironmental records and age estimates for this period (see Corcoran *et al.* 2011, 145-9 for the most recent assessment). The elevation of the deposits identified during this study, however, would perhaps suggest channel infill features of Late Glacial date is a more appropriate interpretation. Similar channel deposits occurring within the valley floor gravel were most recently identified during borehole work at the Olympics Park in Stratford (Fig. 8.2), spanning both the Windermere Interstadial (warm phase) and Loch Lomand Stadial (cold phase) at *c* 11,000 -13,000 BP (Corcoran *et al.* 2011, 150).

Early–mid Holocene (Fig. 8.4)

The surface of the Pleistocene deposits described above would have defined the topography of the early Holocene landscape, which in turn would

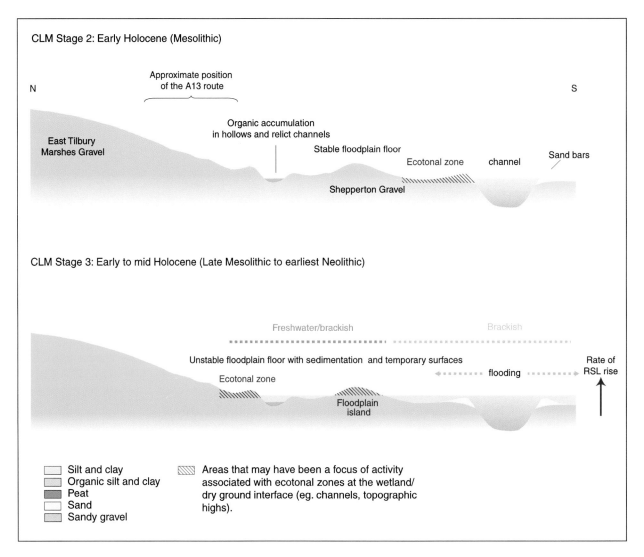

Fig. 8.4 Cultural Landcape Model (CLM) Stages 2 and 3

have influenced patterns of later sediment accumulation. During CLM Stage 2 (Bates and Whittaker 2004; Fig. 8.4) following climatic amelioration but prior to sea-level rise attaining near present day levels, the area is likely to have been characterised by relict Late Glacial features, but with a stable channel within the old Late Glacial main channel. The floodplain of the river adjacent to the main channel would have stabilised with the development of the Holocene vegetation. Local pockets of sediment accumulation are likely to have accrued during this time in channels and hollows on the gravel surface, for example at Bramcote Green (Thomas and Rackham 1996). A key ecotonal area probably existed adjacent to the main Thames channel and floodplain tributaries. Higher ground would have provided additional landscape resources within different environments.

During CLM Stage 3 (Bates and Whittaker 2004; Fig. 8.4) sea-level rise resulted in inundation of the former dry land surface and began to influence sedimentation and fluvial dynamics within the

valley floor area. As the sea-level rose, channel stability will have decreased causing the start of flooding of low-lying areas. The floodplain surface is likely to have become unstable due to widespread flooding and rapid sedimentation. Minerogenic sedimentation probably characterises this phase. While sediment accumulation during this stage will have begun under freshwater conditions, it would have been subsequently transformed by the onset of estuarine conditions as marine inundation occurred. During this period the ecotonal zone between wet and dry ground will have migrated inland and risen in datum across the flood surface. Thus wetland environments began to expand at the expense of the dry ground areas. Temporary landsurfaces may have existed within the flood area but these are likely to have been ephemeral and of local significance only. Activity would probably have remained focused on channel marginal situations and areas of the floodplain not inundated. Later more extensive inundation would eventually focus activity on the floodplain margins and any

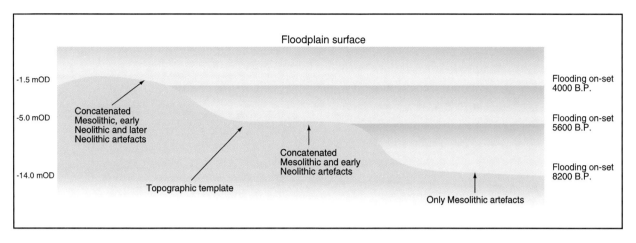

Fig. 8.5   A model for temporal separation of artefact assemblages below the floodplain surface, after URN and URS (1999)

remnant islands of sand and gravel within the floodplain.

Deposits relating to these landscape stages were identified throughout the A13 route corridor. They can be variously described as blue grey or light brown clays, silts or sandy silts and sands, sometimes well sorted, weakly laminated sands grading upwards into silts, with occasional gravel clasts. In general they lie between the basal fluvial gravels and the overlying organic complex.

The presence of a weathered horizon and associated archaeological remains at the upper contact of the sandy facies at Prince Regent Lane, Movers Lane and Woolwich Manor Way indicates that the sands at these locations were exposed as a land-surface prior to inundation. The landscape associated with this horizon, after climatic amelioration but prior to the onset of sedimentation onto the topographic template, is assumed to have been one of relative stability. There would have been minimal sediment deposition and little chance of stratigraphic development, resulting in the concatenated assemblages of Mesolithic and Neolithic artefacts in low lying areas, with the addition of artefacts from later periods at higher elevations, where burial by sedimentation occurred later (Fig. 8.5).

At Canning Town a series of blue grey clay silts or sandy silts (CT3) were recorded at the base of TP29. These pre-date *c* 3600 cal BC and appear to have accumulated in freshwater conditions, in or adjacent to an active channel. The deposits included opercula of the freshwater mollusc *Bithynia* as well as the remains of bank vole, amphibians and cyprinid (the carp family). At Prince Regent Lane in the western part of the site, blue grey clay-silts or sandy-silts (PRL2) beneath the organic complex also accumulated under freshwater conditions, evidenced by the presence of oogonia (calcified fruiting bodies) of stonewort and water flea eggs. Investigation of the top of the sequence in the 'sump' at Freemasons Road indicated that an environment of damp alder carr

and sedge had developed prior to around 2000-2300 cal BC.

A possible early phase of marine incursion was recorded at both Woolwich Manor Way and Movers Lane. At Woolwich Manor Way deposits beneath the main peat body contained pollen of the goose-foot family, which includes species found in saltmarsh environments (Plate 20). This, together with dinoflagellate cysts, sponge spicule fragments and a single example of the brackish diatom *Cyclotella striata*, hint at the proximity of intertidal conditions. Radiocarbon age determinations from the overlying peat suggest that the deposits accumulated during the late Mesolithic period, prior to about 4600 cal BC. In the eastern palaeochannel at Movers Lane (TP39) a gradual change from sand to organic silt accumulation suggests a shift to slow moving conditions during the Mesolithic, prior to about 4000 cal BC. Although pollen was poorly preserved, the presence of goose-foots, together with dinoflagellates, perhaps suggests some marine influence with local saltmarsh and some coastal woodland. Estuarine conditions were not recorded at the Roding Bridge site, located between Woolwich Manor Way and Movers Lane, probably due to the much higher elevations recorded from the surface of the Pleistocene gravels.

Mid Holocene (Fig. 8.6)

CLM Stage 4 (Bates and Whittaker 2004; Fig. 8.6) is characterised by apparent fluctuating sea-levels in which alterations between organic and inorganic sedimentation dominate the area. A major expansion of freshwater wetlands is associated with this phase and the temporary emergence of surfaces to or above flooding level will have stimulated the growth of organic sediments and led to peat growth. The ecotonal zone between wetland and dryland continued to move inland, causing loss of topographic variation. During times of peat accumulation complex boundaries between peat

Plate 20   Saltmarsh, Fambridge, Essex (photo by Andy Roberts)

and non-peat wetland ecosystems will have emerged within the wetland. Wetland would now dominate in the floodplain area as dry ground zones shrank rapidly.

Inter-bedded peat or organic deposits were recorded extensively along the A13 route. These deposits in general represent alder carr wetland (Plate 21) with phases of minerogenic input, up-profile becoming reedswamp and brackish marsh-land. Radiocarbon dates for the accumulation of these organic deposits broadly place them within the Neolithic and Bronze Age. This compares well with the model for estuary contraction at around 4900-1250 cal BC proposed by Long *et al.* (2000) and data from nearby Crossness, where the channel was estimated to have contracted from 4700m to 670m between 3600-2000 BC (Devoy 1979). The sequences also broadly fit within the time range for Devoy's Tilbury III (3550-2050 BC) and IV (1450 BC-AD 200) peat.

Considerable variation occurs, however, within and between route sections within this organic complex, with peat formation occurring within different timeframes at differing elevations. This may be a response to local factors. It is likely that pools of water existed on the floodplain between stands of alder, willow and hazel. Peat will have built up non-uniformly as pools were gradually filled in and new pools formed. Seasonal flooding, and probably an increase in river levels generally,

may have deposited sediment, particularly in those locations adjacent to tributaries.

At Canning Town, on the floodplain of the River Lea, deep organic silt and peat units (CT4) accumulated over a period of about 2500 years between *c* 3650 to 1210 cal BC, from the early Neolithic to middle Bronze Age period. At Prince Regent Lane, located at a higher elevation at the interface between the terrace edge and the Thames flood-plain, the peat/organic silts (PRL4) were much reduced in thickness. Radiocarbon dates suggest accumulation here occurred over a significantly shorter period of time of about 1500 years. The earliest organic sedimentation in the vicinity of Freemasons Road appears to have occurred in the slightly lower lying hollows, followed by more widespread peat formation. Radiocarbon dating of the base of the peat in the 'sump' sequence suggests that accumulation occurred between about 2300 and 800 cal BC. At Woolwich Manor Way peat and organic sediments (WMW4) varied considerably along the route corridor. A lower woody peat and an upper amorphous peat were noted towards the west, replaced by more minerogenic sediments to the east where this group of sediments wedged out against the rising gravel surface. Radiocarbon dates from the thickest sequence in TP1, at the western extent of the route section, indicate accumulation between about 4600 and 1450 cal BC, from the late

Plate 21   Flooded alder carr, Brownsea Island, Poole Harbour (photo by David J Glaves)

Mesolithic to middle Bronze Age. The peat appears to have accumulated throughout the Neolithic and Bronze Age, gradually encroaching onto the higher ground to the east. At Movers Lane radiocarbon dates from peat deposits (ML4) in TP39 indicate that accumulation at this location occurred between *c* 4000 to 900 cal BC; from the early Neolithic to the late Bronze Age.

Late Holocene (Fig. 8.6)

CLM Stage 5 (Bates and Whittaker 2004; Fig. 8.6) is characterised by the final submergence of the former floodplain topography and the loss of much of the floodplain diversity. Typically organic sediment

growth appears to cease after topographically elevated areas became buried, and brackish water conditions dominated. Sporadic occupation for economic use of the floodplain will have continued through hunting/shell fish gathering as well as use of the river and tributaries for transport purposes. Eventual land reclamation and drainage allowed occupation of the land for farming and habitation.

Sediments associated with this phase of landscape development were recorded at all of the A13 sites, evident by the accumulation of predominantly minerogenic silt-clays from the latter half of the 2nd millennium BC. These deposits occurred in every profile examined and represent an ingress of tidal waters as a result of rising sea levels.

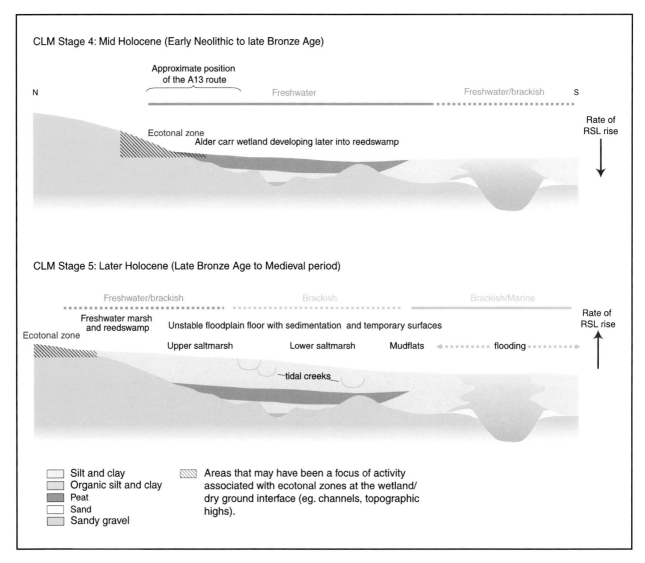

CLM Stage 4: Mid Holocene (Early Neolithic to late Bronze Age)

Approximate position
of the A13 route

N   Freshwater   Freshwater/brackish   S

Rate of
RSL rise

Ecotonal zone
Alder carr wetland developing later into reedswamp

CLM Stage 5: Later Holocene (Late Bronze Age to Medieval period)

Freshwater/brackish   Brackish   Brackish/Marine

Rate of
RSL rise

Freshwater marsh
and reedswamp   Unstable floodplain floor with sedimentation and temporary surfaces

Ecotonal zone

Upper saltmarsh   Lower saltmarsh   Mudflats   flooding

tidal creeks

Silt and clay
Organic silt and clay
Peat
Sand
Sandy gravel

Areas that may have been a focus of activity
associated with ecotonal zones at the wetland/
dry ground interface (eg. channels, topographic
highs).

Fig. 8.6   Cultural Landsape Model (CLM) Stages 4 and 5

The onset of minerogenic sedimentation at Freemasons Road (PRL5) dates from the late Bronze Age to early Iron Age. The pollen from the 'sump' sequence at Freemasons Road, immediately above the peat interface, shows little change apart from a slight rise in pollen of the goosefoot family, which includes species that grow on saltmarshes. However, several erosion channels cutting into the top of the peats in the main excavation area contained common sponge spicule fragments, as well as marine and brackish diatoms, which suggests encroaching estuarine conditions. The upper part of the alluvium from the excavations was not analysed in detail but pollen work from the evaluation stage in T23 indicated the gradual development of open saltmarsh vegetation, with freshwater marshes on the inland edge. Foraminifera and ostracod evidence suggests mixed brackish and freshwater conditions, in which the introduction of freshwater species probably derives from influxes of freshwater from

streams draining the inland marshes. On the higher ground at Prince Regent Lane this sedimentary complex directly overlay Pleistocene colluvial deposits, but also sealed ditches of Roman date. This implies that the higher ground remained relatively dry ground well into the historical period.

At Woolwich Manor Way, minerogenic sedimentation (WMW5) occurred slightly earlier during the middle to late Bronze Age. Accumulation appears to have continued throughout the later prehistoric and into the historic period with evidence of Roman occupation occurring within the alluvium in T15 and TP13 in the east of the site. The environmental evidence indicates that these deposits similarly formed in a predominantly open estuarine environment, with tidal creeks and saltmarsh, although high in the tidal frame with freshwater environments co-existing nearby. A similar change is in evidence at Movers Lane with the deposition of clay silt (ML5) across the whole site, sealing the earlier palaeochannels and the middle and late Bronze Age features on the higher terrace.

The nature and speed of landscape change
(Fig. 8.7)

Despite the apparent variation in the date and elevations for the main period of peat accumulation, Figure 8.7 (updated from Bates and Whittaker 2004) illustrates that the onset of accumulation at the three key A13 sites generally compares well with other sites in the vicinity (the location and details of each site is presented in Table 8.2 and Fig. 8.2). For a more comprehensive review of data derived from unpublished grey literature reports the reader is referred to Batchelor (2009) and Chapter 10. The plot (Fig. 8.7) demonstrates a steep trend associated with rising sea-level prior to 6000 BP, with the gradient reducing following sea-level attaining close to modern elevations. Calculation of the slope of regression lines allows a time-depth model to be produced which can be used to estimate the speed at which dry ground areas were lost to the expanding wetland front during the mid Holocene. This model was applied by Bates to the Barking Reach area, immediately to the east of Movers Lane (Fig. 8.2), demonstrating 75% of dry ground was lost in low lying areas of about -6m to -3m OD over around 700 years during the later Mesolithic period (4700-4000 cal BC, approximately 4.3mm/year

datum) (Bates 1998; 1999; Bates and Whittaker 2004). With reference sites at higher elevations, including A13 sites, the plot broadly shows the slower rate of expansion of the wetlands onto higher terrace edge locations from approximately -3m to 0m OD over a period of around 2500 years from the beginning of the Neolithic to middle Bronze Age (1.2mm/year datum). These figures, although approximations, suggest the loss of dry ground areas to the encroaching alder carr and associated changes in flora and fauna may have been perceptible to local communities within a few generations.

Evident at all of the A13 sites was a rising water table within the upper parts of the peat profiles followed by a change to minerogenic sedimentation during the later prehistoric period. This development has been recorded at many other East and Central London sites and represents a gradual change from a predominantly freshwater regime to a tidal river (see Sidell et al. 2000). The primary factors initiating this change may be attributed to increases in the rate of sea-level rise combined with isostatic downwarp (Devoy 1979; Fairbridge 1983; Shennan 1987 cited in Sidell et al. 2000, 109). However, the precise timing of this change at individual sites is most likely to have been influenced by more local factors such as the location of palaeochannels, elevation and position relative to the main Thames channel.

Table 8.2 Radiocarbon age estimates for selected sites in the Lower Thames where age estimates are available for contexts overlying non-compressible sediments (after Bates and Whittaker 2004)

Site	Elevation mOD	^{14}C yr BP	Lab code	Reference
Tilbury	-13.32	8170±110	Q1426	Devoy 1982
Ebbsfleet Valley	-0.7	4540±40	Beta-108114	Wenban-Smith et al. forthcoming
Ebbsfleet Valley	-2.32	4926±35	NZA-29080	Wenban-Smith et al. forthcoming
Broadness	-8.57	6620±90	Q1339	Devoy 1982
West Thurrock	-8.45	6450±120	IGS-C14/153	Devoy 1982
Stone	-8.82	6970±90	Q1334	Devoy 1982
Slade Green Relief Road	-2	4390±70	Beta-726204	Bates and Williamson 1995
Crossness	-5.3	5850±70	Beta-76991	Pine et al. 1994
Dagenham Vale (HS1)	-3.88	5751±40	NZA-16264	Bates and Stafford forthcoming
Ripple Lane Portal (HS1)	-3.75	5773±40	NZA-28794	Bates and Stafford forthcoming
Movers Lane (A3)	-0.6	3950±35	SUERC-25572 (GU-19431)	This volume
Movers Lane (TP39)	-1.9	4680±35	SUERC-25567 (GU-19426)	This volume
Woolwich Manor Way (A2)	-1.3	4265±35	SUERC-25563 (GU-19425)	This volume
Woolwich Manor Way (T16)	-3.13	5460±80	Beta-152740	This volume
Woolwich Manor Way (T17)	-3.19	5510±70	Beta-152741	This volume
Woolwich Manor Way (TP1)	-3.65	5630±60	Beta-147956	This volume
Freemasons Road (Sump)	-0.6	3745±35	SUERC-24600 (GU-18961)	This volume
Fort Street, Silvertown	-2.52	4750±70	Beta-93683	Wilkinson et al. 2000
Fort Street, Silvertown	-3.3	5660±100	Beta-93689	Wilkinson et al. 2000
Westmoor Street	-0.3	3280±80	Beta-81970	Bates unpublished
Borax Works	-8	6850±70	Beta-76200	Bates unpublished
Canning Town	-1.5	4030±60	Beta-70248	Bates unpublished
Bellot Street	-0.6	3600±70	CIB-325	Unpublished archive
West Ferry Road	-3.2	5460±80	Beta-84317	Pine et al. 1994
Phoenix Wharf	0.3	3110±40	BM-2766	Sidell et al. 2002

Plate 22   *Thames Barrier at Woolwich (photo by Herry Lawford)*

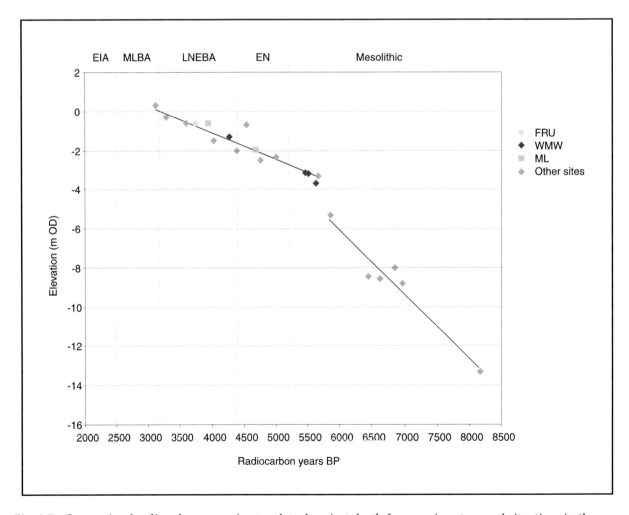

Fig. 8.7   Conventional radiocarbon age estimates plotted against depth for organic onto gravel situations in the Lower Thames (mid estuary) area (after Bates and Whittaker 2004)

Plate 23   Flood defences at Barking Creek on the River Roding (photo by Lars Plougmann)

At Crossness, located well into the floodplain on the opposite side of the Thames to the A13 sites, estuarine conditions are evident much earlier; from the late Neolithic at 2800-2400 cal BC (Devoy 1979). Immediately adjacent to the current Thames channel a sequence from the Isle of Dogs was dated to the early Bronze Age at 2200 cal BC (Wilkinson 1995). The middle to late Bronze Age dates from the A13 sites probably relate to their position at higher elevations, close to the margins with the terrace edge. Similarly late dates were apparent during the investigations associated with the construction of High Speed 1 to the east (formerly known as the Channel Tunnel Rail Link); at Ripple Lane Portal, Dagenham and East of Ferry Lane, Rainham the onset of brackish water conditions was apparent from the middle Bronze Age to middle Iron Age (Bates and Stafford forthcoming). In central London evidence from sites along the Jubilee Line Extension indicates the development of full tidal conditions from the late Bronze Age (c 1000 BC), leading Sidell et al. to suggest an average movement of the tidal head upstream from Crossness of 5.4m a year (Sidell et al. 2000, 109; 2004, 41).

Deposition of estuarine sediments, however, which may represent earlier episodic inundations, was noted during the late Neolithic (c 2800-2550 cal BC) period at both the Union Street and Joan Street sites in Southwark (ibid). Similar evidence for estuarine flood events was noted within the parts of the peat sequences at Woolwich Manor Way, for example in TP1, which contained rare valves of the marine and brackish water diatoms (*Pseudostelligera westii, Cyclotella striata, Diploneis didyma* and *Actinoptychus senarius*) as well as sponge spicule fragments. The building of the trackways during the latter half of the Bronze Age, such as those recorded along the A13 at Woolwich Manor Way and Movers Lane, may be seen as a response by local communities to increasingly wet conditions and seasonal flooding to maintain access routes though the marshes. However, the evidence at Movers Lane suggests repeated episodes of high energy flooding, erosion and sand deposition in close proximity to active channels during this period. It is possible that some of these flood events may be related to higher magnitude tidal surges, to which historically the Thames estuary is particularly vulnerable. It should be noted, however, that prior to extensive floodplain reclamation the river is likely to have been much wider and shallower than it is today. During the 1st century AD the tidal range is likely to have been approximately 2m and the width of the river at high water was close to a kilometre (Graham 1978, Milne et al. 1983 cited in Sidell et al. 2000, 17). Extensive areas of flanking marsh and creek systems along the estuary are likely have facilitated the dissipation of flood waters. Drainage and reclamation through the construction of embankments from the medieval period onwards has, however, substantially narrowed the width of river. This together with an increased depth due to dredging activities has resulted in an increase in tidal flow and funnelling effect, producing a modern tidal range of up to 7m in central London (Haughey 2008). During the medieval period there are numerous historical records of flood events affecting the Thames estuary. A period of increased storminess during the 13th to 15th centuries caused repeated breaches of the river walls. Recurrent flooding affected the lands of the Abbess of Barking, and other breaches occurred near Rotherhithe and in the stretch of the Thames between Woolwich and Greenwich (Galloway 2009). The devastating flood of 1953, caused by a tidal surge in the North Sea, affected extensive areas of the Thames Estuary and was one of the factors that led to the construction of the Thames barrier at Woolwich (opened in 1982) and maintenance of around 300km of associated sea defences. As recently as September 2000, however, the River Roding overflowed its defences and flooded 320 properties in the Wanstead and Woodford areas of East London. Since the 1980s, growing awareness of global warming and sea-level rise has led to a reassessment of coastal defences along the estuary with alternative strategies focused on managed realignment schemes in Kent and Essex and increased flood storage capacity.

Vegetation patterns and human influences
(Fig. 8.8)

Information on vegetation patterns along the route is largely gleaned from the pollen assemblages recovered from the A13 sites (see Haggart, Peglar and Druce in Appendix 3), although more site-specific data is provided by other categories of material such as macroscopic plant remains (Pelling in Appendix 3) and insects (Smith in Appendix 3). The earliest deposits that produced useful information date from the late Mesolithic to early Neolithic, from sequences at Woolwich Manor Way and Movers Lane. The sequence at Freemasons Road is a little later, dating from the early Bronze Age.

Mesolithic woodlands

Evidence for the vegetation of this area of the Thames Valley in the earlier part of the Holocene has been reviewed in Sidell *et al.* 2000 and more recently by Batchelor 2009; suffice to say sites with good pollen preservation are sparse. Overall it appears that an initial phase of birch and pine woodland was superceded by the mid Holocene with lime, oak, elm, hazel and alder, which is evident at sites such as Hampstead Heath and Runneymede Bridge (Scaife in Sidell *et al.* 2000, 111). Prior to its decline, associated with later prehistoric clearance, lime was of great importance and there is increasing evidence to show that as well as being a major constituent of the woodland on better drained sandy soils of the terraces, lime may also have been growing in damp woodland on peaty substrates (ibid) and this may have been the case in the early phases of peat development at Woolwich Manor Way where

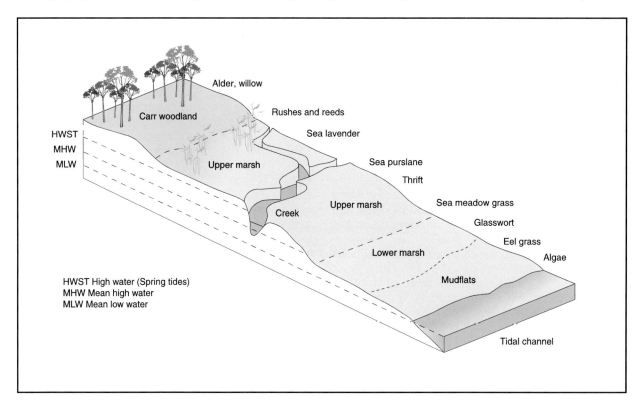

Fig. 8.8   Generic model of wetland zones

high levels of lime pollen have been recorded (Haggart in Appendix 3).

Late Mesolithic to early Bronze Age alder carr

Along the A13 alder carr wetland environments appear to have developed in the low-lying areas from very early in the sampled sequences and are associated with deposition of both the lower minerogenic alluvium and the main period of peat formation. At Woolwich Manor Way the sequence begins in the late Mesolithic period, prior to 4580-4350 cal BC (Beta-147956: 5630±60 BP), which is the date from the base of the main peat unit in TP1 in the western part of the site. The pollen assemblages from the lower alluvial deposits beneath the peat, although poorly preserved, suggest a wetland environment was present in the western part of the site (Haggart in Appendix 3). The eastern part of the site, which lay at higher elevations, remained relatively dry ground and this is reflected in the poorly preserved waterlogged plant remains recovered from the sandy palaeosol and the large assemblage of charred emmer wheat (Pelling in Appendix 3). Locally the environment appears to have been initially rather open with the total herb pollen reaching 73%. The vegetation was dominated by sedges and grasses, with some bracken and ferns. As the alluvium became more organic approaching the interface with the overlying peat, alder began to dominate the assemblages (60% TLP). This, along with willow and hazel, suggests a carr environment with perhaps oak growing at higher elevations. However, the occurrence of pollen of the goosefoot family, together with dinoflagellate cysts, sponge spicule fragments and a single example of the brackish diatom *Cyclotella striata,* hint at the proximity of intertidal conditions. Increasing wetness and the formation of alder car is also suggested by the improved preservation of waterlogged plant remains, with the remains of alder and seeds from plants typical of wet grassy ground such as rushes, sedges, celery-leaved crowfoot and gypsywort (Pelling in Appendix 3). The very base of the peat contained unusually high percentages of lime pollen (> 30% TLP). The pollen grains of lime, however, are very resistant to decay which tends to mean it is well-represented in mineral soils. This together with the presence of fungal spores indicative of dry mesotrophic conditions suggests initially a rather dry alder carr environment. The main body of the peat was dominated by alder, oak, and hazel, with lime at low but constant frequencies; sedges and grasses were few. This suggests that the alder carr became very dense. It is during this period that early Neolithic activity was occurring on the higher ground in the vicinity of T15. Sporadic occurrences of yew, buckthorn and viburnum (probably *Viburnum lantana,* wayfaring tree) pollen occur, a finding mirroring that of Scaife, who comments on the species richness of fen carr peats during the Neolithic and early to middle

Bronze Age at the Union Street and Joan Street sites in Southwark (Scaife in Sidell *et al.* 2000). At Woolwich Manor Way the pollen assemblages from the late Neolithic to early Bronze Age peat, from the excavation areas further to the east, produced similar results to TP1 but also a diverse range of seeds of wetlands plants: sedges, crowfoots, water dropwort and water pepper/mite. Disturbed ground species were also present and included chickweeds, black nightshade and brambles (Haggart and Pelling in Appendix 3).

The pollen sequence analysed from TP39 at Movers Lane begins in the early Neolithic period, in an organic silt at the base of the main peat bed, dated to 3960-3770 cal BC (SUERC-25568: 5055±35 BP). Similar to Woolwich Manor Way, tree and shrub pollen dominated, with alder again being the most abundant. Other important trees included lime, oak and hazel. Ferns were also present and charcoal particles were quite high. Overall this suggests that during the early Neolithic, freshwater alder carr was growing locally in wet places and along riverbanks, with deciduous woodland on the drier ground, but as at Woolwich Manor Way the alder carr eventually became quite dense (Peglar in Appendix 3).

The presence of yew (*Taxus baccata*) in the pollen sequences is of particular note. Yew was also utilised in some of the Bronze Age timber trackways at Woolwich Manor Way as well as the platform structure at the adjacent Golf Driving Range site (Carew 2010, Goodburn 2003b). A small scatter of yew wood chips was recovered from Bronze Age deposits at Movers Lane and an axe trimmed section of yew at Freemasons Road (see Chapter 10). Yew was apparently a major component of coastal woodland at this time and timber has been identified at several floodplain sites within Greater London, for example at Wennington (Sidell 1996), Dagenham (Divers 1994) and Beckton (Meddens and Sidell 1995; Scaife 1997). Sidell (1996) has suggested that yew was an important woodland taxon, and that the low pollen representation was due to taphonomic factors and Scaife (2000) goes on to suggest suggests that this species rich alder carr/coastal woodland may have no modern analogue. Yew is also frequently found within lowland wetland coastal and estuarine peat in Belgium, Germany and The Netherlands (Deforce and Bastiaens 2004). Across Europe there is a recognised shift in yew from lowland wetlands to upland dryland during the Holocene, which may be attributed to a change in ecological preference (Pelling in Appendix 3).

There is little evidence from the A13 sites for human impact on vegetation of the area during the Neolithic period. The analysed pollen profiles do not show a marked elm decline despite the two profiles from TP1 at Woolwich Manor Way and TP39 at Movers Lane potentially containing sediments spanning the event. An early Neolithic elm decline has been recorded at other sites in the region and constitutes a broadly synchronous event dated to around 4300-3800 BC (see discussion of Scaife in Sidell *et al.* 2000, 112). It is a now widely accepted view, first proposed by Girling for Hampstead Heath, that the demise of elm was mainly due to a disease carried by the elm bark beetle *Scolytus scolytus,* although the spread of the disease was probably aided by Neolithic woodland clearance (Girling and Grieg 1977; 1985; Grieg 1989; 1992). The absence of evidence on the A13 sites may be due to the floodplain location where local site conditions such as increased waterlogging and alder carr formation diluted the influence of nearby dryland tree taxa including elm. However, this is hard to reconcile with a date for an elm decline from nearby Silvertown which was placed at 5070 ± 70 BP (Wilkinson *et al.* 2000).

There was some tentative evidence in the pollen record of cereal cultivation from the early Neolithic onwards. However, the similarity of cereal pollen with some wild grasses such as *Glyceria* (sweet-grasses) means that the evidence remains equivocal (Haggart in Appendix 3). At Movers Lane cereal-type pollen was identified in the basal part of the peat in TP39 dated to the early Neolithic (*c* 4000-3600 cal BC) and here there was some also evidence for open areas with grassland, possibly used for pasture prior to the alder carr becoming quite dense (Peglar in Appendix 3). An early decline in lime pollen, along with other trees was also noted at the junction of the silty peat and wood peat, dated to 3600-3360 cal BC, although this could be attributed to human activity it could also have been related to increased water levels. The latter interpretation was also suggested for an lime decline observed in early Neolithic peat deposits from the Ebbsfleet Valley (Huckerby *et al.* in Wenban-Smith *et al.* forthcoming). Alternatively the thick alder carr may have prevented other pollen from reaching the site. The lime decline is normally associated with the Neolithic/Bronze Age activity and this is thought to have led to the absence of lime in the Thames valley at this time (Devoy 1979; 1980; 2000; Scaife in Sidell *et al.* 2000; Scaife in MoLAS 2001; Scaife 2006; Wilkinson *et al.* 2000; Druce in Appendix 3). In the Thames Valley there is an increasing body of evidence at a number of sites suggesting an earlier temporary decline in lime during the early Neolithic (Huckerby *et al.* in Wenban-Smith *et al.* forthcoming). In TP1 at Woolwich Manor Way cereal-type pollen was also present in low frequencies in the upper levels of the peat dated to between the early Neolithic and early Bronze Age (3400-1500 cal BC), and the recovery of an assemblage of charred emmer wheat from T15 at Woolwich Manor Way provides clear evidence for cultivation in the vicinity. At Freemasons Road, although the sediment sequence is a little later, the basal alluvial deposits pre-dating 2300-2000 cal BC also produced cereal type-pollen. An increase in fern and bracken spores and pollen of grassland plants

accompanied by a temporary decline in lime pollen may suggest a clearance episode (Druce in Appendix 3).

Reedswamp, sedge fen and marsh environments of the 2nd millennium BC

There is evidence towards the top of the peat of increasingly wet conditions and more open environments developing in many of the sequences examined during the first half of the second millennium BC. This is evident at Woolwich Manor Way from increases in pollen of plantains (including sea plantain) and pondweeds. This period is also characterised by a gradual decline in arboreal pollen, most notably alder and oak, and an increase in pollen of grasses and goosefoots as well as seeds of meadow buttercup and rushes, suggesting more open areas of damp grassland (Haggart in Appendix 3).

At Movers Lane the upper part of the peat also shows a rapid increase in herbs and fern spores and a concomitant decrease in tree and shrub pollen, mainly due to a large drop in alder, and increases in grasses and sedges (Peglar in Appendix 3). The plant assemblage provided evidence for alder (seeds and cones); wet ground species such as water-dropwort, fool's water-cress, gypsywort, watermint, common spike-rush, branched bur-reed, crowfoots, waterworts, water-plantain, red-shank, meadowsweet, sedges and rushes suggest marshy grassy conditions, and a small number of seeds of duckweeds and caddisfly larval cases may point to some open bodies of water. The drier ground species were relatively limited but indicate a background of scrubby vegetation, ruderal and disturbed habitats with plants such as bramble, fat hen, stinging nettles, orache, knotgrass, cinquefoils, chickweed/ stitchworts, black nightshade and thistle growing in the vicinity (Pelling in Appendix 3).

At Freemasons Road alder carr gave way to damp species-rich sedge fen and grassland developed immediately at the site. Freshwater pools and streams were prevalent with green algae, aquatics, and bulrushes (Druce in Appendix 3). The macroscopic remains produced broadly similar results to the pollen: seeds and cones of alder and fruit of branched bur-reed indicate carr or fen conditions. Aquatic species included crowfoots, water-plantain, water-pepper and occasional seeds of duckweed, as well as oogonia (calcified fruiting bodies) of stonewort and the larval cases of caddisfly. Seeds of waterside vegetation which might have included species growing within the shallow muddy water include branched bur-reed, club-rushes, water dropwort, fool's water-cress, gypsywort and watermint. Seeds of elder and bramble may indicate shrubby disturbed ground. Certainly disturbed habitats and nitrogen-rich soil are suggested by fat hen, stinging nettle, black nightshade, hairy buttercup and docks. Wet or damp grassland is indicated by meadow species, including possible meadow rue, ragged robin, and buttercups (Pelling in Appendix 3).

The changing hydrological conditions at the sites during the 2nd millennium would undoubtedly have affected the local vegetation in terms of the reduction of alder, encroachment of wetter conditions onto drier ground and more open conditions developing as a result of a reduction in the local alder canopy. The more open environment is likely to have increased the pollen catchment by allowing pollen from plants growing on the dryland, which was previously masked by the abundant alder pollen, to be better represented. Further increases in cereal-type pollen during this period, along with an increase of microscopic charcoal and seeds of disturbed ground species such as nettle and bramble, may point to increased clearance and cultivation on the nearby higher terraces, although as mentioned above the distinction between cereal-type pollen and the pollen from some wild grasses found growing in freshwater and coastal situations is problematic. The evidence from the plant remains at all three sites is equally enigmatic as seeds from disturbed, open and wet ground with some aquatic plants have all been recorded. At Freemasons Road, along with cereal type pollen, a significant decline in lime woodland on the surrounding slopes was evident during this period, accompanied by a decline in fern spores and a slight increase in those from bracken. The latter may be indicative of increased grazing (Behre 1986) or alternatively recent burning episodes, as bracken is known to rapidly invade areas cleared by fire (Druce in Appendix 3). The presence of small numbers of 'dung beetles' (eg Plate 24) and 'chafers' may also suggest that some of the landscape in the vicinity was cleared of woodland or used as pasture (Smith in Appendix 3). At Movers Lane there was a small background assemblage of charred plant remains, a significant quantity of charcoal in some samples, and waterlogged plant remains suggestive of scrubby vegetation and disturbed ground.

Plate 24 Dung beetle (Aphodius granarius) *modern specimen and elytra (photo by Professor Mark Robinson)*

The interpretation of environmental proxies identified in estuarine and fluvial situations, particularly pollen, is not easy. The sources of the pollen are likely to be widespread and grains will have arrived on site in a variety of ways. Some pollen is likely to have come from the local plant communities, while wind dispersed pollen will represent plants from further afield and grains may also be transported by water from both river and sea. The local human and animal populations may also have introduced pollen and other plant and invertebrate remains into the sediments. At Woolwich Manor Way, Movers Lane and Freemasons Road the evidence is perhaps best summed up in the insect report which states that 'one major difficulty with these faunas and their archaeological circumstances is the degree to which they can be used reliably to reconstruct woodland surrounding the site' (Smith in Appendix 3). The same could be said of both the pollen and other plant remains when used to distinguish individual plant communities in isolation, but when considered together with the insects they suggest the nature of both the very local wetland and the surrounding dryland vegetation.

Chapter 9: Prehistoric occupation at the terrace edge

The location, date, and nature of the evidence
(Fig 9.1)

Introduction

Direct evidence of human activity was identified at three of the five sites investigated: Prince Regent Lane/Freemasons Road, Woolwich Manor Way and Movers Lane. All three of these sites are located at the edge of the gravel terrace and Thames flood-plain, although close to the confluences of the Rivers Lea and Roding. Reconstruction of the pre-historic topography and environment has demon-strated the presence of shifting wetland and palaeochannel zones as well as areas of higher drier ground, which would have influenced the location, date and nature of activities carried out at the sites (see Chapter 8).

Figure 9.1 is a summary of the distribution of archaeological remains, the periods represented and some indication of the associated topography and environments of deposition. The periods repre-sented by the archaeology span the Mesolithic through to the post medieval period, although the most substantial evidence for occupation dates to the 2nd millennium BC and includes several impor-tant timber structures and trackways identified at all three sites. Aside from the timber structures, however, only a relatively small number of associ-ated features and deposits recorded on the sites were of undoubted anthropogenic origin and a significant proportion of the artefact assemblages, particularly those dated to the earlier periods, showed signs of abrasion and redeposition by later human agency and alluvial processes.

The prehistoric artefact assemblages are dominated by items of worked wood, pottery, worked and burnt flint (Table 9.1, Plate 25 and Appendix 2) and are considered relatively large for the London region when compared with similar recently investigated sites in the Thames floodplain (see for example Holder 1998). Generally faunal remains were poorly preserved at Woolwich Manor Way and Movers Lane, although a modest assem-blage was recovered from Bronze Age deposits at Prince Regent Lane/Freemasons Road. No metal-work or glass was recovered from any of the sites apart from occasional recent items such as iron nails. Seven pieces of fuel ash slag were recovered from Bronze Age features at Movers Lane, although

Table 9.1   Summary of route-wide artefact assemblages

Material	Prince Regent Lane	Woolwich Manor Way	Movers Lane	Total
Prehistoric pottery (no.)	147	264	408	819
Roman pottery (no.)	1	604	1	606
Fired clay (no.)	2		18	20
Unfired clay (no.)	53			
Worked stone (no.)			3	3
Worked flint (no.)	595	233	820	1648
Burnt flint (kg.)	47.5	6.7	>93	
Animal bone (no.)	36	-	473	
Human bone (no.)	-	-	4	4
Human bone cremated (kg)	-	-	0.189	0.189
Jet (no.)			1	1

0   50 mm

1:1

Plate 25   A series of flint points from the A13 sites

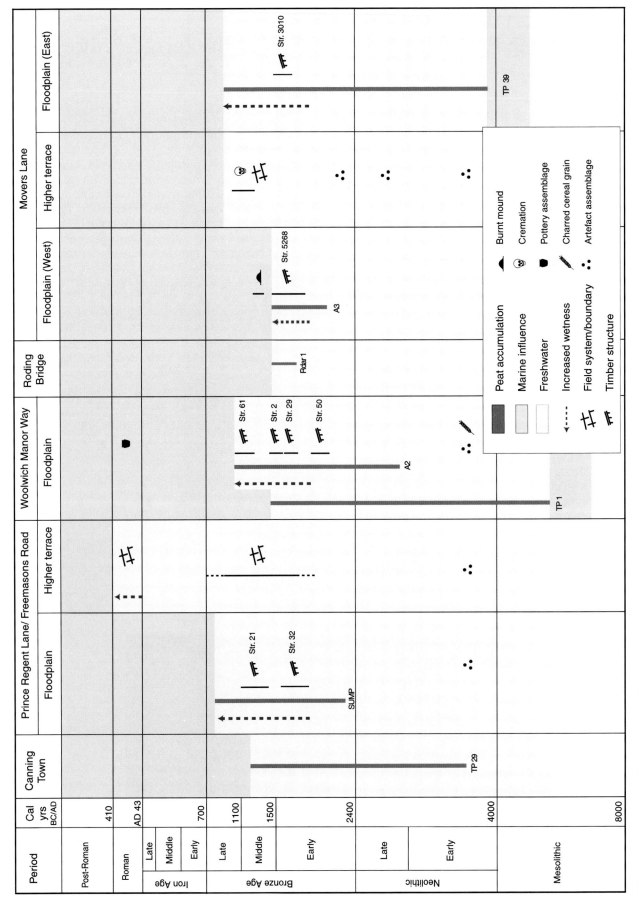

Fig. 9.1 Summary of route-wide archaeology

none clearly derives from metalworking. A very small quantity of fired clay was also recovered from the same site and although none of these fragments were diagnostic, a few had traces of surfaces and could be structural in origin. Significantly, a fragment of jet from Movers Lane is thought to be part of a belt slider dated to the earlier part of the Neolithic (Sheridan in Appendix 2).

Flint points (Plate 25)

a. **Mesolithic rod-shaped microlith** from Movers Lane (MOE00, unstratified) (Fig. A2.3, 13),
b. **Mesolithic/early Neolithic obliquely truncated blade** from Woolwich Manor Way (WMW00, 2005, SF8) (Fig. A2.3, 6),
c. **Early Neolithic leaf-shaped arrowhead** (unfinished?) from Woolwich Manor Way (WMW00, 2001) (Fig. A2.3, 5),
d. **Late Neolithic petit tranchet arrowhead** from Movers Lane (MOE00, 60) (Fig. A2.3, 15),
e. **Early Bronze Age barbed and tanged arrowhead** from Movers Lane (RIR01, 1033) (Fig. A2.3, 16)

Analysis of the distribution and date of the prehistoric pottery assemblages along the route demonstrates that the majority belongs to either early Neolithic plain bowl and decorated styles or middle to late Bronze Age Deverel-Rimbury/PDR styles with much smaller quantities from other periods (Fig. 9.2; Barclay and Rayner in Appendix 2). The largest overall assemblage was retrieved from Movers Lane (408 sherds), followed by Prince Regent Lane (264 sherds) and Woolwich Manor Way (147 sherds). Although the differences may well be a reflection of the scale of the excavations carried out at Movers Lane compared to the other sites, there are clearly differences in date between the sites. Neolithic pottery, which also included smaller quantities of Peterborough Ware and Grooved Ware, was most abundant at Movers Lane and to a lesser extent at Woolwich Manor Way, whereas assemblages were sparse at Prince Regent Lane. Pottery of late Neolithic to early Bronze Age date was generally very sparse at all three sites and the larger number of Beaker sherds at Woolwich Manor Way are attributed to a single vessel (Plate 26, Fig. A2.1, 17). Conversely, middle to late Bronze Age pottery was most abundant at Prince Regent Lane, followed by Movers Lane and was very sparse at Woolwich Manor Way.

Evidence of activity for the later periods, from the 1st millennium BC onwards, was relatively sparse at all sites. Some activity appears to have continued into the Iron Age at Freemasons Road and on the higher ground at Prince Regent Lane a series of possible Roman linear features may represent the remains of boundary or drainage ditches. At Woolwich Manor Way Roman activity is presented by spreads of occupation material containing signif-

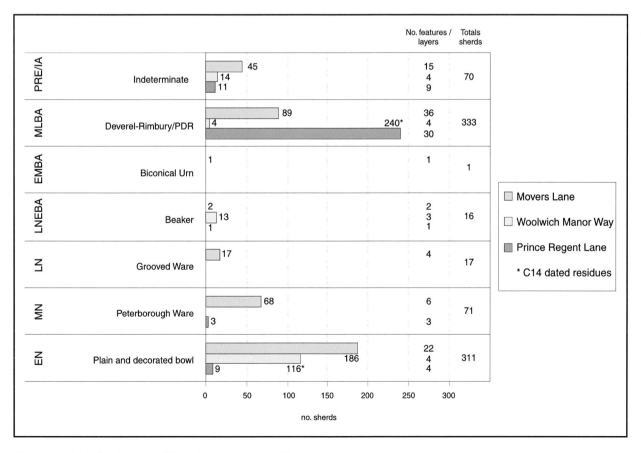

Fig. 9.2 Distribution of prehistoric pottery assemblages

0   50 mm

1:1

Plate 26   Beaker pottery, Woolwich Manor Way (Area 2), context 28

icant amounts of pottery, perhaps laid down in an attempt to consolidate the wet marshland surface. Apart from very occasional sherds of medieval pottery evidence of activity following the Roman period was largely absent.

Mesolithic (8500–4000 BC)

The majority of evidence dated to the earlier periods along the A13 route is represented by artefact scatters, much as reworked material in later deposits and features. The Mesolithic assemblage comprised occasional items of worked flint perhaps indicating only transient activity associated with the maintenance of hunting equipment (Bishop in Appendix 2). Diagnostic items include a microlith from Movers Lane and a micro-burin from Prince Regent Lane. No other certain Mesolithic material was identified although a significant proportion of the overall assemblage was characteristic of the blade-based industries of Mesolithic or early Neolithic date.

The sparseness of material is not atypical and occasional Mesolithic flintwork has been recorded at other sites in the vicinity attesting to persistent activity along the river margins (see Lacaille 1961; MoLAS 2000). The importance of tributary valleys during this period has been highlighted by work in the Colne Valley at Uxbridge to the west of the City (Lewis with Rackham 2011) and this is reiterated by the findings of recent excavations in the valley of the River Beam, Dagenham, which produced *in situ* scatters of early and late Mesolithic date, sealed beneath alluvium (OA 2011). Evidence of activity is also emerging in the Lower Lea, for example at Stratford Market (Hiller and Wilkinson 2005, 36-8) and Carpenters Road (Corcoran *et al.* 2011, 172). In general much of the material from the larger assemblages in the Lower Thames area is early in date. However, dense scatters of later Mesolithic worked flint suggest more intense areas of occupation down stream of the City; for example the scatters from the

Erith Spine Road on the south bank of the Thames may represent a late Mesolithic production site manufacturing microliths and tranchet axes (Bennell 1998) as does the site at Tankhill Road at Purfleet (Leivers *et al.* 2007).

It is possible that further *in situ* evidence of activity associated with former dry land surfaces is preserved further into the floodplain towards the main Thames channel, beneath the thick alluvium and peat deposits (see Fig. 8.4, CLM Stage 2). During the later Mesolithic period, however, estuarine inundation (evident at Woolwich Manor Way and Movers Lane) and an increasingly unstable surface would probably have affected the nature and intensity of activities carried out on the floodplain, which probably focused on ecotonal zones at the wetland margins and drier floodplain islands (see Fig. 8.4, CLM Stage 3). The latter is demonstrated by the evidence recovered from the Royal Docks Community School site, some 500m to the south of the A13/Prince Regent Lane junction. Here Mesolithic activity, which included three microburins and a microlith (along with Neolithic and Bronze Age evidence, see below) was recorded on the dry land surface of two small sandy islands within the floodplain (Holder 1998; Corcoran *et al.* 2011, 57 and 172).

Early Neolithic (4000–3000BC)

The wetland zone appears to have migrated sufficiently inland to impinge on the terrace edge area occupied by the A13 route by the beginning of the 4th millennium BC, which may go some way to explaining the more abundant evidence for activity during this period. This activity is largely reflected in the artefact assemblages; the pottery and flintwork, as opposed to structural remains. Although a number of potential features contained Neolithic artefacts, the often irregular shape would suggest that the majority are of natural origin with the artefacts probably being reworked from contemporary ground surfaces close by. A series of features recorded at the base of the excavated sequence at Freemasons Road were initially thought to be of Neolithic date on the basis of occasional pieces of worked flint. This included a possible rectilinear enclosure and a series of postholes. Subsequent radiocarbon dating and stratigraphic analysis, however, suggests these features are more likely to be Bronze Age. The residual aspect of much of the artefact assemblages clearly limits detailed discussion of the nature of the activities carried out during the Neolithic. Extensive although not particularly dense spreads of early Neolithic pottery and lithic material were identified from the weathered sands at all three sites (Bishop, Barclay and Rayner in Appendix 2) although only at Woolwich Manor Way did these remain relatively undisturbed by later alluviation and human activity (see below).

The earliest Neolithic pottery assemblage from the A13 sites comprises 311 sherds which collectively could be accommodated within the Mildenhall style of the decorated bowl tradition of the mid 4th millennium BC (*c* 3650-3350 cal BC) which is generally distributed across eastern England but also occurs in north Kent (Barclay and Rayner in Appendix 2 and see also Gibson and Leivers 2008; Barclay and Stafford 2008). This pottery would be broadly contemporaneous with the assemblages recovered from the causewayed enclosures at Orsett and Staines (Kinnes 1978; Robertson Mackay 1987). Small assemblages of early Neolithic pottery have also been recorded at the Royal Docks Community School, Prince Regent Lane (Rayner 1997) and at Brookway, Rainham (Holder 1998, 10), while the pottery from Yabsley Street, Blackwell (Raymond 2008), Erith Spine Road (Bennell 1998) and Clapham (Densem and Seeley 1982, fig 5) belongs to the earlier Carinated Bowl tradition (4000-3650 cal BC: Herne 1988; Barclay 2008). In addition 71 sherds, representing a minimum of six vessels, were also assigned to the developed Peterborough Ware style (Mortlake), although most of the material (59 sherds) was recovered from a single deposit (5074, Movers Lane). Mortlake Ware belongs to the period 3350-2850 cal BC (Barclay 2008; Peter Marshall pers comm; Gibson and Kinnes 1997) and is considered to have developed out of the Ebbsfleet and decorated bowl styles of the mid-4th millennium cal BC. Comparisons can be made with the pottery recovered from the ring ditch at Staines Road, Shepperton (Jones 2008) noted as mostly Mortlake Ware and from the outer ditch of the Staines causewayed enclosure, classified as Ebbsfleet Ware (Whittle in Robertson-Mackay 1987, 90 and fig 52, 175-185). There are a considerable number of occurrences (75 sites) of Peterborough Ware from, in particular, the west London area (Cotton 2004, fig. 15.5), although finds from the east side of Greater London are by contrast relatively sparse. River finds of Mortlake Ware are well known and include the bowls from Mortlake, Hammersmith and Putney, while other finds are known from foreshore and eyot contexts

(Holgate 1988; Cotton and Johnson 2004; Cotton 2004).

With reference to the lithic assemblage (Plate 27; Bishop in Appendix 2), core reduction is represented at all three sites but high proportions of retouched implements and useable flakes indicate that tool use was an important element of the activities conducted. The proportion of retouched tools and utilized blades compared to knapping waste was high, even for a 'domestic' assemblage (Wainwright 1972, 66) perhaps suggesting these items were manufactured elsewhere. This is also supported by a large number of flakes and blades whose raw materials were not matched by any of the cores present. The raw materials used appear to have been collected from a number of locations as well as from the immediate vicinity. It also appears that, as well as some cores being brought to the site, others were being taken away for use elsewhere. A number of activities appear to be indicated and the retouched and utilized implements suggest a degree of specialisation. Simple edge-trimmed flakes and serrated pieces, some exhibiting polish, suggest an emphasis on cutting tasks that probably included the processing of silica-rich plant materials such as cereals and perhaps rushes from the wetland zone. Scrapers were also present in numbers; these may indicate hide processing (Bradley 1978). Hunting is indicated by an almost finished arrowhead from Woolwich Manor Way (Fig. A2.3, 5), and other possible arrowhead blanks at Prince Regent Lane indicate manufacture (eg Fig. A2.3, 1).

Early Neolithic worked flint (Plate 27)

a. **Bifacially worked flake** (arrowhead blank?) from Freemasons Road (FRU01, 106, SF167) (Fig. A2.3, 1)
b. **Denticulated scraper** from Woolwich Manor Way (WMW00, 1517, SF3) (Fig. A2.3, 2)
c. **Worn serrated blade** from Woolwich Manor Way (WMW00, 2008, SF138) (Fig. A2.3, 3)
d. **Serrated blade-like flake** from Woolwich Manor Way (WMW00, 2008, SF216) (Fig. A2.3, 4)
e. **Exhausted blade core** from Woolwich Manor Way (WMW00, 2005) (Fig. A2.3, 7)
f. **Utilised flake** from Woolwich Manor Way (WMW00, 2008, SF78). (not drawn)
g. **Utilised blade** from Woolwich Manor Way (WMW00, 2008, SF109) (Fig. A2.3, 10)
h. **Utilised flake (piercing)** from Woolwich Manor Way (WMW00, 2008, SF91) (not drawn)

The remains recovered in T15 at Woolwich Manor Way included a substantial assemblage of early Neolithic charred cereal grain and chaff, mainly from emmer wheat (Plate 28; Pelling in Appendix 3). This was associated with charred hazelnut shell, charcoal (Barnett in Appendix 3), pottery (Barclay and Rayner in Appendix 2) and worked and burnt flint (Bishop in Appendix 2), located on a buried land surface sealed by peat.

0   50 mm

1:1

Plate 27   Early Neolithic worked flint from the A13 sites

Further much smaller scatters of material were identified in equivalent deposits in adjacent trenches (TP13 and T16) and T17 produced a small concentration of burnt flint. This area was latterly preserved *in situ* so was not the subject of further more extensive excavation. The remains in T15 were concentrated in a sondage cut into the base of the north-east end of the trench in an area measuring *c* 1.8 x 2.4m. A further sondage in the south-western end of the trench of similar size produced fewer artefacts. Overall, the landsurface produced 67 sherds of pottery assigned to the early Neolithic and 102 worked flints. Micromorphological analysis suggests the surface was significantly disturbed by trampling and/or cultivation (Macphail, Appendix 3). In certain respects the evidence is reminiscent of the early Neolithic midden deposits excavated at Great Arnold's Field, Rainham (Howell *et al.* 2011, 24-35), at Eton Rowing Lake in the Middle Thames Valley (Allen *et al.* 2004, 91 and forthcoming) and perhaps the Stumble on the Blackwater Estuary in Essex (Heppell 2006; Murphy 1989; Wilkinson *et al.* submitted), although with such a small sample area at Woolwich Manor Way it is difficult to speculate further. At the Great Arnold's Field site Mildenhall type pottery appeared to have been incorporated into a charcoal-rich midden deposit pushed into the fill of the ring ditch (Howell *et al.* 2011, 24-35). At 3770-3630 cal BC (SUERC-24597: 4890±35 BP) and 3630-3360 cal BC (SUERC-24830: 4685±45 BP)

respectively, the radiocarbon dates for the cereal grain at Woolwich Manor Way and the charred residue adhering to a pottery sherd perhaps suggest that the activity represents a series of visits to the same spot, perhaps a favoured point in the landscape, by communities who were presumably also utilising areas of the adjacent gravel terrace (J. Cotton pers. comm.).

Overall, the quantity of material recovered along the A13 route suggests a substantial level of activity during the early Neolithic along floodplain and river margins. The fact that that material appears to have formed small spreads or scatters may reflect a series of short-lived episodes, with the emphasis on mobility and temporality comparable with the wider regional evidence. Substantial activity in a similar topographic position, occupying the ecotonal zone between terrace and floodplain, was located further downstream at the site of Brookway, Rainham (Meddens 1996). Here, the evidence comprised flint knapping debris, pits, a possible post built structure, a gravel surface and a hearth, associated with Mildenhall type pottery. To the west the riverside site at Runnymede provides some of the best evidence for more permanent occupation, dated to about 4000-3500 BC and includes one or more rectangular stake built structures with midden deposits (Needham 1991). On the floodplain, some of the earliest evidence for Neolithic occupation, several centuries earlier than that at Woolwich

Manor Way and other sites, derives from the excavations at Yabsley Street, Blackwall, on the Isle of Dogs, a little to the west of the A13 route (Coles *et al.* 2008). Here a grave and other evidence of occupation was located on a sand and gravel bar beneath alluvium. The grave contained a crouched female inhumation, a fragment of Carinated Bowl pottery and worked flint, including a knife. An oak retaining plank within the grave was dated to 4220-3970 cal BC (KIA-20157: 5252 ± 28 BP) and the charred plant assemblage, similar to that recovered from Woolwich Manor Way, indicates that both cereal cultivation and collection of wild plant remains took place (see below).

Unfortunately apart from a couple of stray axe finds, little is known for the early Neolithic period from the block of higher terrace gravels between Plaistow and Barking which has largely been lost to modern development. Evidence from the wider area predominantly comprises dispersed pits and small artefact scatters often associated with tree throw holes. More substantial evidence derives from monument sites that may have served as communal meeting places for ceremonial, funerary and perhaps more 'domestic' activities. Approximately 10km downstream, at Rainham, these include the ring ditch at Great Arnold's field, a possible length of causewayed ditch at Southall Farm, and a ditched avenue that may represent a long mortuary enclosure at South Ockenden (Howell *et al.* 2011, 35). Similar clusters of monuments are known further east, including the causewayed enclosure at Orsett, Thurrock (Hedges and Buckley 1978; Brown 1996). Both sites at Great Arnold's Field and Orsett appear to have been in use from around the middle of the 4th millennium BC, contemporary with the activity recorded on the A13. On the western fringes of Greater London, a

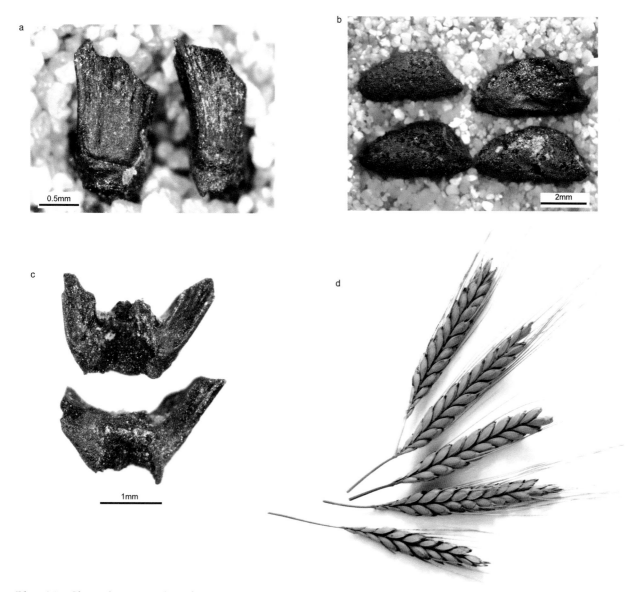

Plate 28   Charred emmer wheat from Trench 15, Woolwich Manor Way a - rachis-internode, b - grain, c - spiklet fork, d - modern ear of emmer (photo by Wendy Smith)

large cluster of monuments constructed on the higher ground overlooking the floodplains of the Thames and Colne points to this area as being a major ceremonial centre during this period. These monuments include the causewayed enclosure at Yeoveney Lodge, Staines (Robertson-Mackay 1987) and the segmented ring ditch at Staines Road Farm, Shepperton, along with the series of cursus and other monuments excavated around Heathrow Airport (Framework 2010).

Late Neolithic to early Bronze Age (3000-2000BC)

In general, evidence of later Neolithic and early Bronze Age activity is sparse in East London although struck flints and pottery have been identified on the floodplain at the Royal Docks Community School and elsewhere in the area (eg Coles *et al.* 2008; Bishop forthcoming; MoLA in prep). At Fort Street, Silvertown, a wooden trackway over marshy ground was dated to 3340-2910 cal BC (GU-4407: 4410+-60) (Crockett *et al.* 2002, Fig. 1.5, 2). More extensive activity dating to this period has, however, been recorded upstream in north Southwark (Ridgeway 1999; Proctor and Bishop 2002; Sidell *et al.* 2002). On the gravel terrace some activity continued at Great Arnold's Field, Rainham, with the deposition of Peterborough Ware in one of the fills of the ring ditch and later Beaker pottery in the central pit (Howell *et al.* 2011, 36). This reuse of earlier monuments is a pattern mirrored at

several other sites including Orsett (ibid). In west London activity is represented by pits, sited away from monuments, containing Peterborough and Grooved Ware pottery, transverse arrowheads and scapers and charred remains of wild plants such as hazelnuts, crab apples and sloes (Cotton 2000, 19).

In terms of artefactual material, activity during the 3rd millennium BC is attested along the A13 by the recovery of a transverse arrowhead and a barbed and tanged arrowhead from Movers Lane (Bishop in Appendix 2; Fig. A2.3, 15 and 16; Plate 29). A small scatter of knapping debris of possible early Bronze Age date was also identified at Movers Lane, along with a number of small and invasively retouched scrapers, suggesting some form of occupation, but there was little further evidence of intensive flint use during these periods at the other sites. Many of the scrapers from Movers Lane were broadly comparable to the 'thumbnail' types, typically of later Neolithic or early Bronze Age date and frequently associated with Beaker period settlements (Edmonds 1995, 140-141).

Late Neolithic to early Bronze Age worked flint (Plate 29)

a. **Semi-invasively retouched blade** from Movers Lane (MOE00), 121(Fig. A2.3, 14)
b. **Extensively reduced multiplatform core** from Movers Lane (RIR01, 3005)(Fig. A2.3, 17)
c. **Thumbnail scraper** from Movers Lane (RIR01, 3005) (Fig. A2.3, 19)

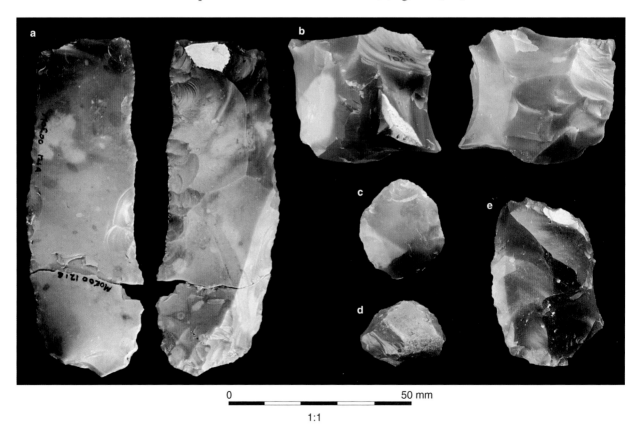

Plate 29   Late Neolithic-early Bronze Age worked flint from the A13 sites

d. **Thumbnail scraper** from Movers Lane (RIR01, 3005) (Fig. A2.3, 18)
e. **Edge trimmed flake** from Movers Lane (RIR01, 3005) (Fig. A2.3, 20)

The pottery assemblage included 17 sherds of Grooved Ware from Movers Lane, some of which closely resembled other Durrington Walls style pottery from the Middle and Upper Thames Valley (Barclay and Rayner in Appendix 2). Grooved Ware from southern England has a date range of 2900-2400/2200 cal BC (Garwood 1999). Fifteen Beaker sherds and one fragmentary vessel were also recovered from the excavations. The vessel, which probably represents a placed deposit, had been inverted in the peat alongside Trackway 29 at Woolwich Manor Way and belongs within Clarke's East Anglian group (1970) which is generally distributed around the Lower Thames and across the adjacent counties of Essex, Kent, Norfolk and Suffolk. As with Grooved Ware, Beaker pottery was, until recently, rare within the Greater London area (Clarke 1970, maps 1-10), however, it is now better represented especially in East London (J. Cotton pers. comm.). Small assemblages of Beaker pottery have been recorded at the Royal Docks Community School (Rayner 1997) and in the Rainham area, at Great Arnold's Field (Smith 1964; Howell *et al.* 2011, 36-7) and Rainham Football Ground (Costello 1997).

Bronze Age (2000-800BC)

A change in the abundance and nature of activity along the A13 route appears to occur towards the end of the early Bronze Age period, during the second quarter of the 2nd millennium BC, consistent with the regional evidence for a period of agricultural intensification (Yates 2007). This is particularly apparent on the West London gravels around Heathrow where parts of the landscape were divided into field systems with droveways and waterholes, forming 'identifiable' farmsteads (Framework 2010). In Southwark and Bermondsey dense patchworks of marks in the subsoil have been interpreted as ard marks (Sidell *et al.* 2002, 35-7). Few settlement sites have so far been located in east London, isolated pits and artefact assemblages have been found in the Lower Lea and Roding Valleys. At Rainham, a late Bronze Age ring work associated with buildings, field systems and cremation burials was excavated at Scott and Albyn's Farm, on the terrace overlooking the Ingrebourne River (Guttmann and Last 2000). Nearby, and on lower lying ground on the floodplain, evidence for animal husbandry was found in the form of a wattle enclosure fence (Meddens 1996). Further evidence of field systems has also been identified further up the Ingrebourne Valley at Hornchurch Aerodrome and Hacton Lane, Upminster (MoLAS 2000; Howell *et al.* 2011).

Three trackways and a platform structure, invariably occurring towards the top of the peat

sequences, were recorded at Woolwich Manor Way (Chapter 5, Figs 5.6 and 5.8) and two trackways were recorded at Movers Lane, along with a number of smaller stake built structures (Chapter 7, Figs. 7.9, 7.11 and 7.13). At Freemasons Road a double row of substantial oak piles may represent the remains of a wooden footbridge or jetty (Chapter 4, Figs 4.7 and 4.8 and Chapter 10, Fig. 10.5). The timber structures are discussed in more detail in Chapter 10; suffice to say the earliest was Trackway 50 at Woolwich Manor Way dated to the latter half of the 3rd millennium BC (Fig. 10.1). The 'bridge' structure at Freemasons Road, Trackway 29 at Woolwich Manor Way, and both trackways at Movers Lane date to the early to mid 2nd millennium BC. The overlap in the radiocarbon dating suggests that some of these structures may have been contemporary. Trackway 2/14 and platform structure 61 at Woolwich Manor Way are a little later dating to the latter part of the 2nd millennium BC. The trackways were fairly simple structures, invariably comprising concentrations of round-wood laid across the marshland surface. They were probably quite short-lived and, given the light construction, were probably only used for human foot traffic. However, some variation did occur; one of the trackways at Movers Lane incorporated wattle hurdles and at Woolwich Manor Way a trackway was constructed of a heterogeneous mix of wood suggesting a number of repairs, and included a possible fragment of a log boat or perhaps a large trough. A number of similar trackway structures have been recorded in the immediate vicinity, most notably those from the Beckton 3D, Beckton Nursery and Golf Driving Range sites adjacent to Woolwich Manor Way (Fig. 1.5; 4, 5 and 6; Fig 5.5, Fig. 10.3, BEC). The sediment and environmental evidence indicate that the structures found along the A13 were constructed during a period of increased wetness. This was a prelude to a major period of marine incursion and is consistent with the evidence from the other sites in the area (see Chapter 8). The broadly north-south orientation, at right angles to the gravel terrace, would suggest the structures may have been built to maintain access to the floodplain which during this period could have included drier floodplain islands as well as saltmarsh areas that may have been present towards the main Thames channel (Chapter 8, Fig. 8.6, CLM Stage 4). This may have been to exploit a range of natural resources; plant collection, hunting, fishing and waterfowling and/or the herding of animals to seasonal pasture (Plate 30 and see Chapter 10 for more detailed discussion).

The timber piled structure at Freemasons Road, located at the confluence of the Thames and Lea (Fig. 10.3), is amongst the most substantial known in the region. In comparative terms the piles are very similar to those from the late Bronze Age palisade alignments found on the Runnymede Bridge site bordering the Middle Thames, west of London (Needham 1991; 1992), although the Free-

Plate 30   Cattle grazing modern saltmarsh (photo by Jim Champion)

masons Road piles are generally a little larger in diameter. It is only at the Vauxhall Thames foreshore site that larger dated Bronze Age piles have been found in the region (Haughey 1999; Sidell *et al.* 2002, 29-30; Webber 1999), although a structure of similar arrangement has been excavated in the Ebbsfleet Valley further downstream (Wenban-Smith *et al.* in prep; Figs 10.2 and 10.6.). It is perhaps noteworthy that, in contrast to the trackways structures excavated at the other sites; the 'bridge' structure at Freemasons Road is orientated on an east-west alignment. Recent topographic modelling work in the Lea Valley suggests that during the early Bronze Age a large floodplain island may have existed immediately to the east of Freemasons Road and it is possible the structure linked the drier ground of the terrace to this island (Fig. 4.8b; Corcoran *et al.* 2011, 56 and fig. 108).

Based on radiocarbon dating, the piled structure at Freemasons Road may have been associated with a series of features located on a slight rise in the marsh surface immediately to the north. The features, comprising a series of gullies and postholes, may represent some form of enclosure perhaps associated with the corralling of animals (Chapter 4, Fig. 4.7, EMBA). However, apart from the enclosure at Freemasons Road, none of the timber structures can be directly related to features

recorded on the higher drier ground. At Movers Lane a 'burnt mound' deposit and associated pits located on the edge of the western palaeochannel appear to post-date trackway construction dating to the latter half of the 2nd millennium BC (Chapter 7, Figs. 7.14 and 7.15), as does the cremation deposit and series of linear features that may define a boundary or form part of a drainage or field system (Chapter 7, Fig 4.7, MLBA). A later phase of activity is also evident at Freemasons Road where a dense series of stakeholes were located (Chapter 4, Fig. 4.12). The pattern of stakes is difficult to interpret, probably as a result of repairs or modifications, but could represent the remains of animal pens or drying racks (see Chapter 10). Linear features recorded on the higher terrace at Prince Regent Lane may represent the remains of a field system (Chapter 4, Fig. 4.5).

In terms of the pottery assemblage only a single sherd from Movers Lane could be assigned an early or middle Bronze Age date (Barclay and Rayner in Appendix 2). A total of 333 sherds, however, were assigned a middle to late Bronze Age date (1500-900 cal BC). Both Deverel-Rimbury (1500-1150 cal BC) and post-Deverel-Rimbury (PDR) plain ware (1150-900 cal BC) forms were present. The Deverel-Rimbury pottery is mostly represented by relatively thick-walled sherds that are typical of Bucket Urn forms and, more rarely, by thinner walled sherds more characteristic of Globular Urns. Several vessels are thought to belong to the later 2nd millennium BC and may be considered as either transitional between the Deverel-Rimbury and post-Deverel-Rimbury (PDR) traditions (1200-1100 cal BC) and/or belong to the initial PDR 'plain ware' phase (1150-950 cal BC) (Barclay 2001, 138-9; Barclay 2008, 96; Needham 1996, 2007). These assemblages tend to be characterised by simple straight, slightly splayed or ovoid-sided jars with simple flattened or rounded rims. Well-developed shouldered forms such as cups, bowls and jars (see Barrett 1980, fig 5:1-5, 12 and 14) are generally absent at this stage, being introduced and becoming more common from the late 11th and early 10th centuries BC onwards. Comparable assemblages include material recovered from Stanwell (O'Connell 1990, fig 28 and 53) to the west of the City, from Gravesend, Kent (Barclay 1994) and further afield at Weston Wood, Surrey (Russell 1989 fig 11, 25), Pingewood Berks (Bradley 1983-5) and Eynsham, Oxon (Barclay 2001).

The quantities of struck flint, largely recovered from Prince Regent Lane and Movers Lane, demonstrates that flintworking continued to play an important role in activities during the Bronze Age, complementing the use of metal tools (Plate 31; Bishop in Appendix 2; Fig.A2.3). The material was present in quantity in the fills of palaeochannels and alluvial deposits where it may have been eroded in or dumped as refuse from adjacent drier areas. Flintworking was associated with the burnt mound feature at Movers Lane and other accumulations of struck flint may suggest that a degree of middening was occurring. The range of activities to which the struck flints were put is not easily discerned, but comparable assemblages were recovered during the excavations at the Royal Docks Community School (MoLA in prep.). There, a similar range of implements is present and micro-wear analysis suggests that these were predominantly used to scrape, cut and pierce hides. Features interpreted as hide drying racks were also recorded and it was suggested that the site might represent a specialist hide-processing location, taking advantage of the abundance of water and possibly the peat, which can act as a tanning agent. Features that contained significant quantities of burnt flint were interpreted as cooking pits, and it may be that these too were associated with hide preparation. Much of the burnt flint found during the A13 excavations was widely dispersed, probably reflecting background waste from hearths. However, substantial quantities were recovered from the burnt mound feature at Movers Lane and significant concentrations were also present within peat deposits at all of the A13 sites,

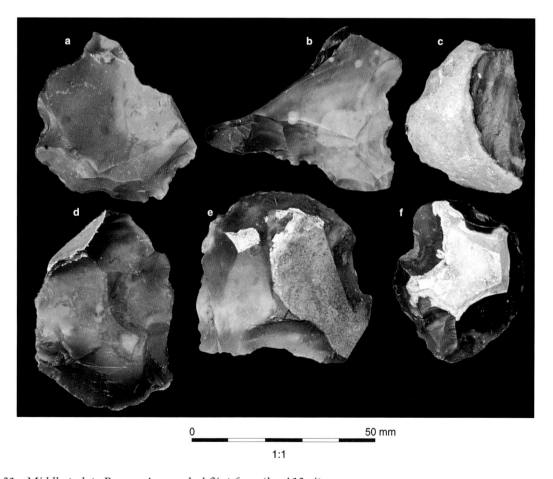

0   50 mm

1:1

Plate 31　Middle to late Bronze Age worked flint from the A13 sites

suggesting that activities resulting in the systematic burning of flint were more widespread (see below and Bishop in Appendix 2).

Middle to late Bronze Age worked flint (Plate 31)

a. **Late Bronze Age core tool (piercer?)** from Freemasons Road (FRU01, 32) (Fig. A2.3, 23)
b. **Late Bronze Age denticulated flake** from Movers Lane (RIR01, 5083) (Fig. A2.3, 26)
c. **Late Bronze Age edge trimmed flake** from Movers Lane (RIR01, 5189) (not drawn)
d. **Late Bronze Age retouched wedge-shaped flake (chopping tool?)** from Movers Lane (MOE00, 516) (not drawn)
e. **Scraper** from Freemasons Road (FRU01, 102) (not drawn)
f. **Scraper** made on a bulbar end from Movers Lane (RIR01, 5189) (not drawn)

Later periods

Evidence of occupation along the A13 from the beginning of the first millennium BC onwards was relatively sparse and overall suggests low-level activity perhaps occurring on a seasonal basis. At Freemasons Road a small assemblage of burnt flint and animal bone was found associated with the upper alluvial sequence, in addition to a possible area of burning and a small pit containing late Bronze Age to early Iron Age pottery. These remains were sealed by a further layer of alluvium, the surface of which displayed evidence of possible poaching by cattle hooves (Chapter 4, Fig. 4.15). A series of linear features may represent drainage ditches or modification of a series of natural channels. This scarcity of evidence is probably a reflection of the increasingly tidal nature of the floodplain (see Chapter 8, Fig. 8.6, CLM Stage 5), which is also evident in quantity of late Bronze Age and Iron Age metalwork deposited in riverine contexts, possibly as votive offerings (see below). Evidence from sites in the vicinity, however, suggests the drier ground of the terraces were heavily utilised (J. Cotton pers. comm.). Late Bronze Age to early Iron Age ring works are known at Leyton and South Hornchurch, with another large sub-rectangular enclosure at Heathway, Dagenham. Aggregated Iron Age settlements have been located in some numbers east, west and south of the city (see Framework 2010; Howell 2005; Howell *et al.* 2011), culminating in the construction of major enclosures at Uphall Camp on the River Roding (Greenwood 2001) and the possible oppidum at Woolwich Arsenal across the Thames to the south.

Evidence of Roman activity was largely restricted to the Woolwich Manor Way site. Here, a relatively large assemblage of late Roman pottery was recovered from the upper alluvial sequence. The assemblage was associated with a series of disturbed alluvial layers and gravelly deposits that may represent an attempt to consolidate the wet marsh surface (Chapter 5, Fig. 5.11) in close proximity to a putative Roman Road. A series of linear features of probable Roman date, perhaps the remnants of a field system or boundary marker, were also recorded on the higher terrace at Prince Regent Lane (Chapter 4, Fig. 4.5). It is possible this may reflect the expansion of field systems off the terrace immediately to the north, which may in turn reflect a wider series of re-alignments and expansions of field systems in the region, visible at places like Heathrow and elsewhere (J. Cotton pers. comm.).

Subsistence and economy

Cereal cultivation

With one notable exception there was very little direct evidence for cereal cultivation from the sites along the A13 during the prehistoric period. There was some evidence in the pollen record of cereal from the early Neolithic onwards (see Chapter 8 and Druce, Haggart, Peglar in Appendix 3). However, as stated previously, the similarity of cereal pollen with some wild grasses, particularly barley-type, means that the evidence remains equivocal. At Woolwich Manor Way an important assemblage of charred emmer wheat grains and chaff dated to the early Neolithic period was recovered from T15 (Plate 28; Pelling in Appendix 3). Micromorphological analysis also indicated that the buried soil which was associated with the assemblage had been subject to disturbance that may be attributed to either trampling and/or ploughing/cultivation (Macphail in Appendix 3). The retouched implements in the early Neolithic flint assemblages also suggest an emphasis on cutting tasks that probably included the processing of silica-rich plant materials such as cereals (Bishop in Appendix 2).

Apart from the assemblage recovered from Woolwich Manor Way, the scarcity of evidence of Neolithic cultivation is not unusual for the Thames Valley, even at sites like Runnymede where there is abundant evidence for more permanent settlement. Although ard marks have been recorded in the soils beneath Neolithic monuments further afield (Morigi 2011), the examples recorded on the south bank of the Thames in Southwark tend to be later in date (see below). With reference to charred assemblages, the earliest remains in the vicinity of the A13 sites are an indeterminate cereal grain and a glume of emmer wheat (*Triticum dicoccum*) from the Yabsley Street grave (Robinson in Coles *et al.* 2008). A possible sherd of Carinated Bowl from the MI6 site near Vauxhall also bears an indeterminate cereal impression (Milne *et al.* 2011, 288), as does an impression on a sherd of Mildenhall pottery (possibly of 'naked barley') from the midden deposit at Great Arnold's Field (Howell *et al.* 2011, 34). Some carbonised cereals were recovered from the Runnymede site and single grains have been recovered from Neolithic pits on the West London gravel terraces and further upstream (MoLAS 2000).

0   10 mm

5:1

Plate 32   Early Neolithic charred bread, made from barley, from Yarnton, Oxfordshire

Assemblages include hulled barley (*Hordeum* sp.), emmer wheat and free-threshing wheat, the latter probably a bread wheat (*Triticum aestivum*). At Eton, however, in the Middle Thames, a notably rich assemblage of early Neolithic grain was recovered from midden material (Allen *et al.* 2004, 91 and forthcoming). We may assume that the cereal was used for a number of foodstuffs, such as bread, porridge and perhaps beer. Of note are the charred remains of barley bread recovered from a pit at Yarnton in the Upper Thames Valley (Plate 32; Morigi 2011, 247).

The significance of cereals in the diet of Neolithic people, particularly in relation to the importance of collected woodland resources, is still a topic of debate (see Moffett *et al.* 1989; Robinson 2000; Jones 2000; Jones and Rowley-Conwy 2007). It is notable that the charred plant remains from the Yabsley Street grave also included seeds of hawthorn, mallow and fragments of hazelnut shell (Robinson in Coles *et al.* 2008) and charred hazelnut shell was also recovered from the assemblage in T15 at Woolwich Manor Way (see discussion below). Rich deposits of cereal grain, while rare, do demonstrate that cereals were probably more widespread than the archaeology tends to suggest, but that for some reason they survive in good numbers only occasionally. This might include the scale of agricultural production, processing methods and erosion of archaeological features (Pelling in Appendix 3).

Although there is good evidence for increasing agricultural intensification from the middle Bronze Age period in the Thames Valley (Lambrick 2009; MoLAS 2000, Yates 2007), direct evidence specifically of cereal cultivation from the A13 sites was again sparse and restricted to occasional indeterminate fragments of charred grain. A small charred assemblage from the middle to late Bronze Age peat at Prince Regent Lane (layer 43, T23) included grains of wheat (*Triticum* sp) and a spikelet fork of spelt wheat (*T. spelta*). Cereal-type pollen, wheat and possibly barley, however, were recorded with increased frequency in middle to late Bronze Age deposits at several sites. This included the main period of peat formation at Freemasons Road, as well as the peat associated with the trackways in Area 2 at Woolwich Manor Way and Area 3 at Movers Lane. Only a small portion of the linear features was exposed on the higher ground at Prince Regent Lane and Movers Lane. These could represent field boundaries, though they could equally have been used for stock control as for cultivation. The absence of evidence for cultivation may be partly related to the position of the A13 sites immediately adjacent to the floodplain where activities are likely to have been seasonal or at least semi-permanent and focused on the exploitation of natural resources provided by the wetland zone, with the marshland edge probably used for grazing of livestock. Increasingly wet conditions during this period means it would have been highly likely any crop cultivation and processing would have taken place on the higher, drier, ground.

In the wider region, cultivation of cereals is evident in the pollen spectra at a number of sites dated to this period along with remains of co-axial or 'Celtic' field systems identified through excavation and aerial photography. There is now good evidence that the higher islands within the floodplain in Southwark and Bermondsey were cultivated in the mid second millennium, with possible ard marks recorded at sites such as Phoenix Wharf, Lafone Street and Wolsey Street (Sidell *et al.* 2002, 35-7). However, the usually crisp definition of these marks suggests that the episodes of cultivation were likely to have been short-lived.

Animal husbandry

Unfortunately the faunal assemblages recovered from the A13 sites were comparatively small (Strid and Nicholson in Appendix 3). Furthermore, since much of the diagnostic artefactual material from the earlier periods was found within later contexts it is difficult to ascertain the importance of the accompanying fauna. More can be said of the animal remains recovered from more securely dated Bronze Age contexts. The assemblage of domesticated species recovered from Freemasons Road, for example, included cattle, sheep and/or goat and pig (Fig 9.3).

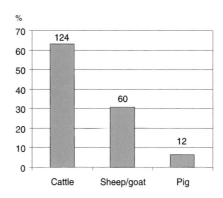

Fig. 9.3   Quantification of bones of cattle, sheep and pig from Bronze Age contexts at Freemasons Road, by number of identified fragments

Cattle were the most numerous taxa and certainly wetland pastures suit cattle far better than sheep. Most of animals appear to have been sub-adult or adult at the time of death. While not all skeletal elements were represented, bones from meat-rich body parts as well as meat-poor body parts were present which may suggest that domesticates were butchered on or close to the site. Butchery marks were recorded on a number of bones from all of the domesticates present in the assemblage. Most of these were cut marks deriving from disarticulation and marrow extraction, but chop marks on the basal part of one cattle and one goat horn core suggest utilisation of horn for horn-working. As stated above, the Bronze Age flintwork from the A13 sites is very comparable to that recorded at the Royal Docks Community School where activities involving specialised hide processing were indicated. This could point to a thriving hide working industry located along the edges of the marshes, possibly associated with the widespread agricultural re-organisation in the region during this period, much of it appearing to focus on animal husbandry (see discussion in Bishop, Appendix 2).

Exploitation of natural resources

The only real direct evidence for the collection of wild foodstuffs on the A13 during the Neolithic derives from the occupation horizon at Woolwich Manor Way where a number of charred hazel nut shells were found in association with the cereal grain. As previously stated, the route-wide flint assemblages included high proportions of retouched implements that included many simple edge-trimmed flakes and serrated pieces, some exhibiting polish, suggesting an emphasis on cutting tasks that probably included the processing of silica-rich plant materials (Avery 1982, 38; Grace 1992; Bradley 1993; Donahue 2002). As well as cereals these may have included rushes that would no doubt have been abundant in this riverine area. Hunting maintenance activities are indicated by an almost finished arrow-head from Woolwich Manor Way, whilst other possible arrowhead blanks are present at Prince Regent Lane (Figs. A2.3.5 and A2.3.1) indicating their manufacture and recalling similar activities recorded at Tank Hill Road and further upstream of the Thames at Dorney (Lamdin-Whymark 2001; Leivers *et al.*. 2007, 26 and fig 20). With reference to exploitation of the local woodlands, the small charcoal assemblage from the early Neolithic occupation surface at Woolwich Manor Way attests to the collection of a range of local woody material probably for domestic hearth fuel (Barnett in Appendix 3). Identified taxa included hazel, pomaceous fruit wood (Pomoideae), cherry-type (*Prunus* sp., a group including wild cherry and blackthorn) and also the only charred representation of elm.

Evidence for the collection of wild plants or indeed the exploitation of fish, game or wildfowl in the Bronze Age faunal assemblages is notably absent. The only wild fauna tended to be rodents and amphibians. Whether this is a true absence or a reflection of the small size of the assemblages or, in the case of fish remains, issues of preservation, recovery and even taboo/cultural choice, is unclear. It seems unlikely that local communities would not have taken some advantage of the range of plants and animals that are likely to have been present in the wetlands. However, the evidence suggests that activities such as the hunting of game and fishing had become rare within the Thames Valley during the later prehistoric period: very few faunal assemblages include wild species. Flint arrowheads do not appear to have been produced into the middle Bronze Age and metal spears appear to have functioned either as status symbols or as weaponry (Lambrick 2009, 155). Collection of wild plant foods does not appear to have contributed significantly to the diet, with the evidence restricted to occasional charred hazelnut shells and edible tubers (ibid).

For the later periods there is substantial evidence from both the waterlogged wood and the charcoal assemblages to indicate that a moderate range of woody types were selected and used on the A13 sites (Barnett in Appendix 3). The concentrations of alder and hazel are likely to reflect both their local availability and their increased productivity due to coppicing. These species indicate the use and management of both the wetland alder carr in the immediate area and of the slightly drier mixed open woodland beyond the floodplain edges. At Movers Lane the charcoal assemblages indicate that both alder and hazel were important, the latter accounting for around 80-95% of the pieces recovered from the burnt mound and associated pit. Fragments of pomaceous fruit wood, oak, willow/poplar, elder, cherry-type and alder were also found in these contexts. This mix of wood types is likely to reflect local gathering of fuel wood but with stands of (potentially managed) hazel particularly targeted. The importance of hazel in the wood charcoal is not reflected in the waterlogged wood assemblages from contemporary contexts, suggesting there was deliberate selection of hazel for fuel and a preference for alder to use in structures likely to be periodically submerged. Alder wood is indeed known for its durability under water (Edlin 1949, 23; Gale and Cutler 2000, 34). At Freemasons Road layer 49, an organic deposit that accumulated around the base of the early to middle Bronze Age piled structure, produced a charcoal assemblage dominated by alder but also oak, with smaller quantities of hazel. Ash, pomaceous fruit wood and six pieces of lime/linden (*Tilia* sp.) were also recovered, the latter the only representation of the taxon in this analysis.

Species identification of the waterlogged wood from the timber structures demonstrated primarily the use of alder but also a range of other tree and shrub types. The dominance of alder and importance of willow/poplar points to use and management of wetland alder carr and the use of slightly drier marginal mixed open woodland is indicated by the presence of oak, hazel, holly, elm and ash. While management of stands is clearly shown by the presence of coppiced pieces (see Chapter 10) the range of taxa utilised may also suggest some casual opportunistic exploitation. The use of alder, hazel and willow for structural components of Neolithic and Bronze Age wetland trackways is commonly reported in the UK, in the Somerset Levels for example, with the use of larger tree types such as ash and oak for planks and large stakes (see discussion in Barnett, Appendix 3). More unusual is the use of yew and holly in the trackways at Woolwich Manor Way, the former also found within worked wood spreads at Freemasons Road. As previously stated (Chapter 8) yew appears to have been an important component of the Bronze Age wetland margins in the region, while the Bronze Age flora at West Heath showed an increase in holly within the existing mix of oak, lime and hazel.

Waterways as routeways and boundaries

During the prehistoric period the waterways would have existed as corridors through areas of dense woodland and inhospitable territory, providing access both to inland areas of southern England, as well as the North Sea. Major north-south tributary valleys, such as the Lea, may have also acted as corridors linking the Thames with the East Anglian zone (Needham and Burgess 1980, 453). Excluding the River Medway, the River Thames and its tributaries drain a catchment area of approximately 4,995 square miles (12935.77 km²). The Thames rises in the Cotswolds and flows within a broad valley for about 338km (210 miles) across Gloucestershire, Oxfordshire and Berkshire, before entering Greater London. Currently the lowest 105km (65 miles) from Teddington Lock in West London are tidal, although during the Bronze Age the tidal head was located further downstream in the vicinity of Westminster (Sidell *et al.* 2000; 2004). It is clear the River Thames played a central role in the lives of past local communities, as it does today. As well as providing a diverse range of natural resources, the river would have also facilitated movement through the landscape, communication between different groups, the opportunity for trade and exchange and a conduit for the spread of ideas, technology and innovations.

Evidence of exchange networks during the Neolithic and Bronze Age in Britain, particularly of exotic items, is well attested; large numbers of stone axes recovered from the Thames originate from Cornwall, Westmorland, Wales, Ireland and Europe. The fragmentary Neolithic belt slider recovered from the A13 investigations at Movers Lane represents a prestigious item made from jet that probably originated from Whitby on the north-east coast (Sheridan in Appendix 2). By the middle Bronze Age the Lower Thames appears to have developed

as a centre for bronze production and consumption. Items recovered from the region commonly include weaponry: narrow blade rapiers, spearheads and shields. The metalwork demonstrates a marked European influence and some items may have been directly imported from the continent. This includes broad-bladed swords of Rosnöen type and leaf shaped flange-hilted swords of Hermigkofen and Erbenheim types (MoLAS 2000, 87).

Inland waters were probably navigated using hide covered coracles and canoes as well as dugout logboats. An example of a logboat, discovered in the 19th century in peat deposits on the Erith marshes, also contained a Neolithic polished flint axe (MoLAS 2000). On the A13 at Woolwich Manor Way it has been suggested a fragment of worked wood incorporated into the structure of 'platform' 61, dated to the middle to late Bronze Age at 1270-1040 cal BC (SUERC-24504: 2945±30 BP), may derive from a dugout logboat (Chapter 5, Fig 5.10c). Wooden paddles have also been recovered, including the late Bronze Age example from Canewdon in the Crouch estuary, Essex dated to 1225-998 cal BC (Wilkinson and Murphy 1986; 1995, 152-7). The basic logboat would probably have required modification for sea travel, such as the fitting of outriggers or the pairing of two boats, to give them the extra transverse stability and freeboard, although no evidence of this has ever been recovered on British sites (McGrail 1990, 32). However, evidence for an advance in the technology of water transport, unique to Britain, is exemplified by Bronze Age sewn plank boats such as those found at Dover, Kent (Clarke 2004) and in the Humber estuary (Wright and Wright 1939; Wright 1990; Wright *et al.* 2001; Van de Noort *et al.* 1999). It is widely accepted that this type of craft was probably used for seafaring (Clark 2004 in van de Noort 2006; McGrail 2001; van de Noort *et al.* 1999). Experimental studies have shown that these craft would have the potential to cross the North Sea and could possibly have been propelled by sail as well as by paddling (Crumlin Pedersen and Trakadas 2003; Gifford and Gifford 2004; Kaul 2004). As well as a routeway, the River Thames is likely to have represented a formidable natural east-west barrier, particularly in its lower reaches and estuary where it was not easy to bridge or ford. The Bronze Age piled bridge structure recorded at Nine Elms, Vauxhall is situated at the point at which the river first becomes fordable, as well as being close to the furthest point upstream at which the river was tidal (Haughey 1999; Sidell *et al.* 2002, 29).

With the growth of the port at *Londinium* the River Thames, and indeed the River Lea, remained important trade and communication routes, alongside the developing network of roads that included the main routes to Lincoln (Ermine Street) and Colchester. The Roman crossing point, which was essential for both commercial and military reasons, was situated in the vicinity of the modern London Bridge. Crossing points also existed where the

Colchester Road crossed the River Lea at Old Ford and Stratford (Corcoran *et al.* 2011, 184). Where it was not easy to bridge or ford the Thames, it is possible a number of ferry points were in use during this period (Fig. 9.4). The alignment of East Ham High Street and Woolwich Manor Way reputedly marks the line of a Roman road leading from the higher ground to the north, perhaps to a ferry crossing at North Woolwich, which is of at least medieval origin. The alignment of Green Street, Boundary Road and Stansfeld Road, slightly to the west may indicate the position of another routeway towards Ham Creek (the Blackwall Basin), a natural harbour which silted up during the 19th century. Finds of black samian ware pottery, roof tile of 3rd century date and a dugout canoe, recorded by Whitaker and Spurrell in 1890 during construction of the Royal Albert Dock, may indicate the presence of a Roman harbour here (Arch. Journal, vol. xlvii p.170 cited in Hanson 1996). Further downstream, at Higham, Kent, a Roman causeway running north to the Thames, opposite East Tilbury, also suggests a ferry point, and further out into the estuary a ferry crossing may have existed between the Kentish flats at Whitstable and the Maplin Sands to the north (Cracknell 2005, fig. 62). That the river served as a political and defensive boundary between different tribal groups is very evident during the later periods through the distribution of late Iron Age coinage and accounts of the Roman campaigns of

the late 2nd century BC. Major tributaries would also have been significant landscape features dissecting territories north-south. The course of the River Lea marks the historical boundary of the counties of Middlesex and Essex, but as early as the 9th century AD a treaty between King Alfred of Wessex and the Dane, Guthrum, established it as the boundary between the kingdom of Mercia and the Danish territories to the east (Corcoran *et al.* 2011, 10).

Burial and ritual activities

There was relatively little evidence for funerary activities on the A13 sites. A late Neolithic to early Bronze Age barbed and tanged arrowhead and the semi-invasively flaked knife, both from Movers Lane, are finely made and this may hint at their use as prestigious implements, these types sometimes being associated with funerary practices (Bishop in Appendix 2; Plate 25, e; Plate 29, a; Fig. A.2.3, 14 and 16). The recovery of two Beaker sherds (Plate 26) and the jet belt slider at this site, although not associated, may conceivably have originated from disturbed burials in the vicinity, for which there is slight evidence in the form of scraps of human bone. The human remains recovered from the A13 sites were restricted to Movers Lane. They included five tiny fragments of redeposited disarticulated human bone; all comprised fragments of long bone shafts

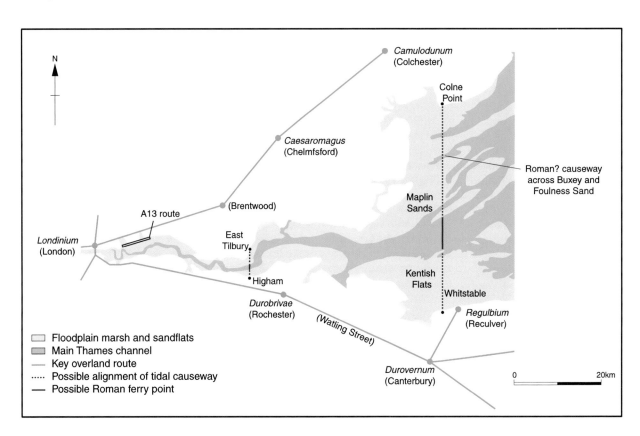

Fig. 9.4 Key routeways along the Thames estuary during the Roman period and postulated crossing points (after Cracknell 2005).

recovered from Bronze Age layers, together with a Bronze Age cremation (1207) of an adult, probably male (McKinley in Appendix 3; Fig. 7.8 Area 2). Since the cremation comprised only around 33% of what would be expected if all the remains were present, and charcoal was absent from the deposit, it is likely that the cremation comprised redeposited pyre debris rather than a complete cremation burial. The cremated bone has been dated to 1260-1010 cal BC (SUERC-24290: 2920±30 BP). Little further can be said of these remains other than the cremation clearly demonstrates that burial was taking place at the site during the late Bronze Age.

The jet belt slider recovered from Bronze Age alluvial deposits at Movers Lane (Sheridan in Appendix 2, Fig. A2.4) constitutes an exotic artefact that formed part of a set of prestige objects during the second half of the fourth millennium BC, although it is also possible it was a curated/'heirloom' object and its electrostatic properties may have afforded it special significance (J. Cotton pers comm). Its watery association is clear, but whether it represents a votive deposit, originally placed in or beside the river, or else the last traces of an eroded funerary deposit is uncertain. Votive deposition would accord with the practice attested further upriver at Basildon (Fig. A2.5 no. 24, Table A2.19).

The Thames is well-known for the large number of later prehistoric votive river finds, particularly metalwork. Of note are the two side-looped copper alloy spearheads associated with the piles of the 'bridge' structure on the foreshore at Vauxhall (Cotton and Wood 1996, 14-16 and fig. 7, nos. 22a and b; Haughey 1999; Sidell *et al.* 2002). Ritual deposition is known from alongside other prehistoric causeways and trackways across wetlands, but more frequently later in the Bronze Age, such as at Flag Fen (Pryor 1991). The inverted Beaker found within the peat deposits alongside trackway 2/14 at Woolwich Manor Way probably represents a 'placed' deposit (Chapter 5, Fig 5.8; Barclay and Rayner Appendix 2, Fig. A2.1, 17). As previously stated the vessel belongs within Clarke's East Anglian group (1970) and is unlikely to be early within the sequence of Beaker pottery (2450-1700 cal BC), although it could belong to the final centuries of the third millennium BC (after 2250 BC; see Needham 2005, fig 13). Two radiocarbon dates were obtained from trackway 2/14; the first from evaluation TP9 at 1880-1520 cal BC (Beta-153984: 3390±60 BP) and the second from the Area 2 excavation at 1610-1430 cal BC (SUERC-24292: 3230±30 BP). These dates suggest the pottery could be contemporary with the trackway. The second date range is perhaps a little late in the Beaker sequence although it is possible the vessel could represent a curated item.

With reference to the piled structure at Freemasons Road, the artefact scatters from organic layer 49 that accumulated around the piles during the construction and use of the structure (Chapter 4, Fig 4.8) appeared, on initial examination, to be of a wholly domestic character: wood working debris,

pottery and animal bones. The animal bones included cattle, sheep and/or goat, pig and dog and, with the exception of two dog mandibles and probably a skull and atlas vertebra, no bones were articulated. The bones were relatively few in number and no specific body parts were over-represented. Butchery marks on cattle and sheep/goat bones indicate food waste, although it is difficult to tell whether this would be from ordinary meals or from feasting (Strid and Nicholson inAppendix 2). The presence of a dog atlas, skull and two articulating mandible halves suggests that these may have been part of a single dog's head, the bones becoming disarticulated by water movements. It is conceivable that the head had ritual connotations: at Flag Fen, articulated and semi-articulated skeletons of dogs and disarticulated human remains suggest ritual depositions, possibly related to funerary rites (Halstead *et al.* 2001, 348-350). However, dog bones with butchery marks have been found on some Iron Age sites, suggesting that in this later period dogs were occasionally exploited for their meat (Maltby 1996, 23-24) and eating of dogs may have been practiced in the Bronze Age as well, for dietary, ritual or medicinal purposes (*cf.* Pasda 2004, 44-45). Dog remains in later Bronze Age flood deposits at Freemasons Road included a single, disarticulated atlas with transverse chop marks on the ventral side of the neural arch, indicating an attempt at decapitation, although for what purpose is unclear.

The occurrence of yew (*Taxus baccata*) in the pollen, plant and waterlogged wood assemblages has been discussed in Chapter 8. Yew was utilised in some of the Bronze Age timber trackways at Woolwich Manor Way as well as the platform structure at the adjacent Golf Driving Range site (Carew *et al.* 2010; Goodburn 2003b). A small scatter of yew wood chips was recovered from Bronze Age deposits at Movers Lane and an axe trimmed section of yew at Freemasons Road (see Chapter 10). Yew is an evergreen wood and it is possible it may have had special, perhaps spiritual, significance for local communities (see Coles 1998). An example of the use of evergreen wood in a non-utilitarian context is the case of the Dagenham idol, found in floodplain deposits during the construction of the Ford Motor Works in 1922. Originally identified as Scots Pine (*Pinus sylvestris*) radiocarbon dating places it in the late Neolithic to early Bronze Age period at 2351-2139 cal BC (Coles 1990) which is broadly contemporary with Trackway 50 at Woolwich Manor Way.

With reference to the Bronze Age timber structures generally, one feature that has been observed, from around 1500 BC, is the apparent reuse of sewn-plank boat fragments in trackway and bridge structures associated with votive deposits. These offerings include a rapier at Testwood Lakes near the Solent (Fitzpatrick *et al.* 1996), an amber bead at Caldicot and human skulls at Goldcliff, in the Welsh Severn estuary (Nayling and Caseldine 1997) and bronzes at Brigg (McGrail 1981; 1997; 2000). Van de

Noort (2006) discusses the evidence in terms of 'rituals of travel', suggesting that from the middle Bronze Age reuse of boat fragments in structured deposits, within or near river crossings, reflects the idioms of transformation and regeneration which are well established for this period (see Brück 2001). No deposits indicative of ritual activity were recovered in direct association with the possible logboat or trough fragment incorporated into Platform 61 at Woolwich Manor Way (Fig 5.10c), although the structure was only partially excavated as it extended beyond the limit of construction impact.

Concentrations of burnt flint are a feature of prehistoric settlement sites and provide evidence for the use of heated stones for various activities such as cooking (Lambrick 2009, 179-180). However, some sites produce much larger quantities of burnt flint and include the much debated and enigmatic class of monuments commonly referred to as burnt mounds. Burnt mounds are more generally dated to the middle and later Bronze Age and they are often found adjacent to water courses. In the classic form they appear as a crescent-like or circular mound of burnt stone often associated with a central trough, probably used to boil water with heated stones (Raymond 1987). The variety of activities that have been suggested for these features include cooking, possibly for communal feasting (O'Kelly 1954; Barber 1990), the processing of fleeces (Jeffery 1991), salt production (Barfield 1991), brewing (Wilkins 2011, 29-30) or the generation of steam for sweat lodges and purification rituals (Barfield and Hodder 1987). A few examples have been found in the Greater London area. The example from Phoenix Wharf, Bermondsey also included a 'boiling pit' and a series of stakeholes, possibly representing a revetment or windbreak, and was interpreted as a possible cooking site (Bowsher 1991; Sidell *et al.* 2002). In common with many other sites, the feature identified at Movers Lane did not really produce the quantity of faunal remains one would perhaps expect of 'domestic' settlement activity. It was, however, associated with a number of pits also filled with burnt flint and the close proximity of the western palaeochannel at Movers Lane clearly provided a ready source of water. The micromorphological analysis detected remnants of burnt bone that could indicate activities associated with food preparation, however there was also evidence for mixing by trampling of an often muddy substrate and evidence for alluvial inwash. This could suggest the material was simply deposited at this location in an effort to stabilize the river bank.

Chapter 10: Aspects of the
Bronze Age Timber Structures

Chronology and function (Figs 10.1-10.4)

The evidence retrieved from the A13 fits within the general regional pattern of an increase in the construction of timber structures along the floodplain wetland margins during the 2nd millennium BC. Aside from the 'bridge' structure at Freemasons Road, three trackways and a possible platform were recorded at Woolwich Manor Way, and a further two trackways at Movers Lane. In addition a number of smaller stake built structures were recorded at all three sites. The dating of the A13 structures is largely based on radiocarbon dating of the worked wood, supported by the analysis of woodworking technology. Unfortunately all attempts to date larger oak wood samples (both natural and humanly worked) by dendrochronology failed. In the case of the 'bridge' structure this was due to the fact that the timbers used for the piles were from rather fast grown oaks with too few annual rings. The earliest structure appears to have been built at Woolwich Manor Way where radiocarbon dates on roundwood from Trackway 50 date construction to the second half of the 3rd / earlier part of the 2nd millennium BC (see Fig. 10.1 and Appendix 1.2), the bridge structure at Freemasons Road, Trackway 29 at Woolwich Manor Way, and both trackways at Movers Lane date to the early to mid 2nd millennium BC. The overlap in the radiocarbon dating suggests some of these structures may have been contemporary, although when all the dates are combined together they are not statistically consistent. Trackway 29 and platform structure 61 at Woolwich Manor Way are a little later, dating to the latter part of the 2nd millennium BC.

The pile alignment at Freemasons Road can be compared with a number of other similar structures excavated in the Thames Valley. The closest parallel based on form is the middle Bronze Age pile group excavated in the Ebbsfleet Valley (Wenban-Smith *et al.* forthcoming). Obvious comparisons can also be drawn with the middle and late Bronze Age pile groups excavated at Vauxhall (Haughey 1999; Sidell *et al.* 2002, 29) and further upstream at Eton (Allen *et al.* forthcoming, Lambrick 2009, 232). The radiocarbon dates suggest that the structure at Freemasons Road is one of the earliest and may well have been contemporary with the larger Vauxhall structure (Fig. 10.2). At T=0.1 at 1df, the dates on the two structures are statistically consistent (chi-squared test using Beta-152738 and Beta-122970). Reconstruction of the contemporary topography at

Freemasons Road tends to support the interpretation that this structure was a footbridge bridge or jetty running from the higher ground out into a wetland zone during a period of increasing wetness. Recent topographic modelling work in the Lea Valley suggests that during the early Bronze Age a large floodplain island existed immediately to the east of Freemasons Road and it is possible the structure linked the drier ground of the terrace to this island (Fig. 4.8b; Corcoran *et al.* 2011, 56 and fig 108).

The dates for the A13 trackways tend to be slightly earlier than a number of Bronze Age structures recorded in the immediate vicinity which appear to post-date 1500 cal BC (Figs 10.3 and 10.4). Further afield there are a number of other Bronze Age trackways and some, such as Bramcote Green in Bermondsey have produced pre-1500 cal BC dates (Thomas and Rackham 1996). There are also possible

Plate 33 Neolithic trackway exposed during excavations at STDR4 in the Ebbsfleet Valley

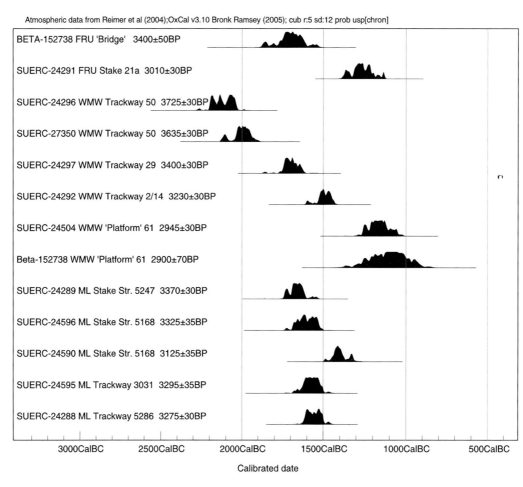

Fig. 10.1 Radiocarbon chronology of the A13 timber structures

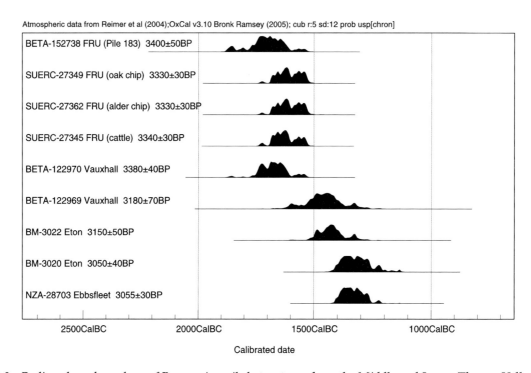

Fig. 10.2 Radiocarbon chronology of Bronze Age piled structures from the Middle and Lower Thames Valley

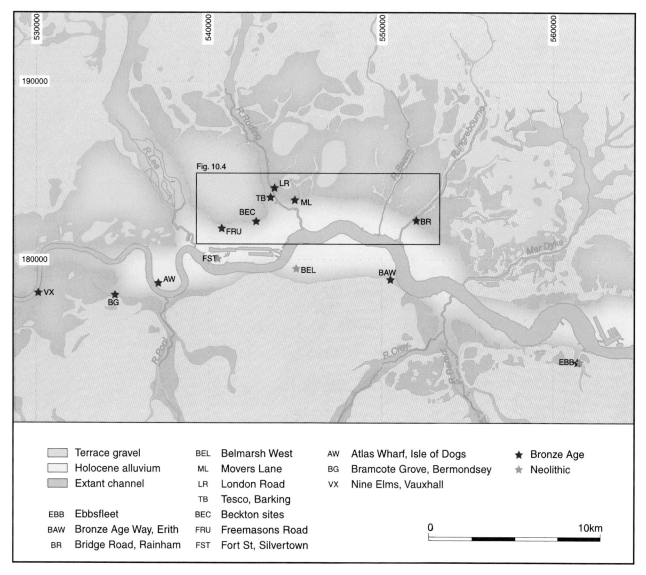

Fig. 10.3   Location of excavated timber structures from Central and East London

early examples, such as Fort Street, Silvertown (Crockett *et al.* 2002), Belmarsh (Hart 2010) and structures in the Ebbsfleet Valley (Wenban-Smith *et al.* in prep) that attest to a tradition of trackway building stretching back to into the Neolithic period (Fig. 10.3; Plate 33).

At Woolwich Manor Way, the trackways lie in close proximity to previously recorded structures at Beckton Nursery and Beckton 3-D (Meddens 1996) and the Golf Driving Range (Carew *et al.* 2010). At the latter site the calibrated date from an earlier platform structure appears to overlap with the dates for Trackways 50 and 29 at Woolwich Manor Way (Fig. 10.4). Although the age-ranges span a considerable time frame (max. around 600 years, min. 130 years) perhaps suggesting repairs to the structures, the youngest date for Trackway 50 and the two older dates from the platform passed a chi square test and are statistically consistent (T=4.9 at 2df). In addition the projection of the alignment of trackway 29 points directly to the platform structure

suggesting they may well have been directly related (Fig. 5.5). The dates for the platform and the date for Trackway 29 are also statistically consistent (T=7.5 at 3df). The trackway structures at the other nearby Beckton sites (Beckton Nursery, Beckton 3D) and the Golf Driving Range coincide with the building of the latest trackway 2/14 at Woolwich Manor Way (Fig. 10.4). All dates from these structures appear to be statistically consistent and could be considered broadly contemporary. Modelling the dates (using OxCal. 4.17) helps to refine the age ranges, providing a modelled start for the phase of 1672-1420 cal BC and an end of 1484-1136 cal BC, with the most likely age range for the date of these structures of about 1450-1390 cal BC.

The building of the trackways, an activity which appears to have significantly increased during the 2nd millennium BC, was clearly a means of accessing the floodplain wetlands. The apparent repair and possible replacement of trackways, particularly at Woolwich Manor Way, suggests that the construction and maintenance of these structures retained some relevance with the changing hydrology of the area and suggests that defined and established access routes into the marshland were respected and maintained. However as their points of origin and destinations are unknown it is difficult to speculate further. The palaeoenvironmental evidence from the A13 sites indicates that construction broadly coincides with rising water levels and a change from predominantly alder carr to a more open environment of sedge fen, reedswamp and marsh. Further into the marsh, closer to the Thames foreshore it is likely that saltmarsh environments existed. Access to the floodplain may have been required to exploit the range of natural resources

that must have been abundant in such environments: plants for medicinal purposes or reeds for basketry and thatching, as well as activities such as hunting, fishing and waterfowling. However, as previously stated there is little evidence of such activities from sites along the A13 or the Thames Estuary in general during this period. Alternatively the trackways may have been used for herding of animals to seasonal pasture on the marshes. Given the light construction, the trackways themselves were probably only used for human foot traffic with the herd wading alongside through the wetter areas. The role of animal husbandry, particularly of cattle, in the local subsistence economies of the region is well attested.

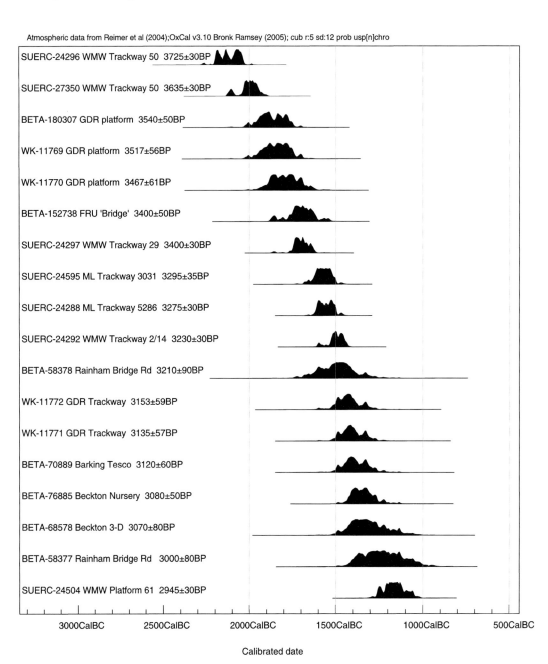

Atmospheric data from Reimer et al (2004);OxCal v3.10 Bronk Ramsey (2005); cub r:5 sd:12 prob usp[n]chro

Fig. 10.4   Radiocarbon chronology of Bronze Age timber trackways in East London

Construction methods

Freemasons Road 'bridge' (Fig. 10.5)

Form

The Freemasons Road 'bridge', a double pile alignment, was the most substantial wooden structure found during the A13 project. No elements of the upper works of the structure were found, although the oak sliver chips from the organic silt that accumulated around the base of the piles (layer 49) do suggest that the trimming of large oak planks of the sort likely to have been used in a walkway had occurred close-by. The reconstruction presented in Figure 10.5 is tentative and has been based on the use of a range of joints and materials documented in Bronze Age timber structures from south-east England. Other possible assemblies can not be ruled out, but axe hewn tusk tenons on the tops of piles for carrying cross planks with socket joints are known in the Bronze Age and later simple trestle type structures. At Swalecliffe in Kent, for example, a substantial cleft plank was supported by two piles with elongated tusk tenons at the base of a waterhole or well (Masefield *et al.* 2003, 66) and another larger example of a tusk tenoned pile comes from Flag Fen (Pryor 1991, fig. 79). Having established a moderately rigid trestle it would have been relatively easy to lay down cleft planks or half logs to form the longitudinals and walkway. There is no evidence of the use of lashings or wooden pegs in such situations so they have not been used in the illustration.

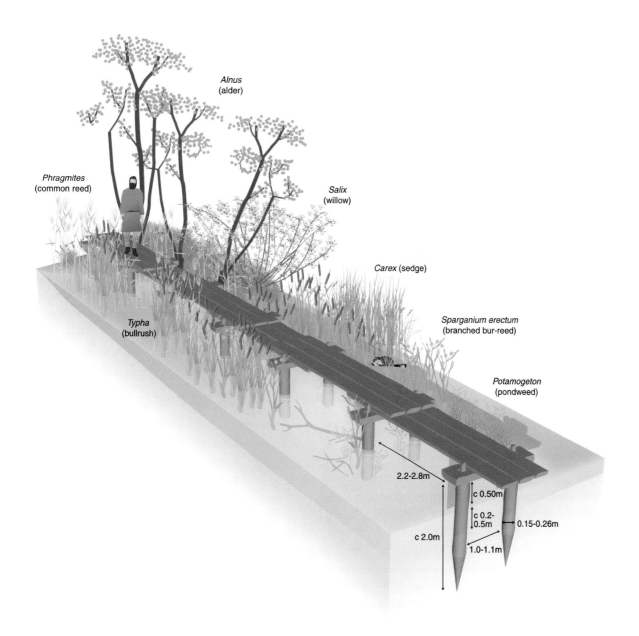

Fig. 10.5   Reconstruction of the Freemasons Road 'bridge'

Comparison of scale

The making, moving and driving of such piles was a substantial undertaking, but not unique in the Thames Valley and estuary floodplain (Cromarty *et al.* 2006; Haughey 1999; Lambrick 2009; Wenban-Smith *et al.* in prep.). In terms of scale, at around 150-260mm diameter the Freemasons Road piles were a little larger than most other piled structures of similar date. A relatively close parallel is the double pile alignment from Ebbsfleet, Kent which appears to have carried a footbridge over a tributary channel (Fig. 10.6). This structure was slightly later in date, at 1410-1220 cal BC (NZA-28703: 3055±30 BP). Here the round oak log piles, 105mm to 150mm in diameter, were set in pairs roughly 1m apart; approximately the same spacing as at Freemasons Road, although the spacing of each pair was a little greater at about 3m rather than 2.2m-2.8m (Wenban-Smith *et al.* in prep.).

The Bronze Age pile groups excavated at Vauxhall (Haughey 1999, Sidell *et al.*, 29) and further upstream at Eton (Lambrick 2009, Allen *et al.* forthcoming) appear to be larger and the arrangement of piles a little less regular. This may have been due to the structures spanning wider, faster flowing water courses and a longer lifespan requiring some maintenance. At Eton two roughly parallel rows of oak timber piles were set about 1.5m–2m apart with the pile diameters averaging 200mm to 230mm, although some were much larger at up to 420mm. The radiocarbon dates for two piles were, respectively, 1530-1300 cal BC (BM-3022: 3150±50 BP) and 1420-1200 cal BC (BM-3020: 3050±40 BP). The Vauxhall structure was even wider; here, the massive piles were set roughly 4m apart with diameters of up to 600mm and could clearly have accommodated wheeled vehicles. Radiocarbon dates on two piles span a considerable period of time; 1770-1530 cal BC (Beta-122970: 3380±40 BP) and 1630-1290 cal BC (Beta-122969: 3180±70 BP). Although there is an overlap in the dates ranges, it is possible that some of the piles had been replaced.

The logistics behind the building of the bridge

One of the authors (DG) has some experience of working with fresh oak logs of the size and growth rate used in the bridge and of working with middle Bronze Age replica tool kits and low-tech aids such as pole levers and this is drawn upon here (Goodburn 2004). The original height of the piles is impossible to reconstruct accurately, however, as water levels along the Thames floodplain edge at this time are unlikely to have been higher than about +1.5m OD, a length of perhaps 2.5m to 3.0m seems adequate to support a decking level above high water levels. This means, if 3m long, the largest freshly cut piles would have weighed around 0.12 tonnes. Whilst a pile this size could be manoeuvred by two adults, to carry or drag the log any distance might take four. In addition, small increases in log diameter make exponential increases in weight. Freshly cut green oak logs of medium to fast growth can weigh as much as about 1.073 tonnes/m³ and generally do not float (Millett and McGrail 1987, 106). This means, unless they were transported by boat as is known in a few cases for stone in the Bronze Age, that water was probably not used to move them. If the piles were around 3m long, many parent trees would have produced two piles. The largest butt log of at least one would have been cleft into sections for the cleft piles. It is likely that the suggested longitudinal planking would have been carried into place by two people during periods of low water level. However, if they were of great width and thickness a team of four might be needed for planks of 3.5m in length, which is long enough to overlap at each end.

The driving of the piles

The driving of piles using percussive rams and medieval documentation of rams of various forms is now well known, at least to archaeologists (Watson *et al.* 2001, 120). This led one of the authors (DG) and other archaeologists to make a simple piling ram to drive piles about the size of the average pile known at Freemasons Road. The occasion was provided by the Channel 4 Time Team investigations of the Vauxhall Bronze Age piled structure. The ram comprised a pole tripod lashed at the head with a greased 'dumb sheave' (a block of ash with two smoothly gouged holes, one for suspension and one for the ram rope). The ram was a 0.7m length of oak log *c* 350mm in diameter, with a pierced projection similar to those seen on the Shardlow Bronze Age logs (on display in Derby Museum). It took four people to position the tripod and three to haul the ram log up and let it drop onto a pile. This was set in a starting hole, and supported by forked poles. The experimental piles were only about 1.6m long. With longer piles a taller heavier tripod would have been needed which might have required a crew of six adults to move. Something similar may have been possible using a natural fibre rope in the summer time, during low water levels at Freemasons Road.

Experimental work, however, at the Loch Tay Scottish Crannog Centre suggests that another less labour intensive method may have been use to set the piles in place if the sediments were soft enough. Nicholas Dixon, Barrie Andrian and their team were able to set long log piles of about the diameter of the smaller examples at Freemasons Road by twisting them, almost screwing them into place in the loch bed just off shore (Dixon 2004, fig 28). In that technique the pile is reared vertically and guyed in place with rope then one person on a light temporary scaffold turns the pile back and forward using a lashed on cross bar. The turning action liquefies the wet silts surrounding the pile tips allowing them to sink. They can be set as much as 0.7 to 1.0m deep by this method (B. Andrian, Scottish Crannog Centre, pers. comm.).

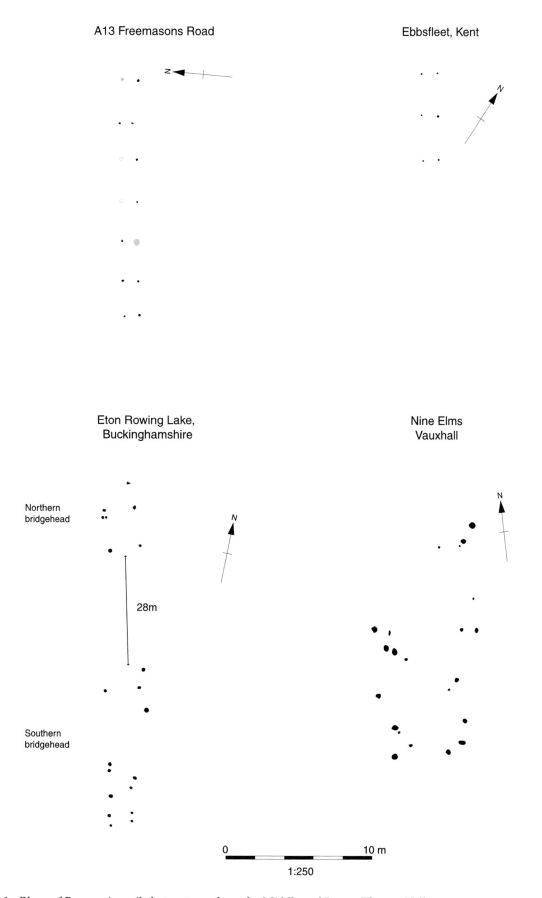

Fig. 10.6 Plans of Bronze Age piled structures from the Middle and Lower Thames Valley

The work force required

As a result of this, all that can be tentatively suggested is the minimum size of the work force required to build the Freemasons Road footbridge. Clearly a larger team could have built the structure much faster. The limited experiments in possible Bronze Age piling methods indicate that the work force could have been at the scale of the extended household rather than a huge communal effort. However, if the structure was built by one extended household rather than a village sized community it would have taken many weeks to build allowing for all the stages in the work required from felling to erection on site. Although some of the woodworking debris found on site might have been the debris left from the finishing of planking for the super-structure of the bridge, no chips from trimming and pointing the piles were found and this most likely took place elsewhere. Hewing the tips a few days or weeks ahead of setting them would have made the piles lighter to move and allowed the tips to dry, thus hardening the surfaces prior to setting.

Tool kits

The implied tool kit used for the woodworking needed to build this bridge is a simple one comprising one or more axes to fell and buck the parent trees and make the pile points; logs would also have been required for skidding the timber and as poles for moving and temporary shoring. Other items that must have been included are ropes, a maul and some wooden wedges for cleaving some of the piles and the super-structure elements. The socket joint holes in the implied cross planks would have been cut using narrow bladed axes and or adzes as the tool mark studies of such joints in other timbers shows (Orme and Coles 1983, 41; Goodburn 2003a, 66).

The stake alignments

The mainly roundwood stake alignments found during the A13 project were simple structures. Once the roundwood material was felled, lopped and bucked a variety of point types were hewn, with small Bronze Age axes of varied form, but all far smaller and lighter than most used since the Iron Age. Roundwood to be woven ('weavers') would have been handled in a similar way, although it may have been cut to longer lengths. The stakes were used to support horizontal elements mainly woven round them as in 'wattle work'. When the wattle work was laid flat in water-logged deposits it is often preserved and here we are able to move beyond the examination of pointed stake ends and examine weave patterns. The wattle hurdles used as a trackway surface at Movers Lane were a distinctive, quickly woven but rather weak, version of the 'slew' weave. The slew weave involved weaving three or four weavers together in and out behind the originally upright

stakes. Where paired stake lines have been found, for example at Freemasons Road, these may represent either a phase of repair or possibly the use of a form of 'dead hedging' where wood branch and stem debris was held between pairs of stakes. Finally, it is also possible that stake lines may have been used to support nets or sheet materials such as bark or natural fibre matting.

Evidence for more specialised older work parties

The level of skill and strength needed to carry out these types of work is modest and well within the abilities of all adults and many children from the age of perhaps five or six years upward. It seems very likely that the building of such simple round-wood structures would have been a whole family affair in Bronze Age Greater London. This is not true, however, of the weaving of complicated weaves or with the use of large diameter weavers where adult strength in arms and shoulders is required. Where stake alignments included cleft timber stakes and large timbers, for example at Movers Lane Area 3, Woolwich Manor Way Platform 61 and elements of Structure 32 (the 'bridge') at Freemasons Road, they imply the logistics and complexity of the work would have reached a different level. The work required physical strength as well as knowledge of larger trees and woodworking skills. This would most likely have been carried out at a greater distance from home and hearth. It may even have been in areas of wildwood where predatory animals might also be found. We might reasonably suggest that it is probably the case that the work parties involved in this included mainly adult men and some older children.

Tool kits

For most of the stake alignments found on the A13 project the tool kit required was meagre; an axe and a large mallet or 'maul' would be all that was needed apart from a chopping block or log end to trim the stake points on. If cleft material was involved a set of wooden wedges and possibly a chisel would also be required. The chisel would be used to cut fibrous slivers in the narrow clefts made during log cleaving.

Evidence of repairs

Clearly the prolonged use of a site in a similar way is indicated by archaeological evidence of repairs to wooden structures or even rebuilds. Such evidence is typically found in wooden property boundaries on waterlogged urban sites, where wattle fence lines are often found superimposed in virtually the same place on the same alignment. In relation to stake alignments from the A13 project, only the rather mysterious stake groups at Movers Lane (Str. 5168 and possibly Str. 5144) probably show signs of the repair or rebuilding of a stake built structure on the same alignment. This is particularly true of Structure 5168 which had a great density of varied stakes, including larger and smaller roundwood and even some cleft timber examples (see Fig. 7.11 and 7.12c).

The trackways

The restricted range of trackway forms found on the A13

Of the five wooden trackways recorded, four were what has been loosely termed brushwood tracks made of roundwood dumped lengthwise (Trackways 50, 29 and 2/14 at Woolwich Manor Way and Trackway 3031 at Movers Lane). Structure 5268 at Movers Lane was a hurdle trackway (Fig. 7.11; Plate 17). In national terms the brushwood tracks were the simplest requiring only the felling, lopping and bucking of poles, coppice stems and some branchwood. The key issue for the builders was moving the material and laying it end to end to form a moderately level walkway. Such trackways represent a modest investment of labour and materials if short in length. However, when extending over hundreds of metres many tons of material would have been required. This trackway type can be paralleled widely in Britain and Ireland from the Neolithic onwards (Coles and Orme 1980a and b; Coles and Orme 1985; Raftery 1990). The fact that Trackway 3031 at Movers Lane (Fig 7.9; Plate 15) and Trackway 2/14 at Woolwich Manor Way (Fig.

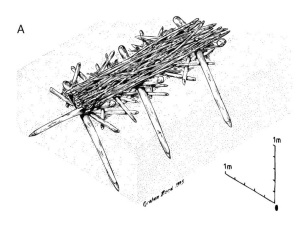

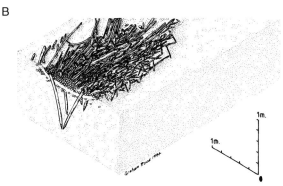

Fig. 10.7   Artist's reconstruction of Bronze Age trackways from Beckton 3-D and Beckton Nursery (from Meddens 1996)

5.8; Plates 9 and 10) included some heterogeneous and even burnt material suggests that the settlements associated with the routeways were close at hand. This is because short and irregular heterogeneous material could be easily carried and dumped at low points in the trackways which seems an unlikely practice for work at a distance.

The wattle hurdle structure at Movers Lane, Trackway 5268, represents a somewhat more elaborate, though lightweight, construction. Having made the hurdle panels out of thin, pliable, rods on dry land they could be laid out rapidly to form a light fairly level trackway. Coppicing is fundamental to the production of such fine rods for this particularly light, regular weaving. The quick multi-weaver 'slew' weave is not exactly paralleled but similar multi-weaver weaves are known from several of the Derryoghil Bronze Age hurdle trackways and on the Thames floodplain at Erith (Raftery 1990, 24; Bennell 1998, 29). No trace of trackway elements with rail logs, cradling stakes or planks were found, although these are known from several other Bronze Age prehistoric wetland sites in Britain, Ireland and elsewhere in north-west Europe. In the immediate vicinity cradle structures are known from the Beckton 3D and Beckton Nursery sites (Fig. 10.7 a and b).

Evidence for trackway repairs

The wattle hurdle surface of Trackway 5268 at Movers Lane had been laid as at least three layers of wattlework, with the uppermost surviving only in very disturbed condition. It is possible that each layer represents annual or biennial doubling-up repairs as the hurdle broke or sank into the bog. In the mixed brushwood of Trackway 3031 from Movers Lane, roundwood of various sizes seems to have been laid in distinct groups as if filling in hollows suggesting phases of repair. In the heterogeneous brushwood Trackway 2/14 at Woolwich Manor Way the poles, rods and logs were accompanied by an assortment of more extensively worked and sometimes weathered timbers, such as a radially cleft oak pale, a weathered ash half log and branch material which may well have been laid as *ad hoc* repairs.

'Platform' 61 from Woolwich Manor Way and some parallels

The term 'platform' in prehistoric wetland archaeology covers a wide range of often ill-defined types of structures; from solidly made structures with timber poles, logs, uprights, through to small spreads of irregular cut roundwood. Structure 61 appears to represent the north-east corner of a fairly solid horizontal spread of cleft logs, poles and smaller material including reused oak plank fragments. A series of stakes were also found driven apparently around the eastern and northern edges of the platform, possibly the remnants of a fence surrounding it (Fig. 5.6, SW corner). Another slightly earlier platform was found just to the south of this structure on the Beckton Golf Driving Range. However, this was more lightly built comprising a layer of possible cut yew stems and branches covered with a layer of close set alder logs (Carew *et al.* 2010; Goodburn 2003b). Platform 61 was mainly made of much larger section material set close together, a little like the log and branch floors of later prehistoric buildings excavated from the eroding edges of the Lower Severn Estuary (Bell and Caseldine 2000, 88). It also broadly resembles the more heavily constructed parts of the Atlas Wharf 'platform' found on the Isle of Dogs, which was of similar date (Goodburn 1998). Unfortunately the trench at Woolwich Manor Way could not be extended southwards to expose more of the structure to ascertain whether it might have supported a dwelling for example. Although the evidence is limited such a function is possible.

Woodworking debitage as an indicator of activity

For a great many years archaeologists have excavated and studied stone tool making debris as standard practice. Sometimes stone tool specialists are able to refit stone flakes showing roughly what had been made where the debris spread lay, in other words the 'debitage' is diagnostic of particular knapping activities and in broad terms the production of certain types of stone artefact. It is less well known that the targeted sampling and study of different types of wood chips and other working debris can provide similar information (Meddens and Beasley 1990, 243; Goodburn 1996, 241). Several finds of woodworking debris, or what might be loosely called wood chips, were made during the A13 investigations which have provided extra insights into the behaviour of those that occupied the area. They have also shed some light on the technological aspects of the woodworking carried out at certain locations, and the range of species being worked. Probably the most important, from a forensic point of view, were the distinctive elongated slivers from smoothing large cleft oak timbers found in layer 49 at Freemasons Road. Apart from some broken fragments in the platform (Str. 61) at Woolwich Manor Way no wide cleft planks were found *in situ*. Using experimental parallels it has been suggested that the debris may have derived from trimming parts of the Freemasons Road bridge superstructure, particularly walkway planking. A smaller scatter of yew wood chips at Movers Lane (Area 3) again suggested the working of timber not used on the site itself, although several items of worked yew wood were found at Woolwich Manor Way and the nearby Beckton Golf Driving Range site (Carew *et al.* 2010).

Bronze Age double pointed sticks; note on a recurring class of wooden artefact

The A13 project produced two mysterious objects of radially cleft wood that resemble each other, and a larger example from beside a Bronze Age trackway was found at Erith on the southern edge of the estuarine flood plain. It should be noted that all these objects were found lying horizontally, not used as some form of stake. At Freemasons Road object 32 was made from an axe trimmed cleft section of yew, 0.44m long by about 25mm square and carved to a point at both ends (Fig. 4.14). Next to trackway 2/14 at Woolwich Manor Way another similar object was found, radially cleft and 0.56m long, 37mm wide and about10mm thick and pointed at both ends (Fig. 5.9, f). The possible parallel from Erith was around twice as large; a radially cleft and double pointed stick of alder, about 1.11m long, 60mm wide and 30mm thick. These objects have similar form and were found in similar contexts but there is little other evidence to point to their function. A role in the drying, smoking and/or cooking fish is possible, although evidence for the exploitation of fish resources is otherwise lacking (see above, Chapter 9) this could extend to other cuts of meat (Fig. 10.8). In the damp temperate climate of the Pacific north-western coast of America Native Americans used to cook opened up cleaned fish held flat by flat pointed stick(s) threaded through slits in the body. The assembly was then set, near up right, leaning slightly over a small fire (Stewart 1984, 84). The fish would be cooked or even smoked and dried using this method, which relies mainly on radiant heat. Today a modernised version of the method, with the fish nailed to a board, is still practiced in the Pacific north-western region.

Raw materials, treescapes and Bronze Age woodmanship (Fig 10.9)

In any situation past or present, the materials selected for different types of structural work are dictated by a combination of factors such as: local availability, itself a result of natural conditions and often human management of the land, the structural characteristics of the species, and often seemingly irrational cultural prejudices. Clearly for these sites the most important natural factor influencing the availability of certain species is the degree of waterlogging and distance to drier land. These factors varied through time and across locations on the A13 project. Environmental archaeologists have been identifying waterlogged wood samples and tree pollen to species or group for over half a century (Godwin 1956; Coles and Orme 1985). Ever since the beginnings of work by Rackham and others in the early 1970s on ancient systems of woodland management or 'woodmanship', seeking evidence for tree management practices such as coppicing, pollarding and other systems has been a key aim of wetland archaeology. In coppicing, young trees are repeatedly harvested as regrowth from an established root system or 'stool'; in pollarding the regrowth springs from higher up a stem out of reach of browsing animals. Each system produces many

Fig. 10.8   Artist's reconstruction of a cooking scene using double pointed sticks (by M Gridley)

young pliable rods (Rackham 1976, 20). Rackham clearly defined a series of terms to describe ancient forms of woodmanship that shaped the landscape or 'treeland'. Prior to the early 13th century AD early treescapes in England were often a distinctive mosaic of managed tree-land forms ranging from orchard and hedgerow trees to areas of more or less unmanaged wildwood. Regarding the A13 project, the concern is therefore not just with the range of species used but also whether the parent trees were subject to a woodmanship practice or not. Due to the cultural and practical selection criterion used by early woodworkers other strands of evidence have also to be considered. For example, the pollen study shows that linden (lime: *Tilia* sp.) was common on the dry land bordering the wetlands but virtually no trace of it was found in the examined worked roundwood or timber

Based on field identifications of the larger stems cross checked with the microscopic identifications, species used as larger structural timber in the round or cleft included one of the two native oaks (or both) with a little ash, alder and elm. A much wider range of species were used as poles, cut branches, and smaller rods, including in order of magnitude: alder, ash, willow/poplar, and less commonly yew, hazel, oak, elm and a single pole of holly.

Only a small proportion of the material excavated was of likely to have been of wildwood origin, in other words being derived from large old trees and typically narrow ringed (that is 2mm wide annual rings or narrower) and straight-grained (Goodburn 1991). It seems that any stands of trees growing in wildwood type conditions were probably a little distance away from the wetland edge zone where various forms of managed treeland and farmland dominated (Fig. 10.9). Oak timber having wildwood characteristics was found as occasional radially cleft stakes at Movers Lane (for example stake 5244, sample 1125) and in the elongated trimming slivers found at Freemasons Road derived from timbers that were not found on site (layer 49). However, the vast bulk of material clearly derived from more open forms of treeland where trees could put on moderately or very wide rings. The process that opened up the woodland was probably frequent fellings although the opening of the wildwood through hurricanes and flash flooding might also have been a factor. The oak piles of the bridge or jetty found at Freemasons Road varied between about 150mm and 200mm in diameter with around 50-70 rings but also include a few cleft timbers from larger diameter fast grown logs up to about 450mm in diameter (for example pile 79). As some of the piles were a little knotty it is likely that they were cut from a log taken well above the base of the tree. It is possible that some or all the above grew in managed woodland with

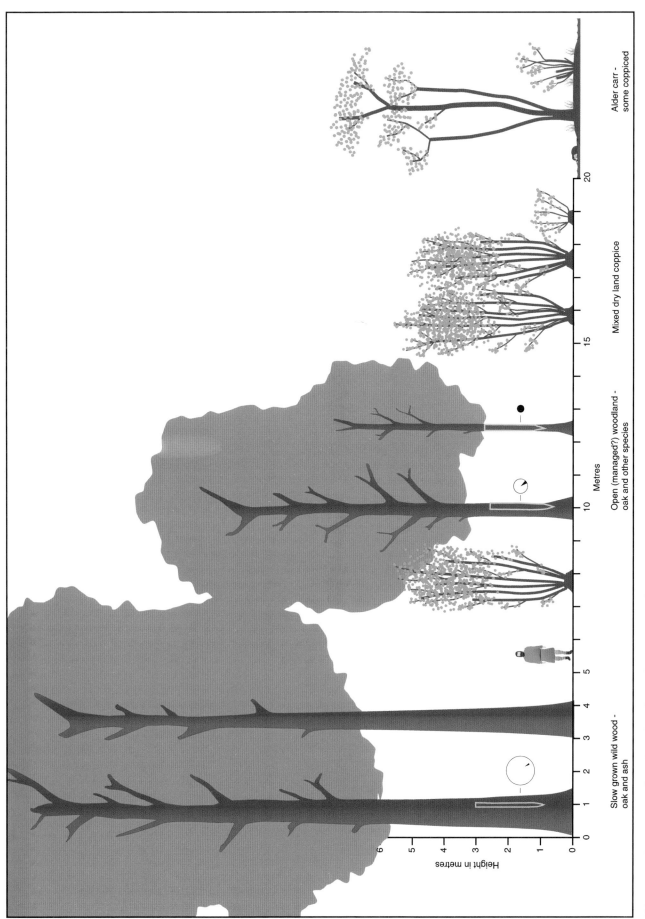

Fig. 10.9   Parent trees for selected timbers of Bronze Age date

Plate 34   Coppiced hazel woodland (photo by Michael J Spiller)

small timber trees and coppice ('coppice with standards' still common in parts of the south-east today) (Plate 34).

The fine, regular young roundwood weavers, *c* 25mm max diameter, in wattle trackway 5268 at Movers Lane were clearly derived from coppiced woodland, in this case mainly of alder. Similar, slightly larger material, also of alder, was used at Movers Lane for stake structure 5247, while a bundle of regular small rods dumped by trackway 3031 was mainly of a mix of alder and willow or poplar. The presence of a small beaver dam on the site shows that we should not assume that all the coppiced material was necessarily evidence of human woodmanship; some areas may well have been cut and maintained by beavers. The coppice derived from species more typical of slightly drier land such as ash, elm and hazel was presumably growing on the drier edges of the wetland or even a little distance up on the gravel terraces. The yew wood elements found probably came from the now extinct wetland yews that were once common in the floodplain wildwood around 2000 BC (Goodburn 1998). The almost total lack of the use of easily worked linden (lime) wood, evidenced in the pollen sequences, is difficult to explain, but perhaps there were cultural prejudices against its use.

From the woodworkers point of view the woodmanship practices employed and the ecotonal

natural environment produced woody materials of many sizes, shapes and species to suit different functions. In a real sense the woodmanship was part of their traditions of woodworking and it is almost certain that the same people were both woodsmen (possibly including children and women in the lighter work) and woodworkers. This contrasts with today, in most cases, when a woodworker buys a timber of a certain size made by someone else from logs supplied at a distance by others, so that the connection between end user and landscape is broken.

Technical details on the recording and analysis of waterlogged wood assemblages

Tool marks, tool kits and dating in relation to some other key Bronze Age assemblages

The level of the preservation of tool marks was disappointing for most of the woodwork found during the A13 project, bearing in mind the very fine preservation of some prehistoric wetland woodwork excavated in the region, such as at Beckton Golf Driving Range (Carew *et al.* 2010; Goodburn 2003b). The general lack of very well-preserved marks was due to various factors such as compression by overburden, ancient weathering, localised drying before full excavation and in some cases hurried excavation and poor wrapping prior to recording. However, some information on the form, size and method of use of Bronze Age axe type tools was recorded which enables some comparisons to be made with toolmarks recorded in other assemblages spanning the Bronze Age. Here we are concerned only with marks on the larger roundwood and timber used where fairly complete tool marks might be expected. Also, for the vast majority of the A13 material, the preservation was not good enough to identify the signatures left by the unique pattern of nicks on individual axe blades.

Although it was soon recognised during work in the Somerset Levels in the 1980s that axes of different periods, from the Neolithic to Iron Ages, left different marks (Orme and Coles 1983, 32), the realisation that the key difference was in the size of the facets and width of the stop marks (or 'jam curves') came later (O'Sullivan 1997). Although the smoothness of the facets and angle of the cut are also factors worth consideration and there are marked differences in these features between stone and metal worked material from the early Bronze Age, these are of much less importance. O'Sullivan, working systematically on prehistoric wetland woodwork from central Ireland, was able to show that there were distinctive changes in the size of the best preserved marks found in assemblages over time from the Neolithic to Iron Ages. Working on material from Oak Bank Crannog in Loch Tay, Sands (1997) was able to take tool mark recording further and distinguish late Bronze Age from early

Iron Age axe marks as well as carry out innovative work on comparing individual axe signature marks. It is now clear that there are predictable trends in the sizes of the largest axes or adzes that groups of woodworkers used through time (Goodburn 2003a, 104; 2004, 129; Webley and Hiller 2009). This is, of course, entirely unremarkable as it has long been known that there were substantial changes in Bronze Age axe forms and that blade width was a key factor. Clearly in any one period there are smaller and larger tools but the working assumption here is that in the vast majority of cases the woodworkers would use the largest heaviest tool for the heaviest jobs such as felling trees over pole size and heavy duty hewing. Thus, near or fully complete axe facets and stop marks can be correlated with broad date ranges in the Bronze Age of early, middle and late, so far the correlations have

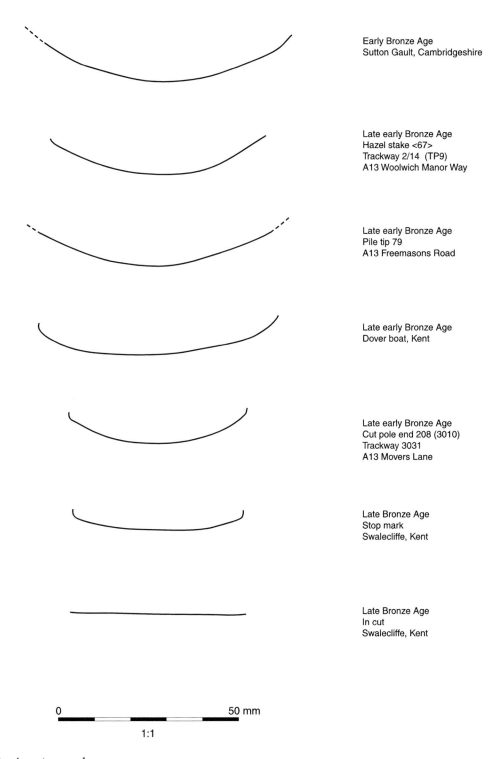

Early Bronze Age
Sutton Gault, Cambridgeshire

Late early Bronze Age
Hazel stake <67>
Trackway 2/14 (TP9)
A13 Woolwich Manor Way

Late early Bronze Age
Pile tip 79
A13 Freemasons Road

Late early Bronze Age
Dover boat, Kent

Late early Bronze Age
Cut pole end 208 (3010)
Trackway 3031
A13 Movers Lane

Late Bronze Age
Stop mark
Swalecliffe, Kent

Late Bronze Age
In cut
Swalecliffe, Kent

0   50 mm

1:1

Fig. 10.10 Axe stop marks

proved reliable with assemblages dated by radio-carbon and tree-ring matching. One notable exception is the partially excavated pile from the middle Bronze Age Vauxhall Bridge now at the Museum of London, where the widths of the facets of the upper parts are narrow and more typical of the late Bronze Age. However, hitherto very little detailed recording of elements of that structure has been possible.

In the case of the Freemasons Road assemblage the pile tips were fairly well preserved and once all of them had been cleaned and recorded the largest nearly complete facets and stop marks could be seen. They were moderately rounded and 65mm wide, implying the use of an axe blade about 70mm wide, which is typical of the middle Bronze Age but at the smaller end of the early Bronze Age spectrum. Similar marks were documented on the Dover Boat (Goodburn 2004, 129, Fig. 10.10). Some of the larger wood chips from the site also implied the use of blades about 70mm wide. However, one of the piles (pile 80), had facets only about 35mm wide indicating the use of a second, much smaller, implement Initially smaller marks were found on the two least well preserved piles and a late Bronze Age date was suggested demonstrating the need to examine as much of the material as possible.

From Woolwich Manor Way there were no nearly complete facets that could be compared, although a fine partial signature survived on one piece of worked yew. Most of the worked material was small roundwood, or had been weathered in antiquity. Similar problems prevented the survival of a range of crisp and clear facets and stop marks from Movers Lane; most of the worked material was small roundwood and the larger material was generally weathered with eroded facets. However, in a few cases fairly well-preserved axe marks did survive such as on the end of a pole from Trackway 3010 (sample 208) which bore a very rounded axe stop mark, 50mm wide, which was from a deep blow and seemed fairly complete. Such a mark would be typical of the larger end of the late Bronze Age spectrum fitting the narrow rounded cutting edges/blades of nearly all socketed axes (Goodburn 2003a, 104). However, radiocarbon dating of the trackway produced a date in the early to middle Bronze Age and this may be another example of a lack of fit of the tool mark to radiocarbon date. An intrusive stake tip 5108 (sample 1000) was found driven through the upper part of the wattle hurdle trackway (Str. 5268) clearly from some way above. The axe facets were small, rounded and only up to 35mm wide which would be best matched in the late Bronze Age (Goodburn 2003a, 104).

The limits of previously existing terminology for describing cut roundwood ends

By the beginning of the A13 project a commonly adopted terminology had gradually evolved to describe the forms of the cut ends of worked roundwood so common in Bronze Age wetland assemblages. The terms described three main categories that all cut roundwood was supposed fall into (O'Sullivan 1997, 307):

1. The chisel form, with one oblique face forming the point or end
2. The wedge form, with two oblique cut faces forming the point or end
3. The pencil form, with multiple oblique cut faces forming the point or end

However, recording work during the A13 project and for other smaller assemblages of Bronze Age woodwork from London shows that the tripartite categories are inadequate with many examples falling outside. The most common exception was pointed or cut roundwood ends formed by cutting two adjacent oblique faces, as exemplified in stake 67 from TP9 at Woolwich Manor Way (Fig. 5.9g). This feature was also noticed by the pioneering prehistoric wetland investigators in the mid 1980s (Coles and Orme 1985, 26), but a simplified schema then gradually evolved. The reason for shaping points or cut ends leaving two adjacent facets becomes apparent when coppice rods are cut for making replicas of early roundwood structures. This was clearly demonstrated by D. Goodburn during the reconstruction of section of the Erith Bronze Age wattle hurdle trackway for Bexley Museum with middle Bronze Age tools. Similarly it was experimental works that led Coles and Orme to the same conclusion.

Many coppice shoots curve tightly in at their base to form a curved butt to the stem (Rackham 1976, 21). If the stem is cut low the simplest way of making a point is to form it with two adjacent oblique faces. If the stem is cut higher then chisel, wedge and pencil forms are more likely to be convenient. A variation on the point of two adjacent faces is one where a third face is also slightly cut so as to taper in, similarly dealing with the curving ends of many coppice stems. Thus, these two categories can be added to the checklists used during the recording of early roundwood found on archaeological sites. None of these issues apply to straight stems grown from seed known as 'maidens'. Ultimately the experience of the A13 woodwork recording has refined recording terminology for smaller roundwood and aided a more subtle understanding of woodworking processes and woodmanship in the Bronze Age of south-east England.

Chapter 11: Concluding comments

by Frank Meddens, Stuart Foreman, Martin Bates and Damian Goodburn

Physical limitations of the investigation

Managing impacts to archaeological deposits within a busy urban environment, alongside a major road construction project, presented numerous logistical challenges, which were addressed by the road engineers through ingenious and innovative ways. For instance, the preservation of the important Neolithic site identified by evaluation trenching at Woolwich Manor Way was achieved by using light-weight polystyrene fill in the road embankment construction, thus substantially reducing the frequency of concrete piles required to support the structure. The nature of the working environment meant that investigations were for the most part limited to relatively small windows where there was a demonstrable below ground impact from construction activity. This can be frustrating for archaeologists who naturally wish to explore the full extent of a site or feature, but is a necessary constraint on developer-funded archaeology. In most cases this should mean that the unexcavated portions of those sites are preserved *in situ* and available for future investigation should the opportunity or need arise. The important Neolithic site at Woolwich Manor Way, for example, was briefly glimpsed in an evaluation trench and subsequently preserved for posterity. On the A13 project some of the key excavation areas were defined by the extents of flyover abutments, which were very small areas indeed, comparable in size with evaluation trenches. The most extensive deep investigation was the coffer dam excavation at Prince Regent Lane (Freemasons Road Underpass) in which a substantial Bronze Age piled structure was found. The extent of the cofferdam was largely dictated by the plan of the new underpass (although informed by evaluation trenching results).

The scope of investigation was also limited to areas where reasonable prospects existed for intact archaeological deposits. Disturbance caused by construction of the existing A13 and the extent of 20th century development on either side of the road meant that these areas often lay in narrow strips of surviving intact deposits, flanked on either side by truncated, disturbed or inaccessible deposits. The relatively undisturbed areas were identified initially on the basis of desk-based studies and geotechnical investigations, and then refined by excavating archaeological test pits and trenches during the Phase I and II evaluation. Geophysical survey methods were not a viable option due the disturbed nature of the ground, the depth of overlying deposits and the often ephemeral character of archaeology in alluvial environments (such as prehistoric waterlogged wooden structures).

A third limiting factor was the physical difficulty in accessing some of the deeper deposit sequences. The most significant waterlogged archaeological deposits were found along the margins of palaeochannels, buried beneath variable depths of alluvium and made ground. The project lies on the periphery of Greater London, in an area which was predominantly undeveloped marshland and agricultural land until the latter part of the 19th century. Nevertheless deep modern made ground was a significant obstacle in some areas (where covered by the existing A13 road embankment, for example). The engineering efforts required to reach the archaeology in these cases meant that the archaeological work was both costly and potentially hazardous. The deposit sequences were not universally deep however; in areas where the terrace gravels lay very close to the present ground surface, the width of the new road was stripped of topsoil to expose quite extensive sections of the terrace surface, in ground conditions comparable in most respects with investigations in rural dry land environments. The least effective interventions proved to be the Watching Brief work. This can be explained both by the inevitable constraints on access and visibility, and the nature of the alluvial deposits, in which it was often difficult to recognise features even when conditions were ideal. The difficulties of creating a coherent archaeological record under general Watching Brief conditions are well-known.

Contribution of the archaeological data to regional research

In spite of the practical limitations the particular topographical niche occupied by the A13 corridor, skirting the northern edge of the Thames flood-plain, offered valuable insights from an archaeological and palaeoenvironmental point of view, which have fully repaid the time, money and effort invested in the archaeological work. The extensive presence of waterlogged sediment sequences offered exceptional potential for the recovery of organic materials of various periods in stratified alluvial and archaeological deposit sequences. The formal excavation areas and evaluation trenches, taken together, provide a rare series of comparatively large scale investigations for the Lower

Thames in the London region, linked by a common project design and geoarchaeological research framework.

The archaeological discoveries range from the Mesolithic through to the post-medieval period, although material from the 2nd millennium BC was most commonly encountered, in the form of timber structures and in particular trackways. This volume therefore marks an outstanding contribution to our understanding of the prehistory of the Lower Thames area, particularly the Bronze Age. Together with other recent large scale investigations within the Thames Floodplain in London, such as High Speed 1 (formerly the Channel Tunnel Rail Link), the Jubilee Line Extension and the Lea Valley Mapping Project, the A13 investigations have helped to clarify the sequence of inundation of the Thames floodplain caused by sea-level rises during the Holocene, shedding particular light on the reactions of Bronze Age communities to these landscape changes. The data is most immediately relevant to the narrow but important topographical zone occupied by the A13 corridor, at the interface between the marshland occupying the valley floor and the gravel terrace to the north. However it also contributes to discussions of contemporary cultural landscape changes beyond the floodplain. As observed throughout the region, there is a widespread change, between the Neolithic and the middle Bronze Age (broadly the late 3rd and early 2nd millennium BC) from a landscape focused on dispersed ceremonial monuments to an agricultural landscape, which in some areas is characterised by a formally delineated environment comprising co-axial field-systems associated with stock management and pastoralism (Pryor 1998; Yates 2001). The different types of archaeological data from the Thames floodplain provide a complementary view of this phase of settlement transformation.

Regional sea-level and climate studies

This volume also presents multi-proxy palaeoenvironmental evidence from a series of radiocarbon dated sediment sequences from the margins of the Thames floodplain. Apart from the important information that these provide for the landscape context of the associated prehistoric archaeological finds (discussed in detail in this volume) these represent valuable additions to the Holocene palaeoenvironmental record for southern Britain, particularly given their close association with significant, radiocarbon dated, *in situ* archaeological structures. The relationship between sea-level rise, climate change and cultural change are complex and multi-factorial, and the subject of current debates which lie largely beyond the scope of this study. Suffice it to say, the changes in landscape during the Neolithic and Bronze Age, as noted in the A13 environmental sequences and other projects in the Thames Estuary, are likely to be related to more widely observed fluctuations in climate across Britain and north-west

Europe, which have yet to be satisfactorily resolved (Brown 2008, 1-18).

Prehistoric archaeology in the Lower Thames floodplain

Until the explosion of development-led archaeology in the 1990s, knowledge of prehistoric human activity in the floodplain of the Lower Thames and its tributaries in the London area was limited, comprising occasional tantalising glimpses, such as the discovery of significant quantities of metalwork, mostly weaponry from the river itself, and occasional other finds such as the Dagenham idol unearthed in 1922 (Coles 1990, 326). In addition there were references to wooden structures, interpreted as crannogs or pile dwellings of uncertain date which had been found in the later 19th century on the River Lea, during the excavations of the Maynard (Smith 1907), Warwick (Needham and Longley 1980), Banbury and William Girling reservoirs. The extent and nature of the peat beds found in the floodplain alluvium had been remarked upon at least as early as 1721 by John Perry in his account of the stopping of the Dagenham Breach. In this work Perry not only refers to the extensive presence of brushwood in the peats, he also mentions widespread finds of hazelnuts and yew trees and occasional finds of deer antlers in these deposits. He also describes the basic sequence of clays overlying peats, which in turn lay on top of blue clays over gravels and sand (Perry 1721).

The A13 project has contributed some new data to add to models of Mesolithic and Neolithic landscape evolution in the Lower Thames Valley, but has produced relatively limited archaeological evidence from these periods. Other recent projects in the region, such as High Speed 1, have been more forthcoming in this respect (Bates and Stafford forthcoming). Nevertheless the identification of elements of a buried Neolithic landscape, including artefacts and components of carbonised wood in a varied range of woods, charred hazelnut shells and the cereal crop remains at Woolwich Manor Way offer rare glimpses of Mesolithic and Neolithic human activity within the floodplain. When set alongside other contemporary evidence in the vicinity (summarised in Chapters 1 and 9) it is clear that the A13 Neolithic finds contribute significantly to regional discussions of this period. The Neolithic evidence, such as it is, appears generally compatible with patterns in south-east England more generally, in supporting suggestions of low density, moderately mobile, seasonally based activities, with a preference for ecotonal locations along channel margins. The cereal crop remains from Woolwich Manor Way contribute evidence to current debates concerning the chronology, extent and context of arable cultivation in the Neolithic. The jet belt slider from Movers Lane contributes to debates concerning long-distance movement of individuals and groups, and exchange mechanisms.

As the edges of the Thames floodplain have been periodically pushed inland and upwards by rising sea levels, areas of earlier prehistoric dry-land or terrace edge activity have been inundated, sealing archaeological sites beneath layers of alluvium. The line followed by the A13 appears to correspond broadly with the edge of the floodplain as it was in the Bronze Age. More extensive Mesolithic and Neolithic remains may well be preserved in equivalent former terrace edge situations in the Thames floodplain to the south of the A13 corridor or along the margins of tributary channels, masked by thick layers of later alluvium. Locating ephemeral Mesolithic and Neolithic sites by currently available survey methods in such deep sequences is notoriously challenging. Physical access is logistically difficult and extremely costly due to the depth of overlying deposits. In general only exceptionally large construction projects offer opportunities for archaeological excavation in this environment. Exceptionally dense concentrations of artefactual materials are likely to be preferentially detected in these situations (for example Tank Hill Road on High Speed 1, Bates and Stafford forthcoming).

Because of these difficulties, development-led investigations have increasingly focussed on modelling the alluvial deposit sequences by various geoarchaeological methods. Current approaches emphasise modelling the inundation of the Thames floodplain in the early Holocene and attempting to identify the shifting ecotonal locations that seem to have been favoured by prehistoric communities. The most likely locations for prehistoric occupation sites in particular periods can be suggested by identifying areas of what would have been higher drier ground in terrace edge situations in the Mesolithic and Neolithic. (Bates and Stafford forthcoming). Buried landscape features such as palaeochannels can also be identified and investigated by such methods; such features may have attracted prehistoric activity and acted as sediment 'sumps' which provide optimum conditions for the preservation of organic artefacts, structures and palaeoenvironmental evidence.

The A13 investigations have produced a remarkable record of the efforts of communities of the 2nd millennium BC to adapt to landscape change as the terrace edge migrated northwards and became wetter during the Bronze Age. The appearance of trackways at numerous locations was presumably driven by a need for continued or increased access through the alder carr wetlands. The structure at Freemasons Road, comprising a double row of substantial timber piles, undoubtedly constitutes the most significant Bronze Age structure uncovered in the A13 work and represents one of the largest structures of its kind in the London region. The distribution of Bronze Age trackway discoveries in the East London marshes, including a high concentration of wooden trackways and platforms in the Beckton area and a limited number of other apparent focal points, suggests that the need for

access was not evenly distributed across the floodplain.

Taken together the evidence suggests a phase of intensive but unevenly distributed exploitation of the Thames marshes throughout the Bronze Age. The main period of trackway construction appears to begin in the late 3rd millennium BC and continue to the late 2nd millennium. The dating of individual structures is often very broad, but it is possible to discern a peak in trackway related radiocarbon dates from the A13 project in the middle period of the 2nd millennium. 1500 BC coincides broadly with a period of cultural transformation across the region in the middle and late Bronze Age, seen as the point of transition to a later prehistoric world of sedentary communities, field systems and hillforts, large scale polities within complex social hierarchies and increasingly intensive agricultural and craft production (Bradley 2007, 178-202). The extent to which this transformation reflects a peak in population levels is unclear. Part of the explanation for the appearance and distribution of the trackways may be increasing population pressure in certain ecotonal localities during the first half of the 2nd millennium BC, leading to increased exploitation of the marshland environments in their immediate vicinity.

A number of key questions surrounding the trackways remain unanswered, as investigations have tended to be focused in the relatively shallow alluvial sequences near the terrace edge. Why are more trackways found in some areas than others? Proximity to a major settlement focus on the gravel terrace is one possibility. There may be as yet unknown factors which made this part of the river valley particularly attractive to Bronze Age communities. We know that the trackways ran from the terrace edge deep into the marshes, but as yet we have little notion of where they ended. Did they terminate in the marsh, or continue as far as the Bronze Age foreshore of the Thames?

Further work is also needed to relate the trackway evidence to contemporary settlement and economic exploitation on the adjacent gravel terraces. Even in this period, which is the richest in terms of archaeological evidence, no certain evidence for settlement was found in the A13 sites. However the density of remains at certain locations, particularly at Prince Regent Lane (Freemasons Road Underpass) is particularly striking when compared with the typically ephemeral and dispersed nature of Bronze Age settlement remains in dry-land contexts in south-east England. The range of features encountered, including wooden trackways and platforms, a piled timber structure, post and stake holes, pits and ditches, animal bone, pottery, struck and burnt flint, suggests that these sites are likely to have been located in close proximity to settlement sites, probably located on the adjacent gravel terrace. The varied character of the wooden trackways, and the inclusion of burnt material in their construction at both Woolwich

Manor Way and Movers Lane, point to significant, possibly seasonal habitation in the immediate vicinity of these sites in the Bronze Age. The investment in substantial timber structures, such as that at Freemasons Road, surely implies a need for frequent passage through the terrace edge landscape and may suggest more permanent settlement in the near vicinity. Unfortunately the impact of 19th century and later development along the line of the A13 is likely to have severely damaged or removed much of the evidence for these postulated terrace edge sites. In particular the construction of the Great Northern Outfall Sewer is likely to have had a significant adverse effect on the survival of archaeology along the inferred line of the Bronze Age terrace edge, although bands of relatively undisturbed deposits are likely to survive, as discovered in the A13 corridor. The areas of high potential indicated by the A13 project suggest priority targets for any future development-led investigations that may be required in the area.

Some evidence has been recovered for economic exploitation of the marshes in the Bronze Age. The A13 data, especially the worked wooden structures, provide evidence for woodland management (such as coppicing for firewood and building materials). The pollen evidence indicates increasingly open conditions and a decline in alder carr woodland in the late 3rd and early 2nd millennium, which could result either from increasingly wet conditions or impacts from livestock grazing (or a combination of the two). There is a small but gradually accumulating body of evidence for the presence of livestock, particularly cattle, in the former Thames marshes from the Neolithic into the Iron Age (see for example Carew *et al.* 2010; Jarrett 1996; Crockett *et al.* 2002). From the A13 sites, fragments of cattle and sheep/goat bone of late Bronze Age date came from ditch fills at Prince Regent Lane. Butchered cattle and sheep bones, part of a pig skull and a piece of a cattle skull came from a flood deposit at the same site. There was also a buried surface of late Bronze Age / early Iron Age date present here which included possible poaching by cattle hooves, and a possible hoof print was identified at the Movers Lane site (this volume). The small Bronze Age wattle fenced enclosure at the Bridge Road site in Rainham is likely to have been for stock management (Meddens and Beasley 1990, 243). Many sites in the area have occasional evidence for the presence of dung beetles from Bronze Age contexts, but their numbers in each instance are so low that they cannot be used as evidence for domesticated herd animals in the marshes. The Bronze Age ditches on the gravel terrace margin at the Prince Regent Lane site may have had a purpose similar to the enclosed fields found at Fengate in Lincolnshire, close to the former dryland margin of the fen (Pryor 1998). These are interpreted as the enclosed winter pastures for cattle, which, during the summer months would have been fattened up on the marshes. A gap in the record for cereal pollen in the

later Bronze Age at the Golf Drivers Range has been interpreted as evidence that stock management became increasingly important at this time, as flooding increased and trackways were constructed to maintain or improve access to the marshland (Carew *et al.* 2010), although cereal-type pollen is present further up the profile, when conditions were at least as wet. Cereal-type pollen was, however, present in later Bronze Age samples from Woolwich Manor Way, although there are known difficulties in identifying cereal type pollen as opposed to wild grasses in coastal wetlands, as discussed in Chapter 8. As is generally the case during this period in the British Isles, there is no evidence for the exploitation of wild wetland resources such as fish and birds (Carew *et al.* 2010).

The recovery of several tiny human long bone fragments, from alluvial layers which contained Bronze Age material, is of interest, although the evidence is clearly very slight and reworking of earlier material is a clear possibility. The evidence for relocation and redistribution of skeletal remains has been noted elsewhere and it has been suggested that veneration of the skeletal remains of ancestors may have played an important part in the lives of Bronze Age communities (Brück 1995; Halstead *et al.* 2001; Owoc 2001; Parker Pearson 1999). Prehistoric human long bones and skulls, whole as well as fragmented, have been noted as selectively occurring in placed deposits, practises which are also found in Iron Age and Roman contexts (Butler 2006, 38-44; Harding 1985; Merrifield 1987) as well as in the case of skulls found in the river Thames (Bradley and Gordon 1988; Edward, Weisskops and Hamilton 2010).

Many of the research questions posed in advance of the project, particularly those related to the historic periods, from Roman times on, have not been addressed to any great extent, as significant remains and datable palaeoenvironmental evidence from these periods were rarely encountered in the A13 sites and did not represent clear settlement or other focii. Rising sea-level in the Thames Estuary in later prehistory is likely to have shifted the line of the terrace edge in a northerly direction, beyond the limits of the A13 investigations. The traces of Roman and later activity encountered along the A13 are largely confined to elements of field systems found on spurs projecting from the gravel terrace into the floodplain. The relative scarcity of Roman, medieval or post-medieval archaeological sites within the A13 sites is somewhat surprising as the archaeological sites at Prince Regent Lane/ Freemasons Road Underpass, Woolwich Manor Way and Movers Lane lie along local historic routeways and at natural river crossing points.

Methodological issues

The adoption of a geoarchaeological approach has benefited the project in two distinct areas:

1. Through the implementation of a seamless strategy of investigation from desktop assessment through field evaluation to excavation and analysis
2. As an aid to interpretation in the field during assessment and excavation and to contextualise the archaeology of the route corridor within the framework of the local and regional environment.

There is little doubt that the adoption of a geoarchaeological framework for the project aided progress by providing a common theme for all stages of the investigation. The identification of sediment bodies likely to contain archaeological remains and the location of that archaeology was in part a function of following this approach. The complex interaction of different organisations at various stages of the project required a common thread to keep the investigations focussed on defined objectives, particularly at times when switching between excavators with differing levels of expertise and familiarity with the archaeology of East London, which might otherwise have impacted detrimentally on the project. A similar approach was adopted within the High Speed 1 project (Bates and Stafford forthcoming).

Secondly the geoarchaeological framework provided a basis for training and informing field staff during the excavation process. This was particularly important given the complex nature of the primary stratigraphy, which was largely controlled by natural sedimentation processes. Such conditions are familiar to the minority of field archaeologists who are accustomed to working routinely in alluvial environments, but are unfamiliar territory for many. In these circumstances it is often common practice for field archaeologists to resort to semi-interpretative 'descriptions' of deposits or to simply cease excavation when 'natural' is reached. Clearly within the context of the floodplain such an approach is flawed and limits the excavators ability to interpret the sequence.

A third avenue of geoarcheological benefit was available to the project but, for a variety of reasons, was not adopted. Although much important information about the sediments and sequences was obtained during the field and laboratory investigations, these investigations were not always conducted at a scale commensurate with the original questions posed by the excavators and archaeological analysts. The reasons for this are in part a function of cost rather than absence of evidence, as well as difficulties in pinpointing those parts of the sequences that could address the questions.

An important characteristic of this project is the extent to which it has proved possible to compare directly palaeoenvironmental evidence for landscape change with archaeological evidence at both a site-specific and a landscape level. The intention of the authors in writing this volume has been to write a report which is relevant to field archaeologists who find themselves working in alluvial environments, as well as to palaeoenvironmental and geoarchaeological specialists. Some of the decisions made in presenting the data, such as the use of interpretative graphics, and inclusion of common species names in the main report text, are intended to make the data more accessible to non-specialists.

Lessons learned

It is worth highlighting key areas where lessons can be learned for the benefit of future projects, particular those in alluvial environments:

With regard to the waterlogged wood, the usual problems of wetland archaeology had to be faced in an urban setting where the zone of construction impact on archaeological deposits was linear and restricted. Many of the excavation areas were relatively small, which caused problems in interpreting some of the timber and roundwood structures. Chief amongst these was the probable corner of a substantial artificial timber platform at Woolwich Manor Way (Str. 61).

Although specialists attended on-site as required, in certain respects unfamiliarity of many of the field staff in some of the special features of prehistoric wetland archaeology, such as the distinguishing of wood chips from bark fragments, inevitably caused some waste of resources. At the initial post-excavation stage time was spent cleaning and checking many kilograms of bark fragments for worked material. This highlights the importance of regular site visits by specialists and targeted staff training.

The most successful method of wrapping lifted woodwork for recording and sampling off-site was to place all but the smallest items in doubled ziplock bags, were first wetted and then tightly wrapped in light, black rubbish bin liners of fine plastic which clings to the wet wood. Then the worked wood was wrapped in heavier duty rubble sacks and double labelled. The inner membrane was thus protected by the tough outer covering. Material wrapped in cling film was the least well-protected and the extra handling required to unwrap this material both tended to damage the material, and was very time-consuming time. It is strongly recommended that wrapping with cling film is not used in future similar projects.

As with waterlogged wood, wherever possible, assessment and analysis of waterlogged bulk and monolith samples should proceed swiftly, since once removed from the ground delicate waterlogged material is prone to degradation and decay. Experience from palaeoenvironmental analyses in connection with this project and others with long delays between collection and final analysis, has demonstrated significant reduction in the range of pollen and plant remains present after a delay of a year or more. In some cases on the A13 project, alternative monolith sample sequences had to be selected for detailed analysis due to the deterioration or loss of key samples between the assessment and analysis phases. Any sampling undertaken should be in accordance with a written site-specific sampling strategy, with clearly stated aims, formulated within the context of the overarching project design and based on specialist advice. The responsibility for collecting, documenting, sub-sampling and curating sample material needs to be clearly set out and managed at each stage. Samples should be kept cool and dark, and stored following the latest English Heritage guidelines.

SPECIALIST APPENDICES

Appendix 1: Scientific dating results

The results of the radiocarbon dating programme are given in Tables A1.1-A1.4 and Table A1.5 presents the results obtained by Optically Stimulated Luminescence dating of sediments (OSL) (see Chapter 2).

Radiocarbon dating *by Rebecca Nicholson*

Thirty samples of bulk organic sediment, wood and charcoal were processed by Beta Analytic Inc., Florida, USA (lab. code Beta) for conventional radiometric dating or (in the case of Beta-152742 only, see Table A1.3) AMS dating. Subsequently, during the post-excavation analytical phase 34 samples of wood, sediment, charred grain, cremated bone and charred pot residues were submitted to the Scottish Universities Environmental Research Centre (lab. code SUERC (GU)) in East Kilbride, Scotland for Accelerator Mass Spectrometry (AMS) dating. Unfortunately two dates on charred residues adhering to potsherds failed, including potsherd SF12 from FRU01 (GU-18957; context 17) and a potsherd from TGW00 TR23 (GU-18955; context 38).

Where sediment (peat) samples were processed by Beta Analytic they were combusted and dated by Liquid Scintillation Spectrometry (LSC). In some cases, wood was extracted from the peat and this was dated rather than the submitted sediment. For sediment samples processed for AMS dating by SUERC, the laboratory standard methodology was used and the humic (alkali soluble) fraction was extracted and dated. The radiocarbon results are quoted in accordance with the international standard known as the Trondheim convention (Stuiver and Kra 1986). They are conventional radiocarbon ages, where 0 BP is the year 1950 (Stuiver and Polach 1977; Mook 1986). All dates have been calibrated using datasets published by

Reimer *et al.* (2004) and the computer program OxCal (v3.10) (Bronk Ramsey 1995; 1998; 2001) with the end points rounded out to 5 or 10 years. The calibrated date ranges cited in the tables, as in the text, are those for 95.4% (2σ) confidence.

OSL dating *by Edward Rhodes and Rebecca Nicholson*

A suite of 7 sediment samples, from two sections from Prince Regent Lane and Movers Lane, were collected. Samples CT1 and CT3 (see Table A1.5) were collected from a section exposed in the east edge of TP66 at the junction of the A13 with Prince Regent Road. Sample CT1 was from context 204, a sandy horizon 2.08m below the ground surface. Sample CT3 came from context 212, a sandy silt 2.75m below the ground surface. Samples CT4 and CT6 were collected from the south edge of TR6 at Movers Lane. Sample CT4 came from context 514, within sandy horizon 0.8m below the ground surface. Sample CT6 came from context 515, a sandy silt with pebbles, at 1.20m below the ground surface.

Optically Stimulated Luminescence (OSL) dates based on sand-sized quartz grains from these four samples were measured. Equivalent dose (D_e) determinations were made using a single aliquot regenerative dose (SAR) technique. Uranium (U), thorium (Th) and potassium (K) concentrations were determined *in situ* using sodium iodide gamma spectrometry. The cosmic dose rate contribution was estimated as a function of geomagnetic latitude, altitude and overburden using the formulae of Prescott and Hutton (1994). The *in situ* water content of each sample was measured and used to calculate dose rate attenuation. Full methodological details and a discussion of the results are available in the site archive.

Table A1.1 Radiocarbon results from Prince Regent Lane and Freemasons Road

Lab code	Event code	Context	OD(m)	Material	δ13C ‰	Conventional 14C yr BP	Calibrated date at 2σ (OxCal 3.10)	Period
Beta-154891	PGL00 T23	Weathered sand (20)	-0.35	Wood	-25.0	3340±70	1870BC (1.6%) 1840BC, 1780BC (93.8%) 1450BC	EMBA
Beta-153982	PGL00 T21	Ditch (46) [48] <11>	-	harred plant remains	-25.0	1770±60	120AD (95.4%) 410AD	ROM
Beta-154892	PGL00 T23	Top of peat (63)	-0.43	ood	-25.0	3280±50	1690BC (95.4%) 1440BC	EMBA
Beta-154893	PGL00 T23	Pile 182 Str.32	-	ood (oak)	-25.0	3400±50	1880BC (6.5%) 1840BC, 1830BC (83.9%) 1600BC, 1590BC (4.9%) 1530BC	EBA
SUERC-24604 (GU-18962)	FRU01 Area A	Peat (2) <111>	-0.32	diment	-28.4	2800±35	1050BC (95.4%) 840BC	LBA
SUERC-24600 (GU-18961)	FRU01 Area A	Peat (2) <112>	-0.6	diment	-26.7	3745±35	2280BC (7.5%) 2240BC, 2230BC (87.9%) 2030BC	EBA
SUERC-24599 (GU-18960)	FRU01 Area B	'Enclosure' gully (198) [199] <165>		on oak wood	-26.0	3445±35	1890BC (95.4%) 1660BC	EBA
SUERC-24598 (GU-18959)	FRU01 Area B	Pot (125) SF150		Charred residue	-24.5	3020±35	1400BC (90.3%) 1190BC, 1180BC (5.1%) 1130BC	MBA
SUERC-24831 (GU-18958)	FRU01 Area A	Pot (9) SF3	-	Charred residue	-	2740±45	1000BC (95.4%) 800BC	LBA
SUERC-24503 (GU-18859)	FRU01 Area A	Peat (2) <112>	-0.48	Sediment	-28.3	3435±30	1880BC (95.4%) 1660BC	EBA
SUERC-24291 (GU-18858)	FRU01 Area B	Stake 334 Gp 21a	-	Wood (hazel)	-27.6	3010±30	1390BC (95.4%) 1120BC	MBA
SUERC-27349 (GU-20652)	FRU01 Area A	Layer 49 'sliver' wood chip	-	Wood (oak)	-25.6	3330±30	1690BC (95.4%) 1520BC	EBA
SUERC-27345 (GU-20651)	FRU01 Area A	Layer 49 mandible	-	Bone (cattle)	-22.5	3340±30	1690BC (94.0%) 1520BC, 1730-1710 (1.4%)	EBA
SUERC-27362 (GU-20675)	FRU01 Area A	Layer 49 wood chip (93)	-	Wood (alder)	-28.0	3330±30	1690BC (95.4%) 1520BC	EBA

Table A1.2   Radiocarbon results from Woolwich Manor Way

Lab code	Event code	Context	OD(m)	Material	δ13C ‰	Conventional 14C yr BP	Calibrated date at 2σ (OxCal 3.10)	Period
Beta-152741	WMW00 T17	Base of peat (2069)	-3.19	Wood	-28.2	5510±70	4500BC (95.4%) 4230BC	LMeso
Beta-147954	TGW00 TP1	Top of peat <M3/86>	-2.04 to -2.13	Sediment	-27.8	3330±60	1760BC (93.6%) 1490BC, 1480BC (1.8%) 1450BC	(late) EBA - MBA
Beta-147955	TGW00 TP1	Middle of peat <M2/85>	-2.92 to -3.02	Sediment	-28.3	4410±70	3340BC (95.4%) 2900BC	ELN
Beta-147956	TGW00 TP1	Base of peat <M1/84>	-3.66 to -3.76	Wood	-28.9	5630±60	4600BC (95.4%) 4340BC	LMeso
Beta-152738	TGW00 TP8	Trackway 1531 (=29), intrusive from 'platform' 61?	-	Wood	-26.0	2900±70	1310BC (95.4%) 900BC	MLBA
Beta-152739	TGW00 TP9	Wood (1523) <68>, residual	-	Wood (*Taxus baccata*)	-25.7	3830±60	2740BC (94.5%) 2130BC	EBA
Beta-152740	WMW00 T16	Base of peat (2078)	-3.13	Wood	-29.2	5460±80	4460BC (78.5%) 4220BC, 4210BC (16.9%) 4050BC	LMeso
Beta-153983	WMW00 T15 EN	Layer (2008) <25>	-0.4	Charred plant remains (grain + charcoal)	-25.0	4850±100	3950BC (95.4%) 3350BC	
Beta-153984	TGW00 TP9	Trackway stake <64>	-	Wood (*Corylus*)	-25.0	3390±60	1880BC (95.4%) 1520BC	EBA
SUERC-24292 (GU-18860)	WMA02 Area 2	Trackway 2/14 (21) <3>	-	Wood (*Alnus*)	-27.6	3230±30	1610BC (7.2%) 1570BC, 1560BC (88.2%) 1430BC	EMBA
SUERC-24296 (GU-18861)	WMA02 Area 1	Trackway 50 (49) <11>	-	Roundwood indet.	-25.3	3725±30	2210BC (95.4%) 2030BC	EBA
SUERC-24297 (GU-18862)	WMA02 Area 1	Trackway 29 (62) <19>	-	Wood (*Fraxinus*)	-26.7	3400±30	1770BC (95.4%) 1610BC	EBA
SUERC-24504 (GU-18863)	WMA02 Area 1	Platform' 61 (63) <21>	-	Wood (*Corylus*)	-28.1	2945±30	1270BC (95.4%) 1040BC	MLBA
SUERC-24830 (GU-18954)	WMW00 T15	EN pottery sherd (2008)	-	Charred residue	NA	4685±45	3630BC (14.8%) 3570BC, 3540BC (80.6%) 3360BC	EN
SUERC-24597 (GU-18956)	WMW00 T15	Layer (2008) <25>	-0.4	Charred grain (*Triticum dicoccum*)	-24.0	4890±35	3770BC (95.4%) 3630BC	EN
SUERC-25562 (GU-19424)	WMA02 Area 2	Sandy peat <2B>	-0.73	Sediment	-28.4	3645 ± 35	2140BC (95.4%) 1910BC	EBA
SUERC-25563 (GU-19425)	WMA02 Area 2	Sandy peat <2A>	-1.3	Sediment	-28.2	4265±35	2930BC (83.7%) 2860BC, 2810BC (10.3%) 2750BC, 2720BC (1.3%) 2700BC	LN
SUERC-27350 (GU-20653)	WMA02 Area 1	Trackway 50 (49) <11>	-	Wood (*Alnus*)	-25.0	3635±30	2130BC (12.5%) 2080BC, 2050BC (82.9%) 1900BC	EBA

Table A1.3   Radiocarbon results from Movers Lane

Lab code	Event code	Context	OD(m)	Material	δ13C ‰	Conventional 14C yr BP	Calibrated date at 2σ (OxCal 3.10)	Period
Beta-147957	TGW00 TP39	Top of peat <30> 0.17-0.27m (superseded by GU-19428)	-0.94 to -1.04	Sediment	-28.3	3040±60	1440BC (95.4%) 1120BC	MBA
Beta-147958	TGW00 TP39	Middle of peat <34> (superseded by GU-19429)	-1.20 to -1.45	Wood	-28.3	3220±70	1690BC (94.3%) 1370BC, 1340BC (1.1%) 1320BC	EMBA
Beta-147959	TGW00 TP39	Base of peat <29> (superseded by GU-19426)	-1.87 to -1.97	Sediment	-27.7	4490±70	3370BC (90.2%) 3000BC, 2990BC (5.2%) 2920BC	EN
Beta-152742	MOE00 T5	Beaver dam (838)	-	Wood	-28.3	3010±40	1390BC (95.4%) 1120BC	MBA
Beta-152743	MOE00 T5	Beaver dam (838)	-	Wood	-28.5	2970±70	1400BC (95.4%) 1000BC	MLBA
Beta-152744	MOE00 T13	Peat (811) <137>	-0.13	Wood	-29.2	3230±70	1690BC (95.4%) 1380BC	EMBA
Beta-152745	MOE00 T13	Peat (811) <134>	-0.13	Wood	-29.2	3120±60	1520BC (94.2%) 1250BC, 1240BC (1.2%) 1210BC	MBA
SUERC-24288 (GU-18855)	RIR01 Area 3	Trackway 5268	-	Wood (Alnus)	-27.5	3275±30	1630BC (93.1%) 1490BC, 1480BC (2.3%) 1450BC	MBA
SUERC-24289 (GU-18856)	RIR01 Area 3	Stakehole Str.5247 <36>	-	Wood (Alnus)	-27.5	3370±30	1750BC (91.1%) 1600BC, 1580BC (4.3%) 1530BC	EMBA
SUERC-24290 (GU-18857)	RIR01 Area 2	Cremation (1208) Gp. 1207 <25>	-	Cremated bone	-21.1	2920±30	1260BC (3.6%) 1230BC, 1220BC (91.8%) 1010BC	EBA
SUERC-24590 (GU-18950)	RIR01 Area 3	Stakehole Str.5168 SF1145	-	Wood (Alnus)	-27.5	3125±35	1500BC (3.4%) 1470BC, 1460BC (92.0%) 1310BC	MLBA
SUERC-24594 (GU-18951)	RIR01 Area 3	Burnt mound (5083) Gp. 5264 <7>	-	Charcoal (Corylus /Alnus type)	-26.5	3070±35	1430BC (95.4%) 1250BC	MBA
SUERC-24595 (GU-18952)	RIR01 Area 2	Trackway 3031 (3010) <54>	-	Wood (Alnus)	-28.9	3295±35	1680BC (95.4%) 1490BC	EMBA
SUERC-24596 (GU-18953)	RIR01 Area 3	Stakehole Str.5168 SF180	-	Wood (Corylus /Alnus type)	-27.1	3325±35	1690BC (95.4%) 1510BC	EBA
SUERC-25567 (GU-19426)	TGW00/TP39	Base of peat <29>	-1.91 to -1.93	Sediment	-27.5	4680 ± 35	3630BC (8.0%) 3590BC, 3530BC (87.4%) 3360BC	EN
SUERC-25568 (GU-19427)	TGW00/TP39	Organic silt below peat <29> 0.40-0.42m	-2.27 to -2.29	Sediment	-28.1	5055 ± 35	3960BC (95.4%) 3770BC	EN
SUERC-25569 (GU-19428)	TGW00/TP39	Top of peat <30> 0.13-0.14m	-0.90 to -0.91	Sediment	-28.7	2860 ± 35	1130BC (95.4%) 910BC	LBA
SUERC-25570 (GU-19429)	TGW00/TP39	Middle of peat <30> 0.48-0.49m	-1.25 to -1.26	Sediment	-28.1	3330 ± 35	1730BC (1.1%) 1710BC, 1690BC (94.3%) 1510BC	EBA
SUERC-25571 (GU-19430)	RIR01 / A3	Peaty sand (5154) <40>	-0.38 to -0.39	Sediment	-28.2	3625±35	2130BC (9.5%) 2080BC, 2050BC (85.9%) 1890BC	EBA
SUERC-25572 (GU-19431)	RIR01 / A3	Organic sand (5215) <40>	-0.58 to -0.62	Wood	-27.1	3950±35	2570BC (95.4%) 2330BC	LNEBA

Table A1.4 Radiocarbon results from Canning Town and Roding Bridge

Lab code	Event code	Context	OD(m)	Material	δ13C ‰	Conventional 14C yr BP	Calibrated date at 2σ (OxCal 3.10)	Period
Beta-147960	TPAR 29 M4	0.30-0.42 Top of peat (FT3)	-0.79/ -0.89	Sediment	-28.3	3120±60	1520BC (94.2%) 1250BC 1240BC (1.2%) 1210BC	MBA
Beta-147961	TPAR 29 M7	0.27-0.37 Base of peat (FT3)	-1.94 / -2.04	Wood	-27.9	4720±70	3640BC (95.4%) 3360BC	EN
Beta-147962	TGW00 IRAR1	6.2-6.29 Top of peat (FT3)	-1.24 / -1.33	Wood	-27.5	3650±70	2210BC (94.0%) 1870BC 1850BC (1.4%) 1810BC	EBA
Beta-147963	TGW00 IRAR1	6.49-6.56 Base of peat (FT3)	-1.53 / -1.60	Sediment	-28.7	3560±70	2140BC (4.1%) 2080BC 2060 (90.1%) 1730BC 1720BC (1.2%) 1690BC	EBA
Beta-147964	TGW00 IRAR3	5.86-5.97 Organic lens in clay-silts (FT1)	-1.74 / -0.85	Sediment	-27.6	3730±70	2350BC (95.4%) 1930BC	EBA
Beta-147965	TGW00 IRAR3	6.65-6.62 Upper peat (FT3)	-1.42 / -1.50	Wood	-27.8	4480±70	3370BC (89.1%) 3000BC 2990BC (6.3%) 2920BC	EN
Beta-147966	TGW00 IRAR4	5.62-5.685 Base of peat (FT3)	-2.46 / -2.56	Wood	-27.8	4650±70	3650 (88.3%) 3300BC 3250 (7.1%) 3100BC	EN
Beta-147967	RDAR 1	4.3-4.35 Top of peat	-0.60/ -0.65	Sediment	-28.7	3180±60	1610BC (95.4%) 1310BC	EMBA
Beta-147968	RDAR 1	4.6-4.65 Base of peat	-0.90/ -0.95	Sediment	-28.1	3220±80	1690BC (95.4%) 1310BC	EMBA
Beta-147969	RDAR 4	5.81-5.87 Peat	-1.36/ -1.42	Wood	-29.5	3050±70	1460BC (95.4%) 1080BC	MLBA

Table A1.5 Optically Stimulated Luminescence dating results

Lab code	Field code	Age estimate code	Site	Event code	Context	Result yr BP
X408	CT1	OxL –1106	Prince Regent Lane	TGW00 TP66	(204)	15800+/-840
X410	CT2	OxL – 1107	Prince Regent Lane	TGW00 TP66	(212)	16300+/-820
X411	CT3	OxL – 1108	Movers Lane	MOE00 T6	(514)	15800+/-850
X412	CT4	OxL - 1109	Movers Lane	MOE00 T6	(515)	23900+/-1300

Appendix 2: Artefactual materials

Prehistoric pottery *by Alistair Barclay and Louise Rayner* (Fig. A2.1)

Three route sections (Movers Lane; Prince Regent Lane and Woolwich Manor Way) produced a total of 819 sherds (7680g) of prehistoric pottery, ranging in date from early Neolithic to Iron Age (Table A2.1). However, most of the pottery can be assigned to the phase of the early Neolithic when decorated bowl was current (3650-3350 cal BC) and to the Deverel-Rimbury and plain ware phases of the mid to late Bronze Age (1500-900 cal BC). Overall the assemblage is characterised by a high degree of brokenness and although featured sherds are quite numerous, the number of reconstructible profiles is relatively low. The overall condition of the assemblage is poor with most sherds exhibiting post-depositional surface damage.

Method

The assemblage was analysed using a standard system developed for the recording of prehistoric pottery and in accordance with the guidelines of the Prehistoric Ceramics Research Group (1992). The assemblage was quantified by sherd count (fresh breaks excluded where possible) and by weight (g). Featured sherds were noted and a selected record was made of decoration, surface treatment, average sherd thickness, diameter, firing colour, the presence of food residues and condition. Fabrics were recorded using a standardised alpha-numeric coding system where letters are assigned to the principal inclusions (A=sand, F=flint, G=grog, S=shell) and a number is used to differentiate varia-tions in the frequency and size of inclusions. In the absence of featured sherds dates were assigned on the basis of fabric analysis. The data was entered on to a Microsoft Access database.

Fabrics

Fabric descriptions are listed in Table A2.2. All of the fabrics recorded indicate that local resources were involved in production. Typically the early and middle Neolithic fabrics are predominately tempered with angular (?knapped) flint inclusions, while grog (broken pottery/fired clay or clay) is used in the fabrics of late Neolithic and early Bronze Age pottery. Calcined flint (burnt and crushed often with a blocky texture) is the temper of choice during the mid-late Bronze Age. The pattern of long-term fabric use, change and choice mirrors that of other sites within the Thames Valley. The occurrence of flint as an inclusion in much of the pottery, in partic-ular material of early-middle Neolithic and middle-late Bronze Age date, introduces the possibility that a relative small proportion of the assemblage has been assigned an incorrect date.

Charred residues and radiocarbon dating

Carbonised residues assumed to derive from the burning of food during cooking were observed on a number of vessels of early and middle Neolithic date and mid-late Bronze Age date. Five vessels with charred residues were selected for radiocarbon dating (Table A2.3). Two of the samples (context 17 sf12 from FRU01 and context 38 from TGW00 T23) failed. The other results are discussed below.

Table A2.1   Prehistoric pottery, breakdown of the assemblage by site

	Prince Regent Lane		Movers Lane		Woolwich Manor Way		Total	
	No. sherds	Weight	No. sherds	Weight	No. sherds	Weight	No. sherds	Weight
Early Neolithic – plain and decorated bowl	9	48g	186	1388g	116	918g	311	2354g
Middle Neolithic – Peterborough Ware	3	37g	68	477g			71	514g
Late Neolithic- Grooved Ware			17	159g			17	159g
Late Neolithic/Early Bronze Age- Beaker	1	8g	2	15g	13	120g	16	143g
Early/Middle Bronze Age – Biconical Urn			1	7g			1	7g
Mid-Late Bronze Age – Deverel-Rimbury/PDR	240	3419g	89	907g	4	22g	333	4348g
Indeterminate Prehistoric and Iron Age	11	56g	45	53g	14	46g	70	155g
Total	264	3568g	408	3006g	147	1106g	819	7680g

Style, form and decoration

Early Neolithic

A total of 311 early Neolithic sherds (representing a minimum of eight vessels) were recovered from three of the route sections (Freemasons Road, Movers Lane and Woolwich Manor Way, Table A2.1). Many of the sherds were assigned an early

Neolithic date on the basis of fabric and, therefore, it is possible that a proportion of these are in fact 'plain' Peterborough Ware, while others could be of mid-late Bronze Age date (see above).

Nine sherds (48g) were recovered from six contexts (49, 52, 81, 101, 118 and 136) at Freemasons Road. Featured sherds include a rolled rim from 136 and a decorated body sherd, possibly from a Mildenhall

Table A2.2 Prehistoric pottery, fabric descriptions

Code	Description
Early Neolithic	
A1/EN	Hard sandy fabric tempered with colourless and white quartz grains
AF1/EN	Hard sandy fabric tempered with colourless and white quartz grains and rare small angular flint
AF2/EN	As above but with slightly coarser (1-3 mm) flint inclusions
F1/EN	Hard fabric with generally well sorted small angular flint (1-2mm)
F2/EN	Hard fabric with sparse ill-sorted small to medium angular flint (1-3mm)
F3/EN	As above but with flint grits up to 7mm
FA2/EN	Hard fabric with sparse ill-sorted small to medium angular flint (1-3mm)
FA3/EN	As above but with flint grits up to 7 mm
LS2/EN	Soft fabric with lenticular plate-like voids probably from leached shell
Middle Neolithic	
F2/MN	Similar to F2/EN
F3/MN	Similar to F3/EN
F4/MN	Similar to F3 but with much coarser flint inclusions
FG3/MN	Similar to F3 but with the addition of rare angular grog
Late Neolithic	
AG1/LN	Hard fabric with sparse quartz sand and rare grog
F1/LN	Hard fabric with sparse fine angular flint- possibly not of this date
G1/LN	Hard fabric with sparse small subangular grog
GFA1/LN	Hard fabric with sparse subangular grog, rare fine angular flint and rare coarse quartz sand. The presence of voids indicate that some organic material has been lost (leached shell or burnt out plant matter)
Late Neolithic/early Bronze Age	
AG1/LNEBA	Hard fabric with sparse quartz sand and rare grog
GA1/LNEBA	Soft fabric with rare subangular grog and rare quartz sand
FGA2/LNEBA	Hard fabric with sparse fine to medium flint, rare grog and rare quartz sand
VG1/LNEBA	Vesicular fabric (?leached shell) with rare subangular grog
Early middle Bronze Age	
FG3/EMBA	Hard fabric with sparse small to coarse calcined flint and rare medium to coarse angular grog
Middle-late Bronze Age	
F1/MBA,MLBA,LBA	Hard fabric with common to dense fine calcined flint
F2/MBA,MLBA,LBA	Hard fabric with moderate to common small to medium (1-3mm) calcined flint
F3/MBA,MLBA,LBA	Hard fabric with moderate small to coarse (1-6mm) calcined flint
FGP3/MBA	Hard fabric with moderate to common small to coarse (1-6mm) calcined flint, sparse subangular grog and rare natural clay pellets
FA2/LBA	Hard fabric with moderate to common small to medium (1-3mm) calcined flint and rare quartz sand
Iron Age/indeterminate prehistoric	
S1/PREH	Soft sometimes brittle fabric tempered with small and often quite dense fine shell platelets. Sometimes leached
S2/PREH	Similar to above but with coarser shell platelets
NAT/PREH	No added temper/temper free fabrics

style bowl, from context 81 (SF98) (Fig. A2.1, 7).

One hundred and eighty six sherds (1388g) were recovered from Movers Lane: most were plain body sherds. The only featured sherds were two rolled rims, one recovered as a redeposited find from Grooved Ware pit 5142 (SS16) (Fig. A2.1, 5), and the other from 3004 (SF175). Of the plain body sherds notable concentrations of pottery came from T8 context 628 (44 sherds), context 121 (43 sherds), T1, context 11 (21 sherds) and context 1094 (22 sherds).

One hundred and sixteen sherds (918g) were recovered from Woolwich Manor Way. Most of the pottery was recovered from 2008 with a few additional sherds coming from 2007, 2013 and as unstratified finds from area 3 and T15. Featured sherds included a shouldered bowl (Fig. A2.1, 1), an everted rim (Fig. A2.1, 6) and a neck sherd. Three sherds from 2008 had been either overfired or refired. The shouldered bowl had sooty and charred residue below the rim and had therefore been used as a cooking pot. The neck sherd (2008 SF82) is from a fine black burnished bowl with thickened surface broken just below the rim. A thickened semi-rolled rim (Fig. A2.1, 2) from 2008 is decorated with rows of `horseshoe`-shaped motifs probably made with the articular surface of a bird or small mammal bone to give oval-shaped impressions. Rims of similar type and with this decoration occur within decorated bowl assemblages from south-east England (for example from Spong Hill: Healy 1988). There is also an expanded rim with oblique incised decoration and internal vertical burnished lines (Fig. A2.1, 3) and a plain everted rim (Fig. A2.1, 4).

Collectively the pottery could be accommodated within the Mildenhall style of the decorated bowl tradition of the mid 4th millennium cal BC (c 3650-3350 cal BC) that is generally distributed across eastern England but is also found in north Kent (see Gibson and Leivers 2008; Barclay 2008). This pottery would be broadly contemporaneous with the assemblages recovered from the causewayed enclosures at Orsett and Staines (Kinnes 1978; Robertson Mackay 1987). Small assemblages of early Neolithic pottery have been recorded at the Royal Docks Community School, Prince Regent Lane (Rayner 1997) and at Brook Way, Rainham (Holder 1998, 10) while the pottery from Yabsley Street, Blackwell (Raymond 2008), Erith Spine Road (Bennell 1998) and Rectory Grove, Clapham (Densem and Seeley 1982, fig 5) belongs to the earlier Carinated Bowl tradition (4000-3650 cal BC: Barclay 2008; Barclay and Case 2007; Herne 1988).

Middle Neolithic

Seventy one sherds (514g) can be assigned to the developed Peterborough ware style (Mortlake) on the basis of form, decoration and fabric. A minimum of six vessels are represented in total with material recovered from three route sections sites (Prince Regent Lane, Freemasons Road and Movers Lane: see Table A2.1) with most of the material (59 sherds) recovered from a single deposit, 5074, from Movers Lane (see below), a context that also produced a fragmentary jet belt slider (Sheridan, Appendix 2).

A small impressed decorated sherd came from context 95 (T21) at Prince Regent Lane and two

Table A2.3   Prehistoric pottery, selected sherds with charred residue submitted for radiocarbon dating

Site code	Lab code	Context	Date	Form	Fabric	Sample	Result BP	cal. BC
WMW00 (T15)	SUERC-24830 (GU-18954)	2008	Early Neolithic	Closed shouldered bowl	F3/EN	Soot and charred residue on exterior surface below the rim	4685±45	3630-3570 (14.8%), 3540-3360 (80.6%)
FRU01	GU-18957	17 (SF12)	Mid-late Bronze Age	Rim form a bipartite jar	F2/MLBA	Internal charred residue	sample failed	-
FRU01	SUERC-24831 (GU-18958)	9 (SF3)	Mid-late Bronze Age	Lower part of a small jar with flint-gritted base	F2/MLBA	Internal charred residue on body wall	2740±45	1000-800 (95.4%)
FRU01	SUERC-24598 (GU-18959)	125 (SF150)	Mid-late Bronze Age	Fragmentary jar. Rim, body and base sherds have thick encrusted residues on the interior surface.	F2/MLBA	Base sherd-internal residue	3020±35	1400-1190 (90.3%), 1180-1130 (5.1%)
TGW00 (T23)	GU-18955	38	Mid-late Bronze Age	Rim from a jar	F2/MLBA	External charred residue	sample failed	-

sherds with impressed twisted cord decoration came from contexts 40 (SF46) and 49 (SF114) from Freemasons Road.

The majority (68 sherds) of the Peterborough Ware sherds were recovered from Movers Lane. This includes three rims (Fig. A2.1, 8-10), a shoulder and a small number of decorated body sherds (not illustrated). One of the rims, from 5016, is from the same vessel as that from 5074 (Fig. A2.1, 8). A small decorated (bone impressed) everted rim could be from an Ebbsfleet style vessel (Fig. A2.1, 11).

The fragmentary remains (55 sherds) from at least three Mortlake Ware vessels manufactured from a coarse flint-tempered fabric (F3/MN) were recovered from context 5074 (Movers Lane). All three vessels (Fig. A2.1, 8-10) are represented by a small number of decorated rim, shoulder and/or body sherds. All three vessels can be described as closed shouldered bowls, although their rim forms and decoration show a degree of variation. One vessel (Fig. A2.1, 9) has a short slightly out-turned thickened rim with typical squared profile. The exterior surface and possibly the rim-top are decorated with short lengths of impressed twisted cord, while the interior rim surface carries an incised lattice motif. A second vessel (Fig. A2.1, 10) has an out-turned rim with an internally expanded lip. The surfaces of the rim and the exterior body surface are decorated with rows of short lengths of impressed twisted cord. Black residue, possibly charred, was observed on the interior rim surface, within most of the crescentric impressions. A third vessel (Fig. A2.1, 8) (same vessel as rim fragments from 5016) has an expanded slightly T-shaped and out-turned rim that is decorated with deep neck pits (finger-tip impressed) and rows of short lengths of impressed twisted cord. The interior neck surface is also decorated with twisted cord impressions, while the outer surface of the neck, shoulder and upper body are decorated with alternating horizontal bands of pinched finger-tip and twisted cord impressions. Beneath the shoulder the body is mostly decorated with horizontal rows of rusticated finger-pinching. A few of the small sherds from this context appear to have been heat damaged, possibly through over-firing or refiring. Unfortunately these sherds can not be assigned to one of the vessels with any certainty although they are in a similar fabric. In addition, from 1109 there was a thick-walled sherd (20mm) probably from near the base of a Mortlake style bowl with faint impressed (?finger-tip) decoration, a shoulder sherd with twisted cord maggot impressions (Fig. A2.1, 13) came from context 60, a rim with twisted cord impressed decoration from context 1094 (Fig. A2.1, 12) and two sherds with indeterminate impressed decoration also came from 1094.

The bowls recorded from the A13 are different in character from the mostly plain pottery recovered from deposits at Ebbsfleet which, at around 3550-3300 cal BC, are of slightly earlier date (Burchell and Piggott 1939; Barclay and Stafford 2008). The closed bowl forms, relatively short necks, slightly heavy rims and profuse use of impressed decoration indicate that the Movers Lane vessels belong more within the Mortlake than the 'developed' Ebbsfleet style. Similarities can be made with the pottery recovered from the ring ditch at Staines Road, Shepperton (Jones 2008) which is noted as mostly Mortlake and from the outer ditch of the Staines causewayed enclosure which is classified as Ebbsfleet ware (Whittle in Robertson Mackay 1987, 90 and fig 52: P175-185).

Mortlake ware belongs to the period 3350-2850 cal BC (Barclay 2008; Barclay and Case 2007; Peter Marshall pers comm; Gibson and Kinnes 1997) and is considered to have developed out of the Ebbsfleet and decorated bowl styles of the mid-4th millennium cal BC. There are considerable finds (75 sites) of Peterborough Ware from, in particular, the west London area (Cotton 2004, fig. 15.5), although finds from the east side of Greater London are in contrast relatively sparse. River finds of Mortlake Ware are well known and include the bowls from Mortlake, Hammersmith and Putney, while other finds are known from foreshore and eyot contexts (Holgate 1988; Cotton and Johnson 2004 and Cotton 2004).

Late Neolithic

Seventeen sherds (159g) of Grooved Ware were recovered from Movers Lane (contexts 1052, 5142, 5169 and 5189). Featured sherds are rare and include a rim and a body sherd with grooved decoration from 5189 (Fig. A2.1, 14) and a small decorated body fragment from context 5169. The pottery from contexts 1052 and 5142 can only be assigned to the Grooved Ware style on the basis of fabric and appearance. However, the relatively thick-walled sherds (11-13mm) with lightly oxidised outer surface and fabric tempered with grog, quartz sand and rare flint closely resemble other Durrington Walls style pottery from the middle and upper Thames valley. Both contexts contain flat base sherds and body sherds with aplastic paired finger-tip impressions (Fig. A2.1, 15-6). The pottery is certainly different in fabric and appearance to sherds of Peterborough ware and Beaker from the A13. The pottery from 1052 could all be from a single vessel, while that from context 5142 occurred alongside residual sherds of early Neolithic bowl (including a neck sherd and semi-rolled rim: Fig. A2.1, 5). The decorated pottery from context 5189 is different in fabric and appearance to the probable Durrington Walls sherds that are described above, although the herringbone pattern and simple rim could also be accommodated within this style (Longworth 1971). Grooved Ware from southern England has a date range of 2900-2400 cal BC (Garwood 1999; Barclay and Marshall 2011).

Beaker

A total of 15 sherds and one fragmentary vessel were recovered from three of the route sections (Freemasons Road, Movers Lane and Woolwich

Manor Way: Table A2.1). The most significant find is the upper portion (approx. half the rim) from an East Anglian style or globular-shaped vessel with zonal decoration (combed bands) (Fig. A2.1, 17) that came from a layer of peat (28, SF1 and SS4), Woolwich Manor Way. The vessel fragment had been inverted and may have been placed within the peat. Residue from the inner surface of the vessel consisted of post-depositional root matter (identified by Ruth Pelling). Two further sherds were recovered from this route section, part of a base fragment (context 01) and an all-over-comb impressed body sherd from T15 context 2007 (Fig. A2.1, 20). Three sherds were recovered from Movers Lane, a base sherd with worn ?comb impressions from 1074 area A2 (Fig. A2.1, 18); a second sherd from the same context tempered with flint could also be Beaker, and two refitting sherds from context 3005 (Fig. A2.1, 19). A single sherd from Freemasons Lane (49 SF77) is from the neck of a probable 'barbed wire' impressed decorated Beaker (Fig. A2.1, 21). It is from a straight or gently shouldered vessel rather than the globular form of the East Anglian style (Clarke 1970).

Beaker pottery was until recently rare within the Greater London area (Clarke 1970, maps 1-10). However, it is now better represented especially in east London (Jonathan Cotton pers comm). Small assemblages of Beaker pottery have been recorded at the Royal Docks Community School, Newham (Rayner 1997), New Road, Rainham, (Doherty 2010), Great Arnold's Field, Rainham (Smith 1964; Howell *et al.* 2011) and further afield at Langford Road, Heybridge where a complete Beaker and some Beaker sherds were recovered (Langton and Holbrook 1997).

With the exception of the vessel fragment, the assemblage is too small to warrant lengthy discussion. The base from 1074 could be from a globular shaped vessel, while the sherds from 3005 appear to be from a vessel with relatively sharp carination. The latter when considered with the occurrence of probable all-over-comb decoration could potentially be from an early type of vessel. The fragmentary vessel belongs within Clarke's East Anglian group (1970), which is generally distributed around the lower Thames and across the adjacent counties of Essex, Kent, Norfolk and Suffolk (*ibid* map 4). This style of vessel is unlikely to be early within the sequence of Beaker pottery (2450-1700 cal BC), although it could belong to the final centuries of the third millennium BC (after 2250 BC- see Needham 2005 and fig 13).

Early/middle Bronze Age

A single sherd (7g) from Movers Lane (context 649) could be of early or middle Bronze Age date on the basis of its appearance and fabric (FG3). This type of fabric is sometimes associated with Biconical and sub-Biconical urns that belong to the end of the early Bronze Age and/or start of the middle Bronze Age period (1800-1400 cal BC).

Mid to late Bronze Age

A total of 333 sherds (4273g) can be assigned a mid-late Bronze Age date (1500-900 cal BC) (see Table A2.1). Featured sherds indicate that both Deverel-Rimbury (1500-1150 cal BC) and post-Deverel-Rimbury (PDR) plain ware (1150-900 cal BC) forms are present. The Deverel-Rimbury pottery is mostly represented by relatively thick-walled sherds (10-20 mm) that are typical of Bucket Urn forms and, more rarely, by thinner walled sherds more characteristic of Globular Urns. The latter includes a rim (Freemasons Road context 105) (Fig. A2.1, 23) and a decorated (combed) body sherd (Freemasons Road, context 81, SF98) (Fig. 22). Numerous sherds (35, 942g) from the base of a Bucket Urn were recovered from Prince Regent Lane (3677) and a single sherd came from T21 context 91. Base sherds, a cordoned sherd and various body sherds were recovered from context 11 T1 and T9 contexts 532, 1005, 1012, 1021, 1033, 1074-5, 1160 and 5038 at Movers Lane. A second base sherd was recovered from Freemasons Road (context 81) and other Bucket Urn sherds came from contexts 303, 105, and 141.

Several vessels are considered to belong to the later 2nd millennium BC and may be considered as either transitional between the Deverel-Rimbury and post-Deverel-Rimbury (PDR) traditions (1200-1100 cal BC) and/or belong to the initial PDR 'plain ware' phase (1150-950 cal BC) (Barclay 2001, 138-9; Barclay 2008; Barclay and Case 2007; Needham 1996, 2007). These assemblages tend to be characterised by simple straight, slightly splayed or ovoid-sided jars with simple flattened or rounded rims (Fig. A2.1, 24-30). Well-developed shouldered forms such as cups, bowls and jars (see Barrett 1980, fig 5:1-5, 12 and 14) are generally absent at this stage being introduced and becoming more common from the late 11th and early 10th centuries onwards. Comparable assemblages include material recovered from Stanwell (O'Connell 1990, fig 28 and 53) to the west of the City, from Gravesend, Kent (Barclay 1994) and further afield at Weston Wood, Surrey (Russell 1989 fig 11, 25), Pingewood Berks (Bradley 1983-5) and Eynsham, Oxon (Barclay 2001).

At Freemasons Road the fragmentary remains of several plain vessels of probable splayed, straight or slightly ovoid form were recovered. Featured sherds include a small number of flattened or squared rims (Fig. A2.1, 27-8: contexts 107 and 125) and base sherds some with deliberately added flint grit and/or a slight 'foot' (Fig. A2.1, 25, 29-30: 9, 107 and 125). One vessel from context 17 (SF12) has a slight bipartite profile (Fig. A2.1, 26). Three simple rims from contexts 1033, 5019 and 5085 at Movers Lane could be from similar vessels to those described above. Charred residues within the bases and on the interior surfaces of a number of body and rim sherds indicate that these vessels were used to cook food over a hearth or within an oven. A fragmentary vessel from Prince Regent Lane (Fig. A2.1, 24) is of similar form to the above but has a

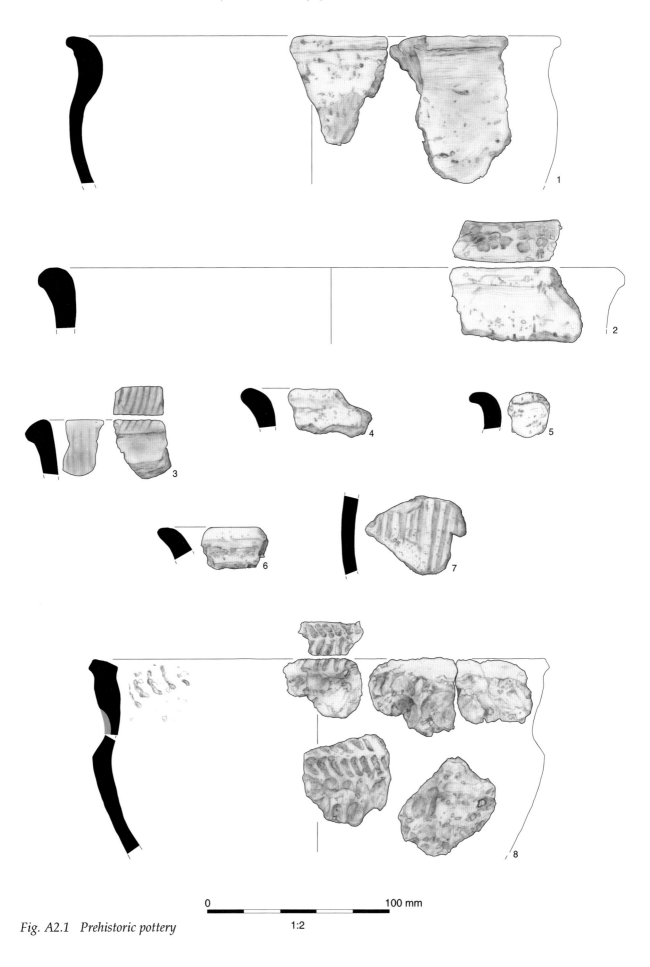

Fig. A2.1 Prehistoric pottery

0   100 mm

1:2

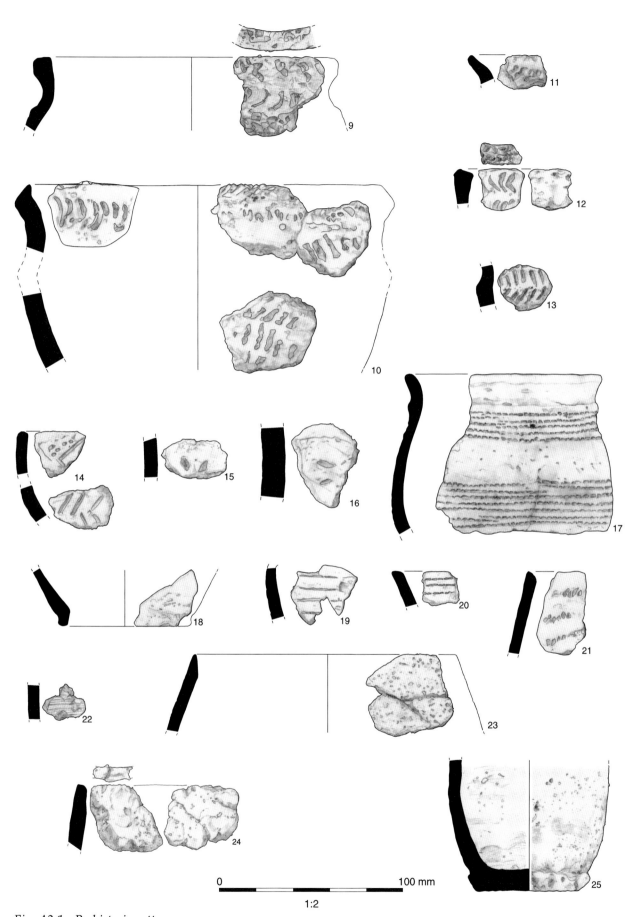

Fig. A2.1 Prehistoric pottery

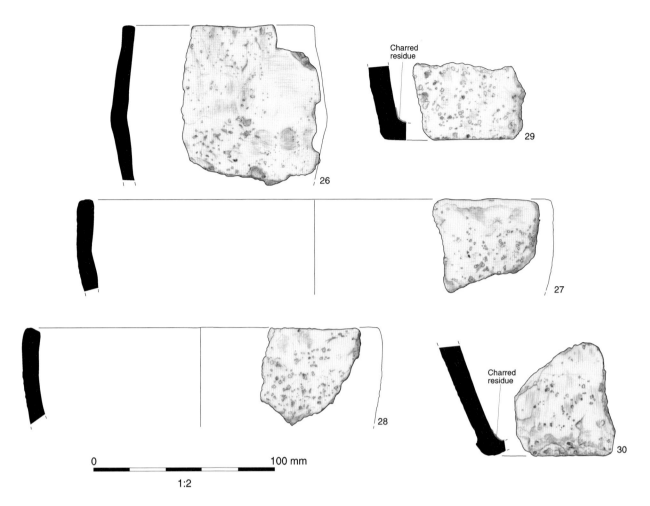

Fig. A2.1 Prehistoric pottery

notched rim. This type of vessel is also considered to be of Mid-Late Bronze Age date and can be paralleled at Gravesend (Barclay 1994, fig. 10:8) and further afield at Eynsham, Oxon (Barclay 2001) and Pingewood Berks (Bradley 1983-85, 27).

Iron Age and indeterminate prehistoric

A total of 70 sherds (155g) are of indeterminate prehistoric date; all are featureless body sherds and some may actually belong within the Iron Age. The latter includes five sherds in shell-tempered fabrics (S1-2) from Freemasons Road (contexts 47, 72, 74 and 81) and Prince Regent Lane (T23, context 63).

Illustrated catalogue (Fig. A2.1)

Early Neolithic

1. **Plain bowl, rim and shoulder sherds from a shouldered bowl of closed form** (142g). Fabric F3/EN. Colour: ext. black; core dark grey; int. dark grey to black. Burnished surfaces. Condition good. External charred residue and sooting below rim. Sample of the residue radiocarbon dated to 3630-3360 cal BC (Table A2.3). Woolwich Manor Way, T15, 2008.

2. **Decorated bowl, thickened rim sherd with impressed oval (bird/small mammal bone) decoration from a large bowl of uncertain form.** Fabric FA2/EN. Colour: ext. black to reddish brown; core dark grey; int. black. Condition good. Woolwich Manor Way, T15, 2008.

3. **Decorated bowl, externally expanded rim with oblique incised decoration on the rim and faint vertical marks on the interior.** From a **Mildenhall style bowl** of probable neutral form. Fabric FA1/EN. Colour: black throughout. Burnished surfaces. Condition good. Woolwich Manor Way, T15, 2008.

4. **Plain bowl, everted rim from a bowl of uncertain form.** Fabric FA2/EN. Colour: ext. and int. light yellowish-brown; core dark grey. Condition worn. Woolwich Manor Way, T15, 2008.

5. **Plain bowl, semi-rolled rim possibly from an S-profiled bowl.** Fabric F3/EN. Colour: ext. and int. greyish-brown; core grey.

Condition very worn. Movers Lane, 5142, SS16.

6. **Plain bowl, everted rim sherd** (8g), **originally burnished.** Fabric. Colour: ext. and int. dark grey; core grey. Condition worn. Woolwich Manor Way, T15, 2008, SF121.

7. **Decorated body sherd** (18g) **with shallow, wide vertical tooled lines and a burnished outer surface.** ?Early Neolithic, **Mildenhall style.** Fabric F1/EN. Colour: ext. greyish-brown; core and int. dark grey. Condition worn. Freemasons Road, 81, SF98.

Middle Neolithic

8. **Mortlake ware bowl, rim and shoulder sherds** (37, 195g) **from a closed bowl.** Fabric F3/MN. Colour: ext. greyish-brown to reddish-brown; core grey; int. greyish-brown to reddish-brown. Condition worn. Movers Lane, 5074 and 5016.

9. **Mortlake ware bowl, rim and shoulder sherds** (7, 40g) **from a closed bowl.** Fabric F3/MN. Colour: ext. greyish-brown; core black; int. greyish-brown. Condition worn. Movers Lane, 5074.

10. **Mortlake ware bowl, rim and shoulder sherds** (3, 69g) **from a closed bowl.** Fabric F3/MN. Colour: ext. reddish-brown; core black; int. greyish-brown. Condition worn. Movers Lane, 5074.

11. **?Ebbsfleet Ware, out-turned and everted rim with impressed bone decoration.** (1, 5g). Fabric F2/EMN. Colour: ext. and int. reddish-brown; core black. Condition worn. Movers Lane, 1189.

12. **Mortlake ware bowl, rim sherd** (5g) **from a closed bowl.** Fabric F3/MN. Colour: ext. greyish-brown; core and int. black; Condition worn. Movers Lane, 1094.

13. **Shoulder sherd** (6g) **from a small bowl decorated with impressed twisted cord 'maggots'.** Fabric F2/MN. Colour: light reddish-brown throughout. Condition worn. Movers Lane T1, 060.

Late Neolithic

14. **?Durrington Wall style, rim and body sherd from the same vessel with impressed grooves.** Fabric GVFA1/LN. Colour: light reddish-brown throughout. Condition worn. Movers Lane, 5189.

15. **?Durrington Wall style, body sherd with aplastic finger-nail impressions.** Fabric GFA1/LN. Colour: ext. dark reddish-brown; core black; int. grey. Condition worn. Movers Lane, 5142.

16. **Body sherd with aplastic finger-nail impressions.** Fabric GFA1/LN. Colour: ext. light reddish-brown; core and int. black. Condition good. Movers Lane, 1052. ?Durrington Wall style.

Beaker

17. **Approximately 50% of the rim and upper vessel of a globular shaped East Anglian type vessel.** Decorated with horizontal zonal decoration that consists of combed lines-rectangular toothed comb up to 43mm long. The rim is simple and out curves, below which is a plain cordon. Fabric VG1/LNEBA; Colour: ext. grey-reddish-brown; core black; int. greyish-brown. Condition worn. Organic matter adhering to the pottery surface is post-depositional and consist of roolets (id: Ruth Pelling). Woolwich Manor Way, 28 SF1 and SS4.

18. **Base sherd from a globular shaped vessel.** Possible worn ?comb impressions. Fabric: GA1/LNEBA. Colour: reddish-brown. Condition worn. Movers Lane, 1074.

19. **Two refitting comb impressed sherds broken at the shoulder of a carinated vessel.** Fabric: GFA1/LNEBA. Colour: ext. brown; core and int. black. Condition worn. Movers Lane, 3005.

20. **Late Neolithic/Early Bronze Age, Beaker ?upper body sherd** (3g) **with all-over-comb impressions.** Fabric FGA2/LNEBA. Colour: ext. and int. brown; core black. Condition average. Woolwich Manor Way, T15, 2007.

21. **Upper body/neck sherd decorated with short lengths of whipped cord similar impressions to barbed wire but lacking the axial incised line.** Fabric: AG1/LNEBA. Colour: ext. brown; core and int. black. Condition worn. Freemasons Road, 49, SF77.

Mid-late Bronze Age

22. **Small sherd with combed decoration, possibly from a Globular Urn.** Fabric F2/MBA. Colour: black throughout. Burnished. Condition fair. Freemasons Road, 147.

23. **Rim from a closed vessel, possibly a Globular Urn.** Fabric F2/MBA. Colour: ext. reddish-brown; core and int. grey. Interior surface had been smoothed, exterior surface is missing. Condition poor. Freemasons Road, 105.

24. **Rim and body sherds from a probable straight-sided jar with simple notched rim.** Fabric F2/MBA. Colour: ext. brown; core and int. black. Condition poor. Charred residue on

interior surface. Radiocarbon sample failed (see Table A2.3). Prince Regent Lane, T23, 38.

25. **Lower part of a small jar with flint-gritted base**. Fabric F3/MLBA. Colour: ext. and core black and int. grey to brown. Internal charred residue on a number of sherds. Sample produced a date of 1000-800 cal BC (see Table A2.3). Freemasons Road, 9, SF3.

26. **Rim and shoulder sherd from a bipartite jar.** Fabric F2/MLBA. Colour: ext. greyish-brown; core and int. dark grey. Condition fair. Charred residue on interior surface. Radiocarbon sample failed. Freemasons Road, 17, SF12.

27. **Rim, body and base sherds possibly all from the same vessel.** Simple squared rim, poss straight sided form, flint-gritted base. Fabric F2/MLBA. Colour: ext. reddish-brown; core black and int. grey. Charred residue on a number of sherds. Freemasons Road, 107, SF137-8.

28-30. **Rim, body and base sherds from at least two vessels.** Simple squared rim, poss straight sided form, flint-gritted base. Fabric F2/MLBA. Colour: ext. reddish-brown; core black and int. grey. Charred residue on a number of sherds. Produced a radiocarbon date of 1400-1190 cal BC (90.3%) (see Table A2.3). Freemasons Road, 125, SF150.

Roman Pottery *by Edward Biddulph (Fig. A2.2)*

The Roman pottery assemblage comprised some 600 sherds, weighing 11kg. Almost the entire assemblage was from Woolwich Manor Way. A single

fragment was collected from Prince Regent Lane. The assemblage was quantified by sherd count, weight, and estimated vessel equivalents (EVE). Museum of London form and fabric codes (Marsh and Tyers 1978; Symonds and Tomber 1991, 94-6) were used as the primary system, although forms were cross-referenced to the Chelmsford typology (Going 1987), which serves as a standard corpus for much of the region.

Prince Regent Lane

A large base fragment (weighing 75g) in Oxford colour-coated ware (OXRC) was collected from deposit 39, a fill of ditch 58. The base was identified as a dish (Young 1977, type C45). The form was produced in the Oxford region from AD 240. Oxford's colour-coated products are recorded in London from this date, but did not arrive in quantity in London and Essex until AD 350 (Symonds and Tomber 1991, 67, 73, 77; Going 1987, 3).

Movers Lane

A single sherd of sandy grey ware (SAND) dating broadly to the Roman period was recovered from gravel layer 832.

Woolwich Manor Way

Forms and fabrics

The assemblage was dominated by sandy grey wares (SAND), which took a 62% share of the assemblage by EVE. None of the pottery could be assigned specifically to source, but the majority is likely to be of local origin. Products recorded in the fabric included necked and bifid-rimmed jars (2G,

Table A2.4 Roman pottery assemblag

Fabric	Sherds	% sherds	Weight (g)	% wt	EVE	% EVE
BB1 Black-burnished ware, category 1	21	3%	225	2%	0.58	13%
BHAD Reduced Hadham ware	15	2%	190	2%	0.15	3%
COAR Coarse-tempered fabrics	211	35%	8506	75%	0.81	18%
MHAD Much Hadham oxidised ware	2	<1%	9	<1%	0	-
NVCC Nene Valley colour-coated ware	4	1%	9	<1%	0	-
OXID Miscellaneous oxidised wares	15	2%	95	1%	0.08	2%
OXIDF Miscellaneous fine oxidised wares	7	1%	37	<1%	0.03	1%
OXRC Oxford red/brown colour-coated ware	1	<1%	4	<1%	0	-
RWS Unidentified white-slipped wares	1	<1%	12	<1%	0	-
SAMCG Central Gaulish samian ware	1	<1%	4	<1%	0	-
SAMEG East Gaulish samian ware	4	1%	65	1%	0.12	3%
SAMLG South Gaulish samian ware	1	<1%	1	<1%	0	-
SAND Miscellaneous sandy grey wares	317	52%	2074	18%	2.83	62%
SESH South Essex shelly ware	1	<1%	4	<1%	0	-
SHEL Miscellaneous shelly ware	2	<1%	30	<1%	0	-
VRW Verulamium-region white ware	3	<1%	24	<1%	0	-
TOTAL	606	-	11289	-	4.6	-

Table A2.5   Roman pottery from context groups 1514 and 2009, AD 240-350, Woolwich Manor Way

Fabric	Bowl	Bowl-jar	Dish	Jar	Storage jar	Total	% total
BB1			0.10	0.42		0.52	13%
BHAD				0.1		0.1	2%
COAR				0.7	0.03	0.73	18%
MHAD						*	
NVCC						*	
OXID					0.08	0.08	2%
OXIDF						*	
SAMCG						*	
SAMEG	0.05		0.07			0.12	3%
SAND	0.05	0.23	0.15	2.08		2.51	62%
VRW						*	
Total	0.10	0.23	0.32	3.3	0.11	4.06	-
% total	2%	6%	8%	81%	3%	-	-

2T and 2W—Going types G24 and G28) and plain-rimmed and bead-and-flanged dishes (4J and 4M—Going types B1 and B6), which were manufactured at kiln sites along the south coast of Essex between the 2nd and 4th centuries, for example at Mucking (Jones and Rodwell 1973), Orsett (Cheer 1998, 98-9) and Dagenham (Biddulph 2007). Other forms included a high-shouldered necked jar (2N—Going type G20) dating to the early Roman period and a 2nd-century reed-rimmed bowl (4A—Going type C16). Other reduced wares arrived during the 3rd and 4th centuries from potteries in Much Hadham, which were responsible for a groove-rimmed dish (4J—Going type B3) and bifid-rimmed jar in a relatively fine fabric with burnished surfaces, and Dorset, which produced splayed-rim cooking-jars (2F—Going type G9) and flanged and plain-rimmed dishes (4G226, 4J, 4M—Going types B1, B5, B6) in handmade black-burnished ware (BB1). Coarse-tempered fabrics (COAR), reserved for large storage jars (Going types G42-44), took the second largest share of the assemblage, contributing 18% by EVE. The fabrics contained a similar mix of inclusions, typically sand and flint, but both reduced and oxidised vessels were recorded, the latter being more common. A sherd of South Essex shelly ware (SESH), dating from the mid 1st to mid 2nd century, may also have belonged to a storage jar. The miscellaneous shelly ware (SHEL) included a piece possibly from the Harrold kilns in Bedfordshire, whose products were exported widely in the 4th century.

Oxidised wares were otherwise poorly represented. A smaller storage jar (Going type G45) was made in the oxidised equivalent of sandy grey ware (OXID) while a beaker was seen in fine oxidised ware (OXIDF). Both probably had a local origin, as did the single sherd of white-slipped oxidised ware (RWS). Two sherds were identified as Much Hadham oxidised ware (MHAD), a fine fabric that arrived, like its reduced ware equivalent, during the later 3rd and 4th centuries. The fabric was largely

contemporary with Oxford red/brown colour-coated ware (OXRC), which was also present in small quantity. Nene Valley colour-coated ware (NVCC), dating from the late 2nd to late 4th century, was marginally better represented; no forms were identified from rims, although one body sherd was probably from a beaker. Three white-ware sherds (VRW) arrived from the Verulamium region between AD 50 and 160.

Imported products were represented entirely by samian, which contributed 3% to the assemblage by EVE. Most sherds were identified as East Gaulish samian (SAMEG). Two forms were recorded: a Drag. 37 decorated bowl, probably from the Blickweiler factory, and a Drag. 31 dish, possibly from La Madeleine; both dated from the late 2nd century. A single body sherd from a Drag. 33 cup in Central Gaulish samian (SAMCG), dating to the 2nd century, was recorded, while a chip of an unidentified South Gaulish samian (SAMLG) vessel was also present.

Chronology

The presence of South and Central Gaulish samian, Verulamium-region white ware, and South Essex shelly ware indicates later 1st and 2nd-century occupation in the vicinity of the Woolwich Manor Way site. However, no context group is certain to date earlier than the mid-3rd century, confining deposition at site to the late Roman period. Two relatively large groups illustrate the main trends in chronology and supply. Context 2009, a dump over a metalled or consolidation surface, contained almost 200 sherds. Jars dominated the group, but dishes made an important contribution. Deposition from the mid-3rd century is likely. The latest piece was an incipient bead-and-flanged dish (Going B5) in black burnished ware dating from *c* AD 240 to 300/330. An East Gaulish ware dish was probably deposited after the currency of the form (up to AD 240), but it need not have been out of use for very long. The assemblage from context 1514, a possible midden spread, was larger than that of 2009 and contained a wider range of material. Jars similarly dominated the group, but dishes were restricted to a single bead-and-flanged vessel. Bowls were marginally better represented than dishes, although vessels present were residual. The dish and bowl-jar (cf. Going 1987, 21-2), supported by Much Hadham ware and Nene Valley colour-coated ware, date deposition to after AD 250 and up to the mid 4th century, but it is possible that groups 1514 and 2009 were contemporaneous.

The late Roman emphasis recorded at Woolwich Manor Way is only occasionally matched in assemblages in the region. Mucking's kilns III to V, whose products may well have reached Woolwich Manor Way, were fired from the late 3rd and into the 4th century (Jones and Rodwell 1973, 39). In contrast, over half of the assemblage at Dagenham Beam Washlands belonged to mid-Roman contexts, although early and late Roman pottery was represented (Biddulph 2007). Most pottery from the Stratford Market Depot site dated to the 1st or 2nd-centuries; the presence of Mayen ware, Alice Holt grey ware, Portchester 'D' ware and Oxford products – largely absent at Woolwich Manor Way – also points to later 4th-century activity (Smith 2005, 34-5). A similar assemblage was recovered from Ship Lane, Aveley. Some 40% of the pottery from that site was recovered from deposits dated to the early Roman period. Later 2nd to 4th-century material was present, but in quantities that suggested a reduction in the scale of activity. A final ceramic phase was recorded, assigned to the late 4th century or first half of the 5th century when supply became dependent on major regional industries as local production ceased (Martin 2002, 139, 145). Given Stratford and Aveley's strong early- and latest-Roman emphases, and Dagenham's strong mid Roman phase, the Woolwich Manor Way assemblage fills something of a late Roman gap in the sub-regional ceramic sequence.

Pattern of deposition

The condition of the pottery was variable, as the assemblage comprised a mix of larger pieces and very small fragments. The mean sherd weight for the assemblage as a whole was 19g, but this ranged from 4g in context group 2003 (a dumped deposit) to 31g in group 2009. The pottery from group 1514 had a mean sherd weight of 14g. There was no clear correlation between context type and condition; the mean sherd weight of pottery from alluvial deposit 2010 was 8g, compared with 21g within alluvium 2011. Similarly, the fill of ditch 1508 contained pottery with a mean sherd weight of 16g, while the pottery from a fill of ditch 2002 had a weight of 5g. Context groups were small, containing on average 47 sherds; removing groups 1514 and 2009 reduces

the figure to 13 sherds. These factors suggest that, with the exception of the material from 1514 and 2009, the pottery was incidental to the process of deposition, generally being incorporated accidentally within redeposited soil. Given their size, groups 1514 and 2009 are more likely to represent deliberate dumps of cultural material, although the lower mean sherd weight of group 1514 suggests that the groups did not necessarily derive from the area of occupation; we may note too that the proportion of identified residual pottery was slightly higher in 1514.

Pottery use and status

The dominance of jars suggests that the vessel class served multiple functions, including storage, cooking and dining, and points to low-level adoption of forms, such as dishes and mortaria, that typify continental-style dining practices. The absence of mortaria from the albeit small mid and late Roman assemblage at Aveley hinted at an 'impoverished' community there too. In contrast, 46% of the late Roman group from Dowgate Hill, London by EVE was identified as dishes. At Chelmsford, dishes accounted for almost 20% of the Phase 6 (AD 260-310) assemblage (Going 1987, table 10). These figures compare with 8% in groups 1514 and 2009 combined. Similarly, mortaria, including late Roman Oxford forms, accounted for 7.5% of the assemblage by rim count at the nearby Stratford Market Depot (Smith 2005, 34), while Nene Valley and Oxford mortaria were present at the Dagenham Beam Washlands site (Biddulph 2007), but were entirely absent at Woolwich Manor Way. That said, the presence of a possible Much Hadham ware flagon at Woolwich Manor Way – represented by body sherds only – in context-group 2004, and decorated samian Drag. 37 bowl and dishes in various fabrics, suggests that the inhabitants were familiar with certain continental practices and had access to appropriate material.

Little evidence of vessel use was encountered. No fragments were obviously burnt or encrusted with soot or other deposit. The Drag. 37 bowl from group 1514 had a worn rim, while the Drag. 31 dish from 2009 had abraded surfaces, but it seems likely that the wear was caused by the conditions of deposition, rather than use.

Illustrated catalogue (Fig. A2.2)

Context 2009, dump over metalled surface. Group date: AD 240-300/330

1. **Hook-rimmed jar** (2W), fabric SAND

2. **Storage jar** (2V), fabric COAR

3. **Plain-rimmed dish** (4J), fabric SAND

4. **Bead-rimmed dish** (Drag. 31), fabric SAMEG, possibly La Madeleine

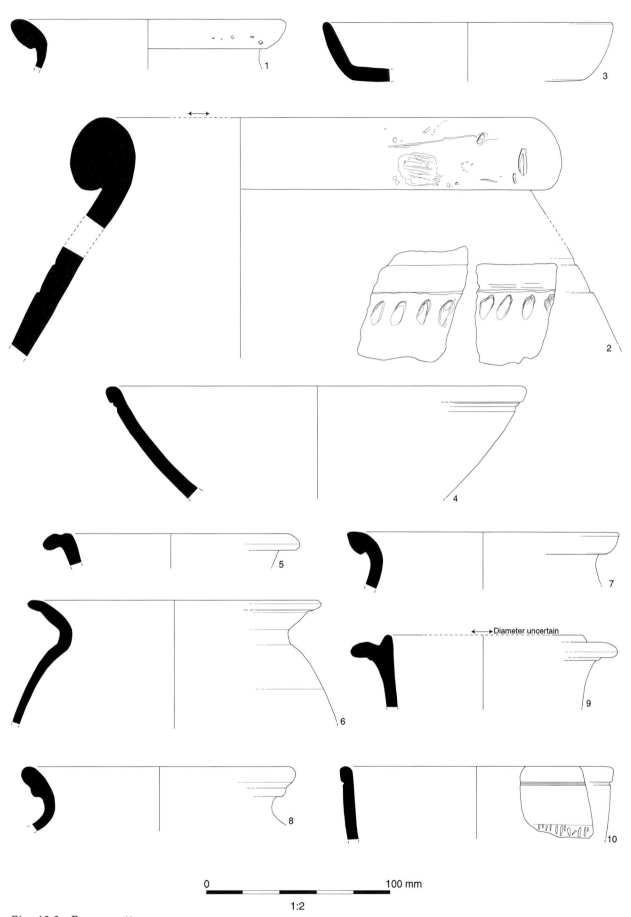

Fig. A2.2   Roman pottery

5. **Incipient bead-and-flanged dish** (4G226), fabric BB1

Midden spread 1514. Group date: AD 250-350

6. **Jar with everted rim** (2F), fabric BB1

7. **Hook-rimmed jar** (2W), fabric SAND

8. **Bifid-rimmed necked jar** (2G), fabric SAND

9. **Bead-and-flanged dish** (4M), fabric BB1

10. **Decorated bowl** (Drag. 37), fabric SAMEG, probably Blickweiler

Lithics *by Barry John Bishop* (Fig. A2.3)

Struck flint and burnt flint was recovered from three of the sites along the A13 Thames Gateway Scheme that witnessed extensive excavation: Prince Regent Lane, (PRL),Woolwich Manor Way (WML) and Movers Lane (ML).

This report incorporates and builds upon separate reports that were written for the purposes of assessing the archaeological research potential of the material following the main phases of investigations; the material from PRL, WMW and the initial evaluation at ML was compiled by the present author whilst the material recovered from the main excavation at ML was assessed separately by Wessex Archaeology. The assessment reports, which in many cases contain detailed descriptions of the material, are available from the archives. The lithic material from all of the phases of archaeological excavation including the evaluations and watching briefs was subsequently re-examined in preparation for compiling this report.

This report provides a summary description of the lithic material from each site. It continues with a description of raw material use and the typological and technological characteristics of the assemblages as a whole in order to provide an impression of the

changing approaches taken to flintworking along the route of the A13. It concludes with a discussion of the nature, extent and significance of flint-working in this part of London and how this reflects on wider schemes of inhabitation and landscape use along the terrace edge.

Prince Regent Lane

A total of 595 struck flint and over 47kg of burnt flint were recovered from the investigations at Prince Regent Lane. The majority of this lithic material was recovered during the main phases of excavation at Freemasons Road Underpass (FRU) (Table A2.6, Fig. A2.3, Plates 27 and 31). Struck flint and burnt flint was present in all but one of the evaluation trenches with no apparent decline in density along the zone of investigations, indicating that prehistoric lithic-using activities were undertaken over a long stretch of the terrace edge. Further struck flint and burnt flint was recovered during a number of Watching Briefs that were conducted during the construction works, although due to the nature of this work it was not possible in most cases to relate the artefactual material to specific contexts or to assign any observed features to an overall stratigraphic sequence.

Burnt flint

Burnt flint was found throughout the depositional sequence and testifies to the persistent use of hearths at Prince Regent Lane, even during wetter periods of peat formation and alluvial deposition. Many contexts produced burnt flint; it was mostly widely dispersed and found in relatively small quantities, suggestive of the incorporation of background waste from hearth settings. Some concentrations, such as those found in the weathered sands horizons during the excavation at Freemasons Road (FRU01), may indicate the positions of such hearths. A few contexts did

Table A2.6 Lithics, quantity of material from Prince Regent Lane by intervention phase

	Blade/narrow flake Core	Flake Core	Conchoidal Chunk	Blade	Broken Blade	Blade-like Flake	Flake	Broken Flake	Rejuvenation Flake	Micro-burin	Chip	Retouched	Total Struck	Hammerstone /Pounder	Burnt Flint (No.)	Burnt Flint (Wt:g)
Evaluation No.	1	5	15	4	2	7	38	10			9	14	105	1	882	6953
Evaluation %	1.0	4.8	14.3	3.8	1.9	6.7	36.2	9.5			8.6	13.3	100			
Excavation No.	9	32	25	27	5	16	126	76	9	1	45	29	400	1	2757	34661
Excavation %	2.3	8.0	6.3	6.8	1.3	4.0	31.5	19.0	2.3	0.3	11.3	7.3	100			
Watching Brief No.	3	4	5	11	2	3	37	10	1		8	6	90	0	711	5883
Watching Brief %	3.3	4.4	5.6	12.2	2.2	3.3	41.1	11.1	1.1		8.9	6.7	100	0.0		

produce relatively significant quantities, such as the upper fill of ditch 28 (LBA/EIA, FRU01) or the second fill of palaeochannel 22 (LBA/EIA, FRU01), both of which contained over 2kg of burnt flint which may have derived from the deliberate disposal of hearth waste. The largest quantities of burnt flint, however, were recovered from the peat horizons. Over 20kg was recovered from Bronze Age peat at Freemasons Road and significant quantities were also present in the peat recorded during the evaluation, particularly that in T23, but also within the other trenches. Further significant quantities were recovered during the Watching Brief, with over 6kg recovered from contexts 3654 and 3679. Although this later material is not closely contextable, the material was noted as coming from dark organic layers, which most likely equate with the peat formations recorded during the evaluation and excavation.

Although the quantities of burnt flint present in the peat varied spatially, it was widely distributed and it did not appear to represent specific hearth locations. Instead, it mostly consisted of large, heavily and uniformly burnt fragments and appeared to have been dumped *en masse* into the peat. The activities surrounding the creation and deposition of this material are not easily explained. Considerable quantities of burnt flint were also deposited on a linear alignment into similarly dated peat formations at the Hays Storage Depot in Dagenham and were interpreted as 'hard core' consolidation dumped onto the peat in order to allow access across it (Meddens 1996, 326). There were no indications that the burnt flint at Prince Regent Lane formed a linear alignment or that it could have aided the traversing of the peat. It is perhaps more comparable to the quantities that are produced as burnt mound accumulations where flint or other stones are deliberately burnt, such as was identified at Movers Lane (see below), and it may therefore represent the spill-over from such activities.

Struck flint

Struck flint was recovered from throughout the depositional sequence, including anthropogenic features but principally from alluvial deposits. Many of the characteristically earlier pieces are edge chipped and abraded, indicating prolonged trampling and redeposition. The later pieces are generally in a better condition and although no certain *in situ* knapping has been identified, a greater proportion of these may have been discarded directly into features or onto adjacent surfaces and incorporated shortly after.

Mesolithic and early Neolithic activity

Indication of the earliest presence at the site is provided by a residual micro-burin from MBA ditch 183; these are characteristically Mesolithic and derive from microlith manufacture although in some cases they may have been used as tools (for

example Donahue 2002). No other certain Mesolithic material was identified although a significant proportion of the overall assemblage was characteristic of Mesolithic or Early Neolithic industries. This material was concentrated within the weathered sandy soils found across the site although similar material was also recovered from later features and deposits, its condition suggesting that it had been redeposited, probably also from the weathered sands. It was perhaps most clearly represented in the weathered sands exposed in the base of the excavations at Freemasons Road (Fig. 4.6). Here the struck flint was concentrated on the western side of Area B and suggested a discrete scatter that continued to the west. A number of these pieces are likely to have been struck off of the same cores but no refitting exercises were conducted. The struck flint from the weathered sands showed no co-relation with the main concentrations of burnt flint, which were located in the northern part of Area B, hinting perhaps at the location of a disturbed hearth.

Technologically, the material from the weathered sands is blade based; blades form nearly 15% of this assemblage and blade-like flakes a further 10%. The two cores from the sands comprise an opposed-platformed blade core and a globular flake-core that had been reused as a hammerstone or pounder. Overall, this assemblage is characterised by a relatively low proportion of unusable knapping waste with a concomitant high proportion of retouched pieces, which amount to over 16%, and potentially useable flakes, which contribute a further almost 40%. This would suggest that, although some core reduction was occurring, the assemblage primarily represents tool use rather than production. The majority of the retouched component from the sands consists of scrapers (60%) with edge-retouched cutting flakes and blades also well represented (Table A2.7). Complementing these latter pieces, a number of the potentially useable flakes and blades exhibit micro-wear damage that would be compatible with them having been used for cutting soft- to medium-hard materials. A bifacially worked flake from context 106 (FRU01, Fig. A2.3.1; Plate 27, a) may indicate attempts at arrowhead manufacture and other possible arrowhead blanks were found as residual material in later phases such as flood deposit 125 (FRU01) and peat layer 101 (FRU01).

The material from the features that cut the sands includes a number of blades and blade-like flakes but these generally appear to have been residually incorporated. Pit 188 (FRU01), for example, contained 16 pieces but these are made from a variety of different raw materials, are generally very fragmented and include many burnt pieces. Retouched pieces from these features consist of two edge-retouched flakes, both probably used as corti-cally backed knifes (FRU, 162 and 66), a side-and-end scraper (FRU, 66), a bifacially worked flake (FRU, 168) and an invasively retouched flake (FRU,

Table A2.7   Lithics, retouched implements from Prince Regent Lane, all phases

Intervention	Total Retouched	Edge retouched flake	Edge retouched blade	Bifacially/invasively retouched flake	Serrated Blade	Serrated Blade-like flake	Notched Flake	Piercer Blade	Piercer flake	Long end scraper	End scraper	Crude Scraper	End and side scraper	Circular scraper	Side scraper	Scraper fragment	Combined Knife/scraper	Invasively retouched flake	Arrowhead blank
Evaluation	14	1		3			1		1		2		3			2	1		
Excavation	29	4	1		1	1		1	1	3	6	1	4	1	1			1	3
Watching Brief	6	2		2				1	1				1			1			

141). The last two possibly represent very early stages in arrowhead manufacture although this is not certain. The material from comparable deposits excavated during the evaluation was broadly similar. Suggestions of *in situ* flintworking were provided by a blade and a flake from the sands in T24 (09), which had clearly been struck from the same core.

Bronze Age

The first evidence for a change in flintworking technology occurs within deposits dated/phased as middle to late Bronze Age. It is clear that there is an element of residuality amongst this material but nevertheless, much of this material is technologically consistent with later 2nd millennium industries. The typological and technological characteristics of theses assemblages from FRU are discussed in more detail below.

Small quantities of struck flint were present in some of the features cutting the surface of the sands in Area B (FRU) but larger quantities were present in the overlying flood layer (FRU, Area B, deposit 125). This material is in a variable condition and was clearly chronologically mixed. There are many early pieces, including a possible arrowhead blank, a core tablet and a few blades, but most of the assemblage consists of crudely produced thick flakes and irregularly and minimally reduced cores, typical of industries dateable to the middle Bronze Age and after. It contains few useable flakes and only two retouched items but higher quantities of trimming flakes, flake fragments, cores and core shatter, suggesting that the assemblage primarily represents the disposal of unwanted knapping waste. All three of the cores consist of small angular fragments of rounded pebbles with flakes removed rather randomly and opportunistically, mostly using cortex or thermal planes as striking platforms, and all exhibit many incipient Hertzian cones indicating unsuccessful attempts at removing flakes. Similar material was found amongst the debris from around the piled wooden structure (Str. 32, Area A). Here, the largest assemblage came from

layer 49 and also consists mostly of preparation flakes, flake fragments and cores, with few useable flakes and no retouched pieces present, suggestive of waste discard rather than tool use. This impression is repeated with the assemblage from pit 75 (Area A), which produced ten pieces although most of these consist of small flakes, flake fragments and core shatter, along with a minimally reduced core made from a thermally fractured pebble. This is also consistent with knapping waste with little evidence for actual tool use or discard.

Many of the features recorded during the evaluation, such as ditches 92 (T21) and 129 (T25) and pit 96 (T21), contained small quantities of knapping waste and crude but useable flakes, indicating sporadic flintworking and tool use may have been occurring in their vicinity.

The largest quantities of struck flint from PRL came from the main peat formations recorded at FRU This produced considerable quantities of burnt flint and struck flint, comprising nearly a third of the struck material recovered during the excavation. It demonstrates that despite the seemingly unfavourable conditions as indicated by peat formation, activity involving the use or discard of lithic material was occurring close by. It was found throughout the excavated areas but was concentrated in the southern areas of excavation furthest from presumed drier land and suggests the peat was actually traversed rather than debris just thrown in from its edges. Most of the struck material is characterised by rather thick, often cortical flakes, and cores consisting of minimally reduced shattered-pebble fragments. Actual knapping is testified by the quantities of preparation flakes, flake fragments, cores and undiagnostic core shatter, although a high retouched component is also present. This comprised five scrapers, a possible scraper sharpening flake, two piercers, a blunted-back knife, a serrate and another possible arrowhead blank (Fig. A2.3, 23; Plate 31, a and e). Some are undoubtedly residual, such as the serrate and the possible arrowhead blank, but the dominance of scrapers and, to a lesser extent, the piercers and knife suggest activities such as hide processing were occurring in the vicinity. Spatially, only minor differences are apparent amongst the struck flint of the northern and southern areas. The northern area did contain higher proportions of useable flakes but fewer retouched implements than were present than in the south. This may indicate different activities occurring, although the size of the assemblages would preclude drawing any definitive conclusions. The silt-clay alluvial layers overlying the peat also contained struck flint and burnt flint. This is significantly less than that found within the peat although sufficient to demonstrate cultural activity continuing in the vicinity, possibly during drier periods. Half of the struck flint comprises cores; these were all made using rounded pebbles, many of which are thermally fractured. Most are minimally reduced and three may have been primarily intended as core tools, as suggested by the small size of the flakes removed. No retouched pieces were present. The distribution of burnt flint declines to the south, with a noticeable concentration within grid square 105/215. This may indicate the presence of a hearth or cooking pit but it is perhaps more likely that the burnt material had been dumped or eroded in from the north.

The peat accumulations and palaeochannels investigated during the evaluation also contained both earlier and later material. The earlier material was probably eroded from adjacent surfaces whilst the later material may indicate activity continuing during their formation. There was little evidence of actual core working amongst the earlier material but potential refittable flakes, cores and frequent trimming and primary flakes and chunks were noted amongst the later material, such as from layers 44/49 (T21).

A few of the features that were cut into these alluvial deposits contained struck flint or burnt flint, the struck flint being dominated by thick flakes and crudely reduced cores. Much of this was found in small quantities and is likely to represent background waste, but an exception to this was the material present in the upper fill of ditch 28 (FRU, 27) which comprised 16 struck flints and over 2kg of burnt flint. The struck flint include most of the stages from the reduction sequence and similarities in the cortex and flint colour suggest that the bulk of this may have originated from a few discrete knapping episodes, although no refittable pieces were identified. It is possible that this material was redeposited from the underlying alluvial deposits but it is perhaps more likely that that the upper fills of this ditch were used for the disposal of waste, including burnt flint and the products from limited knapping episodes.

Another possible exception was the material from the second fill of palaeochannel 22 (FRU). This contained over 2kg of burnt flint and eleven struck pieces, including four cores. Two of the cores are minimally reduced, with small flakes removed from thermally fractured pebbles or possibly even large

flakes; one consists of a more extensively reduced rounded pebble while the fourth consists of a flint nodule arguably obtained directly from the chalk (rather than from a secondary source) which has only a few flakes removed. This last piece is somewhat puzzling; it had clearly been imported to the site and may represent a 'tested nodule' or cached piece of raw material. Its shape, which is mostly formed by narrow nodular protuberances, would preclude any extensive reduction and it would seem that the effort expended in bringing it to the site would have been unproductive in terms of its knapping potential. It is quite possible, therefore, that the piece fulfilled some function other than supplying raw material for flint knapping. The depositional history of this assemblage is also uncertain. It may have been redeposited into the palaeochannel through erosion of earlier deposits although some similarities in the technology, flint colour and cortex type may at least tentatively suggests that it represents an homogenous assemblage deliberately dumped into the palaeochannel.

Woolwich Manor Way

A total of 233 struck flints and just under 7kg of burnt flint fragments were recovered from the investigations at Woolwich Manor Way (WMW). Virtually all was recovered during the evaluation with only three struck flints and 681g of burnt flint retrieved during the excavation of the wooden structures.

The lithic material was present in all of the three principal deposits that were identified; the weathered sand horizons, the overlying peat formation and the post-prehistoric deposits and features that cut in to the peat (Table A2.8; Fig. A2.3, 2-7, 10; Plates 25 b and c; Plate 27 b-h). The bulk of the struck flint and a small quantity of burnt flint came from the weathered sand horizons, occupation upon which can be dated to the early Neolithic. Significant quantities of struck flint were also recovered from the overlying peat formation and the post-prehistoric features. The condition of this material and its typological and technological similarities with the material from the weathered sands suggests that the bulk of it probably derives from the same broad phase of activity and may have eroded or been displaced from comparable near-by deposits.

Burnt flint

Distribution of the burnt flint shows a different depositional pattern to that of the struck flint. Whilst it was also present throughout the depositional sequence, the largest quantities came from the peat horizons followed by the post-prehistoric features (see Table A2.8). The burnt flint from within the weathered sands consists of small variably burnt pebbles, typical of incidentally burnt flint clasts and indicative of small campfires or hearth settings. The quantities from the later phases,

Table A2.8   Lithics, quantification of material from Woolwich Manor Way

	Blade/Narrow flake Core	Flake Core	Conchoidal Chunks	Blade	Broken Blade	Blade-like Flake	Flake	Broken Flake	Rejuvenation Flake	Chip	Retouched	Total Struck	Burnt Flint (No.)	Burnt Flint (Wt:g)
Weathered Sands No.	0	2	7	18	9	11	59	3	3	4	9	125	21	185
Weathered Sands %	0.0	1.6	5.6	14.4	7.2	8.8	47.2	2.4	2.4	3.2	7.2	100		
Peat No.	2	2	3	9	7	4	30	0	1	1	5	64	290	4336
Peat %	3.1	3.1	4.7	14.1	10.9	6.3	46.9	0.0	1.6	1.6	7.8	100		
Post-Prehistoric Deposits No.	2	0	3	5	8	3	17	0	1	0	5	44	189	2190
Post-Prehistoric Deposits %	4.5	0.0	6.8	11.4	18.2	6.8	38.6	0.0	2.3	0.0	11.4	100		

however, consist of larger pieces that were generally more heavily and uniformly burnt. This would be more typical of the deliberate burning of flint, a practice documented from the Mesolithic through to the historical period. In this instance it is comparable to the pattern seen at PRL, where large quantities of deliberately burnt flint were deposited into the peat during the Bronze Age and possibly has a comparable origin to the masses of burnt flint identified as forming a 'burnt mound' accumulation at ML. The stratigraphic position and radiocarbon dates for the peat that produced the largest quantities of burnt flint (WMW, 2070) in T17, may actually indicate activity dating to the later Mesolithic period and recalls the similar, although more extensive, deposits recorded at Spine Road in Erith or Tank Hill Road in Purfleet (RPS Clouston 1997; Leivers *et al.* 2007).

Struck flint: the early Neolithic flint scatter

The material from the weathered sands probably represents relatively well-preserved surface deposited material. Most came from T15 with only single pieces recovered from the weathered sands in T13 and Area 2. The burnt flint from the sands had

a slightly wider distribution, being also present in T16 and Area 1. This restricted distribution is suggestive of a discrete spread or dump of cultural material, centred in the vicinity of T15. The full knapping sequence is represented and similarities in the raw materials used suggest that many pieces may have come from the same cores, although no pieces could be successfully refitted. The material is mostly in a good, sharp, condition although around a third of the pieces show some edge chipping or rounding, there is a relatively high degree of breakage and around 10% of the struck assemblage is burnt. The somewhat variable condition of the assemblage and the lack of refits means that it is not entirely clear whether it represents a more-or-less *in-situ* knapping scatter or a dump of curated or 'middened' material, such as those recorded at other sites along the margins of the Thames, for example by Lamdin-Whymark (2008). The possibility that the assemblage had experienced some redeposition is supported by the fact that, although the full sequence is represented, there is a paucity of small chips and shatter which should be present in considerable numbers had the area witnessed *in situ* knapping.

Table A2.9   Lithics, retouched implements from Woolwich Manor Way

	Total retouched	Edge retouched flake	Serrated flake	Serrated blade	Serrated blade-like flake	Notched blade	Bifacially flaked knife	Truncated blade	Piercer blade	End scraper	Denticulated Scraper	Combined knife / scraper	Leaf-shaped Arrowhead / blank
Weathered sands	9		2	1	1	1				1	2	1	
Peat	5	2		1	1		1						
Post-prehistoric deposits	5				1			1	1	1			1

The material from the weathered sands is technologically homogeneous and similar to the bulk of the material recovered from the peat and the later features. It is predominantly blade-based. Blades contribute over 21% and blade-like flakes a further 8.8% of the assemblage from the weathered sands, and even higher proportions are present amongst the material from the peat and later features. The flakes and blades are generally small, few complete pieces attained dimensions of over 50mm and over half of the complete flakes and blades from the weathered sands are under 30mm long and 20mm wide. The typological and technological characteristics of the struck flint from the weathered sands are described in more detail below.

Only two cores were recovered from the weathered sands, both manufactured from locally available raw materials and abandoned after a few flakes had been removed. Six others were recovered from the peat and later features; all had been extensively reduced, producing blade and narrow flakes.

The flakes and blades suggest that many of the cores used had been brought to the site and any still-serviceable cores appear to have been taken away for use elsewhere, the cores remaining at the site being exhausted or unsuitable for further flake production (eg WMW00, 2005: Fig. A2.3, 7 and Plate 27, e). The flakes and blades had mostly been removed from small single-platformed cores. Interestingly, many of the flakes and blades retain narrow bands of cortex along one of their lateral edges, which may have aided their handling and potential use as cutting flakes. Nine retouched implements were recovered from the weathered sands, representing a relatively high 7.2% of the assemblage from these deposits. Similarly high percentages of retouched implements were recovered from the overlying peat and the post-prehistoric deposits (Table A2.9). The retouched pieces from the weathered sands are dominated by serrated pieces and scrapers, two of the three present being denticulated types (WMW00, 2008: SF138 and SF216; Fig. A2.3, 3-4; Plate 27, c-d). A similar range is seen amongst the retouched pieces from the peat and post-prehistoric features. Of interest are an unfinished leaf-shaped arrowhead from WMW (WMW00, 2001: Fig. A2.3, 5; Plate 25, c) and an obliquely truncated blade WMW (WMW00, 2005: Fig. A2.3, 6; Plate 25, b). Although this latter piece could technically comprise a microlith and therefore indicate a Mesolithic presence at the site, it is perhaps more likely to represent a piercer made using a snapped blade.

Struck flint: use-wear

During the excavations the potential suitability of the struck flints for displaying micro-wear traces was realised and a large proportion of the struck flints were bagged separately and not washed. It subsequently became apparent that the material from the peat and post-prehistoric features had been largely redeposited and it was decided that these would not be conducive for micro-wear analyses. Although it is not certain if the assemblage from the weathered sands was strictly *in situ*, it is in sufficiently good condition to warrant low-power micro-wear analysis following the methodology of Tringham *et al.* (1974). Many of the struck flints from the weathered sands are in a sharp condition but others had experienced some abrasion from movement within its sandy burial matrix and micro-spalling from factors such as trampling and settling, which precluded positive identification of deliberate use-wear.

In total, 86 randomly selected flakes and blades from the weathered sands were examined for potential micro-wear traces. Of these, six are formally retouched and display damage demonstrating they had been used (2 scrapers and 4 serrates), 37 are either burnt or exhibit random and sporadic edge damage considered to be caused by post-depositional processes, such as being shaken with other flakes, during excavation or through trampling (Newcomer 1976; Moss 1983), leaving 43 pieces in sufficiently adequate condition to enable the identification of potential micro-wear traces. Of these, 24 pieces (55.8%) show no evidence of having been used, although it is entirely possible that some or all had been used but not for tasks or for sufficiently long enough to leave traces.

Six types of micro-wear have been identified on the 19 pieces (44.2%) that do show evidence of potential use (Table A2.10). The precise causes of this damage cannot be determined but it is possible to suggest the kinds of actions and materials that may have been involved. Bifacial spalling is most likely to occur through longitudinal cutting- or sawing-type motions, whilst unifacial spalling is most likely to be produced from working the flint's edge at transverse angles to the material, such as through scraping, whittling, shaving or planning. Multifaceted spalling is caused by rotational movement on the tips of converging edges, such as might be caused by using the pieces for piercing. The types of material worked may be suggested by the severity of damage occasioned to the flake. The heaviest spalling, which included a degree of edge crushing, would most likely be caused by working hard materials, such as seasoned wood, bone or antler, whilst light or medium damage could have been caused by working softer materials such as meat, skin, plants or soft wood. The edge rounding observed on one flake may have been caused by the prolonged cutting of materials that have an abrasive element, such as silica-rich plants that include cereals, grasses and rushes. Other flakes from the peat deposits also exhibit clear traces of edge rounding.

The results suggest that a number of activities are represented. Most commonly indicated are cutting, whittling or scraping soft to medium materials, as represented by 12 of the 19 utilized pieces, followed by the scraping of harder materials, represented by four pieces, with piercing

Table A2.10   Lithics, results of the micro-wear analysis on the struck flint from the weathered sands from Woolwich Manor Way

Edge wear description	Blade	Blade Fragment	Blade-like Flake	Flake	Flake Fragment
Medium bifacial micro-spalling and edge smoothing				1	
Light bifacial micro-spalling	1		1		
Heavy unifacial micro-spalling and edge crushing	2			1	1
Medium unifacial micro-spalling		1		5	
Light unifacial micro-spalling	1		1	1	
Multifaceted micro-spalling around a point	2		1		
Total	6	1	3	8	1

indicated by three pieces. Nearly all of the utilization traces were recorded on lateral margins with a few flakes exhibiting micro-wear on their distal termination where this provided a suitably long stretch of the required edge. The three pieces used for piercing all had micro-wear traces on their converging distal ends.

The types of activities indicated broadly complement the range of retouched types, which are dominated by cutting and scraping-type tools. No piercing tools are present amongst the assemblage from the weathered sands but piercers are present amongst the material from the peat and post-prehistoric deposits. Blades and flakes with acute converging distal ends would make good piercing tools without modification and thus may be under represented among formal tool inventories. The proportions of pieces displaying edge wear and the range of activities represented is broadly comparable to that recorded for a similarly dated assemblage from Ebbsfleet (Lamdin Whymark forthcoming a).

Movers Lane

The investigations at Movers Lane (ML) resulted in the recovery of 820 struck flints (Table A2.11; Fig. A2.3; Plates 25, 29 and 31). The majority of these, 573 pieces, were recovered during the main excavations (RIR), with the remainder recovered during

the preceding evaluation (MOE). Considerable quantities of burnt flint are also present. By far the largest came from a single feature, a deposit of burnt flint possibly originating from a burnt mound feature at RIR.

Burnt flint

The greatest quantities of burnt flint from any of the A13 investigations were present as deposit 5264, from which over 82kg (including material recovered during the evaluation, MOE 56/516) was collected. Two associated pits (RIR 5084 and 5088) produced a further 5kg. This deposit clearly represents the dumping of large quantities of deliberately burnt flint close to the palaeochannel and represents important evidence for pyrotechnical activities during the later Bronze Age, it being comparable to a number of 'burnt mound' accumulations found along the margins of the Thames and its tributaries, (see for example Bowsher 1991 and Moore *et al.* 2003).

The majority of the remaining burnt flint recovered during the investigations at ML was distributed in small quantities within a wide range of contexts and this most probably represents general background waste and redeposited material from the burnt flint spread (RIR, 5264). A few features contained higher quantities (RIR, layer 5192 and gully 5159), which may represent the deliberate discard of hearth waste.

Table A2.11   Lithics, quantification of material from Movers Lane

Intervention	Blade/narrow flake Core	Flake Core	Conchoidal Chunk	Blade	Broken Blade	Blade-like flake	Flake	Broken Flake	Rejuvenation Flake	Chip	Retouched	Total Struck	Hammerstone/pounder	Burnt Flint (No.)	Burnt Flint (Wt:g)
MOE No.	1	12	22	22	9	12	108	32	1	13	15	247		1034	5235
MOE %	0.4	4.9	8.9	8.9	3.6	4.9	43.7	13.0	0.4	5.3	6.1	100			
RIR No.	6	19	41	29	17	19	215	147	6	19	54	573	1	?	>88kg
RIR %	1.0	3.3	7.2	5.1	3.0	3.3	37.6	25.7	1.0	3.3	9.4	100	0.2		

Struck Flint

The assemblage from ML is chronologically mixed and was clearly manufactured over a long period, with chronologically diagnostic pieces indicating activity occurring at the site from at least the later Mesolithic and continuing into the latter part of the Bronze Age. It was recovered from a variety of contexts with the majority of pieces present within various naturally formed alluvial deposits, including the fills of palaeochannels. The condition and technological characteristics of much of this material suggests that it had been produced over a long period and subsequently washed or eroded in during the formation of these various deposits.

Struck flint was also present in a wide range of features of prehistoric date although usually only in small numbers and, as with the assemblages from the alluvial deposits, in many instances the material's condition and technological characteristics suggests that it originated from earlier phases of activity at the site and had been residually incorporated. The assemblage mostly consists of undiagnostic flakes and pieces of knapping waste, which combined with the problems of widespread residuality, meant that only a few features contained assemblages of good interpretational value. No evidence of any intentional or patterned deposition was identified and, in general, the material suggested incorporation through casual loss and accidental redeposition.

Struck flint: Mesolithic and early Neolithic

The earliest activity at the site is indicated by the presence of a rod-shaped microlith of later Mesolithic date (Jacobi 1978; Switsur and Jacobi 1979), recovered from unstratified contexts from Movers Lane T5 (MOE00: Fig. A2.3, 13; Plate 25, a). No other unequivocal Mesolithic material is present but a high proportion of the overall assemblage, probably more than half, is the product of a blade-based technology of probable Mesolithic or early Neolithic date. Two flakes, one of opaque grey flint and the other of opaque brown flint (RIR01, 1064 and MOE00, 774), have polished dorsal surfaces and indicate the reuse of at least two Neolithic polished implements, most probably axes. There is

also a high proportion of Mesolithic or early Neolithic retouched implements amongst the overall assemblage, these being comparable to the range of tools identified at PRL and WMW, including simple edge-retouched blades, serrated implements and various types of scrapers (Table A2.12).

Although Mesolithic or early Neolithic struck flint was widely present across the site, few features of this date could be identified as containing *in situ* or directly associated assemblages. The features initially identified as Neolithic during the assessment stage did sometimes contain struck flint of broadly contemporary date, such as tree-throw hollow 1093 (RIR01) which contained 15 struck flints, including a serrated blade exhibiting silica polishing, a small long-end scraper with blunted margins, and a badly thermally-flawed opposed-platformed core. However, as with the assemblages recovered from the other 'Neolithic' features, these pieces were manufactured from many different raw materials and their condition would indicate that they had been exposed for some time before being deposited into the feature. It is certainly possible that this material originally comprised scatters located along the terrace edge, comparable to those identifiable at PRL and WMW, although much of it had been evidently been disturbed.

Struck flint: later Neolithic/Early Bronze Age

Activity dating to the later Neolithic is represented by a petit-tranchet type transverse arrowhead (Green 1980) recovered from a later Bronze Age layer (MOE00, 60; Fig. A2.3, 15), whilst Beaker/early Bronze Age industries are indicated by the presence of a finely made Sutton B or Conygar Hill type barbed and tanged arrowhead (ibid.) from the reworked brickearth in Area 2 (RIR01, 1033: Fig. A2.3, 16; Plate 25, e). No other truly diagnostic pieces from these periods were identified but there is a high proportion of scrapers amongst the overall assemblage and, whilst scrapers are notorious difficult to date, a number of these are small, oval or circular in shape and with semi-invasive retouch around a good proportion of their circumference. Such characteristics are most commonly encountered in later Neolithic and early Bronze Age examples, as exemplified by the 'thumbnail' types

Table A2.12 Lithics, retouched implements from Movers Lane

Intervention	Total Retouched	Edge retouched flake	Edge retouched blade	Serrated Flake	Serrated Blade	Serrated Blade-like flake	Notched Flake	Bifacially flaked Knife	Microlith	Flakes from polished implement	Piercer Blade	Piercer flake	Long end scraper	Scraper fragment	End scraper	End and side scraper	Circular scraper	Side scraper	Denticulated Flake	Barbed and Tanged Arrowhead	Transverse Arrowhead
MOE	15	2		1	3	1	4	1	1	1					1						1
RIR	54	16	6		7		1			1	1	3	3	1	3	4	2	3	2	1	

that these closely resemble. A further possible implement of this period is a semi-invasively flaked knife made on a large curved blade and with a finely facetted striking-platform, recovered from Neolithic or early Bronze Age pit (MOE 121, Fig. A2.3, 14; Plate 29, a). This is a rather unusual implement but is perhaps most closely matched with the elaborate knives of the later Neolithic or early Bronze Age, such as the plano-convex types.

Again, no cut features of this date contained what could be reliably considered as contemporary flintwork. Some, such as hollow 1171 (RIR01) contained a few pieces with later Neolithic or early Bronze Age characteristics but the general paucity of diagnostic implements and the real possibility of residuality means that no integral assemblages were identified from any of the cut features. A small remnant of alluvium (RIR01, 300), however, contained potentially related struck flint and may represent a scatter or dump of knapping debris and discarded tools (RIR01, 3005, Fig. A2.3, 17-20; Plate 29, b-e). The assemblage consists of two refitting decortication flakes, three scrapers, an edge trimmed flake and a globular flake core. None of the flintwork is particularly chronologically diagnostic but two of the scrapers are typical of later Neolithic and early Bronze Age types whilst the core would not be out of place in assemblages of this date.

Struck flint: middle and late Bronze Age

Despite the paucity of diagnostic pieces and the problems of residuality, it is clear that a significant proportion of the overall assemblage retains characteristics of later prehistoric industries, those dating to the latter part of the second and the first millennium BC.

As with the overall assemblage, much of this was recovered from the later Bronze Age alluvial deposits, some of which contained significant quantities of struck flint, although in all of these cases there were many earlier pieces also present. The later material's condition suggests that, on at least some occasions, active channels and wet areas may have been used to dump the struck flint, although no discrete deposits were noted and much of this material may have been eroded into the alluvium along with the earlier pieces. A possible exception to this may be the struck flint recovered from around the wooden structures in the eastern palaeochannel (RIR 3001). The underlying primary silt-clays within this palaeochannel (RIR 3003) produced an assemblage of 29 pieces, which includes a narrow flake core and several blades, three of which had been trimmed along their edges. The majority of these are of Mesolithic or early Neolithic date and the assemblage is predominantly in a good condition, suggesting that, if not dropped directly into the channel as it was infilling, they must have been washed in from a near-by land surface. From the peat overlying the wooden structures is a small assemblage comprising 26 struck

pieces. Some of these are similar to the material from the lower silt-clays, such as a further edge-retouched blade, but most consist of small thick flakes along with two irregularly reduced flake cores, one of which may have been used as a scraper. These are likely to be at least broadly contemporary with the structures although whether these too were residual or represented activities associated with the construction and use of the structures is less certain.

Contemporary activity beside the palaeochannels is somewhat better attested. The burnt flint spread (RIR 5264, contexts MOE 56, 516; RIR 5017, 5018 and 5083) contained 61 struck pieces including a few with early characteristics that had been burnt, but most were technologically homogeneous and typical of later 2nd millennium BC industries. These include many 'squat' flakes with the retouched implements being limited to a notched flake, two large denticulated flakes and two crudely edge trimmed flakes. There are two cores that had had a few flakes removed along one edge, resulting in wedge-shaped pieces which may have been used as tools. Many of these pieces were made from similar pieces of raw materials and a lot of small chips and fragments of knapping shatter are present, suggesting that the deposit may represent waste from both knapping and tool use, although refitting was not successful and most pieces did show some post-depositional abrasion. The deposit also produced a large (465g) weathered but unrolled flint nodule, reminiscent of that from one of the palaeochannels (FRU 22) at PRL (see above).

A large artefact scatter was located within the eastern palaeochannel (RIR 5142). This produced 90 struck flints, nearly all consisting of 'squat' flakes and crudely worked flake cores, the latter mostly consisting of split rounded pebbles each with a few flakes removed, some of which may have been intended as core-tools. Retouched pieces consist of three irregular scrapers, a long angular chunk of flint that had been modified to form a large spur-like piercer, and an edge trimmed blade-like flake, possibly a blunted-back knife, that may be residual. Recalling the nodule from the burnt deposit 5264, there is also a large fragment from a 'bullhead bed' nodule, along with a flake that refitted onto it.

Features associated with the later Bronze Age occupation rarely produced more than a few struck pieces and the material from those that did usually included evidently earlier pieces, with the overall condition of the struck flints indicating a high degree of residuality. This is evident amongst most of the 25 pieces recovered from ditch 620 (MOE 630) although in this case the presence of three refitting fragments from a core, probably a scraping-type core tool, may indicate flint use occurring in the vicinity whilst the ditch was open. Contemporary flint use may also be indicated by the assemblage from pit 5188 (RIRR). The 16 pieces included a number that, whilst not actually refittable, may have derived from the same core. These include an irregular flake core, a scraper with retouch truncating the flake's bulbar end and three thick edge-trimmed flakes. Pit 814 (MOE) also produced an unweathered flint nodule weighing just under 2kg that must have been obtained directly from the chalk. It has a few flakes removed but is otherwise intact and comparable to the other two nodules recovered from Bronze Age deposits at the site (see above).

Characteristics of the lithic industries

Raw materials

The raw materials used for the lithic assemblages at the three sites all consists of flint but this varied considerable in texture and quality. They can be divided into two basic types, both of which were represented at all three sites. The first comprise small smooth-rolled pebbles and cobbles of coarse-grained 'sugary' or 'stony' cherty flint of a variety of colours. Due to the presence of thermal faults and the frequent presence of impurities, these tended to shatter rather than flake cleanly, restricting the possibility of prolonged or systematic reduction. The limitations in their flaking ability appear to have been offset by their ubiquity within the local gravel terraces, as should one piece fail it could easily be replaced. The second type comprises nodular fragments of black, brown or grey translucent or mottled 'glassy' flint with a thick rough cortex, and include flint from the 'Bullhead Beds' (Shepherd 1972). These also contain thermal flaws but are generally of superior knapping quality. They may have been harder to source. Some, such as a distinctive speckled grey flint found at WMW, may have been obtained directly from the chalk. Most, however, had cortex indicative of origins within derived deposits but which had not experienced any significant alluvial rolling (Gibbard 1986). It suggests that a number of different sources were exploited, including localised patches within the local terrace gravels, glacial tills which occur to the north of the site and mass-weathered chalk deposits which are present about 15km to the east at Purfleet or a similar distance to the south along the North Downs. All sources would have been easily accessible via the Thames and its tributaries.

Where it has been possible to assess chronological preferences in the different types of flint used, it is evident that there is some overlap. The early Neolithic assemblages from the weathered sands at WMW and PRL include good quality flint from a number of different sources but these are complemented with pebbles from the local terrace deposits. The later assemblages from PRL and ML, most of which was of later Bronze Age date, are dominated by the use of the locally available pebble flint, although occasional use of the better quality types is evident, this possibly even involving the reuse of

cores and large flakes encountered as relict material from the earlier occupations at the sites.

One intriguing aspect of the later Bronze Age assemblage is the presence of three large and unrolled flint nodules found in different contexts at ML and a similar nodule found at PRL. Each have at most a few flakes removed and are not further worked. They are all of different types of flint and must have been imported to the site. They were unlike the raw materials used for the contemporary struck flint assemblage, which predominantly used low knapping quality pebbles and cobbles from the local terrace deposits. It is possible that they were residual from earlier periods of activity, perhaps representing 'caches' of raw material, as they were comparable to the raw materials used for the Mesolithic or early Neolithic industries. Alternatively, there may be a less prosaic explanation for their presence. Imported but more-or-less unworked nodules appeared to have been intentionally deposited in pre-Iron Age pits at Lefevre Walk in Bow (Brown *et al.* forthcoming) as well as at the late Iron Age site at Iwade in north Kent (Bishop and Bagwell 2005). In the latter case, some of the nodules are very fragile and it is clear that these had been deposited with some care and formality. Prosaic explanations for their deposition are hard to reconcile and it is possible that they represent symbolic or metaphorical objects or materials used in ceremonial practices.

Technology

Mesolithic and/or early Neolithic flintworking was identified at three of the A13 sites and at PRL and ML substantial later Bronze Age industries were present. In order to attempt an exploration of differences in the approaches taken to flintworking from these periods, full metrical and technological analyses were considered for each assemblage. Unfortunately most of the sub-assemblages from the sites are either too small in size or contain a high degree of residual material, rendering them unsuitable for such analyses. Exceptions to this are the artefact spread from the weathered sands at WMW, which provide an integral and well-dated early Neolithic assemblage, and to a lesser extent, the assemblages from the later phases at FRU. At FRU there are noticeable differences between the assemblages from the weathered sands, which are predominantly early in date but with a significant admixture of later pieces, and the later deposits, which although still somewhat contaminated were predominantly of Bronze Age characteristics. It was therefore decided to analyse the earlier and the later phases separately. It should be noted, however, that none of these sub-assemblages are numerically very large and therefore may be prone to a degree of statistical error. Despite this and the possible residuality for some of the material from FRU, a number of interesting trends became apparent during the analyses and it is considered worthwhile to report on these here.

Table A2.13 Lithics, basic flake typology

Types	WMW (2008) % (n = 86)	FRU Weathered sands % (n = 81)	FRU Later deposits % (n = 175)
Blade	29.1	19.8	9.1
Blade-like Flake	11.6	12.3	12.6
Flake	59.3	67.9	78.3

Flake typology

Table A2.13 shows that the high proportions of blades recovered from WMW is not matched by the earlier phases of FRU but there are nevertheless over twice as many blades present in the earlier phases than in the later phases at FRU. Blade-like flakes remained more-or-less consistent across all of the assemblages

Flake shape and size

In order to obtain a more accurate impression of the shape and size range of the assemblages it is necessary to exclude all flakes broken subsequent to manufacture. It is likely that thin and slender flakes would be most prone to post-manufacture breakage and these are likely to be under-represented. Thicker flakes, notably decortication and core shaping ones, are likely to be over-represented, as well as miss-hit flakes that came out thicker than intended, either through thermal flaws or simply by mistake. Nevertheless, all complete flakes and blades flakes from the two sites were measured according to Saville (1980) and their average size given in Table A2.14.

The metrical data confirms that, whilst there is significant variability in the size of flakes and blades, they are on average small with the flakes and blades from WMW being smaller than those from FRU. This is confirmed by the size distribution range; of the material from WMW, over half of the complete flakes and blades are under 30mm long (57.6%) and 20mm broad (50.7%). Although still predominantly small, the figures for the later phases

at FRU show that only 38.3% are under 30mm long and 15.7% under 20mm broad. There are thus more longer and significantly more wider flakes in the later phases at FRU than at WMW. The pieces from the early and late phases at FRU are much more comparable, with the earlier material being on average only marginally longer and narrower. One of the most notable aspects of this is the small size of the raw materials used for both the early and late industries. It is argued that the later industries utilized rounded pebbles available in the vicinity (see above), the size and low knapping quality of which would inevitably result in small flakes. The raw materials used for the earlier industries include better quality raw materials that would have been available in larger sizes. Nevertheless, it appears that only small pieces were being brought to the site, presumably as these were more easily transportable. The greater efforts required to procure these may also favour the resultant cores being worked more efficiently and extensively than more-easily obtainable raw materials, which would also result in more smaller flakes being produced.

Following the standard work by Pitts (1978a and b) and Pitts and Jacobi (1979), the shape distribution of all measured unmodified complete flakes was established by dividing their breadths by lengths and these were compared to a sample of dated assemblages as given in Pitts (1978b, 194) and as modified from Pitts and Jacobi (1979, 166) (Table A2.15).

The flakes and blades from WMW are reasonably comparable to the figures given for the sample of later Mesolithic and early Neolithic industries. The

Table A2.14 Lithics, average metrical values

Measurement	WMW (2008) (mm) (n = 73)	FRU Weathered sands (mm) (n=55)	FRU Later deposits (mm) (n = 127)
Length Max.	63	58	70
Length Min.	9	20	10
Length Ave.	31.2	37.9	35.4
Breadth max.	60	56	79
Breadth Min.	5	5	4
Breadth Ave.	22.4	29.3	30.9
Width Max.	17	18	24
Width Min.	1	2	1
Width Ave.	5.8	8.5	8.4
Breadth/Length ratio Max	1.60	1.54	1.92
Breadth/Length ratio Min	0.22	0.30	0.07
Breadth/Length ratio Ave.	0.77	0.80	0.91

Table A2.15   Lithics, flake shapes (breadth divided by length ratios)

Reference	Suggested Date	Breadth/Length Ratio %					
		<0.2	0.2-0.4	0.4-0.6	0.6-0.8	0.8-1.0	1. 0+
WMW (2008) (n = 73)	Early Neolithic	0	13.6	25.4	22.0	10.2	28.8
FRU Weathered sands (n = 55)	Early Neolithic/M-LBA	0	3.6	25.5	23.6	21.8	25.5
FRU Later phases (n = 127)	M-LBA	0.8	1.6	15.8	20.5	26.8	34.6
Pitts	Early Mesolithic	2	43	27	13	6.5	9
Pitts and Jacobi	Early Mesolithic	1	34.5	26	15	9.5	14
Pitts	Later Mesolithic	0.5	15.5	30.5	22	14.5	17
Pitts and Jacobi	Later Mesolithic	0.5	13	27	22.5	14	23.5
Pitts	Early Neolithic	0	11	33	27.5	14.5	13
Pitts	Later Neolithic/Bronze Age	0	3	16	25	23	33

material from the early phases at FRU contains fewer blades and narrow flakes than the assemblage from WMW but more than in the later assemblages from FRU. The material from the later phases at FRU did correspond to the figures given for the later Neolithic and Bronze Age assemblages given by Pitts but showed an even greater proportion of very wide flakes present. This may indicate that the commonly noted tendency for flakes to become wider from the Mesolithic through to the early Bronze Age continues throughout the Bronze Age. However, all of the assemblages contain greater numbers of wider flakes than might be expected from their suggested dates, which may reflect the limitations of the small pieces of raw materials that were utilized.

Technological attributes

Table A2.16 shows the incidence of different striking platform types. Cortical striking platforms, indicative of the earlier stages in core reduction and suggestive of shorter reduction sequences and less emphasis on core preparation, remain fairly constant across the assemblages with slightly higher proportion present in the early phases of FRU than at WMW. Unmodified flake and dihedral striking platform types are noticeably less well represented at WMW than in both phases at FRU where they are equally represented and contributed nearly half as many. Complex striking platforms, those that had

been trimmed or facetted, are correspondingly more frequent at WMW than within the FRU assemblages although there are slightly more amongst the earlier phases than the later at FRU. There were also greater proportions of shattered platforms amongst the FRU material from all phases, these suggesting less control over reduction and poorer quality raw materials. The average thickness of striking platforms is significantly less at WMW than at FRU, with those from the earlier phases being slightly thinner than those from the later phases.

Table A2.17 shows that the types of bulb of percussion present are in similar proportions at WMW and the earlier phases at FRU, which stand in contrast to those found in the later phases at FRU, and there is a corresponding lower proportion of pronounced types. The pronounced types are associated both with hard hammer working and less control over flaking.

It also shows that there are few differences between the majority of distal termination types in the early and later phases at FRU but the material from WMW contains significantly higher proportions of feather-type terminations and corresponding fewer hinged types. Feather distal terminations are associated with good control over flake detachment and hinged types with less successful removals. Plunged distal types are less diagnostic; they can be associated with deliberate attempts to rejuvenating the core but can also reflect

Table A2.16   Lithics, striking platform type and thickness

Type	Striking Platform Type		
	WMW (2008) % (n = 72)	FRU Weathered sands % (n = 74)	FRU Later deposits % (n = 159)
Cortical	9.7	12.2	13.8
Dihedral	1.4	4.0	3.2
Trimmed	55.6	33.8	30.8
Faceted	6.9	5.4	2.5
Flake Scar	20.8	36.5	37.1
Shattered	5.6	8.1	12.6
	Striking Platform Thickness		
Average (mm)	2.7	3.6	4.0

Table A2.17   Lithics, bulb of percussion and distal termination type

	Bulb of Percussion Type		
	WMW (2008) % (n = 72)	FRU Weathered sands % (n = 70)	FRU Later deposits % (n = 160)
Diffuse	57.0	59.9	48.8
Pronounced	43.1	40.0	51.2
	Distal Termination Type		
Feather	71.6	48.4	48.5
Hinged	19.6	25.8	29.3
Plunged	4.3	8.1	8.6
Retouched	1.4	12.9	8.6
Stepped	3.1	4.8	5.0

a lack of control over flake detachment. The increased numbers present at FRU may suggest the latter cause is more likely here. The frequency of stepped termination reflects the degree of thermal flawing of the raw materials. Retouched distal terminations were commonly present within the FRU material and much more infrequent at WMW. This reflects the greater number of scrapers and other tools at FRU which have had their distal ends modified, whilst serrates and edge trimmed flakes and blades, which are more likely to be modified along their lateral edges, dominated the tool inventories at WMW.

The patterns of flake scars on the dorsal faces of flakes reflects on the nature of previous removals and are indicative of the strategies and approaches used to reduce cores. Table A2.18 shows that unidirectional removals are the most common types at WMW and both the early and later phases at FRU where they formed around half of all types. The greatest differences between the sites is between the proportions of parallel scars, which are noticeably more common at WMW than at FRU, and multidirectional scars, which are much more common at FRU. Parallel scars, as with opposed scar patterns, indicate an ability to repeatedly produce narrow flakes and are closely associated with blade production. Multidirectional scars suggest an opportunistic approach to flake production, with the random use of any available platform. Most of the orthogonal dorsal scar patterns were found on core tablet type rejuvenation flakes, these being most common amongst the material from WMW.

Summary of flintworking approaches: choices and changes

The principal findings from the metrical and technological analyses suggest that there is a significant difference between the early Neolithic industries present at WMW compared to the predominantly later Bronze Age material from the later phases at FRU. More surprising perhaps is the only marginal differences apparent between the material from the earlier and later phases at FRU. Some differences were noted, the earlier material tends to be more similar to WMW than the later material suggesting that there are higher proportions of earlier material within the earlier phases than the later, but also that a significant quantity of 'intrusive' later material may also be present.

The early Neolithic material from WMW demonstrates good control over flake detachment, including evidence for the preparation and rejuvenation of cores with the intention of producing a series of uniformly shaped narrow flakes and blades. The detached flakes typically exhibit narrow and complex striking platforms and often have parallel lateral margins and dorsal scars. This maximises the productivity of the core and there is evidence that imported cores were worked down to a small size. Both blade and flake cores from this period were identified. Some of the smaller flake cores may have produced blades earlier in their productive lives; others may have been intended to produce large sturdy flakes, such as those required for arrowhead manufacture. Some had shattered during reduction and others had been discarded when exhausted.

Table A2.18   Lithics, dorsal scar patterns

Dorsal Scar Pattern	WMW (2008) % (n = 85)	FRU Weathered sands % (n = 75)	FRU Later deposits % (n = 150)
Multidirectional	8.2	20.0	28.7
Opposed	2.4	5.3	0.7
Orthogonal	3.5	1.3	2.7
Parallel	34.1	22.7	20.0
Unidirectional	51.8	50.7	48.0

Later Bronze Age flintworking at FRU is characterised by an ad-hoc and expedient approach to obtain serviceable edges and involved the rather haphazard reduction of unmodified pieces of raw material until sufficient suitable edges were obtained (cf Saville 1990; Brown 1991; Herne 1991; Young and Humphrey 1999; Ballin 2002). This results in the production of variable but frequently short and wide flakes comparable to Martingell's 'squat flakes' (Martingell 1990). They tend to have wide, cortical or simple-flaked, acutely angled striking platforms, thick bulbs of percussion and frequent hinged distal terminations. Flaking sequences tend to be short, resulting in high proportions of cortex remaining on the dorsal surface, whilst dorsal scar patterns tend to be either unidirectional or multidirectional, reflecting short reduction sequences and the use of fortuitous, randomly aligned platforms. Some flakes suggest the use or the 'anvil' or bi-polar reduction method, often associated with the exploitation of small pebbles, particularly during the later Bronze Age (Saville 1990). Retouched implements are numerous but limited in range to edge-retouched flakes, simple scrapers and thick piercing tools, with one of the principal aim of reduction appearing to focus on the production of sturdy but sharp cutting flakes.

Most of the cores of this period were unsystematically reduced using cortical or thermal plains as striking platforms. There is little evidence for core preparation or attempts at maintenance or rejuvenation and often only a handful of flakes had been removed from any particular platform. A few had been more extensively reduced, sometimes using a 'keeling' technique, but again, only with a few removals from any particular platform and with few long knapping sequences evident. This haphazard approach results in many cores exhibiting incipient Hertzian cones from failed attempts at flake detachment. These were often abandoned when quite large, mainly due to severe hinge/step fracturing but often, once a few suitable flakes had been procured, it appears that the core was no longer needed and consequently discarded. In many cases, however, the cores may have been intended to serve as tools. Differentiating core tools from true cores is rather subjective but the former have flake removals that seem to indicate that modification of the raw materials was the aim, rather than the production of flakes. They have produced flakes that are considered too small for any effective use and they sometimes exhibit battered and worn edges suggesting a use for chopping or heavy scraping.

Discussion: the production and use of struck flint along the A13 route

Numerous archaeological excavations over the past few decades have now been conducted along the wetlands of east London, demonstrating an intensity of interest in the floodplain margins and the marshy areas that developed there from the Mesolithic to the end of the prehistoric period (Meddens 1996; Cotton 2000; Kendall 2000; Greenwood *et al.* 2006). Much of this evidence survives below and within Holocene alluvial deposits, with worked flint often forming an important element of the evidence for human activity. Much of this work has yet to be fully published and the nature of this occupation and the role of flint industries remain poorly understood. The excavations reported here therefore provide a welcome opportunity to explore a few of the questions relating to the nature, extent and significance of flint industries within this area.

Struck flint was recovered from all three of the A13 sites where intensive excavation was conducted. It demonstrates activity along the terrace edge from at least the later Mesolithic period through until the later parts of the Bronze Age. The earliest evidence of activity is provided by a microlith from ML and a micro-burin from PRL, both of which are typological markers for the Mesolithic period. No other certain Mesolithic material was identified and, by themselves, these pieces can only indicate transient activity, perhaps associated with the maintenance of hunting equipment. The extent to which this seemingly ephemeral activity may have been typical, however, remains less certain. On the southern banks of the Thames, potentially vast quantities of very late Mesolithic flintwork were discovered at Erith Spine Road (very little was actually excavated but it appeared to be present in dense concentrations across a wide area) (RPS Clouston 1997; Bennell 1998). There, relatively low proportions of retouched implements were present and the struck flint accumulations were interpreted as representing a 'production' site, where tools such as microliths and tranchet axes were manufactured from the locally outcropping chalk-flint for use elsewhere (Taylor 1996 in RPS Coulson 1997). Further scatters of late Mesolithic flintwork, including microlith and transverse axe manufacturing waste, were found across the river from Erith at Tank Hill Road in Purfleet (Leivers *et al.* 2007). Elsewhere, numerous finds of isolated implements or small scatters of flintwork are suggestive of persistent activity along the river margins (eg Lacaille 1961; Lewis 2000a; Bradley 2005; Bishop forthcoming; MoLA in prep.). The combined evidence suggests that during the later Mesolithic the banks of the Thames were used for a variety of pursuits and, in some places, witnessed intense occupation and the prolific production of flint artefacts.

A similar pattern of activity can be traced into the early Neolithic with numerous sites in the vicinity providing characteristic struck flint (eg Lewis 2000b; Cotton 2000; Coles *et al.* 2008; Bishop forthcoming; MoLA in prep.). In many of these cases, diagnostic Mesolithic and early Neolithic struck flints have been found in close proximity suggesting that similar patterns of landscape use were maintained across the transition.

Extensive although not particularly dense spreads of early Neolithic lithic material were identified from within the weathered sands at all three A13 sites, although only at WMW did these remain relatively undisturbed by later alluvial and human activity. The nature of these assemblages is broadly comparable. Core reduction is represented at all three sites but high proportions of retouched implements and useable flakes indicate tool use was an important element of the activities conducted. The retouched implements include many simple edge-trimmed flakes and serrated pieces, some exhibiting polish, suggesting an emphasis on cutting tasks that probably included the processing of silica-rich plant materials (Avery 1982, 38; Grace 1992; Bradley 1993; Donahue 2002). These may include cereals, which were found at WMW, but other candidates include rushes that would no doubt have been abundant in this riverine area. Also well represented are scrapers, including denticulated types. Scrapers are frequently associated with hide processing, an activity often conducted close to rivers (Bradley 1978), although it has also been suggested that denticulated pieces may have been involved in plant processing (Brown 1992), possibly complementing the uses that were put to serrates. Micro-wear analysis on the Neolithic struck flint assemblage from the Royal Docks Community School, located to the south of PRL, suggests that a variety of tasks were conducted, including the processing of silica-rich plants and woodworking (MoLA in prep.). Hunting maintenance activities are indicated by an almost finished arrowhead from WMW whilst other possible arrowhead blanks are present at PRL, indicating their manufacture and recalling similar activities recorded at Tank Hill Road and further upstream of the Thames at Dorney (Lamdin-Whymark 2001; Leivers *et al.* 2007).

The early Neolithic assemblages identified during the A13 investigations suggest extensive use of the river foreshore although at least at PRL and WMW the material seems to have been formed into relatively small spreads or scatters that may reflect a palimpsest of short-term residencies strung along the river margins. This would fit into a much wider view of Neolithic settlement that acknowledges the importance of a variety of modes of mobility and temporality (Edmonds 1999; Whittle 1997; Pollard 1999).

The lithic material may reference the wider use of the landscape in other ways. The raw materials used appear to have been collected from a number of locations as well as from the immediate vicinity. A number of activities appear to be indicated but the retouched and utilized implements indicate that a degree of specialisation may have been occurring. It suggests that particular activities may have been organised at a landscape level, with different places being preferred for different tasks. The assemblages represented the full reduction sequence, indicating that core reduction and tool production were occur-ring on-site. Nevertheless, it may also be significant that the quantity of knapping waste was relatively low in respect to the proportion of retouched pieces, which may be considered particularly high even for a 'domestic' assemblage (Wainwright 1972, 66) and these were complemented by high proportions of unmodified flakes and blades that had been utilized. This may indicate that the on-site production of struck flint is under-represented in comparison to that being used, and that tools and useable flakes and blades manufactured elsewhere were being brought to the site. This is also supported by a large number of flakes and blades whose raw materials were not matched by any of the cores present. In addition it appears that, as well as some cores being brought to the site, others were being taken away for use elsewhere. Taken together, these strands of evidence suggests that the various stages in flint production, use and discard, the *'chaine operatoire'*, were also organised on a landscape scale, being undertaken at different times and places and with different stages being emphasised at different locations (cf Ingold 1993; Edmonds 1997; Conneller 2008; McFadyen 2008).

Later Neolithic and early Bronze Age activity is generally less visible in east London than during previous and subsequent periods although contemporary struck flints have been identified at the Royal Docks Community School and elsewhere in the area (Coles *et al.* 2008; Bishop forthcoming; MoLA in prep), and more extensive activity during this period has been recorded downstream in north Southwark (Ridgeway 1999; Proctor and Bishop 2002; Sidell *et al.* 2002). At the A13 sites, later Neolithic activity is attested by the recovery of a transverse arrowhead at ML and a barbed and tanged arrowhead from the same site indicates that activity continuing into the early Bronze Age/ Beaker period. The nature of the activity is hard to assess. A small scatter of knapping debris of possible early Bronze Age date was identified at ML along with a number of small and invasively retouched scrapers, suggesting some form of occupation, but there was little further evidence of intensive flint use during these periods at the other A13 sites. Many of the scrapers from ML were broadly comparable to the 'thumbnail' types, typically of later Neolithic or early Bronze Age date and frequently associated with Beaker period settlements (Edmonds 1995, 140-141). The barbed and tanged arrowhead and, to a lesser extent, the semi-invasively flaked knife, are finely made and this may hint at their uses as prestigious implements, these types sometimes being associated with funerary practices.

There is much greater evidence of flint use associated with the later Bronze Age occupations identified at PRL and ML. These occupations coincide with the onset of wetter conditions and a renewed interest in the east London peatlands, with numerous wetland and dryland sites now having been identified (Meddens 1996; Greenwood *et al.*

2006; Yates 2007). Many of these have produced flint industries although, given the general intensity of occupation, struck flint does not in general seem to play such a prominent role in the material inventories as it may have done previously. Nevertheless, the quantities of struck flint recovered from PRL and ML was sufficient to demonstrate that it continued to play an important role, perhaps complementing the increasing availability and significance of metal tools. Much of the struck flint recovered from Bronze Age deposits at WMW was probably derived from earlier levels but at PRL and ML relatively large quantities were present within alluvial deposits and the fills of cut features. As is often the case with later prehistoric assemblages, formally retouched forms were limited to simple edge retouched flakes and irregular scrapers (for example Herne 1991; Young and Humphrey 1999), with the production of sharp but unretouched flakes often being one of the principal aims of reduction. In other cases, it appears that raw materials were worked specifically to make core tools, the shape of these suggesting their use as chopping and scraping implements.

The range of activities to which the struck flints were put is not easily discerned, but comparable assemblages were recovered during the excavations at the Royal Docks Community School (MoLA in prep.). There, a similar range of implements is present and micro-wear analysis suggests that these were predominantly used to scrape, cut and pierce hides. Features interpreted as hide drying racks were also recorded and it was suggested that the site might represent a specialist hide-processing location, taking advantage of the abundance of water and possibly the peat, which can act as a tanning agent. Features interpreted as cooking pits that contained significant quantities of burnt flint were also identified and it may be that these too were associated with hide preparation. The evidence from the Royal Docks Community School is very comparable to that recorded at PRL and ML and it is possible that similar, rather specialised, activities were also occurring. If so, this does suggest a flourishing hide working industry located along the edges of the marshes. This may have been associated with the widespread agricultural re-organisations that the region witnessed, much of it appearing to focus on animal husbandry (see Meddens 1996; Guttmann and Last 2000; Yates 2007) and it is tempting to speculate that such production may have contributed to the creation of surpluses and was possibly implicated in the complex networks of exchange that were becoming increasingly important throughout the Bronze Age (Rowlands 1980; Needham 1993; Kristiansen and Larrson 2005; Yates 2007; Needham 2007).

The lithic material was present in some numbers in the fills of palaeochannels and alluvial deposits where it may have been eroded in or dumped as refuse from adjacent drier areas. Flintworking was associated with the burnt mound feature at ML and

other accumulations of struck flint may suggest a degree of middening was occurring. Many of the later Bronze Age features also provided small quantities of contemporary flintwork although, in general, this material probably reflects the incidental incorporation of general background waste. It does, nevertheless, suggest the sporadic but persistent manufacture and use of struck flint at the sites, the small quantities within any particular features suggesting that flint was probably only knapped and used as the occasion required. Raw materials were obtained and struck flint manufactured, used and discarded, all with some immediacy, in and around the settlement and field-systems. This can be contrasted with the convoluted patterns of resource acquisition, mobility and landscape-wide task allocation that characterised the early Neolithic assemblages.

The quantities of burnt flint found during the excavations are also of interest. Much of this was widely dispersed, reflecting the presence of background waste accruing during hearth use. However, substantial quantities were recovered from the burnt mound feature at ML and further significant concentrations were also present within peat deposits at all of the A13 sites, suggesting that activities resulting in the systematic burning of flint were more widespread. Burnt mound accumulations or pits containing significant quantities of burnt flint have frequently been identified along the terrace edges in east London, from comparable topographic situations in north Southwark; see for example Bowsher (1991) and Heard (2000) as well as further afield, such as along the Fen edge in Cambridgeshire (Healy 1996; Edmonds *et al.* 1999; M. Knight pers. comm.). There certainly seems to be a widespread correlation between the pyrotechnical activities responsible for the generation of large accumulations of burnt flint and wetland margins, although it is less certain what sort of activities would have required the deliberate burning of such quantities. Although there are no reasons to suppose that a single cause was responsible for all, perhaps the most favoured explanations see the burning of flint as being connected with cooking activities, its scale suggesting communal efforts, perhaps associated with feasting or ceremonial practices. Other explanations regard it as the residue from saunas (Barfield and Hodder 1987) and a variety of industrial processes, including leather making, wool processing, and most recently brewing have been put forward to account for its generation (see Hedges 1975; Barfield and Hodder 1987; Barfield 1991; Jeffery 1991; Dunkin 2001; Wilkins 2011). Whatever the activities were that generated the burnt flint, it is possible that on some occasions the accumulations may also have additionally served in less mundane capacities. Before becoming covered with vegetation or buried with alluvium they would have been highly visible along the skyline and may have acted as cultural or landscape markers (Edmonds *et al.* 1999, 70), perhaps demarcating

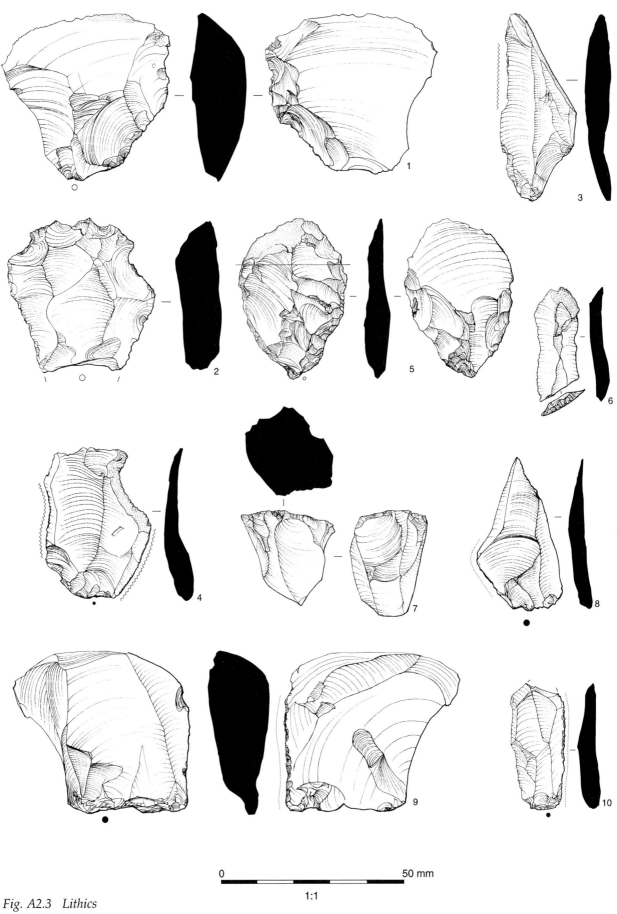

Fig. A2.3   Lithics

50 mm

1:1

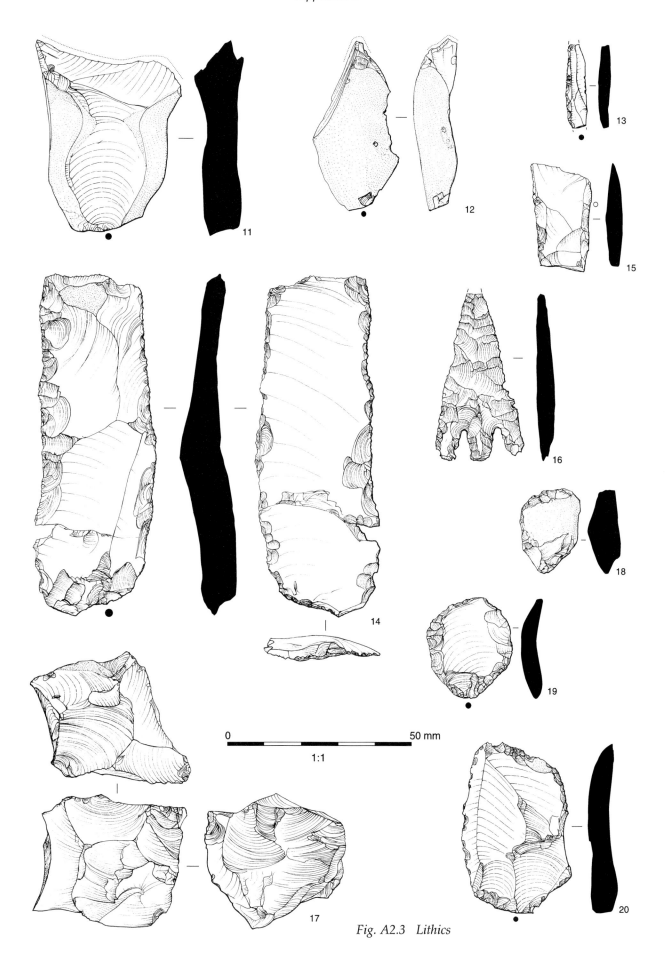

Fig. A2.3   Lithics

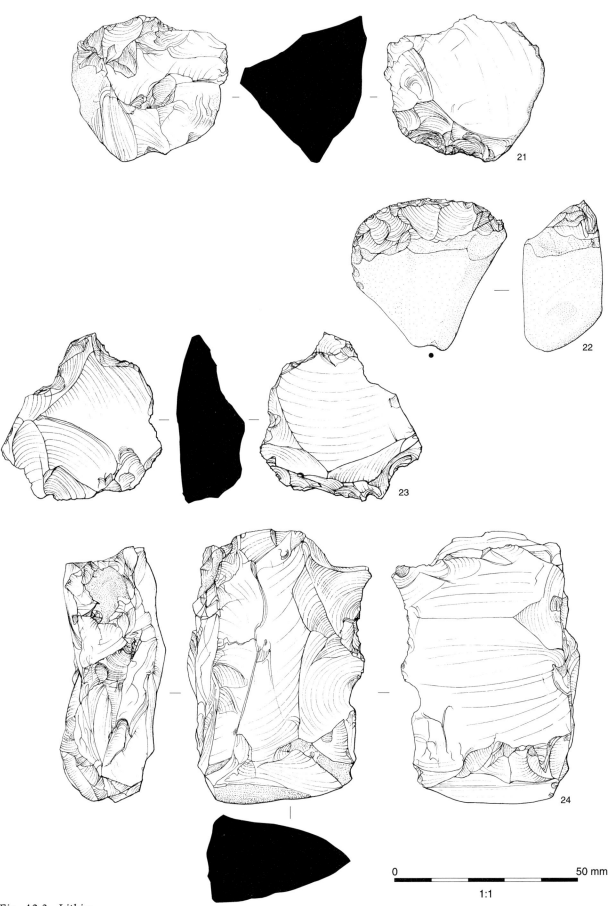

Fig. A2.3   Lithics

dryland and wetland or acting as some form of territorial or tenurial boundaries. Many burnt mound accumulations, including the example at ML, were quickly subsumed beneath alluvium or rising waters, and it is conceivable that they may have been involved in a spiritual or symbolic response to the encroaching wetlands, which were rapidly inundating traditionally held lands.

Illustrated catalogue (Fig. A2.3)

1. **Bifacially worked flake (arrowhead blank?).** Early Neolithic. Freemasons Road (FRU01), 106, SF167

2. **Denticulated scraper.** Early Neolithic. Woolwich Manor Way (WMW00), 1517, SF3

3. **Worn serrated blade.** Early Neolithic. Woolwich Manor Way (WMW00), 2008, SF138

4. **Serrated blade-like flake.** Early Neolithic. Woolwich Manor Way (WMW00), 2008, SF216

5. **Leaf-shaped arrowhead (unfinished?).** Early Neolithic. Woolwich Manor Way (WMW00), 2001

6. **Obliquely truncated blade.** Mesolithic/early Neolithic. Woolwich Manor Way (WMW00), 2005, SF8

7. **Exhausted blade core.** Early Neolithic. Woolwich Manor Way (WMW00), 2005

8. **Utilised flake** – heavy unifacial damage left lateral dorsal. Early Neolithic. Woolwich Manor Way (WMW00), 2008, SF189

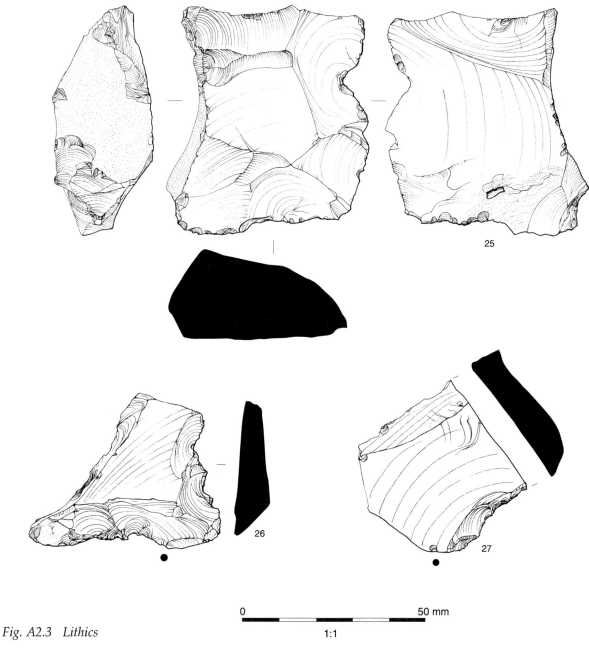

0   50 mm

1:1

Fig. A2.3 Lithics

9. **Utilised flake** – heavy unifacial damage, left lateral ventral. Early Neolithic. Woolwich Manor Way (WMW00), 2008, SF115

10. **Utilised blade** – heavy unifacial damage, right lateral dorsal. Early Neolithic. Woolwich Manor Way (WMW00), 2008, SF109

11. **Utilised flake** – heavy unifacial damage, distal dorsal. Early Neolithic. Woolwich Manor Way (WMW00), 2008, SF102

12. **Utilised flake** – piercing. Early Neolithic. Woolwich Manor Way (WMW00), 2008, SF74

13. **Rod-shaped microlith**. Mesolithic. Movers Lane (MOE00), unstratified

14. **Semi-invasively retouched blade**. Late Neolithic. Movers Lane (MOE00), 121

15. **Petit tranchet arrowhead**. Late Neolithic. Movers Lane (MOE00), 60

16. **Barbed and tanged arrowhead.** Early Bronze Age. Movers Lane (RIR01), 1033

17. **Extensively reduced multiplatform core**. Early Bronze Age. Movers Lane (RIR01), 3005

18. **Thumbnail scraper**. Early Bronze Age. Movers Lane (RIR01), 3005

19. **Thumbnail scraper**. Early Bronze Age. Movers Lane (RIR01), 3005

20. **Edge trimmed flake**. Early Bronze Age. Movers Lane (RIR01), 3005

21. **Core tool – denticulated scraper?** Late Bronze Age. Freemasons Road (FRU01), 103

22. **Scraper**. Late Bronze Age. Freemasons Road (FRU01), 105.

23. **Core tool – piercer?** Late Bronze Age. Freemasons Road (FRU01), 32

24. **Wedge shaped core- core tool?** Late Bronze Age. Movers Lane (RIR01), 5083

25. **Wedge shaped core- core tool?** Late Bronze Age. Movers Lane (RIR01), 5083

26. **Denticulated Flake**. Late Bronze Age. Movers Lane (RIR01), 5083

27. **Edge trimmed/denticulated Flake**. Late Bronze Age. Movers Lane (RIR01), 5083

The jet belt slider, Movers Lane *by Alison Sheridan* (Fig. A2.4)

Description

Fragment, in two conjoining pieces, representing around a third of a subrectangular belt slider with a squarish end, flat top and central oval perforation. Its inner and outer surfaces are, like its end, slightly convex (Fig. A2.4). It is 34.9mm long, 9.3mm wide

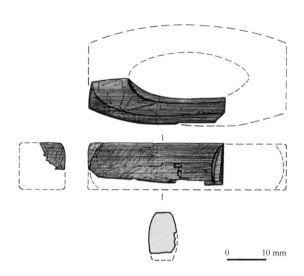

Fig. A2.4   Jet belt-slider, Movers Lane

and 10.2mm thick, but would originally have measured around 51 x 25 x 11mm. It is black, and made of soft Whitby jet, whose woody texture is clearly visible in the fracture surface; it has broken along and across the grain and there is a crack across the hoop (soft jet is particularly prone to cracking). The broken end of the hoop has a convex fracture surface. The surfaces have been carefully smoothed but there are faint, fine striations on all of the surfaces, from where the object had been shaped by rubbing against (or being rubbed by) an abrasive surface such as fine sandstone prior to its final smoothing (the horizontal and diagonal striations on the perforation surface are perhaps more likely to relate to this smoothing process, rather than to the initial cutting- and scraping-out of the perforation). There are no obvious signs of wear. The surfaces are matte but whether they had originally been polished and have lost their sheen post-depositionally is unclear. Found damp and in a fragile condition, the slider was kept wet while post-excavation examination took place. This has precluded the possibility of undertaking compositional analysis (eg by X-ray fluorescence spectroscopy) but there is no doubt, from the macro- and microscopic examination, that the materal is jet. Given that the only significant source of usable jet in Britain is to be found around Whitby (and that around a third of all known sliders have been found in and around Yorkshire, including an unperforated roughout) this is most likely to be the material's source area.

Discussion

Belt sliders of jet and similar-looking materials are a distinctive, and exclusively British, middle Neolithic artefact type. In her review, Isla McInnes (1968) listed 17 examples and mentioned two further, but cruder, slider-like objects, from Hal[l]myre in the Scottish Borders and Scawton in North Yorkshire. Today, the total has risen to 29, including one allegedly found in an Anglo-Saxon grave on 'Hambleton Moor' discussed below; these are listed in Table A2.19 and their distribution shown in Figure A2.5. The additions to McInnes' list reinforce trends in the geographical pattern. Overall, there is a marked tendency towards coastal and riverine finds and there are two clusters: one in North Yorkshire, within 50km from the source of the jet in the Whitby area (Nos. 9–12 and 14–17 in Table A2.19) and the other (Nos. 22–28) encompassing the Thames and Wessex, with three finds (Nos. 22–24) on the Upper Thames gravels, and with the Movers Lane slider (No. 26) closer to the mouth of the river. The wide geographical spread of the overall distribution reminds us of the extensive networks of contacts that must have been operating during the currency of the sliders, and the importance of maritime connections is underlined not only by the east coast distribution but also by the remarkable series of finds along the western seaboard from Cornwall to Skye (although see Table A2.19 regarding the latter find).

Contextually, one slider (No. 10, Boltby Moor) is from a settlement site; twelve or thirteen are associated in some way with funerary monuments; and six are from watery contexts – peat bogs, rivers or the immediate vicinity of rivers. The association with water is strengthened if one includes the eight funerary and stray finds from close to rivers or to the sea. With the exception of the Clyde cairn at Beacharra, where the slider had probably accompanied a secondary interment in a communal chamber tomb, and the sub-megalithic funerary chamber in Gop Cave, which had housed the remains of 14 individuals, the funerary contexts tend to feature individual, crouched or flexed inhumations of adult males, under round or oval barrows or within ring ditches. At Barrow Hills the male was accompanied by a female; at Linch Hill the single 'female' has recently been re-identified as male: see Table A2.19 for details. That the sliders were regarded as precious and prestigious items is indicated by their rarity and by this association with funerary monuments that privilege specific individuals; the associated artefacts, such as a waisted flint 'Seamer' axehead from Whitegrounds, reinforce this impression. As for the context of the Movers Lane slider, its watery association is clear, but whether it represents a votive deposit, placed in or beside the river, or else the last traces of an eroded funerary deposit is uncertain; no specific association with the five fragments of disarticulated human bone from the same context (layer 5074) need necessarily be assumed. Votive deposition would accord with the practice attested further upriver at Basildon (No. 24).

The sliders vary in length from *c* 36mm (at Aldro, No. 15) to possibly about 120mm (probably from Luce Sands, No. 8) and in overall shape from squat and broad (as at 'Hambleton Moor') to long and slender (as at Balgone). As McInnes pointed out (1968, 137) to some extent the variation in shape can be accounted for by the nature of the raw material:

the squat form of the Hal[l]myre slider, for example, follows the shape of the jet beach pebble from which it had been made.

The raw material has been confirmed through macro-/microscopic examination by the author, backed up in several instances by compositional analysis, to be jet in twelve, possibly thirteen cases. Most of the remainder may well also be of jet. Only six out of the 29 are definitely of jet: four from Scotland, one from Wales and one from Giant's Hills 1 long barrow, Skendleby, Lincolnshire, are definitely not of jet, and in all but one of those cases (a broken roughout from Ogmore-by-Sea, Vale of Glamorgan, No. 21) a black, jet-like material has been used, to emulate jet as closely as possible. One can thus answer Terry Manby's question (1974, 98) about whether they had all been made by a single craft specialist or workshop: this appears not to have been the case. However, one cannot rule out the possibility that the same person, or few people, had made several, if not most, of the jet examples; McInnes and Manby were correct to point out the degree of skill required to manufacture these objects. Given that other middle Neolithic items such as 'Seamer' axeheads and 'Duggleby' adzes of flint are likely to be the products of specialist manufacture in Yorkshire (Manby 1974; Manby *et al.* 2003, 53), then specialist jetworking at this time around the Whitby source area, is entirely possible (and indeed would be consistent with the discovery of an unperforated roughout at Fylingdales, to the south of Whitby – the closest find to the source of the jet). Some variation in the quality of manufacture was noted by McInnes, who pointed out that the squat, knobbly jet examples from Hal[l]myre (No. 4) and Scawton (No. 12) are more crudely worked than the other jet examples. Similarly, among the non-jet examples, she noted that 'The edges of the central opening [of the Giant's Hills, Skendleby example, No. 18 are] very crudely gouged out and unfinished' (McInnes 1968, 142), while cut-marks had been left visible on the Scottish examples from 'Wigtownshire (?)' (= probably Luce Sands, No. 8), from Balgone (No. 2) and from 'probably south-east Scotland' (No. 5; note that the Balgone example is better finished than the others). The Ogmore roughout had broken and been abandoned during manufacture. As for the example from beside the Glinzier Burn (No. 6), it may be that this was unfinished, since the 'central opening [was] roughly cut and incomplete' (ibid., 143). It is particularly unfortunate that its raw material cannot be checked, as the item is in private hands, although from its description it may have been of jet, thus suggesting importation in unfinished form.

Whether these objects had actually been used as belt sliders, to retain the loose end of a belt, is a moot point although the consistency of their position with regard to the body, at the hip (Nos. 14, 16, 23, 28) clearly indicates some kind of belt-related use: the Linch Hill example was found 'against the left forearm'. Where use-wear has been identifiable, it has taken the form of locally-heightened polish to the outer edges of the perforation on both sides, rather than polish to the interior surface of the perforation, or to one external surface as might be expected from its use as a slider, with one side rubbing against a garment. The observed pattern of wear could conceivably have been caused by the use of the objects as fasteners, with one side attached to a belt and the other end of the belt being threaded through it; however, attachment in that way would actually minimise the visual impact of the artefact, and for this reason seems unlikely. Suspension from a belt, in the manner of a Japanese *netsuke*, is another possibility but again, more wear to the interior of the perforation would be expected. Of limited assistance to this issue is the fact that a very similar-shaped object, of bone, is known from an Iron Age context at All Cannings Cross and is featured in the Wiltshire Heritage Museum website (registration number DZSWS:2006.1.35). It may be, of course, that the objects were not old enough when buried to have acquired distinctive use-wear traces.

The associated artefacts fall within a relatively narrow range. Ceramic associations are limited to three findspots (excepting the Beacharra chamber tomb, where the pottery pre-dates the deposition of the slider) and in each case it has been Peterborough Ware, in its Mortlake style at Gop Cave and at Movers Lane, and in a northern British congener, the Rudston style, at Boltby Moor (see Barclay and Rayner, this publication, on the Movers Lane pottery). A fourth site, Handley Down barrow 26, Dorset, has also produced Peterborough Ware (almost all Mortlake style), from the ditch fill and the mound covering the grave. At none of these sites, except perhaps Boltby Moor, was the pottery closely associated with the sliders, but a general contemporaneity can arguably be assumed, particularly in the light of the available radiocarbon dating evidence for the sliders and the pottery, reviewed below. Furthermore, a tendency for southern English Peterborough Ware to be found in riverine locations, especially the Thames, reminiscent of some of the slider findspots, has been noted by several commentators including Cotton and Johnson (2004) and Hey *et al.* (2011, 380). The lithic associations are often of distinctive, high-status artefact types: a Seamer axehead at Whitegrounds, and partly-ground flint knives at Barrow Hills and Linch Hill (the latter associated with a woman) and an all-over-ground/polished flake knife at Gop Cave. The leaf-shaped flint arrowhead at Barrow Hills may not have been as prestigious as the large, lozenge-shaped arrowheads found elsewhere in middle Neolithic single graves, some accompanying ground/polished knives (Kinnes 1979), but it may have been accorded special status by virtue of its context – unless, of course, it had been inside the man's body; it had been disturbed by an Anglo-Saxon *Grubenhaus* (see Table A2.19 for other, less closely associated flint artefacts.) As for other associated material, excepting the animal bones

noted at several findspots, mention should be made of the bone skewer pin found at Gop Cave, albeit not directly associated with the sliders.

As for the date of belt sliders, one can safely discount McInnes' claim for a brief currency 'in the second quarter of the second millennium' (1968, 142) which was based on a false premise. The dating evidence can be reviewed under three headings: i) dated human remains directly associated with the sliders, plus other relevant dated human remains; ii) dates relating to associated artefact types; and iii) dates relating to other artefact types forming part of a suite of high status middle Neolithic grave goods. Each will be considered briefly below, as will Ian Kinnes' claim (2004, 107) that the 'Hambleton Moor'slider is of Anglo-Saxon date.

Dated human remains directly associated with the sliders

Two recently-obtained radiocarbon dates for the individuals from Linch Hill (No. 22) and Handley Down barrow 26 (No. 28) together with three dates for individuals from Gop Cave (Nos. 19, 20) provide valuable additional information to add to the data from Whitegrounds (No. 15) and Barrow Hills (No. 23). The Whitegrounds date of 4520±90 BP (see Table A2.19 for details) produced a broad range of 3500–2920 cal BC, although its 1σ version narrows the range to 3360–3090 cal BC. The Barrow Hills skeletons' dates, of 4120±60 BP and 3860±50 BP for the male and female respectively, are both late and mutually inconsistent and may reflect the poor quality of the dated bone. It may be that the four dates obtained from antler from the surrounding ditch, which calibrate to between 3360–3030 cal BC and 3335–2700 cal BC (except for one date with a much greater standard deviation), provide a more accurate assessment of the age of the grave and its slider (see Bradley 1992, 138; Garwood and Barclay 1999, 278 and Hey *et al.* 2011, 397, 398 for a discussion of the Barrow Hills dates). The Linch Hill skeleton has produced a date of 4760±30 BP (3640–3380 cal BC; Mike Parker Pearson pers comm.) while the Handley Down Barrow 26 skeleton has been dated to 3310–2910 cal BC (4410±30 BP: Mike Allen pers. comm.). Finally, although not necessarily associated with either of the two sliders from that chamber, three individuals from Gop Cave have been dated to 3100–2900 cal BC, with one date possibly extending as early as 3300 cal BC (Rick Schulting pers. comm.). Overall, and with the exception of the Linch Hill individual, this dating evidence could be taken to indicate a *floruit* for jet and jet-like belt sliders between around 3350 and 2900 BC.

Dates for associated artefacts

As discussed in Barclay and Rayner's report on the Movers Lane pottery (above), the Mortlake style of Peterborough Ware appears to belong to the period 3350–2850 BC, which accords well with the skeletal dating evidence reviewed above. Furthermore, the

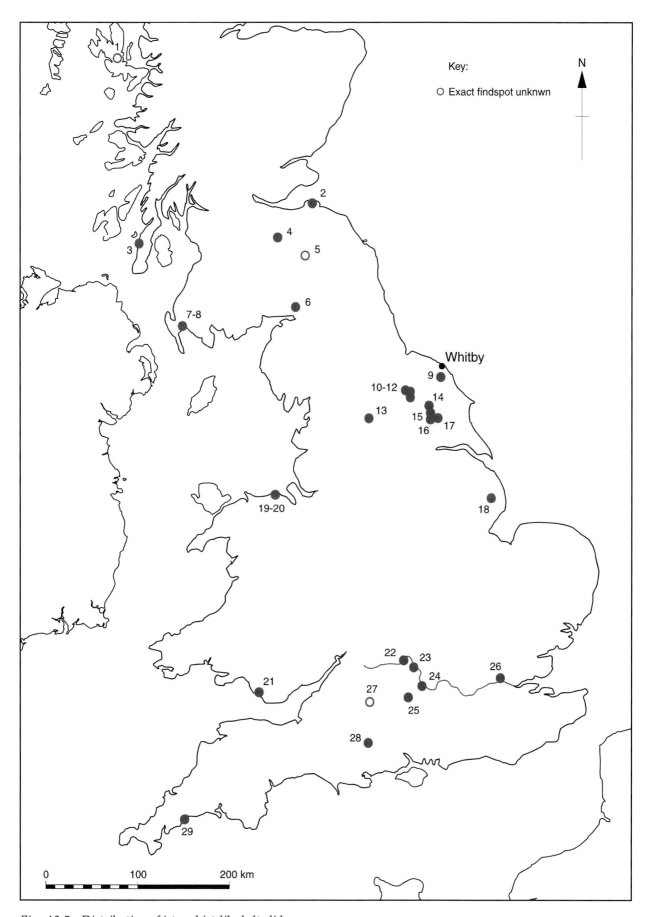

Key:

○ Exact findspot unknwn

N

Fig. A2.5   Distribution of jet and jet-like belt sliders

Table A2.19   List of jet and jet-like belt sliders

No.	Findspot	Context, associations	Dimensions (mm, L x W x Th where available)	Material ID: macroscopic, by whom*	Confirmed by analysis? by whom?*
1	Skye	No information; presumably stray find	77 x 18.9x16.5	Shale (JAS, MD)	XRF (MD)
2	Balgone, near North Berwick, East Lothian	In peat, 6–8 ft (1.83–2.44 m) deep, with 1 ft (0.3 m) more of peat below; close to outlet of ancient lake. Human bones and bones, antlers and tusks of animals; 'Several of the animal bones appear to have been formed into cutting implements'	97.8 x 20.9 x 13.4	Cannel coal or shale	XRF (MD)
3	Beacharra, Argyll & Bute	In blocking material in chamber of Clyde cairn (3rd compartment from entrance); early-to-middle Neolithic pottery, flint flake	84.8 x 22.5 x 10	Jet (JAS)	-
4	Hal[l]myre, Newmains, Scottish Borders (Peeblesshire)	Stray find	48 x 31 x 17	Jet (JAS)	XRF (LT)
5	Probably South-East Scotland	No information; presumably a stray find	35.6 x 15.9 x 9.9 (fragment)	Cannel coal or shale (JAS)	XRF (MD)
6	Glinzier, Dumfries & Galloway	In peat, 4 or 5 ft (1.22 – 1.52 m) deep in 'a very solid peat moss beside the Glinzier Burn'	93 x 32	Probably jet, to judge from McInnes' description	-
7	Luce Sands, Dumfries & Galloway	No information; presumably stray find	15.1 x 20.8 x 12.5 (fragment; less than ¼ present)	?Poor-quality jet (JAS, MD)	-
8	Probably Luce Sands, Dumfries & Galloway	No information; probably stray find	65 x 15 (McInnes says 67 x 19). (Fragment; original L might have been *c* 120)	Probably cannel coal (JAS)	-
9	Fylingdales, North Yorkshire	Barrow? Or stray find – see comments	117.7 x 28.8 x 14.3	Jet (JAS, MD)	-
10	Boltby Moor east of Boltby Scar, North Yorkshire	Settlement. Peterborough Ware (Rudston style); lithics include ground flint knives	30.4 x 20.3 x 16.8 (fragment; probably between ¼ and ⅓ present)	Jet (JAS, Terry Manby)	XRF (SK)
11	'Hambleton Moor', North Yorkshire	Recorded as having been found in a cist with an iron spearhead, of Anglo-Saxon date	41.7 x 34.3 x 35.7	Jet (JAS, MD)	-

196

References (see McInnes 1968 for further references)	Current location	Comments; dates (calibrated using OxCal 4.1; 2σ values cited)
McInnes 1968, no. 13; Clarke *et al.* 1985, 238, no. 13, fig. 3.36, bottom; Wilson 1851, 300	NMS X.FN 43	Find location: Wilson 1851 states 'found in th Isle of Skye'; according to Clarke *et al.* 1985, 238, 'Early accession records do not confirm Skye as the place of discovery'. Photograph caption in Clarke *et al.* 1985 incorrectly lists this as being at top of the photo
McInnes 1968, 12; Struthers 1866	NMS X.FN 164	Mislabelled as FN 162 on object
McInnes 1968, no. 10; Clarke *et al.* 1985, 238, no. 12, fig. 3.36, top	Campbeltown Museum	Photograph caption in Clarke *et al.* 1985 incorrectly lists this as being at bottom of the photo
McInnes 1968, no no.; fig. 29.15	Hunterian B.1914.472	McInnes' account is confused: she omits to list it and cites its illustration under the entry for Gop Cave. Made from a water-rolled beach pebble, minimally modified. Measurements given are those taken by author; Hunterian Museum on-line catalogue says 50 x 33 x *c* 20
Unpublished	NMS X.1998.1 (part of)	From collection of Walter Mason, Selkirk
McInnes 1968, no. 11	In private possession	Possibly an unfinished roughout: according to McInnes, 'Outside brilliantly polished but central opening roughly cut and incomplete'
Unpublished	NMS, X.BH [number between 8208 and 8429]	This is not the missing piece of No. 8
McInnes 1968, no. 14; www.futuremuseum.co.uk	Stranraer WIWMS Museum 1945.144A	Findspot given as 'Wigtownshire?' by McInnes. Material given as jet in the Stranraer Museum website entry, but macroscopically it seems more likely to be of cannel coal or shale. This is the example listed by McInnes as coming from a collection from Castle Kennedy; website entry (inf. Stranraer Museum) states that it had been collected, probably from Luce Sands, by Wigtownshire antiquary Rev R. Anderson. John Pickin (Stranraer Museum) adds (pers. comm..) that Anderson had probably acquired it during the 1920s/1930s. He lived at The Manse, Castle Kennedy.
Unpublished	British Museum 1902.02-16.4	Roughout, unperforated. Note: this is the closest find to the source area of jet around Whitby. It is part of a set of material acquired from the sale of Thomas Boynton's collection, which included material collected by Mr Marshall, the owner of Fyling House, who explored barrows in the area. It is unknown whether the roughout came from a barrow or was a stray find (Terry Manby pers comm.)
Manby 1974, 95; Manby *et al.et al.* 2003, 51, fig. 18	Private hands (T. Lord Collection, currently c/o T. Manby)	'..north-east of Boltby Scar camp (SE 510862 area) an extensive Rudston style assemblage..was salvaged by T. [Tot] Lord in 1959 from an old quarry-like hollow, perhaps a collapsed mouth of a sink-hole or a 'windypit' (Manby *et al.* 2003, 87)
McInnes 1968, no. 9	British Museum 1882.0323.41	See text for discussion of the date and context of this slider. Terry Manby (pers comm.) has suggested that it resembles a macehead in miniature, and has added that 'Hambleton Moor' does not exist as a place name, although the findspot will lie within the Hambleton Hills, which stretch north-south for around 25 km

Table A2.19   List of jet and jet-like belt sliders (continued)

No.	Findspot	Context, associations	Dimensions (mm, L x W x Th where available)	Material ID: macroscopic, by whom*	Confirmed by analysis? by whom?*
12	Scawton, North Yorkshire	Stray find	63 x 48 x 23	From photo on website, could well be jet (JAS)	-
13	Blubberhouses Moor, North Yorkshire	Stray find	No dimensions recorded	Jet ('shiny black jet') (Terry Manby)	-
14	Whitegrounds, North Yorkshire	In small of back of adult male, 25–30 years old, crouched, under round barrow constructed over Early Neolithic oval barrow. Seamer axehead. Calf jaw and pig humerus found in wood-covered pit immediately below body	73 x 17 x 16 (from illustration in Brewster 1984; L confirmed in Clarke *et al.* 1985)	Described by excavator as of jet; from from photograph in Clarke *et al.* 1985, fig. 3.35, seems plausible	-
15	Aldro 177, North Yorkshire	In disturbed round barrow, *c* 25 cm below surface, a little north of the barrow's centre; barbed and tangedflint arrowhead and small flaked flint knife 'close by', but probably later; disturbed remains of two unburnt skeletons at the base, near the centre	36.1 x 21.5 x 15.25	Jet (JAS)	-
16	Painsthorpe 118, near Thixendale, North Yorkshire	Crouched skeleton of old person, primary grave under round barrow; animal vertebrae and jaw fragment with tooth of ox; disarticulated human bones. Slider found close to left hip	73 x 24 x 18.6	Jet (JAS)	NAA (GB)
17	Riggs 16, North Yorkshire	On old ground surface below a round barrow, 2 ft (0.6 m) from crouched skeleton of child, also on old ground surface	70 x 14 x 13 (Th measured from Mortimer's illustration)	Not seen by JAS; described as jet by Mortimer (1905, 177) and presumed jet	-
18	Giants' Hills long barrow 1, Skendleby, Lincolnshire	Upper fill of ditch of long barrow. Beaker at same level in ditch; Beaker pottery in primary ditch fill and in mound	71 x 19 x 21	Not jet (JAS, AW)	XRF (MD, DH): shale or cannel coal
19, 20	Gop Cave (x 2), Flintshire	Cave, sub-megalithic funerary structure with remains of 14 crouched unburnt bodies. Mortlake-style Peterborough Ware; all-over ground flint flake knife; quartz pebbles; skewer pin; burnt animal bones. According to Boyd Dawkins (1901, 330), the 2 sliders and the ground flint knife were found 'in one group'	i) 54 x 22 x 16; ii) 70 x 29 x 27 (as published by Boyd Dawkins)	'Jet or Kimmeridge shale', according to Boyd Dawkins	-
21	Ogmore-by-Sea, Vale of Glamorgan, Wales	Stray, among other partly-worked items of the same local stone	50.9 x 29.8 x 15.6	Locally-available fine-grained soft stone	SEM (MD)
22	Linch Hill (burial 1), Stanton Harcourt, Oxfordshire	Crouched skeleton of young adult (see comment for sex) in pit at centre of double ring ditch; part-ground flint knife, used. Knife and slider found 'against the left forearm'	46 x 27 x 23	Jet (GB; also Dr H.J. Plenderleith, cited by Grimes)	XRF (GB)

References (see McInnes 1968 for further references)	*Current location*	*Comments; dates (calibrated using OxCal 4.1; 2σ values cited)*
Elgee 1930, 112, pl. XVIII, fig. 3; McInnes 1968, 137 ; www.teesmuseums.com	Dorman Museum, MIDDM: 1910.232 Middlesbrough	According to McInnes, like Ha[l]lmyre, of much cruder manufactur than the rest. Is certainly squat like Hal[l]myre and 'Hambleton Moor', and also shares with Hal[l]myre the grooving, on either side of the perforation, that differentiates the ends from the central section. Could have been made from a pebble of jet. Photo on website suggests it has been polished to a medium to high sheen, especially at one end (where it may have been enhanced by wear)
Unpublished; Terry Manby pers comm.	Unknown; stolen from finder	Three fragments, found through fieldwalking by the late Joe Davis
Brewster 1984; Clarke *et al.* 1984, no. 31, fig 3.35	Malton Museum P 117.1	[14]C date: 4520±90 BP (HAR-5587) 3500–2920 cal. BC
McInnes 1968, no. 6; Mortimer 1905, 73, fig. 154	Hull & East Riding Museum KINCM. 1942.175	Wear-polish around outer edges of perforation
Bussell 1976; McInnes 1968, no. 8; Mortimer 1905, 127, fig. 320; Thurnam 1870, fig. 206	Hull & East Riding Museum KINCM: B.118/349:42	
McInnes 1968, no. 7; Mortimer 1905, 177, fig. 445; Sheppard 1929, no. 445	Hull & E Riding Museum	McInnes shows it as having part of one end missing, whereas Mortimer and Sheppard show it as intact; McInnes' L measurement of 70 tallies with the L shown in Mortimer's illustration.
McInnes 1968, no. 3	British Museum 1935 04-12 0067	Radiocarbon dates from this monument relate to material in the mound (Kinnes 1992, 38), not to the secondary ditch fill
Boyd Dawkins 1901; McInnes 1968, nos. 15, 16	Last known location Manchester Museum; not found when curator contacted by JAS	It is unclear which of the individuals had been associated with the sliders. Three C14 dates for three of the individuals were obtained by Rick Schulting (Schulting & Gonzalez 2007) but these were affected by a laboratory problem at Oxford Radiocarbon Accelerator Unit and have been withdrawn; three replacement dates have produced results grouping between 3100 and 2900 cal BC, with one possibly extending as far back as 3300 cal. BC (though possibly subject to the 4th millennium calibration plateau). There is no guarantee that these date the sliders. More dates are planned (Schulting pers comm.)
Mary Davis pers comm.	National Museum Wales, unreg	Roughout
Bussell *et al.* 1982; Grimes 1960, 154–64; McInnes 1968, no. 4	Ashmolean Museum 1945.99	The 'warping and crazing' upon drying, described by Grimes, is characteristic of soft Whitby jet. L.F. Cowley (in Grimes 1960, 168) identified the sex of the individual as female, but re-examination of the remains by Prof Andrew Chamberlain has led to a re-identi fication as 'possible male, because it had a mix of male and female morphological features but the male ones predominated'. This individual has recently been C14-dated for the Beaker People Project: SUERC-26192 (GU-19938) 4760±30 BP, 3640–3380 cal. BC. (Date cited courtesy of Prof Mike Parker Pearson)

Table A2.19   List of jet and jet-like belt sliders (continued)

No.	Findspot	Context, associations	Dimensions (mm, L x W x Th where available)	Material ID: macroscopic, by whom*	Confirmed by analysis? by whom?*
23	Barrow Hills, Radley (near Abingdon), Oxfordshire	On hip of adult male crouched skeleton (age 30–35) in pit under oval barrow; leaf-shaped flint arrowhead. Beside adult female crouched skeleton (age 30–35) , with partly ground flint knife in front of her head	55 x 11 x 13 (dimensions from illustration)	Described in publication as 'shale or jet'	-
24	Basildon, Berkshire	Found on dump beside towpath of Thames Conservancy dredgings, so presumably originally in Thames	50 x 24	Described as jet by McInnes 1968; from Reading Museum photo, breakage pattern is consistent with jet (JAS)	-
25	Near Newbury, Berkshire	In peat, 8 ft (2.44 m) deep in a 12 ft (3.66 m)-thick peat bed; bones of red and roe deer and cave bear	93 x 19	Described as being 'of highly polished jet' in J Brit Arch Assoc XVI, 1860, 323	-
26	A13 Movers Lane, Barking, Essex	From *c* 150 mm thick deposit of alluvial clay sealing Neolithic features cut into terrace gravels; large assemblage of Mortlake-style Peterborough Ware pottery	34.9 x 9.3 x 10.2 (Fragment; est. original dimensions *c* 51 x 25 x 11, to nearest mm)	Jet (JAS)	-
27	Wiltshire?	No information, but assumed to be barrow	38 x 20.6 x 14.9 (including lump of consolidant, which has added *c* 1 mm to L and Th). Much of one side missing	Jet (JAS, AW)	-
28	Handley Down barrow 26, Dorset	Crouched skeleton under round barrow Slider found at hip. Peterborough Ware (almost all Mortlake style) in mound and in ditch fill; Beaker pottery at higher level in ditch fill	76.5 x 19.9 x 20.7	Jet (GB)	XRF (GB)
29	Pentewan tin streamworks, Cornwall	Found on old land surface, below 14.6 m of streamworks overburden, 'on a lavel with hazels, oaks etc.'	L 67	-	-

References (see McInnes 1968 for further references)	Current location	Comments; dates (calibrated using OxCal 4.1; 2σ values cited)
Bradley 1992	Ashmolean Museum	Male skeleton C14-dated to 4120±60 BP (BM-2707, 2880–2500 cal. BC) and female skeleton dated to 3860±50 BP (BM-2708, 2470–2150 cal. BC), but believed to be unreliable, as bones in poor state. Seem anomalously late, and since both individuals appear to have been buried together, would have expected dates to be closer to each other. Antler deposits in the ditches have produced dates of 4500±50 BP (BM-2391, 4420±70 BP (BM-2393), 4320±130 BP (BM-2390) and 4330±80 BP (BM-2391), calibrating to between 3360–3030 and 3335–2700 cal. BC (3360–2590 in the case of BM-2390). See Bradley 1992, 138, Garwood and Barclay 1999, 278 and Hey *et al.* 2011 for discussion
McInnes 1968, no. 2	Reading Museum 1962.132.1	Small part of one side missing
McInnes 1968, no. 1	Society of Antiquaries of London	
This publication	c/o Oxford Archaeology	
Annable & Simpson 1964, no. 131; McInnes 1968, no. 5	Devizes Museum DM 1469 (Brooke Collection)	High sheen around most of perforation edge on both sides could relate to use-wear, although no obvious use-wear signs in interior of perforation. The Brooke Collection was acquired in 1916; a reference to the slider by John Thurnam in 1871 (p. 513) makes it cleat that it had previously been in Sir Richard Colt Hoare's collection at Stourhead: 'In the Stourhead collection, but from what barrow does not appear, is a broken oblong object, an inch and a half in length, a sort of link or slider, perhaps for securing the belt. A perfect slider here figured, very similar in form, from a barrow at Thixendale, East Riding, Yorkshire, is in the Mortimer collection; and one smaller, from the peat, near Newbury, Berks, has been recently added to the museum of this Society [i.e. the Society of Antiquaries of London].'
Bussell *et al.* 1982; McInnes 1968, no. 2	Salisbury Museum 2c4 16	Skeleton recently C14-dated for Dr Mike Allen, as part of the English Heritage-funded Wor Barrow Project; date cited courtesy of Dr Allen: SUERC-33328, 4410±30BP, 3310–2910 cal. BC (Allen *et al.* in prep, A date with Wor Barrow: the life and death of the Wor Barrow people, Antiquaries Journal). Slider split and fell apart on the day after discovery, but fragment analysed; its decomposition is typical of what often happens with soft jet. (Pitt Rivers noted that even the woodgrain in the jet had been visible, and reports that an exact wooden copy of the slider was made)
Penhallurick 1986, 178, fig. 82	Lost	Found 1790; recorded (by William Copeland Borlase) 1871; since lost. from Borlase's engraving, is clearly of a black material and may be jet

available dating evidence relating to the Rudston regional style of Peterborough Ware, sparse though it is (Manby *et al.* 2003, 55; Vyner 2011, 242–3) suggests a similar currency. As regards the dating of partly, and fully-ground/polished flint knives, a category of artefact as discussed for example by Manby (1974), Kinnes (1979), Bradley (1999) and Hey *et al.* (2011, 445), a recently obtained radiocarbon date for skeletal remains associated with a partly-polished flake knife from the rich middle Neolithic round barrow grave at Liff's Low, Derbyshire, also falls within the same time span 3350–3100 cal BC (SUERC-26173: 4510±30 BP) (Jay 2010, 128). Whether any of the aforementioned recently-obtained dates for human remains from Gop Cave (3100–2900 cal BC) date the all-over ground flake knife found there is uncertain, but the possibility cannot be ruled out. Two fully-ground flint knives from Yorkshire, more neatly rectangular than the Gop Cave flake knife, have also recently been dated from associated human remains. One from Aldro barrow C75 (Mortimer 1905, 74, fig. 156) is associated with a date of 3320–2920 cal BC (OxA-V-2199-32: 4422±30 BP) (Mike Parker Pearson pers. comm.) while the other, from Duggleby Howe (Burial D) is associated with a date of 3090–2890 cal BC, modelled as 2980–2885 cal BC (OxA-16747: 4344±33 BP) (Gibson and Bayliss 2009, table 1 and 69).

Dates for comparable material from rich middle Neolithic graves

Belt sliders and partly-ground/polished flint knives form part of a set of objects found in rich middle Neolithic graves, others of which include antler maceheads, edge-polished flint axeheads and large leaf- and lozenge-shaped flint arrowheads. This material has been discussed by several authors, including Fiona Roe, who coined the term 'Macehead Complex' (1968), and Ian Kinnes, who tried to tease out chronological groupings among assemblages from Neolithic round barrows (Kinnes 1979 (his 'Stage D'); Kinnes 2004; cf. Hey *et al.* 2011, chapters 12, 14 and 15 on the Thames middle Neolithic graves). Recent radiocarbon dating programmes have helped to clarify the absolute dating of this material, with the Loveday *et al.* 'antler maceheads dating programme' placing that artefact type within the bracket 3500–2900 BC (Loveday *et al.* 2007); Mike Parker Pearson's *Beaker People Project* providing the aforementioned dates for Linch Hill, Liff's Low and Aldro barrow 175; and Alex Gibson and Alex Bayliss' project on the Neolithic round barrows of the Upper Great Wold Valley, Yorkshire, providing further valuable dates, especially for Duggleby Howe (Gibson and Bayliss 2009; 2010). In addition to the aforementioned flint knife date for Duggleby Burial D, of greatest relevance to the current discussion is their date for Duggleby Howe Burial G, associated with (*inter alia*) a waisted, edge-polished adze-head (the eponymous 'Duggleby adze') which offers a counterpart to the waisted, edge-polished axehead ('Seamer axe') from Whitegrounds (mean of OxA-17243, GrA-33104 and

SUERC-13939: 3335–3025 cal BC, modelled as 3345–3210 cal BC at 94% (4473±19 BP). See Gibson and Bayliss 2009, 68, on the fact that the associated, dated antler macehead was old when buried).

Taken together, this dating evidence points strongly to a currency of *c* 3350–2900 BC for jet and jet-like belt sliders, with the Linch Hill date suggesting that some may have been in use earlier. This period falls, of course, on a plateau in the radiocarbon calibration curve (*c* 4400 BP), although the recent Bayesian modelling of the Duggleby Howe dates suggests that it may be possible to address that issue and refine the chronology a little further. At present the only date which does not fall within that time frame is the one from Linch Hill (although the Whitegrounds date overlaps with it at the 2σ probability level), Finally, as for the attribution of the 'Hambleton Moor' slider to a post-Neolithic date by virtue of its alleged association, in a cist, with an Anglo-Saxon iron spearhead (Kinnes 2004, 107; McInnes 1968, 143): three points need to be noted. Firstly, as McInnes pointed out, details of the discovery of this object are not clearly recorded, and its findspot location is uncertain. Secondly, a recent *corpus* of Anglo-Saxon belt fittings (Marzinzik 2003) includes nothing remotely resembling the 'Hambleton Moor' artefact, either in form or in material. The same is true of the finds from the many Saxon graves in east Yorkshire investigated by Mortimer (1905): Kinnes had suggested that it had been a toggle rather than a slider, but again no parallel of Anglo-Saxon date suggests itself. Thirdly, as Terry Manby has pointed out (pers comm.) the object resembles a miniature waisted stone macehead of a type that is very likely to have been in use between 3500 and 2900 BC. Therefore, if the findspot genuinely was an Anglo-Saxon cist grave, and this is not certain, then one cannot rule out the possibility that the deceased had been buried with an ancient *objet trouvé*: 'Hambleton Moor' lies at the heart of the Yorkshire slider distribution.

Conclusion

In conclusion, the Movers Lane belt slider constitutes a prestigious, exotic artefact that formed part of a set of high status objects during the period *c* 3350–2900 BC and its presence at Movers Lane is consistent with middle Neolithic depositional practices.

Fired and unfired clay finds *by Lorraine Mepham, Charlotte Thompson and Louise Rayner*

Perforated clay balls and a loomweight from Trenches 23 and 21 Prince Regent Lane (PGL00) by Louise Rayner

Two ceramic beads or perforated clay balls, one of which was complete were recovered from the late Bronze Age to early Iron Age alluvial deposits overlying the main phase of peat formation in T23 (context 16, samples 1 and 2). Both beads are in a dark fabric with sand quartz inclusions, which gives a rough finish to the surface. The beads are crudely formed, sub-rounded and on the complete example has an off-central perforation. The maximum diameter of this bead is *c* 12mm.

The beads are not intrinsically datable but examples of similar artefacts are known from the late Bronze Age site at Runnymede Bridge (for example Needham and Spence 1996, fig. 99 C37, although this bead is larger in size) and from Danebury Iron Age hill fort (for artefacts classified as beads and perforated clay balls). Two examples from Danebury are more comparable in size to these beads (Cunliffe 1984, fig 7.44, no. 7.12 and 7.13).

Also examined from this site, is a fragment of loomweight from a late Bronze age deposit in T21 probably a cylindrical type, which are generally ascribed a Bronze Age date. The loom weight fragment is indicative of more settled activity than evidenced by the pottery alone, so is an important find.

Unfired clay from Freemasons Road Underpass (FRU01) *by Charlotte Thompson*

A total of 53 pieces of unfired clay, weighing 938g were recovered from 16 contexts (Table A2.20). All of the pieces were much abraded. The assemblage was recorded to Museum of London Specialist Services standards, established in accordance with the guidelines outlined by the Prehistoric Ceramics Research Group (PCRG 1992, revised 1995). The pieces were examined using a x20 binocular microscope and recorded by fabric, form and condition, and was quantified by 'fragment count' and weight.

The unfired clay objects are all made from a soft silty/sandy fabric that is crumbly or powdery to the touch. Almost all of the pieces have very rare coarse crushed calcinated flint inclusions; occasionally the fabric contains organics and this gives the matrix a vesicular appearance. The assemblage is much abraded, which is due to the crumbly nature of the fabric and the fact that the pieces are unfired.

No forms could to be distinguished due to the abraded nature of the assemblage. However, the unfired clay is likely to have been either weights such as loom or thatch weights, or to have been used for daub. It is worth noting that no piercing typical of clay weights have been found, and as no original surfaces are left it is not possible to see impressions of wattle or organics that would be present if the clay had been used for daub. However, given the abraded nature of the pieces, it is more than likely that such indications have simply not been preserved.

A piece from layer 32 has a marbled-effect fabric from clays being poorly mixed. This is of interest as it indicates that certain clays and inclusions were chosen and then mixed, showing that some degree of selection was used in the preparation of the clay

Table A2.20   Unfired clay from Freemasons Road Underpass

Context	Sample	Count	Weight (g)	Comments
9		1	45	Slightly off-coloured chunk of unfired clay. Rare very coarse flint incls
9		3	66	Largest piece has very coarse (7mm) rock and sub angular flint incls
25		1	13	Has one flat, unabraded surface. Clusters of fine bright red (iron rich?) incls. Very sandy
27	16	5	1	Very scrappy pieces
27		4	1	Small, scrappy pieces
32		2	40	Probably from same object. Coarse iron rich clay pellet incls
32		3	55	Largest piece has marbled effect from poor mixing of clay. Two smaller pieces have very rare coarse flint incls
32		1	19	Abraded, powdery piece. Rare coarse flint incls
33	55	1	3	Vesicular, abraded piece. Organic incls
47		3	57	Chunky pieces - two join. Very rare very coarse flint incls
49		1	6	Some accretion on exterior
49		1	15	V. smooth, worn lump of clay. Slightly sooted at one end. Occasional coarse flint incls
49	101	2	3	Small, abraded pieces. Rare coarse flint incls
52		5	293	Probably from same piece. Large chunks. One lightly sooted
54		4	36	Very abraded and rounded. Very rare coarse flint incls
66		2	4	Small, scrappy pieces
66		1	5	Crumbly/powdery lump of clay
69		4	25	Largest sherd has iron rich clay mixed in and occasional coarse flint incls. Two smallest sherds are brittle
74	102	1	3	Small, smoothed piece
81		4	154	Probably from one object. Largest piece has one flattened side with white accretion on it. Possibly building material
105		1	32	Tatty and very abraded piece
141		2	56	Abraded lump of clay
212		1	6	Crumbly. Full of organic incls and quartz

so as to attain a particular consistency, hardness or perhaps colour.

It is interesting that contexts 47, 49, 52, 74, 81, 105 and 141 contain both unfired clay objects and prehistoric pottery. In this regard, it is more than likely that the entire assemblage of unfired clay objects is prehistoric in date.

Due to the enigmatic nature of these pieces, it is not possible to establish their original form and function, although it is likely that they were used as building materials (such as daub or as thatch weights) or as loomweights.

Fired clay from Movers Lane (RIR01) by Lorraine Mepham

A very small quantity of fired clay (18 pieces, 294g) was recovered, deriving in small quantities from various features and deposits across the site (ditch 1198, alluvial deposits 1018/1021 and 5070, peat deposit 5263, gully 5159 and clay deposit in palaeochannel 5271). None of these are diagnostic, although a few have traces of surfaces; most if not all fragments are likely to be structural in origin.

Appendix 3: Environment and economy

Pollen from Freemasons Road Underpass
by Denise Druce (Fig. 4.3, A3.1)

Introduction

The site at Freemasons Road Underpass revealed a buried Neolithic to Bronze Age weathered land surface with flint artefacts plus a number of cut features sealed by peat. Radiocarbon dates retrieved from the top and bottom of the peat indicate accumulation commenced at 2230-2030 cal BC (SUERC-24600: 3745±35 BP) during the early Bronze Age. The top of the peat, which provided a date of 1050-840 cal BC (SUERC-24604: 2800±35 BP) during the late Bronze Age, was sealed by a layer of bluish grey clay alluvium probably deposited as a result of a rise in relative sea-level. The features associated with the deposits appear to be situated on the periphery of settlement; an early to middle Bronze Age structure forming a double row of substantial timber piles may have provided access across an area of wetland.

A number of monoliths taken from T23 and Area A, during the Phase II and Phase III works at Freemasons Road Underpass, were assessed for their pollen potential (A. Haggart in Gifford and Partners 2001a; 2003b). The Phase II pollen assessment looked at the potential of all the various sediment units present in the sequence, the Phase III assessment concentrated on the organic deposits associated with the piled structure, including its interface with the overlying minerogenic deposits. The assessment demonstrated that pollen was well preserved through peat and upper alluvial deposits but less well preserved in the other deposits investigated, particularly the basal deposits. This preliminary study showed an environment of lime and hazel woodland giving way to alder carr and saltmarsh conditions probably related to a period of sea-level rise in the Thames estuary during the later Holocene (related to Devoy's Thames III (1979) or Model Stage 4 and 5 of Bates and Whittaker 2004). In addition, the assessment showed indications of the known decline in lime woodland in the area, which has been associated with Bronze Age anthropogenic activity, and also indicated possible arable activity in the vicinity.

Further pollen work on the Freemasons Road Underpass deposits was recommended to provide a detailed record of landscape change in the area associated with both regional environmental parameters, such as fluctuations in relative sea-level, and with more local, perhaps anthropogenically driven, landscape changes at the dryland/wetland interface. The results may also be compared with other recent pollen studies from the Thames Valley, such as those from excavations carried out in advance of the Channel Tunnel Rail Link (Andrews *et al.* 2011; Bates and Stafford forthcoming; Wenban-Smith *et al.* forthcoming). Five monoliths taken through a section from the sump area just outside Area A revealed a similar sediment sequence to that observed in T23. Three overlapping monoliths, samples 111, 112 and 113, were chosen for full palynological investigations (Fig. 4.3).

Methodology

Detailed lithological descriptions and sub-sampling of the monoliths used in this study were carried out by the author. Each monolith was cleaned and described in the laboratory. Eighteen sub-samples were taken in total, and of these, six came from the upper part of the organic silty sand (layer 5), two came from the highly organic silty sand (layer 4), nine came from the peat deposit (layer 2), and one came from the uppermost minerogenic deposit (layer 1). The two lowest sub-samples, taken at -0.83m and -0.93m OD respectively from the silty sand deposit layer 5, contained very few pollen grains and are therefore not included in the results. The remaining 16 sub-samples provided the data for the pollen diagram (Figure A3.1), where the depths are expressed as metres (m) OD and the data as percentages of the total land pollen and spore sum (sumP). Aquatic taxa and other palynomorphs and charcoal particles are presented as percentages of sumP + sum of the category to which they belong. Calculations and diagrams were made using the programs TILIA and TILIA-GRAPH in TGView (Grimm 1990). The pollen diagram was divided into five pollen assemblage zones (PAZ), and these were placed by visual examination of the pollen curves.

Sub-samples of a standard size (1ml in volume) were prepared for pollen analysis using the standard technique of heating with hydrochloric acid, sodium or potassium hydroxide, sieving, hot hydrofluoric acid, and Erdtman's acetolysis to remove carbonates, humic acids, large particles, silicates, and cellulose, respectively. The samples were then stained with safranin, dehydrated with tertiary butyl alcohol and mounted in 2000 centistoke silicone oil (Method B of Berglund and Ralska-Jasiewiczowa (1986)). Tablets containing a known number of *Lycopodium* spores were added to the known volume of sediment at the beginning of the preparation so that pollen and spore concentrations could be calculated (Stockmarr 1971). Pollen was counted from equally spaced traverses across whole slides at a magnification of x400 (x1000 for critical examinations) until a minimum sum of 500 terrestrial pollen and spores was reached, if possible. Identifications were aided by a pollen key (Moore *et al.* 1991) and a small modern reference collection held by OA North. Cereal-type grains were defined using the criteria of Andersen (1979). Indeterminate grains were recorded using groups based on those of Birks (1973) as an indication of the state of pollen preservation. Charcoal particles >5 microns were also recorded following the procedures of Peglar (1993). Other identifiable inclusions on the pollen slides (including: fungal and algae spores, remains of dinoflagellate cysts, foraminfera) were also registered. Plant nomenclature follows Stace (1997).

Pollen results: the 'sump sequence'

PAZ1: -0.75 to -0.68m OD (layer 5, organic silty sand)

Arboreal pollen is relatively well represented at the very base of this zone with values of *c* 75% total land pollen and spores (referred to hereafter as TLP). *Alnus glutinosa* (alder) and *Corylus avellana* (hazel) maintain consistent levels during this zone, both with values of around 20 to 25% TLP. *Tilia cordata* (lime) has a similar value of 25% at the base of this zone, but subsequently declines to about 15% TLP, which is reflected in the summary pollen curve. *Quercus* (oak), *Pinus sylvestris* (Scots pine), cf. *Taxus baccata* (yew) and *Ulmus* (elm) are also represented in low numbers. Poaceae (grass) pollen is initially poorly represented but increases to 20% TLP in the middle of the zone. *Cerealia*-type (cereal-type) pollen is also recorded at the very base of this zone, however, the similarity of cereal pollen with some wild grasses, such as *Glyceria* (sweet-grasses), means that the evidence for cereal cultivation at this time is uncertain. The diversity of the herbaceous assemblage is relatively low and includes *Taraxacum*-type (dandelion-type) and *Plantago*-undiff. (plantain), which both have values of *c* 5% to 7% TLP. Other herbaceous taxa include *Aster*-type (daisy-type), *Plantago lanceolata* (ribwort plantain) and *Rubiaceae* (bedstraw). Low values of Cyperaceae (sedge), Caryophyllaceae (pink family), *Potentilla*-type (cinquefoils), and *Ranunculus*-type (buttercups) are recorded in the top of the zone. Undifferentiated *Pteropsida* (fern) spore values peak to values of *c* 15% in the middle of this zone, and *Pteridium aquilinum* (bracken) spores increase to about 10% TLP at the top of this zone. Some pollen grains from aquatics, such as *Lemna* (duckweed) and *Potamogeton* (pondweed) are present, but in very low numbers.

PAZ2: -0.68 to -0.60m OD (layer 4, highly organic silty sand)

Arboreal pollen values increase in this zone, attaining values of about 80% TLP, and this increase is most marked in values of *Tilia*. The rise in arboreal pollen is accompanied by a decrease in herbaceous pollen to less than about 10% TLP. Poaceae show a marked decline in this zone, attaining values of less than 5% TLP compared to a peak of around 20% TLP in the preceding zone. *Plantago*-undiff increases slightly at the top of this zone.

PAZ3: -0.60 to -0.48m OD (layer 2, humified peat)

After the peak in arboreal pollen to about 80% TLP in Zone 2 values very gradually decrease to around 60% TLP during this zone. *Alnus* and *Corylus* values remains relatively constant at about 20 to 30% TLP and 10 to 15% TLP respectively, *Tilia* values, however, decrease from about 20% to 10% TLP at the top of the zone. Additional arboreal pollen grains include low numbers of *Hedera helix* (ivy), *Rosaceae* undiff. (rose family) and *Salix* (willow). The suite of herbaceous pollen remains relatively restricted and numbers decrease during this zone, attaining values of no more than *c* 5% TLP. In contrast, however, *Pteropsida* spores increase dramatically from about 10% TLP to about 40% TLP. *Potamogeton* values increase slightly in the middle of this zone.

PAZ4: -0.48 to -0.38m OD (layer 2, humified peat)

Alnus pollen values increase to about 40% TLP at the base of this zone but then decrease to *c* 10/15% TLP in the upper half. *Corylus* and *Tilia* both decrease in value, and *Tilia*, especially, continues to show the most marked decline reaching values of less than 5% at the top of the zone. As in the preceding zone, *Quercus* pollen values fluctuate slightly but still represents no more than *c* 5% TLP at its highest value. The suite of other arboreal pollen taxa remains largely unchanged and at low values. *Fraxinus*, however, is no longer present, but occasional grains of *Fagus sylvatica* (beech) are recorded in the bottom half of this zone. The diversity of herbaceous pollen increases substantially and both Poaceae and Cyperaceae show marked increases from less than 5% TLP in the previous zone, to values of about 20% TLP in this zone; herbaceous pollen representing roughly 50% to 60% TLP at this time. *Aster*-type, *Taraxacum*-type, and *Ranunculus*-type pollen values increase very slightly, while *Plantago lanceolata* pollen increases to about 10% TLP and *Plantago major/media* (great/hoary plantain) pollen also becomes better represented. Other herbs appear for the first time in the record, many of them restricted to this zone only. They include cf. *Alchemilla* (lady's-mantle), *Apium*-type (marshworts), *Artemisia* (mugworts), *Cirsium/Carduus* (thistles), *Thalictrum* (meadowrue), *Centaurium* (centauries), *Fallopia convolvulus* (black-bindweed), *Filipendula* (meadowsweet), *Caltha palustris* (marsh marigold), *Rhinanthus*-type (yellow-rattle), *Rumex acetosa*-type (sorrel), and *Urtica* (nettle). *Cerealia*-type pollen is recorded once more, this time accompanied by occasional grains of

Avena/Triticum-type (oat/wheat) and *Hordeum*-type (barley-type) pollen. *Pteropsida* spores show a marked decline in this zone, decreasing to values of less than 10% TLP. *Pteridium*, however, increases from less than 5% TLP to about 10% TLP in the top half of this zone. Aquatic pollen increases slightly and both *Typha angustifolia/Sparganium* (lesser bulrush/bur-reeds) and *Typha latifolia* (bulrush) are recorded for the first time; the former reaching values of around 10% TLP plus aquatics. The occurrence of non-pollen palynomorphs such as green algae and fungal spores also increases in this zone.

PAZ5: -0.38 to -0.13m OD (layer 2, humified peat and layer 1, blue-grey clay)

Arboreal pollen values decrease further to about 10% TLP in this zone and *Tilia* disappears from the record altogether. Both *Alnus* and *Corylus*, however, increase slightly at the very top of this zone. The herbaceous component remains relatively uniform, representing around 30% TLP. However, herb diversity is much reduced compared to the preceding zone. Poaceae and Cyperaceae pollen continue to dominate the herbaceous assemblage, at values of 10% TLP and 15% TLP respectively. Occasional grains of *Cerealia*-type, *Hordeum*-type, and *Cannabis/Humulus* (hemp/hop) are recorded in the middle of this zone. The number of *Pteropsida* spores increases dramatically reaching values of approximately 50% TLP. The number of aquatic pollen grains decreases in this zone, as do the number and diversity of algae and fungal spores.

Interpretation and discussion

The pollen data in the earliest zone (PAZ1), which stratigraphically relates to the late Neolithic/early Bronze Age weathered sand (layer 005), indicates a local environment of damp alder carr and sedge, with lime, hazel and oak woodland growing on the drier slopes or interfluves. Areas of disturbed or lightly grazed ground are indicated by the presence of dandelion and plantain. There is evidence of possible cereal cultivation with the presence of one or two cereal-type pollen grains at –0.75m OD. However some wetland and marine grasses such as floating sea-grass (*Glyceria fluitans*) and sea barley (*Hordeum marinum*) produce very similar pollen grains. The decrease in arboreal pollen and corresponding increase in grass pollen suggests possible clearance; although lime woodland appears to be most affected as both alder and hazel appear to show very little change (possibly evidence for a first lime decline?).

A mid Holocene decline in lime pollen has been recorded in many diagrams from southern England and is thought to be caused by anthropogenic activity (Turner 1962). Normally associated with late Neolithic/Bronze Age activity, which saw the more-or-less complete removal of lime from the Thames valley landscape (Devoy 1979; Sidell and Wilkinson 2004; Wilkinson *et al.* 2000) there is

increasing evidence for earlier, temporary, periods of decline (Huckerby, Peglar and Verrill in Bates and Stafford forthcoming). However it is unclear whether these episodes were anthropogenically driven or caused by rising water levels (or both?). The marked but temporary decline in lime during PAZ1 at this site, occurred some time before 2230-2030 cal BC (see date of base of peat PAZ3 below), and commensurate with its decline is a spread in ferns, bracken and grassland. It is quite possible that its early decline here was as a result of increased clearance or grazing pressure on drier ground.

The second zone (PAZ2) corresponds with the development of the organic silty sand (layer 004). The pollen data indicates a recovery in the lime (and hazel) woodland on drier ground and a corresponding decline in areas of grassland and bracken. The locally growing alder carr shows very little change at this point, subsequently any local disturbance caused by nearby activity is not yet apparent.

The pollen data within the third zone (PAZ3, peat layer 002) indicates a period of relative stability with a slight increase in oak to the detriment of hazel at the start, but a very steady decline in woodland generally. As with the decline in woodland at the base of the diagram, lime (and this time oak) appears to be the most affected and ferns take advantage of the lighter conditions on the woodland floor. A slight increase in pondweed suggests increased wetness, plus increased waterlogging is also indicated by the onset of peat development. A radiocarbon date at -0.60m OD at the base of the peat (see Appendix 1.1) produced an early Bronze Age date of 2280-2240 (7.5%) and 2230-2030 (87.9%) cal BC (SUERC-24600: 3745±35 BP).

PAZ4 (peat layer 002) shows the period of most change and records a decline in the local alder and hazel woodland alongside a significant decline in lime woodland on the surrounding slopes. The decline in woodland is accompanied by a decline in ferns and a slight increase in bracken, which may indicate increased grazing (Behre 1986). There is also evidence for nearby cereal cultivation. Damp species-rich sedge/grassland developed immediately at the site and freshwater pools and streams are prevalent with green algae, aquatics, and bulrushes. This increase in wet conditions may be as a result in a rise in the water table associated with Devoy's Thames III (1979) period of estuary expansion, although there is very little evidence of encroaching salt-marsh conditions at the site at this time. A radiocarbon date at -0.48m OD at the base of this zone (see Appendix 1.1) produced an early Bronze Age date of 1880-1660 cal BC (SUERC-24503: 3435±30 BP). This corresponds extremely well with the piled timber structure (Str. 32) and the linear 'enclosure' gully (Gp.199) in the northern coffer dam. Open conditions are maintained during PAZ5 (peat layer 002 and silty clay layer 001), however, a slight regeneration in alder and hazel is indicated at the very top of the diagram; lime, however, has more-or-less disappeared from the record altogether. A local sedge-dominated, relatively species poor environment has developed at the site, and ferns have spread on the adjoining slopes. This encroachment of ferns may indicate a period of possible abandonment at the site. A radiocarbon date at -0.32m OD towards the top of the peat produced a late Bronze Age date of 1050-840 (95.4%) cal BC (SUERC-24604: 2800±35 BP). Although the stratigraphy shows a shift from peat to clay, apart from a slight rise in goosefoot pollen, which includes species that grow on saltmarshes, there is very little in the pollen assemblage to suggest a major increase in saline conditions as yet, although the sedimentary changes seen here are likely to be related to shifts in the morphology of the river during a period of estuary expansion (Devoy 1979).

Conclusion

The pollen and dating evidence shows that peat development at the pollen site took place during the late Neolithic, probably as a result of increased waterlogging due to estuary expansion. Although

there is evidence for an earlier, temporary clearance episode (a first lime decline), the most marked change in the pollen record, linked to a significant decline in woodland (a second lime decline) and the development of grassland and pasture, with evidence of cereal cultivation, is almost synchronous with the date of the Bronze Age piled structure and possible enclosure (see PAZ4 above). At the same time, the pollen evidence indicates the development of reedswamp with freshwater pools and streams immediately at the site, which would support the view that the wooden piled structure was a possible bridge, platform or jetty.

The pollen evidence from Freemasons Road Underpass is consistent with the other pollen sites from the A13 roadscheme and with other London sites such as those from Bramcote Green (Thomas and Rackham 1996; Sidell and Wilkinson 2004), Silvertown (Wilkinson *et al.* 2000; Sidell and Wilkinson 2004) and STDR4 in the Ebbsfleet Valley (Druce, Peglar and Huckerby in Wenban-Smith *et al.* forthcoming). All of which show a Neolithic and early Bronze Age landscape of mixed deciduous woodland dominated by lime with an understorey

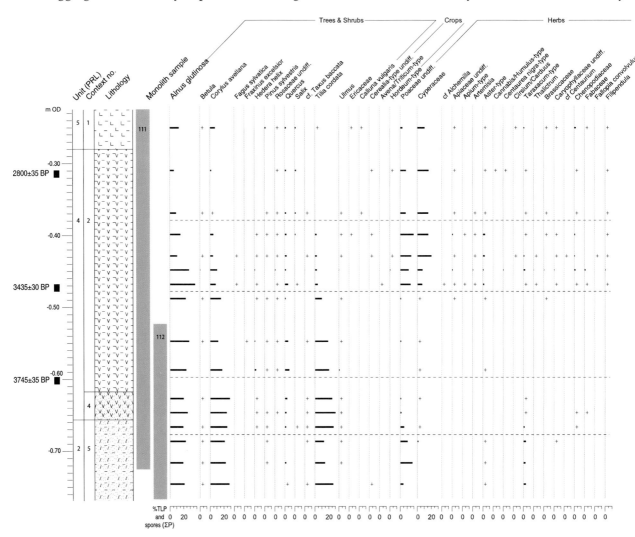

Fig. A3.1 Pollen percentage diagram, Freemasons Road Underpass

of ferns growing on drier ground, and alder carr growing in wetter locations. The Movers Lane diagrams also show at least two periods of lime decline, which is commensurate with increasing evidence of grassland, pasture and cereal cultivation. Like the evidence from Freemasons Road, the (final) lime decline at Movers Lane and other London sites, sees an almost complete removal of lime from the landscape. This coincides with a marked increase in Bronze Age occupation and associated construction. Underlying and, no doubt, influencing this activity is a period of estuary expansion and increased waterlogging.

Pollen and diatoms from Woolwich Manor Way
by Andrew Haggart (Figs 5.3, A3.2-3.10)

Introduction

Two sequences were submitted for detailed analysis of pollen and diatoms from Woolwich Manor Way. The first derived from a deep sequence of alluvial and peat deposits sampled in TP1 during the evaluation stage at the far western extreme of the site

(Fig. 5.3). This sequence was initially assessed in 2001 (Haggart in Gifford and Partners 2001b) and was sampled by four monoliths (M1-M4) covering 3.5m of the stratigraphy between -4.23 and -0.73m OD, but with a gap in the coverage of 0.35m between -2.48 and -2.13m OD. The second sequence derived from the detailed excavation of Area 2 focusing on the peat deposits associated with trackway 2/14 (Fig. 5.3). This sequence was assessed in 2003 (Haggart in Gifford and Partners 2003a) and sampled by two monoliths (M2A and M2B) totalling 0.94m in length between -1.32 to -0.38m OD. Particle size analysis was also conducted on some of the samples from both sequences, along with geochemical analysis on the trackway sequence to aid in the interpretation of the assemblages.

Methodology

The pollen samples were prepared using standard extraction techniques. A known number of exotic *Lycopodium* spores in tablet form were added to 1cm^3 of fresh sediment allowing pollen concentration

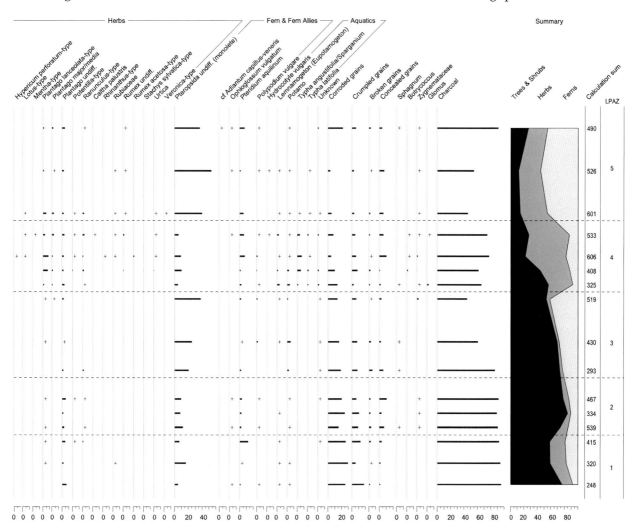

Fig. A3.1 *Pollen percentage diagram, Freemasons Road Underpass (continued)*

values to be derived (Stockmarr 1971). The samples were then deflocculated overnight in a sonic bath using calgon and passed through sieves of 180μm and 10μm. The larger sieve is designed to remove coarser plant debris and the smaller sieve allows fine silt and clay-sized particles to pass through but retains the pollen-sized fraction. The samples were then mixed with a non-toxic heavy liquid, sodium polytungstate, made up to a specific gravity of 2.0. At this specific gravity, the organic component, including pollen, floats and the majority of the mineral component sinks, enabling physical separation. This procedure reduces degradation of pollen grains during extraction from mineral sediments and represents a significant and safer advance on the former use of Hydrofluoric acid to digest the mineral fraction. Following separation, the samples were subjected to standard acetolysis procedures to remove cellulose, (Erdtman 1960) then stained with safranine and mounted on slides using glycerine jelly. The slides were scanned at 400x magnification until a total of 400 total land pollen grains (TLP) were reached. In the Trench 2 profile at 2 levels (0.45m and 0.55m) 100 and 241grains were counted, bringing the average down to 348 ±116. In the TP1 profile at three levels; 3.55m, 4.75m and 5.15m were below the 400 target reducing the average to 356 ± 89. All pollen and other significant content including microscopic charcoal fragments were recorded. Pollen identifications were made using Moore, Webb and Collinson (1991), Reille (1992) and the reference type slide collection at the University of Greenwich. Nomenclature follows Bennett (1994), Bennett, Whittington and Edwards (1994) and Stace (1991). The preservation of each determinable grain counted was also recorded under the categories amorphous, corroded, broken, folded or well preserved whilst indeterminable grains were also categorised using the first four categories above to which a fifth, concealed, was added.

For the diatom analysis hydrogen peroxide (30%) was added to the samples to remove organic material. The samples were allowed to stand and the reaction took place at room temperature. After several days, when the effervescence had stopped and the samples had settled, the supernatant liquid was decanted and replaced with distilled water. A random sample was transferred using a disposable pipette to a coverslip covered in distilled water and allowed to settle and dry. The coverslip was then fixed on a microscope slide using Naphrax diatom mountant. Slides were scanned at x 1000 magnification. The lowest number of diatoms counted was 144 at 3.05m and the highest 458 at 2.85m, overall averaging 300 ± 100 per slide. Identifications were made with reference to Cleve-Euler (1951-55), Hartley (1996) Hendey (1964), Hustedt (1930-61), Krammer and Lange-Bertalot (1986) and van der Werff and Huls (1957-64). Use was also made of the following electronic resources: ADIAC (1998-2001), the ANSP Algae Image Database and Kelly *et al.* (2005). Nomenclature follows Williams *et al.* (1988)

and the University College London (UCL) Amphora checklist.

Particle size analysis was undertaken by laser diffraction on a Malvern Mastersizer 2000 in wet dispersion mode, the organic material having previously been removed by digestion in 30% concentrated hydrogen peroxide. Samples for geochemical analysis were oven-dried overnight then crushed to a powder in a ball mill. They were then transferred to glass tubes and dried overnight at 105°C. For the major and trace elements a lithium metaborate fusion process was used prior to ICPMS and ICPOES analysis.

Test pit 1

The stratigraphy comprised a basal sandy flint gravel with well rounded flint clasts between 5.60m and 5.35m. Overlying this was a dark greyish-brown silty clay with carbonate patches which gives way to a 40mm thick layer of clayey silt at 5.08m. Above the clayey silt was a more organic, very dark grey clay-silt with visible plant fragments which is in turn succeeded by 2m thick very dark brown silty peat at 4.80m. This peat bed is variable in nature ranging from true peat to silty peat. In places there are abundant wood fragments and occasional pockets of dark greyish-brown organic silt. Between 4.50m and 4.40m in the base of monolith 2 there was an extremely dry and cemented peat suggesting a period of desiccation and compaction.

The peat layer has been AMS dated in three places (see Appendix 1.2); towards the base between 4.68m and 4.78m (4580-4350 cal BC; Beta-152740: 5630±60 BP) in the middle between 3.94m and 4.04m (3350-2890 cal BC ; Beta-147956: 4410±70 BP) and towards the top of the layer between 3.06m and 3.16m (1750-1490 cal BC; Beta-149754: 3330±60 BP). Above the peat, at 2.80m, was a dark greyish-brown silt to clay-silt, more organic toward the base, which in turn was overlain by a yellow-brown oxidised clay-silt. Above 1.00m is modern made ground.

Particle size

Twelve samples were analysed for particle size by laser granulometry between 2.90m and 1.85m within the upper part of the main peat bed and the overlying silty clay (Fig. A3.2). There was little difference between samples, most were categorized as poorly sorted fine and medium silts with clay content varying between 9% and 16%. The lowermost sample within the upper part of the main peat bed at 2.9m (-1.88m OD) does contain a small proportion of sand, which is hard to explain. The radiocarbon date in the upper part of the main peat bed suggests this happened after 1750-1490 cal BC. Evidence from Trench 2 at higher altitudes (-0.96m OD) suggests there was incorporation of sand, perhaps from trackway traffic or local soil erosion at this time. It is possible therefore that some reworked sand was transported to lower altitudes and incorporated into the peat at TP1

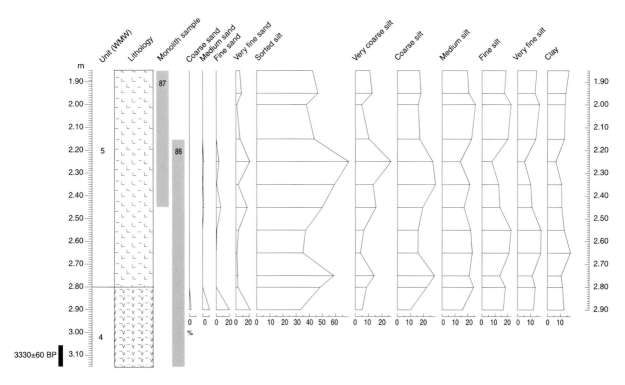

Fig. A3.2   Particle size distribution curves by size classes, TP1, Woolwich Manor Way

Because particles below about 10μm in equivalent spherical diameter (fine silts and clays) flocculate and aggregate at the freshwater/saltwater boundary in estuaries and modern particle size methods such as laser granulometry measure a particle's disaggregated size, what is actually measured may not be meaningful to reconstructing the depositional environment (McCave *et al.* 1995a).

These authors considered the 10μm limit to be much more meaningful in terms of sedimentary processes than the traditional 2μm boundary between clay and silt or even the 63μm boundary between silt and sand. It led them to define the 'sortable silt' mean, which is the average size of the 10–63μm fraction. They suggested that this is the size fraction that varies in response to hydrodynamic processes at the sea bed and from which relative changes in current speed can be inferred. They used this proxy successfully to map palaeocurrent fields in the North Atlantic (McCave *et al.* 1995b).

Figure A3.2 also contains the average 'sorted silt' curve, the average of the 10-63μm fraction for each sample. There appear to be two main peaks in the 'sorted silt' curve equating to 2.75m and 2.25m, the latter of which is accompanied by a rise in the very fine and fine sand category, which might relate to slightly higher energy in the depositional environment.

Diatoms

Fourteen levels were prepared for diatom analysis between 3.05m within the upper layers of the main peat bed to 1.85m within the upper silty clay.

Preservation was variable and in six of the levels it was not possible to obtain a meaningful count. The remaining eight levels are shown in Figure A3.3. On the diagram the diatoms are grouped from left to right according to their ecological codes of Hustedt (1953) as compiled by Denys (1991/2). On the left are fully marine polyhalobous diatoms which give way to this brackish mesohalobous forms and then to largely freshwater oligohalobous types.

The diagram (A3.3) is divided into two diatom assemblage zones, above and below the diatom-barren zone between 2.85m and 2.35m. The boundary has been arbitrarily placed halfway between at 2.60m.

WMWTP1 A 3.05m–2.60m (-2.03 to -1.58m OD)
The diagram is dominated by the brackish form *Cyclotella striata* with an average of 46% total diatoms (TD). The largely freshwater *Pinnularia* genus occurs in frequencies between 8-11% and there are declines in the marine forms *Plagiogramma van-heurckii* and *Rhaphoneis amphiceros*. Total numbers of taxa are low, at about 35 per level.

WMWTP1 B 2.60m- 1.85m (-1.58m to -0.83m OD)
Cyclotella striata again dominates with an average of 31% but there are many more taxa present, ranging from 46 to 70 and averaging 53. Prominent polyhalobous forms include *Opephora marina* and *Rhaphoneis amphiceros* whilst oligohalobous diatoms include *Cocconeis disculus* and *C placentula* and *Gyrosigma acuminatum*.

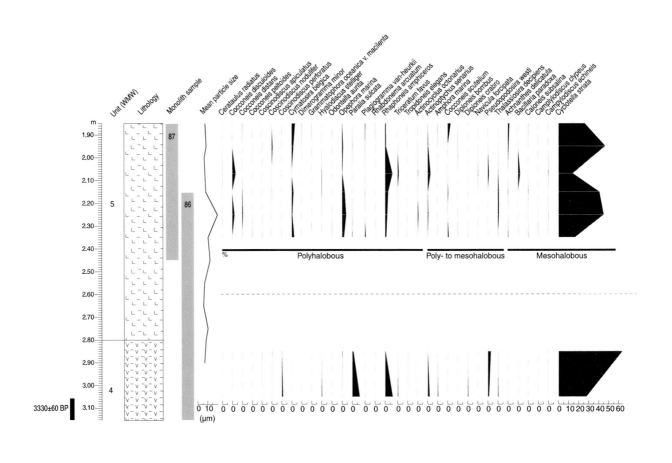

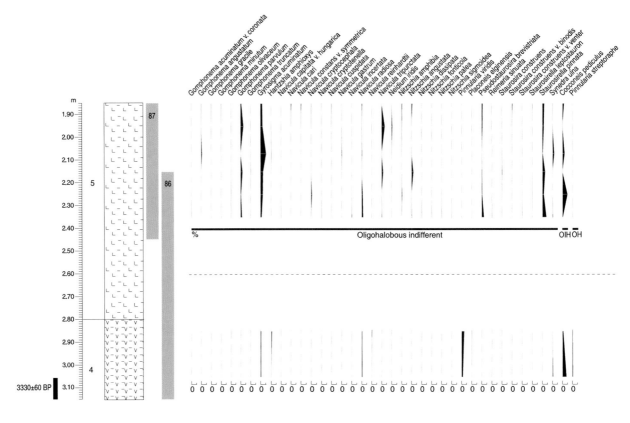

Fig. A3.3   Diatom diagram from TP1, Woolwich Manor Way

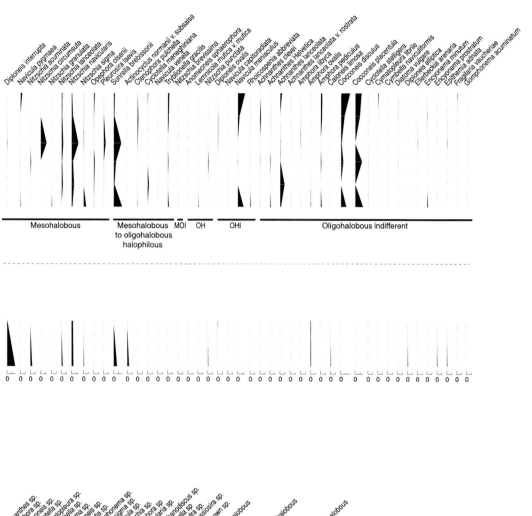

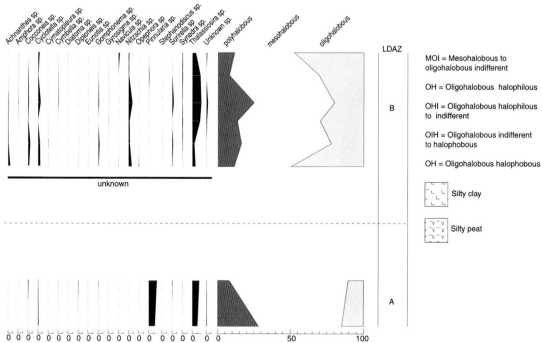

Fig. A3.3   Diatom diagram from TP1, Woolwich Manor Way (continued)

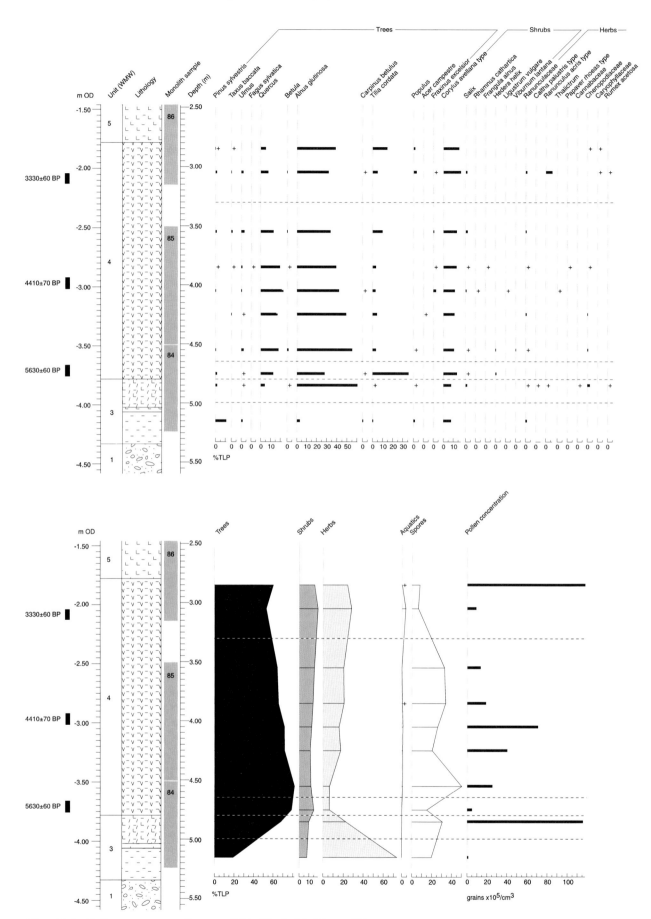

Fig. A3.4   Pollen percentage diagram, TP1, Woolwich Manor Way

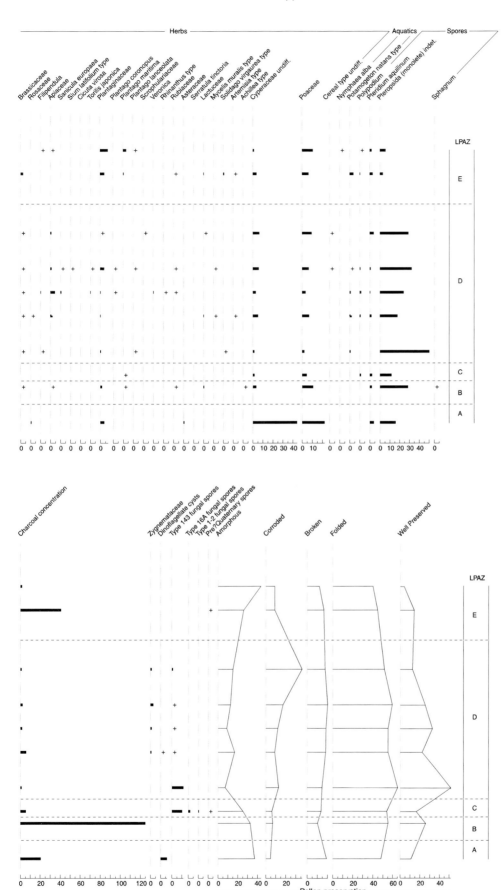

Fig. A3.4   Pollen percentage diagram, TP1, Woolwich Manor Way (continued)

The most abundant diatom in the lowermost count at 3.05m is *Cyclotella striata*, an estuarine planktonic form, common in tidal channels (Vos and de Wolf 1988) and often abundant in the spring plankton (Hendey, 1964). The presence of *Diploneis interrupta* at 8% suggests the presence of saltmarsh nearby. *D. interrupta* is a brackish aerophile whose life habit is epipelic, living freely on the substrate. It inhabits the upper part of saltmarshes at or just below the Mean High Water Spring Tide level (Innes *et al.* 1996; Vos and de Wolf 1998). This would be in accord with the rise in Plantaginaceae including *P. maritima* in the upper part of the pollen diagram. *Cyclotella striata* then rises to 64% TD at 2.85m suggesting an increase in saline conditions.

The second diatom assemblage zone within the upper silty clay is again dominated by *Cyclotella striata*, while *Thalassiosira* sp. averages 6% throughout the zone. This form has been placed in the unknown category because they are hard to identify to species level using light microscopy (Belcher and Swale 1986). However the majority of species in this genus are found in the marine plankton (Round *et al.* 1990; Hendey 1964).

Overall the diatoms suggest deposition in a marine-brackish environment, probably a tidal muflat. However there may be subtle changes evident. *Cyclotella striata* frequencies are only 16% at 2.35m (Fig. A3.3) and oligohalobous diatoms such as *Navicula menisculus*, *Cocconeis disculus*, *C. placentula* and *Staurosirella pinnata* rise in prominence. While the first three have quite wide salinity tolerance, *S. pinnata* is a freshwater species often found attached to sand grains in freshwater lagoons, lakes, pools and ditches. The oligohalobous diatoms total 57% at this level possibly suggesting an increased freshwater influence.

Cyclotella striata frequencies rise to 45% at 2.25m and then fall to 14% at 2.07m. This time the decline in *C. striata* seems to be accompanied by a rise in marine planktonic forms such as *Rhaphoneis amphiceros*, *Triceratum favus* and *Actinoptychus senarius* suggesting an increased marine influence. The decline in mesohalobous forms *Nitzschia circumsuta*, *Nitzschia navicularis* and *Surirella brebissonii* from 2.07m seems to be mirrored by an increase in oligohalobous forms such as *Navicula menisculus*, *Cocconeis disculus* and *C. placentula*.

Pollen

Ten levels were counted for pollen between 5.15m and 2.85m (Fig. A3.4) and five local pollen assemblage zones have been described.

PAZA: 5.15m–5.00m (-4.13m to -3.98 m OD)
This zone comprises a single count within the dark greyish-brown silty clay that overlies the basal sandy gravel. The zone is dominated by Cyperaceae (44%) and Poaceae (22%) followed by undifferentiated monolete fern spores (16%) and *Pteridium*. *Pinus sylvestris* is the largest contributor to total tree pollen, but reaching only 11%.

PAZB: 5.00m–4.80m (-3.98m to -3.78m OD)
Again this zone comprises a single count at 4.85m within the very dark grey clay-silt unit which lies just below the main peat bed. *Alnus glutinosa* frequences rise to dominate at 60%TLP with subsidiary *Quercus* at 11%. Other notable features are the fall in Cyperaceae and Poaceae to 4% and 11% respectively. This level has the highest microscopic charcoal concentration and total pollen concentration also shows a peak at 115 x 10³ grains / cm³.

PAZC: 4.80m–4.65m (-3.78 to -3.63m OD)
This zone consists of a single count at 4.75m within the basal layers of the main peat bed. It is unusual in that it has very high *Tilia* frequencies (36% TLP) which exceed those of *Alnus glutinosa* which falls to 28%. The zone is characterised by a very low pollen concentration of 5 x 10³ grains/ cm³. Fungal spores of type 16A and 143 are also present.

PAZD: 4.65m–3.30m (-3.63m to -2.28m OD)
This zone comprises five levels within the base and middle of the main peat bed. *Alnus glutinosa* pollen rises to 55% then falls to 34% through the zone. *Quercus* rises to a peak of 22% TLP at 4.05m then declines thereafter. *Tilia* frequencies are consistently low through the zone, averaging just 5%. Cyperaceae and Poaceae are also at uniformly low frequencies, averaging only 4% and 6% respectively. Cerealia-type pollen is present in low frequencies in the upper two levels in the zone at 3.85m and 3.55m.

PAZE: 3.30m–2.85m (-2.28 to -1.83m OD)
Quercus representation continues to fall to 5% by 2.85m. *Alnus glutinosa* and *Tilia* frequencies show a slight resurgence to 39% and 14% TLP. Also of note are the rises in Ranunculaceae, Brassicaceae and Plantagniaceae pollen and the aquatic *Potamogeton natans*-type towards the top of the main peat bed.

Cyperaceae and Poaceae dominate the first pollen zone, with total herb pollen reaching 73% and total tree pollen only reaching 19%. This might suggest a fairly open environment, however total pollen concentration is extremely low, the lowest of all levels counted, at 1.36 x 10³ grains/cm³ and the total pollen count at 127 TLP was also low. No diatoms were encountered either, presumably due to post-depositional dissolution, but the presence of dinoflagellate cysts in the dark greyish-brown silty clay may suggest marine conditions existed at or near the site. *Pinus sylvestris* is the dominant tree pollen type and is often over-represented in estuarine clays (Godwin 1975).

Alnus glutinosa dominates the second assemblage zone and the presence of *Salix* and *Corylus avellana*-type suggests alder car had become established at the site with secondary willow and hazel and perhaps oak at slightly higher elevations. Systematic scanning of diatom slides indicated rare occurrences of sponge spicule fragments and a single example of *Cyclotella striata*, a brackish diatom. This, together with the presence of Chenopodiaceae pollen hints at the proximity of intertidal conditions.

The third pollen assemblage zone is rather an anomaly, very high *Tilia* percentages in excess of 30% TLP is unusual. *Tilia* is insect-pollinated and despite high pollen production rates, its pollen percentages recorded in peat or lake deposits are often considered to underrepresent the actual proportion in the contemporary flora. However on the other hand it is highly recognisable and even in a damaged or fragmented condition it can be recorded. It also is very resistant to decay so tends to be preserved where conditions are in general unfavourable for the preservation of other pollen types. According to Godwin (1975) this tends to make *Tilia* pollen well-represented in mineral soils and in assemblages where the proportion of derived pollen is high. No diatoms were encountered during scanning but rare sponge spicule fragments were present.

Of note here is the presence of Type 16A and Type 143 fungal spores at this level. Van Geel *et al.* (1981) suggest the fungus producing the Type 16A asco-spore seems to indicate dry mesotrophic conditions. Blackford *et al.* (2006) suggest it to be an indicator of heathland and dry woodland conditions. Type 143 has been attributed to *Diporotheca* sp. (van Geel *et al.* 1981) a mildly parasitic fungus, which favours eutrophic to mesotrophic conditions. Prager *et al.* (2006) have reported Type 143 as being abundant in dry leaf litter of alder carr.

Taken together these two fungal spore types might suggest the environment to be dry alder carr. Under these conditions oxidation could lead to the destruction of less resistant pollen and the over-representation of the more robust *Tilia* grains. A similar feature has been recorded in the lower layers of a comparable peat bed *c* 1.5km to the south east, at the University of East London Campus, borehole 108 (Haggart 2007) perhaps suggesting a more regional lowering of the watertable.

The main peat bed between 4.55m and 3.55m is dominated by *Alnus glutinosa*, *Quercus* and *Corylus avellana*-type with *Tilia* at low but constant frequencies. Cyperaceae and Poaceae are also in low numbers at the site is likely to have been dense alder carr with willow and hazel. Sporadic occurrences of *Taxus baccata* (yew), *Rhamnus cathartica* (buckthorn) and *Viburnum* sp., probably *V. lantana* (wayfaring tree) pollen occur in this fen peat, a finding mirroring that of Scaife (2000) who comments on the species richness of fen carr peats during the Neolithic and early to middle Bronze Age at the Union Street and Joan Street sites. Yew was apparently a major component of coastal woodland at this time, as shown by common macrofossil remains in the coastal woodland preserved on the foreshore at Erith (Seel 2000). Scaife (2000) suggests that this species- rich alder carr/coastal woodland may have no modern analogue.

Slides were prepared for diatoms at 4.25m and 3.85m but they were not countable. Rare valves of the marine form *Pseudostelligera westii* were noted at 4.25m. At 3.85m two brackish diatoms *Cyclotella striata* and *Diploneis didyma* were present along with the marine planktonic form *Actinoptychus senarius* and rare sponge spicule fragments.

Spores of Zygnemataceae rise to 3% TLP at 3.85m and then decline. These spores are derived from a type of green algae commonly found in stagnant, shallow (less than 0.5m) and mesotrophic fresh water (van Geel, 1976) suggesting a higher fresh watertable between 4.25m and 3.55m.

Quercus pollen continues to decline in the upper-most pollen zone to 5% by 2.85m, probably reflecting regional forest clearance. *Alnus glutinosa* and *Tilia* pollen frequencies rise slightly, but the main feature of the zone is a rise in Plantaginaceae including *P. maritima* and also an increase in *Potamogeton natans*-type suggesting a rising watertable probably triggered by encroaching marine conditions after 1760-1450 cal BC (Beta 147954: 3330 ± 60 BP).

Area 2

The stratigraphy comprises a basal mid-greyish brown fine to medium sand (Neolithic sands, context 25) overlain by a black sandy peat (25/28), the lower part of which has been dated to 2930-2700 cal BC (SUERC-25563: 4265±35 BP). The sandy peat is in turn succeeded by a very dark grey to black silty clayey peat with woody fragments (28). Above this lies a woody peat containing the late early Bronze Age – middle Bronze Age trackway. A hazel stake from the trackway has been dated to 1880-1520 cal BC (Beta-153984: 3390±60 BP) while a sample of alder roundwood gave an age of 1610-1430 cal BC (SUERC-24292: 3230±30 BP). Overlying the trackway is a layer of humified silty peat ranging in colour from black to very dark grey (1), the upper part of which has been dated to 2140-1910 cal BC (SUERC-25562: 3645±35 BP). This date appears anomalous since it is several centuries older, yet overlies the upper surface of the trackway peat by 0.15m. Two possibilites arise: either the trackway has subsided relative to the peat in which it is presently encased or the peat sample used for dating has been contaminated by older carbon. The silty peat is in turn overlain by a very dark grey silty clay (26). The uppermost deposit is an orange brown and grey mottled silty clay (26) with iron-staining along former root channels.

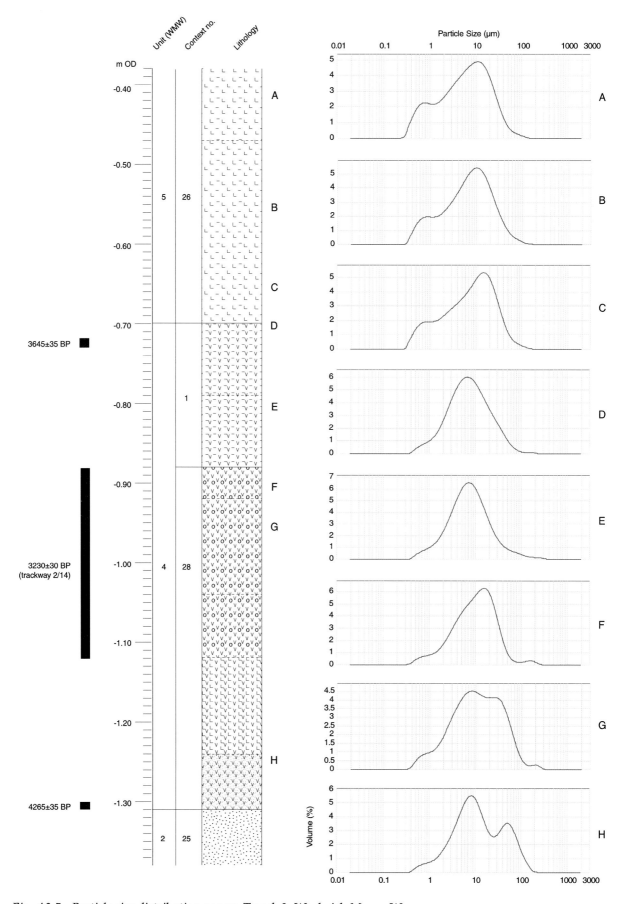

Fig. A3.5   Particle size distribution curves, Trench 2, Woolwich Manor Way

Particle size

Size is one of a number of properties of sediment particles that affects their entrainment, transport and deposition. As such particle size analysis can provide clues to sediment provenance, transport and deposition and can be used as a general measure of the energy present in depositional environments.

Taken as a whole, there is a fining-upwards sequence through the two monoliths. The lowermost sample from 0.87m within the lower black sandy peat is a bimodal, poorly sorted, sandy medium silt (Fig. A3.5) with peaks at 50μm (very coarse silt) and 8μm (fine silt) respectively. The bimodal distribution and sand content of 10.5% could suggest a degree of reworking of the basal Neolithic sands. The following sample at 0.58m is within the trackway wood peat. It again shows a bimodal distribution with peaks this time at 30μm and 8μm and a lower sand content of 5.6%, again perhaps suggesting inclusion of the sand by a different process from that by which the fine silt was deposited.

The fining-upward sequence within the mineral fraction continues through the trackway peat and overlying silty peat in samples at 0.53m, 0.43m and 0.33m. There are progressive peaks in coarse and medium silt, fine silt and very fine silt through these

three samples and the mean grain size falls from 16 to 12μm. There is a marked change in the character of the particle size distribution in the upper samples, with a doubling of the clay fraction between 0.33m and 0.28m; Fig. A3.6). The percentage clay content of the three uppermost samples averages 20.5%.

Geochemistry

Eleven samples were taken for geochemical analysis. Figures A3.7-A3.9 show changes through the profile in major oxides, other major elements and trace elements. Most of the curves have a similar shape which probably reflects the changing concentration of silt and clay. The typical shape, as exemplified by the curve for Al_2O_3 in Fig. 3, is a rise to a small peak within the base of the woody trackway peat at 0.72m–0.74m and then a fall to a minimum at 0.57m–0.59m within the middle unit of the trackway peat. Thereafter there is a rise through the overlying silty peat and into the upper silts and clays.

Two notable exceptions, however, are silicon (Si) and zirconium (Zr) which show the reverse, with a peak in lowermost sandy peat and another in the middle unit of the trackway peat. The most common minerals of these elements, silica (quartz) and zircon are extremely resistant to weathering and concentrations tend to build up in soils.

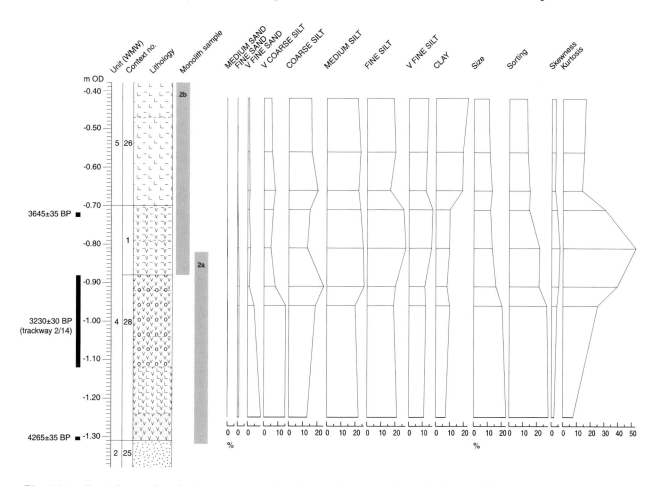

Fig. A3.6   *Particle size distribution curves by size classes, Trench 2, Woolwich Manor Way*

The lower peak in these curves could relate to partial reworking of the basal Neolithic sands and their incorporation within the lower sandy peat. The upper peak could reflect the inclusion of sand and soil into the woody trackway peat via trackway traffic and/or inwash, as also suggested by soil micromorphological analysis.

Another notable feature of the geochemical analysis is the fivefold increase in Pb concentrations in the upper three samples (Fig. A3.8) to an average of 21.3 ppm. A problem exists however in defining what 'natural' background levels of Pb are for this time and location. A core through pre-Industrial Medway mudflat sediments suggests 'natural' levels vary between 10–20 ppm (Cundy *et al.* 2005). A figure of 20 ppm for background levels has also been used in pollution studies of Essex and Medway saltmarshes (O'Reilly Wiese *et al.* 1995; Spencer 2002). This suggests the raised Pb levels may be slightly above background levels.

Levels for natural soils seem to be a bit lower with Emsley (2001) quoting a range between 0.7-11 ppm. A recent study of palaeosols underneath Bronze Age burial mounds in Denmark produced similar figures with natural Pb concentrations ranging from 3 to 11 ppm (Elberling *et al.* 2010). However, these authors also noted, in line with previous studies, that Pb concentrations tend to increase with decreasing particle size, owing to the affinity of metals to bind with clay particles. They found a significant relationship between the proportion of clay and Pb concentrations and produced a regression equation which enabled the estimation of natural background levels based on % clay content.

Using a similar approach but with a far smaller sample, if the levels below 0.35m are assumed to be 'natural', a regression of clay particle size against Pb concentration extrapolated to the 'elevated' values suggests they are higher than would be expected from the increase in clay concentration alone. This could be taken as an indication that the increase in lead levels may be partly due to prehistoric/historic industrial activity or modern contamination and partly due to increasing clay content.

Diatoms

Diatom preservation was extremely poor throughout the column; their scarcity and poor preservation state suggesting post-depositional dissolution of silica. Reinvestigation of the diatom slides after the assessment phase showed that the basal sample at 0.87m within the lower sandy peat contained several examples of a small marine *Thalassiosira* sp. all of which had an orange colouration, suggestive of iron staining. Fragments of sponge spicules and *Pinnularia*, a predominantly freshwater genus, were also present. The lower sandy peat appears to be a mixed deposit with two context numbers (28/25). It

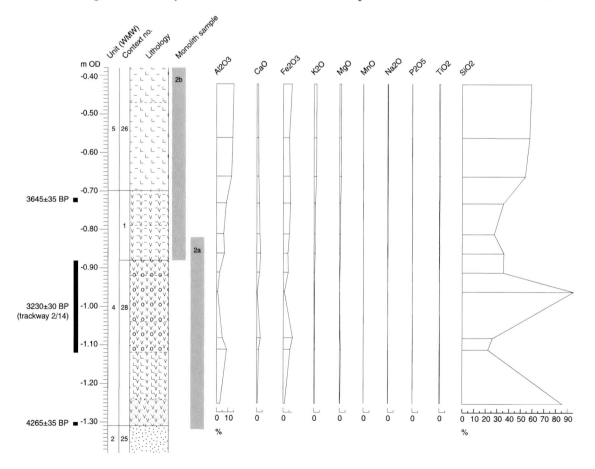

Fig. A3.7   Major oxides, Trench 2, Woolwich Manor Way

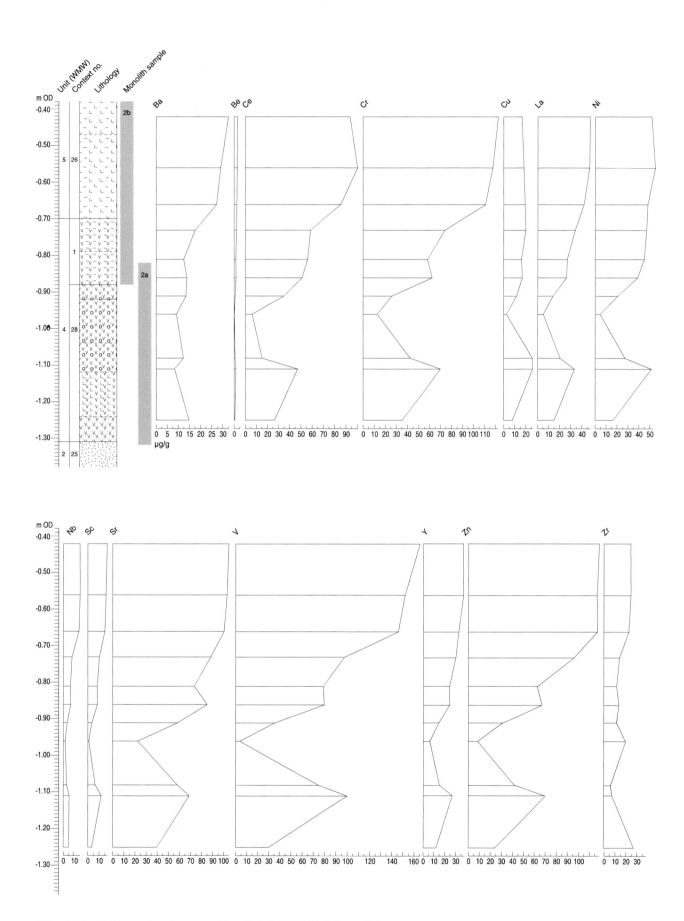

Fig. A3.8   Other major elements, Trench 2, Woolwich Manor Way

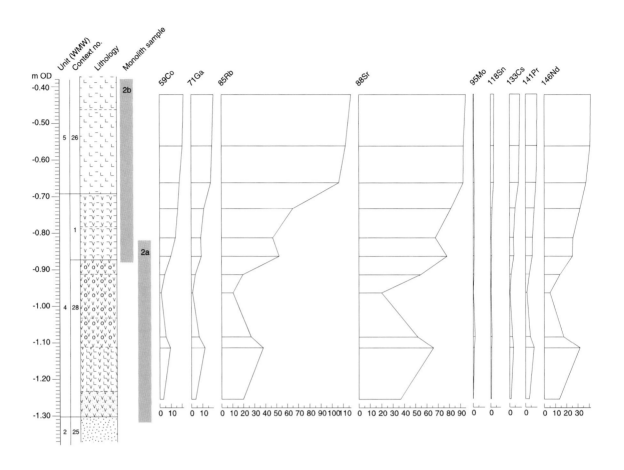

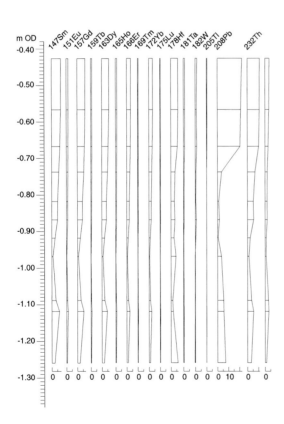

Fig. A3.9   *Trace elements, Trench 2, Woolwich Manor Way*

seems likely therefore that the sand component of this sample (10.5%) may well have been derived from reworking of the underlying Neolithic sands.

At 0.45m within the silty peat above the trackway there were a few examples the brackish form *Cyclotella striata*. At 0.43m again there were a small number of *Cyclotella striata* and poorly preserved *Navicula navicularis* valves. Within the upper organic clay silt *Cyclotella striata* was again present, if badly preserved, with a well preserved example of the fully marine form *Triceratum favus* at 0.28m.

Pollen

The column can be divided into two pollen assemblage zones (Fig. A3.10):

WMWT2A 0.85m–0.44m (-0.47 to -0.06m OD)
This lower zone is dominated by *Alnus glutinosa* which reaches a peak of 58%TLP at 0.71m and averages 42% through the zone. Also prominent is *Quercus* which declines from 25% to 19% and *Corylus avellana*-type at 10%. *Tilia* also has low but consistent percentages of about 6%. Also of note is the rise in *Potamogeton natans*-type to about 5% at 0.45m. Throughout the zone, trees and shrubs dominate with 80% and 11%TLP respectively.

WMWT2B 0.44m–0.04m (-0.06m to 0.34m OD)
Compared to the lower zone, while still dominated by *Alnus glutinosa*, it is at a lower frequency of 31% TLP. Other trees such as *Quercus* and *Tilia* (most probably *T. cordata*; Godwin 1975) decline in importance as well. There are complementary rises in the frequencies of grasses and sedges, Chenopodiaceae, Plantaginaceae and *Pteridium*. Cerealia-type also has a continuous presence.

Interpretation

The basal Neolithic sands were not directly sampled but it is likely that the high medium and fine sand content in the lower sandy peat derives from a reworking of these sands. The oxidised *Thalassiosira* sp. and sponge spicule fragments may suggest the Neolithic sands originally had a marine origin and were then subjected to subaerial weathering and oxidation prior to waterlogging and peat formation.

This sequence of events may have a correlative at Purfleet where Wilkinson and Murphy (1995) describe an estuarine sediment containing poorly preserved marine diatoms which underwent a considerable period of subaerial weathering during which time a soil formed, stable woodland vegetation developed and a woodland molluscan fauna also became established. This may well record a fall in sea level during Devoy's (1979) Tilbury III regression. The subsequent rise in sea level during the following Thames III period triggered a rise in watertable that killed the trees yet preserved them. Tree roots at the base of the wood peat overlying the rubified soil at

Purfleet are dated to 4503–4262 (68% confidence; Wilkinson and Murphy 1995) which is very similar to the date on the base of the sandy peat of 2930-2700 cal BC (SUERC-25563: 4265 ± 35 BP) in Trench 2.

The presence of *Alnus glutinosa* in such high percentages suggests an alder carr formed at the site. *Quercus* and *Tilia* were probably components of drier woodland at slightly higher elevations. The rise in frequency of *Potamogeton natans*-type pollen and aquatic pollen in general to 0.45m suggests a rise in the fresh watertable. The trackway therefore seems to have been built in a largely wooded environment, an alder carr with hazel and willow under conditions of rising groundwater table.

The fall in pollen concentration between 0.71m and 0.45m may also be informative. Pollen concentration is a function of the pollen rain, sedimentation rate and pollen preservation. If we assume the pollen rain from local, extralocal and regional sources did not vary by much during the formation of the trackway peat and there are no major changes in pollen preservation (Fig. A3.10) then it suggests there was an increase in peat sedimentation rate until ultimately the trackway was abandoned just prior to the arrival of marine conditions at the site.

Marine conditions at or near the site are suggested by the organic-walled foraminifera, dinoflagellate cysts and the brackish water diatom *Cyclotella striata*. There is also a rise in the representation of Chenopodiaceae pollen. The Chenopodiaceae or goosefoot family is a large one with 7 genera and perhaps up to 32 species that are native or probably native to the British Isles (Stace 1991), so viewed alone its diagnostic value is limited. However some genera such as *Atriplex* (oraches), *Salicornia* (glassworts) and *Suaeda* (sea-blites) contain species that are often dominant members of saltmarsh communities.

Taken together with the rise in the clay fraction, the rise in Poaceae and presence of brackish diatoms, it is likely the transition from silty peat to upper silty clay represent a change from marginal marine, perhaps saltmarsh environments to less organic intertidal mudflats.

Cerealia-type pollen is present in all but two samples. Tweddle *et al.* (2005) have recently commented on the difficulty of separating Cerealia-type pollen from wild grasses and suggest that only *Secale cereale* (rye) pollen can generally be identified to species level, while pollen from the other cultivated genera *Avena* (oats), *Hordeum* (barley) and *Triticum* (wheat) cannot be confidently separated from some wild grass species, many of which are potentially present in the coastal zone (Behre 2007). A recent paper by Joly *et al.* (2007) suggests a limit of 47µm for grain diameter and 11µm for annulus diameter was best at discriminating between the two groups, putting a minimum of large grass pollen types into the Cerealia-type group and this approach has been adopted here. Using the keys of Andersen and Küster in Tweddle *et al.* (2005) and the grain sizes in Andrew (1984) one grain at 0.43m has provisionally

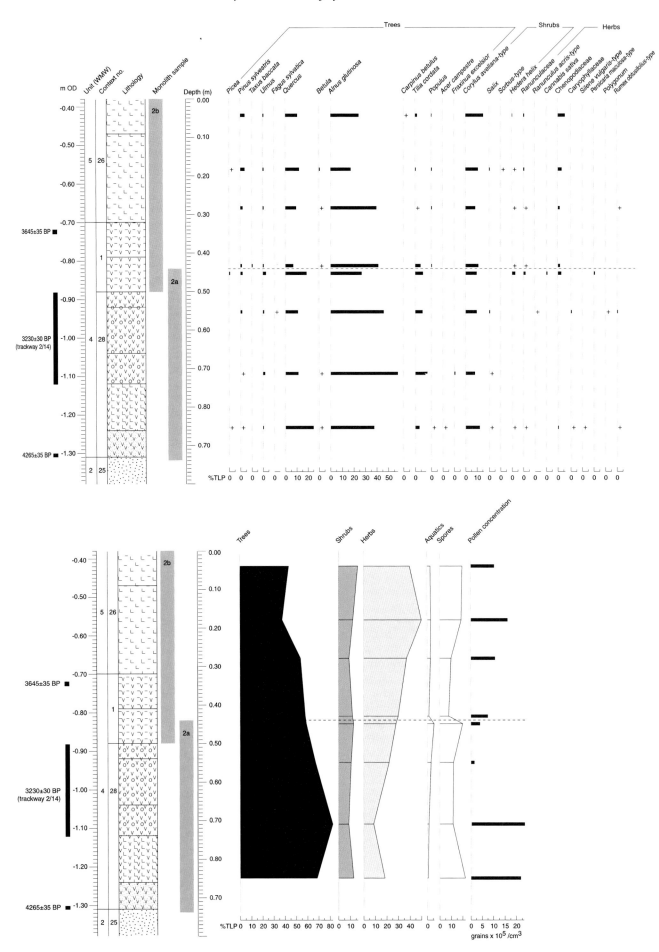

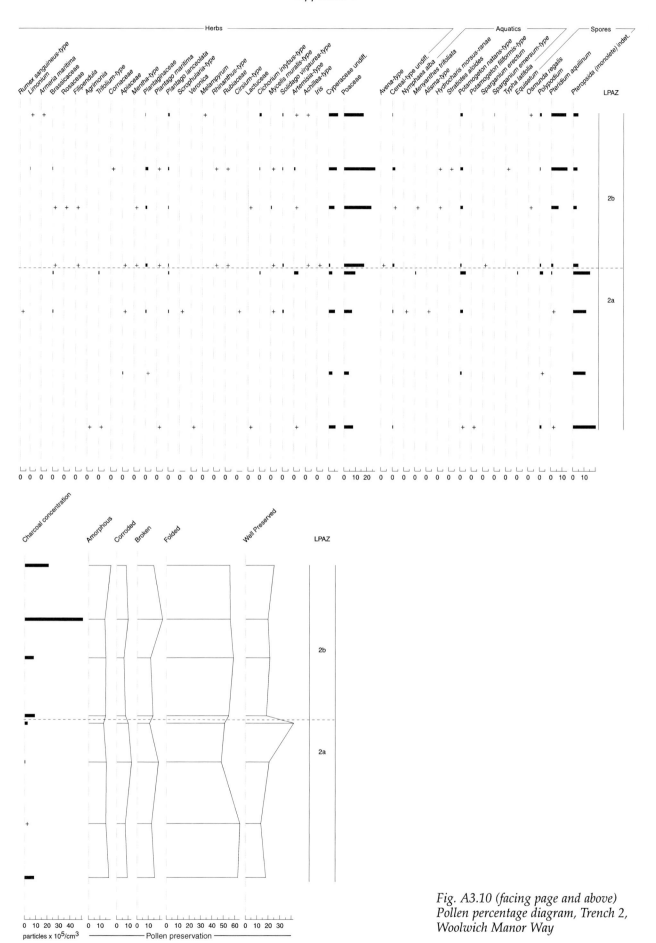

Fig. A3.10 *(facing page and above)*
Pollen percentage diagram, Trench 2,
Woolwich Manor Way

been attributed to *Avena* type which includes *Triticum* spp. on the basis of its maximum diameter, annulus diameter and pore diameter.

Because cereal pollen is not widely dispersed it is likely that cereal cultivation took place in the vicinity of the site, perhaps on slightly higher and drier ground. However there is the proviso that samples from the silty peat above 0.50m and especially in the overlying silty clay will have a waterlain component.

The radiocarbon date on the upper contact of the silty peat of 2140-1910 cal BC (SUERC-25562: 3645±35) seems to be anomalous in that it is older than the trackway it overlies. The two possibilites mentioned earlier are that the trackway has subsided and now lies at an altitude below its original position, or that the sample has been contaminated by older carbon. Assuming the date should be about 3200 BP, it would take about 5% contamination by inert carbon to age the sample by 400 years (Lowe and Walker 1997). The high Pb concentrations in the upper three levels do suggest the sediment may be contaminated, however the high silt and clay proportions in the samples would preclude much downward leaching of contaminants

Pollen from Movers Lane *by Sylvia Peglar* (Figs 7.4-7.5, A3.11-3.13)

Introduction

After assessment of many monoliths from Movers Lane junction with the A13 (Scaife in Wessex Archaeology 2003) three sections were chosen for full pollen analysis: one from the Area 3 palaeochannel, one from the adjacent trackway and (Fig. 7.5) and one from an 'offsite' sequence (Fig. 7.4). It was hoped that the 'offsite sequence' (TP39) would provide a background vegetational and environmental history during the middle Holocene into which the sequences associated with the trackway and sand bar could be slotted.

Methodology

Standard volumes of the sediment samples were prepared for pollen analysis using a standard chemical procedure, using HCl, NaOH, sieving, HF, and Erdtman's acetolysis to remove carbonates, humic acids, particles >170 microns, silicates, and cellulose, respectively. The samples were then stained with safranin, dehydrated in tertiary butyl alcohol, and the residues mounted in 2000 cs silicone oil (method B of Berglund and Ralska-Jasiewiczowa (1986)). Tablets containing a known number of *Lycopodium* spores were added to the known volume of sediment at the beginning of the preparation so that pollen and spore concentrations could be calculated (Stockmarr 1971). Slides were examined at a magnification of 400x (1000x for critical examination) by equally-spaced traverses across at least two slides to reduce the possible effects of differential dispersal

on the slides (Brooks and Thomas 1967). The aim was to achieve a count of 500 grains of land pollen and spores. Pollen identification, where necessary, was aided using the keys of Moore *et al.* (1991) and a small modern pollen reference collection. Andersen (1979) was followed for identification of cereal-type pollen. Indeterminable and unknown grains were recorded as an indication of the state of the pollen preservation. Other identifiable palynomorphs encountered on the slides were also recorded – vegetative remains, *Sphagnum* spores, fungal spores, dinoflagellate cysts, foraminifera, charcoal particles <170 microns, turbellarian eggs, pre-Quaternary spores, algal remains, *etc*, the inclusion of which can add to the interpretation of the pollen analytical results. Plant nomenclature follows Stace (1997).

The results are presented as pollen and spore diagrams with taxa expressed as percentages of the total land pollen and spore sum (sumP/calculation sum). Obligate aquatic taxa and other palynomorphs are presented as percentages of sumP + the sum of the category to which they belong. Calculations and diagrams were made using the programs TILIA and TILIA.GRAPH in TGView (Grimm 1990). Percentage values of <1% are represented as pluses. Taxa to the left of the 'calculation sum' are included in the calculation sum: those to the right are %s of the calculation sum + the sum of the group to which the taxon belongs.

Trackway 5268, Area 3

Monolith <40>, 0.75m long, was extracted from Trench A3, section 592, covering a series of silts, sands and peat. Ten subsamples were analysed (Fig. A3.11)

Organic sand and peaty sand (0.75–0.40m from top of monolith<40>)

The pollen assemblages from the four subsamples from these two basal sediment units are very similar. They are dominated by tree and shrub pollen (>80% total land pollen and spores (TLP)) most of which is alder *Alnus* (alder) but also with *Tilia* (lime), *Quercus* (oak) and *Corylus* (hazel), and odd grains of *Betula* (birch), *Fraxinus* (ash), *Pinus* (pine), *Taxus* (yew), and *Ulmus* (elm). Ferns (Pteropsida (monolete) undifferentiated (undiff.) are also present. There is very little herb pollen and no evidence of aquatic taxa apart from one grain of *Lemna* (duckweed) in the top sample. Pollen preservation is quite good but pollen concentrations are low. Charcoal particle values are very low.

Such assemblages suggest that these sediments were laid down in a reasonably fast-flowing channel as there are no aquatic taxa present and no small minerogenic particles. Regionally there was mixed deciduous woodland probably dominated by lime growing on the drier soils, with oak, hazel and an understorey of ferns, with alder growing on the wetter soils and along the river channel banks. The very small amounts of elm pollen suggest that these sediments were laid down post 'Elm Decline', a more or less synchronous event probably caused by an infection and dated to about 5000 years BP. It has been dated in the Thames estuary to just earlier than 4850 BP at Mar Dyke (Scaife 1988), 5010 BP at Silvertown (Wilkinson *et al.* 2000) some 5km WSW of Movers Lane, and 5040 BP at Rotherhithe (Sidell *et al.* 1995). Wood from 0.60–0.64m between the two basal subsamples in the basal organic sand has been radiocarbon dated to 2570-2330 cal BC (SUERC-25572: 3950±35 BP). The top of the peaty sand (0.40m) has been dated to 2130-1890 cal BC (SUERC-25571: 3625±35 BP). There is very little evidence for reedswamp or grasslands in the area at this time, and no evidence for human presence

Sandy peat (0.35–0.21m)

Two subsamples were analysed from this sediment. The pollen assemblage from the basal subsample is similar to those from the lower subsamples in the organic sand and peaty sand indicating that there was a lot of woodland, including wet alder carr within the area. However, Poaceae (grass) and Cyperaceae (sedge) pollen values are slightly raised and other herbs characteristic of reedswamp and grassland are present. The upper subsample shows a greater increase in grass and sedge pollen and biodiversity is greatly increased with many more herb taxa represented, herbs making up around 15% TLP. These include taxa which may be associated with grassland *Plantago lanceolata* (ribwort plantain), *Taraxacum*-type (dandelion-type), *Aster*-type (daisy-type) and *Ranunculus acris*-type (buttercup-type). There is a concomitant decrease in tree taxa during this period. There is also an increase in taxa charcteristic of reedswamp and marsh including sedges, grasses, *Alisma*-type (water plantain-type), iris and *Typha* species (bulrushes). Charcoal particle values are low in the basal subsample but very high in the upper subsample.

These assemblages suggest some increasing opening of the woodland around the site with increasing wetlands and grassland, perhaps being used for pasture. Lime values decrease particularly and this may be the 'lime decline' that is found in many diagrams from southern England, for example at 3630 BP at Bramcote Green, Bermondsey (Thomas and Rackham 1996) and is thought to have an anthropogenic cause, although the decline could also be due to rising water levels: lime being intolerant of wet soils. The presence of humans locally is evidenced by the dramatic rise in charcoal particles and the occurrence of cereal growth with the presence of several cereal grains within this unit, including (*Triticum* sp.) emmer/spelt and possibly *Hordeum*-type (barley). However, this latter type can also include pollen from wild grasses found in marine and reedswamp habitats (see Haggart, above).

Wood peat (0.21–0.15m)

This unit is associated with 7m long wattle/hurdle trackway 5268. Only one sample was analysed from this unit and the pollen assemblage obtained is very similar to that of the top subsample in the sandy peat below. There is thus evidence of increasing areas of wetlands and grasslands locally at the time of the trackway being constructed. The trackway has been dated to 1680-1490 cal BC (SUERC-24595: 3295±35 BP).

Clayey silt (0.15–0.00m)

Three subsamples were analysed from this upper unit. They are similar to the subsample from the wood peat below but with increasing herb percentages, particularly grasses, sedges and taxa characteristic of reedswamp and grasslands. There is also an increase in goosefoot family (Chenopodiaceae) pollen towards the top of the sequence. This could either indicate increased arable agriculture, representing weeds growing among cereal crops (which have increased values at the top of the sequence) within the area, or that saltmarsh was growing closer to the site. Charcoal values remain high. The very top subsample includes a few dinoflagellate cysts and foraminifera which are characteristic of brackish/saline conditions. However, it also includes pre-Quaternary grains and many spores of the soil fungus *Glomus*, which may suggest that these taxa have been reworked from earlier sediments.

Western palaeochannel, Area 3

Two monoliths <47> and <48> were taken through organic silty clay and silty clay units associated with a sand bar in Trench A3, Section 568. Monolith <47> went down into a gravelly sand correlated with the occupation deposit, but unfortunately pollen was not preserved in this sedimentary unit (Fig. A3.12).

Organic silty clay (1.14–0.87m from top of monolith <48>)

The basal two subsamples are from monolith <47> and the upper subsample from <48>. Tree and shrub pollen accounts for *c* 40-50% TLP in this unit. About half of this is alder with oak, hazel and a little lime and birch making up the rest. There is also about 40% herb pollen, mainly grass and sedge but with many other herbaceous taxa at small values. A few ferns are present and also a variety of obligate aquatic freshwater taxa including *Potamogeton* (pondweed), duckweed, basal hair cells of waterlily (Nymphaeaceae), and remains of the aquatic green algae *Botryococcus* and *Pediastrum,* together with telmatic species such as bulrushes and iris. Charcoal particle values are high throughout.

Such assemblages are characteristic of a variety of habitats around the site with open water, wetlands including alder carr and reedswamp, grassland with many herbs indicative of pasture and arable land with cereals being grown (emmer/spelt and possibly barley) indicating the presence of humans. This organic silty-clay overlies a gravelly sand which is correlated with an occupational layer. Unfortunately subsamples prepared from this unit

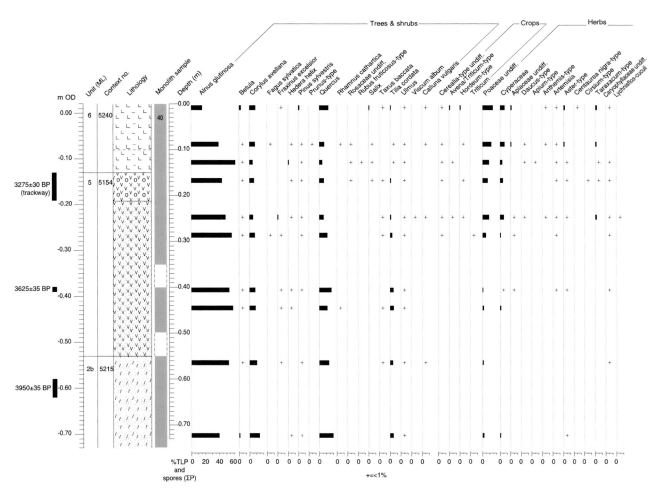

Fig. A3.11   *Pollen percentage diagram, Trackway 5268, Area 3, Movers Lane*

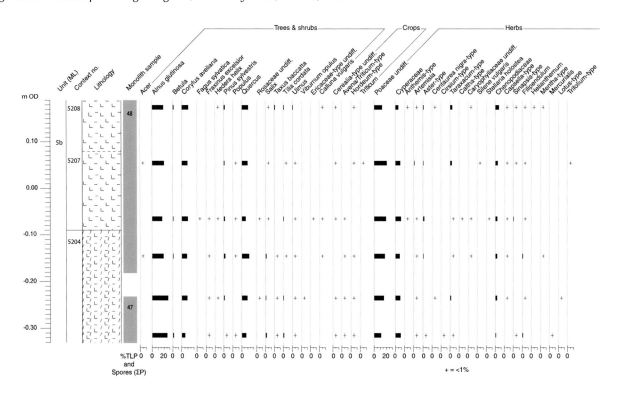

Fig. A3.12   *Pollen percentage diagram, palaeochannel, Area 3, Movers Lane*

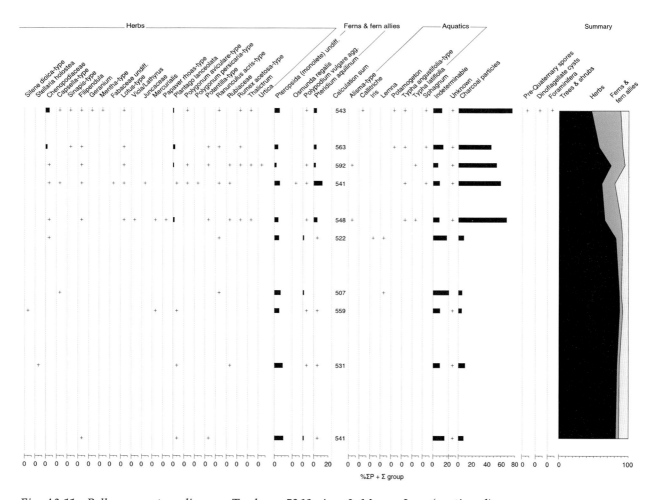

Fig. A3.11   Pollen percentage diagram, Trackway 5268, Area 3, Movers Lane (continued)

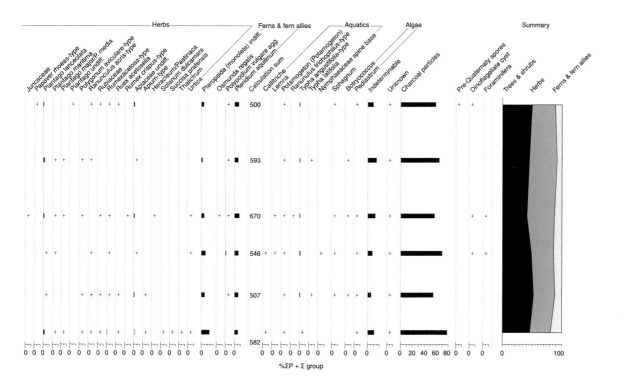

Fig. A3.12   Pollen percentage diagram, palaeochannel, Area 3, Movers Lane (continued)

had extremely low concentrations of badly preserved pollen and could not be analysed. Regionally, deciduous woodland was still extant mainly of oak and hazel with an understorey of indeterminable ferns, *Pteridium aquilinum* (bracken) and *Polypodium vulgare* (polypody fern) which may also have grown on the oaks. Charcoal particle values are high throughout.

Silty clay (0.87–0.57m)

The assemblages from the three subsamples analysed from this unit (monolith <48>) are very similar to those of the unit below, but there is a gradual increase in grasses and other herbs as ferns and deciduous tree taxa slightly decrease. There is also a slight increase in goosefoot family and decrease in sedges towards the top of the monolith, possibly connected with saltmarsh encroaching towards the site. Spores of *Glomus*, pre-Quaternary spores, Dinoflagellate cysts and Foraminifera identified throughout the sequence suggest reworking of older sediments.

The very small values of elm and lime pollen suggest that the sequence postdates the 'elm' and 'lime' declines and would therefore here probably date from <3500 years BP (see below – TGWOO, Trench TP39), the early Bronze Age.

Test pit 39

This is regarded as an 'offsite sequence'. Two monoliths, <29> and <30>, cover the tripartite sequence of clays and silts, peats and clays and silts characteristic of the Thames estuary during the mid-Holocene (Devoy 1979) (Fig. A3.13).

Silty peat (3.95–3.60m)

Four subsamples have been analysed from this unit. Tree and shrub pollen dominate the pollen assemblages (60-80% TLP), particularly alder, averaging 40% TLP. However, other tree taxa are important – lime, oak and hazel all have values of 6-10% TLP. Ferns are also present at *c* 18% TLP and charcoal particles are quite high. The pollen in this sequence was not very well preserved with 18-20% TLP + indeterminable sum, and the assemblages may therefore be somewhat biased with grains that are easily identified even when poorly preserved being overcounted (for example grasses, alder and lime).

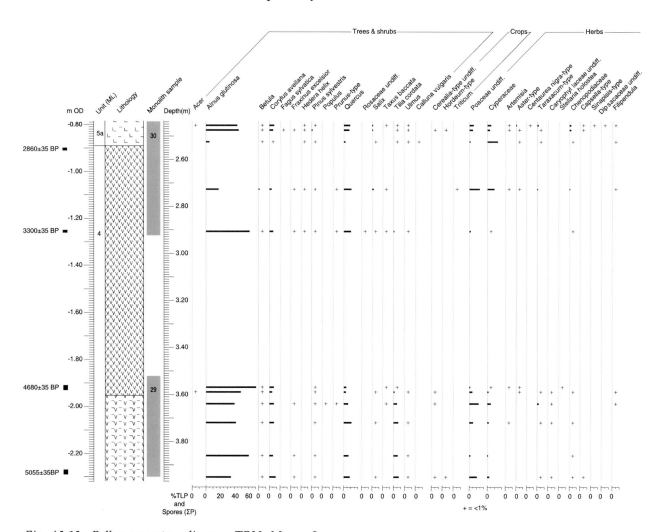

Fig. A3.13   Pollen percentage diagram, TP39, Movers Lane

The pollen assemblages suggest that woodland was prevalent over the landscape, with alder carr in wet places locally and along river banks, and deciduous woodland probably dominated by lime, with oak, hazel and ferns growing regionally on the drier ground. There is no evidence for the growth of freshwater aquatic taxa or of taxa associated with saline water but the growth of alder carr suggests the water around was fresh at the time these sediments were laid down. There were some open areas with grassland, possibly used for pasture, and possible cereal grains which would imply human presence. The base of this unit has been dated to 3960-3770 cal BC (SUERC-25568: 5055±35 BP) which would equate with the early Neolithic. There is very little elm in the assemblages suggesting that this unit is post 'elm decline' but pre 'lime decline' as there are quite high values of lime pollen. The top of the silty peat (humic acid fraction) has been dated to 3630-3360 cal BC (SUERC-25567: 4680±35 BP).

Peat (3.60–2.54m)

Unfortunately, only the very base and near the top of this unit were sampled (top of monolith <29> and most of monolith <30>). The two basal subsamples

and the lower of the two upper subsamples provided pollen assemblages dominated by tree and shrub pollen (alder, oak and hazel but without lime: 85% TLP) with very few herbs and ferns and no aquatics. The junction of the silty peat and peat units therefore mark the 'lime decline' which probably has an anthropogenic cause, but could be due to an increased water level as lime cannot survive on wet ground. The increase in alder could be further evidence of a raised water level. However, it is possible that there may be a hiatus in the sedimentation. The thick alder carr may also be preventing other pollen reaching the site. A subsample (humic fraction) from within the peat at 0.48-0.49m has been dated to the early middle Bronze Age (1690-1510 cal BC (94.3%); SUERC-25570: 3330±35 BP). Although the 'lime decline' was affected by human communities and is therefore not a synchronous event, other sites in the Thames basin have provided dates. The uppermost subsample has increased herb pollen and fern spores and a concomitant decreased tree and shrub value, mainly due to a large drop in alder and increases in grasses and sedges.

The results from this unit thus suggest that alder carr was very prevalent locally at the time of peat

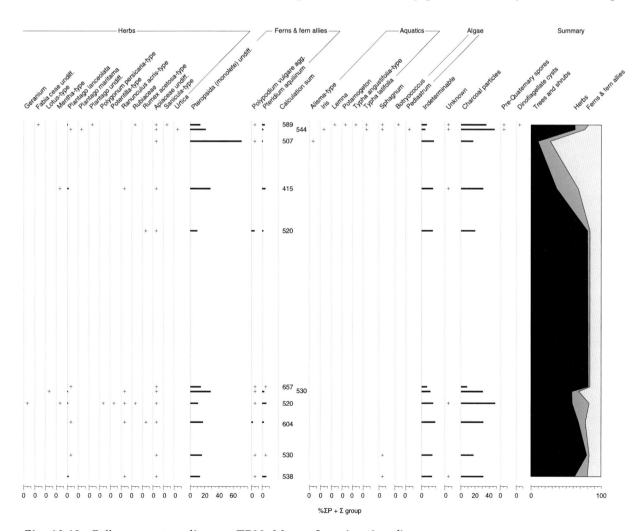

Fig. A3.13   Pollen percentage diagram, TP39, Movers Lane (continued)

formation, and possibly only towards the top of the unit was there evidence for human presence, possibly with some pasturing. There is no evidence for cereal growth in the vicinity although, as above, the large cereal grains may have been filtered out by the dense alder woodland.

Silty clay (2.54–2.44m)

Three subsamples were analysed from this unit. The basal subsample had a very high fern value (>70% TLP) but this could be due to the inclusion of a whole or part fern sporangium in the preparation. Pollen assemblages are again similar to those from the peat, but many aquatic taxa and green algae suggest freshwater wetlands and reedswamps were found locally, possibly due to a rise in water level. In the top subsample a small rise in goosegrass family pollen may indicate that saltmarsh was growing closer to the site.

Interpretation and discussion

The pollen assemblages from the sediments associated with trackway 5268 (Fig. A3.11) show that at the base of the sequence the site was probably in a quite fast-flowing channel with wet ground and channel banks dominated by alder with deciduous woodland with lime, oak and hazel on the drier ground. There is no evidence for other than a freshwater environment at this time. After *c* 3625 radiocarbon years BP woodland taxa begin to diminish (particularly lime) with a corresponding increase in biodiversity and wetland and grassland taxa (grasses and sedges). This suggests that water levels were rising and towards the top of the sandy peat large values of charcoal particles and the presence of cereal pollen grains are evidence of local human presence. An overlying wood peat is associated with a trackway. Trackways have also been excavated at Bramcote Green, Bermondsey (Thomas and Rackham 1996) and correlated with a series of wet boggy areas within the Thames channel. It seems that a rising water level with an increase in wet habitats at our site is also the reason for the building of the trackway here. A few spores of *Sphagnum* (bog moss), not found lower in the sequence, may be further evidence of increasing wetness. Above the wood peat is a clayey-silt unit in which the pollen assemblages are similar to that from the wood peat but with increasing herb pollen indicating increasing open ground (reedswamps and grasslands, possibly being used for pasture) together with cereal production. At the top of the sequence there is possibly some evidence of brackish water influence with dinoflagellate cysts and foraminifera present. However, these may be indicative of reworked sediments, as pollen of telmatic taxa such as grow in reedswamps (bulrushes) and obligate aquatic taxa showing the presence of open freshwater *Potamogeton* (pondweed) and *Callitriche* (starwort) are present.

An underlying unit of gravelly sand was correlated with an occupational level in the sediments associated with a sand bar (Fig. A3.12) but unfortunately it was impossible to obtain pollen analyses from them. However, units of organic silty-clay and silty-clay above the gravelly sand provide evidence of local human presence throughout with high charcoal particle values and the local production of cereals. The landscape was quite open with grassland (possibly pasture) and with some wet habitats, reedswamps and open water. Throughout the sequence analysed there is little change but goosegrass (Chenopodiaceae*)* values are reasonably high and increase upwards. Also odd remains of dinoflagellate cysts and foraminifera are present, possibly evidence for saltmarsh gradually encroaching on the site.

The site at TGWOO trench TP39 (Fig. A3.13) was analysed as an 'offsite' sequence, hopefully to provide a background vegtetational history of the area into which the trackway and sand bar sequences could be slotted. It dates from the beginning of the Neolithic, just after the 'Elm Decline'. The pollen assemblages from the basal sedimentary unit (organic silt) indicate that the landscape was mainly wooded with lime, oak and hazel being the main constituent trees, with an understorey of ferns. However, there is some evidence for some opening of the woodland with herb taxa suggestive of pasture and some cereal grains present. This would suggest that humans were living close by at this time. At the top of the organic silt lime pollen values drop; the base of the peat above has been dated to 3630-3360 cal BC (SUERC-25567: 4680±35 BP). This may be the anthropogenically produced 'lime decline', caused by the trees being cleared as they were on the best soils, or pollarded for cattle fodder (Turner 1962). However, lime is intolerant of wet soils and it's decline here may be due to waterlogging correlated with a rise in sea level. In the upper part of the peat unit tree pollen values decrease further and herbs, particularly grasses and sedges increase. It is difficult to say whether this is due to further clearance by humans or rising water levels. At the top of the sequence there is possibly a small increase in taxa associated with saltmarsh and brackish water which may be indicative of saltmarsh approaching closer to the site.

Ostracods and foraminifera *by John Whittaker*

Introduction

Although no work was carried out on ostracods and foraminifera during the post-excavation analysis stage of the project, the assessment of samples provided a significant body of data that has aided in the characterisation of the environments of deposition associated with the sediments at each site, described in Part 2 of this volume (Whittaker in Gifford and Partners 2000; 2001a; 2001b; 2002; 2003a; 2003b; Wessex Archaeology 2003). For this reason the results of the various stages of assessment for both the evaluations and detailed excavations have been included in this Appendix. Preservation between and within assessed sequences along the route was quite variable, and the negative results from the Phase II investigations at Woolwich Manor Way and Movers Lane and the Phase III investigations at Woolwich Manor Way have therefore been omitted from this report.

Methodology

Each sample was placed in a ceramic bowl and thoroughly dried in a Hotbox (fan-assisted) oven. Boiling water was then poured over the dried sediment, with a little sodium carbonate added to deflocculate the clay fraction. In a few cases a very small amount of dilute hydrogen peroxide was introduced to speed up the breakdown, but always care was taken not to leave the sample in hydrogen peroxide for more than one hour (as long-term exposure is known to have destructive tendencies on the microfauna). Each sample was then washed through a 75μm sieve with hot water and decanted back into ceramic bowl, before final drying in the oven. The dried residues were then stored in small plastic bags before examination under a binocular microscope.

Results and interpretation

Phase 1 evaluation (Canning Town, Woolwich Manor Way, Roding Bridge and Movers Lane)

Twenty four samples from 4 route sections were submitted for microfaunal analysis (Tables A3.1 and A3.2). The lower part of each section examined appears to have been entirely freshwater, even though the samples from a variety of habitats

Table A3.1   Samples examined for ostracods and foraminifera from the Phase I evaluations

Works phase	Site	Trench	Sample	Depth bgl	m OD	Facies	Vol. (g)	Description
I	CT	TP29	3	2.65	-0.45	CT5	56	(205) 2.5Y 4/2 dark greyish brown clay-silt with 10YR 3/6 dark yellowish brown mottles.
I	CT	TP29	4	2.9	-0.7	CT5	41	(204) 2.5Y 4/1 dark grey clay-silt. Occasional 10YR 3/6 dark yellowish brown mottles.
I	CT	TP29	8	4.33	-2.13	CT3	50	(201) 5YR 2.5/1 black well humified peat/silty peat
I	CT	TP29	8	4.45	-2.25	CT3	34	(201) Soft Gley 2 3/5/PB dark bluish grey clay silt
I	WMW	TP1	87/M1	1.85	-0.83	WMW5	38	Dense and firm 10YR 4/2 dark greyish-brown silt to clay-silt.
I	WMW	TP1	87/M1	2.07	-1.05	WMW5	40	as above
I	WMW	TP1	86/M3	2.52	-1.5	WMW5	38	as above, becoming more organic
I	WMW	TP1	86/M3	2.85	-1.83	WMW4	46	10YR 2/2 very dark brown peat varying to silty peat. Peat is moderately well humified in places. In places abndant wood and plant remains Occ. Pockets of 10YR 4/2 dark greyish brown organic silt.
I	WMW	TP1	84/M1	4.95	-3.93	WMW3	46	10YR 3/1 very dark grey clay-silt. Occasional plant fragments.
I	WMW	TP1	84/M1	5.15	-4.13	WMW3	62	10YR 5/2 to 10YR 6/2 dark greyish-brown silty-clay with carbonate patches..
I	RB	Rdar1	na	3.32	0.44	RB5		Dense, brownish grey clay-silt. Massive and structure less. Occ. black mottling. Some Fe staining along old root channels.
I	RB	Rdar1	na	3.68	0.08	RB5		As above
I	RB	Rdar1	na	4.1	-0.34	RB5		Dark brown clay-silt, more organic and softer.
I	RB	Rdar1	na	4.9	-1.14	RB4		Dark grey sandy silt with organic material. Dense and very compact.
I	RB	Rdar1	na	5.13	-1.37	RB2		Grey brown sandy silt, becoming silty then gravelly sand with depth. Dense, massive and structureless.
I	RB	Rdar1	na	5.42	-1.66	RB2		as above
I	ML	TP39	30	2.5	-0.85	ML5	38	Firm 10YR 4/2 dark greyish-brown silty clay.
I	ML	TP39	28	4.15	-2.5	ML3	33	10YR 3/2 very dark greyish brown silt, some sand and organic content.
I	ML	TP39	28	4.25	-2.6	ML3	48	as above
I	ML	TP39	28	4.37	-2.72	ML3	41	as above
I	ML	TP39	28	4.55	-2.9	ML3	47	as above
I	ML	TP39	?	5.15	-3.5	ML2	82	10YR 4/4 dark yellowish-brown medium well-sorted sand. Slight laminations, in places cross bedded. Occasional flint clasts.

Table A3.2   Ostracods and foraminifera assemblages from the Phase I evaluations

| Site | Depth | Unit | Foraminifera | | | Ostracods | | | | | | | | Others | | |
| | | | | | | Brackish | | | Freshwater | | | | | | | |
			Ammonia limnetes (Todd and Bronnimann)	Elphidium williamsoni (Haynes)	Haynesina germanica (Ehrenberg)	Cyprideis torosa (Jones)	Cytherura gibba (Muller)	Leptocythere porcellanea (Brady)	Candona neglecta (Sars)	Candona sp.	Cypria ophtalmica (Jurine)	Darwinula stevensoni (Brady and Robertson)	Limnocythere inopinata (Baird)	Charophyte oospores	Fish bones	Molluscs
CT TP29	2.1	CT5			+	+										
	2.37	CT5	+	+	+						+					+
	2.65	CT3														+
	2.9	CT3														
	4.33	WMW5													+	+
	4.45	WMW5													+	+
WMW TP1	1.85	WMW5	+		+	+		+			+			+		
	2.07	WMW4	+	+	+	+	+	+++	++			+	+	+		+
	2.52	WMW3														
	2.85	WMW3				+										
	4.95	CT5				+										
	5.15	CT5														
RB Irar1	3.32	RB5				++	+				+					
	3.68	RB5														
	4.1	RB5														
	4.9	RB4														
	5.13	RB2														
	5.42	RB2														
ML TP39	2.5	ML5														
	4.15	ML3									+					
	4.25	ML3														
	4.37	ML3									+			+		
	4.55	ML3												+		
	5.15	ML2														

(sandy and calcareous substrates, and rich vegetation) were often barren. There is, however, sufficient evidence from the molluscs, fish remains and Cladocerans, especially at Canning Town (Fig. 3.3) to demonstrate a freshwater origin. Freshwater ostracods were only found at Movers Lane (Fig. 7.4), but it is likely that the very acid organic-rich deposits, in particular, would not only have been non-conducive to the subsequent preservation of calcareous valves but might also signify a generally unfavourable environment. At Movers Lane all that remains in several samples is the chitinous integument of valves of the ostracod (*Cypria ophtalmica*). This ostracod is significantly tolerant of waters high in organic pollution; often stagnant streams and pools. This, then, may give an indication of what the site might have been like throughout the sequence examined.

For the remainder of the samples, from Woolwich Manor Way (TP1, Fig 5.3), Canning Town (TP29, Fig 3.3) and Roding Bridge (Rdar 1, Fig 6.2), the latter part of each section is characterised by a change to brackish water conditions caused by tidal incursion, possibly associated with a small rise in sea-level. The section down to 2.07m bgl at Woolwich Manor Way, to 2.37m bgl at Canning Town and the top sample at Roding Bridge at 3.32m bgl, contain ostracods *Cyprideis torosa, Leptocythere porcellanea,* and/or *Cytherura gibba* (the former two in large numbers), all of which signify the development of muddy, protected brackish creeks. A salinity of between 5% and 10% may be suggested; in salinities lower than that *C torosa* valves are often noded and all the present material, both adult and juvenile, is smooth. That the vast majority of these brackish ostracods were found as carapaces (rather than discrete valves), which also suggests that the populations are *in situ* and not washed in by tidal surges from elsewhere. Some freshwater input into the creeks would still have occurred, as evidenced by some associated freshwater ostracods, but a species such as *Candona neglecta* (the only one commonly present) can itself tolerate low salinities. The interpretation of tidal access is reinforced at these localities by the occurrence of minute foraminifera, which if they were not living *in situ* in salinities close to their limits of tolerance (5%), would have been brought in suspension by the tide from estuarine localities further downstream.

Phase II evaluation (Prince Regent Lane)

Ten samples were submitted from assessment from the Phase II investigations at Prince Regent Lane (Table A3.3). All derive from a series of monoliths (monoliths 103/1, 103/2, 103/3 and 103/4; Fig. 4.3) retrieved from the alluvial sequence in T23 in the western part of the site (adjacent to the Phase III coffer dam excavations)

The slightly organic sand in the lower part of the section was barren of microfauna. There was some plant debris, seeds and oogonia of charophytes. If it is equivalent to the peats found elsewhere then it is presumably freshwater. Higher in the sequence there is a well marked brackish incursion associated

with the onset of tidal influence. This becomes apparent in the sample from 1.02m bgl; the signal is very strong at 0.89m bgl, and was still present at 0.69m bgl. In the uppermost sample, at 0.44m bgl the signal is lost, possibly due to decalcification and/or pollution.

The well-known brackish ostracods *Cytherura gibba*, *Cyprideis torosa* and *Loxoconcha elliptica* all signify muddy, protected brackish creeks (Athersuch *et al.* 1989). Here, and unlike sites investigated during Phase I works (above), they are accompanied by a rich fauna of freshwater ostracods, especially *Sarscypridopsis aculeata* and *Heterocypris salina*, which often live together and have a preference for slightly brackish, small water bodies or coastal pools influenced by marine water; the other taxa represented can also tolerate slightly salty water (Meisch 2000). It is likely, therefore, at this location there were small coastal pools, as well as creeks, that were flooded at high tide by estuarine

Table A3.3   Samples examined for ostracods and foraminifera from Phase II Trench 23 at Prince Regent Lane

Works phase	Site	Trench	Sample	Depth bgl	m OD	Facies	Vol.(g)	Description
II	PRL	23	103/1	0.44	0.81	PRL5	27	(158) dark brownish grey silty clay
II	PRL	23	103/1	0.69	0.56	PRL5	18	(159) light brownish grey silty clay
II	PRL	23	103/1	0.89	0.36	PRL5		(160) mid greyish blue silty clay
II	PRL	23	103/2	1.02	0.23	PRL5		(161)1light brownish grey silty clay
II	PRL	23	103/3	1.13	0.12	PRL5		as above
II	PRL	23	103/3	1.33	-0.08	PRL5		as above
II	PRL	23	103/3	1.53	-0.28	PRL5		(162) mid grey silty clay
II	PRL	23	103/4	1.55	-0.3	PRL5		as above
II	PRL	23	103/4	1.75	-0.5	PRL2		(164) dark grey silty sand
II	PRL	23	103/4	1.95	-0.7	PRL2		(165) light yellow grey silty sand

Table A3.4   Ostracod assemblages from Phase II Trench 23 at Prince Regent Lane

| | | Ostracods | | | | | | | | | | Other | |
| | | Brackish | | | Freshwater | | | | | | | | |
Depth	Facies	Cyprideis torosa (Jones)	Cytherura gibba (Muller)	Leptocythere porcellanea (Brady)	Candona neglecta (Sars)	Candona sp.	Cypria ophtalmica (Jurine)	Heterocypris salina (Brady)	Ilyocypris cf. bradyl (Sars)	Limnocythere inopinata (Baird)	Sarscypridopsis aculeata (Costa)	Charophyte oospores	Molluscs
0.44	PRL5												
0.69	PRL5	+	+	+						+			+
0.89	PRL5	+	++		+++		+	++	+++	+++	+++		+
1.02	PRL5					+					+		
1.13	PRL5												
1.33	PRL5												
1.53	PRL5											+	
1.55	PRL5											+	
1.75	PRL2												
1.95	PRL2												

water during this later phase of Holocene Thames sedimentation.

Phase III excavation, Freemasons Road

Nine samples from four monoliths from the Phase III cofferdam excavations were submitted for assessment. The samples derived from the lower part of the upper alluvium (layer 1) as well as the fill of channel 22 (Section 17, Fig. 4.3). Additional samples were also examined from the basal sandy silts (layers 106 and 76). Ostracods were only preserved in the uppermost sample (0.10m) in monolith 115 (fill 009 of channel 22). These belonged to the *Candona* group of freshwater ostracods and in all cases only fragmentary remains were recovered. These remains were associated with a few earthworm granules. The sample from the upper alluvium (layer 1) in monolith 116 was totally barren. The basal sandy silt produced insect remains and ephippia (egg-cases) of freshwater cladocerans (water fleas) along with abundant fish remains including 3-spined stickleback and eel (S. Parfitt pers. comm.). Apart from the few fragmentary ostracod remains from monolith 115 no other calcareous remains were found in any of the samples. Scales, spines and bone of fish are made of hydroxyapatite (calcium phosphate, not calcite, P. Forey pers. comm.) and therefore the samples would appear to be strongly decalcified.

Phase III excavation, Movers Lane

Eighteen samples, nine each from Areas 2 and 3, were submitted for assessment from the Phase III Movers Lane excavations. These samples were selected from nine monoliths and covered a range of stratigraphic units through both palaeochannels and associated features.

Results from Area 2 were disappointing; no calcareous (or siliceous) microfossils were recorded. The only environmental indication from the main channel deposits came from the peat (layer 3012; monolith 66, 8cm) which contained charophyte oospores. However, the fact that even here the calcareous sheath was missing, leaving only the chitinous inner lining, probably means that this and all the other samples from this sequence are heavily decalcified and/or oxidised. Charophytes (stoneworts) can, however, live in both fresh and brackish-water. In ditch 1038, some ephippia (egg-cases) of cladocerans (water-fleas) were found (monolith 60, 36cm) indicating that this was probably a freshwater habitat.

In Area 3 non-marine ostracods and ephippia of cladocerans, in particular the small channel cut in peat (monolith 38, sample 18, Fig. 7.5) and throughout the basal sands (monolith 55, samples 15-13, Fig. 7.5) suggest that this part of the section was wholly freshwater. However, in the upper alluvium (monolith 51, samples 11 and 12, monolith 52, sample 10) creek-dwelling ostracods, and minute, marine foraminifera occur. The ostracods were clearly *in situ*, the foraminifera would have

been brought in, in suspension with the tide. This, therefore and importantly, signals the onset of tidal conditions, perhaps associated with a rise in sea-level.

Insects *by David Smith* (Fig. A3.14)

Introduction

The insect faunas described here are from the series of open area excavations that occurred along the line of the A13 Thames Gateway improvements during Phase III of the archaeological programme. Material was selected for insect analysis based on two factors. Primarily, it was decided to concentrate on deposits associated with the main archaeological features at these sites, such as trackways and ditches. Secondly, samples were selected based on the degree of apparent preservation. At Prince Regent Lane (Freemasons Road) and Woolwich Manor Way this had been indirectly assessed during the assessment of plant macrofossils (Giorgi in Gifford and Partners 2001a; 2001b; 2002; 2003a; 2003b) and at Movers Lane samples were assessed specifically for insects (Robinson in Wessex Archaeology 2003). This was an extensive investigation and the samples analysed come from various periods as well as sites. These are listed in Table A3.5. It was hoped that an examination of the insect remains from these locations might provide information on the nature of the environment and land use surrounding the sites, and the nature of materials that may have been deposited into the features.

Methodology

The samples were initially processed at the Museum of London Archaeology Service. The samples were divided with part of the sample retained for further analysis and a second part being processed for plant macrofossils. Unfortunately, the retained 'whole earth' samples from Freemason Road and Woolwich Manor Way were not available for insect analysis when the present work programme commenced. The insect analysis described therefore took place on the plant macrofossil flots and residues. The former had been retained over a 250μm mesh sieve and the residues retained over a 1mm mesh sieve. Unfortunately, the use of a 1mm mesh when the residues were processed means that some insect fragments will not have been retained and will have been lost to analysis. However, the material from Movers Lane was processed by Wessex Archaeology where the complete samples had been sieved over a 300μm mesh during a previous assessment for insect analysis. The context details, archaeological description and the weights and volumes of the samples are presented in Table A3.5. During this study the various flot and heavy residues fractions were re-combined and then were processed using the standard method of paraffin

Table A3.5   Context details for the insect analysis

Site	Site code	Period	Context no.	Context type	Sample no.	Vol. soilprocessed by flotation (L)
Prince Regent	FRU01	MBA	146	Fill of ditch 132 (Area B)	143	19
Lane	FRU01	EMBA	72	Posthole fill associated with EMBA double timber post alignment (Str. 32, Area A)	103	19
(Freemasons						
Road)	FRU01	MLBA	125	Flood deposit (Area B)	133	10
	FRU01	MLBA	46	Peat layer	92	9
	FRU01	MLBA	47	Peat layer	99	9
	FRU01	LBA-EIA	37	Fill of ditch 38 (Area B)	52	19
Woolwich	WMA02	EMBA	28	Peat layer under trackway 2/14 (Area 2)	1	2
Manor Way	WMA02	EMBA	57	Peat layer under trackway 29 (Area 1)	23	20
	WMA02	MLBA	1	Peat layer overlying trackway 2/14 (Area 2)	8	9
	WMA02	MLBA	56	Peat layer overlying trackway 29 (Area 1)	22	20
Movers Lane	RIR01	MLBA	1049	Fill of ditch 1038 (Area 2)	6	6
	RIR01	EMBA	3011	Peat associated with trackway 3031 (Area 2)	69	6

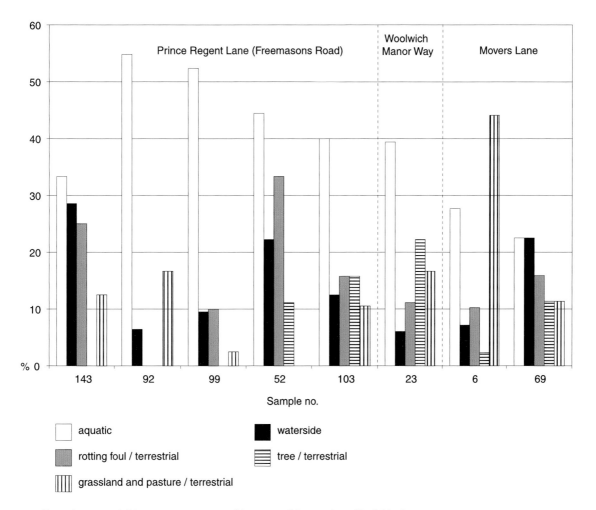

Note: the terrestrial faunas were very small in terms of the number of individuals.
As a result the statistics in this diagram may well over emphasis the dominance of the various ecological groups.

Fig. A3.14   The relative proportions of the ecological groups of Coleoptera recovered from the A13 sites

Table A3.6   The insect assemblages

Site code	Ecological codes		PRL (FRU)						WMW		ML		Plant associations
Sample number		143	103	133	92	99	52	1	23	8	6	69	
COLEOPTERA													
Carabidae													
Leistus ?ferrugineus (L.)		-	-	-	-	-	-	-	-	-	1	-	
Nebria brevicollis (F.)		-	-	-	-	-	-	-	-	-	1	-	
Dyschirius globosus (Hbst.)		-	1	-	-	2	-	-	-	-	1	1	
Bembidion? lampros (Hbst.)		-	-	-	-	-	-	-	-	-	1	-	
Bembidion doris (Panz.)		-	-	-	-	1	-	-	2	-	-	-	
B. guttula (F.)		-	-	-	-	-	-	-	-	-	1	-	
Bembidion spp.		-	1	-	1	-	1	-	-	-	-	-	
Patrobus sp.		-	-	-	-	-	-	-	-	1	-	-	
Pterostichus nigrita (Payk.)	ws	-	-	-	-	-	-	-	-	-	-	1	
Pterostichus minor (Gyll.)	ws	-	-	-	-	-	-	-	1	-	-	1	
Pterostichus spp.		-	-	-	-	-	-	-	-	-	3	-	
Calathus fuscipes (Goeze)		-	-	-	-	1	-	-	-	-	-	-	
Calathus melanocephalus (L.)		-	-	-	-	-	-	-	-	-	-	1	
Agonum sp.		-	-	-	-	-	-	-	1	-	1	-	
Platynus dorsalis (Pont.)		-	-	-	-	1	-	-	-	-	-	-	
Amara spp.		1	-	-	-	-	-	-	-	-	-	1	
Syntomus truncatellus (L.)		-	-	-	-	-	-	-	-	-	1	-	
Halididae													
Haliplus spp.	a	-	-	-	-	-	-	-	-	-	1	-	
Dytiscidae													
Hygrotus spp.	a	-	-	-	-	1	-	-	-	-	1	-	
Hydroporus spp.	a	-	-	-	-	1	-	-	-	-	1	1	
Colymbetes fuscus L.	a	-	1	-	1	1	1	-	-	-	-	-	
Notaris? clavicornis (Geer.	a	-	-	-	-	-	-	-	-	-	-	1	
Agabus bipustulatus (L.)	a	1	-	-	-	-	-	-	-	-	-	-	
Agabus spp	a	-	-	-	-	-	-	-	-	-	-	1	
Acilius spp.	a	-	-	-	-	1	-	-	-	-	-	-	
Gyrinidae													
Gyrinus spp.	a	-	-	-	-	-	-	-	-	-	1	-	
Hydraenidae													
Hydraena testacea Curt.	a	1	1	-	1	-	-	-	-	-	18	-	
Hydraena britteni Joy	a	-	-	-	-	-	-	-	-	-	-	1	
Hydraena spp.	a	-	-	-	-	-	1	-	-	-	9	4	
Ochthebius minimus (F.)	a	-	-	-	4	15	-	-	-	-	6	1	
Octhebius spp.	a	1	5	-	8	30	9	1	-	-	4	1	
Limnebius spp.	a	-	1	-	1	-	-	-	-	-	1	-	
Helophorus spp.		-	1	-	1	8	1	-	-	-	7	-	
Hydrophilidae													
Coelostoma orbiculare (F.)	a	-	4	-	-	1	-	-	-	1	-	3	
Cercyon ustulatus (Preyssl.)	a	-	-	-	-	-	-	-	1	-	-	-	
Cercyon tristis (Ill.)	a	-	-	-	-	-	-	-	-	-	1	-	
Cercyon sternalis Shp.	a	-	-	-	-	-	-	-	7	-	-	-	
Cercyon spp.		-	5	-	-	-	1	1	-	-	-	-	
Megasternum boletophagum (Marsh.)		2	-	-	-	-	-	-	-	-	1	1	
Cryptopleurum minutum (F.)		-	-	-	-	-	-	-	-	-	1		
Hydrobius fusipes (L.)	a	-	3	-	-	1	1	-	2	-	1	1	
Laccobius spp.	a	-	-	-	-	-	-	-	-	-	5	-	
Cymbiodyta marginella (F.)	a	-	-	-	-	-	-	-	-	-	-	1	
Chaetarthria seminulum (Hbst.)	a	-	-	-	-	-	-	-	-	-	-	2	
Histeridae													
Acritus nigricornis (Hoffm.)	df	-	1	-	-	-	-	-	-	-	-	-	
Hister spp.	df	1	-	-	-	-	-	-	-	-	-	-	
Abraeus globosus (Hoffman)		-	-	-	-	-	-	-	-	-	1	-	

Table A3.6   The insect assemblages (continued)

Site code	Ecological codes	PRL (FRU)						WMW			ML		Plant associations
Sample number		143	103	133	92	99	52	1	23	8	6	69	
Silphidae													
Silpha spp.		1	-	-	-	-	-	-	-	-	1	-	
Catopidae													
Catops spp.		-	-	-	-	-	-	-	-	-	1	-	
Orthoperidae													
Corylophus cassidoides (Marsh.)	ws	-	-	-	-	-	-	-	-	-	-	2	
Orthoperus spp.		-	-	-	1	1	-	1	1	-	7	7	
Ptiliidae													
Ptilidae Genus & spp. indet.		-	-	-	-	-	-	-	-	-	2	3	
Acrotrichis spp.		-	-	-	-	-	-	-	-	-	-	1	
Staphylinidae													
Micropeplus staphylinoides (Marsh.)		-	-	-	-	1	-	-	-	-	1	-	
Omalium spp.		-	-	-	-	-	-	-	-	-	1	-	
Olophrum spp.	ws	-	-	-	-	-	-	-	-	-	1	-	
Lesteva heeri Fauv.	ws	-	-	-	-	-	-	-	-	-	-	2	
Lesteva longelytrata (Goeze)	ws	-	-	-	-	-	-	-	-	2	-	-	
Lesteva spp.	ws	-	1	-	-	-	-	-	-	-	1	-	
Trogophloeus bilineatus (Steph.)	ws	-	-	-	-	-	1	-	-	-	-	-	
Trogophloeus spp.		-	-	-	-	1	-	-	-	-	-	1	
Aploderus caelatus (Grav.)		-	-	-	-	1	-	-	-	-	2	-	
Oxytelus rugosus (F.)	df	-	-	-	-	1	-	-	-	-	2	1	
Oxytelus sculpturatus Grav.	df	-	-	-	-	1	-	-	-	-	1	-	
Platystethus arenarius (Fourc.)	df	-	-	-	-	-	-	-	-	-	1	-	
Platystethus cornutus (Grav.)	ws	1	1	-	1	3	-	-	-	-	-	-	
Stenus spp.		1	-	-	4	5	-	-	1	2	2	-	
Stilicus orbiculatus (Payk.)		-	-	-	-	-	-	-	-	-	-	2	
Lathrobium spp.		-	1	-	-	-	-	1	2	-	1	2	
Xantholinus spp.		-	-	-	-	-	-	-	-	-	1	-	
Quedius spp.		-	-	-	-	-	1	-	-	-	-	-	
Philonthus spp.		-	1	-	-	4	-	-	-	-	1	2	
Tachinus spp.		-	-	-	-	-	-	-	-	-	1	-	
Aleocharinidae Genus & spp. Indet.		-	-	-	3	4	-	-	-	1	8	3	
Pselpahidae													
Euplectus spp.		-	-	-	-	-	1	-	-	-	-	-	
Rybaxis sp.		-	-	-	-	-	-	-	-	1	-	-	
Cantharidae													
Cantharis sp.		-	-	-	-	-	-	-	-	-	2	-	
Elateridae													
Agroties spp.	p	-	-	-	-	-	-	-	1	-	4	-	
Adelocera murina (L.)	p	1	-	-	-	-	-	-	-	-	1	1	
Actenicerus sjaelandicus (Müll)	p	-	-	-	-	-	-	-	-	-	1	-	
Athous? haemorrhoidalis (F.)	p	-	-	-	-	-	-	-	-	-	1	-	
Athous spp.	p	-	-	-	-	-	-	-	-	-	-	1	
Eucnemidae													
Melasis buprestoides (L.)	l	-	-	-	-	-	-	-	1	-	-	-	
Throscidae													
Throscus spp.	ws	-	-	-	-	-	-	-	1	-	-	-	
Helodidae													
Helodidae Gen. & spp. Indet.	a	-	1	-	-	-	-	-	2	-	3	-	
Dryopidae													
Dryops spp.	a	-	-	-	-	2	-	-	1	1	1	1	
Oulimnius spp.	a	1	-	-	1	-	-	-	-	-	-	-	
Elmis aenea (Müll.)	a	3	-	-	-	-	-	-	-	-	-	-	
Nitidulidae													
Brachypterus urticae (F.)	p	-	-	-	-	-	-	-	-	-	4	-	*Urtica dioica* L. (stinging nettle)

Table A3.6   The insect assemblages (continued)

	Ecological codes	PRL (FRU)						WMW			ML		Plant associations
Site code / Sample number		143	103	133	92	99	52	1	23	8	6	69	
Cryptophagidae													
Cryptophagus spp.		-	-	-	-	1	-	-	-	-	-	-	
Lathridiidae													
Enicmus minutus (Group)		-	-	-	-	1	-	-	-	-	-	-	
Lithostygnus serripennis Broun		-	-	-	-	-	-	-	-	1	-	-	
Cartodere ruficollis (Marsh.)		-	-	-	-	-	-	-	-	3	-	-	
Corticaria/ corticarina spp.		-	-	-	-	-	-	-	1	-	1	-	
Colydiidae													
Cerylon histeroides (F.)	l	-	-	-	-	-	-	-	1	-	-	-	
Cerylon sp.	l	-	-	-	-	-	-	-	-	-	-	1	
Endomychidae													
Mycetaea hirta (Marsh.)		-	-	-	-	-	-	-	-	1	-	-	
Coccinellidae	-												
Chilocorus bipustulatus (L.)		-	-	-	-	-	-	-	-	-	1	-	Heather (*Calluna* and *Erica* spp.)
Asphidiphoridae													
Aspidiphorus orbiculatus (Gyll.)	l	-	-	-	-	-	-	-	-	-	1	-	
Anobiidae													
Grynobius planus (F.)	l	-	-	-	-	-	-	-	1	-	-	-	
Anobium punctatum (Geer)	l	-	1	-	-	-	-	-	-	-	1	1	
Hadrobregmus denticollis (Crtz)	l	-	-	-	-	-	-	-	-	-	-	1	
Scarabaeidae													
Onthophagus spp.	df	-	1	-	-	-	1	-	-	-	1	-	
Oxyomus silvestris (Scop.)		-	1	-	-	1	-	-	-	-	-	-	
Aphodius sphacelatus (Panz.) or *A. prodromus* (Brahm)	df	-	-	-	-	1	1	-	-	-	7	-	
Aphodius fimentarius (L.)	df	-	-	-	-	1	1	-	-	-	-	-	
Aphodius fasciatus (Ol.) / *A. putridus* Herbst	df	-	-	-	-	-	-	-	-	-	1	-	
Aphodius spp.	df	1	1	-	-	-	-	1	2	-	-	6	
Melolontha melolontha (L.)	p	-	-	-	-	-	-	-	-	-	1	-	
Phyllopertha horticola (L.)	p	-	-	-	-	-	-	-	-	-	5	1	
Chyrsomelidae													
Donacia marginata Hopp	ws	-	-	-	-	1	1	-	-	-	2	1	*Sparganium ramosum* (Erect burr-reed)
Donacia simplex F.	ws	1	-	-	-	-	1	-	-	-	-	-	Range of water reeds and rushes
Donacia spp.	ws	-	-	1	-	-	-	-	-	-	-	-	
Plateumaris sericea (L.)	ws	1	1	-	-	-	1	-	-	-	1	1	Usually on *Carex* spp. (sedges)
Prasocuris phellandri (L.)	ws	-	-	1	-	-	-	-	-	-	-	1	On aquatic Apiacae (Umbellifers)
Agelastica alni (L.)	l	-	-	-	-	-	-	-	-	-	-	-	*Alnus* spp. (Alder spp.)
Phyllotreta spp.		-	-	-	-	2	-	-	-	-	1	1	
Chaetocnema concinna (Marsh.)		-	-	-	-	-	-	-	-	-	1	1	
Scolytidae													
Kissophagus hederae (Schmitt)	l	-	1	-	-	-	-	-	-	-	-	-	*Hedera helix* (L.) (Ivy)
Cuculionidae													
Apion craccae (L.)	p	-	-	-	-	-	-	-	-	-	1	-	*Vicia* species (various vetches)
Apion spp.	p	-	1	-	1	-	-	-	1	-	6	2	
Phyllobius sp.	p	-	-	-	-	-	-	-	-	-	3	-	
Barypeithes spp.		-	-	-	-	-	-	-	1	-	-	-	
Sitona hispidulus (F.)	p	-	-	-	-	-	-	-	-	-	2	-	*Trifolium* species (Clover)
Sitona spp.	p	-	-	-	-	-	-	-	1	-	-	-	
Bagous spp.	a	-	-	-	1	2	-	-	-	-	1	-	

Table A3.6   The insect assemblages (continued)

| Site code | | PRL (FRU) | | | | | WMW | | ML | | | |
| Sample number | | 143 | 103 | 133 | 92 | 99 | 52 | 1 | 23 | 8 | 6 | 69 | |
	Ecological codes												Plant associations
Tanysphyrus lemnae (Payk.)	ws	1	1	-	1	5		-	-	-	8	6	*Lemna* spp. (Duckweed)
Notaris acridulus (L.)	ws	-	-	-	-	1	1	-	-	-	-	2	Often on *Glyceria maxima* (Hartm.) Holmb. (reed sweet-grass) and other *Glyceria* species (sweet-grasses)
Notaris spp.	ws	1	-	-	-	-	-	-	-	-	1	-	
Thyrogenes spp.	ws	-	1	-	-	-	-	-	-	-	-	1	
Curclio spp.	l	-	1	-	-	-	-	-	-	-	-	1	
Leiosoma deflexum (Panz.)	ws	1	-	-	-	-	-	-	-	-	-	-	*Caltha palustris* L. (Marsh marigold)
Alophus triguttatus (F.)	p	-	-	1	-	-	-	-	-	-	18	-	
Limnobaris spp.	ws	-	-	-	-	-	1	-	-	-	-	-	Juncaceae and Cyperaceae (rushes)
Ceutorhynchus contratus (Marsh.)	p	-	-	-	-	-	-	-	-	-	3	-	Associated with Resedaceae and Papaveraceae (migonettes and poppies)
Ceutorhynchus eryisimi (F.)	p	-	-	-	-	-	-	-	-	-	1	-	On *Capsella bursa-pastoris* (L.) Medik. (Shepard's purse)
Ceutorhynchus pollinarius Forst.	p	-	-	-	1	-	-	-	-	-	-	-	*Urtica dioica* L. (stinging nettle)
Ceutorhynchus spp.	p	-	-	-	-	-	-	-	-	-	2	-	
Gymnetron spp.	p	-	1	-	-	1	-	-	-	-	3	-	*Plantago lanceolata* L. (plantain)
Rhynchaenus quercus (L.)	l	-	-	-	-	-	-	-	-	-	1	-	*Quercus* spp. (Oak)
Rhynchaenus sp.	l	-	-	-	-	-	1	-	1	-	-	1	

flotation as outlined in Kenward *et al.* (1980). Insect remains were sorted and identified under a low-power binocular microscope at a magnification between x15 to x45. Where achievable the insect remains were identified to species level by direct comparison to specimens in the Gorham and Girling insect collections housed in the Institute of Archaeology and Antiquity, University of Birmingham.

Results

The majority of the insect remains present are beetles (Coleoptera), with very few individuals of true bugs (Hemiptera) and flies (Diptera) present. A list of Coleoptera recovered is presented in Table A3.6. The nomenclature for Coleoptera (beetles) follows that of Lucht (1987). Column 14 in Table A3.6 lists the host plants for the phytophage species of beetle that were recovered and are predominantly derived from Koch (1989; 1992). The plant taxonomy follows that of Stace (1997).

In order to aid interpretation, where possible, taxa have been assigned to ecological groupings.

The Coleoptera follow a simplified version of the scheme suggested by Robinson (1981; 1983). The affiliation of each beetle species to a particular ecological grouping is coded in the second column of Table 2. The meaning of each ecological code is explained in the key at the base of Table A3.6. The occurrence of each of the ecological groupings is expressed as a percentage in Table A3.7 and in Figure A3.14. The pasture/grassland, dung and woodland/ timber beetle species are calculated as percentages of the number of terrestrial species, as opposed to the whole fauna.

Prince Regent Lane (Freemasons Road)

Posthole 73 (Str. 32, Area A): A moderately sized insect fauna came from the fill of post hole 73 (sample 103) associated with the double post alignment (Str. 32, Fig 4.7). The insect fauna is dominated by taxa associated with slow flowing or standing water such as *Colymbetes fuscus, Hydraena testacea, Ochthebius* spp., *Limnebius* and *Coelostoma orbiculare* (Nilsson and Holmen 1995; Hansen 1986). There is evidence for stands of sedges and areas of duckweed locally. The former is suggested by the

Table A3.7   The relative proportions of the ecological groups of Coleoptera recovered from the A13 sites

| | Prince Regent Lane (Freemasons Road) | | | | | | Woolwich Manor Way | | | Movers Lane | |
	143	103	133	92	99	52	1	23	8	6	69
total number of individuals	21	40	3	31	105	27	5	33	11	195	80
total number of species	18	27	3	16	35	19	5	22	9	76	47
% aquatic	33.3	40.0	0.0	54.8	52.4	44.4	20.0	39.4	18.2	27.7	22.5
% waterside	28.6	12.5	66.7	6.5	9.5	22.2	0.0	6.1	18.2	7.2	22.5
% rotting foul / terrestrial	25.0	0.0	0.0	10.0	33.3	15.8	25.0	11.1	0.0	10.2	15.9
% tree / terrestrial	0.0	0.0	0.0	0.0	11.1	15.8	0.0	22.2	0.0	2.4	11.4
% grassland and pasture / terrestrial	12.5	100.0	16.7	2.5	0.0	10.5	0.0	16.7	0.0	44.1	11.4

presence of *Plateumaris sericea* and *Thyrogenes* spp. and the later by *Tanysphyrus lemnae* (Koch 1992). Given that this is interpreted as a post hole the insect fauna clearly suggest that the feature was probably flooded at some point.

There is also a suggestion as to the nature of the surrounding vegetation and landscape. The 'bark beetle' *Kissophagus hederae* is normally associated with ivy (*Hedera helix*) in woodland. The 'nut beetle' *Curclio* is also an indicator for woodland, as can be the 'woodworm' *Anobium punctatum* which, in addition to its role as destroyer of furniture and structural timbers in settlement, is also associated with dry deadwood in forests and woodlands. Once again, due to the small size of the fauna recovered, care should be taken with the interpretation of these taxa.

Ditch 132, Area B: A small fauna came from middle Bronze Age ditch 132 (sample 143, Figs. 4.7 and 4.11). The fauna is dominated by beetles associated with slow flowing or stagnant water (Table A3.7 and Fig. A3.14). Typical of this environment are the predatory 'diving beetle' *Agabus bipustulatus* and the small hydreanid *Octhebius* (Nilsson and Holmen 1995; Hansen 1986). Similar conditions are also suggested by a number of the phytophages (plant feeding) taxa recovered. The presence of waterside vegetation is clearly indicated by *Donacia simplex* and *Plateumaris sericea* which are associated with *Sparganium ramonsum* (branched bur-reed) and other waterside vegetation, such as *Phragmites* (reeds) and *Carex* (sedges) (Koch 1992). The presence of still water is also suggested by *Tanysphyrus lemnae* which feeds on *Lemna* spp.(duckweed) and by *Liosoma deflexum* which is associated with *Caltha palustris* (marsh marigold) (Koch 1992).

There are also indications that the ditch may have contained areas of sands and gravels, or that water from a fast moving area of river periodically flooded into the ditch. Elmid species such as *Oulimnius* spp. and *Elmis aenea* are normally associated with flowing water crossing over sands and gravels (Holland 1972).

There are hints that some of the landscape around this feature may have been relatively open. The 'click beetle' *Adelocera murina* is commonly

associated with grassy ground and woodland edges. A single *Aphodius* 'dung beetle' was also recovered. However, these aspects of the fauna should not be over interpreted and, in the case of this feature, the plant macrofossils and pollen analysis may give a far better indication of the nature of the surrounding vegetation.

Flood deposit 125 Area B and peat layers 46 and 47 Area A : Three insect faunas come from the 'sandy' layer 125 (sample 133, Fig. 4.13) and peat development (samples 92 and 99) above the early Bronze Age 'bridge' (Str. 32). Once again the vast majority of the insect remains recovered are associated with slow flowing water (Table A3.7 and Fig. A3.14). Again, this is indicated by a range of water beetles recovered such as *Hygrotus* spp. *Hydroporus* spp., *Colymbetes fuscus*, *Acilius*, *Hydraena testacea*, *Ochthebius minimus* and *Coelostoma orbiculare* (Nilsson and Holmen 1995; Hansen 1986). Similar conditions are also suggested by the dryopid *Dryops* spp. and the weevils *Bagous* spp. and *Tanysphyrus lemnae*, the latter species is associated with duckweed (Koch 1992). There also indicators for stands of reed sweet grass, bur-reeds and aquatic hogweeds (Apiacae). This is suggested by the recovery of *Notaris acridulus*, *Donacia marginata* and *Prasocuris phellandrii* which feed on these plants (Koch 1992).

There is limited evidence from the insects that the area around the structure may have been relatively open or that disturbed ground was present. This is suggested by the recovery of *Ceutorhynchus pollinarius* which is associated with *Urtica dioica* (stinging nettle), *Gymnetron* spp. which is associated with plantain *Plantago lanceolata* (plantain), and a single individual of an *Aphodius* 'dung beetle'. However, again, without supporting information from the pollen and plant macrofossils this aspect of the fauna should not be over emphasised.

Ditch 38, Area A: Sample 52 came from ditch 38 (Fig. 4.15). The small insect fauna recovered contains several individuals of the set of water beetles, described above, which are typical of slow flowing water. There is also evidence that a mixed stand of waterside vegetation consisting of *Carex* (sedges), *Sparganium* spp. (bur-reeds) and *Glyceria maxima* (reed sweet grass) grew in the ditch. This is indicated by the 'reed beetle' *Donacia* spp. and the weevil *Notaris acridulus* (Koch 1992). Again, there is evidence for open ground since a number of individuals of *Onthophagus* and *Apion* 'dung beetles' were recovered. A single individual of the 'leaf minor' *Rhynchaenus* spp. was also recovered suggesting there was some tree cover in the area. Once again these aspects of the fauna should not be over emphasised, especially if there is no corroborating evidence from the plant macro fossils and pollen analyses.

Woolwich Manor Way

Only one of the four samples submitted from Woolwich Manor Way produced an interpretable insect fauna. This was from peat context 57 (sample 23) below the trackways in Area 1 (Fig. 5.3). This moderate sized fauna is dominated by species such as *Ochthebius* spp., *Cercyon sternalis*, *Laccobius* spp. and *Dryops* spp. which are all associated with slow flowing or stagnant waters (Hansen 1986).

A few individuals of a number of species associated with deadwood are present. *Melasis buprestoides* is normally associated with dry deadwood of *Quercus* spp. (oak) or *Fagus* spp.(beech) and is today relatively uncommon (Red Data Book notable B) (Hyman and Parsons 1992). However, it is a species that is regularly encountered in prehistoric trackway and wood peat sites in a variety of locations throughout the British Isles (Buckland and Buckland 2006). *Cerylon histeroides* is a small predator which hunts scolytid 'bark beetles' in the deadwood of a range of trees and *Grynobius planus* is a 'woodworm' associated with deadwood and dry timber from a range of hardwood trees. Though these species may indicate the presence of woodland in the area they may also have lived and bred in the timbers of the trackway itself. A single wing case of an *Aphodius* 'dung beetle' was also recovered.

The remaining three samples from Woolwich Manor were either too small to be interpretable or, in the case of sample 22, produced no insect fauna at all. Sample 8 also contained an individual of the lathridiid *Lithostygnus serripennis*. This species is a recent importation from New Zealand with its first record in Britain being in the 1920s (Buckland and Buckland 2006). This, unfortunately, suggests that this sample may have become contaminated during sampling or storage.

Movers Lane

Sample 69 from the peat associated with trackway 3031 (Figs. 7.8 and 7.9) produced a relatively large fauna. The majority of the fauna is again made up of a range of beetles associated with slow flowing water conditions. There are also indications that stands of waterside vegetation existed in the area of the trackway. This is indicated by the recovery of *Donacia marginata* which is associated with *Sparganium* spp. (bur-reed) and the 'reed beetles' *Donacia simplex* and *Plateumaris sericea* which are both associated with a range of sedges, rushes and water reeds.

There were also a few individuals of *Aphodius* 'dung beetles' recovered along with a single individual of the 'garden chafer' *Phyllopertha horticola* suggesting that grassland or meadow was present in the area. There are, again, a number of species which are associated with deadwood such as *Cerylon* spp., the 'woodworms' *Anobium punctatum* and *Hadrobregmus denticollis* and the *Curculio* 'nut weevil'. This may indicate that woodland is present in the local environment and/or that these species were associated with the decaying trackway.

Sample 6 from Movers Lane came from the fill of late Bronze Age ditch 1038 (Fig. 7.9). Once again the insect fauna is dominated by a range of water beetles that are associated with slow flowing or standing water. Typical for these conditions are *Haliplus* spp., *Hygrotus* spp., *Hydroporus* spp., *Hydraena testacea*, *Ochthebius minimus*, *Limnebius* spp. *Cercyon tristis*, *Laccobius* spp. and *Dryops* spp. (Nilsson and Holmen 1995; Hansen 1986). Also present was a single individual of a 'whirligig' *Gyrinus* spp. This beetle is normally associated with still and open water. The small weevil *Tanysphyrus lemnae* was also recovered and is associated with duckweeds.

There are also indications that some of the landscape surrounding the ditch consisted of grassland or pasture. This is suggested by the two 'chafers' recovered, *Melolontha melolontha* and *Phyllopertha horticola*, which both feed as larvae on the roots of grass in open dry pasture (Jessop 1986). *Onthophagus* and *Aphodius* 'dung beetles' again indicate that cattle or other herbivores may have been present in the area. The two 'click beetles' *Adelocera murina* and *Actenicerus sjaelandicus* are often associated with damp grassy areas, disturbed ground and agricultural land (Koch 1989). Disturbed ground is also indicated by the presence of the nitiduliid *Brachypterus urticae* which feeds on stinging nettle (*Urtica dioica*). Similarly, the small 'ladybird' *Chilocorus bipustulatus* is normally associated with heather (*Calluna* spp. or *Erica* spp.).

There is a slight hint that some woodland or trees were present in the area. This is suggested by the 'woodworm' *Anobium punctatum* and the small mould beetle *Aspidiphorus orbiculatus,* both of which are commonly associated with a range of deadwood in a variety of trees. Similarly the 'leaf minor' *Rhynchaenus quercus* is associated with oak trees (*Quercus* spp.).

Discussion

Unfortunately, the individual insect faunas recovered from a range of deposits along the route of the A13 Thames Gateway are often fairly small sized and therefore they should not be interpreted in isolation, but should be used to support pollen and plant macrofossil analyses. It is evident that the majority of the features contained still waters, often associated with a range of waterside vegetation, or, in the case of the trackways, crossed this type of environment.

One major difficulty with these faunas and their archaeological circumstance is the degree to which they can be used reliably to reconstruct woodland surrounding the site. Taken at face value the faunas could suggest that the Bronze Age trackways in particular were located within woodland. However, many of the species recovered could be associated not with woodland but with the rotting timbers of the trackways themselves. Certainly, species such as *Anobium punctatum*, *Hadrobregmus denticollis*, *Melasis buprestoides* and *Cerylon* have occasionally been recovered from trackways and timber structures in the archaeological record before (Buckland and Buckland 2006; Girling 1980; Smith *et al.* 2000). It has been suggested previously that the presence of these or similar species at trackway sites probably indicates that the structures remained exposed on the mire or bog surface for some time. However, this does not seem to have been the case with a number of other trackways, such as those in the Somerset Levels, at Bronze Age Goldcliff, Gwent (Smith *et al.* 2000), and the Bronze Age trackways in London at Bramcote Green (Thomas and Rackham 1996) and Dagenham Hays (Smith 1996), where no wood boring insects were recovered and where it appears therefore that the structures were quickly inundated.

Another factor in all of the samples from the sites examined is that small numbers of 'dung beetles' and 'chafers' are routinely recovered. This may suggest that some of the landscape near to the archaeological features was cleared of woodland or used as pasture. However, given the small size of the faunas recovered it is very difficult to suggest the extent of this clearance. Pollen and plant macro-fossils may provide a better indictor for this aspect of the landscape. Notably, the dates for these sites do match some of the early dates suggested for woodland clearance in the area (Sidell *et al.* 2000; Sidell *et al.* 2002; Thomas and Rackham 1996; Wilkinson *et al.* 2000). One common assumption that is often made when dung beetles are recovered from trackways is that this indicates that cattle may have been driven across the structure. This interpretation of the insect remains is some thing of a fallacy. Dung beetles have a very strong flight potential and are a very routine part of the 'background fauna' found on most archaeological sites (Kenward 1975; 1978). As a result low numbers of them are to be expected on almost any archaeological site and do not necessarily indicate that grazing was very local or that animals were directly involved with the use of any structures on site. High numbers of dung beetles are required before suggesting the presence of cattle with any confidence. Moreover one cannot rule out wild herbivores such as deer.

Locally a number of other insect faunas of similar dates have been recovered; several from trackways. The faunas from Bronze Age Bramcote Green (Thomas and Rackham 1996), Dagenham Hays

(Smith 1996), Beckton (Elias *et al.* 2009) and Belloit Street, Greenwich (Elias *et al.* 2009) were similar to those recovered from the A13 sites. All indicated the presence of still waters, reed beds and a potentially cleared landscape. One exception to this is the fauna from the Neolithic trackway and wood peats from Atlas Wharf (Smith 1999). In this case it is clear that the trackway crossed a major channel of the Thames where fast flowing water predominated and that a dense stand of alder carr and woods surrounded the site.

However, despite the methodological issues with these assemblages, these faunas from the A13 Thames Gateway do generally appear to match the general sequence for the development and change of insect faunas in this part of the Thames Valley (Elias *et al.* 2009; Smith in press).

Charred and waterlogged plant remains *by Ruth Pelling*

Introduction

The excavations along the route of the A13 Thames Gateway Road Scheme have revealed a landscape wide sequence of sediment deposition including mid-Holocene peat formation. Throughout the programme of excavation samples were taken for the extraction of the biological remains in order to trace vertical and lateral patterns in the vegetation and hydrological conditions along the edges of this section of the Thames floodplain. Useful sequences of plant remains have been recovered from Prince Regent Lane, Woolwich Manor Way and Movers Lane, largely relating to the end of the Neolithic and the Bronze Age period of peat formation. The greatest value of the deposits lies in their potential to provide a landscape wide understanding of the sedimentary development and in their comparison with other published sites both locally, and those further up and down river.

Methodology

Systematic sampling across vertical and lateral sequences was undertaken at various locations along the length of the road scheme. The strategy was designed to enable sampling of a wide area and range of deposit types. For each site samples were processed by floatation or wet sieving with the flots collected on a 0.25mm mesh and residues on a 1mm mesh. Flots were kept wet while residues were dried before being sorted for artefacts. Following an initial assessment of the flots (Giorgi in Gifford and Partners 2001a; 2001b; 2002; 2003a; 2003b, Allen and Stevens in Wessex Archaeology 2003) a total of 32 were selected for more detailed study of waterlogged material: 18 from Prince Regent Lane, Freemasons Road Underpass (FRU01), 6 from Woolwich Manor Way (TGW00/WMW00 and WMA02) and 8 samples from Movers Lane (RIR01). Flots selected for more detail examination were first washed through a stack of sieves with water. Each fraction (down to 0.25mm) was scanned under a x10 – x40 stereo-binocular microscope. Species present were identified and item frequency was estimated. Precise counts were not given. While this method limits the potential for quantitative analysis it does enable a greater number of samples to be examined in sufficient detail to characterise the deposits. Nomenclature follows Stace (1997) and species are presented in ecological groups. Item frequency follows a five point scale as follows: 1 = 1-5 items; 2 = 6-25; 3 = 25-100; 4 = 100-500; 5 = >500 or exceptionally abundant. The presence of non-plant remains is also noted. The results are discussed by site and reference is made to the assessment results. As samples were largely related to chronological sequences through flood-plain peats and alluvium rather than distinct archaeological features, the charred and waterlogged plant remains are discussed together in order to explore the temporal and spatial data. Each site is discussed in turn, while an overview section traces the evolution of the wider landscape bringing in both the comparisons between the three sites and data from contemporary sites elsewhere in this section of the Lower Thames Valley.

A number of samples were shown to contain charred plant remains. Following assessment of the material a small number were examined in more detail at analysis level. A total of three samples are discussed from Prince Regent Lane/Freemasons Road Underpass and six samples from Woolwich Manor Way. Charred plant remains (retained in the 0.5mm and larger sieves) were extracted under a binocular microscope at x10 to x40 magnification following standard methods. Identifications were based on well established morphological criteria and by comparison with modern reference material held at Wessex Archaeology. Material is quantified on the basis of grain, seed, chaff item and so on and nomenclature of wild species follows Stace (1997). The results are given in a separate table (Tables A3.8-15).

Prince Regent Lane (Freemasons Road)

A total of 29 samples were taken from 18 deposits during the excavation at Freemasons Road Underpass; these came from a range of features including multiple samples from the peat deposits. Archaeological features sampled included fills of ditches, a channel, a pit and post-hole. Sample volumes range from 10 to 90L, although most were 20 to 30L. The deposits are discussed by period and summarised below. The samples can be characterised by the major plant groups represented, most notably the seeds and catkins of alder, although other species including bur-reed (*Sparganium erectum*) are characteristic of some sample or deposit groups.

The early to middle Bronze Age features

Sample 165 was taken from gully 199 (fill 198) associated with the early Bronze Age 'enclosure' in

Area B (Fig. 4.7). Assessment by Giorgi (in Gifford and Partners 2003b) demonstrated that few biological remains were present other than a few seeds and fruit of mainly aquatic species such as *Lemna* spp. (duckweed), *Chara* spp. (stoneworts), *Alisma* spp.(water plantain) as well as wood and charcoal flecks.

Two samples examined from the fill of ditch 132 in Area B (fill 146, sample 143, Figs 4.7 and 4.11) and posthole 73 associated with the 'bridge' (Str. 32) in Area A (fill 73, sample 103, Fig 4.7) produced very similar assemblages. Both assemblages were characterised by frequent wood fragments, seeds and cones of alder (*Alnus glutinosa*) and fruit of branched bur-reed (*Sparganium erectum*) suggesting a dominant vegetation of alder fen-carr. Aquatic species included crowfoots (*Ranunculus* subgen *Batrachium*), water plantain (*Alisma plantago-aquatica*), water-pepper (*Persicaria hydropiper*) and occasional seeds of duckweed (*Lemna* sp.) as well as oogonia of stonewort (*Chara* sp.) and the larval cases of caddisfly (order Trichoptera). These last three items are particularly indicative of standing water, presumably within the features.

Bankside vegetation which might have included species growing within the shallow muddy water of ditch fill 146 include branched bur-reed (*Sparganium erectum*), club-rushes (*Schoenoplectus* sp.), water dropwort (*Oenanthe aquatica*), fool's water-cress (*Apium nodiflorum*), gypsywort (*Lycopus europeaus*) and water mint (*Menthe aquatica*). Wet or damp grassland is indicated by meadow species including possible meadow rue (*Thalicturum flavum*) and ragged robin (*Lychnis flos-cuculi*) present in the post hole fill (sample 103), while *Juncus articulatus* gp.(rushes) and *Carex* spp. (sedges) and some of the buttercups may have derived from similar habitats.

In addition to the fruits and catkins of alder, seeds of elder (*Sambucus nigra*) and bramble (*Rubus* spp.) were present, which can today be seen in alder carr, but is also a common indicator for shrubby disturbed ground. Disturbed habitats and nitrogen rich soil are also suggested by the presence of fat hen (*Chenopodium album*) as well as stinging nettle (*Urtica dioica*), black nightshade (*Solanum nigrum*), hairy buttercup (*Ranunculus sardous*) and docks (*Rumex* sp.). Other seeds included those of *Viola odorata/hirta* (sweet or hairy violet). Sweet violet (*V. odorata*) is characteristic of shaded and wooded conditions while hairy violet (*V. hirta*) is found within calcareous pastures and open scrub. Either would be possible in this context. Possible food debris is suggested by nutshell fragments of *Corylus avellana* (hazel) from the post hole.

Middle to late Bronze Age flood deposit 125

Two samples (samples 133 and 153) were examined from flood deposit 125 in Area B (Fig. 4.13). The samples produced broadly similar assemblages characterised by wood, alder seeds and catkins, and fruits of branched bur-reed. A similar range of wetland species included crowfoots, water-plantain, pondweeds, duckweeds and stoneworts suggesting shallow, mineral rich water, with caddisfly larval cases suggesting open bodies of still water. In addition seeds of celery-leaved buttercup (*Ranunculus sceleratus*) were present. The wet, marshy grassland type vegetation is represented again by water-pepper, water-dropwort, fool's water-cress, gypsywort, water mint and branched bur-reed with blinks (*Montia fontana* subsp. *chondrosperma*), soft rush (*Juncus effusus* type) and wood-rush (*Luzula* sp.) also present. This last species suggests shady conditions, as may seeds of violets (*Viola odorata/hirta* type). Disturbed and drier habitats are suggested by the presence of elder together with docks, thistles (*Carduus/Cirsium* sp.), brambles, fat hen and stinging nettles.

Middle to late Bronze Age peats

Samples were taken from three locations, all representing sequences through the same middle to late Bronze Age deposit within a roughly 10x10m area. Deposit 32 was located to the east separated from contexts 46 and 47 by a channel truncating the peat. Layer 46 was situated in the south-west and 47 in the north-west. A total of six samples were taken from layers 46 and 47. The assessment demonstrated that the botanical composition of the samples was broadly similar, suggesting homogeneity through the deposit. Detailed scanning was therefore limited to one sample from each layer (samples 92 and 99). Four samples were examined from layer 32.

The deposits are characterised by a significant decline in alder (represented by a single cone bract in layer 46) and *Sparganium erectum*, but an increase in seeds of duckweed (*Lemna* sp), water plantain (*Alisma plantago-aquatica*) and possible crowfoots (*Ranunculus* subg *Batrachium*). The number of seeds and species diversity was also more limited than in the earlier deposits. Degraded wood fragments and a range of mostly aquatic species were present in all the samples, with occasional fragments of charcoal and insects. There is similarly a decline in dry ground vegetation compared to the previous phases: occasional seeds of bramble, elder and violets were the only species represented. The number of seeds of aquatic species, particularly duckweed as well as crowfoots and stoneworts, was significantly increased from previous phases while bank side/marshland vegetation was well represented: common spikerush (*Eleocharis palustris*), water mint and dropwort, marsh pennywort (*Hydrocotyle vulgaris*), spikerush (*Eleocharis* spp.) sedges and rushes were identified. Caddisfly larval cases were noted in one of the samples (Sample 54). Samples examined at assessment were also noted to contain pondweeds (*Potamogeton*), an aquatic plant of slow moving water. Generally these deposits suggest increasingly wet conditions and flooding of the marsh associated with the reduction of the alder carr and the formation of the peat deposits.

A background of drier ground continues to be suggested by seeds of elder, bramble and stinging nettle, although the range and number of ruderal species is decreased from previous phases. The residues produced occasional fragments of bone and burnt flint suggesting human activity on the drier ground.

Late Bronze Age to early Iron Age alluvium and occupation layers

The following samples produced similar results to those described above. Material was limited in layer 31 (Fig 4.15) to occasional wood and charcoal fragments, seeds of *Juncus* sp. (rushes), *Lemna* sp. (duckweed), elder and bramble as well as charred seeds of bramble, ryegrass/fescue type grass seeds (*Lolium/Fescue* sp.) and basal culms/rhizomatous roots. These charred remains suggest some human activity in the area.

A series of samples were taken from the fill of ditch 28 (Figs. 4.3 and 4.15), from a clayey peaty fill context 27 (samples 15, 16 and 50) and the basal peaty silt, fill 33 (samples 44 and 55). The samples from fill 27 produced a slightly more diverse flora. Unsurprisingly seeds of aquatic species and marshland/bankside vegetation dominated, with large numbers of seeds of duckweed, crowfoot, stoneworts and water-plantain/arrowheads (*Alisma* sp./*Plantago-aquatica*/*Sagittaria* sp.) as well as sedges and rushes. Shrubby species indicative of disturbed habitats such as bramble and elder were fairly numerous while seeds of *Fumaria* sp. (fumitory) are also indicative of disturbed or cultivated soils. Wood and charcoal tended to be very fragmentary. The ditch deposits produced a range of aquatics and

A3.8   Samples selected for macroscopic plant remains analysis from Prince Regent Lane (Freemasons Road)

Sample	Context	Context type	Period	Sample volume (l..)
11	18	Fill of natural hollow 19	LBA-EIA	14.5
15	27	Fill of ditch 28	LBA-EIA	19
16	27	Fill of ditch 28	LBA-EIA	19
17	32	Layer (peat)	M-LBA	19
39	31	Layer (peat)	LBA-EIA	19
44	33	Fill of ditch 28	LBA-EIA	19
50	27	Fill of ditch 28	LBA-EIA	19
52	37	Fill of ditch 38/42	LBA-EIA	19
54	32	Layer (peat)	M-LBA	not rec.
55	33	Fill of ditch 28	LBA-EIA	19
81	32	Layer (peat)	M-LBA	19
92	46	Layer (peat)	M-LBA	9
93	32	Layer (peat)	M-LBA	9
99	47	Layer (peat)	M-LBA	9
133	125	Layer (flood deposit)	M-LBA	10
153	125	Layer (flood deposit)	M-LBA	10
103	72	Fill of posthole 73	EBA-MBA	19
143	146	Fill of posthole 146	MBA	19

Table A3.9 Waterlogged plant remains from Prince Regent Road (Freemasons Road)

		Sample	143	103	133	153	17	54	81	93	92	99
		Context	146	72	125	125	32	32	32	32	46	47
		Feature type	ditch	ph	layer	layer	peat	peat	peat	peat	peat	peat
		Period	MBA	EMBA	M-LBA	M-LBA	M-LBA	M-LBA	M-LBA	M-LBA	M-LBA	M-LBA
		Sample Vol (L.)	19	19	10	10	19	?	19	9	9	9
Aquatic/semi-aquatic species												
Ranunculus sceleratus L.	Celery-leaved buttercup		-	-	-	1	-	-	-	-	-	-
Ranunculus Subgenus Batrachium	Crowfoot		3	4	2	3	3	5	2	2	5	2
Alisma plantago-aquatica L.	Water-plantain		2	1	-	1	2	5	-	-	2	1
Alisma plantago-aquatica L. / Sagittaria sp.	Water-plantain / Arrowheads		-	-	1	1	-	-	1	-	-	-
Hydrocotyle vulgaris L.	Marsh pennywort		-	-	-	-	-	-	-	-	-	1
Potamogeton sp.	Pondweeds		-	1	-	1	-	-	-	-	-	-
Lemna sp.	Duckweeds		1	1	2	-	4	1	3	4	3	5
Chara sp.	Stoneworts		1	1	1	-	-	1	-	1	1	1
Wet grass/meadow, marshland												
cf. Thalictrum flavum L.	Common meadow rue		-	1	-	-	-	-	-	-	-	-
Montia fontana subsp. chondrosperma (Fenzl) Walters	Blinks		-	-	-	1	-	-	-	-	-	-
Lychnis flos-cuculi L.	Ragged-robin		-	1	-	-	-	-	-	-	-	1
Persicaria hydropiper/mitis	Water-pepper		-	1	-	1	-	-	-	-	-	-
Oenanthe aquatica (L.) Poiret in Lam.	Fine-leaved water-dropwort		1	2	-	1	2	1	-	-	1	-
Apium nodiflorum L.	Fool's water-cress		1	-	-	-	-	-	-	-	-	-
Lycopus europaeus L.	Gypsywort		1	-	-	1	-	-	-	-	-	-
Mentha aquatica L.	Water mint		1	-	1	1	-	-	1	-	1	1
Juncus articulatus gp.	Jointed rush		1	-	-	-	2	1	2	-	-	-
Juncus bulbosus type	Bulbous rush		-	-	-	-	-	-	-	-	-	-
Juncus effusus type	Soft-rush		-	-	1	2	-	1	-	-	-	-
Juncus sp.	Rushes		-	1	-	1	-	1	1	-	-	3
Luzula sp.	Wood-rush		-	-	-	1	-	-	-	-	-	-
Carex flat (< 2.5mm)			1	1	-	2	-	-	-	-	-	-
Carex trig			1	-	1	1	-	-	-	-	-	-
Eleocharis spp.	Common spike-rush		-	2	1	2	2	2	1	-	1	1
cf. Schoenoplectus lacustris (L.) Palla	Common club-rush		2	-	1	1	-	-	-	-	-	-
Sparganium erectum L.	Branched bur-reed		4	2	2	3	-	-	-	-	-	-
Cultivated ground/Waste places/Dry grassland												
Ranunculus sardous L.	Hairy buttercup		-	1	-	-	-	-	-	-	-	-
Urtica dioica L.	Stinging nettle		1	1	2	1	-	1	-	1	-	-
Chenopodium album L.	Fat-hen		1	-	1	1	-	-	-	-	-	-
Rumex acetosella group	Sheep's sorrel		-	-	-	1	-	-	-	-	-	-

Table A3.9   Waterlogged plant remains from Prince Regent Road (Freemasons Road) (continued)

		Sample	143	103	133	153	17	54	81	93	92	99
		Context	146	72	125	125	32	32	32	32	46	47
		Feature type	ditch	ph	layer	layer	peat	peat	peat	peat	peat	peat
		Period	MBA	EMBA	M-LBA	M-LBA	M-LBA	M-LBA	M-LBA	M-LBA	M-LBA	M-LBA
		Sample Vol (L.)	19	19	10	10	19	?	19	9	9	9
Rumex sp.	Docks		-	1	1	-	-	-	-	-	-	-
Solanum nigrum L.	Black nightshade		1	1	-	-	-	-	-	-	-	-
Sambucus nigra L.	Elder		1	2	3	3	-	1	1	-	-	1
Carduus/Cirsium sp.	Thistles		1	-	-	1	-	-	-	-	-	-
Shady places/woods/hedgerows												
Corylus avellana L.	Hazelnut shell fragment		-	1	-	-	-	-	-	-	-	-
Viola ordorata/hirta L.	Sweet violet		1	-	1	1	-	1	-	-	1	-
Trees												
Alnus glutinosa (L.) Gaertner	Alder cones (female)		2	2	1	3	-	-	-	-	1	-
Alnus glutinosa (L.) Gaertner	Aldet bracts		-	-	-	-	-	-	-	-	-	-
Alnus glutinosa (L.) Gaertner	Alder, seeds		2	1	1	1	-	-	-	-	-	-
Catholic/Not specified												
Ranunculus acris/bulbosus/repens			-	2	-	1	-	-	-	-	-	-
Atriplex sp.			-	-	-	1	-	-	-	-	-	-
Rubus section 2 Glandulosus Wimm. & Grab	Brambles		3	2	3	3	-	1	-	1	1	2
Rosaceae thorns			1	1	1	-	-	-	-	-	-	-
Aphanes arvensis L.	Parsley-piert		-	-	1	-	-	-	-	-	-	-
Small angular Asteraceae			-	1	-	-	-	-	-	-	-	-
Others												
charcoal			-	1	-	-	-	1	1	-	1	1
moss			-	-	-	-	-	-	-	-	-	-
Caddis fly larval cases			1	1	1	1	-	1	-	-	-	-
fungal spores			-	-	-	-	-	-	-	-	-	3
wood fragments			1	1	4	4	-	2	-	2	4	-
degraded wood			-	-	-	-	-	-	3	-	-	3

Table A3.10   Charred plant remains from Prince Regent Lane (Freemasons Road)

	Sample	*26*	*31*	*39*
	Context	*31*	*31*	*31*
	Feature	*Layer (peat)*	*Layer (peat)*	*Layer (peat)*
	Period	*LBA-EIA*	*LBA-EIA*	*LBA-EIA*
	Sample vol (L.)	*not rec*	*not rec.*	*19*
Cerealia indet	Indeterminate grain	1	1	-
Cerealia indet	Culm node	-	-	1
Rubus section 2 Glandulosus Wimm. & Grab	Bramble/Blackberry etc	-	1	1
Lolium/Festuca sp.	Rye-Grass/Fescue	-	1	1

marshland seeds with fragmented and degraded wood including twigs, round wood and bark. Aquatic species include duckweeds, and crowfoots, while the bankside/marshland species included spikerush, rushes and sedges. Drier ground species include stinking nettle, fool's parsley (*Aethusa cynapium*), fat hen, bramble, violet and bugles (*Ajuga* sp.). Occasional seeds and cones of alder were present in the basal deposits of ditch 28.

The single sample from hollow 19 (fill 18) produced a flot containing fragmented wood and silt with a fairly restricted range of marshland and aquatic species. No dry ground plants were identified in the sample. The aquatic species include duckweeds, stoneworts and water-plantain/arrowheads, while gypsywort (*Lycopus europaeus*) and rushes represent marshland or bankside vegetation.

The sample from channel 22 (fill 9, sample 5, Figs 4.3 and 4.15) was not analysed in detail but was assessed by J. Giorgi (Gifford and Partners 2003b). Very limited botanical remains were present beyond small fragments of wood and charcoal and a small number of seeds of while plants including a charred fragment of brome grass (*Bromus* sp.) seed.

Discussion

The deposits from Freemasons Road demonstrate most clearly a presence of alder-carr in the earlier phases which decreases in relation to an increase in wet conditions and rising basal water levels over time. In the earlier phases there is evidence for dry ground and disturbance in the vicinity of the site. There is evidence for standing water (suggested by the caddisfly larval cases as well as the aquatic plants) in part relating to cut features, such as the ditch sampled (feature 146), but also potentially to pools within the alder carr and grassy marshland or possibly cut-off channels. Much of area may simply have been marshy supporting alder trees and plants of disturbed habitats. Some evidence of wet grassland is indicated in the post hole fill associated with the 'bridge' (Str. 32) in Area A (sample 103). This phase also produced possible food debris in the form of hazelnut shell. Throughout these early phases there is evidence for disturbance by humans or livestock in the form of nitrogen loving ruderal species.

The period of later peat formation appears to be characterised by a decrease in drier land species as well as the alder and possibly increased evidence for standing water. This suggests that conditions became too wet for the alder, possibly in association with some clearance and the construction of trackways. Seeds of duckweed in particular become abundant in this phase, although evidence for wet marshland conditions is prevalent. Despite the evidence for disturbed conditions economic species are not positively identified, although both hazelnut and the brambles may have been utilized for food. Occurrences of occasional charred seeds through some of the deposits are indicative of some level of human activity in the area, although they cannot be associated directly with specific activities or activity areas.

Woolwich Manor Way

Samples were taken from Woolwich Manor Way during the Phase II and Phase III investigations. From the Phase II works 18 bulk samples were taken from peats and clay silts. From the Phase III works 8 samples were associated with the trackway, of which 7 were from peat deposits and one from the fill of a ditch/channel. Following assessment of the samples by Giorgi (in Gifford and Partners, 2001b; 2003a) two from Phase II (T15) and four from the Phase III excavations were selected for more detailed analysis.

Four samples were analysed from T15: two from peat layer 2007 (samples 24 and 20) and two for charred plant remains from the underlying weathered sand/palaeosol (samples 21 and 25). This weathered surface produced an early Neolithic artefact spread. Samples from the Phase III works included samples from the peat deposits (context 28) around the Beaker pot in Area 2 (sample 1), and three samples from peat deposits associated with trackway 2 in Area 2 (context 1, sample 8) and trackway 29 in Area 1 (contexts 57, sample 23 and 57, sample 22).

Trench 15 (Phase II works)

Two sequences of four samples were examined from the eastern and western extents of this trench through a series of sandy peat deposits: layers 2008 (palaeosol), 2007, 2006 and 2005 (bottom to top, Fig. 5.3). The assessment demonstrated that the upper most layer (deposit 2005) contained relatively little botanical material other than fragmented wood, charcoal, mosses and a few seeds of sedges and spikerush. The next layer (2006) produced slightly more material including fragmented wood, mosses and seeds of wet and disturbed ground such as sedges and buttercups. The lower two deposits (2008 and 2007) were much more informative and provide a useful insight into the earliest phase of peat formation in the area. They are discussed in chronological order, with the earliest deposit (2008) first.

Layer 2008: Neolithic deposit of emmer wheat (Phase II works) (Plate 28)

The basal deposit of this sequence, layer 2008, consisted of a sandy palaeosol and produced evidence for human activity in the form of a Neolithic artefact scatter. Two samples were taken: sample 21 from the eastern part of the trench and sample 25 from the western end of the trench. Waterlogged preservation was limited in this deposit, consisting of occasional fragments of wood and occasional seeds of buttercup in sample 25. In contrast this deposit did produce abundant evidence in the form of charred plant remains, which were clearly focused in the western extent of the trench being most abundant in sample 25, with flecks of charcoal and occasional grain only turning up in sample 21 from the eastern area.

The charred deposit consists of a large assemblage of charred emmer wheat (*Triticum dicoccum*) and associated spikelet forks and glumes, as well as occasional weeds and hazelnut shell. Preservation of the material was exceptionally good for a deposit of this antiquity. An initial radiometric date on charred grain and charcoal grain from 2008 during the assessment stage provided a date of 3950-3350 cal BC (Beta-153983: 4850 ±100 BP). A second AMS date on a grain of emmer wheat obtained during the analysis produced a date of 3770-3630 cal BC (SUERC-24597: 4890±35 BP).

In total 470 grains were counted. The identification of hulled wheat grains to species is notoriously difficult given the morphological variation possible. Of the 470 grains, only 77 were identified as emmer wheat with any degree of certainty, however, and the majority were identified as *Triticum dicoccum/monococcum/spelta* (hulled wheat) or wheat. A small number of grains showed characteristics of einkorn (*Triticum monococcum*), showing characteristics of having come from single seeded spikelets with a convex ventral surface, high dorsal ridge and laterally narrowed grains. It was not possible to identify the grain as einkorn with any certainty however and they may simply derive from single seeded emmer wheat. The chaff, consisting of spikelet forks and glume bases, provides a much more reliable method of identification. Out of 213 glume bases (where one spikelet fork is composed of two glume

bases), some 57 were positively identified as emmer wheat. No chaff was identified as einkorn. The remaining chaff consisted of glume bases or spikelets which were too damaged or eroded to enable identification. The limited weed flora includes typical ruderal species, mostly spring germinating, which tend to be found associated with early prehistoric cereal remains such as fat hen (*Chenopodium album*), black bindweed (*Fallopia convolvulus*), small seeded medick/trefoil/clover type (*Medicago/Trifolium/Lotus* sp.) and grasses. Given the likelihood that the chaff is going to be underrepresented in the deposit (Boardman and Jones 1990), this deposit is interpreted as a deposit of burnt emmer wheat spikelets and associated weed flora.

Peat layer 2007 (Phase II works)

Two samples were examined from sandy peat layer 2007 (samples 20 and 24) overlying deposit 2008. Waterlogged preservation was much better indicating increased wetness resulting in the accumulation of peat. Both samples produced good sized flots containing wood and moss and a large number of seeds and cones of alder (*Alnus glutinosa*). The wetland component included rushes, bulbous buttercup (*Juncus bulbosus* type), sedges (*Carex* sp.), celery-leaved crowfoot (*Ranunculus sceleratus*), blinks (*Montia fontana* subsp. *chondrosperma*), gypsywort (*Lycopus europaeus*), possible marsh stichwort (*Stellaria* cf. *palustris*) and red shank (*Persicaria maculosa*). This range of species is more characteristic of wet grassy ground rather than open water. Species of waste/disturbed habitat were also present, particularly seeds of common or stinging nettle and bramble (*Rubus* section 2 *Glandulosus*) but also buttercup, fat hen, chickweed, *Aphanes arvensis* (parsley-piert), docks and a single seed of dandelion (*Taraxacum* sp.). Species of *Viola* may have been growing in shadier areas, while some scrub or at least the utilization of wild resources is suggested by a fragment of hazelnut shell. A single seed of yew (*Taxus* sp) was also noted in this sample. Occasional charred grain included possible emmer wheat, conceivably part of the same assemblage picked up in the underlying assemblage from context 2008.

Peat deposits beneath the Bronze Age trackways (Phase III works)

Sample 1 was taken from peat deposits (layer 28) beneath the levels associated with the Beaker pottery and trackway 2/14 in Area 2 (Fig. 5.3). The small flot produced mostly degraded wood and silt and a small flora consisting of wetland plants. Alder was not represented in the samples examined, although limited evidence for alder was recovered from a sample from the same deposit examined at assessment (sample 7, Giorgi in Gifford and Partners 2003a). Identified seeds or fruit included brambles (*Rubus* section 2 *Glandulosus*), water dropwort (*Oenanthe aquatica*), gypsywort (*Lycopus europaeus*), crowfoots (*Ranunculus* subgen *Batra-*

chium) and spikerush (*Eleocharis* spp.). Occasional moss was also noted.

Two samples were taken from the peat below trackway 29 in Area 1 (Fig. 5.3). The lowermost sample (sample 15 peat layer 59) had produced a much richer assemblage. Plant remains noted in the assessment report (Giorgi in Gifford and Partners 2003a) included large quantities of wood and a diverse range of seeds of wetlands plants such as sedges, crowfoots, water dropwort, water pepper/mite, disturbed ground species including chickweeds, black nightshade, goosefoots and brambles, and fragments of hazelnut. The assemblage appears to be comparable to the deposit from the sand/peat interface in trench 15 (layer 2007). The overlying peat (layer 57) produced a limited flora, largely a reflection of the small sample size (1L). The assessment data was generated from a larger flot (20L) and is therefore also referred to. The flots both at assessment and analysis level were found to consist largely of fragmented wood. At analysis level a single seed of yew was the only plant taxa noted, along with fungal spores and the eggs of the water flea. The assessment data recorded by Giorgi (in Gifford and Partners 2003a) included occasional seeds of bramble, water dropwort, and spikerush, as well as a small amount of moss and beetle fragments.

Peat deposits above the Bronze Age trackways (Phase III works)

Both the samples examined were taken from peat deposits overlying the Bronze Age trackways (trackways 2 and 29, Fig. 5.3) in Areas 1 and 2 and are interpreted as being broadly contemporary.

A far richer deposit than layer 56 in Area 1 (sample 22) was recovered from peat layer 1 in Area 2 (sample 8), in part due to a larger sample size (9L), but possibly reflecting the nature of the peat and preservation in Area 2. The deposit was dominated by fragments of wood and evidence for alder (cones and bracts), some of which presumably derives from the trackway itself. A range of fruits and seeds of wet ground species were noted particularly those of water pepper/mite (*Persicaria hydropiper/mitis*), but also *Rumex conglomeratus* (clustered dock), gypsywort, spikerush, branched bur-reed (*Sparganium erectum*) and water plantain (*Alisma plantago-aquatica*). Seeds of meadow buttercup (*Ranunculus acris*) and rushes including soft rush type (*Juncus effusus* type) suggest damp grassland type vegetation. Species of disturbed ground were also present including nettle (*Urtica dioica*) and bramble. Rare seeds of yew (*Taxus baccata*) were again present suggesting it to have been a persistent part of the vegetation in the area of Woolwich Manor Way for a prolonged period.

A much more restricted flora and smaller flot was recovered from the peat deposits in Area 1 (peat layer 56), which is in part likely to be due to the small sample size, although a larger sample was examined at assessment level and produced a similarly limited flora (Giorgi in Gifford and Partners 2003a). The plant remains noted at analysis level were limited to fragmented wood and seeds of nettle. At assessment a slightly greater range of seeds were identified including spike-rush, sedges and brambles. It is possible that conditions in this part of the site were less conducive to good waterlogged preservation of botanical remains. The underlying deposit (layer 57) was similarly limited, while the deposit below that (layer 59) was much richer (see above). Possibly this part of the site was slightly drier.

Vegetation Development at Woolwich Manor Way

The samples from Woolwich Manor Way are particularly useful in that they include samples from Neolithic deposits pre-dating the Bronze Age peat as well as the earliest Bronze Age peat formation. An exceptional deposit was the find of emmer grain and chaff on the sand (layer 2008. T15), beneath the sandy peat sequence which provides evidence for human activity in the area. The differential preservation of grain and chaff is such that chaff tends to be under-represented in archaeological assemblages. This deposit has therefore been interpreted as unprocessed emmer wheat spikelet forks (in which grain and glume bases would appear in equal numbers in a living crop) with associated weeds.

The significance of cereals in the diet of Neolithic people, particularly in relation to the importance of collected woodland resources, is still a topic of debate (Moffett *et al.* 1989; Robinson 2000; Jones 2000; Jones and Rowley-Conwy 2007). Such deposits, while rare, do demonstrate that cereal deposits were probably more widespread than the archaeology tends to suggest, but that for some reason they only survive in good numbers occasionally. This might be as a result of a combination of the scale of Neolithic agricultural production and processing methods, and the subsequent erosion of archaeological features.

The unusual aspect of the Woolwich Manor Way deposit is that it appears to derive from charred spikelets. The majority of Neolithic cereal remains in Britain to date derive from occasional grain, often poorly preserved. There are an increasing number of deposits of spikelets of emmer wheat however, in addition to the exceptional deposits at Balbridie, Grampian region (Fairweather and Ralston 1993) and Lismore Fields (Jones and Rowley-Conwy 2007). A substantial deposit of several thousand emmer spikelets was recovered from a small pit at Westwood Cross, Isle of Thanet, which produced an early Neolithic date of 3800-3650 cal BC (NZA-26510: 4951±35 BP) (Stevens nd). A slightly later date 3650-3100 cal BC (OxA-2299: 4675±70 BP) was recovered from an assemblage of possible emmer spikelets from The Stumble, Essex (Wilkinson and Murphy 1995, 58). A deposit of emmer spikelets and naked barley grain has also recently been dated from a pit at Poundbury, Dorset (Pelling nd.) producing a date of 3766-3637 cal BC (NZA-31070:

Table A3.11   Samples selected for analysis from Woolwich Manor Way

Area/Trench	Sample	Context	Feature type	Period	Sample volume (L.)
T15	21	2008	Sandy Peat layer	EN	15
T15	25	2008	Sandy Peat layer	EN	20
T15	24	2007	Sandy Peat layer	EBA	20
T15	20	2007	Sandy Peat layer	EBA	20
Area 2	1	28	Peat around beaker, below trackway 2	EBA	2
Area 2	8	1	Peat above trackway 2	MBA	9
Area 1	22	56	Peat above trackway 29	MBA	1
Area 1	23	57	Peat below trackway 29	EBA	1

Table A3.12   Waterlogged plant remains from Woolwich Manor Way

	Trench/Area	15	15	A2	A1	A2	A1
	Sample	24	20	1	22	8	23
	Context	2007	2007	28	56	1	57
	Feature/layer	Peat	Peat	Peat	Peat	Peat	Peat
	Period	EBA	EBA	EBA	MBA	MBA	EBA
	Sample Vol (L.)	20	20	2	1	9	1
Alisma plantago-aquatica L.	Water-plantain	-	-	-	-	1	-
Alnus glutinosa (L.) Gaertner	Alder cones (female)	3	2	-	-	-	-
Alnus glutinosa (L.) Gaertner	Aldet bracts	-	-	-	-	3	-
Alnus glutinosa (L.) Gaertner	Alder, seeds	4	2	-	-	-	-
Aphanes arvensis L.	Parsley-piert	3	-	-	-	-	-
Atriplex sp.	Orache	-	1	-	-	-	-
Carex trig	Sedges	2	4	-	-	-	-
Chenopodium album L.	Fat-hen	1	-	-	-	1	-
Chenopodium polyspermum L.	Many-seeded goosefoot	-	-	-	-	1	-
Corylus avellana L.	Hazel nut shell fragment	-	1	-	-	-	-
Eleocharis palustris (L.) Roem.& Schult	Common spike-rush	-	-	-	-	1	-
Euphorbia sp.	Spurge	-	1	-	-	-	-
Juncus bulbosus L.	Bulbous rush	2	-	-	-	-	-
Juncus effusus L.	Soft-rush	-	-	-	-	1	-
Juncus sp.	Rushes	-	-	-	-	3	-
Lycopus europaeus L.	Gypsywort	2	-	1	-	1	-
Oenanthe aquatica (L.) Poiret in Lam.	Fine-leaved water-dropwort	-	-	1	-	-	-
Persicaria hydropiper L.	Water-pepper	-	-	-	-	3	-
Persicaria maculosa Gray	Red shank	-	1	-	-	-	-
Potentilla sp.	Cinquefoils	-	1	-	-	-	-
Ranunculus acris L.	Meadow buttercup	-	-	-	-	1	-
Ranunculus acris/bulbosus/repens	Buttercup	2	3	1	-	-	-
Ranunculus bulbosus L.	Bulbous buttercup	3	2	-	-	-	-
Ranunculus Subgenus *Batrachium*	Crowfoots	-	-	1	-	-	-
Rubus sect. 2 *Glanulosus*	Brambles	1	3	-	-	1	-
Rumex cf. *conglomeratus* Murray	Clustered dock	-	-	-	-	1	-
Rumex sp.	Docks	1	1	-	-	1	-
Sparganium erectum L.	Branched bur-reed	-	-	-	-	1	-
Stellaria media (l) Vill	Common chickweed	1	1	-	-	-	-
Stellaria cf. *palustris* L.	Marsh stichwort	3	-	-	-	-	-
Taraxacum sp.	Dandelion	-	1	-	-	-	-
cf. *Taxus* sp.	Yew	-	2	-	-	-	-
Urtica dioica L.	Stinging nettle	4	-	-	1	1	-
Viola ordorata/hirta L.	Sweet violet	1	1	-	-	-	-
Indet large seed coat		-	-	-	-	-	1
Wood fragments		-	-	-	4	3	-
Coleoptera frags		1	-	-	-	1	-
Fungal spores		-	-	-	-	-	2
Degraded wood and silt		-	-	2	3	-	-
Daphnia (waterflea) egg)		-	-	-	-	-	1
moss		2	-	-	-	-	-

252

4902±40 BP), again early Neolithic so comparable to the Westwood Cross material.

That chaff is rarely recovered from Neolithic assemblages (Robinson 2000) has lead to discussions about storage methods and the suggestion that in the Neolithic crops were perhaps stored as fully dehusked grain (Stevens 2007) in contrast to the later prehistoric period when storage pits are well known. The presence of dated spikelets in pits does raise the question of how crops were stored in the Neolithic and may demonstrate that the absence of chaff on many sites is simply a product of preservation bias. The Woolwich Manor Way deposit is unusual in that it has been recovered from a sand layer, sealed beneath the peat. It is unclear why or how such a deposit would have survived in a context of this type, unless it was originally situated within a subsequently eroded pit.

The weed flora associated with the emmer wheat is limited, consisting of fat hen (*Chenopodium album*), black bindweed (*Fallopia convolvulus*), possible goosegrass (*Galium* sp.), medick/trefoil type (*Medicago/Trifolium/Lotus* sp.) and grass seeds. Seeds of bindweed, cleavers and vetches were recovered at Westwood Cross (Stevens nd), while the Stumble produced goosegrass and vetch (Murphy 1989) and Poundbury produced bindweed and grass (Pelling unpubl). There appears to be a dominance of twinning species which would have been favoured by uprooting. Conditions clearly became wetter towards the end of the Neolithic, as suggested by the formation of peat. The local vegetation at the

Table A3.13   Charred plant remains in samples from Woolwich Manor Way

		Trench No.	*15*	*15*	*15*
		Sample	*24*	*25*	*21*
		Context	*2007*	*2008*	*2008*
		Feature	*Peat*	*Peat*	*Palaeosol*
		Period	*EBA*	*EN*	*EN*
		Sample Vol (L.)	*20*	*20*	*15*
Cereal Grain					
Triticum dicoccum L.	Emmer wheat grain		-	48	-
Triticum cf. *dicoccum* L.	cf. Emmer wheat grain		1	29	-
Triticum cf. *dicoccum/monococcum*	single grained emmer/einkorn		-	12	
Triticum spelta L.	Spelt wheat grain		-	-	-
Triticum cf. *spelta* L.	cf. Spelt wheat grain		-	-	-
Triticum dicoccum/spelta	Emmer/Spelt wheat grain		-	84	1
Triticum sp.	Wheat grain		1	181	-
Hordeum vulgare sl.	Barley grain		-	-	-
Cerealia indet	Indeterminate grain		2	116	1
Cereal Chaff					
Triticum dicoccum L.	Emmer wheat spikelet fork		-	23	-
Triticum dicoccum L.	Emmer wheat glume base		-	11	-
Triticum spelta L.	Spelt wheat spikelet fork		-	-	-
Triticum spelta L.	Spelt wheat glume base		-	-	-
Triticum dicoccum/spelta	Emmer/Spelt wheat spikelet		-	37	-
Triticum dicoccum/spelta	Emmer/Spelt wheat glume base		-	25	-
Triticum sp.	Wheat rachis segment		-	1	-
Cerealia indet	Culm node		-	-	-
Wild Species					
Corylus avellana L.	Hazelnut shell fragments		-	3	-
Chenopodium album L.	Fat hen		-	4	-
Atriplex sp.	Orache		-	-	-
Chenopodiaceae			-	1	-
Galium aparine L.	Goosegrass		-	-	-
cf. *Galium* sp.			-	1	-
Fallopia convoluvulus (L.) Á. Löve	Black bindweed		-	1	-
Rubus section 2 *Glandulosus* Wimm. & Grab	Bramble/Blackberry etc		-	-	-
Medicago/Trifolium/Lotus sp.	Medick/Trefoil/Clover etc		-	1	-
Rubus sp.	Bramble/Raspberry etc		-	-	-
Lolium/Festuca sp.			-	-	-
Poaceae	Grass, small seed (<2mm)		-	1	-
Poaceae	Grass, medium sized seed		-	1	-
Indet leaf bud			-	1	-
Indet seed			-	3	-

Neolithic/Bronze Age transition appears to be characterised by alder carr, as it is at Prince Regent Lane (above) and Movers Lane (below). Wet, mineral-rich open sediments are suggested by herbaceous vegetation, such as sedges, rushes, dropworts, gypsyworts and stoneworts (noted in the assessment of some samples not examined at analysis) which are likely to have been accompanied by alder woodland. The presence of crowfoots, water plantain and the presence of water flea eggs (*Cladoceran ephippia*), suggest some standing bodies of water, although the evidence for this may be less than at Prince Regent Lane and Movers Lane. A background of drier ground ruderal vegetation is also suggested. Also, in contrast to the other sites, evidence of yew was found through the peat deposits at Woolwich Manor Way, both in terms of the fruit or seeds and wood remains. A piece of yew wood from context 1523, sample 68 (wood sample 2, trench 9) submitted for dating gave a radiocarbon date of 2850-2270 (91.5%) and 2260-2200 cal BC (3.9%) (Beta-152739: 3930±60 BP).

The presence of yew is suggestive of drier woodland in the vicinity, although the paucity of the fruit suggests that the trees stood some distance away from the area of the trenches. Both yew and alder wood were identified from the trackway structures (Barnett, Appendix 3, Goodburn this volume).

There appears to be reduction in the presence of alder in the peat deposits associated with the trackways, with the exception of the deposit above trackway 2/14 (peat deposit 1) and an increase in evidence for wet conditions.

Several floodplain sites within Greater London have revealed timber belonging to *Taxus baccata*, such as Wennington Marsh (Sidell 1996), Dagenham (Divers 1994) and Beckton (Meddens and Sidell 1995; Scaife 1997). At Wennington, *T. baccata* macrofossils suggested a local densely covered mixed forest (over 20 tree trunks were recovered from within a trench approximately 20m x 20m), yet the pollen content was low. Sidell (1996) has suggested that *T. baccata* was an important woodland taxon, and that the low pollen representation was due to taphonomic factors. Alternatively, if the woodland was as dense as that suggested by the excavation, and the local conditions (peat) were sufficiently acidic, flowering could have been decreased / inhibited, contributing to the apparently low pollen concentrations. *T. baccata* is also frequently found within lowland wetland coastal and estuarine peat in Belgium, Germany and The Netherlands (Deforce and Bastiaens 2004). Across Europe there is a recognised shift in *T. baccata* from lowland wetlands to upland dryland during the Holocene, which may be attributed to a change in ecological preference.

Movers Lane

A total of 29 bulk samples and 9 samples for waterlogged plant remains were taken during the Phase III excavations at the site. Following assessment of

the sample by Stevens (in Wessex Archaeology 2003) seven samples were selected for closer examination of the waterlogged plant remains (an 8th sample had deteriorated too significantly in storage to be viable for further work). Charred plant remains other than charcoal were limited to the occasional grain in one sample and occasional charred weed seeds and hazelnut shell fragments. Two samples were examined at analysis level although the remains add little to the assessment data.

The samples had suffered some deterioration in storage in the period between assessment and analysis despite storage in IMS in sealed jars. This is seen particularly in the decreased range of species noted in some samples during analysis compared to the assessment (Stevens in Wessex Archaeology 2003). In particular one sample (sample 70 from the peat adjacent to the trackway) had suffered extreme growth of mould rendering it unusable. Generally the range of species remains fairly constant across the site. However, there are some differences between the Movers Lane samples and those from Prince Regent Lane (Freemasons Road).

A series of 29 bulk samples were also taken for charred plant remains. The samples were processed by standard bulk flotation and the flots collected onto 0.5mm mesh sieves with the residues collected on 1mm mesh. The volume of deposit processed for each sample ranged from 5 to 30 litres. An assessment of the flots demonstrated the presence of small quantities of charred seeds throughout the sequence, although in most cases this consisted of one or two charred weed seeds. A fragment of hazelnut shell (*Corylus avellana*) was present in cremation feature 1207. A cereal grain of indeterminate species was noted in pit 1221. These deposits therefore suggest a background presence of activity related to food processing and procurement but produced insufficient material to provide any useful interpretation of the deposits. Charcoal was abundant in a small number of samples and is discussed elsewhere (Barnett, Appendix 3).

Area 2 terrace

Two samples were examined from late Bronze Age ditch 1038 (Fig. 7.8) including sample 6 from the basal fills (context 1049). While the lower fill produced a more diverse flora, both deposits where characterised by an abundance of seeds of stinging nettle (*Urtica dioica*) and bramble/blackberry type (*Rubus* section 2 *Glandulosus*), as well as thorns of Rosaceae type which are likely to have derived from the same species. Seeds of elder (*Sambucus nigra*) were also present in the upper fill (1042, sample 4) and possible dogwood (cf. *Cornus sanguinea*) in the lower fill (1049 sample 6), further suggesting scrubby vegetation. Also present were quantities of wood and the seeds and cones of alder (*Alnus glutinosa*).

Herbaceous species of disturbed habitats were common in the deposits including docks of unknown species (*Rumex* sp.), common toadflax (*Linaria vulgaris*), thistles (*Carduus/Cirsium* sp.), willowherb (*Epilobium* sp.), and, most common of all, stinging nettle. Smaller numbers of seeds of ruderal species included fat hen (*Chenopodium album*), chickweed (*Stellaria media*), plantain (*Plantago major*), parsley-piert (*Aphanes arvensis*), cinquefoils (*Potentilla* sp.), hawkweed ox-tongue (*Picris hieracioides*), smooth sow-thistle (*Sonchus oleraceus*) and dead nettle (*Lamium* sp.). Seeds of greater stichwort (*Stellaria holostea*) and a single seed of three-nerved sandwort (*Moehringia trinervia*) in 1042 (sample 4) suggest shady conditions, again possibly indicative of scrubby vegetation. The high numbers of seeds of some of the ruderal species, particularly nettle, would suggest that plants were growing alongside the ditch, their seeds falling into the wet deposits.

Aquatic species in the upper deposit were limited to occasional seeds of water crowfoot (*Ranunculus* subgen *Batrachium*), duckweed (*Lemna* sp.), rushes (*Juncus* sp.) and possible meadowsweet (*Filipendula ulmaria*). The lower fill (context 1049) produced a more substantial list of species associated with wetter habitats including species suggesting standing water such as pondweed (*Potamogeton* sp.) and duckweed (*Lemna* sp.). More abundant in context 1049, however, were species typical of nutrient rich wet, muddy, marshy or fen conditions, either present within the ditch or around it: celery-leave buttercup (*Ranunculus sceleratus*), crowfoots (*Ranunculus* subgen *Batrachium*), water dock (*Rumex hydrolapathum*), possible clustered dock (*Rumex* cf. *conglomeratus*), gypsywort (*Lycopus europaeus*), water mint (*Mentha aquatica*), fool's watercress (*Apium nodiflorum*), branched bur-reed (*Sparganium erectum*) and one seed of possible yellow iris (cf. *Iris pseudacorus*). This range of species might be growing within the muddy base of the ditch, which may have supported some open water. Caddisfly larval cases further suggest there was some open water in the ditch. There is also slight evidence for damp meadow type grassland including seeds of meadow rue (*Thalictrum flavum*) and ragged robbin (*Lychnis flos-cuculi*). Sedges and rushes further suggest wet or marshy conditions.

The assemblages from the ditch are generally characteristic of scrubby and disturbed habitats that are likely to have been present in the area around the ditch, with evidence for wetter conditions, including standing water within the ditch, as well as marshy grassland type conditions in the vicinity. It is difficult to establish quite how wet the surrounding area was at the time, and it is possible that the very wet conditions only prevailed within the ditch itself.

Area 2, floodplain/palaeochannel area

Three samples were examined from this area including one associated with the root system 3012, and two from peat adjacent to the Bronze Age trackway 3031 (Fig. 7.8). A third sample from the trackway peat had been examined at assessment level but was too badly infested with fungal growth to allow closer examination. Species of wet, marshy conditions dominate although evidence for open water is not strong. Evidence for alder is minimal in these deposits while the scrubby vegetation seen in the Area 2 ditch fills is largely absent, although a background of ruderal vegetation is present.

The sample from the root system was characterised by degraded wood, peat and silt. A fairly restricted flora was represented with small numbers of seeds and only limited evidence for alder. Occasional seeds of cinquefoils (*Potentilla* sp.) and fat hen (*Chenopodium album*) suggest some drier ground. Seeds of thistles (*Carduus/Cirsium* sp.) were also present, although these may derive from bankside species such as marsh thistle (*Cirsium palustre*). Seeds of fine leaved water-dropwort (*Oenanthe aquatica*) indicate quite wet conditions, possibly watery. The remaining species, including water-pepper (*Persicaria hydropiper*), fool's water-cress (*Apium nodiflorum*), branched bur-reed (*Sparganium erectum*), crowfoot (*Ranunculus* subgen *Batrachium*) and red shank (*Persicaria maculosa*), are typical of shallow, nutrient rich water or wet bankside conditions. A small number of fungal sclerotia, including possible charred examples, were also present.

Three samples were taken from the peat associated with the Bronze Age trackway 3031 (context 3011). The lowest sample (sample 70, 30-50cm) had dried out and become mouldy during storage and was consequently not examined further. The assessment demonstrated it to be the poorest of the three samples, consisting of badly degraded peat and wood fragments. Identifiable seeds were limited to a single example of water crowfoot (*Ranunculus* subg. *Batrachium*).

The two samples from the top 30cm of the peat (samples 68 and 69, 0-15cm and 15-30cm) were much more productive. Both samples were characterised by wood fragments as well as degraded peat and silt, with the greater concentration of better preserved wood, including roundwood and twiggy material, in the middle sample (15-30cm). This deposit also produced a slightly more diverse flora, although both samples were seed rich. Species of wet, marshy fen type conditions dominated such as water-dropwort (*Oenanthe aquatica*), fool's water-cress (*Apium nodiflorum*), gypsywort (*Lycopus europaeus*), watermint (*Mentha aquatica*), common spike-rush (*Eleocharis palustris*), branched bur-reed (*Sparganium erectum*), crowfoots (*Ranunculus* subgen *Batrachium*), water-starworts ((*Callitriche* sp.) not recorded in the earlier deposits at the site), water-plantain (*Alisma plantago-aquatica*), red-shank (*Persicaria maculosa*), as well as sedges and rushes. A limited number of seeds of meadowsweet (*Filipendula ulmaria*) were present in the upper deposit (sample 68), typical of wet meadows and common along the edge of alder carr woodland where cover is limited. A small number of seeds of duckweeds (*Lemna* sp.) may point to some open bodies of water, as do the caddisfly larval cases, present in both samples. The wet ground species as

Table A3.14 Samples selected for analysis from Movers Lane for waterlogged plant remains

Area	Sample	Context	Feature	Feature type	Period	Sample volume (L.)
A2	4	1042	1038	Ditch (base)	LBA	1
A2	6	1049	1038	Ditch (base)	LBA	6
A2	29	3004	3012	Root/platform	LBA	1
A2	68	3011	3031	Peat through trackway (0-15cm)	BA	6
A2	69	3011	3031	Peat through trackway (15-30)	BA	6
A2	70	3011	3031	Peat through trackway (30-50cm)	BA	6
A3	34	5147	5159	Gully	BA	30
A3	49	5131	5263	Peat layer	BA	6

Table A3.15 Waterlogged plant remains from Movers Lane

		A2	A2	A2	A2	A2	A3	A3
Area								
Context		1042	1049	3004	3011	3011	5147	5131
Feature		1038	1038	3012	3031	3031	5159	5263
Sample		4	6	29	68 -top	69 -mid	34	49
Feature type		ditch (b)	ditch (b)	Root system	peat	peat	gully	peat
Period		LBA	LBA	LBA	BA	BA	BA	BA
Sample Vol (L.)		1	6	1	6	6	30	6
Aquatic/semi-aquatic species								
Ranunculus sceleratus L.	Celery-leaved buttercup	-	4	-	-	-	-	-
Ranunculus Subgenus *Batrachium*	Crowfoot	1	4	2	4	3	-	2
Callitriche sp.	Water-starworts	-	-	-	1	1	1	3
Alisma plantago-aquatica L.	Water-plantain	-	-	-	2	1	-	4
Alisma plantago-aquatica L./ *Sagittaria* sp.	Water-plantain/ Arrowheads	-	-	-	-	-	-	-
Hydrocotyle vulgaris L.	Marsh pennywort	-	-	-	-	-	-	-
Potamogeton sp.	Pondweeds	-	2	-	-	-	-	-
Lemna sp.	Duckweeds	1	3	-	-	1	-	1
Wet grass/meadow, marshland								
Ranunculus acris L.	Meadow buttercup	-	1	-	-	-	-	-
cf. *Thalictrum flavum* L.	Common meadow rue	-	1	-	-	-	-	-
Lychnis flos-cuculi L.	Ragged-robin	-	1	-	-	-	-	-
Persicaria maculosa Gray	Red shank	-	-	1	-	1	-	-
Persicaria hydropiper/mitis	Water-pepper	-	-	1	-	-	1	3
Rumex hydrolapathum Hudson	Water dock	-	2	-	-	-	-	1
Rumex cf. *conglomeratus* Murray	Clustered dock	-	3	-	-	-	-	-
Oenanthe aquatica (L.) Poiret in Lam.	Fine-leaved waterdropwort	-	-	1	1	2	1	2
Apium nodiflorum L.	Fool's watercress	-	1	1	-	1	-	-
Lycopus europaeus L.	Gypsywort	-	3	-	1	1	1	-
Mentha aquatica L.	Water mint	-	2	-	2	1	-	1
Filipendula ulmaria (L.) Maxim	Meadowsweet	-	-	-	1	-	-	-
cf. *Filipendula ulmaria* (L.) Maxim	Meadowsweet	1	-	-	-	-	-	-
Bidens cernua L.	Nodding bur-marigold	-	-	-	-	-	-	1
Juncus articulatus gp.	Jointed rush	-	-	-	-	1	-	-
Juncus effusus type	Soft-rush	-	1	-	-	-	-	5
Juncus sp.	Rushes	-	1	-	1	-	-	-
Luzula sp.	Wood-rush	1	-	-	-	-	-	-
Carex flat (< 2.5mm)		-	1	-	3	1	1	2
Carex trig		-	-	1	3	2	-	3
Eleocharis spp.	Common spike-rush	-	-	-	1	1	-	3
Sparganium erectum L.	Branched bur-reed	-	2	1	2	2	-	3
cf. *Iris pseudacorus* L.	Yellow iris	-	1	-	-	-	-	-
Cultivated ground/Waste places/Dry grassland								
Ranunculus bulbosus L.	Bulbous buttercup	-	1	-	-	-		

Table A3.15   Waterlogged plant remains from Movers Lane (continued)

		Area	A2	A2	A2	A2	A2	A3	A3
		Context	1042	1049	3004	3011	3011	5147	5131
		Feature	1038	1038	3012	3031	3031	5159	5263
		Sample	4	6	29	68 -top	69 -mid	34	49
		Feature type	ditch (b)	ditch (b)	Root system	peat	peat	gully	peat
		Period	LBA	LBA	LBA	BA	BA	BA	BA
		Sample Vol (L.)	1	6	1	6	6	30	6
Urtica dioica L.	Stinging nettle		5	5	-	2	-		2
Chenopodium album L.	Fat-hen		-	1	1	3	1	1	2
Chenopodium sp.			-	1	-	-	-		
Stellaria media (l) Vill	Common chickweed		-	1	-	-	-		1
Stellaria sp.	Chickweed / Stitchworts		-	-	-	-	1		
Polygonum aviculare L.	Knotgrass		-	-	-	1	-		1
Rumex acetosella group	Sheep's sorrel		-	-	-	-	-		1
Rumex sp.	Docks		-	4	-	-	-		2
Solanum nigrum L.	Black nightshade		-	-	-	1	-		
Lamium sp.	Dead-nettle		-	1	-	-	-		
Linaria vulgaris Mill.	Common toadflax		-	2	-	-	-		
Sambucus nigra L.	Elder		1	-	-	-	-		
Carduus/Cirsium sp.	Thistles		1	3	1	1	-		
Picris hieracoides L.	Hawkweed oxtongue		-	1	-	-	-		
Sonchus asper (L.) Hill	Prickly sow-thistle		-	-	-	-	-	1	
Sonchus oleraceus L.	Smooth sow-thistle			1					
Shady places/woods/hedgerows									
cf. *Cornus sanguinea* L.	Dogwood, fruit		1						
Moehringa trinervia (L.) Clairv.	Three-nerved sandwort		1						
Stellaria holostea L.	Greater stichwort			1					
Viola ordorata/hirta L.	Sweet violet						1		1
Trees									
Alnus glutinosa (L.) Gaertner	Alder cones (female)		2	1			1	1	2
Alnus glutinosa (L.) Gaertner	Aldet bracts			1					
Alnus glutinosa (L.) Gaertner	Alder, seeds		2	3	1		1	3	4
Catholic/Not specified									
Ranunculus acris/bulbosus/repens				1			1		2
Ranunculus parviflorus L.	Small-flowered buttercup								
Atriplex glabriuscula Edmondston	Babington's-orache						1		
Atriplex sp.			1	1		4			
Stellaria cf. *pallida* L.	Lesser chickweed								2
Rubus section 2 *Glandulosus* Wimm. & Grab	Brambles		3	4		1	2	2	3
Potentilla sp.	Cinquefoils		1	1	1	1	1		1
Rosaceae thorns			2	5					
Aphanes arvensis L.	Parsley-piert		1						
Vicia/Lathyrus sp.	Vetches / Vetchlings / Tares								2
Epilobium sp.	Willowherbs			3					
Appiaceae	indet. medium seed		1						
Plantago major L.	Greater plantain			1					
Scruphularaceae	Figwort family			1					
Poaceae mid (2mm-4mm)	grass								1
Poaceae small (<2mm)	grass			1					
Others									
Indet leaf fragments									1
caddisfly larval cases				2			1	1	1
Coleoptera frags			2	1	1	1			2
Fungal spores			1			1	1	1	3
mites									4
wood fragments			4			2	5		
degraded wood and silt				1		3	2		

a whole suggest wet, marshy grassy conditions possibly with occasional open bodies of water, pools and puddles.

The drier ground species were relatively limited, but indicate a background of scrubby vegetation including brambles and ruderal vegetation. Some evidence for alder (seeds and cones) is present in the middle layer (sample 29). In addition there were a range of species of ruderal and disturbed habitats such as fat hen (*Chenopodium album*), stinging nettles (*Urtica dioica*), orache (*Atriplex* sp.), knotgrass (*Polygonum aviculare*), cinquefoils (*Potentilla* sp.), chickweed/stitchworts (*Stellaria* sp.), black night-shade (*Solanum nigrum*) and thistles (*Carduus/ Cirsium* sp.). The viola species (*Viola odorata/hirta*) include species of shady conditions which may occur under the scrubby vegetation.

Area 3

Two samples were examined from Area 3: sample 34 from the Bronze Age peat in gully 5159 (context 5147, Fig 7.11) and sample 49 from the main peat layer 5263 (context 5131).

A limited flora was recovered from the fill of gully 5159 (context 5147) cut through the peat. Most dominant in the flot were seeds and cones of alder and seeds of bramble. A small number of ruderal species of disturbed ground, such as fat hen and prickly sow-thistle were present as were a restricted range of species of wet, muddy or marshy ground such as water-pepper (*Persicaria hydropiper*), water-dropwort (*Oenanthe aquatica*), water mint (*Mentha aquatica*), water-starworts (*Callitriche* sp.) and sedges.

The deposit from the main peat layer produced a rich deposit with large numbers of seeds of many of the taxa. Most abundant were seeds of rushes (*Juncus* sp.), particularly soft rush (*Juncus effusus* gp.), as well as alder seeds and cones and seeds of water-plantain (*Alisma plantago-aquatica*). The assemblage produced strong evidence for marshy wetland conditions such as water-pepper (*Persicaria hydropiper*), water dock (*Rumex hydrolapathum*), water-dropwort (*Oenanthe aquatica*), branched bur-reed (*Sparganium erectum*), duckweeds, sedges and rushes. Occasional seeds of nodding bur-marigold (*Bidens cernua*) were also noted, again a plant of wet ground adjacent to ponds and ditches or marshy fields. Larval cases of caddisfly are indicative of open water.

A range of dry land species was also present, again typical of disturbed, ruderal habitats such as fat hen, chickweed (*Stellaria media),* knotgrass, docks, prickly sow-thistle. A small number of vetches/vetchlings/tares (*Vicia/Lathyrus* sp.) and grasses were present, possibly indicating the presence of grassland.

Discussion

The waterlogged sequences from Movers Lane share many characteristics with the other sites, particularly the deposits from Prince Regent Lane Underpass, suggesting a certain degree of conti-nuity along the extent of the floodplain/gravel terrace margins.

The vegetation suggested by samples from both Area 2 and 3 associated with the onset of peat formation, is characterised by scrubby vegetation, particularly stinging nettle and brambles, with alder carr. The alder woodland appears to have supported an understory of sedges and rushes, with some drier ground shady species such as violets. The wet ground species tend to be more indicative of nutrient rich wet, marshy conditions rather than open bodies of water, with evidence for hay meadow type species such as meadow rue, ragged robin and meadowsweet. The cut features appear to have supported open water as indicated by caddis fly larval cases and higher numbers of aquatic, open water plant species.

The substantial number of ruderal plants associated with disturbed and nitrogen rich soils such as stinging nettle, as well as the limited evidence for charred plant remains, provide evidence for a background of human disturbance, or at least grazing. However there is limited direct botanical evidence for human activity and it is likely that much of this disturbance was on the drier ground of the gravels not directly represented in the excavated area. Evidence for brambles including thorns was abundant in some deposits, particularly ditch 1038, suggesting possible encroachment of drier scrub land onto the edges of the floodplain.

Samples associated with platform and trackway were less productive, but indicate a similar range of wet marshy ground and a background of drier, disturbed habitats, but possibly with less evidence for damp, meadow type grassland and a decline in alder in area 2. Towards the top of the peat deposits above the trackway conditions appear slightly wetter, with a decline in ruderal species, although it is difficult to measure this. This increase in wet conditions and associated decline in alder appears to follow a similar pattern seen at Prince Regent Lane and Woolwich Manor Lane.

Landscape overview

At all three sites a similar pattern of vegetation and hydrological evolution appears to be represented. The sequence broadly follows that seen elsewhere along the Lower Thames. Most of the samples examined fall within a relatively narrow time frame from the late Neolithic to the late Bronze Age.

The earliest deposits represented are the early Neolithic deposits on the sandy silt at Woolwich Manor Way, sealed by overlying peat formation. Evidence for human activity here is derived from the deposit of emmer wheat spikelets. Conditions at this point on the higher ground were presumably relatively dry and there is little evidence for the vegetation prior to the development of the overlying peat.

At all three sites the earliest waterlogged deposits are associated with a vegetation of alder-carr with a fringe vegetation of reeds and rushes, and wet ground species typical of muddy mineral rich deposits. Within the London region alder carr is generally dated to the Early Neolithic to the Middle Bronze Age (Barnett *et al.* 2010; Crockett *et al.* 2002), as it is further up river at Runnymede (Greig 1991) and in the lower Colne Valley at Slough (Wessex Archaeology 2006). At Rainham, there is evidence for clearance and increased agriculture, at the same time as the local environment became wetter, changing from an alder carr to reed swamp (Scaife 1991). This is also the case at Wilsons Wharf (Tyers 1988) and Erith (Sidell *et al.* 1997), where the environment appears to have been opened up and increases in fen taxa occur, along with appearances of cereal pollen and ruderals. It is difficult to establish how dense the woodland is likely to have been from the current deposits, although the deposits from all three sites suggest a background of disturbed and relatively open vegetation.

Some of the cut features and channels clearly supported open bodies of relatively mineral rich water. The presence of yew in Bronze Age deposits at Woolwich Manor Way is of interest. It is a characteristic of a number of sites in London where both the seeds and timber have been identified, for example at Wennington (Sidell 1996), Dagenham (Divers 1994) and Beckton (Meddens and Sidell 1995). The construction of the Bronze Age trackways is clearly associated with increasingly wet conditions and to enable movement across the wetland zone. The wetter conditions with rising basal water levels along the Thames corridor may have resulted in a reduction in alder and a change to reed/sedge fen vegetation prior to the later brackish water conditions. This reduction in alder is dated to the middle to late Bronze Age across London (Merriman 1992, 263; Scaife 2000; 2002; Allen *et al.* 2005, cf. Greig 1991) and appears to be associated with increasing activity within these periods (Meddens 1996), as is presumably seen here. The pattern at all three sites investigated as part of the A13 Thames Gateway Road Scheme fills the well-established sequence of alder carr replaced by a wetter more open landscape during the course of the Bronze Age.

Waterlogged wood: species and age *by Catherine Barnett*

Introduction

A number of key contexts were chosen for waterlogged wood analysis during post-excavation assessment of samples from three sites along the route of the A13: Prince Regent Lane (Freemasons Road), Woolwich Manor Way and Movers Lane. The samples are of worked wood from contexts of Bronze Age date and predominantly derive from the wooden trackway structures. The wood species identifications are presented here and briefly discussed, but this report should be viewed in tandem with the information regarding the wood technology provided by D. Goodburn in this volume.

Methodology

Identification of all waterlogged wood samples recovered was attempted. In the case of samples containing multiple fragments, a minimum of 10 pieces was undertaken. A fine slice was taken from each wood fragment along three planes (transverse section (TS), radial longitudinal section (RL) and tangential longitudinal section (TL)) using a razor blade. The pieces were mounted in water on a glass microscope slide, and examined under bi-focal transmitted light microscopy at magnifications of x50, x100 and x400 using a Kyowa ME-LUX2 microscope. Identification was undertaken according to the anatomical characteristics described by Schweingruber (1990) and Butterfield and Meylan (1980). Identification was to the highest taxonomic level possible, usually that of genus and nomenclature is according to Stace (1997). The results are shown in Table A3.16

Results

As recorded in Table A3.16, a number of fragments had either desiccated or undergone lignitic degradation and so were beyond safe identification. However, a good proportion of the assemblage has been analysed successfully. Young roundwood of alder (*Alnus glutinosa*) clearly dominates the worked wood. However, where samples of bundles of coppiced wood and rod ends were collected, a surprisingly large range of deciduous and evergreen taxa was identified, including willow/poplar (*Salix/Populus* sp, the two being anatomically indistinguishable), holly (*Ilex aquifolium*), hazel (*Corylus avellana*), yew (*Taxus baccata*), oak (*Quercus* sp.) elm (*Ulmus* sp.) and ash (*Fraxinus excelsior*). Larger stakes and logs tend again to be of alder but on occasion were of ash and elm. Since the worked wood derives from chronologically similar structures, they are discussed together below.

Discussion

There are no clear discernible differences in the choices of wood made for the earliest (later early Bronze Age) and latest (late Bronze Age) wooden structures in the three excavated areas, with alder continuing in dominance but with the continued presence of a range of other tree and shrub types. Assuming the woods were all sourced locally, it can be suggested that two habitats were exploited. The dominance of alder and importance of willow/poplar points to the use and management of wetland alder carr, and the use of slightly drier marginal mixed open woodland is indicated by the presence of oak, hazel, holly, elm and ash. While management of stands is clearly shown by the

Table A3.16 Waterlogged wood identifications

Site Code	Context no	Sample/ SF no.	Context type	Grp	Period	Comments (all are medium roundwood 1.5-3.5cm unless stated)	Identification
WMA02	5	-	Log in trackway 14 (cleft)	14	EMBA	large timber	*Alnus glutinosa*
WMA02	6	-	Cleft timber with cut ends in trackway 14	14	EMBA		Desiccated unidentified
WMA02	9	-	Roundwood in trackway 14	14	EMBA		*Fraxinus excelsior*
WMA02	10	-	Timber with 'wedge' type cut end in trackway 14	14	EMBA		*Ulmus* sp.
WMA02	12	-	Cleft half log or trimmed plank in trackway 14 (reused)	14	EMBA	Large stake, slow grown/ narrow rings	*Fraxinus excelsior*
WMA02	13	-	Cut rod possibly of coppice origin in trackway 14	14	EMBA		*Alnus glutinosa*
WMA02	15	-	Tangentially cleft timber in trackway 14	14	EMBA		*Fraxinus excelsior*
WMA02	16	-	Log with lopped branch in trackway 14	14	EMBA		*Alnus glutinosa*
WMA02	18	-	Rod with wedge type cut end in trackway 14	14	EMBA		*Alnus glutinosa*
WMA02	21	ss 3	Roundwood in trackway 14	14	EMBA	rod samples	*Alnus glutinosa* 3 rods, 5 poles; *Salix/ Populus* sp. 1 rod; *Ulmus* sp.1 pole; *Fraxinus excelsior* 1 pole; *Ilex aquifolium* 1 pole
WMA02	21	ss 5	Roundwood in trackway 14	14	EMBA	10 pieces	*Fraxinus excelsior* 5; *Corylus avellana* 1; *Ulmus* sp. 1; *Alnus glutinosa* 1; *Salix/ Populus* sp. 2
WMA02	63	ss 21	Roundwood under large timbers in trackway 61	61	MLBA	numerous small fragments (25% identified)	*Ulmus* sp. 1 large rwd; *Salix/ Populus* sp. 1 large rwd; *Alnus glutinosa* 5; *Salix/ Populus* sp. 3; *Fraxinus excelsior* 1; degraded unid 1
WMA02	20	-	Branch from naturally fallen tree in trackway 29	29	EMBA		*Alnus glutinosa*
WMA02	30	-	Rod with wedge point in trackway	29	EMBA		*Alnus glutinosa*
WMA02	31	-	Rod with pencil point in trackway	29	EMBA		Desiccated unidentified
WMA02	33	-	Stake in trackway 29	29	EMBA		*Alnus glutinosa*
WMA02	36	-	Rod end in trackway 29 with wedge type cut end.	29	EMBA		*Salix/ Populus* sp.
WMA02	51	-	Decayed yew stem In trackway 29	29	EMBA		*Taxus baccata*
WMA02	49	ss 10	Roundwood in trackway 50	50	EBA	numerous small fragments	All desiccated and degraded unidentified
WMA02	49	ss 11	Roundwood in trackway 50	50	EBA	small fragments	Modern root 1; *Alnus glutinosa* 1; cf *Alnus glutinosa* 1; *Quercus* sp.; *Fraxinus excelsior* 2; *Ulmus* sp. 1
WMA02	62	ss 19	Roundwood beneath large timbers in trackway 29	29	EMBA	2 bags of small fragments (c.20% identified)	*Alnus glutinosa* 2 large timbers; cf. *Alnus glutinosa* 1; *Fraxinus excelsior* 1; *Taxus baccata* 1; cf. *Salix/ Populus* sp. 8; *Ulmus* sp. 2; desiccated unid large rwd 2
WMA02	41	-	Log in trackway 61	61	MLBA	large timber	*Ulmus* sp.
WMA02	42	-	Stake not in situ associated with trackway 61	61	MLBA		*Alnus glutinosa*
WMA02	40	-	Stake in situ. may be associated with curved line of stakes to NE of 61	-	MLBA	Large stake 80mm diameter	*Alnus glutinosa*

Table A3.16 Waterlogged wood identifications (continued)

Site Code	Context no	Sample/ SF no.	Context type	Grp	Period	Comments (all are medium roundwood 1.5-3.5cm unless stated)	Identification
WMA02	54	-	Stake *in situ*, may be associated with irregular stake line round 61	-	MLBA	Large stake 80mm diameter	*Fraxinus excelsior*
WMA02	64	-	?Stake	-	EMBA or M-LBA		*Alnus glutinosa*
WMA02	65	-	Cut branch possibly small stake. Poss. associated with trackway 29	-	EMBA	Small rod	*Taxus baccata*
RIR01	1047	-	Fill of ditch 1039	1038	LBA	small pieces	5 Unidentified
RIR01	3009	ss 53	Peat deposit below trackway 3031	-	EMBA	numerous small pieces	*Alnus glutinosa* 1 Rest degraded unid
RIR01	3013	-	Bundle of coppiced wood to one side of trackway 3013	-	EMBA	2 bags of small pieces (25% identified)	*Alnus glutinosa* 5; cf. *Alnus glutinosa* 2; *Salix/ Populus* sp. 1; cf. *Salix/ Populus* sp. 2; *Quercus* sp. 1; unid 3
RIR01	3027	ss 42	Trackway 3031-coppiced bundles	3031	EMBA	several small pieces	Degraded cf. *Salix/ Populus* sp. 3; rest degraded unid
RIR01	5142	ss 16	Sandbank within western channel with artefact scatter	-	LBA	1 bag small pieces (33% identified)	*Salix/ Populus* sp. 1; *Alnus glutinosa* 6; *Alnus glutinosa* 4yr twig<1cm; degraded unid 2
RIR01	5247	ss 36	Stake built structure near trackway 5268 (Area 3)	-	EMBA		*Alnus glutinosa* 2
RIR01	5108	-	Trackway 5268 (Area 3)	5268	EMBA	2 bags small pieces (25% identified)	*Alnus glutinosa* 14 rwd, 1 4yr twig; *Fraxinus excelsior* 1; *Salix/ Populus* sp. 5 rwd, 1 twig; cf. *Salix/ Populus* sp. 6; degraded unid 2
FRU01	27	-	Upper fill of ditch 28	42	post LBA		*Fraxinus excelsior* 2 larger rwd
FRU01	46	sf 67	Sandy silty peat	35	MLBA		*Taxus baccata*
FRU01	48	ss 95	Spread of wood	35	MLBA		Desiccated cf. *Alnus/ Corylus*
FRU01	49	ss 114	Spread of wood 49	31	EMBA		*Taxus baccata* 1 branching twigwood; *Alnus glutinosa* 2 rwd; 8 degraded mature and rwd fragments
FRU01	64	-	Possible timber post	29	EMBA	Large log 110mm diameter	*Fraxinus excelsior*
FRU01	65	-	Plank	33	EMBA		*Alnus glutinosa*
FRU01	85	-	Worked wood part of spread 49	31	EMBA		cf. *Alnus/ Corylus*
FRU01	86	-	Worked wood part of spread 49	31	EMBA		*Taxus baccata*
FRU01	90	-	Worked wood part of spread 49	31	EMBA		*Fraxinus excelsior*
FRU01	91	-	Worked wood part of spread 49	31	EMBA		Desiccated unidentified
FRU01	93	-	Worked wood part of spread 49	31	EMBA		*Alnus glutinosa*
FRU01	94	-	Stake, associated with piled structure	32	EMBA		*Alnus glutinosa*
FRU01	174	-	Part of wood spread 164	22	MBA		cf. *Alnus/ Corylus*
FRU01	175	-	Part of wood spread 164	22	MBA		Unidentified
FRU01	176	-	Part of wood spread 164	22	MBA		*Alnus glutinosa*
FRU01	177	-	Part of wood spread 164	22	MBA		*Alnus glutinosa*
FRU01	185a	-	Post	21d	MBA		*Alnus glutinosa*
FRU01	185b	-	Post	21d	MBA		Unidentified
FRU01	212	-	Posthole 213	21d	MBA		*Alnus glutinosa*
FRU01	335	-	Stake	21a	MBA		*Alnus glutinosa*
FRU01	345	-	Stake	21e	MBA	stake?	*Alnus glutinosa*

presence of coppiced pieces (see Goodburn, this volume), the range of taxa utilised may also suggest some casual exploitation. The selection and use of wood types is considered further in the charcoal report (Barnett, this volume).

The use of alder, hazel and willow for structural components of Neolithic and Bronze Age wetland trackways is commonly reported in the UK, for example in the Somerset Levels where for instance the Sweet Track was constructed of alder and hazel pegs and rails, with oak, lime (*Tilia* sp.) and ash planks (Coles and Coles 1986); the Tinney's track-ways were of alder, hazel and willow brushwood with oak planks (Coles and Orme 1980) and the Meare Heath track was of birch (*Betula* sp.) and alder brushwood with oak stakes (Coles 1980). The use of larger tree types such as ash and oak for planks and large stakes is reported, although often, where present, oak is a more dominant type among the larger stakes and logs than indicated here.

Somewhat more unusual is the use of yew (WMA02 contexts 62 and 65) and holly (WMA02 context 21) within trackways, the former also found within worked wood spreads (FRU01 contexts 49 and 86) and potentially unworked samples at FRU01, these suggesting the yew was growing in/

immediately adjacent to the wetland there. Yew has indeed previously been documented in wetland margins in the region for the Bronze Age, eg at Wennington Marsh (Sidell 1996) and at Erith (Sidell *et al.* 2000), where it was an important component within the submerged forest along with oak, alder and ash. The environment associated with Bronze Age trackways in Beckton was dominantly alder carr (Scaife 1991 in Rackham and Sidell 2000) and oak with alder at Bramcote Green (Thomas and Rackham 1996). The Bronze Age flora at West Heath showed an increase in holly within the existing mix of oak, lime and hazel, which tallies well with its appearance here (Rackham and Sidell 2000).

Charcoal *by Catherine Barnett*

Introduction

A number of contexts were chosen by Oxford Archaeology for wood charcoal analysis during post-excavation assessment of samples from three sites along the route of the A13: Prince Regent Lane (FRU01), Woolwich Manor Way (TGW00) and Movers Lane (RIR01). These contexts range in date from the early Neolithic to the late Bronze Age/

Table A3.17   Charcoal assemblages

Site Code	Area	Sample no	Cxt no	Context type	Grp	Phase
TGW00	T15	21	2008	Palaeosol with artefact scatter formed on surface of sand sealed by peat.		ENEO
RIR01	3	18	5083	Possible burnt mound: black sandy silt clay with abundant burnt flint inclusions by palaeochannel	5264	MLBA
RIR01	3	10	5085	Fill of pit 5084 assoc with burnt flint deposit 5264		MLBA
RIR01	3	20	5154	Peat at edge of western channel. (Late) EBA-MBA trackway sits on its surface	5263	BA
RIR01	3	34	5147	Fill of gully 5159 with burnt daub and charcoal, overlies stake structure	5161	EMBA
RIR01	2B	-	3004	Peat containing burnt flint, wood chips, LBA pot, over drowned root system adapted using brushwood and used as a possible LBA platform adj to trackway		MLBA
FRU01		101	49	Artefact rich organic deposit accumulated around and associated with piled structure (double row oak piles, poss bridge)		EMBA
FRU01	A	82	34	Sandy silt alluvium over the peat that caps the piles		LBA-EIA
FRU01	A	39	31	Dark grey brown, clayey peaty silt at top of piled structure sequence		LBA-EIA

early Iron Age and include layers associated with a Bronze Age piled structure and a possible burnt mound. The results of this charcoal analysis should be viewed in tandem with the waterlogged wood analysis (Barnett above; Chapter 10 above).

Methodology

Up to 100 fragments per sample >2mm were prepared for identification according to the standard methodology of Leney and Casteel (1975; see also Gale and Cutler 2000). Each was fractured with a razor blade so that three planes could be seen: transverse section (TS), radial longitudinal section (RL) and tangential longitudinal section (TL). The pieces were mounted using modelling clay on a glass microscope slide, blown to remove charcoal dust and examined under bi-focal epi-illuminated microscopy at magnifications of x50, x100 and x400 using a Kyowa ME-LUX2 microscope. Identification was undertaken according to the anatomical characteristics described by Schweingruber (1990) and Butterfield and Meylan (1980). Identification was to the highest taxonomic level possible, usually that of genus, and nomenclature is according to Stace (1997).

As shown in Table A3.17, a minimum of 13 tree and shrub types were identified for the contexts as a whole, most being common deciduous types.

Woolwich Manor Way

Early Neolithic

The early Neolithic assemblage from the palaeosol (layer 2008, Fig. 5.3) included hazel, pomaceous fruit wood (Pomoideae), cherry-type (*Prunus* sp., a group containing e.g. wild cherry and blackthorn) and also contained the only charred representation of elm (*Ulmus* sp.). The small but mixed sample is likely to represent domestic hearth fuel.

Movers Lane

Bronze Age-early Iron Age

Alder (*Alnus glutinosa*) proved to be the dominant taxon, forming a large proportion of most of the early, middle and late Bronze Age samples, a phenomenon also found with the worked wood assemblage (Barnett, Appendix 3, above). Interestingly, although alder was found to dominate most

Comments	*Alnus glutinosa*	cf. *Alnus glutinosa*	*Betula pendula/pubescens*	*Corylus avellana*	*Frangula alnus*	*Fraxinus excelsior*	*Hedera helix*	*Pomoideae*	*Prunus* sp.	*Quercus* sp.	*Salix/Populus* sp.	*Sambucus nigra*	*Tilia* sp.	*Ulmus* sp.	Unidentified	Total no. fragments
Small sample of small fresh fragments	-	-	-	1	-	-	-	9	1	-	-	-	-	5	-	16
Large fragmentary sample, some friable c. 10% Identified	11	-	-	79	-	-	-	-	-	2	2	2	-	-	4	100
Medium fragmentary sample, most v mineralised, some vitrified	-	-	-	47	-	-	-	1	1	-	1				9	50
	44	-	-	8	-	1	-	-	-	-	-	-	-	-	4	57
Large sample of fragmentary and mineralised pieces. c. 15% Identified	46	-	4	44	-	3	-	-	-	3	-	-	-	-	-	100
A few large fresh pieces	5	-	-	-	-	-	3 (twig)	-	-	-	-	-	-	-	3	11
Medium-large fresh fragments	20	-	-	2	-	1	-	2	-	23	-	-	6	-	5	59
Sample of v. large pieces incl roundwood 40mm diameter	-	-	50	-	-	-	-	-	-	-	-	-	-	-	-	50
Medium-large fragments, several vitrified. 50% Identified	26 + 2 twig	2	5	-	3 + 1 cf 3yr twig	-	-	1	-	-	-	-	-	-	5 + 5 twig	50

of the later prehistoric charcoal samples, it was not found in the early Neolithic assemblage from the palaeosol at Woolwich Manor Way (layer 2008, T15). Since only a single small charcoal assemblage of this date was available, it is unclear whether this is a true reflection of availability or selection, but a rise in alder carr and widespread fen conditions might be expected in the early Bronze Age of the Thames Basin and is reflected in the pollen assemblages from the late Mesolithic to early Neolithic period at both Movers Lane and Woolwich Manor Way (Haggart, above).

Hazel (*Corylus avellana*) is also important in a number of the assemblages of all ages, and forms *c* 80-95% of the pieces from the possible channel-side middle-late Bronze Age burnt mound and associated pit (RIR01, contexts 5083 and 5085, Figs 7.14 and 7.15). Small numbers of fragments of pomaceous fruit wood, oak (*Quercus* sp.), willow/poplar (*Salix/Populus* sp., the two being anatomically indistinguishable), elder (*Sambucus nigra*), cherry-type and alder were also found in these contexts. This mix of wood types, a minimum of seven taxa, is likely to reflect local gathering of fuel wood but with stands of (potentially managed) hazel particularly targeted. The importance of hazel in the wood charcoal is not reflected in the waterlogged wood assemblages from the same and same-age contexts, suggesting that there was deliberate selection of hazel for fuel and a preference for alder to use in structures likely to be periodically submerged. Alder wood is indeed known for its durability under water (Edlin 1949, 23; Gale and Cutler 2000, 34) and would have made an economic and long-lasting choice for trackway construction.

The charcoal assemblage from the surface of the peat in Area 3 of RIR01, context 5263, has been suggested to be contemporary with the construction and use of the Bronze Age trackway that rests on it. Alder forms 88% of the assemblage, with lesser amounts of hazel and a single fragment of ash (*Fraxinus excelsior*). This compares well with the selection of alder wood shown by analysis of the Area 3 trackways, where alder dominates but is accompanied by small numbers of ash and also willow/poplar pieces.

Middle-late Bronze Age context 3004 is a complex one, comprising a peat over and surrounding the root system of a large tree which is thought to have been adapted and used as a platform with the addition of bundles of brushwood. The peat contained wood chips, pottery and burnt flint. The small charcoal assemblage proved to be of alder with three narrow pieces of ivy (*Hedera helix*). The relationship to the peat and to the possible platform is unclear; it might be from the burning of offcuts and debris from the bundles of coppiced wood or represent an unrelated dump of spent fuel. However, it is suggested the ivy would not have been deliberately chosen for fuel but was attached to the alder wood collected.

The early-middle Bronze Age gully fill, context 5147 is again heavily dominated by alder and hazel but contains small quantities of birch (*Betula pendula/pubescens*), ash and oak. The fill, which overlay structure 5161, contained charcoal and burnt daub. However, the mix of taxa in the charcoal assemblage shows this is unlikely to originate from structural wood; instead it is likely to represent domestic fuel use.

Prince Regent Lane (Freemasons Road)

Early Bronze Age-early Iron Age piled structure sequence

A sample was analysed from (late) early Bronze Age context 49, an organic deposit that had collected around and was believed associated with the piled oak 'bridge' structure (Str. 32). The charcoal assemblage differs somewhat in composition from a sample of similar age at Mover's Lane (context 5147). Alder, hazel and ash are again present, though it is oak that dominates with alder. Ash, pomaceous fruit wood and six pieces of lime/linden (*Tilia* sp.) were also recovered, the latter the only representation of the taxon in this analysis.

A sample from context 34, from alluvium capping the oak piles contained large fresh charcoal fragments including pieces of large roundwood of 40mm diameter. All proved to be of hazel and it is possible these pieces derive from a bundle of coppiced hazel wood related to the structure that was either discarded and burnt or used for fuel, perhaps during construction.

Much of the charcoal from the peaty silt context 31 at the top of the piled structure sequence was vitrified, indicating a high temperature of burn, likely in excess of $>800°C$ (Prior and Alvin 1983). Alder, birch, and pomaceous fruit wood are represented, along with the first appearance of alder buckthorn (*Frangula alnus*). Several pieces of twig wood were found, including alder and alder buckthorn and it may be the assemblage derives from *in situ* burning of vegetation to clear the site or a temporary hearth utilising material immediately to hand.

Discussion

Overall, a moderate range of woody types were selected and used across the three sites. The concentration on alder and hazel is likely to reflect both their local availability and, from the Bronze Age, their increased productivity due to coppicing. As suggested from the results of the waterlogged wood analysis (Barnett, Apppendix 3, above) both the use and management of wetland alder carr in the immediate area and the use of slightly drier mixed open woodland beyond the floodplain edges is indicated by the types identified. The results are somewhat site specific but compare well in broad terms to the findings at Springhead and Northfleet (Barnett 2011) There, alder (and sometimes Pomoideae) dominated the charcoal assemblages of the early and middle to late Bronze Age boiling pits, burnt mounds, pits and hearths and was accompanied by hazel, oak, birch, cherry-type (including bird cherry) in differing quantities. Lime and willow/poplar were rare but field maple (*Acer campestre*), dogwood (*Cornus sylvatica*) and beech (*Fagus sylvatica*) were also found, unlike the A13 sites, suggesting drier, possibly chalky areas beyond the wetland margins were also exploited for wood at those sites.

Animal bone *by Lena Strid and Rebecca Nicholson*

Introduction

This report encompasses animal bones from the adjacent sites Prince Regent Lane (PGL00, Phase II) and Freemasons Road Underpass (FRU01). A small number of bones were recovered from the nearby Bronze Age site at Movers Lane (RIR01) and are discussed briefly at the end of this report. The animal bone assemblage from the Prince Regent Lane and Freemasons Road Underpass comprises 462 refitted fragments from securely dated contexts. The assemblage was recovered from contexts dated from the later part of the early Bronze Age (1690-1520 ^{14}C yr BC) to the late Bronze Age (referred to here as M-LBA) and contexts dating from the late Bronze Age to the Iron Age (LBA-IA). The bones were recovered both through hand collection during excavation and from wet sieved bulk samples, but almost 77% of the recorded bones were hand-retrieved. A full record of the assemblage, documented in a *Microsoft Access* database, can be found with the site archive.

Methodology

Initial assessment of the assemblages was carried out in 2000 and 2003 (Liddle in Gifford and Partners 2000; 2003b; Mepham in Wessex Archaeology 2003). The bones were identified at Oxford Archaeology using a comparative skeletal reference collection, in addition to standard osteological identification manuals. All the animal remains were counted and weighed, and where possible identified to species, element, side and zone. For zoning, Serjeantson (1996) was used, with the addition of mandible zones by Worley (forthcoming 2011). Sheep and goat were identified to species where possible, using Boessneck *et al.* (1964) and Prummel and Frisch (1986); they were otherwise classified as 'sheep/goat'. Ribs and vertebrae, with the exception of atlas and axis, were classified by size: 'large mammal' representing cattle, horse and deer; 'medium mammal' representing sheep/goat, pig and large dog; and 'small mammal' representing small dog, cat and hare. The minimum number of individuals (MNI) was calculated on the most frequently occurring bone for each species, using

Serjeantson's zoning guide (Serjeantson 1996) and taking into account left and right sides.

The condition of the bone was graded on a 6-point system (0-5). Grade 0 equating to very well preserved bone, and grade 5 indicating that the bone had suffered such structural and attritional damage as to make it unrecognisable (Table A3.18).

The age-at-death of the animals was based on evidence from tooth eruption, tooth wear and epiphyseal fusion, using Habermehl (1975) for fusion and tooth eruption, and Grant (1982), Halstead (1985), Payne (1973) and O'Connor (1988) for tooth wear of cattle, sheep/goat and pig. Sex estimation was carried out on morphological traits on cattle pelves, goat horn cores and pig mandibular canine teeth, using data from Boessneck *et al.* (1964), Schmid (1972) and Vretemark (1997).

Measurements were taken according to von den Driesch (1976), using digital callipers with an accuracy of 0.01mm. Large bones were measured using an osteometric board, with an accuracy of 1 mm. These measurements will be available as part of the site archive.

Bone condition

The majority of the bone from the site was in good to fair condition (Table A3.19). The bones from the (late) early and middle-late Bronze Age were slightly less well preserved, which is to be expected given their older age. A total of 4% of the M-LBA and 4.7% of the LBA-IA animal bone fragments had been gnawed. Rodent gnawing was only recorded on one fragment (from a M-LBA context) whereas the other gnaw marks came from from canids or other carnivores. No bones were burnt.

Table A3.18   Bone preservation grading categories

Grade 0	Excellent preservation. Entire bone surface complete.
Grade 1	Good preservation. Almost all bone surface complete. No cracks in bone.
Grade 2	Fair preservation.
Grade 3	Poor preservation. Most bone surface destroyed.
Grade 4	Very poor preservation. No surface structure remaining.
Grade 5	Extremely poor preservation. Unlikely to be able to identify element.

Table A3.19   Preservation level for contexts from the Freemasons Road assemblage.

	N	0	1	2	3	4	5
M-LBA	376	0.8%	35.3%	45.1%	16.2%	2.7%	
LBA-IA	86		58.1%	33.7%	8.1%		

The (late) early and middle to late Bronze Age assemblage

The assemblage from the earlier part of the second millennium BC consisted of 376 bones, of which 177 (47.3%) were identified to taxon (Table A3.20). The domestic mammals included cattle (*Bos taurus*), sheep (*Ovis aries*), goat (*Capra hircus*), sheep or goat (*Ovis aries* or *Capra hircus*) and dog (*Canis familiaris*). The wild fauna included bank vole (*Clethrionomys glareolus*), field vole (*Microtus agrestis*) and frog (*Rana* sp.). One rabbit metatarsal was recovered from layer 47. Since rabbits are burrowing animals, thought to have been introduced by the Normans (Yalden 1999, 158-61) this bone must be considered intrusive and is therefore not considered further.

Domestic species

Cattle dominate the assemblage by number of identified fragments (NISP). Using the calculated Minimum Number of Individuals (MNI) cattle remains the most common species, although they are less dominant compared to sheep/goat and pig. Unfortunately the total number of bones from these three animals is below the recommended cut-off point for intra-species frequency analysis (*cf* Hambleton 1999, 39-40) and so further interpretation of the intra-species frequency would be imprudent. In general, cattle and sheep/goat are the most common taxa in Bronze Age animal bone assemblages in Britain (Serjeantson 2007, 87). Variation in the ratios of cattle:caprines between sites could be dependent on environmental factors; for instance, wetland pastures suit cattle far better than sheep. However, not all selection factors are environmentally determined: as Serjeantson argues (*ibid.*), activities such as feasting and trading secondary products such as wool and dairy products may be at least partly responsible for patterning in faunal assemblages.

Table A3.20   Middle to late Bronze Age bone assemblage from Freemasons Road

	Cattle	Sheep/goat	Sheep	Goat	Pig	Dog	Bank vole	Field vole	Rodent	Frog	Micro-fauna	Small mammal	Medium mammal	Large mammal	Indeterminate
Horn core	2			4											
Skull	4				1	2								5	
Mandible	18	7			2	4									
Loose teeth	11	9					1	1	6						
Atlas	1					2									
Axis		1													
Vertebra													4	6	
Rib													2	13	
Scapula	6	1			1									1	
Humerus	7	3			1	1					2			1	
Radius	9	6				2							1		
Ulna	3					2									
Carpal bones												1			
Metacarpal	10	3													
Pelvis	3	1											1		
Femur	6	3			1										
Tibia	7	6		1	1										
Fibula						1									
Calcaneus	2														
Astragalus	2														
Metatarsal	8	2													
Phalanx 1	4	1			1										
Phalanx 2		1			1										
Sesamoid														1	
Long bone											5		8	12	
Indeterminate														13	107
TOTAL (NISP)	103	43	2	5	9	14	1	1	6	2	16	1	16	61	107
MNI	6	4			1	2	1	1							
Weight (g)	9190	534	59	126	179	275	0	0	0	0	0	0	65	993	405

Table A3.21 Middle to late Bronze Age: mandibular wear stages (MWS) and calculated age at death for cattle (Halstead 1985), sheep/goat (Payne 1973) and pig (O'Connor 1988).

Species	dp4	P4	M1	M	M3	MWS	Estimated age
Cattle	j		e	C		12	8-18 months
	g		b			10	8-18 months
	k		g	C-E		N/A	8-18 months
			g	b		20	18-30 months
			j	f	b	32	30-36 months
				g	f	38	Young Adult
			j	g	f	N/A	Young Adult
				j	g	41-42	Adult
					g	37-49	Adult
Sheep/goat	k		f	E		14	6-12 months
			g	g	d	33	2-3 years
			h	g	e	35	3-4 years
				g	g	36-41	4-6 years
Pig		A	e	c	V	19-21	Subadult

While not all skeletal elements are represented in the small assemblage, bones from meat-rich body parts as well as meat-poor body parts were present. This would suggest that domesticates were butchered on or close to the site.

Judging by the state of epiphyseal fusion, most cattle, sheep/goat and pigs were sub-adult or adult at the time of death. The absence of neonatal remains is likely to be due to taphonomic loss, as bones from neonatal animals are very fragile. A wide range of slaughter ages for cattle and sheep/goat was indicated by the dental evidence (Table A3.21), although the majority of cattle appear to have been slaughtered as sub-adults. Only one pig mandible, from a sub-adult individual, could be aged.

A measurable cattle metacarpal was found to be very large when compared to metacarpals from contemporary British sites published in the ABMAP database (University of Southampton 2003: http://archaeologydataservice.ac.uk/archives/view/abmap), although the number of measureable bones was extremely low (see Table A3.22). The metacarpal was much smaller than those from aurochsen cows, indicating that it belonged to a domestic animal, probably either a bull or an ox.

The dog remains consist of one semiarticulated skeleton and one disarticulated fibula in flood deposit (125); one atlas, skull and two articulating mandible halves in spread (49), discussed further below; and three disarticulated bones in overlying peat deposits (32, 101, 105). These included a butchered atlas, discussed further below. Since the flood deposit (125) was formed later than the spread (49), the dog remains are unlikely to be contemporary. Although the mandible from (125) was incomplete, length and width measurements on the P4 tooth (11.8 and 6.4mm respectively) and M1 (23.8 and 9.4mm: measurements after von den

Driesch 1976 and Phillips et al.. 2009) suggest that the mandibular teeth were of similar size and shape to those from of a modern deerhound (data published in Phillips et al.. 2009) although the partial and fragmented nature of the skull and limb bones meant that estimation of withers height and skull shape could not be made. Data summarised by Harcourt (1974) suggests that dogs in the Bronze Age stood 0.43-0.62m at the withers, but without other measureable bones the height and general body shape of the dog from deposit (125) can not be established. Although the dog would probably fall at the upper end of Harcourt's range it is very unlikely to have been as large as a modern deerhound (this breed stands at 0.7m–0.8m at the withers). It is plausible that the atlas, skull and mandibles in (49) were articulated at the time of deposition, but later disarticulated. Although not all teeth were present, measurements on the mandibular P4 and visual comparison with the mandible from flood deposit (125) indicated a dog of similar or slightly larger size. The fragment of fibula shaft from the same context was also large and hence could have belonged to a wolf rather than a dog, although since the fibula is very fragmented this can not be verified. From visual inspection alone, the bone would appear to have come from a bigger animal than the other dog bones from this context.

Wild species

The only wild fauna in the assemblage were rodents, amphibians and fish. The presence of bank vole, field vole and frog is consistent with a local environment comprising a mixture of open fields and woodlands, interspersed with streams or wetlands (Bjärvall and Ullström 1995). A fin spine from a three-spined stickleback (Gasterosteus aculeatus) from post hole (72) was recorded by J. Liddle during assessment. These fish can be found both in freshwater streams and rivers and in estuarine and coastal waters.

Butchery

Butchery marks were recorded on bones from cattle, sheep/goat, goat and dog. Most of these were cut marks deriving from disarticulation and marrow extraction. Chop marks on the basal part of one cattle (32) and one goat horn core (49) suggest utilisation of horn for horn working. The dog atlas from (105) had transverse chop marks on the ventral side on the neural arch, indicating an attempt at decapitation, but the absence of the corresponding skull means that full decapitation can not be confirmed. It is conceivable that the dog's head may have been used for ritual purposes, but it is also possible that removal of the head was undertaken during butchery of the animal for food. Dog bones with butchery marks have been found on some Iron Age sites, suggesting that in this later period dogs were occasionally exploited for their meat (Maltby 1996, 23-24). Eating of dogs may have been practiced in the Bronze Age as well, for dietary, ritual or medicinal purposes (*cf.* Pasda 2004, 44-45) and it is possible that the skins were used for clothing, though skinning evidence is absent here.

Pathology

A sheep/goat mandible displayed slight bone absorption at the forth premolar/first molar, indicating an infection of the gums. Gum infection is fairly common in livestock populations, and, if severe, can cause mastication difficulties and weight loss (Baker and Brothwell 1980, 153-154).

A note on the bone from spread 49

The bones retrieved from layer 49, an organic deposit that had collected around the piled oak 'bridge' structure (Str. 32), comprised 24 speciable fragments from cattle, sheep/goat, goat, pig, dog and frog (*Rana* sp.). A cattle mandible from this layer was dated to 1690-1520 cal BC (94.0%) (SUERC-27345: 3340±30 BP). With the exception of the two dog mandible fragments discussed above, no bones were articulated. However, the presence of a dog atlas, skull and two articulating mandible halves suggests that these may have been part of a single head, the bones becoming disarticulated by water movements and peat formation.

At the Norfolk Bronze Age sites of Flag Fen and the Power Station Post Alignment site, deposits of articulated and semi-articulated skeletons of dogs and disarticulated human remains suggest ritual depositions, possibly related to funerary rites (Halstead *et al.* 2001, 348-350). This is less likely to have occurred at Prince Regent Lane/Freemasons Road Underpass, as the bones from layer (49) are relatively few in number and no specific body parts are over represented. The presence of gnaw marks suggest that some bones were accessible to dogs or other carnivores. Butchery marks on cattle and sheep/goat bones indicate food waste, although whether from ordinary meals or from more ritualised feasting can not be established from such scant evidence.

Late Bronze Age to Iron Age assemblage

The late Bronze Age to Iron Age assemblage comprised only 86 bones, 35 (47.7%) of which were identifiable to taxon (Table A3.23). Cattle, sheep/goat, goat and pig were represented. No firm identification of sheep was made, but since goats are generally rare on Iron Age sites in comparison to sheep (Maltby 1981, 159-160) it is likely that some or many of the bones are from sheep.

Domestic species

The greatest number of fragments (NISP) was from cattle (Table A3.22), but when calculating the Minimum Number of Individuals (MNI) cattle, sheep/goat and pig were similarly represented. Due to their larger size, cattle were likely to have

Table A3.22 Cattle metacarpal measurements (Bd = Greatest distal breadth) from Freemasons Road and contemporary sites from the ABMAP database.

Site	Phase	Mean	Min	Max
A13 Thames Gateway	M-LBA	59.9		
Crab Farm, Shapwick (Dorset)	EBA	50.4	48.0	52.7
A303, Stonehenge (Wiltshire)	MBA	61.1		
Middle Farm, Dorchester Bypass (Dorset)	LBA	50.8	50.1	51.5

Table A3.23 Late Bronze Age to Iron Age bone assemblage from Freemasons Road

	Cattle	Sheep/goat	Goat	Pig	Amphibian	Micro-fauna	Medium mammal	Large mammal	Indeterminate
Horn core	3	1							
Skull								6	
Mandible	2	2		1					
Loose teeth	2	2							
Vertebra							2	7	
Rib								5	
Humerus	1	1		2					
Radius	1	1							
Ulna	1							1	
Carpal bones	2								
Metacarpal	2								
Femur	1	1							
Tibia	2	1							
Metatarsal	2	1							
Phalanx 1	1								
Phalanx 2	1								
Long bone						3	2	3	
Indeterminate									23
TOTAL (NISP)	21	9	1	3	3	2	2	22	23
MNI	2	2		2					
Weight (g)	1744	133	33	116	0	0	11	352	52

been the main meat provider of the three species and the extremely low number of identified bones renders any comparison of taxon abundance meaningless.

The assemblage contains very few ageable bones and mandibles and it would be folly to try to establish a slaughter age pattern for this assemblage. Nevertheless, the surface structure of the bones indicates all animals were sub-adult or adult at the time of death. However, the absence of neonatal and juvenile bones is likely to reflect taphonomic loss, as the mortality rate of newborn and juvenile livestock would have been high even if none were deliberately slaughtered (Vretemark

1997, 82-83, 88, 95).

A single sheep/goat distal tibia was measured; at a greatest length of 22.3mm this animal is within the size range of caprines from contemporary British sites listed in the the ABMAP database (http://archaeologydataservice.acuk/archives/view/abmap).

Wild species

Fragments of unidentified amphibians, fish and microfauna were again the only non-domestic remains in the assemblage. Hunted animals are normally very rare from British Iron Age sites (Hambleton 1999, 14) and it seems clear that in general game was of minimal dietary significance. The fish bones, identifed by J. Liddle during the assessment from a sample taken from ditch context 41, comprised two fin spines from three-spined stickleback (*Gasterosteus aculeatus*). As above, this fish can be found in both freshwater and saltwater.

Butchery

Butchery marks were found on six bones from cattle, sheep/goat, goat and pig, as well as one unidentified large and one medium mammal. These comprised filleting and disarticulation, as well as marrow extraction. Portioning of the carcass was identified from one paramedially split vertebra from a medium-sized mammal and from one transversly split vertebra from a large mammal. A goat horn core had several chop marks at its base, suggesting utilisation of the horn sheath.

Discussion

Animal husbandry

The two phases of the settlement both yielded very small bone assemblages, which renders intra-site and inter-site comparisons difficult, due to issues of representativity (*cf* Hambleton 1999, 39-40). Indeed, a chronological comparison between the two phases from A13 Thames Gateway is not possible, due to the extremely small number of bones identified to species in the Late Bronze Age/Iron Age assemblage. Nevertheless, the predominance of domestic taxa, mainly cattle, sheep/goat and pig is typical for contemporary sites (Yalden 1999, 100-102).

A comparison of four larger Bronze Age bone assemblages from southern England (Table A3.24) (Bates 2008; Legge 1992; Powell and Clark 2006; Serjeantson 1996) suggests that different animal husbandry strategies were adopted in different areas. Sheep/goat typically comprise around 40% of the three major domesticates by NISP, but at Stansted caprines consitute over 50% of the speciated bone. While the slightly higher relative proportion of sheep/goat bones at Stansted has not been specifically discussed in the report (Bates 2008) and is perhaps surprising given the poorly draining nature of the soils around the sites, it is possible that at Stansted sheep/goat secondary products were particularly important. The compar-

atively large proportion of pig bones at Runnymead and Whitecross Farm may relate to local environments preferentially suited to pig keeping, or unfavourble to ruminants. Alternatively, it is possible that at these sites there was a specialised focus on pig rearing for feasting (although this suggestion is not one favoured by Done (1991, 342-3)). Pigs are very fecund and fast-growing, making them the best of the three taxa for this purpose (Powell and Clark 2006, 110; Serjeantson 2007, 88). Cattle remains frequently dominate the animal bone assemblages of Bronze Age sites in the middle Thames region (Knight and Grimm 2010) while at Grimes Graves, in Norfolk, a predominance of cattle in the Bronze Age in conjunction with a large number of slaughtered calves was interpreted as evidence of a focused dairy economy (Legge 1992).

Although at Prince Regent Lane/Freemasons Road cattle dominated the assemblage, it should be remembered that here the number of identified bones was small and calves were absent, although possibly under-represented due to poor survival and retrieval. Cattle could have provided meat, dairy products and traction, while sheep/goat may have been utilised for meat, dairy products, wool and possibly dung: sheep dung is better than cattle or pig manure for the fertilisation of fields (Serjeantson 2007, 83). Pigs were raised for meat, and consequently slaughtered at or before reaching their full growth. Due to their larger size, cattle would have been the main meat providers.

Ritual or secular?

Bones associated with ritual or ceremonial deposits have not been identified with certainty in the assemblage, although chop marks on a dog atlas from peat deposit 105 representing a decapitation attempt, suggests the possibility of 'ritual' use. However, since no other dog bone could be securely associated with the atlas, the question remains open. Likewise, while it is tempting to see what was almost certainly a disarticulated dog's head in the organic deposit around the piled oak 'bridge' structure (Str. 32) as an example of ritual deposition, the deposit also included bones from domestic ungulates, with no clear over-representation of any skeletal elements (for example, skulls).

Table A3.24 *Percentages of cattle, sheep/goat and pig from Freemasons Road and from four other Bronze Age assemblages in Britain*

Site	No.	Cattle	Sheep/goat	Pig
A13 Freemasons Road	164	62.8%	31.7%	5.5%
Grimes Graves	5094	52.5%	42.4%	5.1%
Runnymede	1531	28.3%	41.5%	30.1%
Stanstead	792	38.4%	50.8%	10.9%
Whitecross Farm, Wallingford	481	22.0%	42.4%	35.6%

A note on the animal bone from Movers Lane

The Movers Lane assemblage comprised 36 bones, of which 11 were speciable. The assemblage was dominated by cattle bones (n:8). Sheep/goat (n:2) and horse (n:1) were the only other animals present. Judging by epiphyseal fusion and bone surface structure all animals were adult or sub-adults when they died. One sheep/goat femur had been sawn through mid-shaft. The edge is smooth, which suggests wear. The distal end would have functioned as a handle. Unfortunately the poor bone surface condition made it impossible to see any wear polishing on the shaft. The femur may have been used to make decorative circular impressions in leather or bark.

Human Bone from Movers Lane *by Jacqueline McKinley*

A small amount of human bone was recovered from Movers Lane and was assessed in 2003. No further work was undertaken.

Cremated human bone was recovered from two contexts (both upper spits) within cut 1207, weighing a total of 189g. The bone is that of an adult ?male; it is well burnt, and quite comminuted: fragments are small and relatively abraded.

In addition, five fragments of redeposited, disarticulated human bone were recovered; all were fragments of long bone shafts and came from sandbank artefact scatter 5142, alluvial deposit 3005 and hurdle trackway 5268.

Micromorphology and bulk analyses *by Richard Macphail and John Crowther* (Fig. A3.15)

Summary

A variety of landscapes and features (palaeosols, occupation soils, burnt mounds, trackways, developing wetland) were studied employing nine thin sections and eleven bulk samples from Movers Lane and Woolwich Manor Way. The Neolithic occupation palaeosol at Woolwich Manor Way formed either by trampling or by cultivation, or through a combination of both processes.

The local Bronze Age landscape had an inferred argillic brown earth soil cover, and fragments of this soil type were found alongside and within a possible terrestrial trackway soil fragment in wooden trackway sediments at Woolwich Manor Way. Evidence of this soil cover was also recorded in palaeosols and at the burnt mound at Movers Lane. Muddy puddles and infills associated with sediment formation, developed along a trackway at Movers Lane; one puddle may speculatively have originated as an animal(?) print. At Movers Lane, occupation soils and the burnt mound were affected by trampling, and by sediment accretion from both occupation disturbance and contemporary alluviation. At the top of the burnt mound occupation

deposits are intercalated upwards within the alluvium, as muddy spreads. Across both sites, ensuing peats were affected by both humification and biological working in places (fluctuating water tables), and alternating and migrating stream flow led to sands (stream flow?) and humic silt (backswamp?) deposition, as local peats were weathered and eroded. These interpretations, however, must remain speculative as sample coverage of the different landscapes and features was small. The report is supported by 3 tables and 27 photos; a CD-Rom with supporting data including 122 digital scans and photomicrographs can be found in the site archive.

Introduction

A series of monoliths from Movers Lane and Woolwich Manor Way were received from Liz Stafford (Oxford Archaeology) in order to analyse the sediment micromorphology and bulk character of prehistoric palaeosols, burnt mounds and trackways onto developing Thames wetland. In addition, the character of the sites and human activities in relationship to rising base levels and marine inundation were investigated.

Methodology

The monoliths were subsampled for nine thin sections and eleven bulk sample analyses (LOI, phosphate-P and grain size; Tables A3.25 and A3.26)

Woolwich Manor Way Monolith 2 was discussed with Andrew Haggart at the Chatham Campus of Greenwich University, from where it was collected after it had been subsampled for diatoms and multi-element analysis.

Bulk analyses

Analysis was undertaken on the fine earth fraction (ie < 2mm) of the samples. LOI (loss-on-ignition) was determined by ignition at $375°C$ for 16 hours (Ball 1964), previous experimental studies having shown that there is normally no significant breakdown of carbonate at this temperature. Phosphate-P (total phosphate) was measured following oxidation with NaOBr using $1N$ H_2SO_4 as the extractant (Dick and Tabatabai 1977), with a slight excess of H_2SO_4 being added initially to neutralise any remaining carbonate. Particle size was determined using the pipette method on < 2mm mineral (peroxide-treated) soil (Avery and Bascomb 1974).

Soil micromorphology

The nine thin section subsamples from monolith series 2, 4, 40, 44 and 47 were impregnated with a clear polyester resin-acetone mixture; samples were then topped up with resin, ahead of curing and slabbing for 75x50 mm-size thin section manufacture by Spectrum Petrographics, Vancouver, Washington, USA (Goldberg and Macphail 2006; Murphy 1986) (Fig A3.15, 1-6). The

Table A3.25 Bulk analytical data

Mono	Context	Description	LOIa (%)	Phosphate-P[b] (mg g⁻¹)	Coarse sand >600 μm(%)	Medium sand 200-600 μm(%)	Fine sand 60-200 μm(%)	Silt 2-60 μm(%)	Clay <2 μm(%)	Texture class
Woolwich Manor Way										
4	2007	Basal peat	9.74*	0.165						
4	2008(u)	Stained sand	1.05	0.059	2.6	47.1	40.0	8.1	2.2	Sand
4	2008(l)	Stained sand	0.618	0.048						
2A	28	Wood peat (trackway)	46.5**	0.415						
Movers Lane										
47	5204	Basal alluvium	4.84	0.251	3.4	42.3	29.6	12.8	11.9	Sandy loam
47	5142	Occupation sands	0.690	0.135*						
44	5121	Stained clays	3.15	0.308	0.8	4.8	5.6	40.0	48.8	Clay
44	5083	Burned mound	4.91	0.588*	3.3	18.9	16.8	42.3	18.6	Sandy silt loam
40	5154(u)	Wood peat (trackway)	27.8**	0.249						
40	5154(l)	Sandy peat upper	29.7**	0.379						
40	5154/52	Peaty sand	17.0**	0.322						

Table A3.26 Soil micromorphology : samples

Thin	Relative	Context	Sediment	MFT	SMT	Voids	Eb clasts	Bt clasts	Trampled clasts	'wetland' clay clasts	Stones
Woolwich Manor Way (WMW) Trench 2 Sample 2 - trackway											
M2A	620-630 mm	28	Wood Peat - trackway	A1	1a1	65%	a-2	a-1	a-1		f
M2A	630-650(665) mm	28	Wood Peat - trackway	B1	1a1	50%	a-5				
M2A	650(665)-700 mm	28	Wood Peat - trackway	C1	1a1	60%					
Woolwich Manor Way (WMW) Trench 15 Sample 4 - palaeosol											
M4A	320-360 mm	2007	Basal peat	B1	1b	55%					
M4A	360-395 mm	2008	Stained sand	D2	2b	35%	a-1				*
M4B	395-470 mm	2008	Stained sand	D1	2a(3a)	30%					*
		2013	Natural sand								
Movers Lane (Western Area 3)(R1R01) Sample 40 - trackway											
M40A	150-230 mm	5154	wood peat - trackway	B2	1a1, 1a2, 1a3	35-70%					*
M40B	230-310 mm	5154	sandy peat upper	B2	1a1, 1a2	45-65%					*
Movers Lane (Western Area 3)(R1R01) Sample 44 - burned mound											
		5122	Laminated clay								
M44A	230-270 mm	5121	stained clays	E1	4a, 4a2(2c etc)	15%				aaa	
M44A	270-310 mm	5083 upper	burned mound	D4	2c, 2b, 4a	20%				aa	f
M44B	340-420 mm	5083 lower	burned mound	D3	2a, 2b, 2c	25%				a*	fffff
		5117	natural gravels								
Movers Lane (Western Area 3)(R1R01) Sample 47 - palaeosol											
M47A	30-110 mm	5204	Basal alluvium with charcoal	E3	4d, 2a	40%					
M47B	110-145 mm	5205	Basal alluvium with charcoal	E2	4b, 4c, 2a	35%					
M47B	145-185 mm	5142	Occup. Sands	D5	4b, 4c, 5a	40%	a-1(large)			a	fff
M47C	185-260mm	5195	Sands/gravels								

nine thin sections included an extra thin section funded by Macphail to try and extend context coverage. Thin sections were further polished with 1,000 grit papers and analysed using a petrological microscope under plane polarised light (PPL), crossed polarised light (XPL), oblique incident light (OIL) and using fluorescent microscopy (blue light – BL), at magnifications ranging from x1 to x200/400. Thin sections were described, ascribed soil microfabric types (MFTs) and microfacies types (MFTs)(see Tables A3.26 and A3.15), and counted according to established methods (Bullock *et al.* 1985; Courty 2001; Courty *et al.* 1989; Goldberg and Macphail 2006; Macphail and Cruise 2001; Stoops 2003). In addition, the quantitative microchemistry of materials within trackway sample M2A were analysed employing SEM-EDAX (Energy Dispersive X-ray Analysis), see Fig. A3.15, 27.

Results

Bulk analyses

The analytical results are presented in Table A3.25. Here, a broad overview is presented of the individual properties analysed. Key features relating to individual samples are highlighted in Table A3.25.

Organic matter (estimated by loss-on-ignition)

The samples exhibit quite wide variability in LOI (range, 0.618–46.5%). The highest values (≥ 9.74%) were recorded in the samples described as including peat, though in several cases the LOI does not appear to match the actual description, for example context 2007 is described as 'basal peat', but with a LOI of only 9.74% clearly contains a high proportion of sand; and the 'wood peat' of context 5154(u) has a slightly lower LOI (27.8%) than the underlying 'sandy peat upper' (29.7%). The remaining samples are largely minerogenic (ie LOI < 5.00%). Of these, the samples from contexts 5204 (basal alluvium) and 5083 (burnt mound), with LOI values of 4.84 and 4.91%, respectively, are notably more organic rich than the others. In the case of the former, significant amounts of charcoal were present, and this will have contributed to the higher LOI.

Total phosphate (phosphate-P)

The phosphate-P concentrations recorded are relatively low (range, 0.048–0.588mg g^{-1}). As might be anticipated, the lowest values were recorded in the three more sandy samples, sands having a low phosphate-retention capacity. Interestingly, context 5142 (occupation sands) has a much higher phosphate-P concentration (0.135 mg g^{-1}) than contexts 2008(u) and 2008(l) (stained sand) (0.059–0.048mg g^{-1}, respectively). Assuming that all three samples have a similar particle-size distribution, then this may indicate some degree of

phosphate enrichment in the occupation sands. Otherwise, only context 5083 (burnt mound) stands out as showing likely signs of enrichment (phosphate-P, 0.588mg g^{-1}).

Particle size

The results are consistent with the field descriptions of the various contexts. In each case the sand fraction largely comprises medium and fine sands (cf. coarse sands), which presumably reflects the character of the alluvial parent materials at these sites.

Overall, the results have demonstrated that there is considerable variability in all three properties analysed. They have enabled better characterisation of the various peaty samples, identified two contexts that show possible signs of phosphate enrichment, and provided detailed insight into the particle-size distribution of selected samples.

Soil micromorphology

Results are presented in Tables A3.26 and A3.15, and illustrated in Fig A3.15, 1-27; results are also supported by a CD-ROM photomicrographic archive (includes EDAX data, and 122 thin section digital scans and photomicrographs). Fourteen sub-units were identified in the 9 thin sections, and 25 characteristics were described and counted.

Woolwich Manor Way, Bronze Age trackway 2/14, Area 2 (sample 2, Fig.5.3)

Context 28; Wood Peat – trackway (M2)

This is layered (sub-units) with different microfacies at 650 (665)-70mm, 630-650 (665)mm and 620-630mm depth (A3.15, 2).

650(665)-700mm: This sub-unit (3) is a partially humified peat and coarse wood-dominated layer, which contains frequent scattered medium sand. Examples of fine burnt flint and coarse wood charcoal were recorded, alongside many ferruginised patches of peat.
This part of context 28 is a peat/wood peat affected by fluctuating water tables, hence peat humification and iron impregnation. Anthropogenic signals include the presence of coarse charcoal and burnt flint, which probably result from overlying trackway traffic and background human activities.

630-650(665)mm: This sub-unit (2) is a medium sand-dominated sediment with small amounts of clast type 1 (Ea horizon soil) and many fine to medium size wood and humified peat fragments. Rare traces of charcoal and rubefied grains are present. *In situ* woody roots, many ferruginised plant remains and relict roots occur. Relict patches of intercalated peat and sand are visible, and this sub-unit has a marked wavy and irregular lower boundary.

It is a mainly minerogenic medium sandy 'alluvium' containing peat and wood fragments, with *in situ* woody roots and trace amounts of charcoal and rubefied grains. Wavy boundary and peat-sand intercalations could imply trampling of this layer.

620-630mm: This uppermost sediment (sub-unit 1) is composed of fine wood and partially humified peat fragments, and contains a scatter of medium sand and few small gravel-size flint and rounded soil (Eb and Bt) and layered humic clay loam clasts (Fig. A3.15, 7-10). This layered clay loam has peat, clay, flint and burnt flint inclusions and a striated b-fabric, and contains rare traces of charcoal. *In situ* woody and monocotyledonous roots are present, alongside minor iron staining (SEM-EDAX investigations found that 'ferruginisation' produced concentrations of 8.10-13.5% Fe [n=4], and one clayey example had also been enriched in phosphate [0.88% P]. Overall, 46.5% LOI and 0.415 mg g^{-1} phosphate-P was recorded. It is a moderately sorted fluvial waterlogged sediment dominantly containing fine partially humified peat and wood fragments, with small flint and presumably local soil clasts. These soil clasts – and an example of humic stained layered clay loam, which contains peat and burnt flint fragments and is probably eroded from a muddy trackway (cf. prehistoric trackway sediments at Stanstead Airport studied through microprobe; Macphail and Crowther, 2005; 2008) – indicate redeposition of trampled and finely fragmented material.

As far as can be judged from this one thin section and bulk sample, it can be suggested that the Bronze Age trackway occupied a fen carr environment where peat formation alternated with alluvial sand deposition; this is also consistent with a geochemical log recording peaks of SiO$_2$ (Andrew Haggart, Greenwich University, pers comm). The trackway and its use is also recorded by the inclusion of soil clasts (Eb and Bt horizon) and 'wetland' clay clasts within the sediments, presumably eroded from local terrestrial soils and wetland, and deposited within in sub-units 1 and 2. In addition, charcoal, burnt flint and a layered fragment of 'trackway' sediment are also present. The peat itself is organic (46.5% LOI), but no remarkable phosphate concentrations (relating to animal traffic?) were recorded (0.415 mg g^{-1} phosphate-P). Inundated sites where waterlogged leaching is common often poorly preserve phosphate concentrations (Thirly *et al.* 2006); an example of phosphate (0.88% P) being fixed with secondary iron was however recorded by SEM/EDAX in the possible terrestrial trackway clast.

Woolwich Manor Way, early Neolithic to early Bronze Age palaeosol, T15 (sample 4, Fig. 5.3)

2008 Stained sand (M4B)

This is a moderately sorted compact coarse silt, fine and medium sand (see Table A3.25), with much fine charcoal and occasional fine burnt flint and quartzite. The fine fabric is weakly humic and contains much very fine charcoal, which thinly coats mineral grains and voids (Fig. A3.15, 11-13); more pure clay void coatings occur rarely. Fine and coarse woody root channels are present, with one channel also being infilled with peaty coarse silt. Weak ferruginisation is recorded throughout.

It is a homogenised occupation soil containing fragmented charcoal and fine burnt flint and quartzite from local burnt mound(s); trampling could have compacted and homogenized this soil as well as producing ubiquitous thin dusty coatings. It is also conceivable that these characteristics could also stem from context 2008 being a ploughsoil (Bronze Age ploughsoils of similar character are recorded from the fens and under Thames alluvium at Bermondsey, London (French 2003; Macphail *et al.* 1990; Merriman 1992; Sidell *et al.* 2000). A rise in the water table led to weak ferruginisation, while overlying wood peat formation is associated with woody rooting.

2008 Stained sand (M4A lower)

The top of the buried soil has a similar character to that in found in M4B below, but in addition, a fine humic pellety fine fabric becomes more common. Fine non-woody roots are partially preserved by ferruginisation. Woody roots become more common. An example of greyish clay void coatings is recorded.

This uppermost 30mm of buried soil records pedogenesis under increasingly moist (and natural topsoil) conditions, with the roots of the extant non-woody vegetation being partially preserved by ferruginisation (perhaps during an intermittent waterlogging stage). Trace evidence of possible marine(?) clay inwash (greyish clay void coatings) appears to have succeeded wood peat formation.

2007 Basal peat (M4A upper)

This partially once-layered, fine and medium sand contains very abundant humified organic matter (humified peat) as organic excrements within thin burrows (Fig. A3.15, 14). Abundant woody roots are present.

Occupation site and palaeosol burial by alluvial sand and wood peat formation is recorded. This sediment probably originally formed as a laminated and intercalated sand and peat, but was affected by a period (or periods) of fluctuating water tables leading to peat ripening and associated burrowing and organic excrement-replacement of the original peat sediment (Avery 1990, 323-325; Bal 1982; Dinç, *et al.* 1976).

The fine and medium sandy palaeosol (2008) and overlying moderately humic (9.74% LOI; Table A3.25) sandy peat (2007) at Trench 15, Woolwich Manor Way studied in thin sections M4A and M4B is a formed of a mature occupation soil and bioworked and humified sandy peat. The 'stained' sand appears to have been trampled, producing well-sorted and finely fragmented charcoal, and thin dusty void and grain coatings that include fine charcoal. Other clay deposition is also recorded, and at least one phase could relate to inundation. No humic topsoil, as such, is present. It can be suggested that this was eroded during phases of alluvial sand and peat formation. The site was affected by fluctuating water tables, allowing soil mesofauna to work the humified peat.

Movers Lane, Bronze Age trackway 5268, western Area 3 (sample 40, Fig. 7.5)

5154 sandy peat upper (M40B)

This is a broadly layered wood peat, with wood fragments and woody roots, and a scattered fine and medium sand component (Fig. A3.15, 1 and 4). Rare fine and very fine charcoal, a burnt flint fragment (Fig. A3.15, 15) and charred humic soil fragment occur. Layers of silty peat sediment occur also as a 5-10mm thick, 15mm-wide, undulating and curved infill (Fig. A3.15, 4, 16-17). The upper sandy peat and peaty sand are humic (29.7% and 17.0% LOI, respectively), but no obvious phosphate-P enrichment is recognised. Broad burrowing, thin organic excrements, and later, abundant gypsum crystal formation, are also recorded.

A sandy wood peat formed that included periodic inwash of fine detrital peat and medium and coarse silt. This silty peat forms incomplete layers and an example of an undulating fine fill. The latter appears to be anomalous and could *possibly* be part of an animal(?) print. One fill includes a charred very coarse sand-size humic sandy topsoil fragment. Rare charcoal occurs throughout the sediment sequence, and one small fragment of burnt flint also testifies to an anthropogenic input. As the detrital peat includes humified peat, it is impossible to recognise if finely fragmented dung is present. The sediments were occasionally burrowed and worked by mesofauna. This level of bioactivity and minor iron-staining records generally continuous waterlogged conditions, with occasional drying out. Gypsum formation probably reflects changed environmental conditions after marine inundation.

5154 wood peat – trackway (M40A)

This is a broadly layered monocotyledonous and wood peat, over humic silt containing detrital fine organic matter. Small amounts of sand and one example of flint gravel, rare fine charcoal and an example of sand-size burnt flint occur. Some infills and one clast are very rich in very fine charcoal.

Monocotyledonous roots and peaty material show strong humification and sometimes strong iron impregnation, compared to (later) woody roots. Minor burrowing, with organic excrements, and abundant gypsum formation is visible. The peaty layer is notably organic with 27.8% LOI.

Layers of detrital organic matter-rich silts and mainly monocotyledonous peat show moderately strong humification and iron impregnation (fluctuating water table). Later(?) woody rooting (wood peat formation) occurred as conditions became permanently waterlogged. Trackway use and fluctuating water tables led to inwash of very fine charcoal-rich silts, along with rare additions of sand, burnt flint and charcoal. Later marine inundation of the site likely resulted in gypsum formation.

Movers Lane, Bronze Age burnt mound 5264, western Area 3 (sample 44, Fig. 7.15)

5083 Burnt mound (M44B1, M44B2)

This a heterogeneous very poorly sorted stony soil deposit with both leached loamy sands (Fig. A3.15, 2, 6 and 18), and humic and fine charcoal rich sandy loam. Upwards, increasing amounts of reddish brown sandy loam-silty clay loam soil, containing fine charcoal, is present, mainly as broad burrow infills (Fig. A3.15, 19). The deposit is very charcoal and burnt flint/chert-rich, and trace amounts of fine burnt bone were found (Fig. A3.15, 20). Very abundant dusty clay intercalations occur alongside thick matrix void coatings; reddish clay infills are also present. Many broad burrows are visible, and moderate iron-staining is recorded. Overall weak phosphate enrichment (0.588mg g^{-1} phosphate-P), a sandy silt loam texture and a 4.91% LOI was measured (Table A3.25).

This is a markedly heterogeneous stony, burnt flint and charcoal-rich burnt mound deposit, formed of once-humic and loamy fine charcoal-rich occupation soils which had developed upwards from leached upper subsoil sands. Traces of fine burnt bone occur as evidence of probable food preparation. The abundance of textural pedofeatures (intercalations and matrix infills) and coarse heterogeneity indicate mixing by trampling of an often muddy substrate; minor likely burrow mixing by earthworms also took place. These mesofauna also mixed rubefied clayey soil from overlying mound deposits. Although these burrows may also possibly be associated with alluvial clay washing through as a record of inundation history, it is additionally considered that the site was likely being affected by ongoing episodic clayey alluviation during the occupation itself. This may have helped thicken the silty clay loam mound above the naturally *in situ* subsoil sands and the natural gravels (context 5117).

Upper 5083 – burnt mound (M44A)

This part of context 5083 is similar to that found in

M44B, below, but is much less stony with smaller burnt flint and less coarse charcoal. Reddish soil as strongly rubefied and finely fissured clay loam and as iron-stained once-humic(?) clayey soil also occur more commonly than below. It is present as clasts and as burrow fills, with some of the latter associated with impure clay void coatings. Intercalations are equally abundant in this very heterogeneous deposit.

Continuing use (trampling) of the site, but with continuing and possibly increasing frequency of clayey alluviation, led to clayey soil accretion over the stony burnt mound itself. Indeed, alluvial clay itself seems to have got burnt/used for hearth construction, and this burnt soil was mixed by trampling and burrowed down-profile. Alluviation may also have led to truncation and reworking of these occupation soils/upper burnt mound; grey alluvium has also been burrowed down-profile. It seems likely that continuing human disturbance occurred, hence the unclear boundary with the overlying stained alluvium (Context 5121).

5121 Stained clays (M44A)

This context is composed of mixed sandy silt loam alluvial soil and clayey alluvial clasts and infills. Some small charcoal and burnt flint and much soil from the underlying burnt mound, including rubefied clay and blackened burnt topsoil, are also present. Muddy pans and infills – some 1-2mm thick – occur, alongside brownish clay infills (Fig. A3.15, 2, 5, 21-22). Iron staining and iron hydroxide infills/plant pseudomorphs occur. This layer records 3.15% LOI, and has a 40.0% silt and 48.8% clay content (Table A3.25)

5121 can be characterised as a muddy slurry of eroded mound material (including burnt soil, charcoal and small burnt flint) and locally trampled(?) silty clay alluvium. Textural pans formed and the deposit as a whole was also earthworm-burrowed at times. Fragments of pure alluvial clayey sediment also occur as sedimentary clasts, while clayey inwash from the overlying alluvial clay is also recorded. The exact origins of this context are not clear, but inundation, erosion and disturbance could have been occurring as the site became wetter and more frequently influenced by clayey alluviation.

Movers Lane, palaeochannel deposit 5142, western Area 3 (sample 47, Fig. 7.5)

5142 Occupation sands (M47B)

These are heterogeneous and, upwards poorly layered, mainly leached medium to very coarse sands and gravels. They contain traces of an argillic clay matrix. The upper layered part includes coarse argillic soil (fine sandy silt loam with clay void and grain clay coatings) clast. There are also poorly bedded sands; one layer is for example relatively rich in medium sand size limonite (weakly-developed gravity separation). Rare traces of burnt flint occur (3.5mm). Many part-humified and iron-stained woody roots (4-8mm) are present. Humic (alluvial) clay contains humified plant fragments, diatoms and phytoliths, while sometimes fine charcoal occurs in relict root channels. In addition, silty clay occurs. One example of void clay coatings formed in this clay was observed. Sands are very poorly humic (0.690% LOI) but may show weak phosphate-P enrichment (0.135 mg g^{-1}).

This context is composed of truncated, disturbed natural sands and gravels which had originally developed an argillic brown sand soil. The last is now evidenced by relict fine matrix material and by a locally eroded coarse (10mm) clast of fine sandy silt loam argillic Bt horizon soil. Occupation led to the inclusion of rare traces of burnt flint, and weakly enriched phosphate-P content (see 5204 below). Woody rooting during fen carr development (and continued occupation) led to inwash of humic clay containing phytoliths, diatoms and sometimes fine charcoal.

5204 Basal alluvium with charcoal (M47B)

These are formed by heterogeneous, intercalated and broadly bedded medium and fine sands and humic silty clay (Fig. A3.15, 23). The homogenised grain size of these two components averages out as a sandy loam (Table A3.25). The sediments contain detrital plant fragments, charcoal (possible charred bark), and include an example of burnt bone (2.5mm), and a 2mm-size burnt sandy soil clast and rare fine burnt flint were also recorded. (The bone fragment seems have attracted fungal activity.)

This basal alluvium is characterised by both low energy humic silty clay and higher energy sands. Included charcoal, burnt bone, burnt flint and a burnt soil example, all testify to the erosion of burnt mounds/occupation soils locally.

5204 Basal alluvium with charcoal (M47A)

The alluvium continues upwards as intercalated and broadly bedded humic clayey silts and clean medium sands. Rare fine charcoal but very abundant very fine to coarse detrital blackened and humified woody plant fragments (up to 6mm) occur – and some are horizontally oriented; phytoliths and diatoms also occur (Fig. A3.15, 25). This humic content, along with clasts of humified peat, have produced 4.84% LOI and 0.251mg g^{-1} phosphate-P content. Fine woody roots seem to be post-dated by monocotyledonous plant roots; the latter are often iron impregnated and associated with iron hypocoatings when penetrating fine sediments. Coarse (1.5mm) prismatic gypsum formation has affected the sediments (Fig. A3.15, 26).

These sediments record alternating deposition of sands and humic silts, with small amounts of charcoal, although abundant humifed (blackened) woody plant material may have appeared charcoal-like in the field. The sediments may be recording rapidly migrating(?) stream flow (sands) and overbank flooding (humic silts), with fen carr wood peat being eroded during this process. Only background human activity (rare charcoal) seems to have been recorded. Changing environmental conditions – marine inundation(?) – led to a monocotyledonous vegetation becoming dominant, and secondary iron and gypsum formation took place.

Discussion

Local soils: modern and ancient soil cover

The A13 route currently runs through urban areas where soils are unmapped. It is possible, however, to extrapolate from the soil cover mapped east of the road route, to suggest that the mid-Holocene soils were typical argillic brown earths (Huckers-brook soil association) or argillic gley soils (Hurst soil association) formed in coarse and fine loamy river terrace drift, which also included gravel (Jarvis *et al.* 1983; 1984). Currently, the margins of the River Thames have a pelo-alluvial gley soil cover formed in marine alluvium (Wallasea 1 soil association); further north of the Thames, tributaries of the Thames are characterised by pelo-alluvial gley soils formed in river alluvium (Fladbury 1 soil association). At Movers Lane and Woolwich Manor Way, the samples studied were selected from sediments that underlie these pelo-alluvial gley soils formed in alluvium. The effects of marine inundation, which can be marked (Boorman *et al.* 2002; Macphail 1994; Macphail 2009; Macphail *et al.* 2010), were apparently only recorded by secondary gypsum formation, for example at Movers Lane (Fig. A3.15, 26) (Kooistra 1978). Waterlogging of the sites due to rising base levels, peat formation and freshwater alluviation, even prior to marine inundation, undoubtedly caused iron depletion and secondary ferruginisation, while loss of phosphate is also likely if in an unstable form; bone fragments may remain but their phosphate content may be reduced (Crowther 2000; Huisman 2009; Macphail *et al.* 2010; Thirly *et al.* 2006).

Thin section sub-sampling of the monoliths allowed the uppermost soil horizons of the Mid-Late Holocene soils to be examined and characterised. At Movers Lane, leached and iron-depleted sandy and gravelly subsoils of the argillic brown earths are recorded below the burnt mound (sample 44; Fig. A3.15, 2, 6 and 18), while the layered and mixed upper 'palaeosol' in sample 47 included a large (10mm) clast of fine sandy silt loam argillic Bt horizon soil. In addition, at Woolwich Manor Way rounded clasts of iron and clay-depleted soil found in trackway deposits are consistent with being fragments of Eb horizon soil that have been eroded from the argillic brown earth cover; a rounded fragment of eroded Bt soil was also recorded in sample 2 (Fig A3.15, 7-8). Argillic brown earth soils have the following horizons: topsoil Ah, upper

subsoil Eb and subsoil Bt. The local presence of these soils and river drift deposits of coarse silts, fine and medium sands is also recorded in the overlying alluvial sediments which contain these grain sizes (Table A3.15; Fig. A3.15, 16-17, 21-22 and 23-24).

Occupation soils and burnt mound

Occupation soils were studied from both Movers Lane and Woolwich Manor Way. At Woolwich Manor Way the early Neolithic to early Bronze Age palaeosol ('stained sand'), is a sand that shows no phosphate enrichment (Table A3.25), but which contains much fine anthropogenic material (burnt flint and charcoal). As discussed earlier, this homogenisation and the presence of dusty clay void coatings (Fig. A3.15, 11-12) can be ascribed to human trampling or cultivation, or both processes (cf. Bronze Age Phoenix Wharf, Bermondsey (Macphail *et al.* 1990; Merriman 1992; Sidell 2003; Sidell *et al.* 2000) (cf. 'equifinality', Goldberg and Macphail 2006, 356). Without a wider sample these speculations cannot be taken further.

At Movers Lane, it can be noted that both the Bronze Age palaeosol (sample 47) and the burnt mound (sample 44) show signs of being both truncated and thickened – the last probably by both trampling and alluviation. Minor phosphate-enrichment was noted in these two occupation deposits (Table A3.25), and traces of burnt bone were recognised in the burnt mound for example, in addition to ubiquitous burnt flint and charcoal (Fig. A3.15, 2, 6 and 19-20). It can be noted that the burnt mound (sample 44) contains coarse charcoal compared to the 'stained sands' at Woolwich Manor Way (sample 4). Microstratigraphic analysis of the burnt mound revealed the movement of red clays down profile, as both wash and burrow-infills. A 'burnt' surface, however, is absent, and has been lost by trampling or alluvial erosion. These red clays (Fig. A3.15, 5 and 19-20) are the likely result of K in ash mobilising rubefied clay, as found in some burnt tree-throw holes and pits (Courty and Fedoroff 1982; Goldberg and Macphail 2006; Slager and Van der Wetering 1977). In addition to trampling, the mound is thickened by clayey alluvium, which is also intercalated with partially trampled spreads of occupation soils (eg. burnt topsoil fragments) in the overlying muddy 'stained clays'. It can also be noted that the burnt mound deposits at Ebbsfleet, Kent were affected by colluviation (Macphail and Crowther forth-coming).

The 'occupation sands' of the palaeosol in sample 47 are truncated and the uppermost deposits included an eroded fragment of Bt horizon material, while overlying sands display a small concentration of sand-size limonite as an example of weak gravity separation (cf. placer deposits). Clearly, this 'old ground surface' was being fluvially worked as water tables rose and flooding took place.

Bronze Age trackway deposits

Trackway deposits were investigated from both sites. Unlike trackways studied elsewhere, such as the Stanstead and Terminal 5 sites at London Heathrow (Framework Archaeology 2006; 2010; Macphail 2003; Macphail and Crowther 2005; Macphail and Crowther 2006; Macphail and Crowther 2008; Macphail and Crowther 2009; Macphail and Cruise 1997-2003), these trackways are constructed of roundwood etc, with one at Woolwich Manor Way (Area 2) being some 1.20m wide and 0.30m thick. In thin section these are obviously rich in woody material, and include peaty sediments; a maximum 46.5% LOI was measured in sample 2. No bulk phosphate enrichment was found in contrast to many terrestrial trackway deposits. Sediments associated with the trackway at Woolwich Manor Way, however, include anomalous amounts of eroded soil clasts (see above) in sandy layers which imply traffic from 'dryland' onto wetland where eroded/ trampled soil was locally reworked (Fig. A3.15. 7-8). Moreover, there appears to be one possible example of iron-stained, and in places phosphate-enriched, terrestrial trackway sediment, which includes peat fragments, charcoal and burnt flint (Fig. A3.15, 9-10 and 27). Terrestrial material was therefore apparently 'tracked-in' along the trackway – probably by people, as the structure is only narrow – and locally reworked by stream flow (Fig. A3.15, 3). Undulating sediment boundaries may also imply trampling effects.

At Movers Lane (sample 40), again sediments within and below the trackway record rare inclusions of anthropogenic materials (examples of burnt flint and charred topsoil (Fig. A3.15, 15-17)). A possible humic silt-infilled animal(?) print was noted (Fig. A3.15, 4 and 16-17), possibly recording muddy conditions, and slowly infilling puddles, along the trackway. At Iron Age Goldcliff, Gwent probable cattle prints along a episodically inundated droveway in the salt marshes, had slowly infilled with impure clayey sediments (Macphail and Cruise 2000). At Movers Lane and Woolwich Manor Way there are too few samples (only 3 thin sections in all) to say more about the use and environment associated with these trackways.

Alluvium

It seems quite clear that the Bronze Age land surfaces were affected not only by flooding and sedimentation, but also by erosion, sometimes all happening whilst the sites were still being utilised (Fig. A3.15, 5-6 and 21-22). Coarse (sandy), fine (silty) and very fine (clayey at Movers Lane burnt mound) sedimentation are all recorded (Table A3.25), alongside wood peat formation for example. Fluctuating water tables are also evidenced by humification (ripening) of peat and its transformation into organic excrements by small invertebrate mesofauna (Dinç *et al.* 1976). Bedded humic silts and non-humic sands occur (Fig. A3.15, 23-25), with the humic silts containing high amounts of detrital humified wood peat and other peat fragments. The exact processes are unknown, but may have included alternating (and migrating) stream flow(?) (sands) and backswamp(?) sedimentation (humic silts) which also testify to weathering and erosion of local peat.

Conclusions

A variety of landscapes and features (palaeosols, occupation soils, burnt mounds, trackways, developing wetland) were studied employing 9 thin sections and 11 bulk samples from Movers Lane and Woolwich Manor Way. The local landscape had an inferred argillic brown earth soil cover, and fragments of this soil type were found in Bronze Age trackway sediments at Woolwich Manor Way; a possible terrestrial trackway soil fragment was also recognised. Evidence of the argillic soil cover was also recorded in palaeosols and at the burnt mound at Movers Lane. Muddy puddles and infills associated with sediment formation, developed along a trackway at Movers Lane; one 'puddle' may speculatively have originated as an animal(?) print.

The early Neolithic to early Bronze Age occupation palaeosol at Woolwich Manor Way formed either by trampling or by cultivation, or possibly through a combination of both processes. At Movers Lane, occupation soils and the burnt mound were affected by trampling and by sediment accretion from both occupation disturbance and contemporary alluviation. At the top of the burnt mound occupation deposits are intercalated upwards within the alluvium, as muddy spreads. Across both sites, ensuing peats were affected by both humification and biological working in places (fluctuating water tables), and alternating and migrating stream flow led to sands (stream flow?) and humic silt (backswamp?) deposition, as local peats were weathered and eroded. These interpretations, however, must remain speculative as sample coverage of the different landscapes and features was small.

Table A3.27   Soil micromorphology : descriptions

Microfacies type (MFT)/ Sample No. Soil microfabric type (SMT)	Depth (relative depth) Soil Micromorphology (SM)	Preliminary Interpretation and Comments

Woolwich Manor Way (WMW) Trench 2 Sample 2 - trackway

MFT A1/SMT 1a1 M2A	620-700mm SM: Moderate homogeneous layers; *Microstructure*: massive, layered: 620-630mm: 65% voids, simple packing voids; *Coarse Mineral*: C:F (limit at 10μm), 100:0, poorly sorted fine and medium sand-size quartz, with few small (1-2.5mm) flint and rounded soil-sediment aggregates (type 1: pale moderately sorted coarse silt and fine-medium sand [eroded natural river terrace soil/weathered Eb horizon]; type 2: brown micaceous silt and sandy loam, with grano-striate b-fabric and humic-staining [eroded subsoil Bt horizon); type 3: brown humic-stained clay with embedded amorphous peat fragments, clay soil clasts, small flint and burned flint, with layered, striated b-fabric (trampled trackway fragment); *Coarse Organic and Anthropogenic*: dominant fine (2-3mm) wood and humified peat fragments (see SMT 1a), with rare fine (1mm) monocotyledonous roots and many medium to coarse (10mm) woody roots; rare charcoal; *Pedofeatures: Amorphous*: occasional ferruginisation of organic material. SEM-EDAX: 'Ferruginisation' produced 8.10-13.5% Fe concentrations (*n*=4), and one example of 0.88% P.	Context 28; Wood Peat – trackway Layered with, 620-630mm: sediment of fine wood and partially humified peat fragments, with scatter of medium sand and few small gravel-size flint and rounded soil (Ea and Bt) and layered humic clay loam clasts. Layered clay loam has peat, clay, flint and burned flint inclusions and striated b-fabric; rare trace of charcoal. *In situ* woody and monocotyledonous roots are present, alongside minor iron staining. (46.5% LOI and 0.415mg g^{-1} phosphate-P was recorded) *Moderately sorted fluvial waterlogged sediment dominantly containing fine partially humified peat and wood fragments, with small flint and local soil clasts. These soil clasts and an example of humic stained layered clay loam, containing peat and burned flint fragments – which is probably eroded from a muddy trackway – indicate redeposition of trampled and finely fragmented material.*
MFT B1/SMT 1a	630-650 (665) mm: 50% voids, simple packing voids, vughs and coarse channels; *Coarse Mineral*: C:F, 95:05, moderately sorted medium and coarse sand-size rounded quartz; rare Clast type 1; trace amounts of micas; *Coarse Organic and Anthropogenic*: frequent to common fine to medium (2-5mm) wood and partially humified peat fragments, with many medium to coarse (10mm) woody roots; rare trace of charcoal and rubefied grains; *Fine Fabric*: SMT 1a1: reddish brown (PPL), generally isotropic or with very low interference colours (relict cellulose)(XPL), black to blackish brown (OIL); very dominant amorphous organic matter with tissue and organ remains; *Pedofeatures: Amorphous*: many ferruginisation of organic material; *Fabric*: relict patches of intercalated peat and sand. Wavy and irregular boundary.	Medium sand dominated sediment with small amounts of clast type 1 (Eb horizon soil) and many fine to medium size wood and humified peat fragments; rare trace of charcoal and rubefied grains. In situ woody roots; many ferruginised plant remains and relict roots. Relict patches of intercalated peat and sand, and marked wavy and irregular boundary. *Mainly minerogenic medium sandy alluvium containing peat and wood fragments, with in situ woody roots and trace amounts of charcoal and rubefied grains. Wavy boundary and peat-sand intercalations could imply trampling.*
MFT C1/SMT 1a	650(665)-700mm: 70% voids, mainly coarse simple packing voids and fissures; *Coarse Mineral*: C:F, 100:0, well sorted frequent medium sand; *Coarse Organic and Anthropogenic*: very dominant coarse	Partially humified peat and coarse wood dominated layer, with frequent scatter of medium sand; examples of fine burned flint and coarse wood charcoal;

wood (25mm), woody roots (10mm) and humified peat (SMT 1a); rare charcoal (4mm) and example of burned flint (2mm); *Fine Fabric:* as SMT 1a1; *Pedofeatures: Amorphous:* many moderate iron impregnation of organic matter.

many ferruginised patches of peat.
Peat/wood peat affected by fluctuating water tables, hence peat humification and iron impregnation; anthropogenic signals include presence of coarse charcoal and burned flint – affects of traffic from above.

Woolwich Manor Way (WMW) Trench 15 Sample 4 - palaeosol

MFT /SMT 1b	M4A upper	320-360mm		2007 Basal peat

SM: Homogeneous; *Microstructure:* massive with very poor layering; 55% voids, simple and complex packing voids, medium to coarse (4mm) root channels; *Coarse Mineral:* C:F, SMT 1b, well sorted fine and medium sand-size quartz; *Coarse Organic and Anthropogenic:* abundant woody root traces; Fine Fabric: SMT 1b: dark reddish brown (PPL), isotropic (mainly interaggregate with coated grain, undifferentiated b-fabric, XPL), very dark reddish to black brown (OIL); very abundant humified amorphous organic matter; *Pedofeatures: Amorphous:* weak trace of ferruginisation; *Fabric:* very abundant thin (250 μm) burrows; *Excrements:* very abundant very thin to thin organic excrements.
Sharp, horizontal boundary.

2007 Basal peat
Poorly once-layered fine and medium sands and very abundant humified organic matter (humified peat) as organic excrements within thin burrows; abundant woody roots.
Site/palaeosol burial by alluvial sand and wood peat formation. This formed probably laminated and intercalated sand and peat, but this was affected by period or periods of fluctuating watertables leading peat ripening and associated burrowing and excrement-replacement of peat.

MFT D2/SMT 2b — M4A lower — 360-395mm — 2008 Stained sand

SM: Generally homogeneous, thin mixing of SMT 1c in topmost few mm; *Microstructure:* massive; 35% voids, fine vughs and closed vughs, with common medium to coarse (7mm) extant root channels; *Coarse Mineral:* C:F, as SMT 2a; *Coarse Organic and Anthropogenic:* many medium to coarse (1-7mm) woody(?) root traces, with rare traces of non-woody fine roots (Fe stained) 1-2mm wide; occasional fine charcoal (max 4mm); occasional fine burned mineral, including weakly calcined flint and quartzite (fine to coarse sand-size, angular); rare trace examples of sand size aggregate mixed type 1/2 (upper Bt/lower Ea); enigmatic greenish clayey material (weathered glauconite/inwashed base-rich clay??); *Fine Fabric:* SMT 2b: dusty and speckled dark brown becoming reddish upwards in places (PPL), mainly isotropic (mainly intergrain aggregate/pellety, undifferentiated b-fabric, XPL), darkish orange brown (OIL); thin humic staining, with many amorphous and charred very fine organic matter *Pedofeatures: Textural:* rare trace of 100 μm thick pale grey finely dusty clay void coatings/infills (same channels as non-woody roots); *Amorphous:* abundant moderate Fe-impregnation of earlier roots and charcoal.

2008 Stained sand
This top of the buried soil has a similar character to that in M4B below, but in addition, fine humic pellety fine fabric becomes more common; fine non-woody roots are partially preserved by ferruginisation. Woody roots become more common. An example of greyish clay coatings is recorded.
This uppermost 30mm records soil formation under increasingly moist conditions, with the roots of the extant non-woody vegetation being partially preserved by ferruginisation (during intermittent waterlogging stage). Trace evidence of possible marine clay inwash – succeeding wood peat formation.

MFT D1/SMT 2a(3a)	M4B	395-470mm		2008 Stained sand

SM: Generally homogeneous, with very dominant SMT 2a and very few 3a; *Microstructure:* massive, with poorly formed fine prisms; 30% voids, fine, sometimes closed vughs, with fine vertical fissures, and with very fine to coarse (1-7mm) extant root channels; *Coarse Mineral:* C:F, SMT 2a: 75:25, moderately poorly sorted coarse silt, fine and medium sand-size quartz (and feldspar), with very few weathered glauconite and mica; very few fine flint gravel present; SMT 3a: C:F 50:50, well sorted coarse silt; *Coarse Organic and Anthropogenic:* occasional very fine to coarse (1-7mm) woody(?) root traces; many fine charcoal (max 2mm); occasional fine burned mineral, including weakly calcined quartzite and flint (fine to coarse sand-size, angular); *Fine Fabric:* SMT 2a: dusty and speckled dark brown (PPL), very low interference colours (intergrain aggregate and coated grain, speckled b-fabric, XPL), darkish orange brown (OIL); thin humic staining, with many amorphous and charred very fine organic matter; SMT 3a: blackish brown (PPL), very low interference colours or isotropic (porphyric, speckled or undifferentiated b-fabric, XPL), dark reddish brown (OIL); very abundant amorphous and sometimes strongly humified organic matter and rare fine charred; *Pedofeatures: Textural:* abundant very thin (25μm) dusty clay, often partially iron-stained grain and void coatings, sometimes containing very fine charcoal; example of 1mm thick fine channel fill of coarse humic silt (SMT 3a); *Amorphous:* abundant weak iron staining and replacement of clay coatings and amorphous infills, rare staining weathered glauconite.

Moderately sorted compact coarse silt, fine and medium sand (see Table A3.25), with many fine charcoal and occasional fine burned flint and quartzite. The fine fabric is weakly humic and contains much very fine charcoal, and thinly coats mineral grains and voids. Fine and coarse woody root channels are present, with one channel also being infilled with peaty coarse silt. Weak ferruginisation is recorded throughout.

This is a trampled occupation soil containing fragmented charcoal and fine burned flint and quartzite (from local burned mound(s); trampling compacted and homogenized this soil as well as producing ubiquitous thin dusty coatings. It is possible that K from ash may have accelerated the formation of these textural pedofeatures. Water table rise led to weak ferruginisation while overlying wood peat formation is associated with woody rooting.

2013 Natural sand

Movers Lane (Western Area 3) (R1R01) Sample 40 - trackway

MFT B2/SMT 1a1, 1a2, 1a3	M40A	150-230mm		5154 wood peat – trackway

SM: Broadly layered with SMT 1a1 (150-190mm) and 1a2 (190-230mm); 5mm patch of of SMT 1a3; *Microstructure:* finely laminated and broadly layered; 55% voids, SMT 1a1: 70% voids, subhorizontal fissures, open vughs and simple and complex packing voids; SMT 1a2: 35% voids, open vughs associated with plant inclusions; *Coarse Mineral:* C:F, as below; very few (example of) gravel-size flint (7mm); *Coarse Organic and Anthropogenic:* rare trace of fine charcoal; example of mediun sand-size burned flint; example of fine charcoal-rich fragmented clasts(s)/infill (5mm) SMT 1a3; abundant (strongly iron impregnated) monocot roots (5mm) and very abundant monocot plant material fragments (tissues and organs; peat); very abundant humified monocot

Broadly layered monocotyledonous and wood peat over humic silt containing detrital fine organic matter; small amounts of sand and one example of flint gravel; rare fine charcoal and an example of sand-size burned flint occur. Some infills/example of clast are very rich in very fine charcoal. Monocotyledonous roots and peaty material show strong humification and sometimes strong iron impregnation, compared to (later) woody roots. Minor burrowing, with organic excrements, and abundant gypsum formation. Peaty layer is notably organic with 27.8% LOI.

and woody(?) OM; many non-iron impregnated (later??) woody roots (7mm) in silty SMT 1a2 layer; *Fine Fabric:* SMT 1a3: very dotted greyish brown (PPL), low interference colours (very open porphyric, speckled (micaceous/fine silty) b-fabric, XPL), grey with black and reddish brown inclusions (OIL): very abundant amorphous OM and plant tissues with abundant fine charcoal; *Pedofeatures: Textural:* occasional humic silt inwash, forming pans(?) or within decaying plant roots(?)(contains rare or very abundant very fine charcoal); Crystalline: abundant small gypsum crystal formation, including typical prisms; *Amorphous:* many amorphous iron staining of plant material; *Fabric:* occasional very broad (2-3mm) vertical burrows; *Excrements:* many very thin (100µm) organic excrements.

Layers of detrital organic matter-rich silts and mainly monocotyledonous peat show moderately strong humification and iron impregnation (fluctuating water table). Later(?) woody rooting (wood peat formation) occurred as conditions became permanently waterlogged. Trackway use and fluctuating water tables led to inwash of very fine charcoal-rich silts, along with rare additions of sand, burned flint and charcoal. Marine inundation of the site resulted in gypsum formation.

MFT B2/SMT 1a1 and 1a2	M40B		

230-310mm

SM: Broadly layered with SMT 1a1 and 1a2; *Microstructure:* massive, broadly layered (15mm) and laminated (10mm); 45-65% voids, medium and coarse root channels; *Coarse Mineral:* C:F, SMT 1a1 – 40/60:60/40 – moderately sorted coarse silt to fine and medium sand, with very few subrounded flint (3mm); SMT 1a2 – 55:45, well sorted medium and coarse silt and very fine sand; *Coarse Organic and Anthropogenic:* rare fine charcoal (max 2.5mm); very abundant wood and woody roots (11mm), lignified bark material; occasional non-woody plant fragments (monocots?); examples of burned flint shard (2mm) and 1mm-size blackened (burned) humic sandy soil; very abundant humified organic matter present – but impossible to identify dung traces – natural humified peaty material present; *Fine Fabric:* SMT 1a2: finely dotted brown and reddish brown (PPL), low interference colours (close porphyric, speckled b-fabric (fine silt ['silasepic'] and fine cellulose plant cells), XPL), orange brown (OIL); humic with very abundant amorphous OM and fine tissue fragments; phytoliths and diatoms present; rare very fine charred OM; *Pedofeatures: Textural:* occasional examples of 5-10mm thick curved and undulating peaty silt infills – 15mm wide (animal trample? and infill??); *Crystalline:* very abundant small gypsum crystal formation, including typical prisms; *Amorphous:* rare amorphous iron staining of plant material; *Fabric:* occasional very broad (2-3mm) vertical burrows; *Excrements:* many very thin (100µm) organic excrements.

5154 Sandy peat upper
Broadly layered wood peat, with wood fragments and woody roots, and a scattered fine and medium sand component. Rare fine and very fine charcoal, a burned flint fragment and charred humic soil fragment occur. Layers of silty peat sediment occur also as 5-10mm thick 15mm-wide undulating and curved infill. Upper sandy peat and peaty sand are humic (29.7% and 17.0-% LOI, respectively); but no obvious phosphate-P enrichment is recognised. Broad burrowing, thin organic excrements, and later, abundant gypsum crystal formation, are recorded.
A sandy wood peat formed that included periodic inwash of fine detrital peat and medium and coarse silt. This silty peat forms incomplete layers and an example of an undulating fine fill, which could possibly be part of an animal print. One fill includes a charred very coarse sand-size humic sandy topsoil fragment. Rare charcoal occur throughout the sediment sequence, and one small fragment of burned flint also testifies to an anthropogenic input. As the detrital peat includes humified peat, it is impossible to recognise if finely fragmented dung is present. The sediments were occasionally burrowed and worked by mesofauna. This bioactivity and minor iron-staining records generally continuous waterlogged conditions, with occasional drying out. Gypsum formation probably reflects changed environmental after marine inundation.

Movers Lane (Western Area 3)(R1R01) Sample 44 - burned mound

MFT E1/SMT
4a/4a2, with 2a,
2c, 2d and 2e

MFT D4/SMT 2a,
2c with 2d and 4a

M44A

230-270mm

SM: Heterogeneous, becoming more homogeneous up-profile (dominant 4a [and more brownish 4a2], with clasts of 2a, 2c, 2d and 2e (as 2d blackened/burned with fine charcoal); *Microstructure:* 15% voids (fine fissures), but with 2-3mm size planar voids separating medium prisms (25% voids); *Coarse Mineral:* C:F, SMT 4a-4a2: 45:55, becoming 20:80 up-profile; well sorted coarse silt with few fine and medium sand; alluvial clay clasts and mound soil clasts also incorporated; *Coarse Organic and Anthropogenic:* rare fine (<1mm) charcoal and burned flint; Fine Fabric: SMT 4a2: speckled pale to darkish brown (PPL), moderately high interference colours (open porphyric, speckled and grano-striate b-fabric (mica present), XPL), orange grey to pale orange (OIL); very weak humic staining and rare relict ferruginised OM, trace of fine charcoal; *Pedofeatures: Textural:* very abundant textural intercalations, with 1-2mm thick silty clay pans and infills marking approximate boundary between 5083 and 5121, and many 2-300µm thick moderately oriented brownish clay (alluvial) infills; *Amorphous:* many Fe broad impregnations and occasional amorphous ferruginisation of plant material and void infills; *Fabric:* very abundant mixing of different soil material and alluvium – possibly muddy slurry of mound and alluvial soil and alluvial clay components; *Fabric:* many broad burrows.

Diffuse, mixed unclear boundary

(5122 Laminated clay)
5121 Stained clays
Mixed sandy silt loam alluvial soil and clayey alluvial clasts and infills, with some small charcoal and burned flint and much soil from the burned mound, including rubefied clay and blackened burned topsoil. Muddy pans and infills – some 1-2 mm thick – occur, alongside brownish clay infills. Iron staining and iron hydroxide infills/plant pseudomorphs occur. (3.15% LOI, 40.0% silt and 48.8% clay recorded)

Muddy slurry of eroded mound material (including burned soil, charcoal and small burned flint), local mobilised silty clay alluvium, forming pans and also being earthworm-burrowed at times. Fragments of pure alluvial clayey sediment also occur as clasts. Clayey inwash from the overlying alluvial clay. The exact origins of this context are not clear, but inundation, erosion and disturbance could have been occurring as the site became wetter and more often influenced by clayey alluviation.

270-310mm

SM: Very heterogeneous (common 2a, 2c, and frequent 2d, very few 4a); *Microstructure:* massive becoming fine and medium prismatic upwards (5204-5142 boundary); 20% voids, mainly very fine and fine fissures, vertical fissures (100-300µm wide); *Coarse Mineral:* C:F, 65:35, poorly sorted coarse silt, fine and medium sand (quartz and quartzite), with few chert (4mm) and quartzite (8mm) gravel; *Coarse Organic and Anthropogenic:* many fine burned flint (4-5mm), occasional coarse (5mm) charcoal; abundant burned soil (SMT 2c or 2d) – as clasts (2-3mm) or burrow fills (5mm); rounded clayey (alluvium) clasts, and burrow infills; *Fine Fabric:* SMT 2c: as SMT 2c, but finely fissured, dark reddish orange brown (PPL), low interference colours (close porphyric, speckled and grano-striate b-fabric, XPL, mica present), orange to reddish orange (OIL); patches of abundant fine charred organic matter (burned subsoil B clay); SMT 4a: rare wide (1500µm) finely speckled greyish

Upper (5083) burned mound
As below in M44B, but much less stony with smaller burned flint and less coarse charcoal. Reddish soil as strongly rubefied and finely fissured clay loam and as iron-stained once-humic(?) clayey soil occur more commonly than below, as clasts and as burrow fills – some associated with impure clay void coatings. Intercalations are equally abundant in this very heterogeneous deposit.

Continuing use (trampling) of the site, but with continuing clayey alluviation, leading to clayey soil accretion over the stony burned mound itself. Alluvial clay seems to have got burned/used for hearth construction, and this burned soil was mixed by trampling and burrowed down-profile. Alluviation may also have led to truncation

brown, impure clay broad burrow infills with rare silt and sand and fine charcoal (open porphyric, speckled and mosaic b-fabric, XPL), grey (OIL), weak humic staining, rare fine amorphous organic and charcoal; *Pedofeatures: Textural:* rare intercalations and embedded grains associated with burned red clay (daub/hearth?); very abundant dusty clay intercalations throughout; rare reddish clay void coatings/infills up to 500μm thick – poorly oriented and partially iron-stained – containing relict fine OM and rare charcoal – phytoliths present; these can occur in burrows infilled with reddish clayey soil (with fine rubefied inclusions); *Amorphous:* many ferruginisation of possibly once-humic soil and also associated ferri-hydrite(?) amorphous iron as void infills; *Fabric:* many broad burrows.

and reworking of the occupation soils/upper burned mound, and grey alluvium has also been burrowed down-profile. Continuing disturbance occurred, hence the unclear boundary with the overlying stained alluvium (Context 5121).

MFT D3/SMT 2a, 2b, 2c   M44B

340-420mm

SM: Very heterogeneous (common SMT 2a, with frequent 2b and 2c – mainly in burrows); *Microstructure:* fine to medium prisms and subangular blocky; 25% voids, moderately accommodated medium planar voids, open and closed vughs; *Coarse Mineral:* C:F, 70:30, very poorly sorted coarse silt, fine and medium sand-size quartz (with mica, feldspar and very few glauconite), with very coarse sand and stone size angular and rounded flint (19 mm); *Coarse Organic and Anthropogenic:* abundant coarse charred wood and charcoal (max 15mm), many burned flint (calcined, cracked, traces of rubefication; max 20mm); traces examples (x3) of sand-size burned bone; example of clayey clast (mica-rich wetland clay?); occasional burned soil (upwards); *Fine Fabric:* SMT 2a – as M4B; SMT 2b – as 2a but, greyish and speckled brown (PPL), grey (OIL); very thin humic coatings and rare to occasional amorphous organic matter and rare fine charcoal (uppermost Ea/Eb horizon); SMT 2c: speckled brown/reddish brown with red inclusions (PPL), moderately low interference colours (close porphyric, speckled b-fabric, XPL), brown and orange brown (OIL); occasional to many fine charcoal (red material is red clay papules) – sometimes very dark and isotropic because of ferruginisation (burned red soil); *Pedofeatures: Textural:* occasional (in uppermost part) thin 50-75 μm reddish clay coatings, some dusty with fine charcoal; generally poorly birefringent (translocated burned clay?); abundant very dusty textural intercalations and pseudo-layering, and embedded grains (form of grano-striate b-fabric) – associated with matrix void coatings up to 500μm thick;

5083 Burned mound

Heterogeneous very poorly sorted stony soil deposit with leached loamy sands, humic and fine charcoal rich sandy loam, and upwards increasing amounts of reddish brown sandy loam-silty clay loam soil, containing fine charcoal and present mainly as broad burrow infills. Deposit is very charcoal and burned flint/chert-rich, with trace amounts of fine burned bone present. Very abundant dusty clay intercalations occur alongside thick matrix void coatings; reddish clay infills are also present. Many broad burrows are present, and moderate iron-staining is recorded. (Weak phosphate enrichment 0.588mg g-1, a sandy silt loam texture and a 4.91% LOI was measured; Table A3.25)

This is a markedly heterogeneous stony, burned flint and charcoal-rich burned mound deposit, developed upwards from leached upper subsoil sands and once-humic and more loamy fine charcoal occupation soils. Traces of fine burned bone occur as evidence of probable food preparation. The abundance of textural pedofeatures (intercalations and matrix infills) and coarse heterogeneity indicate mixing by trampling of an often muddy substrate; minor likely burrow mixing by earthworms also took place. These also mixed rubefied clayey soil from overlying mound deposits/possibly also associated with alluvial clay washing through(?). During occupation, the site was

Amorphous: many weak to moderate ferruginous impregnations; *Fabric:* many broad (2mm) burrows in upper part.

likely being affected by clayey alluviation, helping to thicken the silty clay loam mound above upper subsoil sands and the natural gravels (context 5117).

Movers Lane (Western Area 3)(RIR01) Sample 47 - palaeosol

| MFT D6/SMT 4d and 2a | M47A | 30-110mm | 5204 Basal alluvium with charcoal |

MFT D6/SMT 4d and 2a — M47A

30-110mm

SM: Heterogeneous, intercalated and broadly bedded humic clayey silts (SMT 4d) and medium sands (2a); *Microstructure:* bedded and fine laminated; 40% voids, fissures, open vughs and channels, simple packing voids; *Coarse Mineral:* as M48B; C:F, SMT 4d, 60/80:40/20; moderately well sorted coarse silt and fine sand; *Coarse Organic and Anthropogenic:* rare fine charcoal (1-2mm); occasional fine woody and monocot roots (1-2mm); very abundant detrital humified plant fragments (6mm) and rare coarse clasts of amorphous peat (3mm); Fine Fabric: SMT 4d: speckled and finely dotted dark brownish (PPL), moderately low interference colours (open or close porphyric [according to silt/fine sand content], speckled b-fabric, XPL), pale brown with rare reddish flecks [detrital iron-impregnated OM?] and blackish inclusions (OIL); humic with very abundant fine and medium-size amorphous OM and tissue fragments; fine charcoal, diatoms and phytoliths present; *Pedofeatures: Crystalline:* occasional coarse (1.5mm) gypsum prisms; Amorphous: occasional strongly Fe impregnated fine fabric – associated with non-woody post-woody rooting; *Fabric:* possible rare thin burrows.

5204 Basal alluvium with charcoal

Intercalated and broadly bedded humic clayey silts and clean medium sands (overall mean grain size=fine and medium sandy loam). Rare fine charcoal but very abundant very fine to coarse detrital blackened and humified woody plant fragments (up to 6mm) occur – some horizontally oriented – along with clasts of humified peat, producing 4.84% LOI and 0.251mg g-1 phosphate-P. Fine woody roots seem to be post-dated by monocotyledonous plant roots; the latter are often iron impregnated and associated with iron hypocoatings when penetrating fine sediments. Coarse (1.5mm) prismatic gypsum formation has affected the sediments.

These sediments record alternating deposition of sands and humic silts, with small amounts of charcoal, although abundant humifed (blackened) woody plant material may have appeared charcoal-like in the field. The sediments may be recording rapidly migrating(?) stream flow (sands) and overbank flooding (humic silts), with fen carr wood peat being eroded during this process. Changing environmental conditions – marine inundation(?) – led to a monocotyledonous vegetation becoming dominant, and secondary iron and gypsum formation took place.

MFT E2/SMT 4b, 4c, 2a — M47B

110-145mm

SM: Heterogeneous, intercalated and broadly bedded humic clayey silts (SMT 4b and 4c) and medium sands (2a); *Microstructure:* massive, broadly bedded; 35% voids, horizontal fissures and simple packing voids; *Coarse Mineral:* C:F, 100:0 (sands), 25:75 (silty clay); well sorted layers of fine and medium sand, clayey silts and poorly sorted layers with coarse inclusions; *Coarse Organic and Anthropogenic:* rare woody root traces (4mm); abundant wood charcoal (charred bark?)(1-2mm); examples of 2.5mm-size burned bone (associated

5204 Basal alluvium with charcoal

Heterogeneous, intercalated and broadly bedded medium and fine sands and humic silty clay (mixed average grain size=sandy loam), with detrital plant fragments, charcoal (possible charred bark), and including example of burned bone (2.5mm) and 2mm-size burned sandy soil, with rare fine calcined burned flint.

Basal alluvium includes both low energy humic silty clay and higher energy sands,

fungal material?) and 2mm-size burned (rubefied) sandy soil (see 5083); rare fine calcined burned flint; *Fine Fabric:* as below; *Pedofeatures: Amorphous:* occasional iron-impregnated woody material.

and included charcoal, burned bone burned flint and burned soil examples, evidencing erosion of burned mounds/occupation soils locally.

MFT D5/SMT 5a, 4b and 4c

145-185mm

SM: Heterogeneous (sands and gravels with frequent SMT 5a [argillic fine sandy silt loam soil – as coarse 9mm clast and matrix material] and common SMT SMT 4b and 4c – alluvium); *Microstructure:* massive, channel, poorly layered/laminated (3-6mm thick – includes moderately limonite-rich sand lens); 40% voids, simple packing voids, open vughs and broad channels (4-8mm); *Coarse Mineral:* C:F, 95:05 (sands), 60:40 (argillic loam); very poorly sorted mainly medium, coarse and very coarse sand, with common gravel (13mm); quartz, flint, chert, feldspar, limonite; flint showing both depletion and iron-staining features; *Coarse Organic and Anthropogenic:* rare trace of weakly burned (calcined) flint (max 3.5mm); many 4-8mm woody root traces; *Fine Fabric:* SMT 4b (alluvial clay): yellow brown to dark brown with very dark brown/blackish inclusions (PPL), moderately low to moderate birefringence (open porphyric, speckled and grano-striate b-fabric, XPL), grey with reddish brown and blackish inclusions (OIL); very humic clay (with silt), very abundant blackened and browned tissue fragments and amorphous organic matter; occasional diatoms and phytoliths; rare trace of charcoal; SMT 4c (as 4b – with many very fine charcoal); SMT 5a (argillic fine soil): pale yellowish brown (PPL), moderately low interference colours (close porphyric, speckled and grano-striate b-fabric, XPL), pale yellowish orange (OIL); trace of humic staining in fine voids (relict root channels?); *Pedofeatures: Textural:* abundant thin (25-100μm) well oriented very finely dusty, void and grain clay coatings in 'argillic' SMT 5a clast and within sandy matrix; rare example of thin (50 μm) brownish clay void infilling in SMT 4b 'fill'; *Depletion:* examples of iron depletion from iron-stained flint; *Amorphous:* abundant thin iron grain coatings, fine fabric impregnation, clast hypocoatings and partial ferruginisation of organic inclusions; *Excrements:* possible rare traces of relict iron-replaced very thin excrements in channels.

5142 Occupation sands

Heterogeneous and upwards, poorly layered mainly leached medium to very coarse sands and gravels, with traces of argillic matrix; upper layered part includes coarse argillic (fine sandy silt loam with clay void and grain clay coatings), and poorly bedded sand – one for example relatively rich in medium sand size limonite. Rare traces of calcined burned flint occur (3.5mm). Many part-humified and iron-stained woody roots (4-8mm) occur; humic (alluvial) clay containing humified plant fragments, diatoms and phytoliths, and sometimes fine charcoal occur in relict root channels; silty clay clasts also occur. One example of void clay coatings formed in this clay was observed. Sands are very poorly humic (0.690% LOI) but may show weak phosphate-P enrichment (0.135 mg g-1). *Truncated, disturbed natural sands and gravels which had developed an argillic brown sand soil – now evidenced by relict fine matrix material and as a locally eroded coarse (10mm) clast of fine sandy silt loam argillic Bt horizon soil. Occupation led to the inclusion of rare traces of burned flint, and weakly enriched phosphate-P content (see above). Woody rooting during fen carr development (and continued occupation) led to inwash of humic clay containing phytoliths, diatoms and sometimes fine charcoal.*

Soil Microphotographs and scans (Fig 3.15)

1. Scan of impregnated block 40A=B (Trackway at Movers Lane) that produced thin sections M40A (through peat [P] and humic silt [HS] and M40B (sandy peat [SP]). Block is *c*140mm long

2. Scan of impregnated block 44A+B (Movers Lane; that gave thin sections M44A (laminated clays [LC] and M44B (burnt mound [BM] with calcined flints) at Movers Lane. Block is *c*180mm long.

3. Scan of M2A (Trackway Context 28, Woolwich Manor Way), composed of 1: layer of fragmented wood peat, flint and sediment clasts, 2: sands and soil clasts, 3: wood peat. Frame height is *c* 75mm.

4. Scan of M40B (Trackway Context 5154, Movers Lane)(see 1); broadly layered peat and humic silts containing very abundant fine detrital organic matter. One silty infill may possibly record a small cloven hoof print (Arrow; see 16-17). Frame height is *c* 75mm.

5. Scan of M44A (Context 5121, Movers Lane) (see 2); 'stained clays' composed of alluvium, a muddy slurry of burnt mound material and upper burnt mound containing rubefied clay. Frame height is *c* 75mm

6. Scan of M44B (Context 5083, Movers Lane) (see 2); burnt mound develops upwards from subsoil sands, as fine charcoal-rich loam characterised by coarse flints, burnt flint (BF) and charcoal (Ch). Rubefied burnt soil has been burrowed into the mound from the 'upper mound' (see 5). Frame height is *c* 75mm.

7. Photomicrograph of M2A (WMW, Context 28) showing rounded soil clast of likely upper subsoil Eb in uppermost part of M2A (sub-unit 1 in 3, above). Plane polarised light (PPL), frame width is *c* 4.62mm.

8. As 7 (above), under crossed polarised light (XPL), showing coarse silt and fine and medium sand content of Eb soil clast.

9. Photomicrograph of M2A (WMW, Context 28) showing rounded soil clast of probable 'trackway' soil in uppermost part of M2A (sub-unit 1 in 3, above). Note included burnt peat fragments, flint (BF) and secondary iron impregnation (Fe). PPL, frame width is *c* 4.62mm.

10. As 9, above, under oblique incident light (OIL), illustrating blackish peat fragments, calcined burnt flint and iron staining in voids and around margin of the clast

11. Photomicrograph of M4B (WMW, Context 2008); coarse silt, fine and medium sand with many fine charcoal and examples of burnt mineral grains; dusty grain and void clay coatings occur – see arrow for marked example in 12-13. PPL, frame width is *c* 2.38mm.

12. detail of 11 (see arrow); dark dusty, grain and void coatings. PPL, frame width is *c* 0.90mm.

13. As 12, under OIL. Note reddish burnt mineral grain and fine charcoal in dusty clay coating.

14. Photomicrograph of M4A (WMW, Context 2007); humified and bioworked sandy peat, characterised by thin organic excrements and wood fragments. PPL, frame width is *c* 2.38mm.

15. Photomicrograph of M40B (ML, Context 5154); burnt flint fragment (arrow) and peat. OIL, frame width is *c* 4.62mm.

16. Photomicrograph of M40B (ML, Context 5154); humic silts (HS) in possible 'hoof print' over sand (S) beds (see 1 and 4 above); note – included fragments of peat and charred (blackened) humic sandy topsoil fragment (arrow). PPL, frame width is *c* 4.62mm.

17. As 15, above., under OIL. Note horizontally oriented detrital peat fragments in the humic silts (HS) that may be infilling a 'hoof print', and charred (blackened) topsoil clast (arrow).

18. Photomicrograph of M44B (ML,Context 5083)(see 2 and 6); lower mound with iron-stained flint gravel and sandy soil with little included fine anthropogenic material. PPL, frame width is *c* 4.62mm.

19. As 18, but higher up in burnt mound showing marked heterogeneity and included charcoal (Ch), burnt flint (BF) and inwashed red clay – rubefied and mobilised by burning. PPL, frame width is *c* 4.62mm.

20. As Fig 19, showing rare trace of orange burnt bone (BB); charcoal (Ch) and red clay (RC) as inwash and in burrows, also occur. PPL, frame width is about 4.62mm.

21. Photomicrograph of M44A (ML, Context 5121) (see 2 and 5, above); trampled muddy layers containing red clay (RC), blackened burnt soil (BS), alluvial muddy pans (A) and further mixed (M) layers upwards. PPL, frame height is *c* 4.62mm.

22. As 21. Note red clays (RC), blackend burnt soil (BS), pale alluvial muds (A) and further mixed (M) layers making up these 'stained clays'.

23. Photomicrograph of M47B (ML, Context 5204); broadly bedded humic silty clay and sands. PPL, frame height is *c* 4.62mm.

24. As 23, coarse burnt bone fragment in sandy beds. PPL, frame width is *c* 4.62mm.

25. Photomicrograph of M47A (ML, Context 5204); detail of humic clayey silts, containing phytoliths and diatoms (arrow); PPL, frame width is 0.47mm.

26. As 25; secondary prismatic gypsum crystals, probably recordingeffects of marine inundation of the site.PPL, frame width is *c* 4.62mm.

27. Example of SEM-EDAX analysis on clast within M2 (Woolwich Manor Way, Trench 2, trackway) – see 9-10 above.

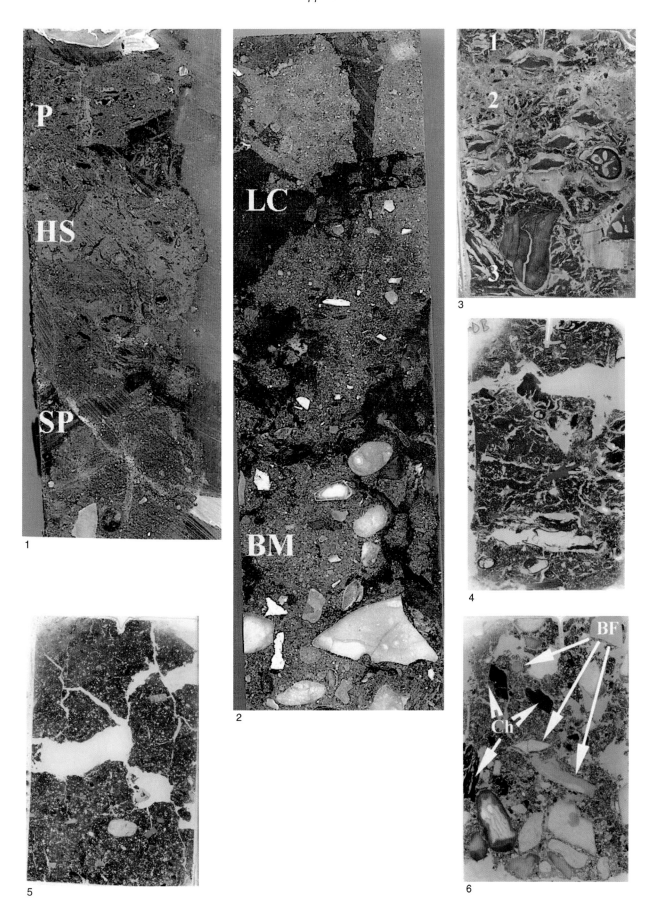

Fig. A3.15   Soil microphotographs and scans

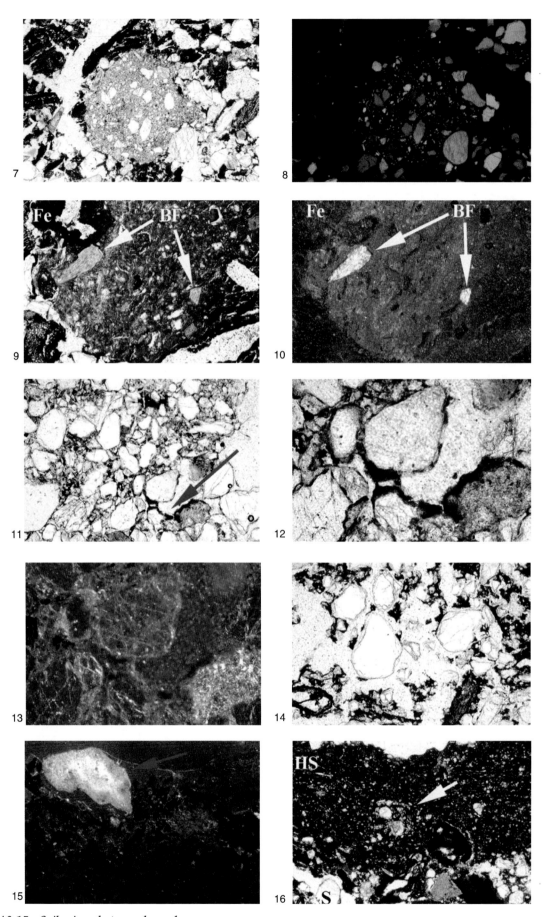

Fig. A3.15   Soil microphotographs and scans

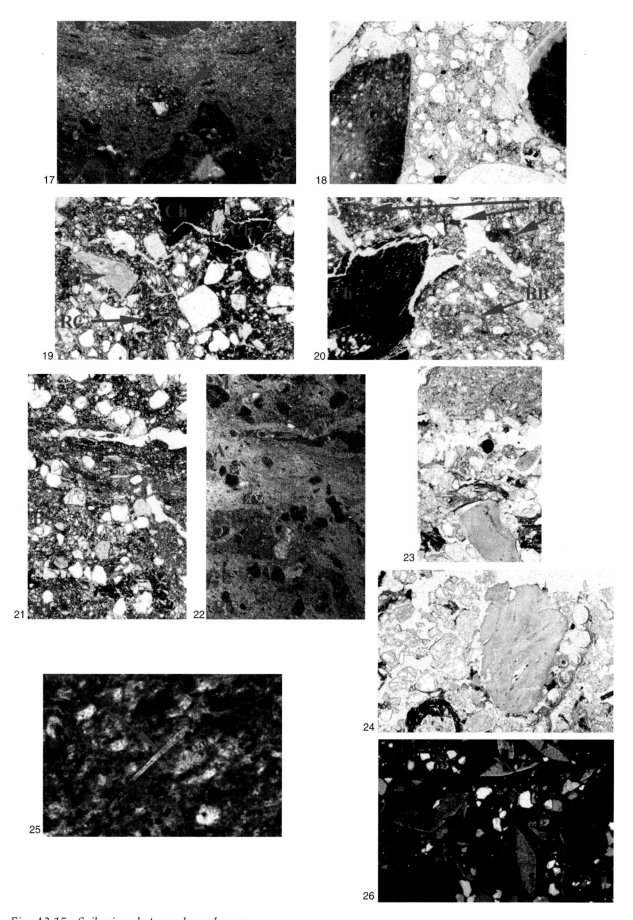

Fig. A3.15 Soil microphotographs and scans

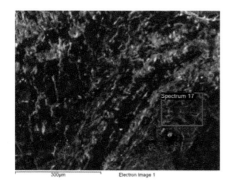
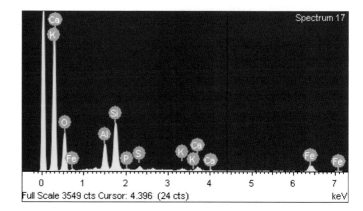

No peaks omitted

Processing option : All elements analyzed (Normalised)
Number of iterations = 3

Standard :
O   SiO2   1-Jun-1999 12:00 AM
Al   Al2O3   1-Jun-1999 12:00 AM
Si   SiO2   1-Jun-1999 12:00 AM
P   GaP   1-Jun-1999 12:00 AM
S   FeS2   1-Jun-1999 12:00 AM
K   MAD-10 Feldspar   1-Jun-1999 12:00 AM
Ca   Wollastonite   1-Jun-1999 12:00 AM
Fe   Fe   1-Jun-1999 12:00 AM

Element	Weight%	Atomic%
O K	49.87	66.82
Al K	10.52	8.36
Si K	21.79	16.63
P K	0.88	0.61
S K	1.81	1.21
K K	1.10	0.61
Ca K	2.47	1.32
Fe K	11.57	4.44
Totals	100.00	

Fig. A3.15   Soil microphotographs and scans

Bibliography

Allen, T, Barclay, A, and Lamdin-Whymark, H, 2004 Opening the wood, making the land: the study of a Neolithic landscape in the Dorney area of the Middle Thames Valley, in *Towards a new stone age; aspects of the Neolithic in south-east England* (eds J Cotton and D Field), CBA Res Rep **137**, 82-98, York

Allen, M J, Scaife, R, Cameron, N, and Stevens, C J, 2005 Excavations at 211 Long Lane, Southwark Part 1: prehistoric Neckinger-side environment in Southwark and its implication for prehistoric communities, *London Archaeol* **11** (3), 73-81

Allen, T, Anderson, L and Barclay, A, forthcoming *The archaeology of the Middle Thames landscape: the Eton College rowing lake project and the Maidenhead, Windsor and Eton flood alleviation scheme, Volume 1: Mesolithic to early Bronze Age*

Andersen, S T, 1979 Identification of wild grass and cereal pollen, *Danmarks Geologiske Undersøgelse, Årbog*, 1978, 69-92

Andrew, R, 1984 *A practical pollen guide to the British flora*, Quat Res Ass Technical Guide 1

Andrews, P, Biddulph, E, and Hardy, A, 2011 *Settling the Ebbsfleet valley: High Speed 1 excavations at Springhead and Northfleet, Kent. The late Iron Age, Roman, Saxon, and medieval landscape. Volume 1: the sites*, Oxford Wessex Archaeology, Oxford and Salisbury

Annable, F K, and Simpson, D D A, 1964 *Guide catalogue of the Neolithic and Bronze age collections in Devizes museum*, Wiltshire Archaeol and Natur Hist Soc, Devizes

Athersuch, J., Home, D J, and Whittaker, J E, 1989 *Marine and brackish water ostracods*, Linnean Society Synopses of the British Fauna (New Series) No. **43**, E J Brill, Leiden

Avery, B W, 1990 *Soils of the British Isles*, CAB International, Wallingford

Avery, B W, and Bascomb, C L, 1974 *Soil Survey laboratory techniques*, Soil Survey Technical monograph **14**, Soil Survey of England and Wales, Harpenden

Avery, M, 1982 The Neolithic causewayed enclosure, Abingdon, in *Settlement patterns in the Oxfordshire region, excavation at the Abingdon causeway enclosure and other sites* (eds H J Case and A Whittle), CBA Res Rep **44**, 10-50, York

Baker, J, and Brothwell, D, 1980 *Animal diseases in archaeology*, Academic Press, London

Bal, L, 1982 *Zoological ripening of soils*, Agri Res Rep, Centre for Agricultural Publishing and Documentation, Wageningen

Ball, D F, 1964 Loss-on-ignition as an estimate of organic matter and organic carbon in non-calcareous soils, *J Soil Sci* **15**, 84-92

Ballin, T B, 2002 Later Bronze Age flint technology: a presentation and discussion of post-barrow debitage from monuments in the Raunds Area, Northamptonshire, *Lithics* **23**, 3-28

Barber, J, 1990 Burnt mound material on settlement sites in Scotland, in *Burnt offerings: international contributions to burnt mound archaeology* (ed. V Buckley), 92-97, Wordwell, Dublin

Barclay, A, 1994 Prehistoric Pottery, in The excavation of a later Bronze Age site at Coldharbour Road, Gravesend (A Mudd), 385-393, *Archaeol Cantiana* **114**, 363-410

Barclay, A, 1999 Grooved Ware from the Upper Thames region, in *Grooved ware in Britain and Ireland*, Neolithic Studies Group Seminar Papers 3 (eds R Cleal and A MacSween), 177-206, Oxbow Books, Oxford

Barclay, A, 2001 Later prehistoric pottery, in A prehistoric enclosure at Eynsham Abbey, Oxfordshire (A Barclay, A Boyle and G D Keevill), *Oxoniensia* **66**, 127-139

Barclay, A, 2002 Ceramic lives, in *Prehistoric Britain: the ceramic basis* (eds A Woodward and J D Hill) PCRG Occasional Publication **3**, 85-95, Oxford

Barclay, A, 2008 Ceramics of the south-east: new directions, South-East Research Framework http://www.kent.gov.uk/publications/environment/serf-paper-neolithic.htm

Barclay, A, and Case, H, 2007 The early Neolithic pottery and fired clay, in *Building memories. The Neolithic Cotswold long barrow at Ascott-under-Wychwood, Oxfordshire* (eds D Benson and A Whittle), 263-281, Cardiff Studies in Archaeology, Oxford

Barclay, A, and Stafford, E, 2008 A radiocarbon dated Ebbsfleet Ware bowl from North Kent, *PAST* **60**, 5-6

Barclay A J, and Marshall, P, 2011 Chronology and the radiocarbon dating programme, in *The Amesbury Archer and the Boscombe Bowmen. Bell Beaker burials at Boscombe Down, Amesbury, Wiltshire*, Chapter 6, Wessex Archaeol Rep **27**, 167-184

Barfield, L H, 1991 Hot stones: Hot food or hot baths? in *Burnt mounds and hot stone technology: Papers from the 2nd international burnt mound conference, Sandwell, 12-14 October 1990* (eds M A Hodder and L H Barfield), 59-67, Sandwell Met. Borough Council, Sandwell

Barfield, L, and Hodder, M, 1987 Burnt mounds as saunas, and the prehistory of bathing, *Antiquity* **61**, 370-379

Barnett, C, 2011 Wood charcoal, in Settling the Ebbsfleet Valley, High Speed 1 excavations at Springhead and Northfleet, Kent. The Late Iron Age, Roman, Saxon and Medieval landscape, Vol. 3, Late Iron Age to Roman human remains and environmental reports (C Barnett, J. McKinley, E Stafford, J Grimm and C J Stevens),113-116, Oxford Wessex Archaeology, Oxford and Salisbury

Barnett, C, forthcoming The charcoal, in Wenban-Smith *et al.*

Barnett C, with Allen, M J, Evans, G, Grimm, J M, Scaife, R, Stevens, C J, and Wyles S F, 2010 A submerged forest with evidence of early Neolithic burning activity and the Tilbury alluvial sequence at Canning Town, East London, *Trans London and Middlesex Archaeol Soc* **61**, 1-15

Barrett, J, 1973 Four Bronze Age cremation cemeteries from Middlesex, *Trans London Middlesex Archaeol Soc* **24**, 111-34

Barrett, J, 1980 The pottery of the later Bronze Age in lowland England, *Proc Prehist Soc* **46**, 297-320

Batchelor, C R, 2009 Middle Holocene environmental changes and the history of yew *(Taxus baccata L.)* woodland in the Lower Thames Valley, unpubl. PhD thesis, Royal Holloway, Univ London

Bates, A, 2008 Animal bone, in *From hunter-gatherers to huntsmen. A history of the Stansted landscape* (N Cooke, F Brown and C Phillpotts), Framework Archaeol Monogr **2**, chapter 32 on CD-ROM

Bates, M R, 1998 Locating and evaluating archaeology below the alluvium: the role of sub-surface stratigraphical modelling, *Lithics* 19, 4-18

Bates, M R, 1999 A geoarchaeological evaluation of the Thames/Medway alluvial corridor of the Channel Tunnel Rail Link, CTRL Union Railways Ltd, unpubl. client report

Bates, M R, and Barham A J, 1995 Holocene alluvial stratigraphic architecture and archaeology of the Lower Thames area, in *The Quaternary of the lower reaches of the Thames* (eds D R, Bridgland, P Allen and B A Haggart), Quat Res Ass, Durham, 35-49

Bates, M R, and Stafford, E C, forthcoming *The Thames Holocene: a geoarchaeological approach to the investigation of the river floodplain for High Speed 1*, Oxford Wessex Archaeol, Oxford and Salisbury

Bates, M R, and Williamson, V D, 1995 A report on the stratigraphic, palaeoenvironmental and archaeological significance of the Slade Green relief road site, unpubl. geoarchaeol service facility technical rep 95/03, Geoarchaeol Service Facility, Univ London

Bates, M R, and Whittaker, K, 2004 Landscape evolution in the Lower Thames valley: Implications for the archaeology of the earlier Holocene period, in *Towards a new Stone Age: aspects of the Neolithic in south-east England* (eds J Cotton and D Field), CBA Res Rep **137**, 50-65, York

Behre, K E, 1986 *Anthropogenic indicators in pollen diagrams*, Rotterdam

Behre, K E, 2007 Evidence for Mesolithic agriculture in and around central Europe, *Veg Hist and Archaeobot* **16**, 203-219

Belcher, J H, and Swale, E M, 1986 Notes on some small Thallasiosira species (Bacillariophyceae) from the plankton of the Lower Thames and other British estuaries (identified by transmission electron microscopy), *Brit Phycological J* **21**, 139-145

Bell, M, Caseldine, A, and Neumann, H (ed.), 2000 *Prehistoric intertidal archaeology in the Welsh Severn Estuary*, CBA Res Rep **120**, York

Bennell, M, 1998 *Under the road: Archaeological discoveries at Bronze Age Way, Erith*, Bexley Council, Bexley

Bennett, K D, 1994 Annotated catalogue of pollen and pteridophyte spore types of the British Isles, unpubl manuscript, Department of Plant Sciences, Univ. Cambridge

Bennett, K D, Whittington, G W, and Edwards, K J, 1994 Recent plant nomenclatural changes and pollen morphology in the British Isles, *Quaternary Newsletter* **73**, 1-6

Berglund, B E, and Ralska-Jasiewiczowa, M, 1986 Pollen analysis and pollen diagrams, in *Handbook of Holocene palaeoecology and palaeohydrology* (ed B E Berglund), 455-484, Wiley, Chichester

Biddulph, E, 2007 Roman pottery, in Beam Washlands, Dagenham, Greater London, NGR 502 836: post-excavation assessment and updated project design (E Biddulph, K Brady, C Champness, B Ford and P Murray), unpubl. report, Oxford Arch., App 1

Birks, H J B, 1973 *Past and present vegetation of the Isle of Skye: a palaeoecological study*, Cambridge Univ Press, London

Bishop, B J, forthcoming, Prehistoric activity, in Brown *et al.* forthcoming

Bishop, B J, and Bagwell, M, 2005 *Iwade: occcupation of a north Kent village from the Mesolithic to the Medieval period*, Pre-Construct Arch. Monogr. **3**, London

Bjärvall, A, and Ullström, S, 1995 *Däggdjur, Alla Europas arter*, Wahlström and Widstrand, Stockholm

Blackford, J J, Innes, J B, Hatton, J J, and Caseldine, C J, 2006 Mid-Holocene environmental change at Black Ridge Brook, Dartmoor, SW England: A new appraisal based on fungal spore analysis, *Review of Palaeobotany and Palynology* **141**, 189-201

Boardman, S, and Jones, G E M, 1990 Experiments on the effects of charring on cereal plant components, *J. Arch. Sci.* **17**(1), 1-12

Boessneck, J, Müller, H H, and Teichert, M, 1964 *Osteologische Unterscheidungsmerkmale zwischen Schaf (Ovis aries Linné) und Ziege (Capra hircus Linné)*, Kühn-Archiv, Bd 78

Boorman, L, Hazelden, J, and Boorman, M, 2002

New salt marshes for old – salt marsh creation and management, in *Eurocoast, Littoral 2002, the changing coast EUCC*, Porto, Portugal, 35-45

Booth, P, Clark, K M, and Powell, A, 1996 A dog skin from Asthall, *International Journal of Osteoarchaeology* **6**, 382-387

Bowsher, J M C, 1991 A burnt mound at Phoenix Wharf, South-East London: A preliminary report, in *Burnt mounds and hot stone technology: papers from the second international burnt mound conference, Sandwell, 12th-14th October 1990* (eds M A Hodder and L H Barfield), 11-19, Sandwell Met. Borough Council, Sandwell

Boyd Dawkins, W, 1901 On the cairn and sepulchral cave at Gop, near Prestatyn. *Archaeol J* **58**, 322–41

Bradley, P, 1999 Worked flint, in *Excavations at Barrow Hills, Radley, Oxfordshire. Volume I: the Neolithic and Bronze Age monument complex* (A Barclay and C Halpin), 211–228, Thames Valley Landscapes Volume 11, Oxford Arch. Unit, Oxford

Bradley, P, 2005 Worked flint, in *Archaeology of the Jubilee Line extension: prehistoric and Roman activity at Stratford Market Depot West Ham 1991-1993* (J Hiller and D R P Wilkinson), 36-38, Oxford Arch/MoLAS

Bradley, R, 1978 *The prehistoric settlement of Britain*, Routledge and Kegan Paul, London

Bradley, R, 1983-5 Prehistoric pottery, in Excavations at Pingewood (ed. M Bowden), *Berkshire Archaeol J* **72**, 17–52

Bradley, R, 1992 The excavation of an oval barrow beside the Abingdon causewayed enclosure, Oxfordshire, *Proc Prehist Soc* **58**, 127-42

Bradley, R, 1993 The microwear analysis, in *Excavations on Redgate Hill, Hunstanton and Tattershall Thorpe, Lincolnshire* (R Bradley, P Chowne, R M J Cleal, F Healy and I Kinnes), EAA **57**, 106-110

Bradley, R, 2007 *The prehistory of Britain and Ireland*, 178–202, Cambridge Univ Press, Cambridge

Bradley, R, and Gordon, K, 1988 Human skulls from the river Thames, their dating and significance, *Antiquity* **62**, 503-9

Brewster, T C M, 1984 *The excavation of Whitegrounds Barrow, Burythorpe Wintringham*, John Gett Publications, Malton

Bridgland, D R, 1994 *Quaternary history of the Thames*, Geological Conservation Review Series, Chapman and Hall, London

Bridgland, D R, 1995 The Quaternary sequence of the eastern Thames basin: problems of correlation, in Bridgland *et al.* 1995

Bridgland, D R, Allen, P, and Haggart, B A, 1995 *The Quaternary of the lower reaches of the Thames*, field guide, Quat Res Ass, Durham

Brooks, D and Thomas, K W, 1967 The distribution of pollen grains on microscope slides, the non randomness of the distribution, *Pollen et Spores* **9**, 621-629

Bronk Ramsey, C, 1995 Radiocarbon calibration and analysis of stratigraphy: The OxCal program, *Radiocarbon* **37**, 425–30

Bronk Ramsey, C, 1998 Probability and dating, *Radiocarbon* **40**, 461–74

Bronk Ramsey, C, 2001 Development of the radiocarbon program OxCal, *Radiocarbon* **43 (2A)**, 355-363

Brown, A, 1991 Structured deposition and technological change among the flaked stone artefacts from Cranbourne Chase, in *Papers on the prehistoric archaeology of Cranbourne Chase* (eds J Barrett, R Bradley and M Hall), Oxbow Monograph **11**, 101-133

Brown, A, 1992 Worked flint – late Bronze Age, in *Reading Business Park: a Bronze Age landscape* (J Moore and D Jennings), 90-93, Thames Valley Landscapes, Oxford Archaeol Unit

Brown, G, 2008 Archaeological evidence for the Roman London to Colchester road between Aldgate and Harold Hill, in *Londinium and beyond. Essays on Roman London and its hinterland for Harvey Sheldon* (eds J Clark, J Cotton, J Hall, R Sherris and H Swain), CBA Res Rep **156**, 82-9, York

Brown, G, Bishop, B, Douglas, A, Leary, J, Ridgeway, V and Taylor-Wilson, R, forthcoming *Crossing the River Lea: from prehistory to Queen Matilda: archaeological excavations at Old Ford, Bow*, Pre-Construct Archaeology Monograph

Brown, N, 1996 The archaeology of Essex *c* 1500-500BC, in *The archaeology of Essex: proceedings of the 1993 Writtle Conference* (ed O Bedwin), Essex County Council

Brown, T, 2008 The Bronze Age climate and environment of Britain, *Bronze Age Review* **1**, November 2008, 1–18, University of Southampton http://eprints.soton.ac.uk/64120/1/BAR1_2008_2_Brown.pdf

Brück, J, 1995 A place for the dead: the role of human remains in late Bronze Age Britain, *Proc Prehist Soc*, **61**, 245-77

Brück, J, 2001 Body methaphors and technologies of transformation in the English Middle and Late Bronze Age, in *Bronze Age landscape. Tradition and transformation* (ed. J. Brück), 149–60, Oxbow Books, Oxford

Brunning, R, 1996 *Waterlogged wood*, English Heritage Guidelines, 2nd edition, London

Buckland P I and Buckland P C, 2006 Bugs coleopteran ecology package (Versions: BugsCEP v761; Bugsdata v709; BugsMCR v20; BugStats v12) [Downloaded December 2006] http://wwwbugscepcom

Bullock, P, Fedoroff, N, Jongerius, A, Stoops, G, and Tursina, T, 1985 *Handbook for soil thin section description*, Waine Research Publications, Wolverhampton

Burchell, J P T, and Piggott, S, 1939 Decorated prehistoric pottery from the bed of the Ebbsfleet, Northfleet, Kent, *Antiq J* **19**, 405-20

Bussell, G D, Pollard, A M, and Baird, D C, 1982

The characterisation of early Bronze Age jet and jet-like material by X-ray fluorescence, *Wiltshire Archaeol Natur Hist Mag* **76**, 27–32

Butler, J, 2006 *Reclaiming the marsh, archaeological excavations at Moor House, City of London*, Pre-Construct Archaeology Monograph **6**

Butterfield, B G and Meylan, B A, 1980 *Three-dimensional structure of wood, a ultrastructural approach*, Chapman and Hall, London and New York

Carew, T, 2003 Bronze Age Beckton, in *Archaeology Matters*, MoL newsletter

Carew, T, Meddens, F, Batchelor, R, Branch, N, Elias, S, Goodburn, D, Vaughan-Williams, A, Webster, L, and Yeomans, L, 2010 Human-environment interactions at the wetland edge in East London: trackways, platforms and Bronze Age response to environmental change, *London and Middlesex Archaeol Soc* **61**, 1-34

Cheer, P, 1998 The kiln pottery, in *Excavations at Orsett 'Cock' enclosure, Essex, 1976* (G A Carter), EAA **86**, Chelmsford, 97-101

Clark, P, (ed.) 2004 *The Dover Bronze Age Boat*, English Heritage, London

Clarke, D V, Cowie, T G and Foxon, A, 1985 *Symbols of power at the time of Stonehenge*, HMSO, Edinburgh

Clarke, D L, 1970 *Beaker pottery of Great Britain and Ireland*, Cambridge Univ Press, Cambridge

Cleve-Euler, A, 1951-55 *Die Diatomeen von Schweden und Finland*, Kungl Svenska Vetensk Akad Handl Ser 4 2:1, 1-163 3:3, 1-153 4:1, 1-158 4:5, 1-255 5:4, 3-231

Coles, B J, 1990 Anthropomorphic wooden figurines from Britain and Ireland, *Proc Prehist Soc*, **56**, 315-34.

Coles, B, 1992 Further thoughts on the impact of beaver on temperate landscapes, in *Alluvial archaeology in Britain* (eds S Needham and M C Macklin), 93-99, Oxbow Monograph 27, Oxford

Coles, B, 1998 Wood species for wooden figures: a glimpse of a pattern, in *Prehistoric Ritual and Religion* (eds A Gibson and D Simpson), 163-173, Sutton Publishing, Stroud

Coles, B, and Coles, J, 1986 *Sweet Track to Glastonbury – the Somerset Levels in Prehistory*, Thames and Hudson, London

Coles, J M, and Orme, B J, 1978 The Meare Heath Track, *Somerset Levels Papers* **4**, 11-46

Coles, J M, and Orme, B J, 1980a *Prehistory of the Somerset Levels*, Exeter

Coles, J M, and Orme, B J, 1980b Tinney's Ground 1978-79, excavation report, *Somerset Levels Papers* **6**, 60-68

Coles, J M, and Orme, B J, 1982 Beaver in the Somerset Levels: some new evidence, *Somerset Levels Papers* **8**, 67-75, Exeter

Coles, J M, and Orme, B J, 1985 Prehistoric woodworking from the Somerset Levels, 3 roundwood, *Somerset Levels Papers* **11**, 25-50

Coles, S, Ford, S and Taylor, A, 2008 An early

Neolithic grave and occupation, and an early Bronze Age hearth on the Thames foreshore at Yabsley Street, Blackwall, London, *Proc Prehist Soc* **74**, 215-233

Conneller, C, 2008 Lithic technology and the chaine operatoire, in *Prehistoric Britain* (ed. J Pollard), 160-176, Blackwell, Oxford

Corcoran, J, Halsey, C, Spurr, G, Burton, E, and Jamieson, D, 2011 *Mapping past landscapes in the lower Lea valley: A geoarchaeological study of the Quaternary sequence*, MOLA Monograph **55**, MoLA, London

Costello, M P, 1997 Prehistoric and Roman material from Rainham: an archaeological watching brief at the former Rainham football ground, 1995, *Essex Archaeol Hist* **28**, 91-102

Cotton, J, 2000 Foragers and farmers: towards the development of a settled landscape in London, *c* 4000-1200 BC, in *London underground: the archaeology of a city* (eds I Haynes, H Sheldon and L Hannigan), 9-34, Oxbow, Oxford

Cotton, J, 2004 Surrey's early past: a survey of recent work, in *Aspects of archaeology and history in Surrey: towards a research framework for the county* (eds J Cotton, G Crocker and A Graham), 19-38, Surrey Archaeological Society, Guildford

Cotton, J, and Johnson, R 2004 Two decorated Peterborough bowls from the Thames at Mortlake and their London context, in *Towards a new Stone Age: aspects of the Neolithic in southeast England* (eds J Cotton and D Field), CBA Res Rep **137**, 128-147, York

Cotton J, and Wood B, 1996 Recent prehistoric finds from the Thames foreshore and beyond in Greater London, *Trans London Middlesex Archaeol Soc* **47**, 33-57

Courty, M A, 2001 Microfacies analysis assisting archaeological stratigraphy, in *Earth Sciences and Archaeology* (eds P Goldberg, V T Holliday and C R Ferring), 205-239, Kluwer, New York

Courty, M A, and Fedoroff, N, 1982 Micromorphology of a Holocene dwelling, *Proc Nordic Archaeometry*, 257-277

Courty, M A, Goldberg, P, and Macphail, R I, 1989 *Soils and micromorphology in archaeology*, 1st edition, Cambridge Manuals in Archaeology, Cambridge Univ. Press, Cambridge

Cracknell, B, 2005 *Outrageous waves: global warming and coastal change in Britain through two thousand years*, Phillimore and Co Ltd, Chichester

Crockett A D, Allen M J, and Scaife R G, 2002 A Neolithic trackway within peat deposits at Silvertown, London, *Proc Prehist Soc* **68**, 185-213

Cromarty, A M, Barclay A, Lambrick, G, and Robinson M, 2006 Whitecross Farm, Cholsey: A late Bronze Age waterfront site, in *The archae-ology of the Wallingford Bypass 1986-92* (eds A M Cromarty, A Barclay, G Lambrick and M Robinson) Oxford Archaeology Thames Valley Landscapes mongr **22**, 9-156

Crowther, J, 2000 The Goldcliff late-Mesolithic site, 5400-4000 cal BC: soil phosphate and magnetic susceptibility studies, in *Prehistoric intertidal archaeology in the Welsh Severn Estuary* (eds M Bell, A Caseldine and H Neumann) CBA Res Rep **120**, 57-58, and 4.16-4.18 on CD, York

Crumlin-Pedersen, O, and Trakadas, A, 2003 *Hjortspring:a pre-Roman Iron-Age warship in context*, Viking Ship Museum, Roskilde

Cundy, A B, Hopkinson, L, Lafite, R, Spencer, K, Taylor, J A, Ouddane, B, Heppell, C M, Carey, P J, Charman, R, Shell, D, and Ullyott, S, 2005 Heavy metal distribution and accumulation in two Spartina sp-dominated macrotidal salt marshes from the Seine estuary (France) and the Medway estuary (UK), *Applied Geochemistry* **20**, 1195-1208

Cunliffe, B, 1984 *Danebury: an Iron Age hillfort in Hampshire*, CBA Res Rep **52**, York

Dalrymple, R W, Zaitlin B A, and Boyd R, 1992 Estuarine facies models conceptual, basis and stratigraphic implications, *J Sedimentary Petrology* **62**, 1130-46

Deforce, K and Bastiaens, J, 2004 The Postglacial history of *Taxus baccata* (yew) in Belgium, in *Abstract book, the Quaternary Research Association third international postgraduate symposium, Royal Belgian Institute of Natural Sciences* (eds V M A Heyvaert and B K Petersen), 82, Belgium Geological Survey, Belgium

Densem, R, and Seeley, D, 1982 Excavations at Rectory Grove, Clapham 1980-1, *London Archaeol* **4**, 177-84

Denys, L, 1991/2 A check-list of the diatoms in the Holocene deposits of the western Belgian coastal plain with a survey of their apparent ecological requirements I: Introduction, ecological code and complete list, *Belgische Geologische Dienst Professional Paper*, **246**, 41

Devoy, R J N, 1977 Flandrian sea-level changes in the Thames Estuary and the implications for land subsidence in England and Wales, *Nature* **220**, 712-715

Devoy, R J N, 1979 Flandrian sea level changes and vegetation history of the lower Thames Estuary, *Phil Trans Roy Soc London* **B285**, 355-407

Devoy, R J N, 1980 Post-glacial environmental change and man in the Thames estuary; a synopsis, in *Archaeology and coastal change* (ed F H Thompson), occasional paper, Society of Antiquaries, new series **1**

Devoy, R J N, 1982 Analysis of the geological evidence for Holocene sea-level movements in south-east England, *Proc Geolog Assoc* **93**, 65–90

Dick, W A, and Tabatabai, M A, 1977 An alkaline oxidation method for the determination of total phosphorus in soils, *J Soil Science Soc America* **41**, 511-14

Dinç, U, Miedema, R, Bal, L, and Pons, L J, 1976 Morphological and physio-chemical aspects of three soils developed in peat in The Netherlands and their classification, *Netherlands J Agricult Sci* **24**, 247-265

Divers, D, 1996 *Archaeological investigations of Hays Storage Services Ltd, Pooles Lane, Ripple Road, Dagenham, Essex*, Newham Museum Service, unpubl rep

Dixon, N, 2004 *The crannogs of Scotland*, Stroud, Gloucester, England

Doherty, A, 2010 The prehistoric pottery, in Bull, R, 105-109 New Road, Rainham, London, RM13, London Borough of Havering, unpubl post-excavation assessment and updated project design

Donahue, R, 2002 Microwear analysis, in Sidell *et al.* 2002

Done, G, 1991 The animal bone, in *Excavation and salvage at Runnymede Bridge 1978: the late Bronze Age waterfront site* (S Needham), 327-342, British Mus Press, London

Driesch, A von den, 1976 *A guide to the measurement of animal bones from archaeological sites*, Peabody Museum of Archaeology and Ethnology, Univ Harvard

Dunkin, D J, 2001 Metalwork, burnt mounds and settlement on the West Sussex coastal plain: a contextual study, *Antiquity* **75**, 261-262

Edlin, H L, 1949 *Woodland crafts in Britain, an account of the traditional uses of trees and timbers in the British countryside*, Batsford, London

Edmonds, M, 1995 *Stone tools and society: working stone in Neolithic and Bronze Age Britain*, Batsford, London

Edmonds, M, 1997 Taskscape, technology and tradition, *Analecta Praehistorica Leidensia* **29**, 99-110

Edmonds, M, 1999 *Ancestral geographies of the Neolithic: landscape, monuments and memory*, Routledge, London

Edmonds, M, Evans, C, and Gibson, D, 1999 Assembly and collection – lithic complexes in the Cambridgeshire Fenlands, *Proc Prehist Soc* **65**, 47-82

Edwards, Y H, Weisskopf, A, and Hamilton, D, 2010 Age, taphonomic history and mode of deposition of human skulls in the River Thames, *Trans London and Middlesex Archaeol Soc*, **60**, 35-51

Elberling, E, Breuning-Madsen, H, Hingea, H, and Asmund, G, 2010 Heavy metals in 3300-year-old agricultural soils used to assess present soil contamination, *European J Soil Science* **61**, 74–83

Elgee, F, 1930 *Early man in North-East Yorkshire*, T Bellows, Gloucester

Elias, S A, Webster, L, and Amer, M, 2009 A beetle's eye view of London from the Mesolithic to the Bronze Age, *The Geol J*, **44**, 537-567.

Emsley, J, 2001 *Nature's building blocks*, Oxford Univ Press, Oxford

Erdtman, G, 1960 The acetolysis method, *Botaniska Tidskrift* **54**, 561-564

Fairbridge, R W, 1983 Isostacy and eustacy, in *Shorelines and Isostasy* (eds D E Smith and A Dawson, A), 3-28, Academic Press, London

Fairweather, A D, and Ralston, I B M, 1993 The Neolithic timber hall at Balbridge, Grampian

Region, Scotland: the building, the date, the plant macrofossils, *Antiquity* **67**, 313-323

Fitzpatrick, A, Ellis, C, and Allen, M J, 1996, Bronze Age 'jetties' or causeways at Testwood Lakes, Hampshire, Great Britain, *Past* **24**, 9-10

Ford, S, 1986 A newly discovered causewayed enclosure at Eton Wick, near Windsor, Berkshire, *Proc Prehist Soc* **52**, 319–20

Ford, S, 1993 Excavations at Eton Wick, *Berkshire Archaeol J* **74**, 27–36

Framework Archaeology, 2006 *Landscape evolution in the middle Thames valley. Heathrow Terminal 5 excavations Volume 1, Perry Oaks*, Framework Archaeology Monogr 1, Oxford Wessex Archaeology, Oxford and Salisbury

Framework Archaeology 2010, *Landscape evolution in the middle Thames valley. Heathrow Terminal 5 excavations Volume 2*, Framework Archaeology Monogr 3, Oxford and Wessex Archaeology, Oxford and Salisbury

French, C, 2003 *Geoarchaeology in action: studies in soil micromorphology and landscape evolution*, Routledge, London

Gale, R, and Cutler, D, 2000 *Plants in archaeology*, Westbury and Royal Botanic Gardens Kew

Galloway, J A, 2009 Storm flooding, coastal defence and land use around the Thames estuary and tidal river c.1250-1450, *J Medieval Hist* **35**, 171-88

Gardiner, J, 2008 On the production of discoidal flint knives and changing patterns of specialist flint procurement in the Neolithic on the South Downs, England, in *Between foraging and farming: an extended broad spectrum of papers presented to Leendert Louwe Kooijmans* (eds H Fokkens, B J Coles, A L Van Gijn, J P Kleijne, H H Ponjee and C G Slappendel), Analecta Praehistorica Leidensia **40**, 235-236, Univ Leiden

Garwood, P, 1999 Grooved ware in Southern Britain: chronology and interpretation, in *Grooved Ware in Britain and Ireland* (eds R Cleal and A MacSween), Neolithic Studies GrOxford Univ. Press Papers 3, 145-176, Oxbow, Oxford

Garwood, P, 1999 The chronology of depositional contexts and monuments (with contributions by A Barclay), in *Excavations at Barrow Hills, Radley, Oxfordshire, Vol I: The Neolithic and Bronze Age monument complex* (eds A Barclay and C Halpin), 275-93, Oxford Archaeological Unit; Thames Valley Landscapes 1, Oxford

Gibbard, P L, 1977 Pleistocene history of the Vale of St Albans, *Phil Trans Roy Soc London* **B280**, 445-483

Gibbard, P L, 1994 *Pleistocene history of the lower Thames valley*, Cambridge Univ. Press, Cambridge

Gibbard, P L, 1985 *Pleistocene history of the middle Thames valley*, Cambridge Univ. Press, Cambridge

Gibbard, P L, 1986 Flint gravels in the Quaternary of Southeast England, in *The scientific study of flint and chert* (eds G De C Sieveking and M B Hart), 141-149, Cambridge Univ. Press, Cambridge

Gibson, A M, and Bayliss, A, 2009 Recent research at Duggleby Howe, North Yorkshire. *Archaeol J* **166**, 39-78

Gibson, A M, and Bayliss, A, 2010 Recent work on the Neolithic round barrows of the Upper Great Wold Valley, Yorkshire, in *Round mounds and monumentality in the British Neolithic and beyond* (eds J. Leary, T Darvill and D Field), 72–107, Oxbow Books, Oxford

Gibson, A, and Kinnes, I, 1997 On the urns of a dilemma: radiocarbon and the Peterborough problem, *Oxford J Archaeol* **16** (1), 65-72

Gibson, A, and Leivers, M, 2008 Neolithic pottery in Neolithic causewayed enclosures and later prehistoric farming: duality, imposition and the role of predecessors at Kingsborough, Isle of Sheppey, Kent, *Proc Prehist Soc* **74**, 245-53

Gifford, E, and Gifford, J, 2004 The use of half-scale model ships in archaeological research with particular reference to the Graveney, Sutton Hoo and Ferriby ships, in *The Dover Bronze age boat in context. Society and water transport in prehistoric europe* (ed. P Clark), 67–81, Oxbow Books, Oxford

Gifford and Partners, 2000 A13 Thames Gateway preliminary archaeological investigations (Phase I), Roding Bridge and Ironbridge-Canning Town, Further Archaeological Works Report, B3295RO8, unpubl client report for RMG (A13) Construction JV

Gifford and Partners, 2001a A13 Thames Gateway preliminary archaeological investigations (Phase II), Prince Regent Lane, Further Archaeological Works Report, B3295RO12, unpubl client report for RMG (A13) Construction JV

Gifford and Partners. 2001b A13 Thames Gateway preliminary archaeological investigations (Phase II), Woolwich Manor Way (Further Archaeological Works Report B3295RO10), unpubl client report for RMG (A13) Construction JV

Gifford and Partners, 2002 A13 Thames Gateway preliminary archaeological investigations (Phase II), Movers Lane (Further Archaeological Works Report B3295RO9), unpubl client report for RMG (A13) Construction JV

Gifford and Partners, 2003a A13 Thames Gateway phase III archaeological works, Woolwich Manor Way (Assessment report on detailed excavation B3295HRO21), unpubl client report for RMG (A13) Construction JV

Gifford and Partners, 2003b A13 Thames Gateway phase III archaeological works, Freemasons Road Underpass (Assessment report on detailed excavation B3295HRO20), unpubl client report for RMG (A13) Construction JV

Girling, M A, 1980 The fossil insect assemblage from the Baker Site, *Somerset Levels Papers* 6, 36-42

Girling, M A, and Grieg, J, 1977 Palaeoecological investigations of a site at Hampstead Heath, London *Nature* 268, 45-47

Girling, M A, Greig, J, 1985 A first fossil record for *Scolytus scolytus* (F.) (elm bark beetle): its occurrence in elm decline deposits from London and their implications for Neolithic elm decline, *J Archaeol Sci* 12, 347-531

Godwin, H, 1956 *History of the British flora*, 1 edn, Cambridge Uni Press, Cambridge

Godwin, H, 1975 *The history of the British flora*, 2 edn, Cambridge Uni Press, Cambridge

Going, C J, 1987 *The mansio and other sites in the south-eastern sector of Caesaromagus: the Roman pottery*, CBA Res Rep **62**, London

Goldberg, P, and Macphail, R I, 2006 *Practical and theoretical geoarchaeology*, Blackwell Publishing, Oxford

Goodburn, D, 1990 *Post-excavation report on woodwork from excavations at Vintners Place, City of London*, Dept Urban Archaeol, unpubl report

Goodburn, D, 1991 Wet sites as archives of ancient landscapes, in *Wet site excavation and survey* (eds J Coles and D Goodburn), 51-53, Exeter

Goodburn, D, 1996 The woodworking evidence, in Thomas and Rackam *et al.*

Goodburn, D, 1999 Assessment of the woodwork, in Atlas Wharf, West Ferry Road, Isle of Dogs, London Borough of Tower Hamlets (ed D, Lakin), unpubl MoL Specialist Services Rep, 33-45

Goodburn, D, 1998 The death of the wildwood and the birth of woodmanship in SE England, in *Hidden dimensions* (ed. C Bernick), University of British Colombia, Vancouver

Goodburn, D, 2003a Prehistoric woodwork, in Masefield *et al.* 2003, 98-105

Goodburn, D, 2003b Summary assessment of the prehistoric worked wood found during excavations at the Becton Golf Driving Range site (GWB02), for Pre-Construct Archaeology, unpubl MoL Specialist Services Report

Goodburn, D, 2004 Assembly and construction techniques, in *The Dover Bronze Age boat* (ed. P Clark), 124-161, London

Grace, R, 1992 Use wear analysis, in Excavations of a Mesolithic site at Thatcham, Berkshire (F Healey, M Heaton and S J Lobb), *Proc Prehist Soc* **58**, 41-76

Graham, A H, 1978 The geology of North Southwark and its topographical development in the post-Pleistocene period, *Southwark Excavations 1972– 74*, **2**, 501-17, London and Middlesex Archaeol Soc and Surrey Archaeol Soc joint publication

Grant, A, 1982 The use of toothwear as a guide to the age of domestic ungulates, in *Ageing and sexing animal bones from archaeological sites* (eds B Wilson, C Grigson and S Payne), BAR Brit Ser **109**, 91-108, Oxford

Green, H S, 1980 *The flint arrowheads of the British Isles: a detailed study of material from England and Wales with comparanda from Scotland and Ireland*, Part I, BAR Brit Ser **75**

Greenwood, P, 2001 Uphall Camp, Ilford – an update, *London Archaeol* **9**, 207-16

Greenwood, P, Perring, D and Rowsome, P, 2006 *From Ice Age to Essex: a history of the people and landscape of east London*, Museum of London/English Heritage

Greig, J R A, 1989 From lime forest to heathland-five thousand years of change at West Heath Spa, Hampstead, as shown by the plant remains, in *Excavations at the Mesolithic site on West Heath, Hampstead 1976-1981* (eds D Collins and J D Lorimer), BAR Brit Ser **217**, 88-89

Greig, J R A, 1991, The prehistoric riverside settlement at Runnymede: the botanical story, in *Excavation and salvage at Runnymede Bridge, Berkshire, 1978* (eds S Needham and D Longley), 234-261, British Museum, London

Grimes, W F, 1960 *Excavations on defence sites, 1939–1945, 1: Mainly Neolithic–Bronze Age*, HMSO, London

Grimm, E C, 1990 TILIA and TILIA-GRAPH, PC spreadsheet and graphics software for pollen data, INQUA, Working Group on Data-handling Methods Newsletter, **4**, 5-7

Guttmann, E B A, and Last, J, 2000 A late Bronze Age landscape at South Hornchurch, Essex, *Proc Prehist Soc* **66**, 319-359

Habermehl, K-H, 1975 *Die Altersbestimmung bei Haus- und Labortieren*, second edition, Verlag Paul Parey, Berlin, Hamburg

Haggart B A, 1995, A re-examination of some data relating to Holocene sea-level changes in the Thames Estuary, in Bridgland *et al. 1995*, 329-338

Haggart, B A, 2007 University of East London Docklands campus: geoarchaeological borehole sampling evaluation, Essex Co Co Field Archaeol Unit

Halstead, P, 1985 A Study of mandibular teeth from Romano-British contexts at Maxey, in *Archaeology and Environment in the Lower Welland Valley* (F Pryor), EAA Rep **27**, 219-224

Halstead, P, Cameron, E and Forbes, S, 2001 Non-human and human mammalian bone remains from the Flag Fen platform and Power Station post alignment, in *The Flag Fen basin: archaeology and environment of a Fenland landscape* (F Pryor), 330-350, English Heritage Archaeol Rep, London

Hambleton, E, 1999 *Animal husbandry regimes in Iron Age Britain: a comparative study of faunal assemblages from British Iron Age sites*, BAR Brit Ser **282**, Archaeopress, Oxford

Hansen, M, 1987 *The Hydrophilidae (Coleoptera) of Fennoscandia and Denmark Fauna* (Fauna Entomologyca Scandinavica 18), Scandinavian Science Press, Leiden

Hanson, I, 1996 Albert Basin, unpubl. archaeological desk-based study, Newham Museum Service

Harcourt, R A, 1974 The dog in prehistoric and early Britain, *J Archaeol Sci* **1**, 151-175

Harding, D W, 1985 *The Iron Age in lowland Britain*, Routledge and Kegan Paul, London

Harding, P, and Gibbard, P, 1983 Excavations at

Northwold Road, Stoke Newington, North-East London, 1981, *Trans London Middlesex Archaeol Soc* **34**, 1-18

Hart, D, 2010 Excavations at Belmarsh West, Woolwich, *London Archaeol*, **12** (8), 203-207

Hartley, B, 1996 *An atlas of British diatoms*, Biopress Ltd, Bristol

Haughey F, 1999, The archaeology of the Thames: prehistory within a dynamic landscape, *London Archaeol* **9** (1), 6-21

Healy, F, 1996 *The Fenland Project 11: The Wissey embayment, evidence for pre-Iron Age occupation*, EAA **78**

Healy, F, 1988 *The Anglo-Saxon Cemetery at Spong Hill, North Elmham, Part VI: Occupation during the Seventh to Second Millennia BC*, EAA **39**

Heard, K A, 2000 Post-medieval tawyers' yard in Bermondsey, *London Archaeol* **9**, 137-143

Hedges, J, 1975 Excavation of two Orcadian burnt mounds at Liddle and Buckquoy, *Proceedings of the Society of Antiquarians of Scotland* **106**, 38-98

Hedges, J, and Buckley, D, 1978 Excavations at a Neolithic causewayed enclosure, Orsett, Essex, 1975, *Proc Prehist Soc* **44**, 219-308

Hendey, N I, 1964 *An introductory account of the smaller algae of British coastal waters, Part V, Bacillariophyceae (Diatoms)*, HMSO, London

Heppell, E, 2006 The Stumble, Essex, in *Archaeological evaluation of wetlands in the Planarch area of North West Europe* (L Dyson, E Heppell, C Johnson and M Pirters), Kent Co Council

Herne, A, 1988 A time and a place for the Grimston Bowl, in *The archaeology of context in the Neolithic and Bronze Age: recent trends* (eds J C Barrett and I A Kinnes), 9-29, Sheffield

Herne, A, 1991 The flint assemblage, in *Excavations at Grimes Graves Norfolk 1972-1976:* Fascicule 3 Shaft X: Bronze Age flint, chalk and metal working (I Longworth, A Herne, G Varndell and S Needham), 21-93, British Museum Press, Dorchester

Hey, J, Garwood, P, Robinson, M, Barclay A, and Bradley, P, 2011 *The Thames through time, the archaeology of the gravel terraces of the upper and middle Thames: the formation and changing environment of the Thames Valley and early human occupation to 1500 BC*, Part 2 Mesolithic to Early Bronze Age, Oxford Archaeology Thames Valley Landscapes Monogr **32**

Hill, J, and Rowsome, P, 2011 *Roman London and the Walbrook Stream Crossing: Excavations at 1 Poultry and Vicinity*, MoLA, London

Hiller, J and Wilkinson, D R P, 2005 *Archaeology of the Jubilee Line Extension: Prehistoric and Roman Activity at Stratford Market Depot West Ham, London 1991-1993*, Oxford Archaeology, Oxford

Holder, N, 1998, *Royal Docks Community School site, Prince Regents Lane* (post excavation assessment and updated project design), unpubl MOLAS Rep

Holgate, R, 1988 *Neolithic Settlement of the Thames Basin*, BAR Brit Ser **194**, Oxford

Holland, D G, 1972 *A Key to the larvae, pupae and adults of the British species of Elminthidae*, Freshwater Biological Association Scientific Publication 26, Freshwater Biological Association, Ambleside

Howell, I, 2005, *Prehistoric landscape to Roman villa; excavations at Beddington 1981-7*, MOLAS Monograph **26**, MoLA, London

Howell, I, Swift, D, and Watson, B, with Cotton, J and Greenwood, P, 2011 *Archaeological landscapes of east London: Six multi-period sites excavated in advance of gravel quarrying in the London Borough of Havering*, MOLA Monograph **54**, London

Huisman, D J, 2009 *Degradation of archaeological remains* Sdu Uitgevers bv, Den Haag

Hustedt, F, 1930-61 *Die Kieselalgen, Deutschlands, Osterreiche und der Schweiz unter Berucksichtigung der ubrigen lander Europas sowie der angrenzenden Meeresgebiete Akad Verlag*, Leipzig

Hustedt, F, 1953 Die Systematik der diatomeen in ihren beziehungen zur geologie und okologie nebst einer revision des Halobien-systems, *Svenske Botankiska Tidskrift* **47**, 509-519

Hyman, P S, and Parsons, M S, 1992 *A review of the scarce and threatened Coleoptera of Great Britain. Part 1*, Joint Nature Conservation Committee, Peterborough

Ingold, T, 1993 The temporality of the landscape, *World Archaeology* **25**, 152-174

Innes, J B, Shennan, I, Twiddy, E J, and Zong, Y, 1996 *The contemporary diatom and pollen flora and foraminiferal fauna of Kentra Bay and Moss SSSI*, Lochaber Scottish Natural Heritage Research, Survey and Monitoring Report SNH/HMSO

Jacobi, R, 1978 The Mesolithic of Sussex, in *Archaeology in Sussex to AD 1500* (ed. P L Drewett), CBA Res Rep **29**, 15-22

Jarrett, C, 1996 Archaeological Evaluation at the East Beckton District Centre, Kingsford Way, Beckton. Unpublished Report, Newham Museum Service Archive Report HE KW 95

Jarvis, M G, Allen, R H, Fordham, S J, Hazleden, J, Moffat, A J, and Sturdy, R G, 1983 *Soils of England and Wales*, Sheet 6 South East England, Ordnance Survey, Southampton

Jarvis, M G, Allen, R H, Fordham, S J, Hazleden, J, Moffat, A J, and Sturdy, R G, 1984 *Soils and their use in South-East England*, Bulletin No 15, Soil Survey of England and Wales, Harpenden

Jay, M, Richards, M, Parker Pearson, M, and Needham, S, 2010 Appendix A – Liffs Low radiocarbon date footnote, in "One of the most interesting barrows ever examined" – Liffs Low revisited (R Loveday and A Barclay) 128–9, in *Round Mounds and Monumentality in the British Neolithic and Beyond* (eds J Leary, T Darvill and D Field),108–129, Oxbow, Oxford

Jeffery, S, 1991 Burnt mounds, fulling and early textiles, in *Burnt mounds and hot stone technology, papers from the second international burnt mound conference Sandwell, 12th-14th October 1990* (eds M.A. Hodder and L.H. Barfield), 97-108,

Sandwell Metropolitan Borough Council, Sandwell

Jessop, L, 1986 *Coleoptera: Scarabaeidae* (Handbooks for the Identification of British Insects 5/11), Royal Entomological Society of London, London

Joly, C, Barillé, L, Barreau, M, Mancheron, A, and Visset, L 2007 Grain and annulus diameter as criteria for distinguishing pollen grains of cereals from wild grasses, *Rev Palaeobotany and Palynology* **146**, 221-233

Jones, G, 2000 Evaluating the importance of cultivation and collecting in Neolithic Britain, in *Plants in Neolithic Britain and beyond* (ed. A S Fairbairn), Neolithic Studies Group Seminar Papers **5**, 79-84, Oxbow Books, Oxford

Jones, G and Rowley-Conwy, P, 2007 On the importance of cereal cultivation in the British Neolithic, in *The origins and spread of domestic plants in Southwest Asia and Europe* (eds S Colledge and J Conolly), 391-419, UCL Institute of Archaeology Publications, London

Jones, M U and Rodwell, W J, 1973 The Romano-British kilns at Mucking with an interim on two kiln groups, *Essex Archaeol Hist* **5**, 13-47

Jones, P, 2008 *A Neolithic Ring Ditch and Later Prehistoric Features at Staines Road Farm, Shepperton*, SpoilHeap Publications, Monogr 1

Jones, A P, Tucker, M E, and Hart, J K (eds) 1999 *The Description and Analysis of Quaternary Stratigraphic Field Sections. Techn Guide 7*, Quat Res Ass, London

Kaul, F, 2004 Social and religious perceptions of the ship in Bronze Age Europe, in *The Dover Bronze Age Boat in Context. Society and Water Transport in Prehistoric Europe* (ed. P Clark), 122–37, Oxbow Books, Oxford

Keith-Lucas, M, 2000 Pollen analysis of sediments from Moor Farm, Staines Moor, Surrey, *Surrey Archaeological Collections* **87**, 85-93

Kelly, M G, Bennion, H, Cox, E J, Goldsmith, B, Jamieson, J, Juggins S, Mann, D G and Telford, R J, 2005 *Common freshwater diatoms of Britain and Ireland: an interactive key*, Environment Agency, Bristol, accessed at http://craticulanclacuk/EADiatomKey/html/indexhtml

Kendall, M, 2000 *The archaeology of Greater London: an assessment of archaeological evidence for human presence in the area now covered by Greater London*, MoLAS Monogr, MoLA/English Heritage, London

Kenward H K, 1975 Pitfalls in the environmental interpretation of insect death assemblages, *J Archaeol Sci* **2**, 85-94

Kenward H K, 1978 The analysis of archaeological insect assemblages: a new approach, *Archaeol York* **19/1**, CBA for YAT, York

Kenward, H K, Hall, A R, and Jones, A K G, 1980 A tested set of techniques for the extraction of plant and animal macrofossils from waterlogged archaeological deposits, *Sci and Archaeol* **22**, 3-15

Kinnes, I, 1978 The earlier prehistoric pottery, in The causewayed enclosure, Orsett, Essex (J

Hedges and D Buckley), *Proc Prehist Soc* **44**, 259-268

Kinnes, I A, 1979 *Neolithic round barrows and ring-ditches in the British Neolithic*, British Mus Press, London

Kinnes, I A, 2004 A truth universally acknowledged: some more thoughts in Neolithic round barrows, in *From sickles to circles: Britain and Ireland at the time of Stonehenge* (eds A M Gibson and J A Sheridan), 106-115, Tempus, Stroud

Knight, S, and Grimm, J M, 2010 Animal bone, in *Landscape Evolution in the Middle Thames Valley. Heathrow Terminal 5 Excavations Volume 2* (J. Lewis, M. Leivers, L. Brown, A. Smith, K. Cramp, L. Mepham and C. Phillpots), section 13 CD-ROM, Framework Archaeology Monogr 3, Oxford and Salisbury

Koch, K, 1989 *Die Käfer Mitteleuropas (Ökologie. Band 1/2)*, Goecke and Evers, Krefeld

Koch, K, 1992 *Die Kafer Mitteleuropas (Ökologie Band 3)*, Goecke and Evers, Krefeld

Kooistra, M J, 1978 *Soil development in recent marine sediments of the intertidal zone in the Oosterschelde – the Netherlands: a soil micromorphological approach*, Soil Survey Papers **14**, Soil Survey Inst, Wageningen

Krammer, K, and Lange-Bertalot, H, 1986 *Die Süsswasserflora von Mitteleuropa 2: Bacillariophyceae 1 Teil: Naviculaceae Gustav Fischer-Verlag*; Stuttgart

Kristiansen, K, and Larsson, T B, 2005 *The rise of Bronze Age society: travels, transmissions and transformations*, Cambridge Univ. Press, Cambridge

Lacaille, A D, 1961 Mesolithic facies in Middlesex and London, *Trans London Middlesex Archaeol Soc* **20**, 101-149

Lambrick, G, with Robinson, M, and Allen, T, 2009 *The Thames Through Time, the archaeology of the gravel terraces of the Upper and Middle Thames: the Thames Valley in late prehistory: 1500 BC-AD 50*, Oxford Archaeology Thames Valley Landscapes Monogr 29, Oxford

Lamdin-Whymark, H, 2001 Neolithic activity on the floodplain of the River Thames at Dorney, *Lithics* **22**, 22-36

Lamdin-Whymark, H, 2008 *The residues of ritualised action: Neolithic depositional practices in the Middle Thames Valley*, BAR Brit Ser 466, Archaeopress, Oxford

Lamdin-Whymark, H, forthcoming a The Late Glacial to Bronze Age flint, in Wenban-Smith *et al.* forthcoming

Lamdin-Whymark, H, forthcoming b The flint, in Bates and Stafford forthcoming

Langton, B, and Holbrook, N, 1997 A prehistoric and Roman occupation and burial site at Heybridge: excavations at Langford Road 1994, *Essex Archaeol Hist* **28**, 12-46

Legge, A J, 1992 The faunal remains, in *Excavations at Grimes Graves, Norfolk, 1972-1976: Fascicule 4 Animals, environment and the Bronze Age economy* (A J Legge), British Mus Press, 15-42

Leivers, M, Barnett, C, and Harding, P, 2007 Excavations of Mesolithic and Neolithic flint scatters and accompanying environmental sequences at Tank Hill Road, Purfleet, Essex, 2002, *Essex Archaeol Hist* **38**, 1-44

Leney, L and Casteel, R W, 1975 Simplified procedure for examining charcoal specimens for identification, *J Archaeol Sci* **2**, 153-159

Lewis, J S C, 2000a The Upper Palaeolithic and Mesolithic periods, in Kendall 2000, 45-62

Lewis, J S C, 2000b The Neolithic period, in Kendall 2000, 63-80

Lewis, J S C, with Rackham, J, 2011 *Three Ways Wharf, Uxbridge. A Lateglacial and Early Holocene hunter-gatherer site in the Colne valley*, MOLA Monograph 51

Liddle, J, undated, A13 Thames gateway DBFO, report on animal bone recovered from Phase III archaeological works, Freemasons Road Underpass (FRU), unpubl rep

Long, A J, Scaife, R G, and Edwards, R J, 2000 Stratigraphic architecture, relative sea-level, and models of estuary development in southern England: new data from Southampton Water, in *Coastal and estuarine environments: sedimentology, geomorphology and geoarchaeology* (eds K Pye and J R L Allen), Geol Soc Special Publ **175**, 253-279, The Geol Soc, London

Longworth, I, and Cleal R M J, 1999 Grooved Ware gazetteer, in *Grooved Ware in Britain and Ireland* (eds R Cleal and A MacSween), Neolithic Studies Group Seminar Papers 3, 177-206, Oxbow Books, Oxford

Longworth, I H, 1971 The Neolithic pottery, in *Durrington Walls: Excavations 1966-1968* (G J Wainwright and I H Longworth), Soc Antiqs Research Rep **29**, London

Loveday, R, Gibson, A M, Marshall, P D, Bayliss, A, Bronk Ramsey, C, and van der Plicht, H, 2007 The antler maceheads dating project, *Proc Prehist Soc* **73**, 381-92

Lowe, J J, and Walker, M J C, 1997 *Reconstructing Quaternary Environments*, Longmans, London.

Lucht, W H, 1987 Die Käfer Mitteleuropas (Katalog) Krefeld, Goecke and Evers

McCave, I N, Manighetti, B, and Robinson, S G, 1995a Sortable silt and fine sediment size/composition slicing: parameters for palaeocurrent speed and palaeoceanography, *Paleoceanography* **10**, 593-610

McCave, I N, Manighetti, B, and Beveridge, N A S 1995b Circulation in the glacial North Atlantic inferred from grain-size measurements, *Nature* **374**, 149 152

McFadyen, L, 2008 Temporary Spaces in the Mesolithic and Neolithic: understanding landscapes, in *Prehistoric Britain* (ed J Pollard), 121-134, Blackwell, Oxford

McGrail, S, 1981 *The Brigg 'raft; and her prehistoric environment*, BAR Brit Ser **89** and Greenwich National Maritime Mus Archaeol Ser 6

McGrail, S, 1990 *Boats and boatmanship in the late prehistoric southern North Sea and Channel*, CBA Res Rep **71**, 32-48, York

McGrail, S, 1997 The boat fragments, in *Excavations at Caldicot, Gwent: Bronze Age palaeochannels in the Lower Nedern Valley*, CBA Res Rep **108**, 210-217, York

McGrail, S, 2000 The boat planks, in *Prehistoric Intertidal Archaeology in the Welsh Severn Estuary* (M. Bell, A. Caseldine and H. Neumann), CBA Res Rep **120**, 77, York

McGrail, S, 2001 *Boats of the World*, Oxford Univ. Press, Oxford

McInnes, I, 1968 Jet sliders in late Neolithic Britain, in *Studies in Ancient Europe* (eds J M Coles and D D A Simpson), 137-144, Leicester Univ. Press, Leicester

Macphail, R I, 1994 Soil micromorphological investigations in archaeology, with special reference to drowned coastal sites in Essex, in, *SEESOIL South East Soils Discussion Group* (eds H F Cook and D T Favis-Mortlock), 13-28, Wye

Macphail, R I, 2003 *Scanian Road profiles (A1316 and A1317): soil micromorphology (with reference to chemistry)*, Lab for Environmental Archaeology, Univ. Umeå, Umeå

Macphail, R I, 2009 Marine inundation and archaeological sites: first results from the partial flooding of Wallasea Island, Essex, UK. Antiquity Project Gallery, http://antiquityacuk/projgall/macphail/

Macphail, R I, Allen, M J, Crowther, J, Cruise, G M, and Whittaker, J E, 2010 Marine inundation: effects on archaeological features, materials, sediments and soils, *Quaternary International, Geology and Taphonomy*, **214**, 44-45

Macphail, R I, Courty, M A, and Gebhardt, A, 1990 Soil micromorphological evidence of early agriculture in north-west Europe, *World Archaeol* **22(1)**, 53-69

Macphail, R I and Crowther, J, 2005 *Stansted Airport Long Stay Car Park and Mid Stay Car Park (BAACP00 and BAAMP00), soil micromorphology, chemistry and magnetic susceptibility*, unpubl rep for Oxford Archaeology

Macphail, R I and Crowther, J, 2006 *Terminal 5, soil micromorphology, chemistry, magnetic susceptibility and particle size analyses*, unpubl rep for Framework Archaeology

Macphail, R I, and Crowther, J, 2008 Soil micromorphology, chemistry and magnetic susceptibility, in *From hunter-gatherers to huntsmen: a history of the Stansted landscape* (N Cooke, F Brown and C Phillpotts), chapter 30 CD-ROM Framework Archaeology Monogr 2, Oxford and Salisbury

Macphail, R I, and Crowther, J, 2009 Soil micromorphology, chemistry and magnetic susceptibility, in *Four millenia of human activity along the A505 Baldock bypass, Hertfordshire* (eds M Phillips, H Duncan and C Mallows), Albion Archaeology, Bedford, 84-85, 122-123, CD-ROM Appendix IV Soils

Macphail, R I, and Crowther, J, forthcoming Soil micromorphology, chemistry and magnetic susceptibility, in Wenban-Smith *et al.* forthcoming

Macphail, R I, and Cruise, G M, 1997-2003 Soil investigation of Area A, in Archaeological excavations in advance of the A414 Cole Green by-pass, near Hertford (ed. T McDonald), *Hertfordshire Archaeol* **13**, 33-35

Macphail, R I, and Cruise, G M, 2000 Soil micromorphology in Bell *et al.* 2000, 267-269 and CD-ROM

Macphail, R I , and Cruise, G M, 2001 The soil micromorphologist as team player: a multianalytical approach to the study of European microstratigraphy, in Earth Science and Archaeology (eds P. Goldberg V. Holliday, and R. Ferring), 241-267, Kluwer Academic/Plenum, New York

Maltby, M, 1981 Iron Age, Romano-British and Anglo-Saxon animal husbandry – a review of the faunal evidence, in *The environment of man: the Iron Age to the Anglo-Saxon period* (eds M Jones and G Dimbleby), BAR Brit Ser **87**, 155-203, Oxford

Maltby, M, 1996 The exploitation of animals in the Iron Age: the archaeozoological evidence, in *The Iron Age in Britain and Ireland: recent trends* (eds T C Champion and J R Collis), 17-27, J R Collins Publications, Univ. Sheffield

Manby, T G, 1974 *Grooved Ware sites in the North of England*, BAR Brit Ser **9**, Oxford

Manby, T G, King, A, and Vyner, B E, 2003 The Neolithic and Bronze Ages: a time of early agriculture, in, *The archaeology of Yorkshire: an assessment at the beginning of the 21st century* (eds T G Manby, S Moorehouse and P Ottaway), Yorkshire Archaeological Society Occasional Paper **3**, 35–116, Leeds

Marsh, G, and Tyers, P, 1978 The Roman pottery from Southwark, *Southwark excavations 1972-74, vol 2*, Southwark and Lambeth Archaeological Excavation Committee, 533-82

Marsland A, 1986, The floodplain deposits of the Lower Thames, *Quarterly J Engineering Geol* **19**, 223-247

Martin, T S, 2002 The late Iron Age and Roman pottery, in A late Iron Age and Romano-British farmstead at Ship Lane, Aveley: excavation on the line of the A13 Wennington to Mar Dyke road improvement, 1994-5 (S Foreman and D Maynard), *Essex Archaeol Hist* **33**, 138-47

Martingell, H, 1990 The East Anglian Peculiar? The 'Squat' Flake, *Lithics* **11**, 40-43

Marzinzik, S, 2003 *Early Anglo-Saxon belt buckles (late 5th to early 8th Centuries AD): their classification and context*, BAR Brit Ser **357**, Oxford

Masefield, R, Branch, N, Couldrey, P, Goodburn, D, and Tyers I, 2003 A later Bronze Age Well complex at Swalecliffe, Kent, *Antiq J* **83**, 47-121

Meddens, F M, 1996 Sites from the Thames Estuary wetlands, England, and their Bronze Age use, *Antiquity* **70**, 268, 325-334

Meddens, F, and Beasley, M, 1990 Wetland use in Rainham, Essex, *London Archaeol* **6**, 242-248

Meddens, F and Sidell, E J, 1995 Bronze Age trackways in East London, *Current Archaeol* **12**, 412-16

Meisch, C, 2000 *Freshwater Ostracoda of Western and Central Europe*, Spektrum Academischer, Heidelberg, Berlin

Merrifield, R, 1987 *The archaeology of ritual and magic*, Batsford, London

Merriman N, 1990 *Prehistoric London*, MoL/ HMSO, London

Merriman, N, 1992 Predicting the unexpected: prehistoric sites recently discovered under alluvium in Central London, in *Alluvial archaeology in Britain* (eds S Needham and M G Macklin), 261-267, Oxbow, Oxford

Millett, M, and McGrail, S, 1987 The archaeology of the Hasholme logboat, *Archaeol J* **144**, 69-155

Milne, G, Batterbee, R, Straker, V, and Yule, B, 1983 The River Thames in London in the mid–first century AD, *Trans London Middlesex Archaeol Soc*, 34, 19–30

Milne, G, Cohen, N and Cotton, J, 2011, London's Top Secret, *London Archaeol* **12 (11)**, 287-89

Moffett, L, Robinson M A, and Straker, V, 1989 Cereals, fruit and nuts: charred plant remains from Neolithic sites in England and Wales and the Neolithic economy, in *The Beginnings of Agriculture* (eds A Milles, D Williams and N Gardner), Symposia of the Association for Environmental Archaeology No 8, BAR Internat Ser **496**, 243-261, Oxford

MoLAS 2000, *The archaeology of Greater London, An assessment of archaeological evidence for human presence in the area now covered by Greater London* (see Kendall above)

MoLAS (in prep) *Later prehistory in the former wetlands of east London*, MoLAS Monogr Ser

Mook, W G, 1986 Business meeting. Recommendations/resolutions adopted by the twelfth international radiocarbon conference, *Radiocarbon* **28**, 799

Moore, P, Bradley, T and Bishop, B, 2003 A late Bronze Age burnt mound site at The Phillimores, Campden Hill Road, Kensington, *London Archaeol* **10** (7), 179-186

Moore, P D, Webb, J A, and Collinson, M E, 1991 *Pollen analysis*, second edition, Blackwell, Oxford

Morigi, A, Schreve D, and White, M (Part 1); Hey, J, Garwood, P, Robinson, M, Barclay A and Bradley, P (Part 2) 2011 *The Thames through time, the archaeology of the gravel terraces of the upper and middle Thames: the formation and changing environment of the Thames Valley and early human occupation to 1500 BC*, Oxford Archaeology Thames Valley Landscapes Monogr **32**

Morris, E, 2004 Later Prehistoric Pottery, in *Green Park (Reading Business Park) Phase 2 Excavations 1995- Neolithic and Bronze Age Sites* (A Brossler, R Early and C Allen), Oxford Archaeology Thames Valley Landscapes Monograph **19**, 58-90

Mortimer, J R, 1905 *Forty years' researches in British*

and Saxon burial mounds of East Yorkshire, A Brown and Sons, London

Moss, E H, 1983 Some Comments on edge damage as a factor in functional analysis of stone artefacts, *J Archaeol Sci* **10**, 231-242

Murphy, C P, 1986 *Thin Section Preparation of soils and sediments*, A B Academic Publishers, Berkhamsted

Murphy, P J, 1989 Carbonised Neolithic plant remains from the Stumble, an intertidal site in the Blackwater Estuary, Essex, England, *Circaea* **6** (1), 1989 for 1988, 21-38

Nayling, N, and Caseldine, A, 1997 *Excavations at Caldicot, Gwent: Bronze Age Palaeochannels in the Lower Nedern Valley*, CBA Res Rep **108**, York

Needham S, 1991, *Excavation and salvage at Runnymede Bridge 1978: the late Bronze Age waterfront site*, British Mus Press, London

Needham, S, 1992 Holocene alluviation and interstratified settlement evidence in the Thames valley at Runnymede Bridge, in *Alluvial archaeology in Britain*, (eds S Needham and M Macklin) Oxbow Monograph **27**, 249-260, Oxbow Books, Oxford

Needham, S, 1993 The structure of settlement and ritual in the late Bronze Age of south-east Britain, in *L'habitat et l'occupation du Sol à L'Age du Bronze en Europe* (eds C Mordant and A Richard), 49-69, Editions du Comité des Travaux Historiques et Scientifiques, Paris

Needham, S, 1996 Chronology and periodisation in the British Bronze Age, in Absolute chronology: archaeological Europe 2500-500 BC (K Randsborg), *Acta Archaeologica* **67**, 121-140

Needham, S, 2005 Transforming Beaker Culture in North-West Europe: processes of fusion and fission, *Proc Prehist Soc* **71**, 171-217

Needham, S, 2007 800BC, the great divide, in *The earlier Iron Age in Britain and the Near Continent* (eds C Haselgrove and R Pope), 39-63, Oxbow, Oxford

Needham, S, and Burgess, C B, 1980 The later Bronze Age in the lower Thames valley: the metalwork evidence, in *The British Later Bronze Age* (eds J C Barrett and R.J.Bradley), BAR, Brit Ser **83** (ii), 437-469, Oxford

Needham, S and Longley, D, 1980 Runnymede Bridge, Egham: A late Bronze age riverside settlement', in *The British Later Bronze Age* (eds J Barrett and R Bradley), , BAR, Brit Ser **83** (ii), 397-436, Oxford.

Needham, S, and Spence, T, 1996 *Refuse and disposal at Area 16 East Runnymede*, Runnymede Bridge Research excavations Volume 2, British Mus Press, London

Newcomer, M H, 1976, Spontaneous retouch, in *Tweede Internationale Symposium Over Vuursteen, Staringia* **3** (ed F H G Engelen), 62-64, Nederlandse Geologische Vereniging

Nilsson, A N, and Holmen, M, 1995 The aquatic adephaga (Coleoptera) of Fennoscandia and Denmark II Dytiscidae, *Fauna Entomologyca*

Scandinavica **35**, E J Brill, Leiden

Noort, R van de, 2006 Argonauts of the North Sea – a social maritime archaeology for the 2nd millennium BC, *Proc Prehist Soc* **72**, 267-287

Noort, R van de, Middleton, R, Foxon, A, and Bayliss, A, 1999 The 'Kilnsea-boat', and some implications from the discovery of England's oldest plank boat, *Antiquity* **73**, 131-5

O'Connell, M, 1990 Excavations during 1979-1985 of a multi-period site at Stanwell, *Surrey Archaeol Collections* **80**, 4-61

O'Connor, T, 1988 *Bones from the General Accident site, Tanner Row, Archaeology of York, the animal bones* Vol **15/2**, York Archaeological Trust/CBA

O'Kelly, M J, 1954 Excavation and experiments in ancient Irish cooking sites, *J Roy Soc Antiq Ireland* **84**, 105–55

O'Reilly Wiese, S B, Bubb, J M, and Lester, J N, 1995 The significance of sediment metal concentrations in two eroding Essex saltmarshes, *Marine Pollution Bulletin* **30**, 190–199

O'Sullivan, A, 1997 Neolithic, Bronze Age and Iron Age Woodworking Techniques, in *Trackway Excavations in the Mount Dillon Bogs, Co Longford, 1985-1991*, Trans Irish Archaeol Wetland Unit 3, 291- 342, B. Raftery, Dublin

Orme, B J, and Coles, J M, 1983 *Prehistoric woodworking from the Somerset Levels: 1: Timbers*, Somerset Levels Papers **9**, 19-43

Owoc, M A, 2001 The times they are a changin': experiencing continuity and development in the Early Bronze Age funerary rituals of southwestern Britain, in *Bronze Age landscapes: tradition and transformation* (ed J Brück), 193-206, Oxbow Books, Oxford

Oxford Archaeology, 2011 Dagenham and Washlands, public realms enhancement, Dagenham, Greater London, NGR TQ 5033 836, archaeological watching brief report and updated project design, unpubl rep

Oxford Archaeology, 2005 A13 Thames Gateway DBFO roadscheme: post-excavation project design, unpubl client rep for RMG (A13) Construction JV

Parker Pearson, M, 1999. *The archaeology of death and burial*, Sutton Publishing, Stroud

Pasda, K, 2004 Tierknochen als Spiegel sozialer Verhältnisse im 8 – 15. Jahrhundert in Bayern *Praehistorika Monographien 1 Praehistorika Archäologischer Verlag*, Erlangen

Payne, S, 1973 Kill-off patterns in sheep and goats: the mandibles from Aşwan Kale, *Anatolian Studies* **23** , 281-303

Peglar, S M, 1993 The mid-Holocene *Ulmus* decline at Diss Mere, Norfolk, UK: a year-by-year pollen stratigraphy from annual laminations, *The Holocene*, **3** (1), 1-13

Pelling, R, nd The charred plant remains from Poundbury, Dorset, unpubl specialist rep for Wessex Archaeology

Pendleton, C, 2001 Firstly, let's get rid of ritual, in Bronze Age landscapes, tradition and transformation (ed J. Brück), 170-178, Oxbow Books, Oxford

Penhallurick, R D, 1986 *Tin in antiquity*, The Institute of Metals, London

Perry, J, 1721 *An Account of the Stopping of Dagenham Breach*, B Tocke for J Peele, London

Phillips, C, Baxter, I L, and Nussbaumer, M, 2009 The application of discriminant function analysis to archaeological dog remains as an aid to the elucidation of possible affinities with modern breeds, *Archaeofauna* **18**, 51-64

Pine, C A, Williamson, V D, and Bates, M R, 1994 A report on the stratigraphy, archaeological and palaeoenvironmental potential of the Crossness Sewage Works, Geoarchaeological Services Facility Site Assessment Report 94/14, Institute of Archaeology, London, 2 vols

Pitts, M W, 1978a Towards an understanding of flint industries in Post-glacial England, *Bulletin of the Institute of Archaeology* **15**, 179-197

Pitts, M W, 1978b On the shape of waste flakes as an index of technological change in lithic industries, *J Archaeol Sci* **5**, 17-37

Pitts, M W, and Jacobi, R M, 1979 Some aspects of change in flakes stone industries of the Mesolithic and Neolithic in Southern Britain, *J Archaeol Sci* **6**, 163-177

Pollard, J, 1999 These places have their moments: thoughts on settlement practices in the British Neolithic, in *Making places in the prehistoric world: themes in settlement archaeology* (eds J Brück and M Goodman), 76-93, Univ College of London Press, London

Powell, A, and Clark, K M, 2006 Animal bone, in *Late Bronze Age ritual and habitation on a Thames eyot at Whitecross Farm, Wallingford: the archaeology of the Wallingford bypass, 1986-92* (eds A M Cromarty, A Barclay, G Lambrick and M Robinson) Thames Valley Landscapes Monograph **22**, Oxford Archaeology, Oxford

Prager, A, Barthelmes, A, Theuerkauf, M, and Joosten, H, 2006 Non-pollen palynomorphs from modern Alder carrs and their potential for interpreting microfossil data from peat, *Review of Palaeobotany and Palynology* **141**, 7-31

Prehistoric Ceramics Research Group, 1992/1995 (1st/2nd edn) *The study of later prehistoric pottery: guidelines for analysis and publication*, PCRG Occ Pap 2, Oxford

Prescott, J R, and Hutton, J T, 1994, Cosmic ray cotribution to dose rates for luminescence and ESR dating: large depths and long term time variations, *Radiation Measurements* **23**, 497-500

Prior, J, and Alvin, K L, 1983 Structural changes on charring woods of *Dictostachys* and *Salix* from Southern Africa, *International Association of Wood Anatomists Bulletin* **4** (4), 197-206

Proctor, J, and Bishop, B, 2002 Prehistoric and environmental development on Horselydown: excavations at 1-2 Three Oak Lane, *Surrey Archaeological Collections* **89**, 1-26

Prummel, W, and Frisch, H J, 1986 A guide for the distinction of species, sex and body side in bones of sheep and goat, *J Archaeol Sci* **13**, 567-577

Pryor, F, 1991 *Flag Fen: prehistoric fenland centre*, London

Pryor, F 1998 *Farmers in Prehistoric Britain*, Tempus, Stroud

Rackam D T, 1994 Prehistory 'in' the Lower Thames floodplain, *London Archaeol* **7**, 191-196

Rackham, J, and Sidell, J, 2000 London's landscapes: the changing environment, in Kendall 2000, 11-27

Rackham, O, 1976 *Trees and woodland in the British landscape: the complete history of Britain's trees, woods and hedgerows*, London

Raftery, B, 1990 *Trackways through time: archaeological investigations on Irish bog roads, 1985-1989*, Headline Publishing, Dublin

Raymond, F, 2008 The pottery, in An early Neolithic grave and occupation, and an early Bronze age hearth on the Thames foreshore at Yabley Street, Blackwell, London (S Coles, S Ford and A Taylor) *Proc Prehist Soc* **74**, 215-233

Rayner L J, 1997, Assessment of the Prehistoric Pottery from the Royal Docks Community School, Newham, Unpubl. report, MoLAS

Reille, M, 1992 *Pollen et spores d'Europe et d'Afrique du Nord*, Laboratoire de Botanique historique et Palynologie, Marseille

Reimer, P J, Baillie, M G L, Bard, E, Bayliss, A, Beck, J W, Bertrand, C J H, Blackwell, P G, Buck, C E, Burr, G S, Cutler, K B, Damon, P E, Edwards, R L, Fairbanks, R G, Friedrich, M, Guilderson, T P, Hogg, A G, Hughen, K A, Kromer, B, McCormac, G, Manning, S, Bronk Ramsey, C, Reimer, R W, Remmele, S, Southon, J R, Stuiver, M, Talamo, S, Taylor, F W, van der Plicht, J, and Weyhenmeyer, C E, 2004 IntCal04 Terrestrial radiocarbon age calibration, 0–26 Cal Kyr BP, *Radiocarbon*, **46**, 1029–58

Ridgeway, V, 1999 Prehistoric finds at Hopton Street in Southwark, *London Archaeol* **9**, 72-76

Robertson- Mackay, R, 1987 The Neolithic causewayed enclosure at Staines, Surrey: excavations 1961-63, *Proc Prehist Soc* **53**, 23-128

Robinson, M A, 1981 The use of ecological groups of Coleoptera for comparing sites, in, *The Environment of man: the Iron Age to the Anglo-Saxon period* (eds M Jones and G Dimbleby), BAR Brit Ser **87**, 251–86, Oxford

Robinson, M A, 1983 Arable/pastoral ratios from insects, in *Integrating the subsistence economy* (ed M Jones) BAR Int Ser **181**, 19-47, Oxford

Robinson, M A, 2000 Further considerations of Neolithic charred cereals, fruits and nuts, in *Plants in Neolithic Britain and beyond* (ed A S Fairbairn), Neolithic Studies Grp Seminar Papers **5**, 85-90, Oxbow Books, Oxford

Roe, F E S, 1968 Stone mace-heads and the latest Neolithic cultures of the British Isles, in *Studies in ancient Europe* (eds J M Coles and D D A Simpson), 145-172, Leicester Univ. Press, Leicester

Round, F E, Crawford, R M, and Mann, D G, 1990 *Diatoms: biology and morphology of the genera*, Cambridge Univ. Press, Cambridge

Rowlands, M, 1980 Kinship, alliance and exchange in the European Bronze Age, in *Settlement and society in the British later Bronze Age* (eds J C Barrett and R Bradley), BAR Brit Ser **83**, 59-72, Oxford

RPS Clouston 1997 Bronze Age way: Archaeological investigations, Unpubl. RPS Clouston Archive Document, Bexley Council

Russell, M J G, 1989 Excavation of a multi-period site in Weston Wood, Albury: the pottery, *Surrey Archaeological Collections* **79**, 3-52

Sands, R, 1997 Prehistoric woodworking: the analysis and interpretation of Bronze and Iron Age toolmarks, *Wood in Archaeology*, Vol 1, Univ. College London, London

Saville, A, 1980 On the measurement of struck flakes and flake tools, *Lithics* **1**, 16-20

Saville, A, 1990 The flint and chert artefacts, in *Brean Down: excavations 1983-1987* (M Bell), 152-157, English Heritage, Hertford

Scaife, R, 1988 Pollen analyses of the Mar Dyke sediments, in Wilkinson 1988

Scaife, R G, 1991 Rainham Marshes, pollen analysis, unpubl. Palaeopol archive rep

Scaife, R, 1997 Assessment of pollen from Beckton, unpubl. Palaeopol archive rep

Scaife, R, 2000 Holocene vegetation development in London, in Sidell *et al.* 2000, 11-117

Scaife, R G, 2002 Vegetation history; pollen and waterlogged plants, in Crockett *et al.*, 2002, 191-203

Schmid, E, 1972 *Atlas of animal bones for prehistorians, archaeologists and quaternary geologists*, Elsevier publishing co, Amsterdam, London, New York

Schweingruber, F H, 1990 *Microscopic wood anatomy*, third editon, Swiss Federal Institute for Forest, Snow and Landscape Research, Birmensdorf

Seel, S, 2000 The Erith buried forest, in *IGCP 437 Coastal environmental change during sea-level highstands: the Thames Estuary field guide* (eds E J Sidell and A J Long), 33-39, Environmental Res Centre, Univ. Durham

Serjeantson, D, 1996 The animal bones, in *Refuse and disposal at Area 16 East Runnymede: Runnymede Bridge research excavations, Volume 2* (S Needham and T Spence), 194-253, British Mus. Press, London

Serjeantson, D, 2007 Intensification of animal husbandry in the late Bronze Age: the contribution of sheep and pigs, in *The earlier Iron Age in Britain and the near continent* (eds C Haselgrove and R Pope), 80-93, Oxbow Books, Oxford

Shepherd, W, 1972 *Flint its origins, properties and uses*, Faber and Faber, London

Sheppard, T, 1929 *Catalogue of the Mortimer Collections of Prehistoric Remains from East Yorkshire Barrows*, A. Brown and Sons, Hull

Sidell, E J, 1996 A13 Thames Avenue to Wennington, Wennington Marsh, Unpubl. MoLAS Archive Rep

Sidell, E J, 2003 The London Thames: a decade of research into the river and its floodplain, in *Alluvial archaeology in Europe* (eds A J Howard, M G Macklin and D G Passmore), 133-143, A A Balkema Publishers, Lisse

Sidell, E J, Scaife, R G, Tucker, S, and Wilkinson, K N, 1995 Palaeoenvironmental investigations at Bryan Road, Rotherhithe, *London Archaeol* **7**, 279-285

Sidell, E J, Scaife, R G, Wilkinson, K N, Giorgi , J A, Goodburn, D, Gray-Rees, L, and Tyers, I, 1997 Spine Road Development, Erith , Bexley (RPS Clouston Site 2649) a palaeoenvironmental assessment, Unpubl. rep MoLAS ENV01/97

Sidell, E J, Wilkinson, K N, Scaife, R G, and Cameron, N, 2000 *The Holocene evolution of the London Thames: archaeological investigations (1991-1998) in advance of the London Underground Limited Jubilee Line Extension*, MoLAS Monogr **5**, Mus of London, London

Sidell, J, Cotton J, Rayner, L, and Wheeler, L 2002 *The Prehistory and topography of Southwark and Lambeth*, MoLAS Monogr **14**, Mus of London, London

Sidell, J, and Wilkinson, K, 2004 The Central London Thames: Neolithic river development and floodplain archaeology, in *Towards a new Stone Age: aspects of the Neolithic in south-east England* (eds J Cotton and D Field), CBA Res Rep **137**, 38-48, London

Slager, S and Van der Wetering, H T J, 1977 Soil formation in archaeological pits and adjacent loess soils in Southern Germany, *J Archaeol Sci* **4**, 259-67

Smith I., 1964, Annual round-up of fieldwork, *Medieval Archaeology* **8**

Smith, D, 1994 The insect remains from the Hays Site, Dagenham, Unpubl MoLAS archive rep

Smith, D, 1996 Insect Analysis, Appendix VI in Divers 1996

Smith, D, 1999 Atlas Wharf, Isle of Dogs: Paleoentomological analysis, Unpubl reps to MoLAS, Univ. Birmingham Environmental Archaeology Services Report 8

Smith, D, Osborne, P, and Barratt, J, 2000 Beetles and evidence of past environments at Goldcliff, in M, Bell *et al.* 2000, 245–260

Smith, D N, in press *Insects in the City: A palaeoentomological perspective on London's past*, Mellen Press, Lampeter

Smith, K, 2005 The Roman pottery, in *Archaeology of the Jubilee Line extension: Prehistoric and Roman activity at Stratford Market depot, West Ham, London, 1991-1993* (J Hiller and D R P Wilkinson), 33-35, MoLAS, London

Smith, R A, 1907 Time keepers of the ancient Britons, *Proc Soc Antiq London* vol. **21**, 319-34

Spencer, K L, 2002 Spatial variability of metals in the inter-tidal sediments of the Medway Estuary, Kent, *Marine Pollution Bulletin* **44**, 933–944

Stace, C, 1991/1997 *New Flora of the British Isles* (1st/2nd edn), Cambridge Univ Press, Cambridge

Stevens, C J, 2007 Reconsidering the evidence: towards an understanding of the social contexts of subsistence production in Neolithic Britain, in *The origin and spread of domestic plants in Southwest Asia and Europe* (eds S Colledge and J Conolly), 375-389, Left Coast Press, Walnut Creek

Stevens, C J, nd Charred plant remains from the excavations at Westwood Cross, Broadstairs, Thanet, unpubl. rep, Wessex Archaeology

Stewart, H, 1984 *Cedar: Tree of life to the Northwest Coast Indians*, Douglas and McIntyre, Vancouver

Stockmarr, J, 1971 Tablets with spores used in absolute pollen analysis, *Pollen et Spores* 13, 614-621

Stoops, G, 2003 *Guidelines for analysis and description of soil and regolith thin sections*, Soil Sci Soc of America, Inc, Madison, Wisconsin

Struthers, J, 1866 Note relative to excavations at Balgone near North Berwick. *Proc Soc Antiq Scot* 6 (1864–66), 107–8.

Stuiver, M, and Kra, R S, 1986 Editorial comment, *Radiocarbon*, 28(2B), ii

Stuiver, M, and Polach, H A, 1977 Reporting of ^{14}C data, *Radiocarbon*, 19, 355–63

Sumbler M G, 1996 *London and the Thames Valley*, British Regional Geology, Brit Geol Survey Keyworth

Switsur, V R, and Jacobi, R M, 1979 A radiocarbon chronology for the early Postglacial stone industries of England and Wales, in *Radiocarbon Dating* (eds R Berger and H E Suess), 42-68, Univ. California Press, Berkeley and London

Symonds, R P, and Tomber, R S, 1991 Late Roman London: an assessment of the ceramic evidence from the City of London, *Trans London Middlesex Archaeol Soc* 42, 59-99

Taylor, H, 1996 Lithics, unpubl. rep in RPS Clouston 1997

Thirly, M, Galbois, J, and Schmitt, J-M, 2006 Unusual phosphate concretions related to groundwater flow in a continental environment, *J Sedimentary Res* 76, 866-877

Thomas, C, and Rackham, D J, 1996 Bramcote Green, Bermondsey: a Bronze Age trackway and palaeoenvironmental sequence, *Proc Prehist Soc* 61, 221-53

Thurnam, J, 1871 On ancient British barrows, especially those of Wiltshire and the adjoining counties (Part II: round barrows), *Archaeologia* 43(II), 285–552

Tringham, R, Cooper, G, Odell, G, Voytek, B, and Whitman, A, 1974 Experimentation in the formation of edge damage: a new approach to lithic analysis, *J Field Archaeol* 1, 171-196

Turner, J, 1962 The *Tilia* decline: an anthropogenic interpretation *New Phytologist* 61, 328-341

Tweddle, J C, Edwards, K J, and Fieller, N R J, 2005 Multivariate statistical and other approaches for the separation of cereal from wild Poaceae pollen using a large Holocene dataset, *Vegetation Hist and Archaeobot* 14, 15-30

Tyers, P, 1988 The prehistoric peat layers (Tilbury IV), in SLAEC 1988 Excavations in Southwark 1973-76, Lambeth 1973-79 (ed P. Hinton), *London Middlesex Archaeol Soc / Surrey Archaeol Soc*, joint publication 3.

van der Werff, A and Huls, H, 1957-74 Diatomeenflora van Nederland 8 parts published privately by A Van Der Werff, Westzijde, 13a De Hoef, (U), The Netherlands

van Geel, B, 1976 Fossil spores of Zygnemataceae in ditches of a pre-historic settlement in Hoogkarspel (The Netherlands), *Review of Palaeobotany and Palynology* 22, 337-344

van Geel, B, Bohncke, S J P, and Dee, H, 1981 A palaeoecological study of an upper late Glacial and Holocene sequence from "De Borchert", The Netherlands, *Review of Palaeobotany and Palynology* 31, 367-448

Varndell, G, 2004 The Great Baddow hoard and discoidal knives: more questions than answers, in *From sickles to circles: Britain and Ireland at the time of Stonehenge*, (eds A M Gibson and J A Sheridan), Tempus, Stroud, 116–22

Vos, P C, and de Wolf', H, 1988 Methodological aspects of paleo-ecological diatom research in coastal areas of the Netherlands, *Geologie en Mijnbouw* 67, 31-40

Vretemark, M, 1997 Från ben till boskap Kosthåll och djurhållning med utgångspunkt i medeltida benmaterial från Skara, Skrifter från Länsmuseet Skara, Nr 25

Vyner, B, 2011 Appendix 1: Ceramics, in *Holes in the Landscape. Seventeen Years of Archaeological Investigations at Nosterfield Quarry, North Yorkshire* (A Dickson and G Hopkinson), 237–270. On-line publication: http://www.archaeologicalplanningconsultancy.co.uk/thornborough/pdf/holes_in_the_landscape.pdf

Wainwright, G J, 1972 The excavation of a Neolithic settlement on Broome Heath, Ditchingham, Norfolk, *Proceedings of the Prehistoric Society* 38, 1-97

Warren, S H, 1912 On a late glacial stage in the valley of the River Lea, subsequent to the epoch of River-drift Man, *Quarterly Journal of the Geological Society* 68, 213-251

Warren, S H, 1916 Further observations on the Late Glacial or Ponders' End Stage of the Lea Valley, *Quarterly Journal of the Geological Society of London* 71, 164-182

Warren, S H, 1938 The correlation of the Lea Valley Arctic Beds, *Proceedings of the Prehistoric Society* 4, 328-329

Watson, M, 1988 Assessment of the archaeological importance of the Royal Albert Docks development, unpubl Rep

Watson, B, Brigham, T, and Dyson, T, 2001 *London Bridge, 2000 years of a river crossing*, MoLAS Monograph 8, London

Webber M, 1999 *The Thames archaeological survey 1996-1999*, London

Webley L, and Hiller J, 2009 A fen island in the Neolithic and Bronze Age: excavations at North Fen, Sutton, Cambridgeshire, *Proc Cambridge Antiq Soc* XCVIII, 11-36

Wenban-Smith, F F W, Stafford, E C, and Bates, M R, forthcoming *Prehistoric Ebbsfleet*, Oxford Wessex Archaeology Monograph

Wessex Archaeology, 2003 A13 Thames Gateway, Movers Lane archaeological investigations (assessment report 50012/ML/PXA/ReV01), unpubl rep for RMG (A13) Construction JV

Wessex Archaeology, 2006 Environmental remains from Coln industrial estate (CBI 06), unpubl client rep. 631101 for L-P Archaeology

Whittle, A W R, 1997 Moving on and moving around: Neolithic settlement mobility, in *Neolithic Landscapes* (ed P Topping), Neolithic Studies Group Seminar Papers 2, Oxbow Monograph **86**, 15-22

Wilkins, B, 2011 Past Orders: the archaeology of beer, *Current Archaeology* **256**, 28-35

Wilkinson, K N, Scaife, R G, and Sidell, E J. 2000 Environmental and sea level changes in London from 10, 5000 BP to the present: a case study from Silvertown, *Proceedings of the Geologists Association* **111**, 41-54

Wilkinson, T, 1988 *Archaeology and environment in South Essex: Rescue archaeology along the Grays bypass* 1979-80, EAA Rep **42**, Essex Co Council, Chelmsford

Wilkinson, T J, and Murphy, P, 1986 Archaeological survey of an intertidal zone: the submerged landscape of the Essex coast, England, *J Field Archaeol* **13(2)**, 177-94

Wilkinson, T J, and Murphy, P L, 1995 *The archaeology of the Essex coast, Volume 1: the Hullbridge Survey* EAA Rep **71**, Essex County Council, Chelmsford

Wilkinson, T J, Murphy, P, Brown, N, and Heppell, E, submitted *The archaeology of the Essex Coast, Volume 2 the Hullbridge Survey*, EAA series

Williams, D M, Hartley, B, Ross, R, Munro, M A R, Juggins, S, and Battarbee, R W 1988 *A coded checklist of British diatoms*, ENSIS Publishing, London

Wilson, D, 1851 *The archaeology and prehistoric annals of Scotland*, Sutherland and Knox, Edinburgh

Worley, F, 2011 Animal bones from Northfleet, in *Settling the Ebbsfleet valley: CTRL excavations at Springhead and Northfleet, Kent – the late Iron Age, Roman, Anglo-Saxon and Medieval landscape* (P Andrews, E Biddulph, A Hardy and A Smith), Volume 2: The finds, Oxford Wessex Archaeology Monograph, Oxford and Salisbury

Wright, D, 1959 *Baskets and basketry*, B T Batsford, London

Wright, E V, 1990 *The Ferriby boats. Seacraft of the Bronze Age*, Routledge, London

Wright, E V, Hedges, R, Bayliss, A, and van de Noort, R, 2001 New AMS dates for the Ferriby boats; a contribution to the origin of seafaring, *Antiquity* **75**, 726–34

Wright, C W, and Wright, E V, 1939 Submerged boat at North Ferriby, *Antiquity* 13, 349–54

Wymer, J, 1991 *Mesolithic Britain*, Shire Publications Ltd

Wymer, J, 1999 *The Lower Palaeolithic Occupation of Britain*, Wessex Archaeology and English Heritage

Yalden, D, 1999 *The history of British mammals*, Poyser, London

Yates, D, 2001 Bronze Age agricultural intensification in the Thames Valley and estuary, in *Bronze Age Landscapes: Tradition and Transformation* (ed J Brück), 139-148, Oxbow Books, Oxford.

Yates, D T, 2007 *Land, power and prestige: Bronze Age field systems in southern England*, Oxbow, Oxford

Young, C J, 1977 *Oxfordshire Roman pottery*, BAR Brit Ser **43**, Oxford

Young, R and Humphrey, J, 1999 Flint use in England after the Bronze Age: time for a re-evaluation? *Proc Prehist Soc* **65**, 231-242

Maps sources

Chapman, J, and Andre, P, 1777 Map of Essex

Milne, T, 1800 Land use map of London and environs

Rocque, J, 1746 Map of London, Westminster and Southwark

Rocque, J, 1754 Map of Middlesex

Index